D0998680

HANDBOOK OF SALES PROMOTION

HANDBOOK OF SALES PROMOTION

Stanley M. Ulanoff, Ph.D.

Editor in Chief

Associate Professor of Marketing (Advertising and Sales Promotion),
Baruch College, City University of New York;
Consultant to Industry and Government

McGraw-Hill Book Company

New York   St. Louis   San Francisco   Auckland   Bogotá   Hamburg
Johannesburg   London   Madrid   Mexico   Montreal   New Delhi
Panama   Paris   São Paulo   Singapore   Sydney   Tokyo   Toronto

Library of Congress Cataloging in Publication Data
Main entry under title:

Handbook of sales promotion.

   Includes index.
   1. Sales promotion—Addresses, essays, lectures.
I. Ulanoff, Stanley M.
HF5438.5.H35   1985   658.8′2   83-25608
ISBN 0-07-065733-5

Copyright © 1985 by McGraw-Hill, Inc. All rights reserved. Printed in the United States of America. Except as permitted under the Copyright Act of 1976, no part of this publication may be reproduced or distributed in any form or by any means, or stored in a data base or retrieval system, without the prior written permission of the publisher.

1 2 3 4 5 6 7 8 9 0   DOC/DOC   8 9 8 7 6 5 4

ISBN 0-07-065733-5

The editors for this book were William A. Sabin and Chet Gottfried,
the designer was Al Cetta,
and the production supervisor was Sally Fliess.
It was set in Zapf Book Light by Byrd Data Imaging Group.
Printed and bound by R. R. Donnelley & Sons Company.

To the Marketing Science Institute and to Alden G. Clayton, its president and managing director, whose early recognition of the rapidly growing importance of sales promotion and whose aid, both academic and financial, have been invaluable.

Content

vii

About the Editor in Chief

Stanley M. Ulanoff (Chapter 1) is an active consultant in the field of marketing (sales promotion, advertising, and public relations). He is an associate professor of marketing at Baruch College, City University of New York, where he previously headed the advertising and public relations division. Prior to taking his present position, he served as the assistant to the president of the State University of New York at Stony Brook and taught part-time at Long Island University, C. W. Post Center, and the State University of New York College at Farmingdale. He has had practical experience as a newswriter; as an advertising copywriter for Cecil & Presbrey; as a promotion copywriter for *The New York Times*; as president of a radio broadcasting station in Springfield, Massachusetts; as a free-lance writer; and as an advertising and public relations consultant. In addition to his academic duties, he has been a consultant to the U.S. Department of Defense and to Compton Advertising, one of the world's largest advertising agencies, where he served as assistant to the president.

Ulanoff has written and/or edited eighteen books on the aerospace industry and on history, most of which have been published by Doubleday and Arco (Prentice-Hall). His textbook *Advertising in America* was first published by Hastings House in 1977. He is the author of many magazine and newspaper articles that appeared in such publications as *Public Relations Journal*, *The New York Times*, and *Newsday*, and he has written research papers for the Marketing Science Institute and other organizations. His honors include *Chevalier dans L'Ordre des Palmes Académique*, awarded by the French government; the Legion of Merit, the Meritorious Service Medal, and the Commendation Medal from the U.S. government; the Conspicuous Service Cross from the state of New York; the American Association of Advertising Agencies Fellowship at Compton Advertising; and the Lewis Kleid Direct Mail Advertising Scholarship. He was named "VIP" (very important professor) by Specialty Advertising Association International on two occasions, and he was the recipient of a Russell Sage Foundation grant and the gold Alumni Distinguished Service Award from Hofstra University. He has been listed in *Who's Who in the East*, *Dictionary of International Biography*, *Contemporary Authors*, *Who's Who in America*, *Men and Women of Science*, *Men of Achievement*, and *Who's Who in Public Relations*.

A graduate of the University of Iowa School of Journalism, Ulanoff earned an M.B.A. at Hofstra University and a Ph.D. at New York University.

During World War II, after graduating from Infantry Officer Candidate School, Ulanoff was successively an infantry and an intelligence officer. He served as a special agent of the Counter Intelligence Corps in Europe, and during 1972 he had commanded the first Reserve unit to perform its two-week annual training at U.S. Army headquarters in Heidelberg, Germany.

Ulanoff served on a special extended tour of duty as the information officer at Fort Drum, New York, in 1974. He participated in and supervised media relations, community relations, the production of radio and TV broadcasts, film and slide shows, and press conferences. A later tour of duty brought him and the unit he commanded to the U.S. naval station at Roosevelt Roads in Puerto Rico on a special assignment. Presently he is a colonel in the Army Reserve.

He is a graduate of the Command and General Staff College and Defense Intelligence Schools, and has completed special courses at the University of Virginia Law School, the California Institute of Technology, the University of Louisiana, and the U.S. Department of State Foreign Service Institute.

Contributors

Donald A. Adler (Chapter 29) is vice president of the Carlson Marketing Group, Inc., and chief operating officer of the Promotion Fulfillment Division. Formerly he served for a period of seven years as president of the Maple Plain Company, Inc., a leading firm in sales promotion fulfillment. His past business experience also includes service as president of St. Croix Corporation, a sporting goods manufacturer, and as general manager of Schaper Manufacturing Company, a producer of games and toys. Adler has a B.B.A. from Spencerian College. He is a veteran of World War II.

Eugene R. Beem (Chapter 14) is associate professor of marketing at Baruch College, City University of New York. Until 1980 he was vice president of economics and corporate development for the Sperry & Hutchinson Company, which he joined in 1958. Between 1954 and 1958 he was assistant professor of business administration at the University of California, Berkeley.

Beem is the coauthor of *Triggers to Customer Action—Some Elements in a Theory of Promotional Inducements*, a 1981 publication of the Marketing Science Institute. An earlier article, "Who Profits from Trading Stamps?" (*Harvard Business Review*, November–December 1957), led to his employment by the Sperry & Hutchinson Company.

Beem received a Ph.D. in economics from the University of Pennsylvania in 1951 and a B.A. from Wooster College in 1942.

Leonard Bierman (Chapter 7) is executive vice president of Marden-Kane, Inc., and has been with the firm since 1966. Earlier, he was employed in the premium and incentive marketing industry. He has been a guest speaker at seminars given by New York University on service station promotions and by the National Restaurant Association on building traffic counts through games and sweepstakes. He has also served as moderator or panelist at various trade functions and meetings.

In 1976, Bierman received the *Advertising Age* first Annual Award of Excellence in Marketing Strategy. In 1983, he won an *Advertising Age* award for one of the eleven best promotions of 1982.

Bierman received a B.B.A. from Baruch College, City University of New York, in 1962.

Russell D. Bowman (Foreword) is vice president for marketing development at John Blair Marketing, New York. Previously he served for ten years as the corporate promotion development manager of General Foods Corp. and as promotion development manager of the Birds Eye Division. He has also served as account supervisor for the Colgate and Clairol accounts at Norman Craig and Kummel in New York and as account executive, copywriter, and media buyer at BBD&O in New York. He has lectured for *Advertising Age*, the Association of National Advertisers, the Premium Merchandising Club of New York, Marketing and Communications Executives International, the Promotion Marketing Association of America, and several colleges and universities.

Bowman is former chairman of the sales promotion policy committee of the Association of National Advertisers. He is a member of the boards of directors of the Marketing Executive's Club of New York, the Promotion Marketing Association of America, and Marketing Communications Executives International. He has written seven feature articles that appeared in *Advertising Age*, *Marketing Communications*, and other trade publications. Bowman is also the author of *Couponing and Rebates*, published in 1980 by Lebar-Friedman.

Roseann Caffaro (Chapter 2) is managing editor of *Premium/Incentive Business Magazine*. She has worked on the magazine since 1977, and each year she supervises the preparation of its *Directory of Premium Suppliers and Services*. She is a member of the Premium Merchandising Club of New York. Caffaro holds an M.A. from Columbia University.

John A. Cleary (Chapter 4) is president and general manager of Donnelley Marketing, a company of The Dun & Bradstreet Corporation, a position he has held since 1979. He began his career with Donnelley Marketing in 1956 as an account executive; later he served as an account supervisor, as regional sales manager, and as vice president for national marketing services. He currently serves on the board of directors of the Promotion Marketing Association of America and the Southwestern Area Commerce & Industry Association of Connecticut.

Cleary earned a B.S. at the University of Illinois College of Journalism and Communications in 1956, and he was also recognized as that year's outstanding journalism graduate.

William J. Corbett (Chapter 12) is director of public relations for Avon Products, Inc., the world's largest manufacturer and distributor of cosmetics, fragrances, and fashion jewelry. He is responsible for Avon's worldwide public relations programs in thirty-two countries.

Corbett is on the Public Relations Advisory Committee of the U.S. Information Agency, he is a member of the international committee of the Public Relations Society of America, and he is the representative of the

International Public Relations Association to the United Nations. He is chairman of the international committee of the New York chapter of the Public Relations Society of America, a member of the National Advisory Board of the Center for the Study of the Presidency, and a member of the board of directors of the Forum for Corporate Social Responsibility.

Prior to joining Avon in 1968, Corbett served as an assistant district attorney of Nassau County, New York, and as a criminal defense lawyer with the Nassau County Legal Aid Society. Corbett is past chairman of the American Bar Association's Ordinance and Administrative Regulation Committee of the Local Government Law Section, a former member of the board of directors of the Public Affairs Council, former communications chairman for the Direct Selling Association, a former adviser to the New York State Joint Legislative Committee on Consumer Protection, and founder of the Hobart & William Smith Colleges Communications Advisory Council.

Corbett is a graduate of Hobart College and has a J.D. from Fordham Law School. He is a former Air Force public relations officer and earned ten military awards, including the Air Force Commendation Medal, for service with Operation Deep Freeze and missions to NATO, the Rio Pact nations, and the United Nations.

Michael J. Cox (Chapter 3) is vice president of marketing at Donnelley Marketing, a company of The Dun & Bradstreet Corporation. Donnelley Marketing is a leading supplier of marketing services to packaged goods manufacturers. Cox joined Donnelley Marketing as a sales coordinator in 1967, and later he served as an account executive with responsibility for major accounts. He was promoted to account supervisor in 1975 and to manager of sales planning and development in 1977; he was appointed to the position of director of marketing in 1980. Cox is also a member of the senior management group responsible for strategic planning. He is a member of the Direct Marketing Association and the Promotion Marketing Association of America.

Cox received an M.A. in marketing from Iona College. He served in the Marine Corps, where he earned the rank of captain during a tour of duty in Vietnam.

Len Daykin (Chapters 5 and 6) is senior vice president of Don Jagoda Associates, a sales promotion firm. Previously he was vice president and director of merchandising at Foote, Cone & Belding. He was honored with the Jesse Neal Editorial Achievement Award in 1971.

Daykin received a B.A. from the City College of New York in 1962, an M.A. from the City University of New York in 1971, and an M.B.A. from Adelphi University in 1981. He served as a first lieutenant in the U.S. Army Reserve from 1963 to 1969.

Harold J. DeVestern (Chapter 18) is regional sales manager in the Premium and Incentive Division of the Bulova Watch Company, Inc., Jackson Heights, New York; he is responsible for sales in the eastern third of the United States. His business experience encompasses more than thirty-five years of management in the sales promotion industry; he has been with Bulova since 1970. DeVestern attended Sampson College. He is a veteran of World War II.

Richard G. Ebel (Chapter 15) is vice president of public relations at Specialty Advertising Association International; he has been with the Texas-based trade association since 1969. Previously, he held editorial, advertising, and public relations positions with the National Moving & Storage Association, the National Association of Retail Druggists, and *The National Underwriter*, an insurance trade newspaper.

He has written articles for *Industrial Marketing* and *Imprint* magazines and is a contributor to the *Book of Knowledge*, published by the Grolier Society. He frequently lectures to college marketing and advertising classes and addresses advertising and sales promotion organizations. He is a member of the American Academy of Advertising and the Public Relations Society of America.

Ebel studied at Northwestern University, from which he graduated with a B.S. in journalism, and at Northern Illinois University, where he earned an M.A. for studies in public relations. He served in the U.S. Army from 1954 to 1956 and was stationed in Japan.

Susan L. Fry (Chapter 2) is editor and copublisher of *Premium/Incentive Business Magazine*, a position she has held since 1976. The magazine deals with advertising and sales promotion, particularly with the use of premiums and incentives of all kinds to stimulate business activity at both the consumer and the trade levels.

She is a member of the Incentive Manufacturers Representatives Association, the National Premium Sales Executives, the Promotion Marketing Association of America, the Premium Merchandising Club of New York (which she served as president in 1979 and 1980), the Society of Incentive Travel Executives, and the New York Business Press Editors; she is an honorary member of the British Institute of Sales Promotion.

Fry graduated cum laude from Allegheny College, where she earned a B.A. in English literature, in 1968. She received an M.A. in communications from the University of Pennsylvania, Annenberg School of Communications, in 1970.

Lynn I. Halbardier (Chapter 21) is manager of media relations at Specialty Advertising Association International; she has been with the Texas-based trade association since 1979. Formerly, she held positions in corporate communications and public relations with the Federal Reserve Bank of Dallas, Employers Insurance of Texas, and the City of Garland, Texas.

She has written articles for *Personnel Journal*, *Association Trends* magazine, and *Show Magazine*. She lectures on specialty advertising to college marketing and advertising classes on behalf of Specialty Advertising Association International.

Halbardier received a B.A. in journalism from East Texas State University and has done graduate work at the same institution.

Jerome Hamberger (Chapter 16) is vice president of David Hamberger Inc., the family display business, where he has worked since 1949. He has held many positions in the company, including those of sales manager and shop manager. He has been a member of the National Association of Display Industries since its inception.

Hamberger earned a B.A. in administrative engineering at the New York University School of Engineering. His college career was interrupted by a two-year stint in the Navy (1944 to 1946), where he worked on radar maintenance in the Pacific theater.

Don Jagoda (Chapters 5 and 6) is president of his own sales promotion firm, Don Jagoda Associates, Inc., in Syosset, New York. He was previously affiliated with the S. Jay Reiner Company and the Hudson Pulp & Paper Corporation.

He is a director of the Promotion Marketing Association of America and of the New York chapter of the Marketing Communications Executives International. He is president of the Premium Merchandising Club of New York and is a member of the National Premium Sales Executives Club. He has also written numerous articles on sweepstakes and sales promotion.

Jagoda has a B.S. from New York University. He served in the U.S. Army from 1951 to 1953.

Richard Kane (Chapter 7) is president of Marden-Kane, Inc., a promotion and marketing services company; it was the first consultant company to specialize in national contests, sweepstakes, and games. Throughout his business career he has written articles and given numerous speeches and presentations on promotional applications.

Kane attended the University of Missouri, where he took prejournalism courses. He served during the Korean War in psychological warfare.

John M. Kawula (Chapter 8) is vice president of the Point-of-Purchase Advertising Institute (POPAI), a position he has held since 1982. From 1974 to 1979 he served as director of public relations for POPAI. Previously he had been vice president of marketing for the Donaldson Marketing Promotion

Group. While with Donaldson, he designed marketing and merchandising programs for a number of leading consumer goods companies, including R. J. Reynolds, Kenner Toys, Airwick Consumer Products, Sheaffer Eaton-Textron, and Seagrams Distilling Company. Before joining POPAI, he also served as promotion and research manager of *The Morning and Evening News*, a New Jersey daily newspaper, and he received numerous awards acknowledging his work in the fields of public relations, community service, and education.

Kawula is the author of two books, and he has served as consulting editor to such trade publications as *Marketing Communications*, *Financial Ad Views*, and *Chain Store Age—Supermarket*. He has lectured in the fields of public relations and creative merchandising at colleges and universities, to service organizations and professional groups, and at corporate seminars throughout the nation.

Robert L. Klein (Chapter 26) is senior vice president of Management Decision Systems, Inc., of Waltham, Massachusetts, and is responsible for the company's Models Development Group, which is a national leader in the development and use of problem-solving models and computer software for business analysis and planning. The Models Development Group is pioneering the design and implementation of new tools for measuring market response and predicting consumer behavior. Klein has been associated with the Models Development Group since its founding in 1970 and is personally responsible for the development of many of its procedures for the design and evaluation of new products.

He is a new member of the Institute of Management Sciences, the American Marketing Association, and the Promotion Marketing Association of America. He is the author of "Using Supermarket Scanner Panels to Measure the Effectiveness of Coupon Promotions," which appeared in *Marketing: Measurement and Analysis 1981*. His articles on new products and market research have appeared in *Advertising Age*, *Marketing News*, and *Household and Personal Products Industry*.

Klein received a B.S. in mechanical engineering from M.I.T. in 1966 and an M.S. from M.I.T.'s Alfred P. Sloan School of Management in 1968. He served for two years as an officer in the U.S. Public Health Service doing management science consulting at the National Institutes of Health.

Robert B. Konikow (Chapter 9) is a self-employed consultant and writer. He has served as public relations counsel for the Exhibit Designers & Producers Association, with whom he helped develop the Trade Show Bureau. He has been active in the trade-show field for many years. In Washington, soon after World War II, he was a founder of a company devoted to visual communication in all media, including exhibits, and he served as account executive and copywriter on many projects. He also managed the division that acted as the official contractor for trade shows held in the Washington area. In 1956, Konikow went to Chicago, where he was managing editor of *Advertising Requirements* (later renamed *Advertising & Sales Promotion*). Here he attended many trade shows and wrote and edited numerous articles on the use of exhibits as a marketing tool.

In 1981, Konikow received the Distinguished Service Award of the National Trade Show Exhibitors Association, "in recognition of his outstanding contribution to improving the effectiveness of the trade show medium." He is the author of several books, including *Discover Historic America* (Rand McNally), *Communications for the Safety Professional* (National Safety Council), and *How to Participate Profitably in Trade Shows* (Dartnell). He is currently working on a book entitled *Exhibit Design*, to be published by the Photographic Book Co. Konikow is a graduate of Harvard University.

Robert Letwin (Chapter 19) is the publisher of *Successful Meetings* magazine and vice president of Bill Communications, Inc., its parent company. He is an authority on meeting and exhibit techniques and has been on the faculty of the Charles Morris Price School of Advertising and Journalism. A featured speaker across the nation, he has conducted seminar sessions from London to Tokyo, and he is a consultant to industry and government on convention and trade-show activities and business potential.

Letwin is a graduate of the Temple University School of Business Administration.

Joseph S. Maier (Chapter 24) is president of Joseph S. Maier & Associates, a sales promotion and creative services agency located in Glen Ellyn, Illinois. He has served many blue-chip clients throughout his career, including Procter & Gamble, Ralston Purina, Alberto-Culver, Oscar Mayer, J. Walter Thompson, International Harvester, Blistex, Abbott Laboratories, Kellogg's, and Allied Van Lines. Before forming his own agency in 1982, Maier was a partner and director of merchandising at Tatham-Laird & Kudner Advertising in Chicago. His fourteen years at this firm were preceded by nine years at the Quaker Oats Company, where he held various positions in sales, sales promotion, and brand management.

Besides his business activities, Maier teaches an introductory course in advertising at Rosary College in River Forest, Illinois. He served as cochairman of first-day activities of the Promotion Marketing Association of America's "Promotion Update '82" forum, where he delivered a major address on group promotions. He also served as a seminar leader on sales and marketing for Allied Van Lines' 1982 convention.

Maier holds a B.A. in communication arts from the University of Notre

Dame and an M.B.A. in marketing from the University of Chicago Graduate School of Business.

Edward D. Meyer (Chapter 25) is a senior vice president and the director of promotion services at Dancer Fitzgerald Sample; he has been with the firm since 1974. He has over eighteen years of experience in agency and client sales promotion and has been involved in every area of consumer sales promotion in virtually every product category. At Dancer Fitzgerald Sample, he has been actively involved in the development and implementation of sales promotion programs for Procter & Gamble, General Mills, Duracell, Wrangler, Life Savers, and Toyota, while directing promotion efforts for all the company's accounts. Meyer previously spent ten years in the sales promotion area at Pepsi-Cola, General Foods (promotion manager of the Kool Aid and pet-food divisions), and Hunt Wesson, where he was director of merchandising.

Meyer is a contributing columnist to *Advertising Age* and a member of the American Association of Advertising Agencies' promotion committee.

Thomas W. Nethercott (Chapter 14) is on the staff of Cranwill Associates, Inc., in New York City. His involvement with trading stamps extended from 1967 through 1981. As research manager at Bigelow Carpets, he observed their effectiveness as an incentive device for retailers of home furnishings. Later, as manager of research studies at the Sperry & Hutchinson Company, he evaluated the role of trading stamps as a promotional inducement over the long term. Prior to his association with Bigelow, he served as marketing analyst at Uniroyal, after gaining earlier experience in retailing at Allied Stores Corporation.

Nethercott is a graduate of the College of William and Mary, where he majored in economics and was awarded membership in Phi Beta Kappa. He received an M.S. in marketing from Columbia University.

Robert A. Robertson (Chapter 10) is founder and president of Game-Show Placements, Ltd., in Los Angeles. Since 1969, his company has provided thousands of products to be used as awards on network and nationally syndicated game shows and has served such companies as Revlon Cosmetics, Chrysler Corporation, Hershey Chocolate Company, Colgate-Palmolive, and GTE-Sylvania, as well as numerous lesser-known companies. His background includes many years as an advertising agency copywriter and account executive.

Robertson is a graduate of Wayne State University, where he majored in journalism. He has also done extensive postgraduate study in Italy and France.

William A. Robinson (Chapter 22) is president of William A. Robinson, Inc., of

Northbrook, Illinois, a firm that has helped many Fortune 500 companies find creative solutions to tough marketing problems. Robinson is an internationally known figure in the fields of advertising and sales promotion. He has lectured around the world and has conducted marketing workshops and seminars in North and South America, Europe, and the Orient. His "Best Promotions" program—cosponsored by Crain Communications, Inc.—has been presented more than 125 times throughout the world since 1972. He has also taught sales promotion classes at the undergraduate and graduate levels at several leading universities, including the University of Florida, Michigan State University, and Northwestern University.

"Robinson on Sales Promotion" is a regular feature in *Advertising Age*, and five volumes of Robinson's annual review of the outstanding work in the field, *Best Sales Promotions*, are now in print. He is coauthor, with Don E. Schultz, of two definitive texts on the industry, *Sales Promotion Essentials* and *Sales Promotion Management.*

Jay K. Shapiro (Chapter 27) is vice president of Hand Tip & Novelty Co., Inc., a New York firm that has been part of the specialty advertising industry since the company's founding in 1900. He joined the company in 1972 as production manager, moved into sales, and served as general manager before becoming vice president in 1977.

Shapiro is a member of the executive board of the Specialty Advertising Association of Greater New York and a former member of the board of the Association of Metropolitan Advertising Specialty Suppliers; he has also served on various committees of Specialty Advertising Association International (SAAI). For the past eight years he has been a member of the SAAI ambassadors program, and he has spoken before advertising and marketing clubs as well as university graduate and undergraduate advertising and business classes.

Shapiro is a graduate of the Executive Development Seminar course cosponsored by SAAI and the University of Wisconsin Graduate School of Business. In 1979 he developed and produced a national advertising campaign for Hand Tip & Novelty Co., Inc., that won the SAAI Gold Pyramid award for excellence, the industry's top promotional award.

Shapiro received a B.S. from the State University of New York College at New Paltz and did graduate work at New Paltz, Adelphi University, and the New School for Social Research.

Fred Sherry (Chapter 13) is now retired and is a gentleman farmer in New Hampshire. He was sales promotion manager for the Grand Union Company from 1960 to 1977, during which time he was a panelist and/or guest speaker at various supermarket industry regional meetings and national conventions. Sherry was also vice president of Food Center Supermarkets, in Peekskill, New York. He has also served as a consultant to the supermarket industry.

Sherry received an L.L.B. in 1937 from Saint Johns University and practiced law for six years. Later he was awarded a J.D. He earned a B.A. at the City College of New York in 1934.

Peter D. Smith (Chapter 28) is the director of incentive marketing for the Consumer/Professional and Finishing Markets Division of the Eastman Kodak Company of Rochester, New York. He is also responsible for Kodak's world-wide sales to U.S. military exchanges and for trade relations with the catalog showroom industry. Prior to assuming his present position, he was the sales manager for Kodak's regional office in Dallas. Among his other responsibilities, during twenty-seven years with Kodak, he has been director of wage and salary administration for marketing, distribution, and staff groups; director of pricing; director of personnel and training, international markets division; product planning specialist for movie products; a member of the general management staff; and a field sales representative.

A Yale graduate, Smith has an M.A. in education from Wesleyan University and was a Sloan Fellow at M.I.T.'s Alfred P. Sloan School of Management, where he received an M.S. in management.

Laurence Peter Stuart (Chapter 11) is senior vice president of marketing and advertising at Wembley Industries, a position he has held since 1979. Before joining Wembley Industries in 1971, he worked as a photographer and as a TV cameraman.

Stuart is a member of the Neckwear Association of America and of the Father's Day Council of the Men's Fashion Association. He is also a board member of the New Orleans chapter of the Leukemia Society and a trustee of the Ronald McDonald House in New Orleans. In addition, he is a consultant to Executive Essentials, a career consulting and management development company, and has been a guest lecturer at Louisiana State University, where he has taught courses in creative selling. Stuart also speaks all over the country on the subject of selling to major department and specialty stores.

He is currently working on two books: a biography of Sam C. Pulitzer, chief executive officer of Wembley Industries, and a book about men's fashions, entitled *Softwear for Success*.

Stuart, born in London, England, has a B.A. in journalism from Louisana State University. He served in the U.S. Air Force.

Howard Stumpf (Chapter 8) is president of the Point-of-Purchase Advertising Institute (POPAI), a position he has held since 1966. Prior to assuming this position, he was manager of the H & D Display Division of Westvaco Corporation and was in charge of that company's nationwide display opera-tions. His duties included bringing together autonomous regional operating units into one national sales and production organization. While with

Westvaco, Stumpf served POPAI as chairman of the board, vice chairman of the board, treasurer, and general chairman of POPAI's 1961 symposium and exhibit. Before joining Westvaco, he was merchandising manager of Wilson Plastics, now a division of Foster Grant, Inc. He earlier served as a field salesman for the Industrial Division of Armstrong Cork Company.

Jay Thalheim (Appendix A) is president and chief executive officer of Thalheim Expositions, Inc., a position he has held since 1960. He has lectured at the University of Pennsylvania, the Promotion Marketing Association of America, the Premium Merchandising Club of New York, and the National Association of Exposition Managers.

He is a member of the National Association of Exposition Managers and is a certified exposition manager. He is also a member of the National Premium Sales Executives, the Premium Merchandising Club of New York, Marketing Communications Executives International, the Promotion Marketing Association of America, and the Friars Club.

Thalheim is a graduate of the Wharton School of Finance of the University of Pennsylvania, where he received a B.S. in 1943. He served in the military from 1944 to 1946.

Richard I. Topus (Chapter 17) is assistant professor of marketing at Long Island University, C. W. Post Center; he was formerly director of graduate studies in business at Hofstra University. From 1958 to 1978 he was employed by Friendship Dairy Products, where he was appointed vice president of marketing in 1963 and became a member of the board of directors in 1974. Topus has established supermarket workshops at, and has been an adjunct member on the faculties of, the State University of New York College at Farmingdale; Long Island University, C. W. Post Center; the Kingsborough Community College of the City University of New York; and Rutgers University.

He has written many articles for the trade press and has been a guest lecturer at Cornell and other universities. He is also a consultant to industry.

Topus has a B.S. and a M.B.A. from Hofstra University. He served in U.S. Army Intelligence during World War II.

Myer S. Tulkoff (Chapter 30) is an attorney with AT&T Technologies, Inc., a position which involves antitrust counseling and education at the manufacturing entity of AT&T. Earlier, he served in the New York office of the Federal Trade Commission. He joined the FTC as an attorney in 1959 and was appointed assistant regional director in 1968. He received the FTC Certificate of Commendation and the Commission's Meritorious Service Award. He is listed in *Who's Who in Government* (first and second editions) and in *Who's Who in American Law* (second edition).

Tulkoff prepared the chapter on FTC organization and procedures in *You and Antitrust*, published by the New York State Bar Association in 1966. He is the author of an article on the fair trade laws (*New York Law Journal*, March 1975), "A Look at the FTC in 1975" (*New York State Bar Journal*, August 1975), "Antitrust Implications of Suggested Retailers' Resale Prices" (*New York Law Journal*, May 27, 1976), and an article on the *Schwinn* case (*New York Law Journal*, June 24, 1976). Tulkoff delivered an address before the 1976 Antitrust Law Symposium of the New York State Bar Association. For a number of years he was a guest lecturer on antitrust law and consumer protection at the American Management Association.

He is a member of the Kentucky State Bar Association, the New York State Bar Association, the Reserve Officers Association, the Civil Affairs Association, the Association of the U.S. Army, and the Kentuckians. He is admitted to practice law in New York and Kentucky; before the U.S. District Court, Southern District and New York; and before the United States Supreme Court.

Tulkoff graduated from the University of Kentucky College of Law, where he was third in his class, and he holds a J.D. He served on the law review and was elected to the Order of the Coif upon graduation. He served two tours of duty in the U.S. Army, as an enlisted person and as an officer, in Japan, Korea, and the United States. He remained active in the Army Reserve from 1955 until 1978, when he retired with the rank of colonel. He was awarded the Meritorious Service Medal with Oak Leaf Cluster, among a number of other decorations and service medals. He is a graduate of the U.S. Army Command and General Staff College and the Industrial College of the Armed Forces.

Nancy Zimmerman (Chapter 20) is managing editor of *Incentive Travel Manager* and *Association & Society Manager*, trade journals aimed at, respectively, incentive travel executives and association executives involved in convention and meeting planning. She is a ten-year veteran of the travel industry, having spent five years as a sales agent with Mexicana Airlines and five years as manager of corporate services for Cardillo Travel Systems Inc., a nationwide chain of travel agencies. Prior to joining the travel industry, Zimmerman worked as a feature writer for the *Everett Herald*, a daily newspaper in Everett, Washington; she has also done free-lance feature writing and ghostwriting.

Zimmerman holds a B.A. in editorial journalism from the University of Washington and an M.A. in Spanish literature from the University of California, Los Angeles.

Robert N. Zoul (Chapter 23) is manager of marketing expense and control at Kraft, Inc.; he is responsible for the expense and budget control areas of advertising and promotion. Zoul has an extensive background in internal auditing for Kraft, General Mills, and Armour.

He is a member of the advertising financial management committee of the

Association of National Advertisers (ANA), and he presented a paper on advertising budget preparation, administration, and control at a recent ANA financial seminar. He has served as a guest lecturer at Roosevelt University for several years under the auspices of the education committee of the Institute of Internal Auditors, covering the subject of internal auditing of advertising and sales promotion.

Zoul holds a B.S. in accounting from Bradley University. He served with the U.S. Army in Korea.

Foreword:
We've Come A Long Way

RUSSELL D. BOWMAN
Vice President for Marketing Development, John Blair Marketing

The concept of incentives, which are a vital part of sales promotion, goes back a long way; perhaps the first incentive was the apple in the Garden of Eden. Sales promotion has always been a factor in our nation's businesses. Posters, premiums, and even business gifts were introduced in colonial days. Premiums offered by soap and soft-drink companies go back to the late nineteenth century. Coupons have their roots in the wooden nickels that owners of general stores used as a selling device.

Reportedly, the first coupon dates back to 1895, when C. W. Post distributed $0.01 coupons good toward the purchase of his Grape Nuts cereal. Today, General Foods, the company that makes Grape Nuts, is one of the leaders in couponing.

Contests and premium offers aimed at children go back a long way too. Before the advent of TV, the best way to reach millions of kids was on radio. During the 1940s, offers for Little Orphan Annie cocoa mugs and Captain Midnight secret decoder rings had children poised by their radios, pencil in hand.

After World War II, when the country was gearing up for the mass production of consumer goods and when new-product introductions were increasing dramatically, sampling and couponing became the more commonly used devices. Advertising revenues were growing (especially with the introduction of TV in the late 1940s), and promotion was still the stepchild when it came to marketing priorities. Market research grew during this period as well, but for every dollar spent on advertising, probably no more than 10 to 20 cents was spent on promotion, and so promotion remained less tangible and much less tested.

As the years progressed, sales promotions often mirrored the times. During the 1960s, T-shirts and other premiums reflected the nation's preoccupation with peace, while other promotions were built around a growing concern for ecology or were based on the "pop art" fad. Meanwhile, consumers were seeing more games and trading stamp plans, as well as sweepstakes that offered more in prizes than the sponsor usually had to give away.

Although sales promotion activity grew modestly throughout the 1950s and early 1960s for the most part, increased expenditures went unnoticed. But during the late 1960s and throughout the 1970s, merchandising and sales promotion underwent changes that led to the state of the art in sales promotion today.

THE STATE OF THE ART IN SALES PROMOTION

We can summarize sales promotion today by saying that it has become more *acceptable*, more *responsible*, and more *tangible*.

More Acceptable. Once the total expenditures for promotion had been established in the early 1970s, the billions of dollars involved brought about a new level of recognition for the business. A provocative article in a 1976 issue of *Harvard Business Review* reported that sales promotion was growing at a faster rate than advertising, and many people considered this a landmark in terms of industry acceptance. Meanwhile, more and more sales promotion executives were becoming an important part of management. A study by the Association of National Advertisers, originally conducted in the 1950s, was repeated twice in the 1970s and showed that the responsibility for sales promotion (especially consumer-oriented efforts) had shifted considerably to the sales promotion department. The acceptance, and consequently the growth, of sales promotion agencies definitely increased during the late 1970s and early 1980s. The 1981 directory of sales promotion agencies in *Marketing Communications* magazine listed 160 such agencies; the 1982 issue listed 230. When the Promotion Marketing Association of America (PMAA) began to run national conferences in the 1940s, about 100 people would show up. During the 1970s, attendance would pass the 200 mark. More than 300 people attended the 1982 two-day conference in Chicago, which cost the average company over $500 a person, and the PMAA probably turned down another 100 whose requests for reservations came in too late.

More Responsible. Like its marketing counterparts, sales promotion has had its credibility problems. Advertisers were faced with regulatory actions in the 1970s because of "deceptive" ads. Retailers were criticized for using "bait-and-switch" techniques and "loss leaders." Sales promotion people had to change sweepstakes rules and the rules governing the advertising of premiums to children. Now, even though there is much less threat from the Federal Trade Commission and consumer groups, companies and agencies are extremely cautious about mailings and sweepstakes rules, and really deceptive sales promotion ads are extremely rare. The PMAA has issued a code of ethics and a set of guidelines concerning both coupons and refunds to help new practitioners in the field. The Direct Marketing Association has published a brochure on mailing regulations in conjunction with the FTC. Network TV stations have been airing animated public service commercials aimed at educating children concerning mail-in premiums, guarantees, and the like. Where problems may exist, the use of objective research is often the solution, such as the coupon studies by the GMA and the recently completed study financed jointly by John Blair & Co. and Donnelley Marketing, illustrating the benefits of couponing for the retailer.

More Tangible.   It's been said that nothing sells like success; we might say that nothing sells like *tangible* success. The difficult economic situation of the mid-1970s and current economic problems have been a true test of results. Couponing has blossomed because it offers an immediate, tangible incentive to the inflation-conscious consumer. For the advertiser, it brings very real results; in some cases, such as coupon promotions launched by fast-food outlets, the results can be measured the next day. The advent of the Universal Product Code and of scanning devices has made it possible to measure the results of a promotion a week after it is launched and to compare these with the results of previous promotions.

One of the most tangible developments of the 1970s was the resurgence of rebates. The now famous Chrysler rebates of 1974 and 1975 resulted in a sales increase of 36 percent for Chrysler, and since other automobile manufacturers followed suit, there was an industry increase of 18 percent. In fact, the reduction of industry stock by over 200,000 units by February 1975 gave Detroit new hope and put thousands of people back to work. Since then, Chrysler has had its problems, but the company has been able to "stick it out," when many predicted that it wouldn't last into the 1980s.

Thus we can say that sales promotion has come a long way, and that it has progressed largely in reaction to the times; however, statistics indicate that it seems to be more or less "inflation-proof." As the gross national product fell, sales promotions, especially coupon promotions, increased. And during previous economically depressed years, sales promotion grew faster than traditional advertising. Then, when the economy and corporate budgets rebounded, sales promotions (again, particularly those involving couponing) increased even more. So, when this happens to our national economy again (which we hope will be soon), we might expect to see another boost in the sales promotion industry.

HANDBOOK OF SALES PROMOTION

The Nature of Sales Promotion

Two of the most publicized and most costly sales promotions of all time consisted of half-fare coupons given by United Airlines and American Airlines, to all passengers, during a three-week period that ended on June 17, 1979.[1] The coupons entitled bearers to a reduction of 50 percent on any round-trip full-fare ticket, within the continental United States, from July 1 through December 15, 1979.

United had just come through a long strike, during which its facilities had been completely closed down. The half-fare coupon was the company's way of reintroducing service. American Airlines, on the other hand, feared the competition and ran exactly the same promotion.

It was estimated that these sales promotion efforts would "cost the [air transport] industry hundreds of millions of dollars."[2] Even if each coupon was valued at $50, with 4 million distributed, this would amount to $200 million. Also, since the coupons could be valued as high as $300 each, the overall cost could be considerably higher. And all this was exclusive of the heavy cost of advertising the promotions on TV, in newspapers, and in other media.

Meanwhile, enterprising individuals met each American and United flight and offered cash to the passengers for the half-fare coupons, and travel agents ran ads offering to buy them for $20 apiece.[3] After the three-week period of coupon distribution had ended, an actual market for them came into being. One Los Angeles commodities firm had an inventory of 10,000 coupons, and they were selling for as high as $75 each, with even higher prices expected.[4] At about the same time, Pan American Airways announced that it would honor both United's and American's coupons.

Airlines continued this type of sales promotion into the 1980s in their struggle to maintain an advantage over their competitors. In fact, the Ralston Purina Co. "of Checkerboard Square," in conjunction with Republic Airways, offered free flights for children as premiums for the purchase of its cereals. The promotion was heralded by advertising and was boldly announced on the front, back, sides, and top of the cereal box: "Kids fly free on Republic with five proof-of-purchase seals from Chex or Honey Bran cereals, with full-fare-paying adults." The offer was good through August 15, 1982, and was honored by the airline from January 15 through November 15, 1982, for domestic flights.

Some of the other airlines offered their own services as an incentive to a segment of the market—"frequent travelers." Business executives who traveled a great deal were able to earn free flights or to upgrade their accommodations or class of service (e.g., to pay for coach but fly first-class) on the basis of the number of air miles they had logged with the particular airline. Pan Am's "ultimate reward" for flying 175,000 miles on its airline was thirty days of unlimited first-class service for two, anywhere the airline flew. And, in the first quarter of 1983, United offered frequent fliers one free trip for six flights totaling at least 8000 miles. This type of sales promotion seeks to attract the "heavy users," the roughly 20 percent of airline customers who account for 80 percent of all air travel. It is also a way to get continuity and to establish brand loyalty—to "keep 'em flying" on *your* airline.

Not to be outdone, Northwest Orient offered a "Way to Go Bonus" that even the infrequent traveler was able to enjoy. For one round-trip in the continental United States costing $200 or more, the traveler could fly to Hawaii for only $99. As a change of pace, Air Florida gave S&H stamps to its patrons.

The preceding are examples of particular sales promotion efforts, but, considering the general lack of knowledge concerning the subject, it is still reasonable to ask, What is sales promotion? Even those who have some experience in the field, including marketing professionals, often confuse sales promotion with advertising, with personal selling, with publicity, and most frequently with the overall term *promotion*. The chapters that follow will answer the question and will place sales promotion in its proper perspective in the economy.

ENDNOTES

1. W. M. Carley, "All's Fare in Love and Airlines' War: Coupons Take Off," *The Wall Street Journal*, June 6, 1979, pp. 1, 35.
2. Ibid.
3. Ibid.
4. Gene G. Marcial, "A New High Flier Tours Most Active on the Big Board," *The Wall Street Journal*, June 28, 1979, pp. 1, 45.

1 What Is Sales Promotion?

STANLEY M. ULANOFF, Ph.D.

Associate Professor of Marketing (Advertising and Sales Promotion), Baruch College, City University of New York; Consultant to Industry and Government

While all of us are familiar with the tools of sales promotion, since we constantly use them and are exposed to them, most of us, even marketing professionals, are hardly aware that they *are* sales promotion devices; for that matter, as stated earlier, most of us do not really know what sales promotion is. This is not surprising, however, when we consider the fact that business executives and academicians did not begin to study the subject seriously until the mid-1970s.

Perhaps it is crass to relate the relevance of a subject to the amount of money spent on it or to judge its importance in terms of dollars, but we live in a society that does just that. In simple terms, in 1981, some $58 billion was spent on sales promotion in the United States. If this fact by itself does not seem impressive, it should take on greater significance when coupled with the fact that approximately $35 billion was the total amount spent on advertising in this country during the same period. Even more striking is the fact that in recent years the total amount of money expended on sales promotion has been increasing at a faster rate than the dollars being allotted to advertising![1]

A comparison of advertising and sales promotion, over a six-year period, clearly indicates the disparity of growth between the two over the period measured. In 1976, $21.7 billion was spent on advertising, as compared with $29.82 billion spent on sales promotion, which had already moved ahead. By 1981, these figures had escalated to $35.68 billion for advertising and $58.14 billion for sales promotion. Percentagewise, in 1976, 42.1 percent of the combined total dollars spent on both advertising and sales promotion was expended on the former, as opposed to 57.9 percent on sales promotion. By

5

1981, the amount spent on advertising had dropped to 38.1 percent, while the figures for sales promotion had jumped to 61.9 percent.[2]

While, in a way, it might seem that sales promotion sprang forth full-grown, like Athena from the head of Zeus (as depicted in Greek mythology), in reality it had been there all along, maturing and blossoming without anyone's realizing it. So, as we have seen, now sales promotion is bigger than advertising and is growing by leaps and bounds.

What, then, is sales promotion? Perhaps the best way to begin answering this question is to give some examples that are readily recognizable to the consumer (no matter what our job, position, or station in life, we are all consumers). The introduction to Part I provided a few examples of sales promotions employed by some of the nation's airlines. Following are a number of others that might be more familiar.

Remember when, shortly before the start of the new year, your insurance agent, plumber, bank, or electrician sent you a calendar on which was prominently displayed the business's name, address, and telephone number? That was a form of sales promotion known as *specialty advertising*. You may have received a ballpoint pen or any of a multitude of other useful specialty advertising items, ranging from Frisbees to coffee mugs to key rings, each given with "no strings attached" and bearing an imprinted advertising message.

Another example of sales promotion, called a *premium*, is the set of dishes that the consumer gets from the supermarket for having saved $300 worth of cash-register tapes within a specified three- or four-month period. Had the supermarket given *trading stamps* instead of honoring the cash-register tapes, the consumer might have chosen the dishes from a catalog of items available for redemption. Some premiums are packed directly into the soap, cereal, or Cracker Jack box. Others are attached to the outside of the package. In order to get some premiums, consumers must mail in a proof of purchase, sometimes accompanied by a specified sum of money—substantially less, however, then they would have to pay for the same item in a retail store. Another form of sales promotion is the *cents-off coupon* you find in newspapers and magazines, in and on packages in retail stores, and sometimes in the mail. Similar to these are *rebates* and *refunds*, a kind of sales promotion discount which is employed by the manufacturer to encourage sales and which is sent directly by the manufacturer to the customer. While the offering of rebates has been, for all practical purposes, the exclusive preserve of manufacturers of consumer products, principally automobiles and major home appliances, a service company recently included rebates in its marketing strategy. Home Lines, a steamship company in the cruise business, offered a $200 rebate for customers booking passage on the *SS Oceanic* during the late summer and fall of 1982.[3] By comparison, cents-off coupons are generally valued at under $1, while rebates have been offered in amounts exceeding several thousand dollars.

Implying that Chrysler Corporation had been bailed out of its financial debacle by the use of rebates, *Newsweek* magazine published a cartoon showing the auto company's board chairman, Lee Iacocca, running for president of the United States. In it, Iacocca explains "Iacoccanomics" by pointing to a poster that has the words *tax cut* crossed out, with *rebate* substituted for them.[4]

Actual samples of products given away in stores or sent through the mail or otherwise delivered to your home are also a type of sales promotion.

Perhaps you have been intrigued by the lure of a trip to Hawaii or some other exotic place offered as a prize in a *sweepstakes*. All you have to do is drop your entry in a box at the retail store or mail it in with a box top, another proof of purchase of the product, or the product's name handwritten on a 3- by 5-inch piece of paper. Or you might enter a *contest* that offers such prizes as cash, a trip, a house, an automobile, or a camera for the best last line to a limerick, the best name for a new product, or the best recipe using a specified product (as in the Pillsbury baking contest). Most contests require that you send in an actual proof of purchase of the product, rather than a handwritten substitute, as in a sweepstakes. Contests also differ from sweepstakes in that winners are chosen on the basis of skill, talent, or ability, while in a sweepstakes the prizes are awarded purely on the basis of chance. Some sweepstakes, like a 1979 Natural Light beer prize promotion, masquerade as contests in that they ask the entrant to employ skill in naming something. However, since the winners are chosen by random drawing and no purchase

FIGURE 1-1. A free sample plus a cents-off coupon. (*Courtesy of Donnelley Marketing.*)

is required, they are really sweepstakes. Both contests and sweepstakes are types of sales promotion.

Similar to sweepstakes are *games of chance*, in which customers are given an opportunity to win a prize each time they make a purchase or visit the place of business. The consumer may be an instant winner or may have to return to the store a number of times in order to win. For example, the customer may be given a card on which is printed a certain letter. The purpose of the game is to collect the letters that spell the name of the product. Let us say that the item is called Duxo. The manufacturer is able to control the number of prizes awarded by simply limiting the distribution of any one of the letters. For example, an unlimited number of D's, u's, and o's could be printed, but only a handful of x's. After five or six visits to the store, customers will probably have several D's, u's, and o's, and they will continue to collect those same letters on subsequent trips—unless they are among the lucky few to

FIGURE 1-2: Steak knives are popular premiums and prizes. Prior to the oil shortage many gas stations gave one knife with each fill-up to encourage repeat purchases. (*Courtesy of Washington Forge.*)

draw an x. Needless to say, the game described here, and a number of variants of it, is a sales promotion too.

Other forms of sales promotion include company-sponsored *sports events*; *athletic equipment* furnished by the manufacturers gratis to famous sports figures; *customized articles of clothing* bearing a company trademark, to be worn by salespeople and other personnel; *free merchandise*, such as clothes, automobiles, and other "props" given to TV programs in return for a mention in the credits; and merchandise supplied to TV game shows to be used as *prizes*. Still other types of sales promotion are *exhibits*, *displays*, and *demonstrations*.

Numerous and varied as these examples of sales promotion are, they represent only a part of the picture. They are just some of the promotions employed by manufacturers and retailers to motivate consumers to buy, including techniques for getting them to try a new product, bringing them into the store, inducing them to keep coming back, and fostering goodwill. Manufacturers also use sales promotion techniques designed to stimulate retailers, wholesalers, and their own sales personnel to sell. All these will be discussed at greater length in the chapters that follow.

HISTORICAL BACKGROUND

Although the precise origin of sales promotion is lost in the depths of antiquity that predate recorded history, it is quite probable that some form of sales promotion was involved in the earliest business transactions, when men and women first began to engage in specialized labor. Prior to that time people were, in a manner of speaking, completely self-sufficient. That is, each family unit provided for all its basic needs, including food, clothing, and shelter. Later it became apparent that some were better hunters than their fellows and that others were better farmers, toolmakers, and so forth. This led to the barter system, as each followed a particular trade. It is highly likely that shortly after this specialization or division of labor took place, farmers might have offered potential customers a bite of one of the carrots or other vegetables they grew. This, in reality, would have been an example of sampling—"Try my product." It is well worth a vendor's time and effort to offer a sample of merchandise free, at a reduced rate, or accompanied by some other incentive, because if customers like the product, they will buy more of it and, the seller hopes, will come back to purchase it again and again.

Sampling is only one of a number of elements that make up what is called the *sales promotion mix*. These will be covered in greater detail later in this chapter and in other parts of the book. However, in delving into the background of sales promotion, we shall discuss a few promotions that have documented histories as well as some of relatively more recent ancestry.

It can be reasonably assumed that premiums, or a primitive form of them, became a part of life long before history began to be recorded. Premiums probably came into existence at approximately the same point in time when samples first emerged upon the scene. The first weapon maker to discover that the customer was more likely to purchase a stone knife from him than from his competitor, because he offered a free arrowhead along with his merchandise, had found the secret of motivation by means of premiums. So much for conjecture, however. More tangible evidence, in the form of written documentation, of the vestiges of premium usage during a later period has been found. Detailed studies of the documents have uncovered facts concerning the merchandising practices of the ancient Greeks and Romans. In Athens, long before the Christian era, purchasers of idols of Zeus, Atlas, Hermes, or other Greek gods received incense, lamps, and drinking cups as free gifts or premiums from the merchants. Other Greek businessmen gave bracelets and jewelry to customers who purchased garments priced above a set minimum.[5]

The practice was continued in ancient Rome, where evidence has been discovered indicating that cosmetics dealers gave their customers relatively expensive gold trinkets that reputedly possessed love powers.[6]

FIGURE 1-3. An ad in a trade publication promoting 7-Up's classic upside-down "un-cola" glass, which was a container premium offered to soda-fountain operators. A glass was given to each customer with the purchase of the beverage. This was a form of direct premium. (*Courtesy of NPSE Foundation.*)

The premium, an inducement to buy, is such a natural merchandising device that indications of its use have also been found in an ancient civilization that thrived in China for thousands of years before the birth of Christ.[7]

The practice continued and was brought to the new world, where it flourished. One common example was storekeepers' informal custom of giving children candy or a few gumdrops when they accompanied their parents to the general store. Lollipops were, and still are, given by barbers to children to induce them to have their hair cut or to stop them from crying in the barber's chair. Adults, on the other hand, were lured by the unique inducement known as the "baker's dozen." The customer paid for twelve rolls and received an additional one free. All other things being equal (and even with some not so equal), you can bet your bottom dollar that most customers bought from the baker who offered the thirteen rolls than from the one who sold the standard dozen. Present-day variants of this type of promotion include offering two extra packs of cigarettes or a lighter with each carton, adding a free bar of soap to a package of three, and including a few extra ounces of fruit juice in a can at no additional cost to the customer. In the old days the word *premium* wasn't even used. A small present given by a merchant to the purchaser of an article was known as a *lagniappe*.

A more recent innovation in the use of premiums is the practice of requiring consumers to collect trading stamps, coupons, or other proofs of purchase in order to obtain the premium. This began in 1851, when Benjamin Talbot Babbitt, a pioneer of many marketing practices, introduced individual packaging to the soap industry. He put a wrapper around each cake of soap. However, women, who were accustomed to having their soap cut for them by the grocer from a long bar, rejected the packaging outright. A lesser man might have peeled off the wrappers and let it go at that, but Babbitt, who had a warehouse full of wrapped soap and few takers, came up with a winning idea. He offered a full-color lithograph suitable for framing—a premium—in exchange for twenty-five of his soap wrappers, and sales soared. Babbitt's idea caught on, and in the latter half of the nineteenth century and the first few decades of the twentieth, a number of variants of his premium innovation appeared. Coca-Cola issued series of nature cards; Church & Dwight, manufacturers of baking soda, published sets of bird cards; the Dixie Cup Company put photos of movie stars on the insides of lids of paper ice-cream cups; English and American tobacco companies inserted soldier cards, depicting fighting men from different countries and different periods in history, in packs of cigarettes; and chewing-gum manufacturers sold their wares with the inducement of colorful cards illustrating American Indians of different tribes, World War I airplanes and heroes, and other subjects of interest to young collectors.

This latter form of sales promotion is the mainstay today of the Topps

Chewing Gum Company, which inserts cards featuring color photos of athletes in each pack of gum. The company produces series featuring football stars, baseball stars, and the stars of other popular sports, and it keeps the cards current from season to season. Topps has gotten this promotion down to a science and contracts with entire teams and leagues, as well as with individual sports figures, for exclusive use of their images in chewing-gum promotions. Some of these cards have become collectors items and are worth hundreds of dollars.

The coupons enclosed in cigarette packages and those given by cigar stores were another twist to premium promotions, which sprang from Babbitt's soap wrappers. The recipient saved the coupons until he had collected enough for the premium he had selected in the company catalog. (We say "he" because women didn't smoke in those days. To paraphrase Virginia Slims, Baby hadn't come a long way yet.) The manufacturer of Old Gold cigarettes was among the first to use a coupon plan, and the company

FIGURE 1-4. Window displays are related to other displays and to point-of-purchase advertising. A good window display can be a work of art, designed to attract the attention of passersby and draw them into the store. (*Courtesy of Jack Daniel's.*)

continues the practice to this day. Other cigarette companies that followed suit include Chesterfield, Raleigh, Bel-Air, and Alpine.

Among the advantages accruing to companies that use coupon plans is the brand loyalty of their customers. Coupon collectors rarely change brands.

A natural outgrowth of the coupon plan was the trading stamp. The stamps issued by trading stamp companies allowed the customer a little more freedom of choice than cigarette coupons and the trading stamps produced by individual retailers. With the latter two the consumer is locked in to a particular brand of cigarettes or a specific retail store. However, trading stamps that are issued by independent stamp manufacturers and are sold to a variety of retail stores allow consumers to obtain their trading stamps (all of which can be redeemed at a central source for premiums from the same catalog) from a number of different outlets.

Trade shows are another form of sales promotion, but not a *consumer* type, and are a very positive means of displaying merchandise to dealers and distributors (and sometimes to consumers, as well). These shows have their roots in ancient times. The early existence of trade shows is well documented in a number of passages in the Old Testament. The Book of Esther describes how, for a period of six months, Ahasuerus, King of Persia, "showed the riches

FIGURE 1-5. The Premium Show at the New York Coliseum. This is an important trade show featuring sales promotion items. (*Courtesy of Thalheim Exposition Management Corp.*)

of his glorious kingdom," much as the late Shah of Iran, his recent successor, did in a magnificent display at Persepolis, Iran, in 1971. Further documentation attesting to the early origin of trade shows can be found in Chapter 27 of the Book of Ezekiel, which tells of the city of Tyre and the "silver, iron, tin, and lead, they traded in their fairs." Since Tyre had been established well over 2000 years before the time of the Hebrew prophet who wrote about it, it can be reasonably assumed that trade shows have been around for a long, long time.

Archaeologists have discovered even more tangible evidence relating to the early beginnings of point-of-purchase advertising, yet another type of sales promotion. The ancient Roman city of Pompeii, located in southern Italy near Naples, was a flourishing port and a vacation resort for the wealthy. Without warning, one day in the year 79, it was literally buried alive under tons of cinders, ash, and lava by a sudden volcanic eruption of Vesuvius. Nearly seventeen centuries later, in 1748, archaeologists rediscovered the city. It was so remarkably preserved by the volcanic ash and cinders that furniture and other household items remained practically in their original state, and point-of-purchase advertising, outdoor advertising, and signs were intact and easily read.

Specialty advertising is of much more recent vintage than sampling, premiums, and trade shows, although we can be reasonably sure that some facets of this form of promotion had their roots in antiquity, as well. The first use of advertising specialties in relatively modern times has been traced back to Auburn, New York, and the year 1845. At that time and in that place an insurance salesman attached his business announcements to calendars that he gave away to both existing customers and potential ones. Since that time, specialty advertising has come to include ballpoint pens, key rings, coffee mugs, new kinds of calendars, and scores of other useful, relatively inexpensive items that carry a printed advertising message and are given freely, with no obligation on the part of the recipient.

Sometimes the advertising specialty is related to the donor's business. By their very nature, road maps given by oil companies and recipe booklets distributed by food manufacturers and processors encourage the recipient to use more of the product being promoted by the manufacturer. Unfortunately, since the onset of the energy crisis the petroleum companies have stopped giving away road maps. This void, however, has been filled by enterprising individuals who sell the road maps in coin-operated machines located at gas stations.

It is interesting to note that despite the passage of time and countless innovations, calendars, with their ability to "sell" for a full year, still represent half of the specialty advertising business.

Although, as has been stated earlier, there are many elements in the sales promotion mix, the aforementioned few should suffice to authenticate the historic background of sales promotion and to establish it as an important and long-standing component of business and marketing.

RELATIONSHIP TO MARKETING

To establish the relationship between sales promotion and marketing, we can say that sales promotion is a component of the latter, once removed. However, to make a family analogy, we might say that sales promotion is a grandchild of marketing.

The Marketing Mix

In this respect, a family tree provides an excellent graphic display. Broken down to its principal elements, marketing has four major subdivisions that make up the marketing mix. To simplify the study of the discipline, they have been called the "four P's": *product*, *place* (distribution), *price*, and *promotion*. Each of these may be likened to a son or daughter in the marketing family and can be depicted as the major limbs of the tree. So when we examine the elements of promotion—which are advertising, personal selling, publicity, and sales promotion—we are looking at the branches or twigs on the limb: the next generation (the grandchildren) of marketing, known in the trade as the *promotion mix* and also as the *tools of selling*.

Marketing itself has been defined in the simplest of terms. In essence it is the movement or passage of goods and services through the channels of distribution from the producer to the ultimate consumer—you.

It is the function of the elements of the promotion mix, including sales promotion, to facilitate or speed the journey of those goods or services along the routes of distribution.

Now we shall explore what they do and how they do it.

Advertising.   The most glamorous elements of the promotion mix are contained in advertising. It is readily known to us through the mass media, which it employs to deliver its message. We see it on TV, in our newspapers and magazines, on outdoor billboards, and in trains, buses, and taxicabs. And we receive it in our mail and hear it on our radios. Although there are others, these, in essence, are the principal media through which advertising informs us and/or attempts to persuade us to do something. Usually we are being asked to buy something, whether it be a product, a service, or an idea.

Advertising is, in fact, the most important means of announcing sales promotions. By definition:

> Advertising is a tool of marketing for communication of ideas and information about goods or services to a group; it employs paid space or time in the media or uses another communication vehicle to carry its message; and it openly identifies the advertiser and his relationship to the sales efforts.[8]

Personal Selling.   While advertising is impersonal and directs its message to a mass market, personal selling, as the term implies, usually involves one saleperson and one customer. However, a number of salespeople can make a presentation to a group representing one company that is a potential buyer, or even to a group of individual buyers representing more than one company.

Personal selling is present at each marketing level, ranging from the salesperson at the local mom-and-pop store through wholesalers' salespeople and manufacturers' sales forces who sell to wholesalers, large retail chains, and other manufacturers. Therefore, at one end of the scale we have the unskilled salesperson who sells a piece of candy for $0.10 and, at the other end, the well-educated, highly skilled sales engineer with an M.B.A. who sells multimillion-dollar computers or four-engine jet aircraft. Taking into account the vast numbers of salespeople at all levels and their salaries, commissions, and expenses in the overall scheme of things, personal selling is more costly than advertising, publicity, and sales promotion, and it commands the biggest share of the promotion dollar.

Personal selling has been defined as:

> The presentation of a product, service, or idea by a salesman in direct contact with his prospect. It covers all types of salesmanship, including telephone selling, and encompasses selling to industry, middlemen, and the ultimate consumer.[9]

Publicity. This element of the promotion mix is in reality an important part of public relations. Public relations has always been considered a tool of management, which calls upon it to interpret and to announce corporate positions and policy as well as to handle consumer, community, employee, and stockholder relations, among other things. While public relations still retains its former management functions, two of its components, publicity and press agentry, play an important role in marketing and in the promotion mix. Publicity, along with advertising, makes known the birth of new products or services and of improvements to them. It accomplishes this end through press releases or news stories sent to the various news and trade media, press conferences, and other media events, and press agentry calls attention to them by other methods.

Along with advertising, publicity is a means of bringing sales promotions to the attention of the public.

Sales Promotion. Essentially, the job of sales promotion, the subject of this book, is exactly what the term implies—the promotion of sales. However, advertising, publicity, and personal selling also promote sales. The definition provided by the American Marketing Association leaves to sales promotion those activities not covered by the other three areas of the promotion mix, as well as various nonrecurring selling efforts that are not ordinarily considered part of marketing. The following is a consolidation of the best definitions of sales promotion, together with some contributions from the author:

Sales promotion consists of all the marketing and promotion activities, other than advertising, personal selling, and publicity, that motivate and encourage the consumer to purchase, by means of such inducements as premiums, advertising specialties, samples, cents-off coupons, sweepstakes, contests, games, trading stamps, refunds, rebates, exhibits, displays, and demonstrations. It is employed, as well, to motivate retailers', wholsalers', and manufacturers' sales forces to sell, through the use of such incentives as awards or prizes (merchandise, cash, and travel), direct payments and allowances, cooperative advertising, and trade shows.

Roger A. Strang, of the University of Southern California, differs with the traditional definitions of sales promotion. He correctly points out that all of them suggest that sales promotion "is a catch-all for all those marketing (promotion) activities which do not fall neatly into advertising, personal selling or publicity."[10] This he believes to be wholly inadequate. The definition he offers is certainly less complicated: "Sales promotions are short-term incentives to encourage purchase or sale of a product or service."[11]

The difference between promotion and sales promotion. By this time it should be perfectly clear that although they are related and the terms are similar, there is a significant difference between promotion and sales promotion. As it has been explained, *sales promotion* is a part or subdivision of promotion. Promotion encompasses all the tools of selling, including sales promotion, and is itself a component of marketing. It is responsible for moving the demand curve upward and to the right by utilizing some or all of the elements of the promotion mix—advertising, personal selling, and publicity, along with sales promotion.

Promotion, then, may be defined as the combined and coordinated efforts of a business, government, political party, nonprofit institution, etc., to sell its goods, services, ideas, or "people." Promotion includes all or any of the tools of selling.

The fine line. While we have been trying to sort out the elements of sales promotion and place each one into its proper, logical niche, it is important to understand that there is often a very fine line dividing the major components of promotion, just as there is a fine line dividing some of the subordinate elements that make up sales promotion. To define sales promotion as consisting of all those promotional efforts which do not belong to advertising, personal selling, or publicity most certainly can add to the confusion and create problems of identity.

Scholars may quibble, for example, over whether specialty advertising is advertising, public relations, or sales promotion. Some claim that point-of-purchase advertising belongs in the category of advertising rather than sales promotion or that trade shows are a part of advertising or personal selling, rather than a part of sales promotion. Others may contend that exhibits and displays, along with the sponsorship of sports and special events, are more closely related to publicity or public relations. Still others hold that direct-mail advertising comes under the aegis of sales promotion rather than advertising. It might also be argued that travel incentives are a form of premium or prize— a service premium rather than a merchandise or product premium. And so it may well be. However, premiums, prizes, and travel incentives still remain under the broad banner of sales promotion.

These arguments notwithstanding, we will settle the question here and now, at least as far as this book is concerned. Trade shows, displays and exhibits, specialty advertising, and point-of-purchase advertising will be considered integral parts of sales promotion and will be thoroughly covered in this volume. And though the sponsorship of sports events might be within the realm of publicity, it has strong sales promotion ramifications and will be discussed as well. On the other hand, direct-mail advertising, an important element of direct marketing, can rightfully be considered a part of advertising and therefore will be left for treatment in the pages of advertising textbooks.

The tools of sales promotion. The reader has already been introduced to most of the elements of the sales promotion mix, but to put them into proper perspective we shall list and describe them here in terms of the specific functions they perform.

The tools of sales promotion are employed primarily by two of the principals of marketing: the manufacturer and the retailer. Although a few of the elements are used in common by each, for the most part the needs of the retailer differ from those of the manufacturer. (Retailers' needs coincide with those of manufacturers when retailers market merchandise on services under their own label, such as A&P's Ann Page products and Sears's Kenmore appliances and Allstate insurance.)

Basically, manufacturers are interested in selling the specific products they manufacture to the wholesaler, to the retailer, and, through them, to the ultimate consumer. The retailer and the wholesaler, on the other hand, want to sell *any* product they carry, and they don't care which manufacturer produced it—unless they, as resellers, are offered inducements by particular manufacturers.

To accomplish these ends, a manufacturer usually engages in three different sales promotion campaigns. One is aimed at inducing the consumer to buy the manufacturer's merchandise at any retail outlet. A second campaign is used to motivate its own salespeople to sell more and to induce wholesalers and retailers to sell its merchandise in preference to the products of other manufacturers. A third effort might be directed at other manufacturers or businesses that are potential users of its products.

In order to influence consumers, manufacturers offer premiums, cents-off coupons, rebates, refunds, samples, sweepstakes, contests, games, point-of-purchase advertising, exhibits, displays, and demonstrations. Campaigns to motivate their own sales forces and those of wholesalers and retailers could include a sales contest based on sales beyond a specified percentage of the previous year's figures, for which the manufacturer would provide incentives in the form of cash, merchandise, or travel. In addition, to woo wholesalers and retailers, manufacturers can offer dealer loaders, trade allowances, business gifts, and push money ("spiffs"), and they can display their wares at trade shows.

Milliken & Company employed a spectacular method of displaying its wares. For close to thirty years the textile manufacturer produced an annual breakfast-show musical extravaganza at New York's Waldorf-Astoria Hotel. In recent years each annual show cost $2 million and featured such movie and TV stars as Ray Bolger, Elke Sommer, Bert Parks, Angela Lansbury, Gwen Verdon, Donald O'Connor, Cyd Charisse, Joel Gray, and Phyliss Diller. Each show, which ran for only thirteen performances during a two-week stand each spring, had an exclusive invited audience of 30,000 ready-to-wear buyers, manufacturers' representatives, and fashion industry executives.

Owens-Illinois, a manufacturer of glass bottles, credits its leadership in glass packaging for soft drinks with "Thirst for Adventures." This innovative sales promotion was a national contest in which bottlers (other manufacturers) created effective retail displays, events, and media campaigns featuring an Owens-Illinois product. There were hundreds of prizes for individuals, and members of the winning bottler's team had a choice of a white-water rafting expedition, an ocean cruise, or a resort vacation.

Retailers' main concerns are to attract consumers to their stores and to encourage them to buy. To this end, like manufacturers, they employ premiums, cents-off coupons, sweepstakes, contests, games, point-of-purchase advertising, and advertising specialties. In addition, retailers can distribute trading stamps.

It should be pointed out that the retailer does not use such sales promotion items as premiums, sweepstakes, contests, and games to encourage the purchase of *specific brands* of products, as the manufacturer does, but rather to encourage overall purchases. For example, a customer may receive a premium from a retailer for total purchases of $35 or more.

Sales promotion which is employed by manufacturers to encourage the movement of products to wholesalers and retailers is called *internal* sales promotion; that which is used to move products from the retailer to the ultimate consumer is known as *external* sales promotion. Internal sales promotion is said to *push* merchandise through the channels of distribution, while external sales promotion *pulls* it through.

SPECIFIC FUNCTIONS OF SALES PROMOTION

As defined, the job of sales promotion has two major functions: (1) to stimulate, encourage, motivate, persuade, and induce people to buy goods and services and (2) to motivate sales personnel to sell. Each of these functions can be further subdivided to fit a number of diverse, yet specific, needs of the individual retailer, wholesaler, or manufacturer, with each function contributing to the overall objective.

To Stimulate Consumers to Buy

1. To increase consumer sales
    a. To increase the frequency of use by present customers
    b. To increase units of purchase
    c. To extend the buying season or use period
    d. To build continuity
    e. To add new customers in the present territory
    f. To add new customers by extending the present territory
    g. To find new uses for a product
    h. To bring traffic to a store
    i. To increase the sale of slow-moving items
    j. To renew interest in a declining product
    k. To add interest to a product that is similar to a competitor's product
2. To foster goodwill
3. To introduce a new brand or product
4. To announce an improvement or change in an established product or its package
5. To counter the sales promotion and marketing activities of a competitor
    a. To meet price competition
6. To determine the effectiveness of consumer advertising
    a. To test the effectiveness of consumer media
7. To increase the effectiveness of consumer advertising
    a. To increase consumers' readership of advertising
    b. To attract consumers' attention

To Motivate Retailers', Wholesalers', and Manufacturers' Sales Forces to Sell

1. To increase sales
    a. To increase the inventories of wholesalers and retailers
    b. To reduce dealer inventories to make room for a new or improved product or package
    c. To gain the cooperation of retailers' and wholesalers' sales personnel
    d. To discourage substitution by retailers and wholesalers
    e. To add impetus to a sales drive
    f. To boost sales of a slow-moving item
    g. To inform retailers' and wholesalers' sales forces of marketing and promotional activities
    h. To boost off-season sales

    i. To increase sales in slow areas

    j. To facilitate the securing of shelf devices and point-of-purchase advertising space from retailers

    k. To add interest to a product that is similar to a competitor's product

2. To train retailers' and wholesalers' sales forces

3. To foster goodwill

4. To introduce a new product

5. To announce an improvement or change in an established product or its package

6. To counter the sales promotion and marketing activities of a competitor

    a. To meet price competition

7. To determine the effectiveness of trade advertising

    a. To test the effectiveness of trade media

8. To obtain a list of potential retail and wholesale customers

9. To increase the effectiveness of trade advertising and sales efforts

    a. To increase retailers' and wholesalers' readership of advertising

    b. To attract retailers' and wholesalers' attention

WHERE IT IS TODAY

Despite the fact that sales promotion has been with us for a long time, only recently has it been recognized as the important element of marketing and promotion strategy that it is. As stated earlier, it presently commands a larger share of the marketing dollar than advertising, and during the last twelve years it has been growing at double the rate of advertising.

Although sales promotion has been characterized as being less organized and less professional than its sibling advertising, it is, according to sales promotion authority William A. Robinson, "coming of age":

> Advertisers are realizing that it takes more than just a nice ad in *Reader's Digest* to attract the customers they need and to make their message stand out from the morass of impressions received every day by the average consumer. More companies are employing marketing communications specialists and sales promotion agencies to accomplish this task.[13]

Robinson also points out that today there is more scientific, long-range planning for sales promotion. Just as has been true of advertising campaigns during the past twenty years or so, sales promotion programs are being subjected to rigorous testing, analysis, and evaluation.[14]

Along with this belated recognition by industry has come interest from among members of the academic community. During 1978 the American Academy of Advertising (AAA), a national professional association of professors of advertising, created a committee to study sales promotion. At the same time the prestigious Marketing Science Institute, in Cambridge, Massachusetts, held conferences on the subject to determine what research was needed to support this long-neglected area of marketing.

Among other things, the results of the AAA committee study on sales promotion showed that more than 82 percent of the colleges and universities surveyed offered courses that covered the subject of sales promotion. While only 5 percent reported teaching courses that dealt primarily with sales promotion, the others said they taught it as part of advertising or marketing. Of equal importance were the responses which indicated that more emphasis should be placed on the teaching of sales promotion and which pointed out the need for an up-to-date textbook (or handbook) on the subject.[15]

Research published by the Marketing Science Institute clearly indicates the tremendous growth of sales promotion and the results of this growth:

> A major conclusion of the study is that there has been a rapid expansion of departments. Almost two-thirds of the surveyed companies had such departments at the division level and 44% of these were established between 1971 and 1977. Like the advertising department, the sales promotion department's role in the planning process was largely consultative and its primary responsibility was to execute promotion programs. However, the more recently established departments were more active in helping to plan sales promotion campaigns, particularly since a number of companies preferred to develop this expertise in-house rather than rely on a sales promotion agency.[16]

Further attesting to the growing importance of sales promotion in both the promotion and the marketing mixes is the fact that today there is hardly a manufacturer of consumer products—ranging from pens and razors to automobiles, recreational vehicles, and houses—that does not cater to the rapidly expanding sales promotion market. Such well-known companies as Eastman-Kodak, Cannon, Van Heusen, Gillette, Bulova, General Electric, General Motors, Hart Schaffner & Marx, Palm Beach, Magnavox, Royal, Rockwell International, and RCA, to name only a few, make their products available for use as premiums; as prizes for sweepstakes, contests, and games; as merchandise redeemable for trading stamps; as business gifts; and as incentive awards for salespeople and dealers. They actively promote these incentive marketing sales by advertising in the trade journals and by publishing catalogs and special price lists (the prices are often the same as wholesalers' or distributors' prices).

A recent innovation in sales promotion, as has already been mentioned, is the reintroduction of rebates and refunds. The reader will note that we say "reintroduction," because that, in effect, is what it is. Rebates and refunds have been around before. In reality they are a form of discount resembling the cents-off coupon. The principal difference is that rebates and refunds are usually of much greater value and are redeemed directly by the manufacturer rather than by the retail store. Another development is the practice of honoring manufacturers' cents-off coupons for 1½ times or twice the printed value. This promotion is being followed sporadically by some supermarket chains. It can be used in lieu of store or retailer cents-off coupons.

SUMMARY

The following list highlights the points of this chapter:

Marketing

Product
Place (distribution) } The Marketing Mix
Price
Promotion

Advertising
Personal selling
Publicity } The Promotion Mix
Sales promotion

a. To induce consumers to buy:
   premiums
   cents-off coupons
   rebates and refunds
   samples
   sweepstakes, contests, and games
   point-of-purchase advertising
   exhibits, displays, and demonstrations
   trading stamps
   advertising specialties

The Sales Promotion Mix

b. To motivate sales personnel to sell:
   sales contests
   incentive travel
   dealer loaders
   business gifts
   allowances
   push money (spiffs)
   trade shows

Sales promotion—an element of promotion, which is in turn a component of marketing—is a very important tool of selling that has been a part of the scene for as long as business itself.

Since it is a composite of many different, and sometimes diverse, elements, sales promotion has until now not been recognized for the powerful economic force that it is. Recent studies, however, have shown that $58 billion—more money than was spent on advertising—was expended on sales promotion during 1981 and that for nearly a decade it has been growing at a much faster rate than advertising.

New interest in sales promotion has also been shown by scholars. A study conducted by the AAA showed that 82 percent of the colleges and universities surveyed teach sales promotion in some form and that a number of them feel that greater emphasis should be given to the subject. One important result of the study was that it indicated the strong need for a textbook that thoroughly covers the subject of sales promotion as a modern practice.

At the same time, the prestigious Marketing Science Institute, which is affiliated with the Harvard Business School, has held a number of conferences on sales promotion and has set up guidelines for further research on the subject.

Sales promotion has become a very complex, sophisticated, and measurable art and science. Unlike the situation in advertising, however, there are relatively few outside sales promotion agencies. There are more than 3500 advertising agencies in the United States, compared with a mere twenty agencies specializing in sales promotion.

ENDNOTES

1. *Marketing Communications Magazine*, September 1982.
2. Ibid.
3. *Travel Age East*, Aug. 2, 1982, p. 4.
4. *Newsweek*, Aug. 2, 1982.
5. William S. Beinecke, Tobe Lecture Series, Harvard University, Cambridge, Mass., Feb. 15, 1962.
6. Ibid.
7. Ibid.
8. Stanley M. Ulanoff, *Advertising in America*, Hastings House, Publishers, Inc., New York, 1977, p. 17.
9. Richard E. Stanley, *Promotion*, Prentice-Hall, Inc., Englewood Cliffs, N.J., 1977, p. 8.
10. Roger A. Strang, "A Note on Issues in Sales Promotion Research," unpublished paper, 1978, p. 2.
11. Ibid.
12. Ulanoff, op. cit., p. 16.
13. William A. Robinson, *100 Best Sales Promotions of 1976/7*, Crain Books, Chicago, 1977, p. 9.
14. Ibid.
15. William B. Goodrich, "Survey on Sales Promotion in Advertising Curriculums," unpublished paper, 1978, pp. 3–5.
16. Roger A. Strang, *The Changing Roles of Promotion Planners*, Marketing Science Institute, Cambridge, Mass., 1978, pp. 37–38.

 Manufacturers' Sales Promotions to Consumers

Manufacturers' sales promotions to consumers are the promotions most familiar to the general public. Since we are all consumers, we benefit from, and are exposed to, these sales promotions. Most of them, like premiums, cents-off coupons, samples, rebates, sweepstakes, contests, and games, fall into the "something-for-nothing" category. (And who doesn't like to get something for nothing?)

In a surprising move, at the beginning of the new model year in October 1982, Chevrolet announced an appealing consumer incentive program. The automobile manufacturer offered free round-trip flights for two on Eastern Airlines to purchasers of new Chevettes and Citations.

Besides the "freebies" and giveaways, there are several other types of manufacturers' sales promotions to consumers. For the most part they tend to announce or call attention to the product or service and its uses. Principal among these are point-of-purchase advertising; exhibits, displays, and demonstrations; and game-show promotions. The latter can also be linked, in a way, to the games, sweepstakes, and contests in the something-for-nothing class.

Another sales promotion technique is the sponsorship of sports events. In this category we have the $400,000 Volvo Masters Tennis Championship. And in golf, alone, PGA tour tournaments are sponsored by Seiko, Isuzu, Honda, USF&G, MONY (Mutual of N.Y.), Manufacturers Hanover, Georgia-Pacific, Miller High Life, Buick, the Bank of Boston, Panasonic, Coors, J.C. Penney, and Chrysler.

With the help of advertising and publicity, together with the mass media, these consumer promotions are designed to pull merchandise through the channels of distribution. In other words, they serve to attract the potential customer to the product or service and to induce that customer to seek it out at the supermarket or other retail outlet.

Premiums:
Versatile Marketing Tools of the 1980s

SUSAN L. FRY
Copublisher/Editor, Premium/Incentive Business Magazine

ROSEANN CAFFARO
Managing Editor, Premium/Incentive Business Magazine

Two different promotions, offering the same premium, can be equally success-ful if, in one case, 250 premiums are redeemed by consumers and, in the other, 5000 are claimed. That's because the promotion planner's goal is not to sell premiums but to market a product by means of a premium offer.

For example, in one promotion a $40 fluorescent lantern was sold through the mail for $25 to consumers who sent in two labels from a jar of barbecue sauce. The relatively costly outdoor-oriented premium didn't have many takers.

But all displays for the barbecue sauce featured an outdoor theme and an actual lantern premium. The premium helped differentiate the barbecue sauce from competitors' products and increased the display's chances of being placed on the supermarket floor, not relegated to the stockroom.

Retailers were happy to take the display lanterns home after the promo-tion ended. This campaign upped display orders—the initial objective of the promotion.

In a second promotion, the lantern was offered free by mail to purchasers of a deluxe sleeping bag, costing $250. The premium made the difference in the buyer's selection of that bag rather than a competitive model.

The $40 suggested retail value of the free lantern also encouraged consumers to trade up from a less expensive bag to realize this savings. Since the promotion planner's goal was to give the product a selling edge over the competition, this program, in which 5000 lanterns were redeemed, was a success.

Premiums can be used to excite the trade, increase coupon redemption, spur multiple purchases, induce trial buys, and define or enhance a product's image. Promotion planners should tell premium suppliers in advance what their goals are. To retain supplier trust, the expected redemption rate should be discussed.

Although some progressive American firms (mainly soap and food companies) began offering premiums in the mid-1800s, it wasn't until after World War II that premium promotions became standard practice for the marketers of most consumer products. New industries, such as the fast-food business, recognized the power of on-the-spot giveaways to build traffic and keep customers coming back. Today, we see point-of-purchase or mail-in offers in car rental agencies and banks.

The unwritten law that mail-in offers should be low-priced was thrown out in about 1972, when Brown & Williamson Tobacco offered a sailboat for $129 in the mail. Nowadays, marketers often allow consumers to charge high-value premiums on their credit cards.

Before discussing major trends in premiums, it is necessary to define the various types of premium promotions. In addition to promotions involving self-liquidators and free mail-in offers, there are at least seven other types. Actual examples, plus definitions, of each of these will be given below. A report on the sums spent on each type of promotion will follow. Then some key trends in the use of these promotions will be examined.

Finally, a step-by-step guide for marketers on how to put together a consumer premium promotion will be presented.

TYPES OF PREMIUMS

In a recent survey of promotion planners, *Premium/Incentive Business Magazine* found that of 218 respondents, 76.1 percent were involved in selecting or testing premiums. The magazine defines a premium as something given away free or at a reduced price, in return for a consumer's performing a specified action—usually the purchase of a product or service.

This definition separates a premium from an advertising specialty, which typically does not require, though it may encourage, a product buy. Proofs of purchase, required by many premium offers, can range from box tops, wrappers, and other trademarks taken from product packages to cash-register receipts, product serial numbers, and Universal Product Code (UPC) symbols.

Package-Related Premiums. Package-related premiums come *with* the product purchased and provide an immediate consumer reward. Such free items may be attached to the outside of packages (*on-pack premiums*) or placed inside packages (*in-pack premiums*). Firms will sometimes turn a new product that they want consumers to sample into an on-pack premium.

When displayed near the product and available free with a purchase, they are called *near-pack premiums*. Near-pack premiums are often incorporated into the same display unit as the product itself. *Container premiums*, the last form of package-related offer, actually hold the promoted product. In this case, the container is different from the product's normal packaging.

In one sales promotion, Father's Day cards were attached to packages of British Sterling gift sets. The on-pack cards were fastened with tabs and slots and could easily be removed by children, who could buy their fathers a present and get a free card at the same time.

About $1 million in videocassette sales can be traced to Mickey Mouse doll in-pack premiums. Valued at $10, the dolls provided Christmas shoppers with an extra present when they bought *A Walt Disney Christmas* videocassette, priced at about $50.

In-pack premiums don't have to be directly related to the product to be successful, as long as the demographics match. A manufacturer of plastic trash bags successfully used Harlequin romance books as in-pack premiums. Buyers of Warner-Lambert's Listermint mouthwash could pick up a free Rand-McNally world map, offered as a near-pack premium, from displays in supermarket health and beauty-aids sections. Promotion planners are still talking about the live goldfish once offered as a near-pack premium by Procter & Gamble.

Container premiums hold the product and function as the product package. Dunkin' Donuts packed twelve sugar cookies into a pumpkin-shaped glass jar for Halloween. A 68 percent display increase was snagged by Summer Sheer hosiery when the manufacturer packaged the stockings in decorative metal canisters.

Continuity Premiums. Continuity premiums come in sets—like glassware or dishes—and motivate consumers to acquire all the pieces in the set over a period of time. Often the first piece is given away free or offered at a very low price, with additional pieces sold at regular prices.

Many supermarkets have offered volumes of an encyclopedia as a continuity promotion. Consumers must return to the store each week to build a complete set. The forerunner of continuity promotions is the trading stamp. Shoppers collect books of stamps and redeem them for premiums shown in catalogs.

An offshoot of the continuity concept is the premium catalog, used by such marketers as 7-Up, General Foods, and Philip Morris. The latter has issued a premium catalog filled with items—some costing hundreds of dollars—tied in with its Marlboro Country advertising theme.

Coupon plans are another form of continuity program. Betty Crocker coupons, redeemable for an array of tableware items, have been placed on General Mills brands since the 1930s. Brown & Williamson recently doubled the value of coupons included on packs and in cartons of its Raleigh and

Belair cigarette brands. The company distributes about 2 billion coupons annually, millions of which are redeemed for merchandise at its redemption center.

Supermarket tape promotions offer one or more premium items in return for cash-register tapes totaling a specific amount. Usually that amount is large enough to make the tape plan pay for itself, since the store profits from extra buying volume week after week.

Referral Premiums. Referral premiums are handed out to consumers by salespeople for referring potential buyers to them. National Home Life Assurance gave bronze medallions to policyholders in return for the names of friends who might be interested in insurance policies.

Point-of-Purchase Premiums. Point-of-purchase premiums are not related to the product package. They are given away, or self-liquidated, at the point of sale. Since the planner's goal is to attract customers to the retail store, these premiums are also called *traffic builders*. Magic King plastic toys, given out with a purchase at a Burger King restaurant, are point-of-purchase premiums.

Hostess Premiums, "Door-Opener" Premiums, and "Bounce-backs." The direct selling industry often employs hostess premiums to thank consumers for holding selling parties in their homes. Person-to-person salespeople may use door-opener premiums to reward potential buyers for letting them into their homes. Bounce-backs are additional premiums that consumers receive with the delivery of a premium they have requested. Bounce-backs are usually offered by mail in conjunction with the delivery of free or self-liquidated items.

SPENDING FOR CONSUMER PREMIUMS

Spending for consumer premium offers, as defined above, amounted to more than $5.3 billion in 1981. That was just about 34 percent of spending tracked by *Premium/Incentive Business Magazine* for premiums and incentives of all kinds. (Clearly, almost two-thirds of incentive expenditures go for offers the consumer never sees: sales incentives; dealer, distributor, and retailer incentives; business gifts; and employee incentives. Total spending for premiums and incentives, in 1981, as reported by *Premium/Incentive Business Magazine*, was $15.6 billion, including just under $2 billion for travel incentives.)

How did marketers allot their consumer premium dollars in 1981? When spending on these offers is taken alone, the pie splits as shown in Figure 2-1.

Self-liquidators accounted for 31.4 percent of consumer premium spending in 1981. Continuity programs took 19.2 percent of the pie, with an additional 7.6 percent allotted for trading stamps. Sweepstakes and contests attracted 13.5 percent of marketers' 1981 consumer premium budgets, while package-related offers (on-pack, in-pack, near-pack, and container premiums) accounted for 10.5 percent. Other premiums given at the point of purchase cost a flat 10 percent of the composite consumer premium budget for all those surveyed. Free mail-in offers accounted for 4.5 percent of spending, the least

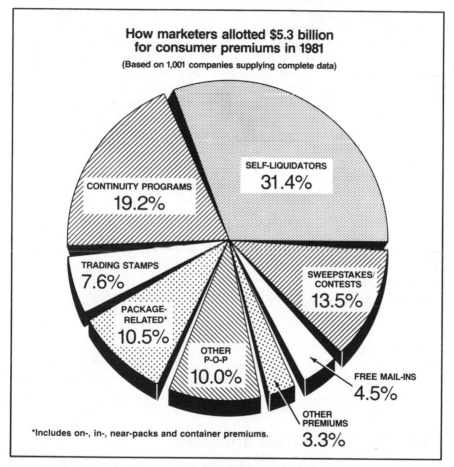

FIGURE 2-1.   How marketers allotted $5.3 billion for consumer premiums in 1981. (*Courtesy of* Premium/Incentive Business Magazine, *A Gralla Publication.*)

amount budgeted for any of the tactics defined. All "other premiums," which include hostess gifts, door-opener and referral premiums, and some bank premiums, accounted for just 3.3 percent of the 1981 consumer premium expenditures pie.

A breakdown of consumer premium spending, projected to the universe of marketers using such promotions, is given in Table 2-1. The growth of each tactic from 1980 to 1981, with projections for 1982, is also tracked.

Spending for self-liquidators amounted to more than $1.6 billion in 1981, with a projected percent increase in 1982. (See Table 2-1.)

Marketers anticipated an 8.5 percent increase in their spending for continuity programs in 1982, bringing expenditures to more than $1.8 billion by year-end. While trading stamps accounted for just under $406 million in marketers' 1981 budgets, the 10.5 percent boost in 1982 budgets for trading stamps is the highest for all premiums except sweepstakes and contests. Budgets for package-related premiums, while marked by an 11 percent boost in 1981 over 1980 levels, were expected to grow just 3 percent in 1982.

TABLE 2-1 Changes in Consumer Premium Spending by Type of Promotion, 1980–1982*

Type of promotion	Expected 1982*		1981	
	Cost, thousands of dollars	Percent change vs. 1981	Cost, thousands of dollars	Percent change vs. 1980
Self-liquidators	$1,826,295	+9.0	$1,675,500	+7.1
Continuity programs	1,112,201	+8.5	1,025,070	+8.6
Trading stamps	448,679	+10.5	405,997	+9.5
Sweepstakes and contests	840,603	+16.6	720,929	+10.9
Package-related premiums†	577,593	+3.0	560,770	+11.0
Other POP premiums	564,423	+6.2	531,472	+10.2
Free mail-in premiums	249,761	+2.9	242,722	+0.4
Other premiums	187,751	+5.3	178,301	+6.4
Total	$5,807,306	+8.7	$5,340,761	+8.4

* As of April 1982.
† Includes in-pack, on-pack, near-pack, and container premiums.
SOURCE: *Premium/Incentive Business Magazine*, A Gralla Publication.

WHY SELF-LIQUIDATORS ARE GROWING

Self-liquidators have shown the most consistent growth rate since *Premium/ Incentive Business Magazine* began tracking consumer premiums in 1974. One reason for this may be that self-liquidators, by definition, pay for themselves, at least in terms of the cost of merchandise offered. (Often, advertising of self-liquidator offers is budgeted separately.)

Consumers are usually asked for enough cash to cover a self-liquidator's cost to the promotion planner, plus shipping and handling charges. The original cost may be way below the usual retail price because the planner bought in quantity. The key is to offer premiums with a high perceived value so that consumers will feel they are saving money by ordering them, or to offer exclusive merchandise or items that will boost the self-image of the recipient.

Buyers of two rolls of Bounty paper towels, two bars of Safeguard soap, and one box of Bounce fabric softener could send away for an Atari video computer system with three game cartridges for $149. The average retail price was $194, so consumers were offered a $45 savings.

The majority of self-liquidator offers are not priced so high. In fact, many marketers resist a price tag higher than $5, depending on the retail price of the product being promoted and its purchase frequency. Pillsbury, for instance, self-liquidated milk mugs for one Slice 'n Bake cookies proof of purchase and a milk-carton stub. Shaped like the Pillsbury Dough-Boy character, the mug provided Pillsbury with ad reinforcement, while the milk-purchase tie-in gave grocers two products to sell in a single promotion.

On the other hand, self-liquidator prices of $20 or less have become common in the marketplace. Some recent winners have included credit-card-size calculators, hot-air corn poppers, and stereo or radio headphones, priced from $9 to $39, with appropriate product proofs of purchase.

TEN TRENDS TO WATCH IN CONSUMER PREMIUMS

Consumer premium promotion, and indeed all promotion, has become more sophisticated in the past ten years. Despite the rise of couponing (accounting for more than half of all consumer promotion spending today), marketers continue to seek out cheap, measurable, and effective ways of moving products to consumers. Premiums, in many cases, fill the bill admirably.

What's new in consumer premiums? The following trends, recently identified by *Premium/Incentive Business Magazine*, should be considered when planning promotions:

1. Rising value of self-liquidators
2. Higher proof-of-purchase requirements for free mail-in offers
3. More options for consumers to combine cash and proofs of purchase when ordering premiums
4. Joint sponsorship of premium promotions by several brands or firms
5. Use of telecommunications with premium offers
6. Use of premiums by industries that are new to this promotion tactic, such as real estate and transportation (airlines and car rental agencies)

7. Use of institutional gift certificates as premiums
8. More integrated premium promotions, involving both the trade and consumers
9. More use of personalization or customizing (e.g., a company logo) on premium merchandise
10. Promotion of premiums based on licensed properties

Some of these trends are discussed below.

Rising Value of Self-Liquidators.   In general, prices of self-liquidators had climbed to about $15 by the 1980s. But premiums in the hundreds of dollars could also be found. Sending in the inner seals from two jars of Folger's instant coffee qualified consumers to order a Magic Chef microwave oven by mail for $239.99. This represented a $100 savings.

Higher Proof-of-Purchase Requirements.   More proofs of purchase are being required to redeem free mail-in offers. This makes the consumer "work harder" to receive the item. Del Monte offered free Country Yumkin plush toys for any combination of sixty labels from Del Monte, Hawaiian Punch, and Chun King products. The toys were shaped like fruit, reinforcing the claim of the nutritious nature of Del Monte foods.

Increased Options for Consumers.   Consumers were also given more options in terms of putting together combinations of sums of money and proofs of purchase to receive a premium. For example, 9-Lives cat food offered a "pocket shopper" that helped organize coupons and shopping lists. Cat lovers could receive this premium free with fifty labels, for $1.95 and twenty labels, or for $3.95 and no labels. A $0.50 postage and handling charge was imposed in all cases.

Joint Sponsorship of Promotions.   A fourth trend has been increasing sponsorship of premiums by a combination of brands or firms. If brands combine budgets, they can make a bigger advertising and promotional splash and thus boost premium redemptions and sales.

Campbell's "Trainload of Good Foods" promotion offered consumers a limited-edition HO scale train set, valued at over $75, for $25.95. To receive the set, consumers had to send eight different proofs of purchase from nine Campbell, Franco-American, and Swanson products. The promotion broke in early October, and consumers had to order by October 31 to ensure Christmas delivery of the train set. This spurred quick purchases of the sponsoring brands.

Use of Telecommunications with Premium Offers.   During the 1980s, use of telecommunications may become commonplace in connection with premium offers, enabling consumers to communicate with promotion sponsors by telephone to order premiums or to obtain a qualifying word or phrase that must appear on their premium order blanks.

In the sweepstakes area, Captain Crunch cereal used a toll-free telephone number so that consumers who found treasure maps packed in their cereal packages could call to find out whether they had won Huffy bicycles.

Use of Premiums by Industries New to the Tactic. A sixth trend has been the adoption of premiums by industries new to this promotion tactic. A purchaser of a Park Ridge condominium in New York City received a free Chrysler LeBaron convertible. In Arizona, anyone who bought a Heritage Terrace home on a certain day was given a free Apple II personal computer system.

Air Florida passengers were surprised to receive books of S&H stamps on intrastate flights. Car rental agencies competed in offering calculators, luggage, and gift certificates.

Use of Institutional Gift Certificates as Premiums. Another trend has been the use of institutional gift certificates offered as premiums. These have included certificates for Wendy's fast-food items, for Sears products and services, and for AT&T telephone equipment and services. Wendy's certificates are redeemable for meals at Wendy's outlets, Sears certificates can be exchanged for merchandise at any Sears store, and AT&T certificates can be used to pay a phone bill or order a new telephone.

More Integrated Promotions. An eighth trend has been the integration of premium promotions within a larger framework. Premiums have been increasingly backed by trade incentives. For example, French's mustard offered a self-liquidator in the form of a Yogi Bear plush toy. The R. T. French firm also adapted its squeeze bottles to look like Hanna-Barbera characters. Its salespeople were inspired by these characters' appearance at the promotion kickoff meeting. Employees participated in a coloring contest, with large plush toys as prizes. Ads and point-of-purchase displays repeated the character theme.

SETTING UP A PREMIUM PROMOTION

Setting up a premium promotion can take as long as a year. Planners should resist the temptation to get an offer on the shelves immediately if sales start to dip. The legal and financial consequences of a poorly planned promotion can be disastrous.

On the other hand, well-planned and well-executed promotions can join with advertising to boost product sales. There are at least twenty steps that promotion planners should consider taking when setting up a premium campaign:

1. Set promotion objectives in terms of measurable results.
2. Decide what type of premium offer will achieve those results.
3. Talk to suppliers and premium representatives when choosing the premium item. Often, suppliers can offer case histories of how successful certain items were in former campaigns. Check retail prices personally.
4. Estimate redemption. Redemption is based on such factors as the premium's cost, the shelf life of the product, buyer demographics, the premium's perceived value, how the premium is advertised, trade support, and the cost of the product.
5. Consult an attorney. Different industries have their own regulations limiting the premiums they can offer. For example, liquor firms may not ask for proofs of purchase in a nationwide promotion. Legal advice is also needed to avoid running afoul of regulations like those concerning the size of the word *free* in premium ads and the way information concerning any handling charges must be stated.
6. Make sure that your factory can accommodate the necessary packaging changes.
7. Consult an advertising or sales promotion agency about designing a campaign theme involving ads, displays, and trade incentives.
8. If possible, pretest the premium. Except for fad items, most premiums will remain popular during the testing period. Tests can consist of focus-group interviews, shopper panels at malls, or regional roll-outs of the actual promotion.
9. Draw up a marketing plan that covers the promotion's goals and execution and clearly defines responsibilities for each phase of the campaign.
10. Put together an order form for consumers. Be sure to state such restrictions as "Offer good while supplies last" and to limit the number of premiums in the ad copy. Otherwise, the requests for free mail-in offers or even self-liquidators could be so great that the budget is left in ruins. Also state the expiration date of the offer. Order forms should contain the sponsoring firm's address and ample room for consumers to write in their own addresses. All terms of the offer should be specified on this form.
11. Arrange for fulfillment (processing and delivery) of the premiums. Many fulfillment houses offer this service and will also warehouse premiums to be shipped.
12. Set up a procedure to deal with customer complaints concerning the premium.
13. When committing for the premiums, arrange for reordering and for a take-back privilege, if possible. Set a launch date.

14. Launch the promotion to the trade at a sales meeting.

15. Start consumer advertising of the premium.

16. Make sure that displays are being erected in stores and that specially marked packages are indeed on the shelves.

17. Keep track of orders sent to the fulfillment house to see whether reordering will be necessary.

18. As orders wind down, tabulate the promotion's results in terms of sales increases, displays erected, premiums redeemed, or units shipped. The introduction of scanning devices in supermarkets may soon help grocers, and in turn manufacturers, calculate the impact of a premium program more quickly and accurately.

19. Evaluate the success of the campaign against the original objectives.

20. Draw up a case history as a guide for future promotions.

3 Promoting with Cents-off Coupons

MICHAEL J. COX

Vice President and Director of Marketing, Donnelley Marketing, a Company of The Dun & Bradstreet Corporation

Cents-off coupons have been used for many years by packaged goods manufacturers to generate trial and stimulate purchases of branded products. As far back as 1895, an entrepreneur named C. W. Post, of Battle Creek, Michigan, was offering such an incentive to consumers for purchasing a ready-to-eat breakfast cereal he had invented and was marketing under the interesting, if somewhat unusual, name of Grape Nuts.[1]

The device the Post Company chose was a "certificate" that consumers clipped or tore from a newspaper or magazine advertisement and then took to a grocer. The certificate entitled the bearer to a $0.01 reduction on the posted retail price of a box of Grape Nuts, and it also assured the retailer of reimbursement for that amount from the manufacturer in return for going along with the plan.

The premise was simple, the promise was straightforward, and everyone stood to gain from taking part in the transaction: Consumers got price breaks for trying an item they might not otherwise have been disposed to buy; grocers sold more Grape Nuts because their customers were asking for it by name; and C. W. Post was able to build sales volume, increase market share, and add new trade outlets for his product.

COUPONING TODAY

Although there have been profound technological changes down through the years in the way we market consumer goods and services in the United States, the essential ingredients of a cents-off coupon promotion—the process by

which the promotion works and the benefits that can accrue to its participants, if the promotion is properly conceived, planned, and executed, of
course—are exactly the same as they were twenty, fifty, or even one hundred
years ago.

Cents-off couponing in the 1980s is but one of several weapons in the
modern marketing manager's sales promotion arsenal. The development of
research and testing techniques, the ability of broadcast and print media to
create brand awareness on a massive scale, the development of manufacturing
and distribution systems for moving products to the consumer, and the
computer's capability of processing and manipulating large amounts of data
in order to select target audiences—all these are factors that actually increase
the potential of a coupon to influence consumer purchasing behavior today.
That, after all, is still couponing's primary purpose, whether the "product"
couponed is a breakfast cereal or an airplane ticket: to trigger sales action that
might not otherwise occur. That is what this chapter is all about. (See Figure
3-1.)

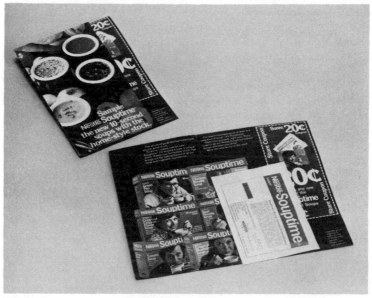

FIGURE 3-1. A cents-off coupon together with a sample of
the product. (*Courtesy of Donnelley Marketing.*)

POPULARITY AND GROWTH

Coupons have always been popular with consumers because they offer something special: immediate cash savings. Retailers like them because they encourage the consumer to make a purchase decision and to act on that decision sooner rather than later or not at all. Manufacturers like them because they appeal directly to the shopper, creating a demand that effectively pulls a product through the distribution pipeline; they allow manufacturers to rely less heavily on the retail trade to help push a product through with cooperative advertisements and store displays, in return for case allowances and other forms of promotions aimed at dealers and sales forces.

The retail trade plays a pivotal role in the couponing process and benefits both directly and indirectly from its cooperation. For honoring coupons almost as a form of legal tender and forwarding them to redemption centers and clearinghouses to be tallied up in reports to the manufacturer, the retail grocery trade alone is paid more than $230 million a year (based on 3 percent redemption × 100 billion × $0.08 per coupon). And there is strong evidence to suggest that couponing adds to retail store sales volume—and profits—by stimulating consumers to make "unplanned" purchases of food and nonfood items with the money saved.[2]

WHAT COUPONS DO

Couponing gives the manufacturer control and flexibility in terms of when, where, and how often a promotion should take place and how large it needs to be to achieve the desired sales and profit objectives for the featured brand. Couponing also serves as a hedge against price controls or guidelines by allowing the manufacturer leeway to competitively lower the price of its products when and where necessary without permanently affecting its overall pricing structure.

Consumer appeal and manufacturer control are the two major reasons for the phenomenal growth of couponing in the United States in recent years. That growth, both in terms of absolute volume and as a percentage of all forms of consumer promotion activity, has been steady since 1973.[3] Through the 1950s and the 1960s couponing regularly accounted for something between one-fifth and one-third of all manufacturer-sponsored consumer-brand sales promotions, sharing the limelight with such other devices as cash discounts, sampling, contests, sweepstakes, and premium offers.[4]

The early 1970s, however, ushered in a new era. It is no accident that the coupon "explosion" that started in 1975 had its origin in the first years of that decade—a period in which high unemployment, inflation, an economic recession, a sudden worldwide oil shortage, and government-mandated wage and price controls (1972) became dominant features of the economic landscape. For the manufacturer, the consumer, and the retailer as well, cents-off couponing had become serious business indeed.

As Table 3-1 shows, by 1981 there were more than 100 *billion* manufacturers' coupons in circulation (not to mention the countless millions circulated by the retail trade), compared with less than half that amount as recently as 1976.[5] Four out of five American families were using them, and more than 1000 packaged goods manufacturers routinely included them in their marketing mix, along with media advertising and trade promotion.[6] From 1978 through 1981, in fact, executives of the nation's leading food manufacturing companies were steadily increasing budget allocations for consumer promotions, of which cents-off couponing had become the largest component, while allocations for media advertising remained steady, and those for trade promotions actually declined during the period.[7]

TABLE 3-1 Percent of Coupons Distributed by Medium*

Solo ROP			
Daily newspaper	36.2	31.1	27.3
Co-op (all)	16.1	17.1	17.7
Sunday paper	9.5	9.0	7.3
Sunday FSI	14.9	18.4	26.2
Magazine	12.2	13.3	11.8
Direct mail	3.2	3.4	3.3
In pack and on pack	7.9	7.7	6.4
Total	100.0	100.0	100.0

* Coupons distributed: 1979, 81.2 billion; 1980, 90.6 billion; 1981, 102.4 billion.
SOURCE: Nielsen Clearing House, Clinton, Iowa.

Coupon promotions work. To understand how they work, and to develop a set of principles to put that understanding to practical use, requires an examination of the various types of coupon delivery systems in use today, a look at their capabilities, and some general commentary on how to mold that information into a strategy for meeting objectives and obtaining results.

TYPES OF COUPONS

There are several types of couponing available to the marketer; each has its strengths and efficiencies. Some offer advantages that relate to specific marketing needs and objectives, while others offer a combination of features whose collective impact has a general effect on brand sales performance. And various coupon vehicles can be used in combination with one another to increase or ensure market coverage.

Perhaps the simplest way to categorize coupon promotional alternatives is according to the method by which they are distributed. There are five basic types of coupons: newspaper coupons, magazine coupons, direct-mail coupons, package-delivered coupons, and coupons delivered direct to the consumer.

Newspaper Coupons

There are four ways to get coupons for a brand into the hands of a newspaper buyer. These are discussed below.

- One is through solo run-of-press (ROP) offers, which in 1981 accounted for about one in five (27 percent) of all manufacturers' coupons circulated in the United States. ROP coupon offers are printed in black and sometimes a second color on the actual page of a newspaper and thus go out to the newspaper's entire circulation, usually on "best food days" (Wednesday or Thursday in most cities), when retailers place their own food ads. Low cost, short lead time (as little as two days), and the fact that an advertisement can be constructed around the coupon are the major features of solo ROP.

- Newspaper "co-op" programs bring a number of manufacturers together to share the cost of one or more ROP pages of coupon offers, distributed on best food days. The cost is slightly lower than that of solo ROP, but the lead time is longer because the sections are brokered, produced, and syndicated far in advance by companies specializing in such activities. The redemption rates tend to be higher than solo ROP redemption rates, probably because the large group of money-saving offers in the newspaper's food section attracts regular consumer attention.

- Sunday supplements such as *Parade*, *Family Weekly*, and *Sunday Metro* are color magazines distributed with Sunday newspapers. These three magazines have the highest circulation of all such supplements and are syndicated among hundreds of dailies across the country. There are also several major local and regional independent Sunday supplements. Coupons can be printed either on the page or in "pop-up" form (printed on heavier stock and glued onto a supplement page). In addition to full color, Sunday supplements offer the advertiser massive coverage with a single media buy. A single coupon promotion appearing in a combination of Sunday supplements can reach a national audience of more than 50 million people—all on the same day.[8]

- Free-standing inserts (FSIs) in 1983 surpassed newspaper solo ROP in terms of coupon distribution by volume (Table 3-1). In 1981 they accounted for about 26 percent of the total. Two years earlier FSIs accounted for less than half of the solo ROP share. FSIs are preprinted in four colors on quality paper stock and are distributed in about 100 Sunday newspapers. Recently they became available on best food days. FSIs offer the user magazine-quality graphics, major market selection, and a wide audience reach of more than 38 million households. The bulk of such inserts are co-ops put together by the four major FSI suppliers. Multiproduct manufacturers occasionally publish their own FSIs.

In general, newspaper-circulated coupons—from solo ROP at the bottom end of the cost scale to FSIs at the top—offer broad coverage at reasonable cost, with lead times that vary from a few days, for solo ROP, to several months, for FSIs. Disadvantages include varying degrees of skipped and duplicated coverage, waste, little audience selectivity, and a high level of coupon misredemption due to a lack of control over the distribution. For quick, mass circulation at low cost, however, they can be very effective.

Newspaper Coupons Offer:

- Market selectivity
- Broad or narrow distribution
- Program flexibility
- Precise timing
- Low distribution costs
- Frequency
- Co-op opportunities
- Retail trade tie-ins

Sunday-Supplement and FSI Coupons Offer:

- Full-color graphics
- Controlled timing
- Market selectivity
- Local, regional, or national options
- Concentrated coverage
- Weekend in-home readership
- Moderate distribution costs

Magazine Coupons

Coupons circulated in consumer magazines, both the on-page and the pop-up varieties, account for about 10 percent of total coupon distribution volume in this country. Magazines offer higher-quality graphics than newspapers, as well as better audience targeting and selectivity, since magazines have editorial content, or "environment," which determines a magazine's audience.

Redemption rates for magazine pop-up coupons are higher than those for FSIs (Figure 3-2). The opportunity for misredemption is much lower than in any other type of newspaper distribution. The trade-offs are a higher cost per 1000 and longer lead times—from one to two months or even more—tied to editorial production. Since retail impact is slow, there is very little opportunity for merchandising magazine coupon promotions with the retail trade because magazines do not have the saturation levels of other media.

Magazine Coupons Offer:

- Full-color graphics
- Editorial environment
- Audience selectivity
- Regional participation
- Pass-along readership
- Longer exposure
- Pop-up coupon option

Direct-Mail Coupons

Direct-mail coupons can be delivered either "solo" or on a co-op basis. This medium can be expensive compared with others, because of added costs for postage and such predelivery necessities as folding, inserting, addressing, and presorting according to mail-carrier routes. However, there are several factors that tend to offset the expense. Direct-mail coupons have the highest redemption rate of all coupons (Figure 3-2). Second, the *quality* of redemptions is higher because there is virtually no misredemption. Postal delivery eliminates duplication and makes organized coupon fraud virtually impossible. The audience selectivity is highly flexible and precise because mailing lists are pulled from a computerized data bank by specific geographic criteria and

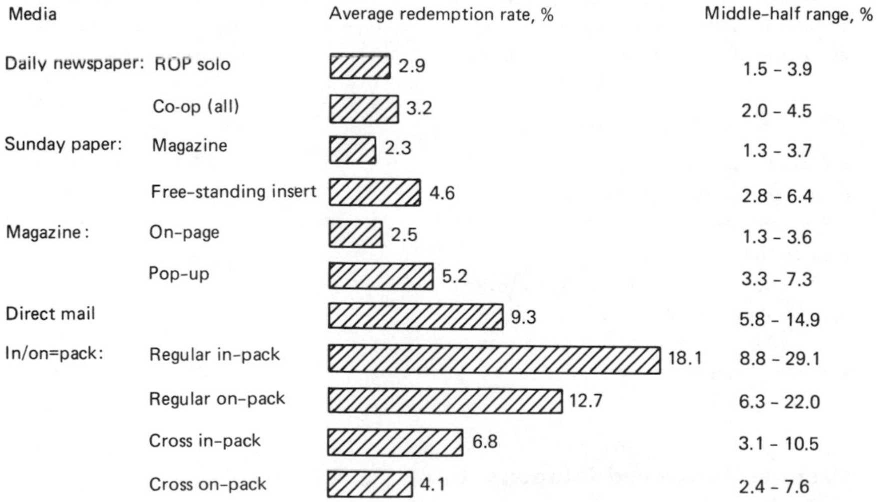

Media		Average redemption rate, %	Middle–half range, %
Daily newspaper:	ROP solo	2.9	1.5 – 3.9
	Co-op (all)	3.2	2.0 – 4.5
Sunday paper:	Magazine	2.3	1.3 – 3.7
	Free-standing insert	4.6	2.8 – 6.4
Magazine :	On-page	2.5	1.3 – 3.6
	Pop-up	5.2	3.3 – 7.3
Direct mail		9.3	5.8 – 14.9
In/on=pack:	Regular in-pack	18.1	8.8 – 29.1
	Regular on-pack	12.7	6.3 – 22.0
	Cross in-pack	6.8	3.1 – 10.5
	Cross on-pack	4.1	2.4 – 7.6

FIGURE 3-2. Coupon redemption rates by media—grocery products.
(*Courtesy of A. C. Nielsen Co.*)

demographic characteristics, e.g., age, income, education, and family size. In effect, coverage can be tailored to fit practically any geographic area, on demographic target.

Solo mailings are particularly useful for companies that need a high impact within very specific sales territories or trading areas, such as auto dealerships, banks and thrift institutions, agencies that supply and service household appliances, and various franchises like fast-food restaurants and hardware stores. For such businesses the coupons can serve one or more purposes: They can promote sales of a specific product, build floor traffic at a particular location (in the case of a premium or limited-time discount offer), and, when used as a direct-response mechanism, build customer prospect lists or even sell goods or services directly. Co-op direct-mail couponing, on the other hand, is more widely used by the manufacturers of grocery products, health and beauty aids, and various nonfood items sold in supermarkets, in chain and independent drugstores, and in mass merchandising outlets. The typical direct-mail co-op has from twenty to thirty-five participating manufacturers. The co-op "ensemble"—typically an envelope full of money-saving coupons printed with high-quality graphics on easy-to-use separate sheets—gets a high degree of consumer attention.

As with other media offering quality graphics and co-op arrangements, lead times are long: ten to twelve weeks at a minimum. And, since product-category exclusivity is of major importance for participating brands, reservations in certain categories must be made as much as a year in advance. Audience reach can be as high as 45 million households, or more than half of all households in the United States. Trial-size product samples can accompany coupons, adding enormous impact to new-product introductions.

Direct-Mail Coupons Offer:

- Direct appeal to consumers
- Demographic selectivity
- Specific area or market focus
- Coverage flexibility
- Consumer attention and awareness
- Total control of distribution
- Consumer, trade, and sales tie-ins
- Product-category exclusivity
- High redemption rates

Package-Delivered Coupons (In/on Pack)

There are several varieties of package-delivered coupons. The most common are those found either stuffed inside or printed on the outside of the product package. "Cross-ruff" coupons are in-pack or on-pack coupons offering cents off the price of a different product, for example, a coupon for a safety razor on a package of blades. "High-value" packs contain coupons for several products, and "instant" coupons are stuck on the outside of the package so that they are immediately redeemable for cents off the posted retail price. All such devices enhance the value of the purchased product at little or no distribution cost to the manufacturer. Each serves a specific promotional objective, and—except for in-pack and on-pack coupons, whose purpose is to generate subsequent or repeat purchases—all forms enjoy a relatively high (11 percent) average redemption rate. One shortcoming is that the coupons reach mostly current users and are therefore poor trial generators. Impact is long-term, and there is little or no merchandising power.

Package-Delivered Coupons Offer:

- Target-audience focus
- Repeat-buying stimulus
- Brand-loyalty reward
- Controlled financial liability
- Low distribution cost
- High response rate
- Point-of-purchase merchandising
- A selling tool to the trade

Direct-to-the-Consumer Coupons

If a cents-off coupon can be handed to practically anyone, in any place, and at any time, why go to the expense of hiring crews of people to distribute coupons by hand when there are a number of alternatives for reaching much larger audiences at a substantially lower cost? The answer is that coupon handouts make the most sense in terms of total control over who gets the coupons and when and where they are distributed.

Like product samples, coupons can be distributed in the store, near the store, from house to house, at high-traffic pedestrian areas, and at special events. In fact, coupons and product samples are often distributed in the same brand promotion to generate trial and provide the consumer with a purchase incentive. When distributed in the store or at special events, personal-contact couponing combined with the distribution of product samples or a product demonstration adds up to a three-dimensional "event" that can move many cases of a product in a very short period of time. Retailers are eager to lend their support because results are quick, dramatic, obvious, and measurable. In-store co-op couponing, in the form of booklets handed out on high-volume shopping days, is one way to achieve results at a lower cost than is involved in solo distribution.

Near-store couponing offers the manufacturer a larger audience and increased selectivity; e.g., distributors can hand the coupons to women only, to teenagers, or to any visually identifiable category of recipients. Users of the product being couponed can be separated from nonusers through a series of questions. (See the section on self-selecting promotions.)

Coupons, like product samples, can be targeted to large audiences with generally similar economic or behavioral characteristics (e.g., train and airline commuters) at specific times of the day, and they can be handed out at events that, by their nature (country-music festivals, jazz concerts, state fairs, and sports events, for example), attract audiences with fairly similar lifestyles, incomes, ethnic backgrounds, and purchasing behavior. To be most effective, personal-contact couponing should be combined with product sampling, but if the face value of the coupon is high and if the retail outlets are nearby, then the coupon will produce dramatic results.

COUPON REDEMPTION

As we shall see later on, coupon redemption is not merely a factor in the sales promotion equation; it is the most important factor of them all, not only because the main objective of the promotion usually is to get consumers to respond, but also because the amount, speed, and pattern of response can tell us some very important facts. The amount of response over a period of time tells us how much the promotion cost to deliver the sales. The speed of response will tell us whether we provided enough lead time and whether the coupons were "in sync" with the advertising campaign and trade promotion activities. The pattern of response, in turn, will give valuable insights into which sales territories, trading areas, neighborhoods, cities, metropolitan areas, or geographic regions responded best to a particular coupon offer or couponing medium.

Among the factors that affect redemption rates for coupons in all media are the following.

Distribution Control. The more steps there are between printing the coupon and getting it into the hands of the consumer, and the longer the time span, the greater the likelihood that the coupon will be lost or misplaced, that there will be a delay in its use, or that it will be improperly used. Beware of printing overruns, unrecorded coupon shipments, unverified receipts, and unexplained interruptions or delays in the handling of bulk quantities of coupons. Some companies go so far as to require a security bond from printers, shippers, and handlers.

Type of Audience Reached. Some couponing schemes are highly selective, and when the "right" sales prospect is reached, redemption rates go up. One example of such selectivity is what marketers call the "self-screening" aspect of handing out coupons to consumers in or near a supermarket. The person who distributes the coupons (and who may also be handing out product samples at the same time) is able to decide who will receive the promotional offer. The distributor can direct the offer primarily to men, to women, or to middle-aged people, for example, and through simple questioning can even determine users and nonusers of a particular product, such as a pet food ("Pardon me, do you own a dog?"). The tendency is for costs to rise along with selectivity, while mass coverage aims at generating redemptions through sheer volume and low unit cost.

Product Usage. If your product is something which practically everyone uses, like toothpaste or soap, then couponing can have a dramatic effect on sales, because there are already so many users in the marketplace. Attention need be directed only to what face value is offered and how to fill the distribution pipeline. It is when usage is less broad for the category that couponing has to work harder. This is particularly true for a product that is completely new—and creates a new category. Coupons work wonders in new-product introductions. Other ingredients, such as product sampling, must be brought into the promotional mix to support the heavy brand-awareness advertising. Extensive trade promotions and consumer promotion will ensure a strong product introduction.

Brand Awareness. The emergence of mass-circulation print and broadcast media as advertising vehicles over the past half century has made it possible for the marketing manager with a large-enough budget and a clever-enough agency to create a considerable amount of awareness practically overnight; it is a matter of total circulation, in the case of print media, or of gross rating points, in the case of broadcast media. However, there is so much advertising in circulation these days that a campaign really has to stand out from the crowd in order to be noticed, remembered, and acted upon.

That's precisely where couponing comes in: to act as a trigger to sales action once brand awareness has been established and the product has been positioned in the consumer's mind. For this reason—the connection between the ad campaign and the coupon offer—successful packaged goods manufacturing companies carry the advertising theme, the concept, the art, and the copy over into their cents-off coupon offers, often creating "mini-ads" in FSIs and direct-mail ensembles.

Brand Loyalty. Because there are so many established brands in almost every product category and because every one of them is competing for market share, today's consumer has become a habitual brand switcher. That's why the marketing manager of today looks not only to brand conquests but also to brand *loyalty*, or repeat purchases, as the twin keys to successful sales performance. Couponing (especially in-pack and on-pack couponing) happens to be the only mechanism that can generate new purchases and, by rewarding brand loyalty, also generate repeat purchases.

Availability at the Retail Level. Suffice it to say that no matter how brilliant the strategy, how creative the ad campaign, or how dramatic and well-timed the coupon offer, if the store manager has not stocked the shelves and the storeroom with the featured brand, it is all for naught. This is the link that retailers as well as manufacturers find most troublesome. When it is missing, everyone loses.

To avoid such situations, you must make sure that the featured brand is "sold in" to the trade and that the coupon promotion is fully merchandised to key buyers, wholesalers, jobbers, and the buying committees of large chain and independent supermarkets, drugstores, and mass merchandising outlets. This can be done through direct contact by the sales force, by mail, and by advertisements in retail trade publications. In relation to the volume of sales that could be affected, the expense can be considered insurance, at the very least, and possibly a very wise investment.

Display Space. A cents-off coupon will "pull" the consumer only so far: usually to the area where other products in your brand's category are on display. If for some reason your brand is not there, consider that shopper to have been conquered on enemy territory. To be truly effective, a couponed product should be given some sort of special consideration by the retailer, unless the container itself is an attention-getter. In addition to its place on the aisle, special displays can be set up for the product at the ends of aisles or in other areas of the store.

Coupon Design. Since most coupons conform to Grocery Manufacturers Association standard sizes, the largest of which is supposed to fit into the bills section of the cash-register drawer, there is little space on the coupon for graphic design. Often there is barely enough space for a headline, the face-value amount, a picture of the product, and the "fine print" spelling out the details. Actually, that's all that really needs to be on the coupon itself. But the art, the copy, and the design of the material surrounding the coupon are a different story. In the case of FSIs, as well as direct-mail coupons delivered on either a solo or a co-op basis, the trend in recent years has been to make the coupon one part of a larger brand advertisement. This creates a dramatic effect, not unlike that of a similarly designed four-color ad appearing in a quality national magazine. In fact, such formats have been known to test higher than magazine ads. (The advertising effect of coupon inserts is discussed more fully below.)

Face-Value/Retail-Price Ratio. There is neither a hard-and-fast rule nor even a rule of thumb as to what the best face-value/retail-price ratio is, and there is not much evidence to suggest that such a ratio would be practical enough to work consistently or that it would apply to a wide-enough range of products if it did exist. There has been an upward trend in face values in recent years, just as there has been in retail prices, so the two are at least loosely connected.[9] For want of a more precise measure, the best kind of estimate to make is one based on experience: What worked last time, and how much did it cost? If there was no last time, then look at other products in the same category: Is it worth the risk to offer a higher face value than the competition, or if the competition is not couponing, can a face value be offered that is just low enough to generate sales while keeping costs in check?

Coupon Usage. In some parts of the United States—particularly the southeast and some sections of the southwest and northwest—couponing has been slow to catch on, partly because of resistance by small retailers in areas not yet fully served by supermarket chains and partly because consumers either didn't receive them or were not in the habit of using them. This has been changing in recent years.

Competitive Activity. If the manufacturer of a competing brand is distributing free samples of the product at the very time your coupons find their audience, this will clearly have an effect on your promotion. In the case of a media advertising campaign, all the world (including the competition) can see it, measure it, and project its cost and direction; a coupon "drop," however, is swift, silent, and all but impossible to track or measure. Generally, by the time a coupon promotion hits, it is too late for the competition to launch any immediately effective countermeasure.

Factors Influencing Redemption Rates

- Control and security of distribution
- Type of audience reached
- Product-usage incidence
- Brand awareness
- Brand loyalty
- Availability at retail
- Display space and location
- Design and appeal of the coupon advertising message
- Ratio of the face value to the retail price
- Coupon usage in the area
- Competitors' activity

MISREDEMPTION

Any discussion of couponing would be less than complete if it did not address head-on the issue of coupon fraud. The scale of the problem can be appreciated by noting that, as total estimated coupon distribution increased more than 400 percent from 1972 to 1982 (23 billion to 100 billion), the annual dollar amount paid out to retailers by manufacturers for face values and retailer handling fees during the same ten-year period increased almost *tenfold*, from $139 million to a staggering $1.3 billion.[10]

Different couponing media have different misredemption rates, of course, which correspond in fairly direct proportion to lack of control over the production and distribution processes. (See Table 3-2.) In other words, the

TABLE 3-2 Misredemption Opportunity by Medium*

	Points	Misredemption opportunity
Newspaper, FSI	8–10	High
Newspaper, co-op	7–10	High
Newspaper, ROP	5–7	High
Magazine, ROP	5	Medium
Magazine, ROP	4½	Medium
Sunday supplement	3–4	Medium
Thematics (magazine insert)	3	Medium
On pack	2	Minimal
In pack	2	Minimal
Direct-mail co-op	1½	Minimal
Direct-mail solo	1	Minimal

* The table depicts the degree of misredemption susceptibility for each medium based on a Point scale of 0 to 10, 0 being no misredemption potential, and 10 being the highest misredemption potential.

lower the control over distribution, the more coupon fraud there will be. The sheer *volume* of coupon traffic and the enormity of potential corporate liability for that volume—some $27 billion in the aggregate[11]—present a tempting opportunity for anyone with an inclination to try to "beat the system" by improperly gathering and obtaining payment for even a tiny percentage of the whole.

There are no hard figures on how much money is paid out each year in bogus claims, because much coupon fraud goes undetected and because until recently such information was less than likely to be announced by manufacturers, distributors, clearinghouses, and redemption agents. Largely because of cooperative industry efforts, as well as the development of increasingly sophisticated systems of detection by manufacturers and redemption agents, coupon fraud has become much more difficult to perpetrate than it was only a few years ago.

What Is Misredemption?

Misredemption can be defined as any attempt to collect coupon handling fees and face values for a brand of product that was not actually purchased from a retailer. For example, "gang-cut" or "mint-condition" coupons may be obtained from printing overruns or removed from unsold or undelivered newspapers.

Who are the perpetrators? Some are otherwise legitimate retailers who insist on abusing the process by trying to collect on illegitimate claims until they are caught and either warned or prosecuted. Others are "storefront" operators who use real or fictitious retailer names and for whom coupon fraud is an ongoing big business. Almost all are organized and involved in large-scale submissions. Abuses by individual consumers, or even small groups of them, are not a substantial part of the problem, since the potential rewards are so minor compared with overall scale. (See Table 3-2.)

A stricter definition is that misredemption is *any* claim for payment for a coupon which, in the manufacturer's opinion, was improperly used. Examples are honoring submissions for the coupon for the wrong size of the couponed product, or even for the right size and brand, but after the offer has expired. Which definition is used is ultimately the business of the manufacturer. Coupon fraud is a crime, at the very least to the extent that such improper claims are submitted through the U.S. mail. (Mail fraud is a felony-class federal offense punishable by a $10,000 fine and up to five years in prison.)

Thanks to the diligence of the U.S. Postal Service and the growing willingness on the part of manufacturers to cooperate in the apprehension and prosecution of such criminals, misredemption is gradually being brought under control. But arrests and convictions, however important they may be as short-term deterrents, are only part of the solution. Various methods of detection that have recently been developed, such as computer tracking and referencing and the use of sequential numbering and optical scanning marks and devices, will be far more effective in making cents-off promotions serve their purpose.

The marketing and sales promotion manager can also play an important part in the prevention process. The following checklists, one for handling redemption requests received directly from retailers and the other for handling submissions received from coupon clearinghouses (which are agencies employed by retailer organizations), will go a long way toward helping planners of coupon promotions stop fraud.

Redemption Requests

1. Is the retailer's operation still active, or has it gone bankrupt? Has the retailer changed to a new line of business?
2. Is the retailer in the appropriate line of business? (For example, a tobacco stand should not be submitting soap- or food-product coupons.)
3. Is the retailer within the coupon distribution area? Coupons for highly targeted promotions are sometimes returned from several different parts of the country.
4. Are the redemption amounts requested—both individually and cumulatively—within the retailer's normal sales volume levels?
5. Do the coupons look valid, or have they all been cut and "aged" by the same process?
6. If the coupons are numbered, are the numbers random or sequential?
7. Considering coupon volume and the date of initial distribution, does a particular retailer's redemption request seem excessive?

In evaluating redemption requests received from clearinghouses, the following checklist, in addition to the one above, should be used.

Redemption Requests from Clearinghouses

1. Is the retailer submitting coupons through several clearinghouses and perhaps directly to the manufacturer as well?
2. Does the clearinghouse submit the coupon submissions by each retailer separately, and are all retailers clearly identified?
3. Has the clearinghouse been audited by the manufacturer or redemption agent?
4. Does the clearinghouse have formal contracts or merely informal agreements with submitting retailers?
5. Do the clearinghouse's contracts with retailers contain a manufacturer's release clause?

Because redemption rates are so important to the effectiveness of couponing, it cannot be overemphasized that the primary responsibility for policing misredemption rests with the manufacturer. As a purely practical matter, the policing begins with careful selection of the couponing vehicle, stringent control of the distribution process, and constant scrutiny by an alert coupon redemption service.

STRATEGY

Marketing managers have one main objective: to generate sales of their products and increase profits. They can achieve this by increasing revenue, reducing costs, or both.

Sales can be increased by undertaking various marketing activities, or value may be enhanced by reducing price, increasing consumer benefits, or improving product quality. Any of these actions will add costs, of course, but such costs can be reduced relative to sales by raising prices, cutting quality, or throttling back on marketing activities. These latter alternatives, in turn, will tend to reduce sales over the long term.

For any promotion there is a certain trade-off or equilibrium that must be established among all the above considerations. The next step is to tip the equilibrium in the direction of meeting concrete brand objectives by tinkering with various elements to achieve speed, economy, and efficiency of effort. Cents-off couponing offers an extraordinary opportunity for this because there are so many elements available for fine tuning: timing, audience selection, brand message, face value, and geographic coverage, not to mention selection of the medium itself.

Couponing in all its variety is a constantly evolving marketing tool because the manufacturers who use it are ever on the lookout for a slight advantage that will produce the desired objectives. New technology is constantly being developed to permit more direct and effective audience impact. The real measure of any marketing activity, however, is how well it fulfills its purpose in today's competitive environment. It is simply not enough to state one's objective as "to increase sales." The professional must go the extra step and say specifically just how that is to be accomplished and from where those sales are supposed to come: new users, new uses, more usage from current customers, changes in purchasing habits, or expanded trading areas.

Having reviewed the various types of couponing media in terms of their relative strengths and efficiencies, we shall now turn our attention to planning and evaluating the coupon promotion.

PLANNING

As with media advertising, cost per 1000 units circulated is a factor for consideration in planning and budgeting, but unlike the situation in advertising, direct results (coupon redemptions) can be compared with program costs to measure real effectiveness at various points in the couponing cycle. Of major importance to the sales promotion manager are such considerations as timing (will the product be available when the coupons drop?), face value (is it high enough to generate action but low enough to make a profit?), and geographic or demographic selectivity (what is the best way to reach the largest possible number of consumers who are most likely and able to respond?).

The ability to reach large audiences and to do so at reasonable cost are only two of several important planning considerations, however. Among the others (see Table 3-3), not necessarily in order of importance, are:

- Lead-time flexibility. (How much production time is involved?)
- Frequency of issue. (How well will this medium fit in with the program schedule?)
- New trial. (What is the objective: new users or maintenance of market share?)
- Impact. (How much retail action will be generated?)
- Targetability. (Can the medium provide geographic and demographic selectivity?)
- Redemption security. (How vulnerable is the medium to coupon fraud?)
- Trade tie-in potential. (Can consumer pull be combined with trade push?)

EVALUATION

The effectiveness of any coupon promotion must be measured against a clear and unambiguous statement of the promotion's objective. If achieving product movement for trade tie-in merchandising is the desired result, for example, the promotion might correctly focus on achieving the broadest possible reach for the lowest possible cost per 1000. Some other considerations are as follows:

- Under any circumstances, it is desirable to project program payments for each major coupon program. This will require some assumptions based on consistent company experience and judgment.
- Start with cost per 1000 gross delivered. Often, this is as far as many marketers go. Delivery is not always the most important cost element, so it should never be overestimated.
- The most important single cost of a coupon promotion is not distribution but redemption, which is easily computed by multiplying the face value of the coupon by the expected percentage redemption of the total circulation purchased. Often company experience is a valuable guideline. However, the actual redemption rate will depend more on the product category (i.e., its usage incidence by the target audience) than on any other factor.
- The percentage discount to selling price, the frequency of coupon use for both the product and the category, product distribution patterns, and similar elements are also important considerations.

In evaluating one promotion against another, it is important to take the above projections even further. To be specific:

- The manager should make an estimate of net-value redemption, which is a projection of the amount of sales that must be guaranteed in order for the coupon to pay back.

TABLE 3-3 Coupon Media Characteristics*

Characteristic	Magazines		Newspapers				Direct mail		Product package		Other	
	On page	Pop-up	ROP co-op	ROP best food day	FSI	Sunday supplement	Co-op	Solo	In pack and on pack	Cross-ruff	Hand-out	Coupon with sample
Lead-time flexibility	3	2	4	5	2	3	2	3	2	1	2	1
Quality of graphics	5	5	1	2	5	4	5	5	2	2	5	5
Demographic targeting	4	4	1	1	2	2	5	5	2	2	4	5
Geographic selectivity	3	3	4	4	3	3	4	5	2	2	5	5
Low cost per 1000	3	2	5	4	3	3	2	1	5	4	1	5
Coupon security	3	3	1	1	2	3	5	5	4	4	4	5
Redemption rates	2	3	2	2	4	3	5	5	5	4	5	5
Market impact	2	3	3	3	4	3	5	5	1	1	4	5
Trade tie-in potential	2	3	4	5	5	4	3	5	1	1	5	5

* 5 is best; 4 is above average; 3 is average; 2 is below average; 1 is least.

- Misredemption estimates are just that: estimates. But are generally accepted redemption-rate ranges based on experience or on generally accepted industry estimates for every coupon vehicle? (See Figure 3-2.)
- Estimates of payout should be made on the basis of trial-to-conversion projections. Projecting these estimates across different couponing vehicles allows comparisons of payback for each one.
- It is possible, in fact desirable, to conduct consumer tests of various types of coupons to determine the optimum coupon face value for a specific product. Note that face values will often test differently from one geographic area to another.
- Financial liability for a specific promotion should be figured (again, by adding face values and handling fees and then multiplying the sum by the expected redemption rate) to arrive at a dollar amount that should be placed in reserve, to be charged to the brand marketing budget when the coupon is dropped.
- Coupons are not meant to operate on their own, or in a vacuum. They are best used in conjunction with other elements of the marketing program to create a greater overall effect than any one of these elements could achieve on its own. In other words, the coupon creates a purchase incentive, but the incentive will be frustrated if the trade has not ordered and is not displaying the product—or if the advertising has not created awareness of the product.

INNOVATIONS AND EVOLUTION

To classify coupon vehicles according to the methods by which they are delivered is to run the risk of oversimplifying the couponing process as well as to ignore the richly diverse variety of couponing devices that are constantly being developed to meet special marketing purposes. Today's tried-and-true vehicles, after all, some of which were practically unheard of ten years ago (FSIs are a case in point), are the end result of constant tinkering and innovation aimed at achieving the goal that inspires and eludes the marketing professional: the perfect solution. It is the search for this solution, in an ever-changing marketplace, which stimulates new ideas and new approaches (many of which fail, only to succeed in another part of the country or in the same place a year or two later) and which has caused the couponing "industry" to evolve into the efficient and enormously popular phenomenon it is today. The process of innovation, change, and evolution continues. Following are some examples of special-purpose coupon promotions that have grown out of the ferment in recent times.

Gift Packages to "Start-up" Consumers. At several times in their lives, almost all people become first-time purchasers of a specific class of product—

for example, college students, newlyweds, new parents, and men and women entering the military service. Because first-time buyers of a class of product are faced with purchasing decisions they have never made before (about such items as health and beauty aids, baby products, and household cleansers), they constitute not only a new and ready market but also an audience upon which brand awareness and product trial can create an indelible impression, leading to repeat purchases and regular usage. There are a number of companies that offer manufacturers a distribution service aimed at such highly targeted audiences, delivering, at rather low cost, coupons, as well as product samples when possible, to college campuses, marriage license bureaus, hospitals, and military installations all over the United States. Coverage can be selected on a local, regional, or national basis. For years, in fact, a marketer of disposable diapers has built and protected a share of the market for its baby diapers through programs centered on hospital maternity wards.

"New-Neighbor" Guides.   Using new telephone listings to locate people moving into new homes, some companies offer, on a co-op basis, to distribute coupons and/or product samples either to specific neighborhoods or to audiences with specific demographic characteristics in a cross section of neighborhoods in cities, counties, or market areas. Coupons are printed in magazine-style tabloid formats or are bound into booklets and sent out via third-class bulk mail. Again, as with the example above, the purpose is to make the participating brand the consumers' first choice when they go shopping.

Self-Selecting Promotions.   A variation on the in-store or near-store coupon distribution theme is one in which the consumer is reached by mail or in a magazine and is asked to fill out a questionnaire in return for getting one or more high-value coupons or a product sample of the promoted brand or brands. Also offered on a co-op basis, this "qualifier" questionnaire elicits information on brand-purchasing behavior and can be used to measure market share, as well as to build a direct-mail list so that samples and subsequent coupon offers can be targeted toward consumers of the promoted brands or even the competition's customers. When printed on the page, or inserted in a magazine, or sent via direct mail, the offer usually combines some inducement for consumer participation with the questionnaire. Sometimes a coupon good for at least one purchase of a product is included so that the consumer returns a poof of purchase along with the completed questionnaire. More often, the consumer is given the opportunity to enter a contest or sweepstakes. Sometimes the consumer is asked to send in a small amount of money, the purpose of which is to ensure that the consumer is "involved" or interested in answering the questionnaire.

In-Store Delivery Systems. One of the more innovative coupon promotions in recent years was a co-op program in which manufacturers' coupons were printed on grocery bags, which were offered free of charge to supermarket chains in return for expanded shelf space and special in-store displays for featured products. This was truly a something-for-everybody scheme; consumers saved money on return trips to participating stores, retailers had a cost-free supply of paper bags as well as a device for keeping customers coming back to their stores, and manufacturers were able to increase sales because the trade and consumer aspects were so well tied together. A major flaw, however, was the vulnerability of the program to the temptation on the part of some retailers to cut and redeem the coupons without having sold the featured products.

More successful is the co-op coupon booklet program in which a marketing company actually hires people and stations them in the store to hand out booklets of coupons on peak traffic days, with special displays and tie-in advertising arranged in advance. In such programs misredemption is minimized, but operating costs are higher because of hiring, training, supervising, and staffing expenses.

The "Self-Destruct" Coupon. Truly a multipurpose device, the self-destruct coupon is actually two coupons printed in such a way as to give prospective purchasers a choice of using one or the other. Consumers can select one unit or a small size of the featured brand, in which case the coupon can be redeemed at a lower face value, or they can choose more than one unit or a larger size of the same brand, in which case the coupon will be redeemed at a higher face value. The effect of making one choice over the other, of course, is to destroy the unused coupon; hence the name. Such devices were popular with manufacturers when they began to appear in the mid-1970s. (See Figure 3-3.)

The manufacturer's strategy is to give consumers a choice of two offers without increasing promotional costs and redemption liability and to get regular users to "trade up" to larger sizes or make repeat purchases. An inherent problem, however, is that consumers tend to cut *both* coupons out and present them to the retailer, whose inclination is to present the one with the larger face value, no matter what size or quantity of the featured brand was purchased, for payment by the manufacturer—which undermines the process.

Other New Ideas in Couponing

The above examples are only a few of the dozens of ways the couponing process can be manipulated to achieve specific marketing goals. When creative thinking is applied to such seemingly routine aspects of coupon promotions as delivery and timing, the variety of possibilities grows even larger. Innovations that have been tried in recent years with varying degrees of success include distribution of coupons in egg cartons with home-delivered milk and even distribution of coupons at movie theaters. Innovations related to the timing (or, more properly, to the duration) of coupon promotions range from "instant" coupons, which are attached to the product and redeemed immediately for cents off the posted retail price, to "timed" offers, in which one coupon is good only in January, another only in February, and so on, the purpose being to encourage repeat purchases. Each of these innovations, in its own way, affords the marketer a greater degree of influence on purchasing behavior, the usual trade-off for which is loss of some degree of security, which can lead to mishandling and reduced effectiveness. Nevertheless, innovation and experimentation must and will continue. Magazine pop-up coupons, for example, were that medium's answer to competition from other couponing media with higher redemption rates. From that idea developed co-opped pop-ups, also bound into magazines, and so-called answer cards, which are also coupon co-ops but are glued to the inside back page of a Sunday supplement.

SUMMARY

In all its variety and for all its strengths as well as its shortcomings, couponing has been with us for a long time and probably will be with us, in one form or another, for a long time to come—not just because it has become "big

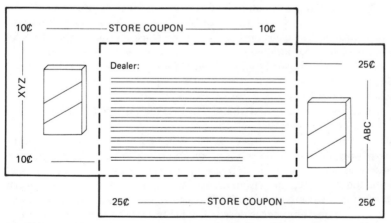

FIGURE 3-3. Self-destruct, or option, coupons. Either one coupon *or* the other can be used.

business" or is merely a long-running fad, but because it works. Unfortunately, because the term *couponing* focuses not on the process but on the device around which the process is built (a simple scrap of paper with no real intrinsic value), those who are unfamiliar with the dynamics of that process tend to trivialize it or to suggest that all those billions of bits of paper are just so much waste—that the enormous investment by manufacturers in brand promotions for thousands of products would be better deployed as direct price reductions to the consumer.

The same argument was made many years ago about media advertising. To believe this, however, is to ignore the fact that we live and thrive in an environment where competition, in the form of new-product development as well as pricing, actually reduces the cost of goods and services over the long run, while it serves to drive inferior and/or costly items off the market. And couponing, as well as the rest of sales promotion and advertising, has become an important and very powerful instrument of competition.

THE PAST AND THE FUTURE

The marketing of consumer goods in this country is profoundly affected by technological change. We have seen how the development of mass-circulation print media and the establishment of broadcast networks turned the concept of national brands into reality many years ago. Improvements in transportation and advances in the manufacture and distribution of products have, in turn, made it possible to produce and deliver enormous quantities of goods to market with remarkable economy and efficiency; hence the development of supermarkets and the formation of retail chains after World War II. The proliferation of products and the explosion of brand advertisements that continued through the 1950s and 1960s set the stage for some type of device that would cut through all the clutter and appeal directly to consumers with an offer they could not afford to turn down. Trade promotions had been tried, but there was only so much shelf space, display area, or trade support available for each store. Trading stamps gained popularity but were not brand-specific, and so they benefited mainly the retailer. Then along came coupons—but they had been there all the time.

Manufacturers and consumers rediscovered coupons in the 1970s partly because of prevailing economic conditions and partly because of the sponsorship of several major companies. Their continued popularity and success as a marketing tool, however, stem from a basic principle that was apparent nearly a century ago: Consumers like and will use coupons because they represent true and immediate value, regardless of the posted retail price; manufacturers like them because they offer a high degree of control over, and flexibility in, retail pricing.

As long as that principle applies, the couponing process can move along with technological change and become more efficient for doing so. As optical scanning devices, for example, are installed in more and more supermarkets around the country, new and different ways of using them are being developed. One application would be to link purchased products to coupon offers, which would go a long way toward eliminating misredemption. Another would be to apply Universal Product Codes to all coupons to make the physical counting of coupons by redemption agents and clearinghouses more efficient. And perhaps a "paperless" coupon could be developed using interactive cable television, received on sets in supermarkets, on which manufacturers could post—and shoppers could accept or reject—electronic coupon offers for immediate redemption.

These and other changes may or may not come about. In the meantime, there are many ways the marketer can use cents-off coupons. In the words of one executive of a major packaged goods company: "I'm not going to say that couponing as we know it will last forever. After all, there were people making predictions thirty years ago that you couldn't run a retail operation without offering credit and home delivery. But I do know that it works; and until something better comes along, we're going to keep on couponing."

ENDNOTES

1. Russell D. Bowman, *Couponing and Rebates: Profit on the Dotted Line*, Lebhar-Friedman Books, New York, 1980.
2. *Cents-off Coupons and Consumer Purchasing Behavior*, report on a study commissioned by John Blair Marketing and Donnelley Marketing and conducted by Burke Marketing Services, Inc., 1981.
3. Bowman, op. cit.
4. Nielsen Clearing House, Clinton, Iowa, 1981.
5. Ibid; Bowman, op. cit.
6. Nielsen Clearing House, Clinton, Iowa, 1982.
7. *Fourth Annual Survey of Couponing Practices*, Donnelley Marketing, Stamford, Conn., March 1982.
8. Bowman, op. cit.
9. Nielsen Clearing House, Clinton, Iowa, 1982.
10. Donnelley Marketing, Stamford, Conn., 1982.
11. Ibid.

Product Sampling

JOHN A. CLEARY
President, Donnelley Marketing, a Company of The Dun & Brad-street Corporation

If cents-off couponing can be called the Mercedes-Benz of sales promotion, then product sampling is certainly the Rolls Royce. Product sampling is, to be sure, a quality vehicle, offering high performance with a track record of proven achievements down through the years. And though it is a highly specialized and sometimes costly mechanism, if used wisely and correctly it can deliver a handsome return on one's initial investment.

WHY SAMPLING?

While large-scale couponing is a relatively new phenomenon, dating from the emergence in the 1920s of national brands and of efforts by soft goods manufacturers to promote the sales of those brands, product sampling has really been with us for centuries. The butcher who offers you a slice of new sausage, the farmer who urges you to try one of the apples displayed by the bushel, the greengrocer who winks as you sample the grapes—each is applying the time-tested theory that if you can be enticed to try the smallest unit of a product that will deliver a meaningful impression, the likelihood of your buying in large, profitable quantities is significantly enhanced. Product sampling based on this simple theory could have existed in the earliest bazaars, which, since they operated on the barter system, didn't even require money.

To a great extent, this is still the basic thrust of any product-sample distribution: to demonstrate a unique product feature or departure. Because the sample is free, the sampling process induces initial trial, which in turn inspires posttrial purchase. In today's competitive marketplace, where conventional media have limited power to support such product claims as "new," "improved," "different," and "unique," an effective sampling campaign can bring an important extra dimension to a product roll-out or reintroduction. But modern product-sampling techniques have to go one step further than the method used by the butcher, farmer, or greengrocer: They must establish, in the consumer's mind, an association between the product and the manufacturer's brand name so that the consumer will follow through and purchase the product. Because of this, the product package—size, physical construction, and graphic design—is an important component of the sampling mechanism. Cost considerations based on these factors are also important ingredients in the ideal sampling "formula," as we shall see below.

Also, because of the massiveness of most sampling roll-outs and the fact that their targets are one step away from the actual point of sale (discussed below), posttrial logistics as well as timing and coordination with advertising strategy are extremely important considerations.

The following comment from the *1969 Annual Report* of the Colgate-Palmolive Co. (New York, 1970, p. 10), while it relates to a special type of product sampling, is nevertheless indicative of one company's faith in the efficacy of the mechanism as a sales promotion vehicle:

> Of all promotional activities, product samples delivered or mailed directly to the home are most conducive to securing consumer trial. Since sampling furnishes an actual demonstration of a brand's ability to perform, customers gained in this manner tend to be more loyal and steady buyers than consumers who try products as a result of other motivation.
>
> Repeated tests verify this conclusion and also disclose that sampling is more efficient when larger sizes are distributed. In many cases, resampling of the same product in a relatively short period of time has proven beneficial to a brand's share of the market. The rapid success of many of our new and revitalized products is attributable largely to this form of promotion.

In short, there is simply no more effective way of generating consumer trial and purchase of a product than by giving away free samples of it, nor is there a better way to revitalize an existing brand, provided that the product is improved or unique enough to elicit favorable consumer response. This is perhaps the most important judgment to be made prior to any product-sampling program, for because of the very nature of the vehicle, a lackluster or "me too" product that is distributed en masse is doomed to certain failure from the start. On the other hand, for the product that can truly demonstrate high value to the consumers who receive it, the results can be phenomenal—again, because of the very nature of the sampling mechanism.

Sampling Compared with Couponing

Couponing tends to increase preplanned purchasing; when shoppers take coupons to the supermarket, in effect they are placing them fairly high up on their shopping list. By contrast, a free sample increases the tendency to buy on impulse. Because it is free, the product sample provides the consumer with an opportunity, even an incentive, to try the product because there is absolutely no cost risk or obligation.

Such trial not only tends to break down consumer skepticism as to the brand's product claims (again, provided they are demonstrably true) but also heightens in-store recognition. Because of these unique but mutually reinforcing characteristics, manufacturers often combine couponing with sampling in the same product roll-out for an effective one-two punch. If proper controls are established to ensure that samples are distributed to the "right" prospects for the product (more on this later), a manufacturer can expect between 50 and 80 percent of the households or shoppers receiving the sample to try the product in very short order. Given the right product and the right conditions, a sales volume can be achieved in a few weeks that might otherwise have taken several years to build.

SAMPLING IN ACTION

An example of just such a success was the introduction of Agree creme rinse and conditioner by the S. C. Johnson Company in 1977. A complete newcomer to the health and beauty-aids field, the firm had for several years enjoyed success with a number of products marketed nationally under the Johnson's wax label. Six months after the Agree debut in the first quarter of 1977, its new creme rinse and conditioner was in the top spot nationally with a market share in the low 20s. The new brand had passed up quality products from Clairol, Breck, Revlon, and Gillette, some of which had been advertising and working at building brand loyalty for years.

There were two major reasons for Agree's success: (1) It was a quality product with universal appeal that was designed to meet a real need and (2) it was quickly and heavily sampled to more than 30 million households on the heels of a massive national advertising campaign. The Agree roll-out is estimated to have cost $14 million, with approximately half that amount allocated for advertising, and the other half for sample distribution and a cents-off coupon offer redeemable with the consumer's initial purchase. Seven out of every ten households receiving the sample got enough Agree (⅝ ounce) for one or two uses, while the other three received a larger amount (2 ounces). The lighter samples were distributed via mail through Donnelley Marketing's

Carol Wright cooperative ensemble mailings, and the heavier ones were mailed solo to especially compiled lists of young females making up a category of potential "heavy users" of the product.

Prior to the Agree roll-out, product-usage incidence of creme rinses and conditioners as reported by Target Group Index (TGI) showed not only a proliferation of brands but also the possibility of a confusion factor on the part of the public as to which of these fifteen or twenty products were creme rinses and which were conditioners. The genius of the Agree strategy was to eliminate such confusion by appropriating to itself both descriptions and then aiming its advertising message as well as its sample distribution to a new, broader category of its own creation: the after-shampoo hair-care market.

It is worthy of note, in studying the Agree campaign, that this so-called axiom was ignored in the interest of reaching a mass national audience quickly with a novel and ultimately effective product claim: that Agree was for everyone—young and old, male and female, people with long hair and people with short hair, and everyone in between. To hedge its bet, S. C. Johnson distributed the heavier samples to the narrow band of potential heavy users too. As to the question of duplication, which certainly did exist in a roll-out on such a scale, cost considerations gave way to the theory that, since it could not be controlled without watering down the impact, whatever duplication did occur would at least serve to reinforce usage among users and nonusers too.

COST VERSUS EFFECTIVENESS

Although the unit cost of sample distribution, which of course includes the cost of the product samples, can on first inspection seem quite high—generally from $0.25 to $0.50 per unit—care should be taken to evaluate effectiveness as well as cost-related efficiency. For just as there may be products and services whose selling points are so clear that they require no actual physical introduction to consumers, there are those which require demonstration for specific reasons having to do with either the product itself or conditions prevailing in the marketplace. In any case, at the outset of any product introduction it is important—and relatively easy—to set up a test-marketing situation to determine just how high is "up" in terms of its selling potential based on demonstration versus other promotion methods. Generally speaking, funds required for sampling need not and should not take away from funds allocated for introductory advertising. But if product sampling *is* funded to some extent at the expense of advertising, a successful sampling campaign—because of its intrinsic effectiveness—will generally justify subsequent higher levels of advertising support for higher brand share than might have been obtained with an advertising-only approach at the outset. Experience indicates that, given these considerations, product sampling often turns out to be the least, rather than the most, expensive of promotion alternatives for maximizing sales, market share, and profits. To carry our automotive analogy even further, there is a remarkable number of old Rolls Royces on the road today because, despite their initial cost, astute buyers saw them as a smart one-time investment.

SAMPLING FOR ESTABLISHED BRANDS

While large-scale sampling can yield dramatic results almost overnight for a product that the consuming public has never heard of, the mechanism is by no means limited to new-product launches or national brands only. A product that has been around for several years but has a low usage incidence can be "introduced" to the public as if for the first time. And the sampling program can be applied market by market to fit the manufacturer's distribution capabilities. High-penetration sampling can also be used to test-market a product prior to extending a company's manufacturing and distribution operations into potential new sales territories.

The S. B. Thomas Company of Totowa, New Jersey, a wholly owned subsidiary of CPC International, combined all three of these strategies with considerable success. By qualifying the rule that one should not sample an established product, the Thomas Company, makers of Thomas' English muffins, embarked on an aggressive, region-by-region product-sampling campaign in 1976 that within eighteen months had tripled sales, doubled manufacturing capacity, opened a score of new markets in the midwest and Pacific regions, and positioned the Thomas brand as the leader in every market it served. Prior to its sampling experience, Thomas had been serving markets within a 450-mile radius of its large—and at that time its only—bakery in northern New Jersey.

The key to the Thomas Company's success was the fact that, although English muffins had been sold in cities in the northeast for a number of years (since 1888 in some areas) and enjoyed a small but loyal franchise of users, the vast majority of the public in these market areas had never tried Thomas' English muffins, even though focus groups and other research devices indicated them to be a unique and demonstrably superior product.

The strategy of the Thomas Company, like that of the S. C. Johnson Company with Agree, was to launch a product-sampling campaign of such massive proportions that the company would at once convert users of "ordinary" breakfast bakery products (such as toast) to its brand, while reinforcing the loyalty of an existing heavy-user core.

The sampling campaign began in Philadelphia with house-to-house delivery of packages of four fresh muffins, an amount calculated to ensure meaningful trial. The retail value of the sample package was approximately

$0.67. The package included a coupon worth $0.07 toward the purchase of the product at the store and a clearly worded statement that the muffins had been baked less than twenty-four hours prior to delivery. The test program proved that even in markets where Thomas' English muffins had top or nearly top brand share, door-to-door product sampling could substantially expand consumer usage of the product category by enabling consumers to taste it at no risk or cost. Category usage, in fact, doubled in several markets and came close to doubling in many others.

The Philadelphia test covered between 60 and 65 percent of households in the metropolitan area, a total of 640,000 households. Concentrating on the city's inner and outer suburban rings ensured maximum impact on neighborhoods whose residents' incomes, education, and lifestyles indicated both the ability and a predisposition to try, and subsequently buy, something new on the basis of perceived product superiority. Upwards of 90 percent of households receiving the muffins tried them within twenty-four hours, and dramatic sales results were immediate. Subsequent to the Philadelphia test, 575,000 samples were distributed in Boston; 112,000 in Providence, Rhode Island; and 155,000 in Hartford, Connecticut. Soon the New Jersey bakery was running at full capacity and there was talk of expansion.

Following its experience with sampling an existing product in the northeast, the Thomas Company in 1976 launched a tightly controlled door-to-door campaign in both northern and southern California to support the proposed construction of a new bakery in Orange County, near Los Angeles. On the strength of the results the plant was opened, and Thomas' English muffins became the number one brand in its category in markets that the plant served in the Pacific region. More recently, a third plant went up in Frederick, Maryland, to serve new markets opened up by product-sampling campaigns in Virginia, West Virginia, and the entire state of Ohio. The Frederick bakery also relieved the New Jersey plant of some production pressure.

An additional illustration of a successful sampling program for an established brand was the in-store taste sampling of a General Foods product, Stove Top stuffing, in 1977. Positioned as a substitute for rice and potatoes, this product was developed to enable the homemaker to create more variety in meal planning. Cents-off coupons were used in the original launch as one ingredient in the overall marketing program. In this case, the couponing program met its objectives, and initial product sales seemed to be good, but after a period of time it was noticed that the usual and expected repurchase did not occur. Follow-up studies indicated that homemakers had been putting the product in the pantry awaiting a special occasion, many of them no doubt associating Stove Top with the holiday turkey. To remedy the situation, General Foods decided to try product sampling through in-store taste demonstrations. Soon afterward, repeat purchases began to occur, and a substantial increase in television advertising was effected to support the higher sales levels.

The point about Thomas' English muffins is that, although the product had been around for more than half a century, very few consumers in the markets in which it was sold could recall ever having tried it—something less than 7 percent, according to a TGI table—while more than 70 percent recalled having tried *some* brand of English muffin. While sampling of an existing product should be undertaken with considerable caution (see the steps outlined below), an "ever-tried" product-usage incidence of 10 percent or less is a fair indicator that the "new-product introduction" approach used by the Thomas Company is a viable strategy.

SAMPLING METHODS

Distribution of consumer products by direct mail and by door-to-door delivery are two of a whole range of sampling methods in use today; each one has either a specific purpose or a special feature that distinguishes it from the rest. The range includes, but is not necessarily limited to, the methods discussed below. (See Table 4-1.)

Samples Delivered to the Home

Solo Direct-Mail Delivery. The chief advantages of solo direct-mail delivery are that it is dramatic, effective, and fast. The manufacturer can select a specific demographic profile or cross section and zero in on it, via preselected mailing lists, with maximum impact. Because of postage and packaging costs, this method is best suited for products weighing 6 ounces or less. (See Figure 4-1.)

Direct-Mail Co-op Delivery. Direct-mail co-op delivery is best for samples weighing 1 ounce or less and is much less expensive than solo mailings because costs are shared with other participating couponers and product samplers. Although there is little flexibility as to timing (co-op mailings go out several times a year on a fixed schedule, but mailings are often booked as much as a year or more in advance), various geographic extensions and demographic modules are available whose costs might be prohibitive in a solo mailing. Co-op distributions typically feature product-category exclusivity (only one brand of shampoo, only one of coffee, etc.) to ensure unintruded share of mind for each featured product.

Newspapers and Free-Standing Inserts. Certain products which are lightweight and flat and which lend themselves to being spot-glued either to

TABLE 4-1 Sampling Techniques

Distribution method	Typical price range	Primary advantages	Primary restrictions
Co-op mail-in offer Co-op mailing or insert offering the consumer a sample upon request	Cost of co-op couponing or insert, $15 to $20 per 1000, including postage	Low cost per 1000	Restricted to ad copy to induce trial. Response approximately half that of a cents-off coupon
Sample in a co-op mailing or insert Co-op mailing or insert giving the consumer a free sample	$40 to $80 per 1000, assuming machine-insertable	Low cost per 1000	Size and weight limitations. Media availability and timing. Limited selectivity compared with solo sampling. Long lead-time requirement
Mail sampling Samples packaged by advertiser and delivered by mail	$80 to $140 per 1000	Lowest-cost *solo* technique. Ability to optimize selectivity using special lists. Timing geared to roll-out needed. Coupon can be delivered with the sample	Maximum gross sample weight 4 to 5 oz for postal distribution cost to be less than cost of house-to-house sampling. Some restrictions resulting from formulation and sample size
In-store sampling	$80 to $120 per 1000 per sampling store day	Excellent strategic weapon. Full coupon redemption in three to four weeks and mostly during the sampling weekend. Particularly strong method where product has unique, easily differentiated taste and/or where demonstration benefits the product. Moves product	Sales-force control of the trade sell-in. Limited sample size. Greater roll-out time than for mail sampling

TABLE 4.1 Sampling Techniques (*Continued*)

Distribution method	Typical price range	Primary advantages	Primary restrictions
		through retail in a highly visible way to the trade	
House-to-house sampling	$200 to $250 per 1000	Items weighing in excess of 4 to 5 oz. High consumer impact. Quick trial of sample	Less selective than mail sampling. Requires close support of field sales force

the newspaper page or to a card insert can be sampled at relatively low cost by this method. Physical requirements limit the range of suitable products to paper goods and granulated or powdered chemicals or laundry detergents, but distribution costs are quite low. The principal costs are those of packaging, attaching, and inserting the product.

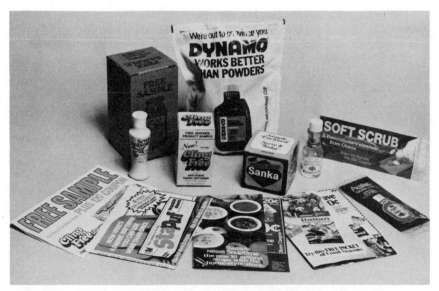

FIGURE 4-1. An assortment of free samples designed for solo direct-mail or house-to-house delivery.

House-to-House Delivery. House-to-house delivery is particularly suited for heavy or bulky samples, since high postage costs would preclude mailing them. The product is delivered ready for immediate trial to the preselected markets, neighborhoods, households, or any combination thereof. Although roll-out takes from six to ten weeks to guarantee 50 percent penetration of the households, house-to-house delivery is similar to direct mail in effect and response.

Sampling at or Near the Point of Purchase

All the above product-sampling methods, while effective in varying degrees in terms of inducing trial of the product delivered, nevertheless have one limitation to which retailers and some manufacturers object; i.e., the very act of sampling takes the customer out of the market—for however short a period of time—during the trial period. Retailers complain that the consumer's brand preference has been "neutralized" in a product category the retailer has advertised and stocked. Since manufacturers are the prime sponsors of product sampling, they like to see the quickest possible "conversion" from trial to purchase. Hence some manufacturers may favor other sampling methods that take place not in the home but closer to the point of purchase, thus ensuring quick conversion.

Sampling Using Prepriced Shippers. Trial-size packages (usually smaller than purchase-size packages) of such high-usage products as toothpaste and shampoo are prominently displayed in the store and offered at an attractive low price—usually from $0.19 to $0.25. This can inspire trial repurchase at a very low cost to the consumer. The prepriced shipper is self-liquidating and motivates consumers to take a sample from the store where the display is located rather than somewhere else. In addition to strong product appeal, success depends on active retail support in terms of prominent space and in-store advertising for the sample display.

In-Store and Near-Store Sampling. On-premises taste sampling of snack foods such as crackers, cheeses, smoked meats, and sausages provides instant high impact and spurs impulse buying, especially when package displays are attractive and prominently placed. Near-store sampling and couponing in shopping centers are variations of this method aimed at directing customers to the store featuring the product being sampled or couponed.

High-Traffic-Area Sampling. Used primarily for sampling and test marketing candy and tobacco products, the objective of high-traffic-area sampling is immediate product trial by large numbers of consumers in the shortest possible time. Hundreds of thousands of samples can be distributed by this method in a matter of hours at relatively low unit cost.

Retailer support. While the above categories of sampling reach consumers at locations where they may be most disposed to buy, i.e., at or near the retail store or at least in a commercial neighborhood, there is an "X" factor that goes with such optimum location: retailer support. Where it is strong, in-store, near-store, and high-traffic-area product-sampling methods (for a limited range of "impulse" products) are both quick and effective. Where it is weak or where the distribution pipeline fails to provide sufficient product to meet demand, these methods fall flat, for once the customer is on or near the premises and has tried the product, a deferred purchase decision is nothing short of a tactical disaster.

Sampling in Specialized Markets

Another form of sampling, which was pioneered by Gift-Pax of West Hempstead, New York, reaches some highly specialized markets. These markets include, but are not limited to, high school and college students (with different packages for males and females), expectant mothers, new mothers, brides, and military recruits. The contents of each package of samples is designed specifically for its particular market. Items generally include pharmaceuticals, beauty and grooming aids, and food, merchandise generally obtainable in supermarkets and drugstores.

Distribution is controlled. For example, each package is given directly by the college or school to the student, by the hospital to the new mother, and by the appropriate institutions to other groups. Not only does this save shipping costs, but the fact that the kit is given by a respected institution adds authority and prestige to each sample in the package.

At the outset of any product introduction or reintroduction for which a trial-by-sampling program might be considered, there are several basic steps that should be taken:

1. Evaluate the need for trial by sampling. Does the product have a unique feature (e.g., taste, texture, or effect) that can best be demonstrated with an actual sample?
2. Determine the "samplability" of the product. Can it be packaged, canned, bottled, glued, stapled, etc., and arrive in the hands of the consumer in usable condition? Can it be mailed, or must it be hand-delivered?
3. Select the most efficient sample size. Too much, of course, is wasteful and costly, but too little (e.g., a detergent sample that will do less than two or three washloads) will not ensure meaningful trial. (See Figure 4-2.) Determine postage costs for solo or co-op mailings and insert costs for other types of distribution.

4. Examine the target audience in terms of your ability to reach it. Not every profile can be hit economically, even with a big budget, but well-defined targets combine efficiency with effectiveness.
5. Select, test, and measure your trial-by-sampling plans and choose your markets according to the most easily measurable plan.
6. Train and establish a sampling supervisor network and reporting system.
7. Alert your sales force for the sell-in to retailers and begin merchandising the program to the trade via newsletters, advertisements, and direct correspondence.

SUMMARY AND TRENDS

Product sampling has become a recognized marketing technique. Gone is the time when only the biggest manufacturers with new brands would dare to use product sampling. Since the days of heavy dependence on product sampling by the soap and detergent manufacturers after World War II, an organized body of knowledge about sampling has come into being, and this knowledge has spread to many other manufacturers (e.g., the S. B. Thomas Company and the S. C. Johnson Company), permitting them to adapt sampling to their unique objectives. Sampling has emerged as one part of the promotion mix

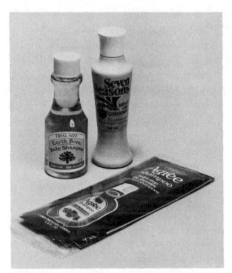

FIGURE 4-2. The sample must be enough for at least two uses.

which is capable of being tested, which has a predictable payout, and which is affordable on a per-customer-gained basis.

The use of product sampling as a promotional tactic will grow in the years to come, first because more manufacturers will need better promotional techniques, and second because experienced marketing managers knowledgeable in promotion are being attracted away from the larger manufacturers by these companies' aggressive and growing competitors.

5 Refunds and Rebates:
Their Time Is Now

DON JAGODA
President, Don Jagoda Associates

LEN DAYKIN
Senior Vice President, Don Jagoda Associates

Refunds and rebates, which are among the basic weapons in the promotional arsenal, have long languished in the shadow of cents-off, store-spendable coupons. In the past decade, however, refunds and rebates have been rediscovered by both marketers and the consuming public. The result is a true example of that gnarled old chestnut: "There is nothing so powerful as an idea whose time has come."

As promotional techniques of rapidly growing importance, refunds and rebates must be understood both in their totality and also as the sum of their parts. What seem on the surface to be relatively simple devices are, on closer inspection, as complex as the most sophisticated of promotional programs. Multiproduct "do-it-yourself" coupons, composed of individual savings stamps to be used at the consumer's option; multifaceted "instant-winner" games with thousands of prizes; and self-screening sampling programs utilizing such economies of delivery as questionnaires in newspaper inserts— all these have nothing on refunds and rebates as flexible, powerful, results-oriented sales promotion tools.

This chapter will begin with a study of refunds and rebates in the academic sense, and then move to a more detailed approach to the subject. Our "menu" shapes up this way:

- A basic definition of refunds and rebates
- The general advantages and disadvantages of refunds and rebates
- The growth of refunds and rebates in terms of marketer use and consumer response
- Various types of refunds and rebates and how to put them to use
- The construction and operating dynamics of refunds and rebates
- Refund and rebate economics and planning

WHAT IS A REFUND?

A refund (or rebate—the terms are essentially interchangeable), as used in promotion today, consists of cash, a check, coupon values, or a product offered to the consumer in return for a proof of purchase of a specified product or service.

There are, however, slight differences of meaning between the terms *refund* and *rebate*. *The Random House Dictionary* defines a refund as a restoration or repayment of money, and a rebate as a return of part of the original payment for some service or merchandise, or a partial refund. Thus, according to both strict English usage and actual promotion practice, what we loosely describe as refunds are in fact more precisely rebates, unless full purchase price is being refunded. But the real world beckons, and it is the way in which refund and rebate programs are served up and advertised to consumers that controls our terminology. The term *rebates* has become more or less synonymous with large "direct-from-the-factory" cash payments or deductions (on automobiles, appliances, etc.), while the term *refunds* is associated with the smaller incentives of cash, checks, or coupons mailed back by packaged goods manufacturers.

To simplify matters, we are going to use the term *refunds* exclusively from this point forward to refer to these programs, large and small, launched by purveyors of goods and services of all types.

OBJECTIVES OF REFUND PROGRAMS

Refund programs share a number of basic objectives with programs featuring store coupons, including those discussed below.

To generate repeat purchases over a specified period of time. Since many refund offers require a number of product proofs of purchase, a refund offer that is alive over an extended period of time can work to create a number of purchase-repurchase cycles, and thus help forge a degree of brand loyalty.

A couponing program can accomplish this goal with a single advertisement that delivers a series of "timed" coupons, with specified months or weeks of use. Fast-food restaurant chains are greatly enamored of this technique, as are the manufacturers of certain packaged goods, including tobacco products and pet foods. As another approach, marketers can simply stage a coupon "blitz," running coupons on a brand repeatedly over a period of weeks or months.

To stimulate multiple purchases over a specified period of time. When a refund offer has a "short fuse," or fast expiration date, and when a number of proofs of purchase are required to qualify for the refund, multiple-purchase activity is created. This can serve to "pantry-load" consumers, pulling them off the market in a particular product category for a period of time and blunting the impact of competitions' sales promotion programs, while creating a sales blip that may be somewhat artificial. Store coupons can accomplish a similar objective with a store-redeemable certificate offering the consumer the chance to "buy three and get one free"—in effect, a 25 percent price reduction that gets four of an item into the consumer's kitchen cupboard at once.

To "billboard" a product line and generate purchases over an expanded product line. Every product line has its "heavy hitters" and "weak sisters." Refunds can force exposure and usage of additional items in a line by creating a purchase requirement consisting of proofs of purchase from specified items, including the most popular and least popular items or varieties in a product line. Consumers are drawn into the offer by the power of the refund and by a purchase requirement involving partly a more popular and hence more frequently purchased item. To complete the purchase requirement, additional varieties or flavors must be bought. Thus, this type of refund is essentially a form of forced sampling.

Coupons can accomplish this objective by offering certain savings on the purchase of two, three, or more *different* varieties or flavors.

To induce consumers to trade up to larger sizes. This objective can be realized by requiring a combination of proofs of purchase, such as net-weight statements adding up to a certain number of pounds, a technique commonly used in pet-food refund programs. In another application, products in a refund program are assigned point values based on size and retail price, and the consumer must accumulate a specified point total in order to receive a refund. One result of this may be a skewing of purchases to larger sizes, since this enables the consumer to obtain the required total more quickly. If larger product sizes are more profitable to the manufacturer or represent a strong consumer commitment to brand loyalty, this may be an important marketing objective that such refunds can meet.

Coupons can work toward a similar objective when a single ad presents a pair of coupons for two sizes of the same product in such a way that either one or the other, but not both, can be used. The coupon for the larger size offers more favorable savings, both numerically and percentagewise, thereby explicitly encouraging consumers to go with the larger size.

To bedazzle the consumer with relatively large numbers. Some refund programs based on purchase requirements can offer savings of $5, $10, and even more. Procter & Gamble has tested long-term refund programs offering ultimate savings of $100. And, of course, the auto makers have become exceedingly reliant on refunds (rebates) of $500 and more on specified models to move out inventory stocks.

Store coupons may not have the ability to command consumer attention with savings in the double digits or more (although a number of brands—

Maytag is an example—have experimented with the concept of large-dollar-value coupons on large-dollar-value items), but a page of packaged product coupons from one manufacturer, or grouped on a co-op basis, can be bannered with featured savings of $2, $3, $4, and the like. When it appears in newspapers, magazines, or inserts with the more workaday solo coupons offering a mere $0.15 or $0.25, the page of $3 coupons will prove to be an attention-getter.

Refund programs also share a number of general objectives with other basic promotional vehicles, including offering promotion variety, providing an additional selling tool in trade presentations, and tying in with advertising messages.

ADVANTAGES OF REFUND PROGRAMS

With all this sameness in objectives, particularly relative to store coupons, what makes a refund program so unique and so right in so many ways for today's marketers? The following are the essential advantages of refund offers over those of other promotional tools.

Drama. Few promotional tools can offer the drama of a refund in terms of consumer savings. Auto makers may have been forced into the use of big refunds to get customers into dealer showrooms, but there is no disputing the effectiveness of these programs in working toward the manufacturers' objectives. In print media, the headline spotlighting refunds of $2, $5, $7, or more on packaged goods can stop consumers in their tracks.

Lack of Trade Involvement. Because the refund is by and large a direct interaction between the consumer and the manufacturer, there is no need for store policies and procedures concerning the handling of refunds, as there is in the case of store coupons. Many classes of retail trade, and small operations within all classes of trade, are not comfortable with, and may not accept, store coupons. The entire reimbursement mechanism required to sort and clear coupons and repay stores for giving consumers their coupon savings, plus handling fees to stores and clearinghouses, is almost entirely absent in the processing of refunds. The retailer gets the full purchase price up front.

The refund's simplicity in terms of bypassing the retailer (while increasing consumers' interest in purchasing the retailer's product) makes this promotional device the answer for outlets with little or no experience in handling coupons.

Minimization of Abuse. There is no opportunity for misredemption in refund offers at the consumer and store levels, since the refund document in an advertisement is not tantamount to cash, as store cents-off coupons are. Therefore, there is far less in the way of large-scale fraud in refund programs at these levels. Abuses may exist if refund processing centers fail to screen and verify each and every refund claim as to proper documentation and required proofs of purchase. In the absence of such screening, refunds are given to anyone who sends in a claim, regardless of the proof-of-purchase requirement. This may mean lower processing costs charged by the fulfillment center, but overall costs to the manufacturer may increase because of the acceptance by the center of incomplete refund claims.

Slippage. Slippage will be discussed in more detail later as a vital component of refund planning and costing-out exercises. But it does represent a distinct—if abstract—advantage of refunds over many other promotional programs. Slippage is exactly what the term implies: consumers fail to complete or send in their refund requirements and thus "slip" out of the program. Additional purchases of the product have been made because of the consumer's *intent* to claim the refund. But the claim is never made—the consumer simply forgets to mail it in, misses the deadline for refund claims, or loses or misplaces the proofs of purchase. And, quite obviously, the more complicated and involved a refund program is in terms of proof-of-purchase requirements, the greater the slippage. Slippage reduces the marketer's liability in terms of refund-claim payment, while generating significant product purchases in association with the refund offer.

Low Relative Cost. Slippage helps make the refund offer far more affordable to the marketer than such "high-intensity" promotional vehicles as product sampling and store-redeemable coupons. Up until recently, the low-cost aspect of refunds has also been attributed to low-level consumer response, especially as compared with coupons. Because with refunds the reward is not immediate, as it is with store coupons, the overall response or redemption rate has been far lower when measured on a percent-of-circulation basis than that of coupons.

Recent data suggest that refunds have been gaining enormously in terms of consumer acceptance and use, while store-coupon usage may be at or near a plateau after more than a decade of heady growth. This increase in refund usage must be factored into marketers' planning in terms of projected program costs. The old benchmark averages of, say, 2.5 percent redemption of coupons offered via print media versus 0.5 percent redemption of refunds may have to go out the window in terms of planning for tomorrow's refund programs.

REFUNDS IN PERSPECTIVE: WHY ALL PROMOTION IS GROWING

The reasons for the growth in all promotional activities are important enough to warrant a digression, since they really are impacting the entire subject of promotion itself.

Long-Running Economic Recession and Inflation. With all of us feeling the pinch, the idea of saving money by means of things like refund offers, free samples, and store coupons has become increasingly appealing. The worse we perceive things to be, the more attractive the larger savings offered in refund programs will seem.

Population Stability. As a result of slowed population growth in the United States, there has been no real net growth in the size of the retail base for years. New stores that open serve to replace older stores that have closed. Many retailers are going out of business or merging with conglomerates. What it really boils down to is a fairly fixed and finite amount of space in which to transact the sale of goods and services.

Competitive Intensity. The slowed population growth and the static retail base have combined to produce a competitive intensity in the marketing arena that borders on science fiction. Manufacturers are pumping out new products—always the lifeblood of packaged goods firms—at a greater rate than ever before. And these new products are being dumped into a market-place that essentially is resisting them. Add to this the counterpressure from private-label and generically labeled goods and the siphoning of a growing percentage of traditional volume by "underground" operations such as flea markets, and the challenge to the manufacturer of branded goods and services stands forth in sharp detail.

Future Shock. The complexity of life, the rapid rate of change, and the instant communication of events via the all-reaching electronic media have produced a short-term horizon, what Alvin Toffler calls "future shock" in his landmark sociological best-seller. We can fly to Europe in four hours, put home budgets on a small computer terminal, and even see products marketed specifically for one pass through the trade. We have no patience with a new product that is slow catching on.

How then can advertising (which relies on a long period of exposure and frequency of message to build awareness of, and desire for, goods and services) be the sole builder of successful marketing case histories?

The answer is that it cannot. Sales promotion is also necessary: to score a rapid sales victory; to convert, even for just one trial, the user of a competitive product; to encourage multiple purchases and increase the frequency of purchases; and to support and enhance the advertising message, focus on the benefits depicted in the advertising, and create some consumer action *now*, before someone else does.

Within the general sphere of sales promotion, such tools as refunds and sweepstakes have shown the sharpest growth in recent years. Store coupons have reached such levels of saturation that their rate of growth, if not the actual number of coupons in distribution, has slowed appreciably. Sampling, as potent a trial generator as it is, has always been held in check by the enormous costs involved in producing and distributing trial sizes. Premiums must be seen in close alliance with product advertising, since the best premiums are devices for cementing a consumer's own vision of a product's positioning.

So the growth of refunds can be attributed to the particular advantages of this type of promotion, detailed earlier, and also to the general conditions that have made promotion of all types a critical element of the marketing mix.

DRAWBACKS OF REFUND PROGRAMS

Obviously, refunds are not the be-all and end-all of promotion. Refunds have certain disadvantages not shared by other promotional vehicles, and in many instances these are the flip side of refunds' advantages. Some of these drawbacks are discussed below.

Relatively Low Response Rate. We are speaking here of refunds versus coupons, since the response rate or redemption of refunds is generally superior to that of premiums and roughly equal to sweepstakes response. The element of slippage is vital in appreciating that refund response rate per se is really the tip of the iceberg.

Delayed Reward. In the promotion arena, the best type of gratification is instant gratification. In coupons, this means being able to save money when purchasing an item. In sweepstakes, it means an instant-winner game in which you know immediately if you are a winner and what prize you have won. In sampling, it is the immediate availability of a small quantity of a product for trial use. In premiums, it is the on-pack, in-pack, or near-pack item that is received at the time the product is purchased.

Refunds are a two-phase promotional tool. First, consumers must make one or more product purchases in order to obtain the required proofs of purchase; then they must submit the proofs of purchase and other required documentation by mail and await a reward that may arrive weeks later. These factors present obstacles to the consumer and account for the existence of slippage in refund offers and the relatively low response rate.

Less Trade Support.   Since refunds do not directly involve the trade, overall trade support tends to be weak. Coupons require involvement of store and headquarters personnel and can visibly influence product movement. Sweepstakes and immediate-reward premiums, when advertised in the media or in the store at the point of purchase, can generate additional traffic in stores and influence product sales. For all the reasons set forth above, refunds do not create this kind of excitement in and of themselves. Thus marketers must make these offers seem exciting by flagging refund availability prominently on packages and by running ads with dramatic headlines, such as "save $5."

Questionable Product Movement.   Refunds generally require multiple proofs of purchase. This tends to make the refund offer something less than ideal when the main promotional objective is to generate new-user trial. Thus it follows that refunds appeal more directly to existing product users, as rewards for brand loyalty. Following this logic, the requirements to qualify for the refund may be right there in the existing product user's pantry, and therefore the results of a refund offer may be both tenuous and hard to measure. In fact, the refund and coupon clubs across the country advise their members to save proofs of purchase from every product they buy and to keep them for use in a future refund program.

The Annoyance Factor.   The delayed nature of the refund reward, plus the necessity of putting something in the mail, tends to be a consumer inhibitor. An additional element is the labor required to extract the required proofs of purchase. In some cases, a jar must be soaked in warm water to remove a label, and in others the contents of a package must be emptied or used up before the required proof of purchase can be "liberated." These factors are related both to the low response rate of refunds and to slippage, which must be considered in assessing refund programs.

GROWTH OF REFUNDS

Despite all their disadvantages, refund programs have grown dramatically in terms of both marketer use and consumer acceptance. The advantages of refund programs and the incredible growth of promotion as a whole far outweigh the negatives.

It was only recently, however—in 1977 and again in 1981—that consumer use of refunds was properly documented. The Nielsen Clearing House conducted surveys that, in the most recent instance, involved a national telephone sample of 1007 respondents on a random basis. This survey showed that in terms of consumer awareness alone, refunds have made important inroads as a promotional tool. (See Figure 5-1.)

As the Nielsen Clearing House points out, "The current awareness level represents a 23% increase over the study three years ago, when 74% of the households interviewed stated they were aware of refund offers. More than 9 of every 10 U.S. households have heard of refund offers." Thus, from a base that we might term one of "latency," the potential for consumer use of refunds is approaching universality.

Figure 5-2 shows the dramatic increase in actual refund use reported in surveys taken in 1977 and 1980, from 27 percent of the respondents to 45 percent. The latter figure indicates that nearly half of those people who are aware of refunds have actually sent in for a refund at some point in time.

A further measure points to the growing use of refunds as a "here-and-now" tool. Figure 5-3 shows the percentage of respondents in a Neilsen Clearing House survey who reported having sent in for a refund at *any* time. The dramatic figure here is the 1980 percentage of consumers reporting that they had sent in for refunds *in the past year*, as opposed to the percentage reporting having done so more than a year earlier. About three-fourths of the consumers reporting using refunds in 1980 had done so within the past year. This points to the increasing appeal of refunds and to their growing ability to generate speedier action than in the past.

Figure 5-4 provides a good barometer of the potential for growth in

FIGURE 5-1. Percentage of households aware of re-fund offers. (*Courtesy of A. C. Nielsen Co.*)

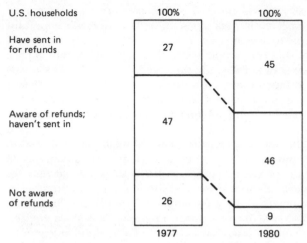

FIGURE 5-2. Participation in refund offers. (*Courtesy of A. C. Nielsen Co.*)

refunding. It indicates how many *separate* refund offers were claimed by those households reporting refund usage in the 1977 and 1980 studies. The growth has all been in the direction of more and more utilization of refund offers. In 1977, 21 percent of the refund-using households claimed they had sent in for

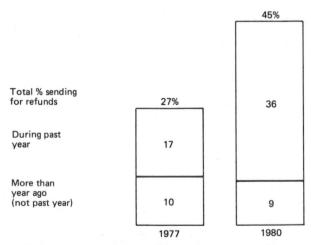

FIGURE 5-3. Percentage of households sending for re- funds. (*Courtesy of A. C. Nielsen Co.*)

four to six refunds in the past year. In 1980, 24 percent reported sending in for four to six refunds. While in both studies the groups claiming to have sent away for seven, twelve, and even more refunds during the previous year represent only a small percentage of the total, they represent a greater percentage of the 1977 total, which is all the more significant because the 1980 refund-using group was much larger than the 1977 group.

Thus, every indication is that more consumers are taking advantage of refund offers more often than ever before. There is no reason to assume that these growth trends will not continue.

The Nielsen Clearing House data also show that refund use is highest among those with annual incomes between $15,000 and $25,000, among people whose weekly grocery purchases cost between $31 and $40, among larger families, and among white female shoppers. On a regional basis, both the southeast and the southwest show markedly lower refund use than other regions of the country, where approximately 50 percent of households take advantage of refund offers.

The quantum leaps made by refunds in recent years are further illustrated by some of the figures emerging from a *Ladies' Home Journal* study of consumer attitudes toward promotion conducted in 1977, the same year in which the initial Nielsen Clearing House report on refunds was published. The *Ladies' Home Journal* study, which consisted of personal interviews with 200 women across the country, found that 73 percent of the sample was, at best,

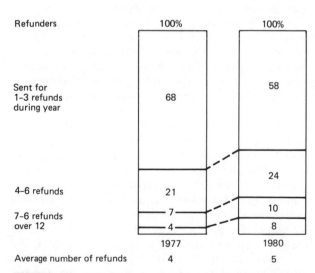

FIGURE 5-4. Number of refunds sent for. (*Courtesy of A. C. Nielsen Co.*)

only somewhat interested in cash-refund offers and that only 13 percent "frequently" sent away for them.

Steadily increasing costs of postage and the "bother" of the refund mail-away-and-wait process were seen as the key inhibiting factors; other significant problems included the delayed-reward effect, the label or proof-of-purchase requirements, and the expiration of a refund offer before the required proofs of purchase could be collected.

TYPES OF REFUND PROGRAMS

Changes in the economy and the mystique of the large dollar amount of refunds have made refund offers the growth medium they are today. Let's now take a look at various types of refunds and how they are put to use.

Cash Refunds. The cash-refund program is the type most easily understood and most universally accepted by the consumer. The refund can take the form of cash mailed back directly from the manufacturer; this method is employed by Smith-Corona and other companies manufacturing relatively expensive, infrequently purchased products.

The consumer pays the regular purchase price to the retailer and obtains a sales receipt to include with the refund-request form in the ad, which stipulates the required proofs of purchase. In a relatively low-volume program, it is far easier for the manufacturer to deal directly with the consumer.

Refunds on more frequently purchased packaged goods are generally handled through recognized processing and fulfillment centers; the Ray-O-Vac batteries $1 cash-refund offer, utilizing George Burns as spokesman, is a good example. The official Ray-O-Vac refund mail-in certificate combined simplicity of language and clarity of offer, while still containing the information for retailers and consumers that is legally required to appear on store coupons.

More recently, highly seasonal merchandise in a wide range of categories has benefited from refunds channeled through professional processing and fulfillment centers; for example, the recent Owens-Corning "Get in the Pink" campaign, which promoted fiberglass insulation, ceiling tiles, and roofing shingles, combined a cash-refund offer with a sweepstakes.

The refund offer featured $10 cash back on fiberglass insulation, $10 back on fiberglass ceiling panels, and $15 back on fiberglass roofing shingles. The advertisement for this refund offer appeared in Sunday supplements on September 12. According to the specifics of the offer, purchase receipts could be dated no later than September 26, and refund claims could be received no later than October 31. This illustrates the short-fuse, product-loading objective of many refund offers, that is, to generate multiple purchases over a short span of time. Marketers rely on this technique when the product in question is seasonal in nature and when the competition may be expected to be running its own promotions. In the case of insulation, ceiling tiles, and roofing shingles, the yearly sales curve peaks in the early fall. Owens-Corning was therefore utilizing its offer to bring consumers into building supply stores to purchase specific products in the quantities required to qualify for the refund.

A $1 Kingsford charcoal cash-refund offer illustrates the way marketers of packaged products use the short-fuse technique. The company's advertisement appeared in Sunday free-standing inserts on June 27. It contained a "Hurry! Offer expires . . ." warning, telling consumers that the offer would be withdrawn on August 15. By requiring proofs of purchase from 40 pounds of charcoal, Kingsford was seeking to create a purchase-repurchase cycle that would defeat competitive promotional activity during the peak summer season; 40 pounds of charcoal is probably all that a typical household needs during the summer.

The two programs described below illustrate the growth of refunds as a promotional vehicle for product categories which rarely, if ever, have been promoted to consumers in the past.

Coleman offered a $4 cash refund as a mailed-back reward for purchasing its Inflate-All air pump, and Joseph E. Seagram & Sons offered a $1.50 cash refund for proof of purchase of its 1.75-liter party size of Seagram's 7 Crown whiskey. The liquor industry in particular has recently begun to appreciate the potency of refunds in moving out special product sizes during peak seasons, and it has accordingly begun to use cash refunds in great numbers and with seasonal regularity.

Coupon Refunds. When the objective of the refund offer is to reward loyal consumers and keep them buying the brand, marketers frequently utilize refunds in the form of store coupons good for free specified sizes or types of the product. This variation may have less impact than the cash refund, since to get the reward, the consumer must select the featured item during another visit to the store. However, using this format reduces the marketer's total dollar liability, since the cost of goods given away relative to the value of the refund coupon will always be less than the cost of an identical refund offer on a cash-back basis. Furthermore, not all the refunded coupons will be utilized by consumers receiving them. In addition, fraudulent claims will be minimized since the refund is good only if the consumer makes an additional purchase of the featured brand.

The wording used in coupon-refund offers must differ from that used in cash-refund offers because the use of the reward is narrowly constrained, as opposed to the universal utility of cash. Thus, such programs can offer *savings* of $1.50, $2, and the like, or they can banner that magic word *free* in the headline.

In one offer, Swift promised the consumer a total of three $0.50 store coupons good toward the purchase of any Swift Premium food product in return for four proofs of purchase from among a number of brands listed. The offer was worded, "Save $1.50."

In two head-to-head competitive offers on plastic bags, both Dow Chemical (Ziploc) and Mobil Chemical (Hefty) commanded consumer attention by making the word *free* the largest graphic element in their advertisements. Dow offered the consumer one free coupon for Ziploc storage bags and one free coupon for Ziploc heavy-duty freezer bags in return for *two* proofs of purchase of each. Dow thereby gained three consumer exposures to each of two products within the same brand family for each completely fulfilled offer. Mobil offered the consumer a coupon good on Hefty Odor Guard trash bags in return for a proof of purchase from *either* Odor Guard trash bags or Hefty medium garbage bags.

The objective here was to reward consumers who were already using Odor Guard trash bags and, more important, to induce users of other Hefty garbage bags to trade up to the more expensive Odor Guard trash bags. This was done by means of the store coupon, which was good *only* for Odor Guard trash bags but was available for proof of purchase of *either* Odor Guard or the lower-cost medium garbage bags. To ram home the Odor Guard benefit, the refund also required consumers to write the answer to "What's missing?" on the refund request certificate. The answer to the question was provided right beneath the line for consumer fill-in, i.e., "odor-causing germs." Getting the consumer to write this phrase manually was superior to virtually any other form of advertising copy or visual, in terms of awareness and recall, that the company could have used. This was a form of "programmed learning"; here, the consumer mentally traded up to the Odor Guard product prior to receiving a coupon refund, which, in effect, resulted in a free sample of the Odor Guard product when the coupon was used.

"Let Us Buy Your . . ." ("LUBY") Refunds. This form of refund can work on either a cash-refund or a coupon-refund basis; it is essentially a strategic device to give advertising copy more impact. The advertisement surrounding a LUBY offer suggests the benefits of another product or products in association with the featured brand. While, on the surface, it seems that a LUBY offer should involve directly related products, that is not always the case.

A Welch's "Popcorn Party" offer yielded the consumer a store coupon worth $0.75 toward the purchase of any brand of unpopped popcorn for three 40-ounce or larger bottles of Welch's bottled grape juice. The association of Welch's grape juice with popcorn reinforced the positioning of the product as one that fits the same usage situations as carbonated soft drinks but is "differently delicious," since it contains no added sugar and is enriched with vitamin C.

Diet 7-Up, allying itself with weight-conscious consumers, offered a $1.50 coupon good toward the purchase of any fresh produce in return for a series of specified proofs of purchase of the product.

Even though offers such as those described above result in store coupons to the consumer, the marketer's liability is increased because the savings are on a "foreign" product; the marketer must accept and pay for the face value, plus the handling, of all coupons coming back through the coupon clearing-house channels.

A LUBY offer can function on a cash-refund basis, as shown by a refund offer involving Dixie plates and cups. The benefit to the consumer was up to $2 worth of free charcoal. In order to qualify for this refund, the consumer was required to submit two proofs of purchase from any Dixie Livingware product and one proof of purchase from any brand of charcoal, *plus* a cash-register receipt indicating the prices of both the charcoal and the Dixie items. The consumer then received in the mail a check for the purchase price of the charcoal, up to $2. The Dixie items and the charcoal were obvious "go-togethers," and, since consumers generally consider charcoal to be a relatively expensive item, the $2 offer looked good all around. The entailments of the offer from the consumer's standpoint (multiple proofs of purchase, cash-register receipt, etc.) were expected to result in a good deal of slippage. Thus it was assumed that there would be an increase in the sales of Dixie products, as a result of the offer, but a reduced amount of refund claims because of incomplete proof-of-purchase materials, loss of register receipts, etc.

A "Free Picnic" offer from Lever Bros.' line of bar soaps demonstrated that a LUBY-refund offer need not pair up only closely related products, such as diet soft drinks and produce, grape juice and popcorn, or charcoal and disposable cups and plates. In this program, which ran from June to September, consumers got back the purchase price up to $1 on a variety of picnic products, including paper napkins, snacks, rolls, and hot dogs. While operating under a "Free Picnic" banner to command attention, each month's free offer was a separate LUBY refund requiring proofs of purchase of featured Lever bar-soap brands and the picnic item of the month.

The relationship between bar soap and picnics is tenuous at best, although Lever Bros. took pains to describe its products as "your favorite summertime bar soaps" in the ad copy.

Escalating Refunds. The escalating refund is a serious attempt to maximize both multiple purchases and continuity of purchases over a specified time period that can be as long as one year or as short as thirty to forty-five days. This type of program offers the consumer an increasingly larger refund based on greater and greater purchase requirements, and is designed to bring to its peak the element of slippage.

A L'Oreal hair-care products offer is an example. In addition to a sweepstakes event, L'Oreal featured "The Great $1—$2—$3 Refund," with $1 offered for one featured product, $2 cash back for two products, and $3 for any two featured products plus a proof of purchase from the higher-priced Excellence hair color, Brush-On Highlights, or Extra Body perm.

A Del Monte "Savings Jackpot" used a slot machine as a device to present escalating-refund savings of from $0.50 to $4. Note that the word *savings* was a tip-off that the refund would be in the form of coupons, not cash. The unique element here was the combination of both specified Del Monte products, as in a Hawaiian Punch requirement at the $0.50 level, and "wild cards," which were the consumer's choice of proofs of purchase from any other Del Monte, Hawaiian Punch, or Chun King products.

In this program, consumers could not only escalate but also accumulate their savings. Thus, if the requirements to get *each* of the increasingly valued refunds were met (a total of sixty labels from specified and wild-card items), the consumer was eligible not only for $7.50 in coupon-refund savings but also for a $2.50 cash bonus, making this a $10 program, as highlighted in the subheading to the "Savings Jackpot" theme. This program operated over a six-month period from late April through the end of October.

A Heinz catsup offer was an escalating-refund program with a twist. Here, the consumer was offered a greater reward based not on additional purchases but on completion of a strategically devised "task." The lower-level offer was $1 worth of Heinz catsup coupons in return for two 44-ounce Heinz catsup proofs of purchase. To get the $2 savings, composed of the $1 worth of Heinz catsup coupons and a $1 coupon good toward the purchase of any brand of hot dogs, the consumer was required to send in two 44-ounce Heinz catsup proofs of purchase, *plus* an illustration of a 44-ounce Heinz catsup bottle cut from a retail grocer's newspaper food ad.

In doing this, Heinz steered the consumer toward supermarket ads in the best-food-day issues of local papers and thus acquired an additional selling tool to present to the trade in terms of retailers' increasing emphasis on Heinz 44-ounce catsup in their own advertising. Since it escalated the $1 savings up to $2 by adding a coupon worth $1 toward the purchase of hot dogs, this program combined elements of escalating-refund and LUBY-refund offers.

Because escalating refunds generally dangle the promise of greater refund size for greater purchase activity, the slippage in such refund programs is intense. The objective is to get consumers to try for the maximum refund level. The greater the number of proofs of purchase required, the greater the level of slippage. The marketer can therefore talk about large total savings and yet be confident that very few consumers will make the required number of purchases, although many will *try* to. And therein lies the benefit.

Double or Bonus Refunds. This type of refund requires the consumer either to perform a special task or to make a second purchase in order to increase the refund value. A double refund is really another variant of the escalating refund; a bonus refund is a totally different device.

A Glad Bags offer from Union Carbide was similar to the Heinz catsup escalating-refund offer described above in that the consumer was offered the opportunity to double a $1 refund. The program required the consumer to submit proofs of purchase from any four of five featured Glad products and also to locate a "Glad refund doubler" symbol in retail grocery ads in local newspapers. Like the Heinz catsup program, this program offered *savings* up to $2, not cash, which limited the marketer's liability.

Westinghouse's "Watt-a-Refund" program was a bonus-refund offer with a dramatic and interesting twist. A bonus refund generally involves an initial purchase to receive a cash or coupon refund *and* a second purchase to take advantage of an additional refund certificate mailed back with the initial refund portion of the offer. Thus a number of discrete purchase and repurchase cycles are generated.

In its program, Westinghouse offered consumers a $1 cash refund for the purchase of three packages of specified types of Westinghouse bulbs. Along with the $1 refund check, consumers received an *additional* refund in the form of a "bonanza" rub-off certificate. A second refund value was hidden under a rub-off device, identical to the ones used in instant-winner games. In this Westinghouse offer, the minimum refund was $1, as in the initial phase of the program, but the maximum refund was as large as $10,000. Regardless of dollar amount, the "mystery refund" was still a refund. In order to claim it—whether $1, $100, $1000, or $10,000—an additional set of three proofs of purchase was required. Thus, Westinghouse combined the excitement of a sweepstakes with the practicality of a refund offer in one program.

Overlay Programs. A number of programs already discussed have illustrated refunds as part of overlay promotions. Simply stated, in an overlay program a refund offer is one of several promotional tools, operating simultaneously and delivered via a common advertisement, used to achieve a number of objectives and strengthen the overall appeal of the total set of programs. Most commonly, an overlay program includes both a store coupon and a refund offer of some type. But the program could also consist of a sweepstakes plus a refund, or even of a sweepstakes, a coupon, and a refund.

When the overlay consists of a coupon plus a refund, the objective is to broaden the appeal of the offer to both existing users and potential new users. When the program combines a sweepstakes and a refund, the central idea is to use the inherent drama and attention-getting power of the sweepstakes to hold and motivate the ad reader, showcasing the refund offer as part of the total program.

A program from Carnation Company's Little Friskies, Chef's Blend, and Fish Ahoy cat foods centered on an escalating refund offering savings of up to

$4, effected as $1, $2, or $4 worth of coupons for increasingly large proof-of-purchase requirements. As an overlay to the refund, a set of $0.25 store coupons, each good toward the purchase of one of the featured brands, was included. These were considered trial generators and "starter" coupons toward the accumulation of the proofs of purchase required for the refund. The coupons expired on December 31, while the refund was good only through September 30 of the same year. This schedule was designed to generate the multiple and repeat purchases required for the refund over a more concentrated period.

IPSO, Inc., marketer of IPSO candies in snap-together boxes, offered a $1 cash refund for four proofs of purchase. The advertisement, which was written to excite and motivate children as well as adults, presented the refund certificate in crystal-clear form. Here a $0.25 starter coupon overlay the "Build-a-Buck" refund offer. In this instance, the starter coupon had no expiration date; the refund offer, however, expired on September 30 following the ad publication date of May 16.

In a free Kingsford charcoal offer, two "outdoorsy" brands—Reynolds wrap aluminum foil and Coca-Cola's Hi-C fruit drink—were featured in store coupons. The refund, effected as a coupon good for a free 10-pound bag of Kingsford charcoal, required proofs of purchase from Reynolds wrap, Hi-C, *and* Kingsford charcoal. The refund portion of the program was on a short-fuse basis, expiring June 15, after a May 23 advertising announcement.

Finally, a $1 cash refund for the proofs of purchase of three different Nabisco cookies provided an overlay to Nabisco's "World Series 1982 Sweep-stakes." The sweepstakes ad caught the reader's attention and presented the lure of exciting prizes with no purchase necessary. The refund provided cash rewards for purchase of the cookies and thus enhanced the value of the total program.

REFUND CONSTRUCTION AND OPERATING DYNAMICS

The official refund certificate, which must accompany required proofs of purchase, sales or cash-register receipts, or other necessary documentation, is the central element of any refund program. Compared with a cents-off store coupon, the official refund certificate is a model of simplicity. It must include the following:

1. Identification of the nature of the refund. In a Kool-Aid offer, for example, the refund consisted of a store coupon good for another canister of the product. This information was presented on one full page of a three-page direct-mail advertising unit.
2. The mailing address to which consumers should forward the refund materials.

3. Information concerning specific proofs of purchase and other documentation required.
4. Space for the consumer's address, including zip code.
5. The expiration date of the offer.
6. Any limitation in terms of duplication by household or family. Most refunds are limited to one per household or family. Computerization of refund requests can eliminate duplicate requests.
7. Information concerning fulfillment of the refund, e.g., "Allow six to eight weeks for processing requests."
8. Any legal disclaimer, e.g., "Void where prohibited, taxed, or otherwise restricted."
9. Any originality requirement, e.g., "Certificate may not be transferred, exchanged, or sold, nor may it be reproduced or copied." This alerts the recipients of coupon and refund newsletters, which mechanically reproduce thousands of coupon, refund, premium, and sweepstakes offers, that only original certificates (and proofs of purchase, for that matter) will be accepted.

An actual proof of purchase is a must in a packaged goods refund offer. The proof of purchase may be an official seal contained on the package, the Universal Product Code symbol and digits cut from the package, a cap liner, or an interior flap, for example. Refund programs, however strategically appropriate, that permit something other than an actual proof of purchase from a package (such as handwritten Universal Product Code numbers plus a cash-register receipt) create what amounts to a license to steal on the part of the consumer. If a product as currently manufactured (e.g., an aerosol product) has no mailable proof of purchase, one must be created.

When refunds are effected in the form of cash, the checks utilized should contain somewhat more information than a standard check. When the refund is for less than $5 or perhaps $10, a check marked "payable to bearer" is the most cost-efficient route for the marketer to go in terms of processing and fulfillment of the offer.

In addition, the refund check should specifically show the limit of the amount for which it can be cashed; this will prevent any attempt at check alteration by the recipient. Also, each check should show a date after which it cannot be cashed. Naturally, the name of the bank, its Federal Reserve number and location, and an account number in magnetic code numbers, plus "reminder" product logos and information, are standard elements of the refund check.

When cash refunds are for more than $5 or $10, as in the Westinghouse "Watt-a-Refund" program (the mystery-refund program detailed earlier), the check should be a typical two-party check. This requires custom imprinting of the name of the refund recipient and the amount of the check (this check can also indicate the topmost limit of the refund offer). Other particulars are the same as those for smaller refund checks, discussed above. When custom-written checks are utilized, window envelopes can save time and duplication of name and address entries in fulfillment and processing.

Finally, when a brand name incorporates a prominent celebrity or licensed character or when the brand is closely associated in advertising with a celebrity or character, a "personality" check may be used for the cash refund. The personality or licensed character "signs" the check, and a likeness of the celebrity also appears on the check. This technique was used in recent years by STP Corp., a manufacturer of automotive engine-additive products. In a refund program, the famous racing brothers Kyle and Richard Petty both signed the refund checks, and their likenesses, along with the STP logo, appeared on the checks.

As another example, the manufacturer of Weather Patrol mittens, which uses a Warner Brothers Bugs Bunny character on its product packaging and in its advertising, gave out $0.50 refund checks featuring the likeness and "signature" of Bugs Bunny.

Personality checks add a certain spice to the refund offer, and they can also help limit the marketer's refund liability because many recipients never cash these checks, preferring to keep them as souvenirs.

THE ROLE OF FULFILLMENT CENTERS

As noted earlier in this chapter, refunds on big-ticket, infrequently purchased items, such as cars and major appliances, may efficiently be handled directly by the sponsoring marketer. When higher-volume products are involved, the handling of a refund program is best left to a professional fulfillment center, just as the majority of cents-off store coupons, sweepstakes, and sampling programs are handled in fulfillment centers featuring the latest in modern handling and reporting techniques.

The professional fulfillment center is geared to:

1. Provide required post-office boxes for the offer
2. Work with the marketer in structuring and debugging the offer before it appears
3. Open a bank account and print refund checks
4. Receive and open mail
5. Screen refund requests for eligibility, proof-of-purchase requirements, sales or cash-register receipts, etc.
6. Post information for reports to be issued to the marketer
7. Check refund requests against prior refunds processed to eliminate duplicate requests
8. Issue refund checks, insert them in envelopes, and address, stamp, seal, and mail the envelopes

9. Provide weekly and monthly activity reports to the marketer
10. Handle "grief" mail from consumers

With refund offers growing in appeal, and hence in volume of response, selection of a fulfillment center that will properly service the program, particularly in terms of refund-claim verification, is vital. Obviously, the cost to the marketer of the fulfillment center's services will vary according to the complexity of the offer and the frequency and complexity of analysis reports to be provided to the marketer by the fulfillment center. Currently, for the full panoply of required services, fulfillment centers charge from $0.35 to $0.55 *per refund request*, plus postage (generally bulk rate). These costs per refund do not include the one-time costs of printing the checks (or coupons) or the costs of opening post-office boxes.

In selecting a fulfillment center for receiving and processing refunds, the marketer should be aware of *all* the costs entailed if a candidate fulfillment center presents costs on an à la carte, or "basic cost plus a few extras," basis, in order to show an inordinately low cost per refund just to get the business. It is a good idea to visit the fulfillment center to make sure that all systems and personnel are in place as promised. (For greater detail, see Chapter 29.)

REFUND ECONOMICS AND PLANNING

When selecting a refund offer to use as a promotional tool, the marketer must address two questions. The first concerns the appropriateness of the refund versus other promotional techniques available, and the second has to do with the cost-benefit relation: What is affordable to the marketer, and what results may be produced? The material presented thus far in this chapter provides a good foundation for marketing executives in the selection and employment of refund offers. You know your product, your budget, and your objectives. You now have a good background for measuring the strengths of a refund program against your objectives, your audience, and the broad canvas upon which your product is doubtless one of several competing for the same target consumers.

Projecting the costs of the refund program and weighing these against the benefits, i.e., increased sales volume of your product, are the crucial final steps in chiseling the refund into the granite of your next year's approved promotion plan.

Unfortunately, this presents a problem, even for marketers who have long experience with refund offers—firms with past results of refund programs down to three decimal points for literally every product in the shop. The problem is that refund offers are going through the roof, and normative data available simply cannot address what will occur in a given refund program today, all other things being equal. The data we have can be only directional at best, not absolute.

Obviously, everything is a variable in planning and projecting refunds. Response will vary, depending on:

1. The featured product's existing position in the marketplace in terms of brand share, total volume, universality of category use, etc.
2. The size of the refund and whether it is in the form of cash or coupons
3. The number of proofs of purchase required
4. In-store, on-package, and advertising media used to deliver the offer
5. The expiration date
6. Overlay programs (coupons, sweepstakes, premiums, etc.)

A lot of this is common sense. Clearly, refunds (along with other promotions) will work best when the featured product is a leader, has a broad volume base to begin with, is in a category enjoying widespread use, and has a high purchase frequency.

A refund offer of less than $1 in today's economy may be considered not worth the consumer's time in terms of collecting and saving the required proofs of purchase, filling in the refund form, and addressing, stamping, and mailing the refund request. The larger the refund, in conjunction with the number of proofs of purchase required, the greater the response to the offer is likely to be.

How much advertising is needed to deliver the offer and whether to use cash refunds or coupon refunds are vital considerations. Heavy use of print media to announce a refund is appropriate if maximum and rapid response among users and nonusers of the featured product is an objective. A cash refund might tip a nonuser over the edge in terms of purchasing the product, whereas a coupon refund might self-limit the program to rewarding and holding existing users of the product (a not inconsiderable objective, given today's competitive climate).

A refund program with a short-fuse expiration date may produce a truly readable response in terms of sales—that "blip in the curve" that all marketers look for. Refund programs operating over a period of six months to one year may not show up on a sales curve at all in any given monthly measuring period, especially if the featured product has strong volume to begin with or has large seasonal swings in volume. In these instances, only the regular refund processing reports testify to the impact of the program over time.

Overlay programs involving refunds plus coupons or other promotional tools often serve to increase, to a degree, the response rate of all the promotional tools combined in the overlay.

The Nielsen Clearing House has estimated response averages for cash-refund offers, based on delivery media. These are shown in the accompanying table.

	Average	Range
Print-media offers	0.5% of circulation	0.1–0.9%
Point-of-purchase offers	2.5% of circulation	1.5–4.5%
In-pack and on-pack offers	5.6% of circulation	1.4–7.4%

Given the burgeoning growth of refunding in the past few years, these response averages, particularly those for print-media offers, are likely to be on the conservative side.

Let's put these historic refund-response norms to work, however, in developing a hypothetical refund cost-benefit analysis. Assume that a brand is planning to offer a $1 cash refund requiring two proofs of purchase and the official refund certificate. The refund will be advertised in a nationally distributed free-standing insert with circulation totaling 36,000,000, plus in-store point-of-purchase refund "take-one" pads, totaling 20,000 stores × 50 certificates per pad = 1,000,000. Media costs and advertising and point-of-purchase production costs are not included in this budgeting exercise.

Now assume that the refund fulfillment center is handling refund redemptions at $350 per 1000 plus bulk postage ($0.109 each), plus $40 per 1000 for custom check printing. According to response averages:

1. Print-media circulation: 36,000,000 × 0.5% response = 180,000 responses.
2. Point-of-purchase circulation: 1,000,000 × 2.5% response = 25,000 responses.
3. Total responses = 205,000 (assuming no duplication by household or family).
4. 205,000 × $1 refund face value = $205,000.
5. 205,000 × $350 per 1000 fulfillment = $71,750.
6. 205,000 × $40 per 1000 for check printing = $8200.
7. 205,000 × $0.109 return postage = $22,345.
8. Total refund costs = $307,295.
9. Total responses × 2 proofs of purchase required per response = 410,000 units moved.
10. Total refund costs divided by total units moved = $307,295/410,000 = $0.749 cost per unit moved.

The $0.75 cost-per-unit-moved figure must be analyzed by the marketer in terms of the product's factory price to the wholesaler or retailer to determine whether the offer is economically feasible. Obviously, a product with a per-unit factory price to the wholesaler or retailer of, say, $0.60 scarcely justifies this program. The marketer of a product with a per-unit factory price of $1.50 must accept what amounts to half price for the sale of these items. But it is crucial to note that this movement may meet the precise competitive objectives the marketer has in running the refund offer, with cost considerations set aside.

Let's go further. Suppose the marketer decides to continue to offer the $1 refund, but to require four proofs of purchase instead of two. The marketer calculates that with these heavier proof-of-purchase requirements, response to the offer both in print media and at the point of purchase will decline by one-third. Thus:

1. Print-media circulation: 36,000,000 × 0.335% response = 120,600 responses.
2. Point-of-purchase circulation: 1,000,000 × 1.68% response = 16,800 responses.
3. Total responses = 137,400.
4. 137,400 × $1 refund face value = $137,400.
5. 137,400 × $350 per 1000 fulfillment = $48,090.
6. 137,400 × $40 per 1000 for check printing = $5496.
7. 137,400 × $0.109 return postage = $14,977.
8. Total refund costs = $205,963.
9. Total responses × 4 proofs required per response = 1,200,328 units moved.
10. Total refund costs divided by total units moved = $205,963/1,200,328 = $0.172 cost per unit moved.

With these heavier proof-of-purchase requirements, while total number of responses has declined by one-third, the number of units moved has increased by 192 percent, while cost per unit moved has declined by 77 percent!

HOW SLIPPAGE AFFECTS THE NUMBERS

We've mentioned slippage often in this chapter as a vital element affecting refund programs. Let's see how it works. Slippage—which occurs when the consumer fails to submit the refund claim—does not increase the marketer's liability, even though the refund offer may have the effect of increasing sales of the product.

According to an A. C. Nielsen consumer survey:

Thirty-three percent of consumers always claim refunds they intend to claim.
Twenty percent of consumers almost always claim refunds they intend to claim.
Thirty percent of consumers occasionally do not claim refunds they intend to claim.
Seventeen percent of consumers almost always do not claim refunds they intend to claim.

We do not present this as the last statistical word on the subject of slippage, but it is obvious that slippage can have a dramatic effect; in fact, in this Nielsen study, fully 67 percent of the respondents reported that they failed to follow through and claim at least *some* refund offers they had intended to claim. Given the amount of total promotional activity in the marketplace, the many offers with which the consumer is bombarded, the complexity of life, and the normal human penchant for disorganization, it is probably safe to assume that you can tack on 40 to 50 percent of movement a brand received in fulfilled refund responses as incremental movement based on slippage. And, logically, the greater the proof-of-purchase requirements, the greater the degree of slippage.

Using the last refund-cost–movement calculation, let us now be conservative and assume a 40 percent slippage factor as an additional element in the calculation:

1. Print-media circulation: 36,000,000 × 0.33% response = 120,600 responses.
2. Point-of-purchase circulation: 1,000,000 × 1.68% response = 16,800 responses.
3. Total responses = 137,400.
4. 137,400 × $1 refund face value = $137,400.
5. 137,400 × $350 per 1000 fulfillment = $48,090.
6. 137,400 × $40 per 1000 for check printing = $5496.
7. 137,400 × $0.109 return postage = $14,977.
8. Total refund costs = $205,963.
9. Total responses × 4 proofs required per response = 1,200,328 units moved.
10. Slippage at 40% = 480,131 additional units = 1,680,459 total units moved.
11. Total refund costs divided by total units moved = $205,963/1,680,459 = $0.122 cost per unit moved.

At a cost of less than $0.15 per unit moved, this program, offering a $1 refund, has even greater potency and cost efficiency than one offering a store coupon worth $0.10 toward one product purchase. That's because the total coupon cost includes the $0.10 face value, plus approximately $0.09 per coupon in handling costs to retailers and the coupon clearinghouse.

In the first example, a 40 percent slippage factor would have brought the cost per unit moved down from $0.75 to $0.54.

Slippage is a true "wild card" in the planning of refunds, but it is not a spectral shadow—it is real, and must be plugged into cost-benefit calculations.

Since the existence of coupon and refund clubs and newsletters has been noted, the subject should be addressed before concluding this chapter. These clubs and newsletters present the details, and in some cases reproduce entry materials, of hundreds of coupon, refund, sweepstakes, and premium programs. Promotion executives should be of two minds regarding these clubs and publications. To the extent that they provide additional exposure for a program to consumers deeply interested in taking advantage of promotional offers, there is a positive aspect to their existence.

However, if these clubs and publications suggest that consumers mass-produce entries and refund certificates from published examples or if they set up "swap clubs" to trade coupon and refund materials, the effect is to subvert the intent and purpose of the marketer's use of the particular promotional offer. The inclusion of a stipulation in refunds voiding all mechanically reproduced refund certificates and proofs of purchase can help control the promotional offer, as we have noted.

We have seen that refunds seem to be on the ascendancy, while store coupons, if not on the wane, have reached levels of distribution and use that make substantial added growth a near impossibility. Refunds are not the answer to every marketer's promotional needs. But they offer flexibility, they can be presented in countless creative ways, and, most important, consumers are actively looking for them. If we still believe that "the customer is always right," then refunds are guaranteed healthy growth in the years to come.

Sweepstakes and Contests: The Bottom Line Is Promotional Excitement

DON JAGODA
President, Don Jagoda Associates

LEN DAYKIN
Senior Vice President, Don Jagoda Associates

Standing head and shoulders above all other promotional vehicles in terms of generating sheer excitement—at both the consumer and the trade levels—are the prize promotions: sweepstakes, contests, and games. The attraction is the chance to win fabulous prizes, ranging from trips around the world to huge sums of cash. Whether consumers actually enter prize promotions or not, the advertising that supports them is among the most compelling, appealing to what may be thought of as greed, but is more realistically defined as self-interest.

And yet, despite the drama and scope of sweepstakes, contests, and games, these promotions, as we shall see, are among the most cost-efficient for the sponsoring marketer. They offer tremendous promotional power on a fixed budget—a combination that, considering all the other factors that have propelled sweepstakes and contests into the limelight, is almost irresistible.

In this chapter, we will precisely define sweepstakes, contests, and games; discuss their growth; outline the advantages and disadvantages of these programs; identify the various formats used; explore the important legal issues involved; and provide some cost guidelines that marketers can use in the planning of these events.

HISTORICAL BACKGROUND

The origin of games of chance is lost in the mists of time, but it's reasonable to assume that they have been a diversion of the human race for centuries. Elizabeth I, queen of Britain, raised capital to defray the costs of harbor repair by inaugurating the English lottery in 1569. But even that was a "recent" usage.

105

Distribution of prizes by lot was used in the entertainments of the Roman emperors and among the feudal princes. The first government lottery is believed to have been held in France in 1520. In the American colonies, many lotteries were authorized by the colonial legislature for such public purposes as the paving of streets, the construction of wharves, and the erection of churches, not to mention the outfitting of the soldiers who served in the Revolutionary War.

In 1890, Congress forbade the use of the mails for lottery purposes, and five years later, following a scandal involving the Louisiana state lottery, it prohibited the shipment of lottery tickets. The decline in lottery fortunes at the end of the nineteenth century was due in large part to the frequency of fraud in their operation. In this century, the first legalized lottery in the United States was the New Hampshire state lottery, established in 1963; it was followed over the years by lottery programs in more than forty states.

In 1981, when the rock group the Rolling Stones toured the United States, concert tickets were made available on a lottery basis, so great was the demand. In 1982, the state of Washington approved a lottery program for fund-raising. And, inevitably, the subject of lotteries has crept into literature; *The Lotteries*, for example, is a 1980 mystery involving the horrors visited upon a winner of a New England state lottery.

Sweepstakes arose essentially as a type of lottery in conjunction with horse races in which one or a few winners took "all the stakes." In medieval England sweepstakes were popular entertainments for tavern patrons. Shakespeare made reference to them as "swoopstakes" in *Hamlet*, to define a mythical random drawing by Laertes to guess the fate of his father, Polonius. Perhaps the most famous sweepstakes in the world is the Irish Hospitals Sweepstakes, which began in 1930 to benefit hospitals in Ireland and has had as many as 10 million entries.

Prize promotions have had their ups and downs in recent decades. Their growth has not been linear, like that of store coupons, nor has it been as explosive as the rise of refund and rebate programs. Sweepstakes and contests have had distinct cycles, and the downside of these promotional programs has always been triggered by a perception of alleged abuses by the sponsors, be they governments or private companies. Eliminating the abuses has historically preceded a new surge in popularity. For example, in the 1960s, according to direct-mail expert Bob Stone, packaged goods marketers, supermarket chains, oil companies, magazines, and catalogs found sweepstakes, particularly lucky-number "preselected winner" events, to be

> . . . a magic elixir for hyping sales at the retail counter and through the mails.
>   But then in the late '60s, a black cloud began to settle over this newfound promotional gold mine. Consumer discontent and the long arms of government regulatory agencies started to descend. Damaging publicity disclosed, for example, that the lure of big prize contests—prize structures of $250,000

and over—was just that. For in many instances—chance being what it is—
only 10% or less of total prize structures were redeemed. And there were
examples of winners being "seeded" into markets particularly important to
advertisers. Legislation designed to stamp out sweepstakes was given serious
hearings.

Cooler heads prevailed and major legal questions were resolved for the
most part. Unfavorable publicity waned as the consumer was assured that all
prizes will be awarded, or if not, that all unclaimed prizes would not be
awarded. Many marketers began to clearly state the odds.... Some of the
users of sweeps shuddered at the new guidelines which brought about
smaller prize structures and odds disclosures. But, not unlike reactions to
truth-in-lending disclosures, the consumer reacted favorably to forthright
sweeps promotion.

The growth of sweepstakes since the modern "reformation" era has been
substantial. In 1977, according to *Incentive Marketing*, total spending on
sweepstakes by marketers amounted to $98 million. Total spending for 1982
was on the order of $172 million—a 76 percent increase in just five years. As
important as total dollar growth for prize promotions is their increasing
utilization in classes of products and in trades that rarely, if ever, used them in
the past: hardware and housewares manufacturers and retailers, auto makers,
banks, and many others.

SWEEPSTAKES AND CONTESTS AS MARKETING TOOLS TODAY

Two of the biggest concerns in the minds of marketers who are planning for
possible prize promotions are the appropriateness of the strategy for the
particular target audience and the question of what a sweepstakes can
actually do.

In truth, it is difficult to gauge the full impact of a sweepstakes. The
number of entries received does not equate to sales, since product purchase
cannot be required. A sweepstakes that is heavily advertised will generate
brand awareness and recall and will do everything else that nonpromotional
product advertising does. The new generation of instant-winner games,
matching games, programmed-learning sweepstakes, and so on, can increase
store traffic to the brand display—and this will impact on sales, but in a way
that cannot be predicted with certainty.

It is probably wisest to think of sweepstakes as a highly dramatic
multilevel element of a brand's *advertising* strategy, since a well-constructed
sweepstakes will have a theme and a prize structure in keeping with the
product and its regular advertising. We use the term *multilevel* to indicate that
the advertising impacts on both the trade and the consumer. The sweepstakes
may or may not be advertised in normal consumer media. But it must get
visibility at the point of purchase, even if only on the product package itself.

The benefits to the trade of utilizing sweepstakes at the point-of-sale materials are that they create in-store excitement, demonstrating the traffic-generating power of media-advertised instant-winner programs. And, increasingly, trade sweepstakes are held that parallel consumer programs relating to use of the point of purchase; these are of direct benefit to store owners, operators, and managers.

The going rule of thumb is that a good sweepstakes will generate entries on the order of 1 to 2½ percent of total circulation of the program, including advertising and in-store point-of-purchase materials. If a marketer must "keep score" via sheer number of entries received, then a multiple-entry sweepstakes may be the answer, since that format is an entry generator of peerless power. But it still cannot be directly related to sales. Benson & Hedges 100s uses multiple entry as a format, not to generate sales, but to multiply and magnify brand awareness, since every single one of the entries must include the handwritten words "Benson & Hedges 100s." The power of sweepstakes advertising lies in the attention paid to it by consumers. The table below shows readership scores for a recent food-product sweepstakes advertisement appearing in a major women's magazine.

	Noted	Read most
Sweepstakes ad	49%	17%
Norm for all food-product ads	46%	9%
Sweepstakes-ad index	107	189

While the sweepstakes ad was noted by 7 percent more readers than other food-product ads in the same issue of the magazine, the dramatic difference is the weight of intensive readership. The sweepstakes ad's rate of "read most" attention on the part of the readership sample was nearly double that of other food ads in the same issue. The wish-fulfillment lure of big cash, travel, or merchandise prizes will get people reading and keep them reading.

Who enters sweepstakes? A recent study of 2000 consumers in all walks of life produced the responses shown in Table 6-1.

As the data in Table 6-1 show, nearly half of the consumers in this study reported that they had entered a sweepstakes at least once in their lives, and nearly one-third reported that, whether they had entered a sweepstakes or not, they had purchased products featured in a sweepstakes ad.

Overall, sex, age, working status of female heads of household, and marital status are not major determining factors in sweepstakes entry. What seems to matter most is the existence of children under 18 in the household, the size of the household itself, and family income, along with the region of the country in which the family lives.

Larger households with young children, families with larger incomes, and people living in the west seem to constitute the most active sweepstakes-entering groups. And, in general, the percentage of consumers reporting purchasing a product in association with sweepstakes programs tracks right along with who is entering. Younger, bigger households with higher incomes tend to buy the featured brand more, as part of the overall sweepstakes program (although this may not be reflected in the use of actual proofs of purchase to enter the sweepstakes itself).

Looking at the big picture, we can see that by and large, the greatest response to a sweepstakes promotion comes from the same audience that is

TABLE 6-1   Participation in Sweepstakes

	Percent who "ever entered" a sweepstakes	Percent who purchased products in association with a sweepstakes offer
Total sample	48.2	28.4
Sex		
Men	44.0	28.4
Women	49.1	28.4
Age		
18 to 34	51.5	32.3
35 to 49	53.3	31.2
50 and over	42.7	23.6
Female head of household		
Working	50.9	28.6
Not working	47.8	27.2
Marital status		
Married	51.2	29.0
Single	46.4	33.8
Children under 18 in household		
One or more	53.3	32.4
None	44.5	25.4
Household size		
One to two persons	41.8	24.0
Three or more persons	53.9	32.4
Annual income		
Under $10,000	42.0	23.1
$10,000 to $14,999	50.5	29.3
$15,000 to $24,999	54.1	34.6
$25,000 and over	54.6	34.8
Domicile		
East	42.6	24.6
Midwest	50.3	31.0
South	46.5	27.0
West	55.7	32.1

more involved with consumer promotions of all types—the so-called heavy-hitter audience consisting of larger, relatively affluent families. For marketers who can use a coupon offer or a refund or rebate offer, the sweepstakes is also an entirely appropriate promotional tool.

CONTEST AND SWEEPSTAKES NEWSLETTERS

For many consumers, entering sweepstakes and contests is something of a hobby, enhanced by the existence of a number of contest newsletters. These newsletters duplicate the official entries, state the rules, and often provide the correct answers to a fill-in-the-blanks question or a series of questions that must be answered in order to qualify the entry. This tends to defeat the marketer's purpose in including "programmed-learning" questions or other tasks, although contest newsletters do provide additional exposure of the program and will certainly significantly increase the number of entries received.

On balance, the newletters do not reach sufficient numbers of consumers to blunt the impact of a prize promotion as an element of advertising and marketing strategy. And, while newsletter subscribers can and do win prizes in sweepstakes and contests, the benefit of the program to the marketer accrues before the event is judged and the prizes are awarded—in the advertising impact, point-of-purchase impact, and overall response.

WHAT IS A SWEEPSTAKES OR CONTEST?

It is important to distinguish between the terms *sweepstakes*, *games*, and *contests*, as currently used in sales promotions launched by private-sector marketers of goods and services and in sweepstakes and lotteries sanctioned by state or local governments in this country. Any sweepstakes or lottery is a prize promotion in which winners are selected by chance. These promotions are governed by three distinct elements: prize, chance, and consideration (or purchase). People purchase lottery tickets, thereby obtaining a random chance to win a prize. Private-sector marketers are not permitted to conduct such a promotion if all three of the basic elements are present; therefore, the one element that can be eliminated is consideration. Without making any purchase, consumers can get sweepstakes entries, mail them to a post-office box or deposit them in a container provided for this purpose, and be eligible to win prizes on a random-chance basis.

Along with their entries, consumers may be asked to submit a proof of purchase from the sponsoring brand or a facsimile (the brand name written on a piece of paper). Because the consumer is offered the option of a facsimile proof of purchase, the legality of the program is preserved. Although consideration is not necessary in order to gain entry to the random drawing, some states have concluded that requiring consumers to visit a store in order to get an entry blank is tantamount to requiring consideration.

All forms of sweepstakes, including the lottery-style instant-winner games that utilize some form of concealment devices, fall under the same strictures. *All* these programs, no matter how complex or how steep the odds, are random-chance events.

A contest, like a sweepstakes or lottery, is a prize promotion; however, in a contest, prizes are awarded not on a random-chance basis but on the basis of a test of skill. For marketers of goods and services, a contest can require a recipe, a photograph, a jingle, or an essay as a test of skill. The winners in such a program are not picked on a random basis. *All* contest entries must be opened and screened, and the judging proceeds according to a weighted set of criteria that are made known to all entrants as part of the contest rules.

Because the element of chance is not operative in contests, they are not governed by the same body of state regulations and decisions that govern sweepstakes. In a contest, consideration, or purchase of a product, can be required for entry. Because skill is involved, contests generate far fewer entries than sweepstakes. In fact, in terms of entries, industry observers rate sweepstakes as anywhere from four to ten times more potent than contests. Because a contest will generate only a fraction of the entries generated by a sweepstakes, many marketers waive any purchase requirement in a contest, even though such a requirement is legal. The idea is to present as few obstacles to entry as possible.

TYPES OF SWEEPSTAKES AND CONTESTS

Recent changes in the entry mechanics of prize promotions, discussed below, relate almost wholly to sweepstakes programs, not contests, since a contest requires a demonstration of skill on the part of the entrant, who mails the entry to a post-office box or deposits it in an on-premises container. The contest, therefore, has remained a basically static type of promotional program in the evolutionary sense. Regardless of the theme, the specific test of skill required, or the prize structure, contest programs, when stripped to the bare essentials, are all pretty much alike.

This does not mean that there is no utility in contest programs. In recipe contests, marketers are trying to tap the creative genius of the American homemaker. Winning recipes may appear on product labels, in printed ads, in TV commercials, or in recipe booklets. In photo contests, winning entries may provide the visual elements for a continuing series of advertisements. An essay-contest winner may be recruited as a corporate spokesperson for the brand or service.

Marketers who need evidence of sales to reassure themselves of the payout nature of promotions they run will select contests over sweepstakes simply because proof of purchase can be required. This may be a penny-wise and pound-foolish decision since contests will generate only a fraction of the entries generated by a sweepstakes. If a sweepstakes entry blank asks for either an actual or a facsimile proof of purchase, the number of *actual* proofs of purchase will far exceed the number generated by a contest identically exposed and advertised to the target audience, simply because the sweepstakes generates so many more total entries.

Therefore, when looking at the various types of prize promotion formats, we see that contests are limited to the standard format in which the consumer obtains an entry blank, either from advertising or from a display at the point of purchase, and mails it in. The various sweepstakes formats are discussed below.

1. In the *standard sweepstakes*, the consumer obtains an entry blank through some print media or at the point of purchase and mails it to a post-office box or deposits it in a handy container provided for that purpose. The drawing to select winners is conducted at a specified later date. This is the old workhorse program we've all known since sweepstakes began. But, given the right product, the right prize structure, and the right advertising support, this type of program can provide the marketer with all the benefits and advantages of the other sweepstakes formats in use today.

2. The Benson & Hedges 100s sweepstakes is, without a doubt, the most famous example of the *multiple-entry sweepstakes*. Because a multiple-entry sweepstakes is like many different sweepstakes combined, each offering a different prize, this format greatly multiplies consumer involvement in the advertising and, not incidentally, mushrooms the number of entries received. In this type of program, a separate entry is required for each prize.

3. The *programmed-learning sweepstakes* is exemplified by Boyle-Midway's "Easy Living Sweepstakes." This format requires the entrant to read the ad and write down the key points. This is an ideal way to ram home a product's benefits as well as to communicate the entire product positioning, while at the same time forcing high consumer involvement.

4. The *automatic-entry sweepstakes* is an increasingly popular format. Prime examples are Listermint's "Suit Your Own Taste" program and Warner-Lambert's "Cut Out for Bermuda" program. The cents-off coupon actually serves as the entry. Before redeeming the coupon, the consumer fills in the name and address area and is thus automatically entered in the sweepstakes, without any fuss or bother. This format provides a strong incentive to consumers to maximize their use of coupons in product purchases.

5. *Matching games* are sweepstakes in which winning entries are preselected; the advertising generally says, "You may already be a winner." The matching device can be a number, symbol, or illustration that the consumer must match up with an identical number, symbol, or illustration on a product

The **Listermint** and New **Listermint Cinnamon**

"Suit your own taste" Sweepstakes!

OFFICIAL ENTRY FORM

Enter me in the "Suit Your Own Taste" Sweepstakes

Check one (✔)

Mail to: Listermint
P.O. Box 2704
Westbury, NY 11591

☐ Listermint Green

☐ Listermint Cinnamon Red

Name_____

Address_____ Apt._____

City_____ State_____Zip_____

NO PURCHASE NECESSARY

Void where prohibited or restricted by law. All entries must be received by OCTOBER 31, 1980.

OFFICIAL RULES · NO PURCHASE NECESSARY

1 Complete the entry form above or on a 3" x 5" piece of paper, handprint your name, address, zip code, and choice of Red or Green Sweepstakes, along with the words, "Listermint Suit Your Own Taste Sweepstakes - Green" or "Listermint Cinnamon Suit Your Own Taste Sweepstakes - Red". Mail to Listermint, P.O. Box 2704, Westbury, NY 11591. Enter as often as you wish, but each entry should be mailed separately and must be received by October 31, 1980.

2 Winners will be determined in a random drawing from among all entries received prior to the end of the sweepstakes. Judging will be conducted by National Judging Institute, Inc., an independent judging organization whose decisions are final on all matters relating to this sweepstakes. Judging will take place by March 15, 1981. Odds of winning are dependent on number of entries received. Only one prize to an individual or household. All prizes are non-transferable and not redeemable for cash. In the event a motor vehicle is won by a minor, it will be awarded in the name of a parent or guardian. The colors of the prizes offered are for representation purposes only. Winners will be given a choice of color offered or any standard color available from the manufacturer. The automobiles pictured are 1980 models; 1981 models will be awarded. For a list of major prize winners, send a stamped, self-addressed envelope to: LISTERMINT SWEEPSTAKES WINNERS, P.O. BOX 2778, Westbury, NY 11591.

3 Sweepstakes open to all U.S. residents except employees and their families of WARNER-LAMBERT COMPANY, its subsidiaries, affiliates, advertising agencies, and Don Jagoda Associates, Inc. Void in Missouri, Maryland, and wherever else prohibited or restricted and subject to all Federal, State, and local laws. Taxes on prizes, if any, are the responsibility of the individual winners. Winners may be required to execute an affidavit of eligibility and release.

X3069

FIGURE 6-1a. **An example of a standard sweepstakes entry form.**
(*Courtesy of Don Jagoda Associates.*)

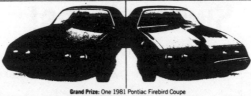

FIGURE 6-1b. A prime example of an automatic-entry sweepstakes. (*Courtesy of Don Jagoda Associates.*)

or in a store display. Where it is difficult to get displays up, the Universal Product Code number, which is on every package, may be used. A matching game can bring potential customers into a store to see whether their entries match, and it provides the kick of letting them know instantly whether they've won.

6. *Instant-winner games* are the most exciting form of sweepstakes today. And, just to reiterate, a game is not a separate type of promotion, but a type of sweepstakes, because the winners are determined by chance.

Games can provide the all-important elements of instant gratification and participation. Is there anyone who can resist rubbing off that magical concealed spot? What Polaroid did for the photography business, games are doing now for sweepstakes. And sales promotion professionals have found an infinite variety of ways to gratify the public's urge to play, while satisfying the client's urge to sell. The major strength of the game is that it can be integrated with the product—on the package or in the package—literally forcing sales.

Making the game pieces work for you is not so simple. How to maintain suspense, how to let losers down gently, how to transmit a positive sales message even to losers, how to encourage repeat entries, and how to maintain the game atmosphere—all are integral factors in sweepstakes games.

There is also the matter of establishing proper controls and security in the production and distribution of game cards and, by the way, of matching-game print entries as well. And there is also a crucial need to observe the fine line of legality, as more regulatory agencies take a closer look at games.

ADVANTAGES AND DISADVANTAGES OF SWEEPSTAKES AND CONTESTS

Advantages

There are five main advantages to running a sweepstakes or contest event.

Fixed Cost. The sweepstakes or contest is one of the few promotions in which you can determine all your costs in advance. The sponsor can establish the budget and tightly control expenditures. Regardless of how many entries are received, the sponsor's liability is limited to the budget established in advance.

Excitement. The sweepstakes or contest has built-in excitement. The basic appeal is to acquisitiveness; everybody wants something for nothing. There is also something of the thrill of gambling because of the element of chance, and yet the consumer is really safe because little, if anything, is being risked. The "big promise"—a car, a trip, cash—is always a surefire attention-getter. Consequently, when executed properly, the sweepstakes or contest literally magnifies the promotion, making it look much bigger than it actually is.

A Selling Tool. Frequently, sales promotion professionals can tell a client that a sweepstakes or contest will succeed or fail *before* the first ad ever appears. Why? Because the number one reason for many prize promotions is simply to give the salespeople more ammunition and enable them to offer the buyer a whole promotion—an *event* that meets the buyer's needs, not merely another price deal.

Increased Display Treatment. It's axiomatic that to increase sales volume quickly, you need to get off-shelf display treatment for your product. The inherent drama and excitement of a sweepstakes or contest and the potential of these programs for increasing store traffic are two of the reasons why many buyers will OK the store displays and support a sweepstakes event.

Increased Ad Impact and Readership. The lure of free prizes makes people read sweepstakes ads. Certainly, the readership scores of these ads are higher than average. By carefully integrating a copy platform into the sweepstakes or contest theme or mechanics, you can further extend the reach of your advertising and thus stretch your advertising dollars.

Probably the best example of this is the now-famous Benson & Hedges 100s sweepstakes, mentioned earlier, which has been conducted by Philip Morris for more than ten years. Instead of an arbitrary number of prizes, there are exactly 100, and each of the prizes is in units of 100, such as 100 pounds of chopped liver, 100 miles of toilet paper, 100 hours in Venice, or 100 cubic inches of Ford Granada. The cumulative awareness of this program has resulted in recent entry totals on the order of four to five million per year—an incredible number.

Disadvantages

The disadvantages of sweepstakes and contest programs are discussed below.

Limited Interest. Only certain types of consumers are interested in entering sweepstakes and contests, although the number is growing.

Difficulty of Testing. Testing a sweepstakes or contest program is difficult unless the test can be conducted regionally and the sponsor can fund a prize structure for the test that is meaningful to potential entrants. In any event, since a sweepstakes or contest must have as much exposure as possible to provide meaningful results, a test program can never be conducted in an atmosphere of secrecy or under "lab" conditions.

Regulations.   Because of federal and state regulations, it is both difficult and unwise to implement a sweepstakes or contest program without the help of a professional sweepstakes and contest organization.

Low-Key Efforts.   In the past, sweepstakes were utilized more as low-key efforts to promote goods and services than as promotional tools to stimulate new-product sales or new-user trial. This disadvantage, however, is largely a thing of the past, for *today* sweepstakes have emerged as a state-of-the-art promotion and as a sophisticated, aggressive marketing tool. Comparing today's sweepstakes with those of, say, five years ago is like comparing a popgun with a laser beam. Sweepstakes have been launched on a true odyssey, powered by a whole galaxy of innovations.

CHANGES AFFECTING SWEEPSTAKES AND CONTESTS

What's the magic potion that turned what was once a relatively passive type of promotion into an aggressive marketing tool? The answer is *change*, specifically in four significant areas.

Regulations.   There has been a definite trend toward easing of federal and state restrictions on sweepstakes. And while implementing these programs still requires significant legal and promotional expertise, marketers are not as handcuffed as they used to be.

Consumer Acceptance.   Today, forty-four states are conducting their own lotteries. This has been a tremendous help in removing the stigma that used to be attached to sweepstakes. Every ad or commercial for a state lottery helps build consumer acceptance of sweepstakes of all types.

Economic Conditions.   Inflation and recession have caused economic hardship among much of the populace. Today, anything that offers the hope of something for nothing is warmly welcomed: cents-off coupons, refunds and rebates, and prizes, prizes, prizes.

Entry Mechanics.   The most exciting change is in the area of entry mechanics, where a whole new dimension has been added: *involvement*. Consumers now do more than just write their names and addresses. Ways have been developed to make participating in sweepstakes and contests more interesting, literally forcing consumers to study an ad, handle the product, and, yes, even *buy* the product.

SWEEPSTAKES PLANNING

While sweepstakes and contests may be as successful in terms of audience response as the other basic promotional tools, planning for a sweepstakes is far more involved. Any prize promotion requires handling thousands of details.

As with any promotion, the success of a sweepstakes depends on blending the many ingredients of marketing. There is no secret success formula for sweepstakes. Each one is different. But there is a pattern of elements that are present in most successful sweepstakes promotions, and there are certain basic issues that must be addressed. The following guidelines can help you avoid some of the pitfalls and plan a better promotion.

Determine the Objectives. Before you can know whether a sweepstakes will do the job, you must analyze the reasons for the promotion and determine what you expect it to achieve. For example, you must decide whether the problem is sales or distribution and whether the promotion is to cover a single product or the full line.

Establish the Markets. The next step is to determine whether the promotion is to be national or regional and to establish who is the audience at which the sweepstakes will be aimed. Both these factors will affect the ad media and the prizes.

Assign Responsibilities. Decide who will be responsible for each facet of the promotion: who will do the planning and create the sweepstakes idea and mechanics. Specify what your ad agency will be responsible for and who will handle the sweepstakes and postsweepstakes details. Decide whether to use the services of a sweepstakes planning organization. Sweepstakes specialists can create sweepstakes ideas; develop the mechanics; draft the rules; arrange for post-office clearance; receive, process, and store entries; judge the winners; arrange for the prizes; and handle all details and correspondence in connection with the prizes, including supervising their delivery. The important thing is to use every available source of assistance to carefully plan and administer the promotion. You want to anticipate problems and eliminate them before they arise.

Develop the Theme. The sweepstakes idea or theme must be integrated with your objectives so that your product will not suffer from being subordinated to the sweepstakes itself. Perhaps you will decide on an "umbrella" theme, such as the Dunkin' Donuts "Party Time" sweepstakes, which tied together the sponsor's anniversary, the association of the product with parties, and the party nature of the sweepstakes.

Another approach is to "spotlight" a specific product feature or benefit and build the sweepstakes theme around it. As was discussed earlier, Benson & Hedges 100s cigarettes focuses on the length of the product in its sweepstakes.

Another effective way of integrating a sweepstakes and the product is to make the product an integral part of the grand prize, as Sunkist did with its "Win a Carload of Oranges" sweepstakes.

Prepare the Entry Mechanics. Should the promotion be a sweepstakes or a skill contest? If getting a lot of entries is important, then a sweepstakes would be best. A sweepstakes is also the simplest form of prize promotion, because winners are selected at random. In a sweepstakes you may request a proof of purchase with each entry, but you must also offer consumers the alternative of not submitting proofs of purchase or of submitting facsimile proofs of purchase.

On the other hand, if you want to be able to require a proof of purchase with every entry, you'll have to go with a skill contest. That doesn't mean you're limited to the old "twenty-five-words-or-less" format. There are also jingle-writing contests, photography contests, and the ever-popular recipe contests. Bear in mind, too, that a clever entry device can sometimes greatly enhance the promotion.

The entry mechanics should spell out the duration of the promotion and the conditions covering participation and judging. In a skill contest, it's especially important to make certain that you establish measurable, judgeable criteria. Most important, keep the sweepstakes and the rules as simple as possible.

Check the Regulations. Although there's some confusion in this area, sweepstakes are perfectly legal. It's lotteries that are illegal for use in connection with consumer goods and services. There are federal, state, and local lottery laws as well as Federal Trade Commission regulations that must be adhered to. And several states now require that sweepstakes be registered and reported. Just make sure that you, your attorney, or your sweepstakes planning firm is up on the latest statutes governing games of chance.

Select the Prizes. The prizes are the heart of the sweepstakes. They should be appropriate for the audience and the time of the year, and they should tie in with the sweepstakes theme. Offer as many prizes as possible so that people will feel they have a better chance of winning. For the supplementary prizes, a variety of merchandise is preferable to cash. Merchandise is more interesting and significant than a small cash award.

Estimate the Costs. Early in the planning stage, firm up estimates of the cost of advertising, production, sales promotion and display material, prizes, handling, and judging.

FIGURE 6-2a. *(Courtesy of Don Jagoda Associates.)*

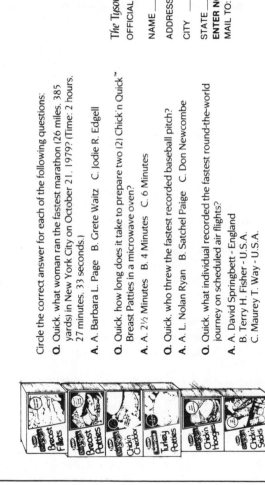

Circle the correct answer for each of the following questions:

Q. Quick, what woman ran the fastest marathon (26 miles, 385 yards) in New York City on October 21, 1979? (Time: 2 hours, 27 minutes, 33 seconds.)

A. A. Barbara L. Page   B. Grete Waitz   C. Jodie R. Edgell

Q. Quick, how long does it take to prepare two (2) Chick'n Quick™ Breast Patties in a microwave oven?

A. A. 2½ Minutes   B. 4 Minutes   C. 6 Minutes

Q. Quick, who threw the fastest recorded baseball pitch?

A. A. L. Nolan Ryan   B. Satchel Paige   C. Don Newcombe

Q. Quick, what individual recorded the fastest round-the-world journey on scheduled air flights?

A. A. David Springbett - England
   B. Terry H. Fisher - U.S.A.
   C. Maurey T. Way - U.S.A.

The Tyson Chick'n Quick™ Super Quick Sweepstakes.

OFFICIAL ENTRY FORM - NO PURCHASE REQUIRED
PLEASE PRINT

NAME _____

ADDRESS _____

CITY _____

STATE _____ ZIP CODE _____

ENTER NOW. SWEEPSTAKES ENDS: JULY 31, 1982

MAIL TO: TYSON CHICK'N QUICK
SUPER QUICK SWEEPSTAKES
P.O. BOX 2707
WESTBURY, N.Y. 11591

FIGURE 6-2b. Chick'n Quick "Super Quick Sweepstakes" exemplifies the "programmed-learning" sweepstakes, with questions to enhance consumer awareness of product benefits and positioning. (*Courtesy of Don Jagoda Associates.*)

Plan the Advertising. If you're going to have a promotion, promote it. Be prepared to devote most of your print space and airtime to the sweepstakes. Use the same media you have used all along. Keep the layouts simple and feature the prizes prominently; they are the carrots you are dangling before your audience.

Get the Sales Force Fired Up. Whether you have your own sales force or sell through brokers, jobbers, distributors, or dealers, the task is still the same: to convince them that the sweepstakes is a sales tool designed to make their jobs easier and help them write more orders. The sweepstakes gives them a change of pace, another reason for asking for a display or an order.

Sell the Trade. Dealer cooperation is essential. Sometimes it's the reason for the whole promotion. Get dealers excited about the impact the promotion will have on consumers and the traffic it will pull into their stores. Set up a trade sweepstakes to run simultaneously with the consumer sweepstakes; this will give dealers an added incentive to cooperate.

Plan the Publicity. Back up the advertising with publicity. Frequently, the sweepstakes idea or the fact that you are running a sweepstakes is news. Send trade publications a publicity story spelling out the details. When it's over, send releases to every prizewinner's hometown paper. Then follow up with "how-we-did-it" articles.

Arrange for Judging the Winners. Whether you're running a sweepstakes or a skill contest, the safest thing is to have the judging done by a professional organization. You want to make certain that the winners are selected fairly and impartially, so leave the judging to the experts.

Check the Major Winners. Just as a precaution, be sure to run a background check on the major prizewinners to ascertain that the entries are their own work and that there is no question about their entries or their eligibility as winners. The judging agency usually will handle this for you.

Announce the Winners. Once the sweepstakes is over, see that the judging is done as quickly as possible and that the winners are announced promptly. You must also send a list of winners to anyone who requests it.

Deliver the Prizes. Nothing creates more ill will than a disappointed prizewinner. Delivery of the prizes should therefore be handled quickly and smoothly.

Analyze the Results. The most important criteria are: How did the sweepstakes affect sales? Did it achieve its objectives? Did it succeed in getting all the displays you wanted? What did the sales force think of the promotion?

Many details are involved in a sweepstakes, but that's true of every promotion. It's vital to bear in mind that a sweepstakes is only a tool. It's what you, your agency, and your sales organization do with it that makes the difference between a mediocre promotion and a bell-ringing success.

Sweepstakes Planning Checklist

Further codifying the total planning and implementation process in a prize promotion would produce a detailed countdown checklist such as the following.

Planning

- ☐ Establish your marketing objectives.
- ☐ Determine your promotion budget.
- ☐ Select a project coordinator.
- ☐ Assign project responsibilities and set up a timetable.
- ☐ Consult a sweepstakes planning organization.
- ☐ Determine which company products will be promoted.
- ☐ Determine the duration of your promotion.
- ☐ Determine the geographic areas that will be involved.
- ☐ Establish a media budget and schedule.
- ☐ Establish criteria for evaluating results.

Theme and Format

- ☐ Develop a theme or unifying concept for your sweepstakes.
- ☐ Select a theme that will appeal to your target audience.
- ☐ Select a theme that reflects your proper product image.
- ☐ Select a theme and format that satisfy your marketing objectives.
- ☐ Select a theme and format that can be easily understood.
- ☐ Give sufficient emphasis to the product being promoted.
- ☐ Consider the possibility that the theme may lend itself to a noncompetitive product whose marketer might be willing to participate in the sweepstakes and share expenses.
- ☐ Develop the theme and word the copy in a manner that clearly reflects whether the sweepstakes is based on skill or on chance.
- ☐ Comply with truth-in-advertising standards. Don't mislead consumers.
- ☐ Submit the theme and copy to the departments whose approval is required—promotion, advertising, legal, etc.

Rules

- ☐ Make sure that everyone involved in planning understands the difference between a legal sweepstakes and an illegal lottery.

☐ Indicate where official entry blanks can be obtained.

☐ Spell out the alternative to submitting proofs of purchase.

☐ State eligibility requirements—who may enter.

☐ Specify whether multiple or mechanically reproduced entries may be submitted.

☐ Establish the deadline for receiving entries.

☐ If you have decided on a skill contest, spell out the judging criteria.

☐ Specify whether a winner may elect to receive cash instead of merchandise.

☐ Indicate the mailing address for submission of entries.

☐ Identify those states in which the promotion is void.

☐ Determine whether affidavits will be required of winners. If so, state this fact.

☐ Make available a list of winners and include the address to which requests for the list should be sent.

☐ Submit rule copy to attorneys for legal approval. Secure post-office clearance.

Mechanics

☐ Select a prize structure appropriate to the theme of the promotion.

☐ Determine the number of prizes to be offered in each category; this will depend on your promotion budget.

☐ Secure illustrations and descriptions of prizes.

☐ Determine who will select the winners. (Using an independent judging organization reinforces credibility and objectivity.)

☐ Comply with the state statutes requiring registration and the filing of a surety bond.

☐ Arrange for verifying and notifying winners and for securing affidavits of eligibility and release.

☐ Secure relevant statistical data—weekly reports of entries received, a breakdown of entries received by media used, etc.

☐ Arrange for orderly and timely shipment of prizes to winners.

☐ File postsweepstakes reports with states requiring such information.

Support

☐ Map your strategy for trade and dealer sell-in.

☐ Prepare the necessary promotional materials for the trade—brochures, letters, trade ads, etc.

☐ Prepare in-store display materials—risers, window streamers, shelf talkers, end-of-aisle displays, etc.

Consider the need for a dealer incentive program:

    ☐ Trade sweepstakes

☐ Case allowance
☐ Advertising allowance
☐ Prepare press releases on each winner for submission to hometown newspapers.
☐ Consider a "pep rally" for field personnel in charge of implementing the program.

SWEEPSTAKES AND CONTEST BUDGETING

As has been pointed out, a critical benefit of a prize promotion is the fixed-cost nature of the event. The fact that there are no major open-ended liabilities in a sweepstakes or contest makes this type of promotion affordable for marketers who cannot accept unlimited liability. A small company, for whom an elaborate program of coupons, samples, or refund offers may be too costly, can successfully launch a sweepstakes and get the desired results. At the other end of the spectrum, a sweepstakes may be ideal for brands in product categories with such high volume and purchase frequency that a coupon drop or refund offer will result in a redemption rate so high that the promotion becomes a victim of its own success, blowing budgets through the roof.

Many sweepstakes and contest programs are overlaid with coupon offers for the sponsoring brand. This has the function of encouraging purchase of the product in association with the sweepstakes and of utilizing media delivery of a sweepstakes or contest ad to provide a direct price incentive to the consumer. In such combination programs, the cost of the add-on promotion device must be budgeted separately from the sweepstakes or contest event itself, and the marketer must use all the data available in planning for the coupon response.

The costs of a sweepstakes or contest event can be grouped as follows:

1. Advertising and point-of-purchase production and media costs
2. Prize costs
3. Administration and judging costs

Advertising and point-of-purchase costs in a prize promotion are no different from those in any other type of promotion, and the result of a greater expenditure on media advertising is also the same. Strong, extensive national advertising and a major point-of-purchase package and sales drive to get the store materials up will result in a much stronger program—whether it's a coupon drop or a sweepstakes. Television and radio support will also increase awareness of the program and add somewhat to the entry rate, but at an increased cost.

Prizes in a sweepstakes or contest are the great variable. We have already crossed the $1 million threshold in private-sector prize promotions, with such events as Dr. Pepper's "Be a Pepper Millionaire" sweepstakes. The various state lotteries have yielded cash prizes as high as $11 million, and this has had an impact on prize promotion planning.

Depending on the product, the theme of the sweepstakes, and the regionality or nationality of the event, a prize budget as low as $25,000 can produce an exciting, results-getting promotion.

While cash prizes may be the most universally accepted and desired, they raise a number of problems and questions for the marketer.

1. Cash prizes may be unexciting, depending on the amounts, the nature of the target audience, and the relevance of a cash prize to the featured product and to the theme of the event. In the case of a sweepstakes aimed at children, for example, cash prizes would be meaningless. Kids want to win trips, bicycles, games, and electronic gadgets. A $1000 cash prize means less to a child than a $500 computer plus a game cartridge.

2. A cash prize cannot be discounted or bartered. A $100,000 cash prize costs the marketer $100,000. The same $100,000 expressed as retail value of merchandise prizes may cost the marketer far less. In fact, when advertising exposure to a potential prize supplier is significant—e.g., when there is extensive national print advertising, point-of-purchase advertising, or even a special 30-second TV commercial—prizes may be offered at little or no cost in exchange for this valuable exposure. It becomes an advertising bargain for the prize supplier and a trade-off for the sponsoring marketer.

3. The tax implications to winners of cash prizes may be considerable. Prizes over $600 must be declared as income. In fact, professional sweepstakes administration and judging organizations report this income directly to the IRS. A cash prize thus may involve a greater tax liability than a merchandise prize.

Administration and judging costs depend on such factors as the complexity of the program mechanics, special printing involved in concealed-device instant-winner games, the need to visit printing or packaging plants to supervise the production and distribution of instant-winner game cards and packages, prize fulfillment, special tabular analyses of entrants, and any creative changes in the original concept and planning of the program. For planning purposes, marketers may estimate that the cost of a typical prize promotion, exclusive of any special printing, will range from $8000 to $15,000.

The total prize promotion package, including administration, prizes, and media and point-of-purchase advertising, could be in the $250,000 to $500,000 range for a national event.

In budgeting for a prize promotion, it's clear that the utilization of a professional administration, implementation, and judging organization is perhaps the least costly element, but it could be the most important one, since independence and objectivity are vital in the proper handling of these programs; a professional service can anticipate problems before they arise, thus helping the marketer avoid them.

For most marketers, a do-it-yourself sweepstakes is entirely possible, but putting clerical people and legal retainers who are relatively inexperienced in this area to work on the event will prove far more costly and cumbersome than letting the professionals do it in the first place, not to mention creating a potential legal nightmare.

CONCLUSION

The final step in sweepstakes and contest planning is the step taken least often—*postprogram evaluation*. It is vital to assess the results of a prize promotion, if only to appreciate properly what these programs can accomplish. Do not simply count entries; evaluate advertising readership, trade cooperation, special displays in stores, and product sell-in *and* sell-through. If the program has accomplished the desired objectives, consider the size, scope, and timing of repeat editions of the event.

Sweepstakes, contests, and games appeal to the dreamer and the gambler in all of us. They can be exciting, potent promotional programs, when properly conceived and handled. They have been with us for centuries, in one way or another, and their use by marketers of goods and services may be just at the threshold of great and important growth.

Games:
"Here's to the Losers"

RICHARD KANE
President, Marden-Kane

LEONARD BIERMAN
Executive Vice President, Marden-Kane

Contests, sweepstakes, and games are prize promotions falling under the shadow of the sales promotion umbrella. In general, the three types of campaigns can be defined as follows:

CONTESTS.   These are promotions involving an element of skill.

SWEEPSTAKES.   These are promotions based on luck or chance; winners are selected by means of a random drawing.

GAMES.   These are continuity-type promotions; they will be discussed more fully later in this chapter.

Before we investigate the different kinds of games that exist, perhaps it would be wise to discuss some of the philosophy that should be incorporated into prize promotions.

"HERE'S TO THE LOSERS"

Frank Sinatra sings a song in which he offers a musical toast that goes, "Here's to the losers." The words seem like a lament, but one of the basic facts of life is that there will always be more losers than winners.

If only the world could be full of winners! But it can't. Simple economics dictate that. Otherwise, no racetrack would ever open again, cobwebs would cover the printing presses that produce lottery tickets, and even Las Vegas, blazing in the Nevada night, would sink into darkness. Everything in the world that revolves around words like "bet!" or "free!" or "win!" or "take a chance!" would come to an end.

So even though we might like to reshape the scheme of things and make this a world of winners, we can't. Reality dictates that more losers have to exist than winners.

In many prize promotions more attention is placed on how the winners will feel than on how the losers will. Such an approach is totally out of balance. A truly successful promotion will always reach the majority, not the minority.

The goal should always be to *make the losers happy*, because there are a lot more of them. Winners are automatically happy, whether they ride away in a brand-new car or sail off to Tahiti; it doesn't really matter whether a winner deposits $5000 or $10,000 in the bank. It's the loser who's standing there with an empty wallet and no dream trip in sight. The loser is really the one we have to satisfy. Successfully integrating into the promotion the element that makes losers happy is the key.

When a company runs a skill contest, awarding prizes on the basis of the entrants' abilities, it's the contestants' own fault that they lose. Not luck. By the same token, in a sales incentive program when a salesperson fails to get the "pot of gold" because someone else did better, it's that person's own selling ability, or perhaps something that is beyond his or her control, that is to blame. Not luck.

But in the case of a promotion based on a random drawing, or even in an instant-winner game, the outcome depends entirely on luck. In such promotional programs you've got to inject, if at all possible, the element that eases the loser's pain.

There are a number of ways to do this; some are very simple, others are sophisticated, and others are still being developed. The past twenty-five years have seen the emergence of a number of landmark developments in, and approaches to, promotions. Combining a cents-off coupon with a sweepstakes is one way of making a loser not feel like a loser after all. This approach isn't applicable to all programs, but when it is, it works effectively.

One of the first "instant" promotions ever run was developed about ten years ago. Every entrant had an equal chance to win. Every entrant! The promotion was based on the almost immutable laws of probability. Let's say that the odds of being an instant winner were 200 to 1, which also meant that for every 200 players, there would be 199 losers. And that was the defeating formula!

Out of every 200 entrants there was one winner; but out of every 200 entrants there were 199 losers. Thus this was really an "instant-loser" promotion. To offset this, the industry developed the "second-chance" concept. An entrant who didn't win instantly still had the opportunity of winning through a continuity-collection device. The person might never really win, but the immediacy of losing was taken away. The blow was softened, so to speak.

Essentially, when you run a promotion built around a sweepstakes, contest, or game, you're selling a dream. The dreams we dream at night end with daybreak and are usually forgotten, but the dreams you sell in print, on TV and radio, or at the point of purchase have to last a lot longer. They cannot end abruptly. The loser can't be left feeling like a loser, a dreamer without a dream.

We've all seen movies in which the hero and heroine walk off hand in hand into the sunset, destined to live happily ever after. Life, unlike a film, is not compressed into two hours or so. Fortunately, we go on. As some news stories have recently told us, even the real winners of a real million dollars can't be guaranteed a happy ending. But that moment when the prize offered in your promotion seems attainable is the moment into which you should put all the magic you are capable of.

To make that momentary dream seem possible, to let your audience feel they can reach out and almost touch that rainbow's end, and to make the losers feel, at least for the moment, that they are walking with the winners—that's the real goal. So perhaps as you go about developing your promotion, you should remember the lyric, "Here's to the losers."

The popular short story "The Lady or the Tiger?" really has no ending, and yet it has delighted readers for generations. As you will recall, the story ends with the hero confronting two doors. One leads to a tiger and certain death; the other, to a beautiful lady and life. The hero opens the door on the right, but what is behind it? We never know, but we can always hope for the best.

That is the way a truly successful promotional program should be designed: to leave our hero facing a door marked "winner" and a door marked "loser," always hoping for the best.

GAMES

Now that we have discussed the philosophy behind prize promotions, let's carefully examine the world of games. The only similarity between a game of chance and a sweepstakes is the fact that they both involve prizes, whether cash or merchandise, which may be won by just a few of the players. The method of participation and the way winners are determined are what distinguish a game from a sweepstakes.

To enter a sweepstakes, all a person generally has to do is fill out an entry blank and mail it to a post-office box or deposit it in a container provided for that purpose. Winners are selected in a random drawing.

In a game, however, one participates by first obtaining a game ticket at the sponsoring outlet. There are no entry blanks to be filled out, mailed, or deposited. In order to be a winner, the player generally has to collect a number of these game tickets in order to complete a phrase, spell a word or words, match the left and right halves of an item, or collect stamps to complete a row or column of numbers (like bingo), pictures, words, etc. The missing word, letter, stamp, or number has been mixed in among the thousands or millions of game cards in circulation, and winning is purely a matter of luck. One has to play the game frequently to have any chance of ever finding the winning card; finding it on the first try is highly unlikely.

In a sweepstakes, as a rule, people may enter as often as they like, as long as they send their entries in separate envelopes, but most people do not enter more than once because of the cost involved. So, theoretically, a person sending in one entry has a far better chance of being a winner in a sweepstakes than in a game.

Now that we have discussed the two major differences—how one participates and how one becomes a winner—let us see who are the biggest users of games. Our discussion will center on two time periods: 1965 to 1970 and 1975 to the present.

Who Uses Games?

From 1965 to 1970 the greatest users of games were the supermarkets and the oil industry (service stations). Some say that the rise in the popularity of games among supermarkets was due to the fact that they needed a type of promotional device other than trading stamps, which were beginning to cost them too much money, approximately 2 percent of sales; others insist that games were introduced by supermarkets who were not using trading stamps but needed something to attract customers. Whatever the reasons, money games with a gambling flavor became popular.

Henry Reichman really pioneered the field in the supermarket industry with a game called "Spell Cash." Store customers simply collected letters, trying to complete the magic word for a big payoff. It wasn't long before the boom was on, and supermarket owners were quick to realize the advantages of games in drawing traffic into their stores. By 1967 there were 215 different games being played in the nation's supermarkets, with horse racing the most popular type. There were as many as fifteen different horse-racing games going on at one time; the most popular was called "Let's Go to the Races."

Shortly thereafter the oil industry realized what games could do to attract customers to service stations, and in 1966 the first oil company game was introduced by Tidewater, now Getty Oil; the promotion was called "Win-a-Check." "Win-a-Check" was a matching game. The motorist received a sealed envelope containing the left or right half of a facsimile bill of a specific denomination. A player who collected both the left and right halves of the same bill won that amount. This game, which was the first of its kind, was so successful that sales reportedly increased by 80 percent. As soon as "Win-a-Check" was introduced, all the major oil companies, including the independents, introduced their own games. The only exceptions were Texaco and Gulf Oil, who never used games during this period. By 1969 there were so many games being sponsored by supermarkets and oil companies that you could hardly tell one from another, and finally they just died out.

In 1974 games started to reappear in supermarkets. However, the fast-food industry (McDonald's, Burger King, Kentucky Fried Chicken, Dunkin' Donuts) replaced the oil industry as a major user of games. As a result of its meteoric rise, this industry began to face the same problems that the service stations faced—a vast number of retail outlets all competing for the same customers, in this instance for people who wanted to eat out occasionally and were looking for a good, inexpensive meal.

Because of the energy crisis, which hit this country in October 1973, and the resultant shortage of petroleum products, there was no need for the oil industry to go back to games to attract customers to their service stations; they could sell just about everything they could pump out of the ground or import.

Since 1974 probably the largest users of game promotions have been the thirteen states that run lotteries to increase revenue for education. A lottery is nothing more than a game; it has the same format as the games used by commercial enterprises, except that in a state lottery, you have to pay to participate, whereas in a game promotion sponsored by a commercial enterprise, law dictates that no purchase be required.

Why They Use Them

We have spoken about supermarkets, gasoline stations, and fast-food operations as the greatest users of games. Why do they use them? When you begin to realize how many thousands of supermarkets, service stations, and fast-food operations there are, you begin to realize that there is intense competition and that they are all offering basically the same thing. When a supermarket has offered low prices as the sole inducement to consumers and has lowered prices as much as possible, games are another thing to try. Therefore, one might ask the question, If everybody is offering games, where does the fantastic increase in sales come from? This increase in sales is garnered from shoppers called "transients." Transients are people who have no loyalty to any particular brand of gasoline, supermarket chain, or fast-food outlet. They shop for bargains, wherever the prices are lowest. It is this group of shoppers that these retail outlets try to attract with a game, hoping to retain a certain percentage of them when the promotion is over. However, after a while, games also reach a saturation point, and they too eventually die.

Cost-Traffic Relationship

The cost of running a game promotion generally runs between ½ and 1 percent of sales. With this type of cost, what percent of increase in traffic does one need in order to pay for the cost of a game? There are really no industry statistics. Each game promoter that you speak to might have a different figure. Some say that a game will increase traffic anywhere from 15 to 40 percent and that there will be a somewhat smaller percentage growth in sales. Others claim a 25 percent growth in traffic with a minimum of a 10 percent increase in sales. Some supermarkets say they need a 15 percent increase in sales to pay for a game. However, in some promotions as little as a 7 or 8 percent increase in sales has paid for the cost of the game. Some operators say that even a 3½ percent increase in sales is sufficient.

It is perhaps interesting to compare this controversial question with a similar one asked in relation to trading stamps. Despite a wide range of estimates, experience over the years has shown that a 12 to 15 percent gain in volume will adequately offset the cost of a trading stamp program; before the days of saturation, most stamp users achieved more than that. Considering that a stamp plan usually costs approximately 2 percent of sales and that games cost about one-fourth that amount, it is realistic to believe that a much smaller gain at the cash register can make a game profitable.

Types of Games

There are two general categories of games. By far the largest consists of paper games: spelling games, matching-half games, and bingo-type games. The two most popular spelling games in the early 1960s were "Spell Cash," mentioned earlier, and "Tigerino," which was created by Marden-Kane. The object of "Tigerino" was to spell *tiger*; by the way, this game carried out the theme of one of the most successful campaigns in the history of advertising: "Put a Tiger in Your Tank." In this game the consumer was given a paper game ticket. The ticket had a black concealment device, which, when removed, revealed one of the letters in the word *tiger*. A consumer who collected all the necessary letters won a prize.

Another type of paper game, which is still very popular, involves collecting matching halves. The first matching-half game was created by the Glendenning Company for the Tidewater Oil Company, and in fact was the first oil company game to hit the market. As mentioned earlier, each time customers went into a Tidewater station, they received the left or right half of a facsimile bill of a specific denomination, from $1 to $1000. A customer who collected matching halves won that amount. The halves were given to the customer in an envelope.

Marden-Kane developed a game for Dunkin' Donuts called "Go for

Dough." The concept was basically the same as that of the Tidewater game. Customers tried to collect matching halves of bills or matching halves of cards showing a specific food product, e.g., a box of doughnuts. However, in this promotion the halves were concealed under a wash- or rub-off concealment device.

The next games to become popular had a bingo format. There were many variations, in which customers collected pictures of presidents, national parks, and endangered species, for example. The primary objective was to complete a row, a section, or a column with whatever the game required. Generally these paper games consisted of six or eight different sections, each of which had a different denomination or value. These sheets were usually handed out with the game tickets during the first four or five weeks of the promotion. In addition to receiving a game sheet each time they visited a service station or supermarket, customers also received a game ticket containing stamps which related to one of the game sections. The stamps were to be pasted or fitted into slots on the game sheet.

The types of games discussed above are the ones most frequently in use today. What all these games have in common is that they are continuity-type games. A consumer can never complete a game during just one visit to the retail outlet; multiple visits are required in order to obtain a sufficient number of game tickets to complete a game section.

PLAY $1,000.00 TIGERINO!

WIN 1¢ TO $1,000.00—3 WAYS TO WIN

Wash off black rectangle GENTLY with water on each Tigerino ticket you collect.

1. Win Instant Cash— When rectangle reveals cash amount, redeem through any participating dealer.

2. Win $1,000.00— Spell [| | | |] in stripes.
If striped letters appear, collect tickets until you spell T-I-G-E-R in 5 striped letters only on one or more tickets.

3. Win $50.00— Spell [| | | |] in solid letters.
If solid letters appear in rectangle, collect tickets until you spell T-I-G-E-R in 5 solid letters only on one or more tickets.

NOTE: When spelling T-I-G-E-R, in striped letters or solid letters, combinations using duplicate letters are not winners. Tickets that are mutilated, tampered with or illegible, are automatically void. All tickets subject to validation by Marden-Kane, Inc., whose decision is final.

RULES: No purchase necessary. Collect a ticket whenever you visit a Humble dealer displaying the Tigerino banner. He will arrange redemption of all prizes. Tigerino can be played by all licensed drivers. Employees of Humble Oil & Refining Company, its dealers, affiliates and subsidiaries, their advertising agencies and their families are not eligible for prizes. Void where prohibited by law. Winning tickets must be redeemed within one month after official end of contest. ©Copyright 1966 Marden-Kane, Inc.

FIGURE 7-1. While all games feature the continuity factor, Tigerino introduced the instant winner. (*Courtesy of Marden-Kane.*)

The big moment is here! It's your chance to cash in on the numbers you've found in Newsday during the past week.

You should have collected seven two-digit numbers, starting last Monday and including the one in today's edition of Sunday Newsday.

Now all you have to do is match them up with the numbers hidden under the wash-off spot below and you win a cash prize —as much as $1100!

Got your seven numbers handy?

Good luck!

GAME #1

PLAY 7 / WIN 11

Match 7 NUMBERS WIN $1100

MATCH 6 NUMBERS WIN $110

MATCH 5 NUMBERS WIN $11

MATCH 4 NUMBERS be eligible for the $11,000 Jackpot

Newsday

Using a moist tissue, rub the spot gently, revealing the all-important numbers.

If you can match five, six or seven of them with your numbers, you're an instant winner! If you can match four, you qualify for the Second Chance Sweepstakes, with a Jackpot Prize of $11,000 to be given away in a drawing after all weekly games are completed.

Are you a winner? Have you qualified for the Second Chance Sweepstakes? If so, read the instructions on the reverse side of this form for your next move.

FIGURE 7-2. This is a game with a second-chance sweepstakes. (*Courtesy of Marden-Kane.*)

In some instances, of course, a particular game piece might reveal an instant winner. Instant prizes were introduced by Marden-Kane in the game "Tigerino," which was created for Exxon. Participants could win anywhere from $0.01 to $1000. There were thousands of $0.06, $0.09, and $0.15 prizes and very few $0.01 prizes. This was done so that a $0.06 prize would have greater impact—it wasn't the least amount promised. In the 1960s the small prizes— $0.06, $0.09, etc.—were not so insignificant as one might think; gasoline was selling for $0.29 a gallon, and a $0.06 prize could be deducted right off the purchase price.

Today the instant-winner feature has become a permanent part of all games. It has been greatly popularized by states which have lotteries. The participants like the immediacy of being instant winners. However, even the state lotteries have added a continuity feature, since there are instant losers as well as instant winners. As long as people continue to play the game, they haven't lost. There are a number of promotional reasons behind the instant-winner format. Basically the objective is to generate excitement in the store, but another purpose is to keep people returning to the store week after week, hoping to get the one missing piece and win the game.

As was mentioned earlier, probably the single most popular game was one called "Let's Go to the Races." This was a TV-type game promotion. Unlike paper games, these games peak every week, with a half-hour wholly sponsored telecast of tapes of horse races. During the previous week, people collect game tickets, hoping to hold the number of the winner in the first, second, third, fourth, or fifth race. Each week a new race is run, and each week new game tickets are distributed. When running a game of this type, extreme care must be exercised in coordinating the correct weekly tickets with the proper TV programs. In some instances TV stations have run a TV race that did not match the tickets given out at the supermarket for that week; the result was havoc. Because of the high cost of TV airtime in the major metropolitan areas, these games are now used primarily in the smaller markets.

Another type of game, pioneered by Marden-Kane, is called the *probability game*. In a probability game every single ticket that is printed is a potential winner. On each ticket are concealed a number of squares, circles, etc. Players can remove only a limited number of concealments, revealing pictures of a person, place, or thing. If all the revealed spaces match, the player has won. The game ticket usually has from ten to forty concealed areas; thus, while each ticket is a potential winner, the probability of uncovering four or five identical items is not very great, considering the number of permutations and combinations that are possible. These games did not become widely popular, largely because of the high cost of manufacturing, security problems, and the potential liability. However, the ticket used in the very first probability game, which was called "Heads or Tails" and was developed for Exxon, contained a latex scratch-off device and was the same type of ticket which is being used today by all the lotteries in the United States.

$1,000		
$ 500	55	1 in 97,800
$ 250	69	1 in 77,960
$ 100	74	1 in 72,690
$ 50	150	1 in 35,860
$ 25	250	1 in 21,520
$ 15	500	1 in 10,760
$ 10	800	1 in 6,725
$ 5	1,500	1 in 3,590
$ 1	2,000	1 in 2,690
	10,000	1 in 540
Product Prizes:		
Values up to 50¢	45,000	1 in 360
TOTALS	60,398	1 in 90

Prize disclosure for the 54 participating A & P stores in Pennsylvania and West Virginia. Game ends Sept. 11, 1976.

Copyright 1976, F.&W' Marketing Marden-Kane, Inc.

FIGURE 7-3. Games and more games.
(*Courtesy of Marden-Kane.*)

PRIZES

For prizes, cash is the odds-on favorite. It has universal appeal and is easier and cheaper to handle than merchandise, which requires storage, shipment, servicing, and replacement if defective. In the fast-food industry, another very popular type of prize is food. It is cheap to give away, and it affords the opportunity to force the trial of new or different products that a company may be introducing. The prize values will generally range from $1 to $1000, the most popular amounts being $5, $10, $25, $100, $500, and $1000.

THE LAW

The laws governing game promotions are very similar to those which govern sweepstakes promotions. There are, however, some notable exceptions. First of all there is the Federal Trade Commission (FTC) rule which governs game promotions in the food retailing and gasoline industries. This is rule 16 CFR 419, which prohibits misrepresenting the chance of winning a prize and forbids the use of any advertising which fails to disclose the number of prizes to be awarded, the odds of winning, the geographic area covered, the number of outlets where entry blanks may be obtained, and the termination date of the game. All game pieces must be mixed and dispensed on a random basis. The game sponsor must report to the FTC and must post in each outlet a list of winners and prizes, the total number of game pieces distributed, and the number of prizes offered and awarded. Successive games must be spaced in time, and a game may not be terminated before all the game pieces have been distributed.

The FTC rule came into being as a result of some abuses practiced by game sponsors and promoters during the 1960s. For example, an average of 10 percent of winners actually received their prizes in many of the oil company promotions. Seeding of game pieces, breaking the game, and thus controlling winnings were common, and sometimes true, allegations. Although the alleged abuses looked worse than they actually were, even Congress saw fit to investigate the whole industry. Supermarket and oil industry representatives and game promoters were called before a special hearing of a subcommittee of the Select Committee on Small Businesses. The results are reported in *The Use of Games of Chance in Gasoline Marketing and Their Impact on Small Business*, which can be obtained from the Library of Congress or the Government Printing Office.

In addition, some states went even further than the FTC in cracking down on the promoters and users of games, especially in the gasoline industry. Six states actually banned all types of game promotions designed to entice customers to purchase gasoline. (See Chapter 30.)

SKILL GAMES

In this chapter we have touched briefly on game promotions based on chance. Since 1975 some game promotions have also taken the form of skill contests, based on knowledge and ability, as opposed to chance. Such game promotions are used primarily by the fast-food industry and consist of three to five multiple-choice questions, the answers to which are concealed. If the consumer picks the correct answer, the word *right* appears under the concealment. A consumer who answers all the questions correctly wins a prize.

If one were to offer prizes of varying degrees of value in a skill contest, one would have to provide for a continuation of run-off questions to those persons who answered all the questions correctly until all were eliminated but one, who would receive the prize of greatest value. Since this would be very expensive and time-consuming, the only thing that one can do to stay within the bounds of the law is to offer everybody a prize of equal value so that there cannot be any "chance" whatsoever in the awarding of the prizes. The cheapest prizes that one can offer that will have any meaning whatsoever to the prizewinner consist of food, such as hot dogs, hamburgers, french fries, or a soft drink. That is the reason why the fast-food industry has used this type of promotion in some instances.

Experience has shown that game promotions of this type do not really do anything to increase traffic to, or sales of, the sponsoring outlet. Such promotions are used basically as another method of couponing and as a way of adding a little fun and excitement to a coupon promotion.

Point-of-Purchase Advertising

HOWARD STUMPF
President, The Point-of-Purchase Advertising Institute

JOHN M. KAWULA
Vice President, The Point-of-Purchase Advertising Institute

There is a long and perilous gap separating the television screen, the sound of the radio, and the newspaper and magazine page from the cash register in the retail store. What happens between the time consumers see or hear an advertisement or commercial and the time they enter the store can tip the balance in determining what they will buy. This is where the other half of the marketing mix—sales promotion and merchandising—goes to work and where point-of-purchase (POP) advertising plays a particularly important role.

POP materials close the gap between where consumer advertising leaves off and sales are made. Defined, POP advertising is the element of sales promotion that concerns itself with signs and displays located in, on, or adjacent to the place where the advertised product or service is available for purchase; it has the fourfold purpose of informing, reminding, persuading, and merchandising. The terms *point of purchase* and *point of sale* are synonymous, although *point of purchase* is the more commonly used term in the United States.

Those who are involved with POP merchandising agree on one point: It is an unusual business. It is a business that can only be labeled "heterogeneous." It covers the entire spectrum of consumer marketing in this country, from calculators and pantyhose to dry cleaning and automobiles.

POP advertising materials run the gamut from the thinnest papers to the heaviest plastic and sheet metals. They can be used for as little as ten days or as long as ten years. The one common denominator is that these signs and displays—purchased by marketers of branded consumer items and services—are seen by shoppers in stores generally not owned or controlled by the advertised brand, and only where the product or service is available.

141

HISTORY

POP advertising has a long and interesting history. Together with outdoor advertising, it could very well be considered the "granddaddy" of all product advertising. Long before the age of printing, traders made themselves known and called attention to their products by means of signs and displays. A milk seller's stall in ancient Pompeii, for example, displayed a terra-cotta sign showing a goat. During the Middle Ages shops in London and Paris exhibited picture advertisements so that servants who could not read might find them.

POP advertising also played an important part in America's early years. The butcher showcasing mutton chops, the baker displaying sweet rolls, and the candlestick maker exhibiting tapers—all made heavy use of signs and in-store displays. One of the earliest forms of POP advertising was the cigar-store Indian (Figure 8-1), which is now only a quaint reminder of the past.

The butcher, the baker, and the candlestick maker are not the same

FIGURE 8-1. A cigar-store Indian. (*Courtesy of POPAI.*)

either. From the Yankee peddler to the general store to the supermarket; from across-the-counter service to self-service; from home delivery to cash-and-carry—each progressive change has brought with it an increased need for more effective in-store merchandising techniques. What the cigar-store Indian did for our grandfathers is still being done today by equally imaginative POP materials. The key is to motivate sales.

POP advertising's recent past is best illustrated by the "Honest Scrap" sign (Figure 8-2), which is a classic in that it attests to the character of the owner. The 3- by 4-foot sheet-metal sign described the business he was in and delivered its message in a split second.

Today new technologies are creating expanded opportunities for companies to attract and interact with consumers at the point of purchase. For example, the Estée Lauder Prescriptives Skinprinter unit (Figure 8-3) used a

FIGURE 8-2. "Honest Scrap." (*Courtesy of POPAI.*)

computer to help department-store beauticians precisely analyze their customers' skin-care needs. First, shoppers were asked to describe their skin qualities by pushing buttons in response to questions about oiliness, elasticity, and other characteristics. After they had answered each question, a readout near the bottom of the countertop display showed color bars, symbols, and letters that "prescribed" the proper skin-care products. The department-store beauticians used brochures provided by Estée Lauder to interpret this code, and they could recommend products that most closely matched the consumer's needs. The brochures were also available from a box located behind the display unit. This enabled consumers to take home the appropriate information, even if the beautician had stepped away from the counter.

Although the "Honest Scrap" sign from the World War I era and the modern Estée Lauder Prescriptives Skinprinter are as different in scope as they are far apart in years, they both performed the basic function of POP advertising in that they brought the consumer, who was in a position to buy immediately, into direct contact with the product or service.

SCOPE OF POP ADVERTISING TODAY

Expenditures for POP advertising in 1983 totaled $6.2 billion. This did not include advertiser dollars spent in-house, salespeople's time and effort, or the cost of warehousing, shipping, and maintaining a sales promotion staff to work with the producers and suppliers who design, create, produce, and sell

FIGURE 8-3. The Estée Lauder Prescriptives Skinprinter unit, by Donaldson Display Company, Inc., South Hackensack, N.J.

the displays and signs to national and regional marketers of branded items and services.

The POP industry, in terms of constant dollars, has recorded continuous growth during the last fifteen years, averaging an annual increase of 12 percent—with the exception of a marginal 4 percent drop in 1974. This is not surprising since the industry and the nation suffered an acute raw-material and energy shortage, manufacturers of consumer products experienced a shortage of merchandise to sell, and all society was caught in an inflationary spiral and worldwide recession. As inflation was brought under control and the free market philosophy began asserting its dynamics, the POP advertising industry once again resumed its growth pattern.

ADVANTAGES OF POP ADVERTISING

Why do advertisers invest in POP materials?

1. Recall is unnecessary. There is no need for consumers to remember that the display is there, and although it may help them recall other advertising messages, the display or sign in and of itself is the medium that spurs the consumer to action.

2. A POP display is found only where the item or service it is advertising is available for sale.

3. Unlike other media, POP advertising is at the right place, at the right time, and for the right audience. Television commercials, by comparison, often play to empty chairs. TV viewership dropped by 1 million homes across the nation in 1980, and the decline in the number of viewers is continuing. Sales of TV sets have also plummeted. In addition, advertisers are facing TV production costs that have risen at a record rate—100 percent in 1980 and 1981 alone. Placement costs are also escalating at an alarming rate, with projections for a one-minute commercial during the 1985 Super Bowl surpassing the $1 million mark. As cable television increases viewer options, the opportunity to use TV to reach mass audiences is declining dramatically. And TV is not alone in its inability to reach consumers in a cost-effective manner. Many ad messages in magazines and billboards are also overlooked. POP advertising, by contrast, addresses itself to consumers when they are shopping. And since consumers generally shop in stores that they can afford—whether they select an elegant boutique or a discount store—the selling messages are highly pertinent to the target audience; there are no empty chairs.

4. The display or sign is providing impact when the consumer is there with cash or credit and is in a buying mood.

5. Shoppers' attention is drawn to the product or service by POP advertising. The special placement of colorful and well-placed display materials sets the product or service apart from other, similar classes of goods or services in the retail outlet.

6. By stressing the special features or advantages of a product or service (which may or may not include special pricing), POP advertising allows consumers to determine the product's value quickly and helps them decide whether to purchase it.

7. When the merchandising unit's concept relates to other advertising messages, the POP display can serve to remind consumers of previous selling messages.

8. After all the advertising and all the presentation of products at the retail level, POP displays are the advertiser's and the retailer's last chance to make the sale.

9. Particularly in the area of frequently purchased items, such as toiletries, food, and motor oil, POP advertising encourages impulse purchases. Shoppers may not have intended to buy a POP-advertised product, but seeing the product in a specially presented display brings it to their attention and encourages them to consider buying it—and to make the decision then and there. What degree of influence does in-store merchandising have on purchases? According to the eighth POPAI–Du Pont study of consumer buying habits, which surveyed the supermarket purchasing patterns of 4000 consumers nationwide, the expenditure of two-thirds of every dollar spent in the supermarket is decided upon in the store. This is a very strong indication of the importance of merchandising factors at the point of purchase.

10. POP advertising can be the deciding factor in a purchase. When shopping for items such as a television set, a stove, or an automobile, consumers are not driven by impulse so much as by a need or desire to find a replacement item that offers better performance than their old one. Since impulse does not play an important role here, POP advertising serves to educate and explain. It helps the shopper reach an intelligent decision concerning product and price range. In the case of automobiles, where there are a variety of body styles, color combinations, and model types available, good showroom POP advertising will help convince the buyer to purchase one type of automobile over another.

11. Consumers' desire to buy something for other members of the family can be triggered by POP advertising.

12. Price specials which should not be overlooked can be brought to the consumer's attention by POP advertising. It creates a feeling on the part of consumers that they cannot afford to pass up a bargain, whether the item really is a bargain or not.

TYPES OF POP ADVERTISING

There are three major categories of POP advertising. The first includes short-term signs and displays which are designed to last only a few weeks. Signs, banners, and bins are examples of short-term units. The usual materials are paper, cardboard, corrugated paperboard, inexpensive plastics, and the like.

The second major category includes long-term displays which have a life of at least three months, but may be designed to last for many years. These units are made of wood, wire, metal, or more expensive plastics. Some may be used as outdoor units.

The third major category includes long-term signs which are maintained in service for many years. For some marketers, outdoor signs are a major vehicle for establishing company image.

SIGNS

Signs have always been extremely important in the general scheme of things. Long before words were written, or even spoken, people used signs to express themselves. Before the cave dwellers learned to communicate orally with more than grunts, they told stories by drawing pictures on cave walls.

From those crude beginnings evolved the written word. Since then, of course, signs have become instrumental in identification, merchandising, and advertising. Our modern-day concept of image projection, brand identification, and advertising continuity is materially aided by signs. Signs keep a company's name and trademark constantly in the consumer's eyes. In fact, the design of a sign can give people a distinct and lasting impression of a company and its products. However, the original and probably most important reason for having a sign is to identify a product, service, or dealership. It tells everyone, "Here is where you buy it."

An effective sign program is an essential part of any marketing effort. Signs perform the vital function of identifying the local establishment where customers can buy nationally advertised goods or services. They bring all a company's marketing efforts into focus directly at the sales outlet. Signs brighten the entire commercial environment and, when illuminated outdoors at night, offer a warm welcome to prospective customers. Furthermore, the more light present in commercial areas at night, the greater the safety of customers and passersby.

Signs include everything from the small plastic or card-stock shelf talkers in supermarkets and discount stores (which may be in use for only twelve shopping days) to the large plastic illuminated units (which may or may not be designed to rotate) at service stations, fast-food restaurants, and department stores. At one end of the spectrum, the price of a sign can be figured in pennies, and at the other end, the expenditure may well be $3500 or more. Signs are one of the most widely used items in the retail environment. A recent study noted that the average supermarket has, at any given time, in excess of 150 signs.

Short-range indoor signs and window signs are generally found in foodstores, drugstores, and hardware stores. These are made of paper and/or card stock. Characteristically, they are bright in color (often multicolored) and use large, bold copy. Usually screen printing or the lithographic process is employed. They are highly visible and highly effective.

Another type of sign is found where major appliances are sold. These displays can be made of fiber poles in either light plastic or heavy card stock. They often incorporate light or motion to point out special features. Many of these sign elements are placed on or around the major appliance. Many manufacturers have developed signs that are quite elegant in appearance and structure for use in television departments. These are long-term in nature, designed to serve a year or more. Many of these signs incorporate moving color or backlighting and are constructed of injection-molded plastic, metal framing, or polyurethane. The last can be molded to look exactly like wood.

Hardware stores and automotive maintenance centers or parts stores are important users of signs that are designed to last for several years. Most of these units are made of metal or vacuum-formed plastic. They can reproduce, in giant form, the particular shape of the product that is being promoted. The buying frequency or buying intensity in these stores is not so great as in drugstores, for instance, and therefore the life span of these signs is extended considerably in such outlets.

Fast-food outlets are one of the prime users of outdoor illuminated signs. For example, the flashing electric sign on a restaurant on Route 66 tells travelers that they can stop for a quick, inexpensive meal. Other restaurant signs indicate whether the establishment is a snack bar, a family restaurant, or a chic nightclub, for example. Characteristically, these signs attempt to inform and persuade the potential customer.

To be seen across vast distances and at high speeds, a sign must leap out at the driver. Most highway signs communicate eye-catching, provocative images that give specific information ("Over a Billion Sold") and directions ("Park Here"). Seen from afar, these signs suggest that we slow down, and they tell us why we should stop and where we should go. For example, McDonald's glowing yellow arches have become a nationally recognized symbol. They signify the same menu and standard of quality wherever they appear, and they are familiar to travelers passing through any town.

Case History: The R. J. Reynolds Overhead Package Merchandiser

How does an advertiser maximize impulse sales at the checkout area without disrupting limited checkout space or displacing existing retailer fixtures or counter displays? R. J. Reynolds's answer was to create an overhead package merchandiser, which used a pole support from the counter or ceiling to maximize the air space above the counter area (Figure 8-4). The unit could be set to merchandise from 78 to 104 brands of cigarettes and to stock up to 1014 packs or 101 cartons.

Each brand was easily identified through front facings in rows that stocked thirteen packs. Drawers slid down to the clerk's level to simplify restocking. Changeable backlighted color transparencies, placed on each side of a consumer interest point, such as a lighted clock, added impact to brand advertising. Brand identification was carried through on the lower-drawer decal panels of pack facings and on two Reynolds-brand twenty-pack displays mounted on each side of the fixture. The unit not only enhanced store decor but also allowed for easy inventory control and adapted easily to varying counter depths and height configurations.

Random retail reports indicated that increases in package sales ranged from 10 to 20 percent after this unit was installed. The overhead package merchandiser also secured complete chain placement, along with placement in stores that previously had not accepted advertiser-sponsored merchandising units.

DISPLAYS

The ability of an attractive display of merchandise to grab customers' attention and prompt them to buy was recognized as an important merchandising tool by merchants of an ancient era. When high walls protected cities from invaders, the only entrance was through the city gates, which became a gathering spot and a profitable marketplace for merchants who, by displaying their wares, attracted travelers to stop and buy. When walled cities were no

FIGURE 8.4 a. The R. J. Reynolds overhead package merchandiser, by H. King & Associates, Ltd., Elmhurst, Ill.

FIGURE 8.4*b*.

FIGURE 8.4*c*.

longer necessary, merchants established shops in the centers of cities and continued to display the goods they wanted to sell.

Today's retailers also realize that customers are likely to buy merchandise they see on display. They use advertising and other types of promotion to precondition the consumer, and they depend upon displays to make the final sale. The successful POP display must embody what has been referred to as "the four I's": impact, identification, information, and imagery. If any of the four is missing, the battle is weakened from the start.

Impact. The impact of the display must be immediate. It must grab consumers' attention and create interest in the product line. It must shout, "Stop, here I am, buy me."

Identification. Bold, vivid identification is also a necessity if the display is to be successful. Without it, the corporate name remains obscure. Identification dramatically links the message to the source.

FIGURE 8.4*d*.

Information. With the advent of new consumer legislation, it is also essential that a sign or display offer relevant, meaningful product information. After all, it is the heart of the message. Information is vital to relate the "whys" of buying the product to consumers: why they should consider switching brands or why they should try a new taste treat, a new detergent, the latest fad in clothing, or even a new tool for the garden.

Imagery. The art of communicating the sales message to the consumer is becoming increasingly complex. As more and more companies compete for attention, the last "I"—imagery—is vital. It is the overall impression that establishes the perceived relevance of the product and says, "Take me to the checkout counter."

Case History: The L'eggs Boutique

Today, L'eggs is the number one seller in the regular, support, and knee-high hosiery categories. In fact, this brand accounts for more than 40 percent of the total pantyhose sales in supermarkets, drugstores, and mass merchandising outlets. Marketing executives at L'eggs give heavy credit for their now-famous story to the impact of their POP display. All L'eggs, packaged in the highly identifiable plastic egg, are merchandised through free-standing or in-line POP display units. It is estimated that more than 80,000 displays currently in retail stores are helping millions of shoppers to make their selections quickly, while providing thousands of retailers with increased profits through outstanding in-store merchandising.

The original twelve-dozen and twenty-four dozen L'eggs boutiques were created at a time when the entire product line consisted of fourteen stock-keeping units (SKUs)—pantyhose and stockings in seven colors each. Over the last thirteen years, line extensions (new colors, styles, and sizes and multipacks) combined with new products (Control Top, Knee-Hi, Sheer Energy, and Sheer Elegance) have increased the L'eggs product line to a present 100 SKUs with a potential of 125 SKUs in the future.

Therefore, L'eggs updated the original egg modular POP display, which first appeared in the marketplace in 1969, and four subsequent "generations" of this distinctive display have appeared in retail outlets across the United States. The modern, sculptured thirty-five-dozen boutique assures high retail visibility and is the result of improved technology and the latest production techniques in plastic and steel (Figure 8-5). Its engineering design allows it to withstand abuse from shopping carts, cleaning machines, etc., and yet its elegant design allows for placement in fine department stores as well.

The boutique is designed for maximum flexibility. Inexpensive vacuum-formed inserts accommodate single packs, multipacks, or any combination of the two. Inserts are interchangeable to permit numerous planogram variations to accommodate varying preferences by regions and will also accommodate unknown future packaging configurations.

The unit's design also maximizes sales. Header cards carry product information and can be easily changed or replaced. Promotional material can be inserted into side-panel shelf edges. Additional POP material can be quickly attached to "floating" logos located on all four sides of the sculptured header. Shelf edges also carry color-coded product information for easier consumer selection.

The sculptured base covers the reinforced concrete support, which affords weight and stability when it is revolved. The base also features a hidden storage capacity for a new, sophisticated computerized delivery and inventory system. This system involves tracking each display in the United States to compile sales figures. The computer will forecast the styles, colors, sizes, etc., that each display will need on a weekly basis. The result will be faster, easier servicing by L'eggs personnel with a savings of over $400,000 annually in servicing time.

This fifth generation in the progression of L'eggs displays will require some 85,000 displays, "billboards" that will create a minimum of 100 million impressions weekly at various retail outlets.

Short-Term Displays

Short-term (temporary) promotional displays are those units which are eliminated after the stock has been depleted through sale and/or those units intended for use for six months or less. These include displays which offer Christmas, Halloween, Easter, or other seasonal merchandise. Short-term promotional displays are generally designed for quick installation. They can be suspended from the ceiling, placed on a counter or floor, positioned in a window, or put in any other area of the retail environment. Design structures take advantage of whatever space exists. Short-term promotional displays are characterized by vibrant colors to attract consumers' attention. The primary purpose of these displays is to stand out in the crowded marketplace and to explain the advantages of the product or service in a split second. Short-term promotional displays have one common objective: to sell items that rank high in impulse purchasing.

Short-term displays, therefore, must be designed to present merchandise so effectively that customers are persuaded to buy goods they had not planned to purchase. They are used to attract three types of customers who come into a store: those who know exactly what they want and where they can find it, those who are interested in a particular item but want to think about it before they buy it, and those who are walking casually through the store.

To be selected as impulse purchases, items must be attractively displayed in a location where they will be easily seen by a large number of people. The display and the product must be adequately labeled and clearly priced so that even the uninterested consumer will also be attracted and influenced.

Case History: The Hartz Pet Gift Center

The Hartz pet gift center (Figure 8-6) gained additional off-shelf space for Hartz Mountain Corporation's entire line of peggable dog and cat products and proved to be a sturdy, disposable, easy-to-assemble mer-

FIGURE 8-5. The modern L'eggs thirty-five-dozen boutique, by The Howard Marlboro Group, New York.

chandising vehicle. The corrugated tower-dump unit enabled retailers to display a maximum amount of product in a minimum amount of space during seasonal promotions.

The center occupied 3 square feet of floor space and gained immediate consumer awareness through giant graphics of a family pet. The dog's wagging tongue caught the attention of consumers in the aisles and led them to the assortment of products on display.

The merchandising unit included injection-molded hook bars that could be easily affixed to the back wall in a choice of nine different lettered locations. The hook bars also accepted wire hooks at predetermined numbered receptacles to hold different mixes of peggable carded items.

FIGURE 8-6. The Hartz pet gift center, by Henschel-Steinau, Inc., Englewood, N.J.

Short-Term Counter Units

Counter units are another form of POP display which can be designed for short-term use. Counter units are highly effective for display of merchandise that customers buy on impulse, and they are ideal for products that come in small packages. Often, the product is shipped in a carton that becomes its own display when the inside panels—protected in shipping and handling—are folded out. These can easily be placed right on the counter, ready to sell, with little inconvenience to the retailer. As a further improvement in design and appearance, a display, with the product in place, may be completely set up in the shipping container. The box is discarded, and the display goes right on the counter.

These units are similar to floor units, except that they are smaller and are intended for use on shelves or counters. Counter displays enjoy widespread use in such retail outlets as drugstores, hardware stores, home improvement centers, candy and tobacco shops, liquor stores, mass merchandising outlets, and department stores. Here they can be placed on counters near the cash register to further attract the attention of shoppers.

Case History: Illinois Bell's "Chicago, My Kind of Phone" Promotion

Illinois Bell's customized "Chicago phone" faceplate for the Exeter phone line was designed to stimulate buying interest and spark impulse purchases of all design-line telephones at Bell Phone Center Stores (Figure 8-7). POP units displayed the Chicago phone and held entry blanks and information for a "Chicago, My Kind of Phone" sweepstakes.

Graphics on the display reinforced the art on the Chicago phone faceplate and helped tie the campaign in with the Chicago Convention and Tourism Bureau's overall campaign to position Chicago as "my kind of town." The artist who designed the Chicago phone faceplate also designed a Chicago poster which was given to Illinois Bell customers who purchased telephones. The Chicago phone was extremely popular, and POP displays proved to be the vital, on-the-spot link providing continuity between a public relations campaign, newspaper and radio ads, and key customer groups.

Checkout counters are an ideal location for some short-term displays. The customer who is waiting to check out will impulsively pick up one or perhaps several of the featured items. This leads stores to use the counter or front-end area to display items they wish to sell quickly. The area surrounding the checkout stand provides a natural setting for POP displays.

Pilferage is also of prime concern to today's retailer. An excellent place to locate small, highly profitable items that are particularly subject to pilferage, such as cards, razor blades, gum, and candy, is at the front counter, where they can be seen by the cashier.

Long-Range or Permanent POP Displays

Permanent displays are those units which are intended to be restocked and those which maintain their position for more than six months. Some permanent displays remain in use for fifteen years or more. Such POP displays serve a myriad of purposes, and the philosophies behind them vary considerably.

Permanent POP displays use a multitude of materials, including sheet aluminum and steel, wire and metal tubing, glass, injection-molded plastic, and wood. A permanent POP display is expensive, so it must do a successful

FIGURE 8-7. Illinois Bell's "Chicago, My Kind of Phone" promotion, by Dynagraphic Merchandising Corporation, Chicago.

job of merchandising the product to consumers. Some of the basic types of permanent POP displays are discussed below.

Department Makers. These displays provide a special attention-getting area for presentation of the product to shoppers. Department makers become a store within a store—almost a boutique.

Displays of this nature are often used when an assortment of colors and sizes of certain products requires a place for stocking related products. Cosmetics, for instance, can be arranged by colors and sizes—for ease and convenience of shopper selection. These displays can be planned for shopping from the front only, from a corner position open on one or two sides, and often from all sides. Rotation is a characteristic of these units. Shoppers are able to stand in one spot and rotate the sections of the display to turn the merchandise around, avoiding the inconvenience of walking around the display.

Department makers serve to control inventory and prevent out-of-stock conditions, and they provide an excellent device for marketing complex lines and related items from the same manufacturer.

Case History: General Electric's Quick-Fix Display

General Electric's Quick-Fix display used a color-coordinated system to attract customers' attention and gain prime floor space for products often categorized as back-room stock (Figure 8-8). Developed for five General Electric and Hotpoint product lines (range, refrigerator-freezer, dishwasher, washer, and dryer), the floor unit contained a complete line of replacement parts as well as detailed installation and repair instructions that helped instill confidence in prospective do-it-yourselfers.

The highly organized system allowed for rapid identification of merchandise and immediate restocking. The unit featured five repair manuals and included ninety-four "most often used" parts in packages color-coded to their respective repair manuals. Illustrated instructions and an estimate of the amount of time necessary to complete the job were included in each package. A gravity-feed capability kept the display looking full and appealing.

The POP program was supported by a comprehensive public relations program that included extensive coverage in both consumer and trade magazines, as well as national media tours for GE Quick-Fix spokespersons. Local dealer co-op advertising allowances and publicity packages were also available.

Display Racks. Display racks are a form of floor stand featuring shelves, pockets, or hooks. They are usually made of wire, are designed for the special display of a group of related items in a subdepartment, and facilitate customer self-selection and/or self-service. Racks may or may not carry an advertising message. This often depends upon a product's packaging and the selling message. The best-known products sold from these displays are carbonated beverages, small cans of paint, cleansers, polishes, etc. Racks are characteristically open and airy. High visibility of the product is the primary key to the usage of racks.

Heavy card stock or corrugated boxboard signs sometimes accompany display racks, especially when seasonal changes are planned; store personnel or a company salesperson can easily remove the holiday promotion and put in a new advertising message—perhaps introducing a new product, a new size, or a product improvement.

Case History: The Bali Bra Boutique

From 1973 to 1980, when the female population was growing by approximately 2 percent a year, the bra market showed a decline in unit sales. One of the reasons for the decrease in sales was thought to be consumer difficulty in making product selections.

FIGURE 8-8. General Electric's Quick-Fix display, by Harbor Industries, Inc., Grand Haven, Mich.

Prior to the introduction of the Bali boutique system (Figure 8-9), bras were featured primarily unpackaged on hangers suspended from standard tubular racks. The result was minimal brand awareness, a low fashion image, soiled products, and inefficient inventory controls (with frequent out of stock conditions), as consumers struggled to find their choice of brands, sizes, and styles.

Some brands of bras were also sold in traditional cardboard packages that offered no product visibility. Therefore, when consumers wanted to see or touch the product, they would open the packages and often fail to put the merchandise back where it belonged.

A new packaging and display system was needed to facilitate fast, easy product selection; to encourage impulse purchases and multiple sales; to minimize try-ons and reduce clerk assistance; and to increase profitability both for the retailer and for Bali.

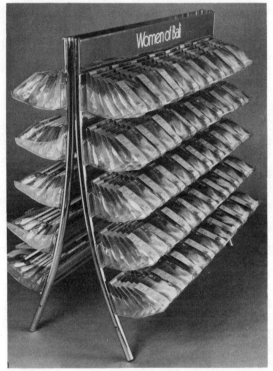

FIGURE 8-9. The Bali bra boutique, by The Howard Marlboro Group, New York.

First, a single see-through plastic package was developed to accommodate each of the bras in the Bali line. Each purselike package was individualized through the insertion of a card showing a picture of the product and giving the pertinent information. The package was designed not only to be functional but also to have inherent appeal to women shoppers.

In a Bali bra boutique, clear plastic sculptured, injection-molded trays accommodate twelve packages and permit excellent product display. Size and style information is visible on all packages in both the top and the bottom positions. Trays engage easily into matching aluminum extrusions on 30- and 60-inch modular boutiques, as well as on wall systems.

The overscale chrome-plated tubular look created an instant fashion environment, and units were successfully placed in all leading department stores and some 15,000 specialty stores. A mirrored header calls attention to the Bali brand and permits the insertion of promotional materials.

Permanent Counter or Shelf Units. Counter or shelf units designed for long-range merchandising often attract the consumer's attention through eye appeal. The materials used in manufacturing these displays are of the highest quality, and the workmanship and style are superior.

Characteristically, permanent counter units are designed around a specific product or product line that is being presented; they are not general-purpose in nature. The mounting, size, or angle of product placement is for one particular piece or product—for instance, a camera, a radio, a fine writing instrument, or a hardware item. The design is not apt to fit any other product.

Consumers rarely pick and choose from these displays because the product being presented is an expensive item and must be protected from loss due to pilferage or customer mishandling. Literature racks are often an important part of these displays. Since these products are not impulse items, consumers have the option of taking home a sales brochure for further consideration and, more important, next-day reinforcement.

Case History: Revlon's Polished Ambers Dermanesse Skin Programmer

To better inform black women about the dermatological variations of their skin compositions, Revlon decided to develop a teaching machine (Figure 8-10). The complicating factor, however, was that this unit could not be electronic, since most department-store cosmetics counters did not have sufficient electric outlets available. And, where such outlets did exist, the wires could have presented a safety hazard to salespeople.

Therefore, Revlon decided to rely entirely on a mechanical, as opposed to an electronic, "computer" designed to function on a balanced-scale principle. Consumers answered the eight questions posed by the machine by sliding a clear plastic chip over the appropriate response. After they had answered all eight questions, they could unlock the balance mechanism by pushing a release button. The resulting scale readout told the consumer which Revlon cosmetics would be best for her.

Since all scales need to be adjusted after a certain period of use, a device was designed for the underside of the computer which could be used to adjust the scale in the field. This could be done easily by the salesperson, who simply turned a screw until the machine's readout lined up with the central balance point.

FIGURE 8-10. Revlon's Polished Ambers Dermanesse skin programmer, by Thomson-Leeds Company, Inc., New York.

Counter and shelf displays often rely on motion and light, and these are used not only to increase attention factors or to provide an aura of elegance and quality but also to turn or highlight the product so that customers can stand in just one place and see the product pass before their eyes. This enables an entire line of watches, cigarette lighters, or fine writing instruments, for instance, to be viewed, and the right choice made more rapidly.

Clocks are often incorporated in these units to provide a handy feature for passing shoppers. Important locations for use of this class of display include taverns which have bar and fountain units as well as cash-register signs, department stores (particularly in the areas where cosmetics and household goods are sold), housewares stores, home improvement centers, discount stores, lawn and garden stores, and a host of other retail store types.

Case History: The Coke Supermarket Clock

The Coca-Cola Company's Coca-Cola brand is often referred to as "Coke" in the marketplace. To "marry" the two trademarks, and also to put primary emphasis on the stronger graphic visibility of Coke, a supermarket clock was developed which was also placed in gymnasiums, movie theaters, and service stations (Figure 8-11). Because these are considered prime locations for soft-drink consumption, the Coca-Cola Company wanted to create a unit that was demonstrably better than those associated with its competition.

Through a new patented process utilizing two panels of plastic, silk-screened with different patterns, a visual effect was created that gave the illusion of motion with no moving parts. The strong Coke logo was immediately seen, while the Coca-Cola logo was less obvious. This very creative and unusual design did exactly what the Coca-Cola Company wanted: It tied the Coke trademark to the Coca-Cola trademark and produced an exciting new type of clock with the illusion of motion.

Most permanent counter and shelf units are not shipped with the product in place, although there are a few examples to the contrary, particularly in the cosmetics field. An elegant appearance is important because these units are placed in the finest department stores as well as in automobile showrooms and other retail establishments.

HOW POP ADVERTISING RELATES TO OTHER MEDIA

The two halves of the marketing picture are advertising and sales promotion (or merchandising). Advertising, whether it is printed, broadcast, or put in the form of skywriting, is a very important part of the marketing mix. Advertising may bring consumers into the store, but the key element of sales promotion—the POP display—brings the product eyeball to eyeball with the consumer.

Marketers who were once dazzled by the glamour of the television giant have been just as dazzled by that medium's rapidly increasing costs, which go up an average of 20 percent per year. This has reduced the length of individual television commercials, increased the number of commercials, and thus reduced exposure and impact.

The reaction to ballooning media costs has been a sudden return to basics by advertisers who want to reach consumers where their dollars are spent. Merchandising—the age-old art of sound marketing, implemented in new ways—can deliver a lot of sell for a relatively small expenditure, perhaps the cost of one network commercial.

The mass media have based their value on cost per 1000 exposures. Since advertisers, advertising agencies, and educational institutions think in these terms, how does POP advertising relate to other media in terms of dollars-and-cents evaluation of the delivered advertising message?

Signs and other permanent POP units surpass all other media in delivering the lowest cost per 1000 exposures:

FIGURE 8-11. The Coke supermarket clock, by Thomas A. Schutz Company, Inc., Morton Grove, Ill.

- An outdoor 3- by 5-foot wall-mounted metal sign that costs $20, provides 500 daily adult exposures, and has a three-year life span has a cost per 1000 of $0.04.
- An outdoor metal curbside sign that costs $50, provides 2500 daily adult exposures, and has a three-year life span has a cost per 1000 of $0.03.
- An in-store permanent product merchandiser or sign that costs $5 to $20, has an exposure range of from 200 to 1000 daily (depending on the type of outlet), and has a one-year life span has a cost per 1000 ranging from $0.03 to $0.37.
- An in-store temporary product merchandiser or sign that costs from $2.50 to $10, provides an exposure range of from 200 to 1000 daily (depending on the type of outlet), and has a two-week life span has a cost ranging from $0.18 to $3.

These figures can be examined against the approximate cost of reaching 1000 adults in other media: A 30-second spot on network TV runs from $4.05 to $7.75, a one-minute radio spot costs from $3.50 to $4.75, a full-page four-color ad in a national magazine costs from $2.50 to $4, and a 1000-line newspaper ad is priced at $3.50 to $4.50. An outdoor painted bulletin runs from $1.25 to $1.50, while a thirty-sheet poster runs from $0.45 to $0.50.

Research indicates that even the best sales messages will be forgotten in three to five days. This may be due to the fact that the average person is barraged with more than 1500 selling messages daily. More than 80 percent of the nation's largest advertisers now use POP materials in conjunction with their overall advertising programs. And studies show that when these materials are linked to an advertising program, public awareness of the entire program can be increased by as much as 500 percent.

POP materials can also be used cost effectively to extend advertising reach and frequency. When combined with a clock, thermometer, calendar, message board, or other feature useful to retail outlets, POP advertising extends the time the materials stay up and further increases their value and economy.

RETAILERS' ATTITUDES TOWARD POP ADVERTISING

Not only has there been evidence of a major shift among national advertisers, but also retailers—the people who must ultimately accept or reject each merchandising aid—are viewing POP advertising in a new light.

Profit-minded retailers over the last several years have been demanding more and more merchandising ideas, programs, and supporting materials. They realize that well-prepared POP advertising will result in sales increases.

The troubled economy has produced an increase in the number of do-it-yourselfers visiting home improvement centers. These consumers were browsing the aisles more than they were buying, and so these outlets turned their stores into idea centers. They instituted "project planning," filling the environment with idea-generating signs and displays. They "turned the consumers on"—stirring their creative impulses and sparking their imaginations—and generated increased sales.

The phenomenon of the do-it-yourselfer is also readily apparent in the petroleum industry. The idea of pumping your own gas or changing your own oil has become quite common. Petroleum companies have recognized this trend and have reacted with the "self-serve" gasoline station. Creative retailers have given the consumer the option of self-service or full service, thereby attracting all market segments. Signs dividing the oil company outlet between full service and self-service are now an integral part of petroleum marketing.

Displays of products manufactured by the big oil companies have also become common in discount stores, hardware stores, and even supermarkets. These offer further evidence of the high sales volume and large profit associated with the do-it-yourselfer.

Case History: The Mobil 1 Promotional POP Program

The Mobil 1 promotional POP program was developed to convince the trade and the consumer that Mobil 1 was "the best motor oil you can buy" (Figure 8-12). The total program consisted of trade brochures, which explained the profit potential and comprehensive support programs; product inflatables; case cards for mass stackings; window units; shelf talkers; brochure dispensers; and consumer information and comparison guides, placed at checkout counters, which explained the benefits of using Mobil 1.

The graphic design appealed to the upper-income do-it-yourself consumer, and the POP materials concisely and simply presented the reason to buy the most expensive motor oil sold.

All the elements in the program worked together to position Mobil 1 as a top-quality product marketed by a top-quality company.

Progressive Grocer magazine has also noted that the food industry has a strong desire for merchandising assistance. Retailers are demanding more and more POP materials, but they do have reservations and restrictions. They realize that well-prepared POP advertising can achieve sales increases—in fact, one study indicated that in some instances sales increases went as high as 400 percent over a product's normal movement. The same report showed that related-item POP displays upped the dollar sales of products by 170 percent or more than the increases realized when the same items were displayed separately.

The *Progressive Grocer* article noted that more than 75 percent of supermarket managers and food-chain executives want more storewide, seasonal, and other special promotional programs. The same number want additional merchandising ideas, and almost as many said they don't have enough display materials.

The Point-of-Purchase Advertising Institute's four-part research study, entitled *Retailers' Attitudes towards P-O-P*, examined current trends and future anticipations in supermarkets, home improvement centers, full-line discount stores, and chain drugstores. This study revealed that 88 percent of all retail outlets use promotional displays, with 36 percent of the store managers reporting more usage than two years earlier. More than 90 percent responded that they employed signs and on-product units. Future needs were evenly split between permanent and semipermanent promotional POP pieces. In the area of collateral POP materials, respondents reported that banners, posters, signs, and shelf talkers would be included in their plans.

GETTING DISPLAYS USED

In order for any promotional material to work for the advertiser, it has to work for the retailer first. If POP advertising as a marketing tool is to flourish—as it has in the last fifteen years—continual strides must be made to provide

FIGURE 8-12. The Mobil 1 promotional POP program, by Case-Hoyt/ Atlanta, Atlanta, Ga.

retailers with what they need, not with what advertisers and suppliers of POP materials think they need.

It is important for marketers and their suppliers of POP materials to analyze the retail environment and to establish a checklist of questions that include the following: Does the retailer have special racks for displaying the materials? Are the racks available in all stores? Will the retailer provide special gondola space to promote the product? What POP materials will the retailer allow to be placed there? Is the retailer concerned about pilferage?

Each retail outlet's requirements are different. For example, cosmetics and fragrances sold through independent drugstores depend upon different POP displays from those used for cosmetics and fragrances sold in the finer surroundings of department stores. The independent drugstore does not have the staff to promote a particular product, so the POP display must serve as a silent salesperson. Successful displays must tell what the product is, what it will do, and what variations are available. They must arouse consumer interest and maintain it until a sale is made. Counter merchandisers are among the major POP materials found in independent drugstores. These retail outlets also use testers, which allow shoppers to sample the product's scent or taste. A tester can be part of the merchandiser or furnished as an independent unit. These stores also accept floor stands holding large amounts of a product, which they otherwise would not have room to stock.

Counter merchandisers and floor stands are not as acceptable to department stores, however. These stores characteristically employ beauty consultants or salespeople to service the consumer and make the sale. Department stores do accept promotional support from the manufacturer, but they are more selective about what will be used and how it will be used. They try to maintain a personalized quality in their cosmetics and fragrance departments. Testers or pedestals of a permanent nature are highly acceptable to department stores.

Remember that a POP display is successful only if it works in the store in which it is placed. After all, that's where the buck changes hands!

CONSUMER BUYING HABITS

The advertiser and the retailer are two sides of the sales triangle. The third side, and perhaps the most interesting one, is the consumer, who today (compared with his or her counterpart of a decade ago) has become more discriminating, more independent in thought, and more individual in taste. The consumer monitors opinions, fashion, and lifestyles and thus provides a dynamic influence affecting a product's success or failure in the marketplace.

Is today's aggressive consumer still influenced by impulse items? Such a question lies at the very root of human behavior, and the POPAI–Du Pont eighth study of consumer buying habits, published in 1977, was designed to monitor and report on this aspect of the consumer's purchasing habits in supermarkets. This study, financed by some fifty national advertisers, was conducted by recording 53,000 purchases made by 4000 shoppers at 200 supermarkets throughout the country and comparing these purchases with what the consumers who made them said they would buy as they entered the supermarket. The intent was to determine what percentage of total purchases was planned before the shopper entered the store and what percentage was influenced by something that happened after entering the store.

Even though the findings of the POPAI–Du Pont study relate to the supermarket, parallels can be drawn for almost any other retail outlet found in today's marketplace.

The study's findings can be compared with those of a similar study conducted by Du Pont in 1965. Shoppers in the 1977 study reported planning more of the items they bought before they entered the store and relying more heavily on both shopping lists and newspaper ads. However, if consumers are now making more shopping decisions at home than they used to, they still make almost two-thirds of those decisions—64.8 percent—in the store. Consumers remain alert for, and act on, such in-store influences as price, new products, and POP displays. In other words, they are still greatly influenced by what they see in the store and how they view what they see.

The 1977 POPAI–Du Pont study revealed some very interesting trends among consumers: less frequent visits to the supermarket, more planning, more systematic approaches to shopping, buying for smaller households, fewer large families, and, incidentally, more elderly people shopping (40 percent of the shoppers in the study were 50 years old or older, and 30 percent were 30 years old or under).

The study reported that the average supermarket shopping experience lasted almost twenty-five minutes, plus an additional seven minutes at the checkout counter. This was several minutes longer than a decade earlier. The total average amount spent was reported to have risen from $8.01 to $17.68, an increase of 121 percent. This is doubly meaningful when viewed in terms of decreasing family size.

The statistics work out to a spending rate of $0.70 per shopping minute. Obviously, it is advantageous to the retailer to keep the shopper in the store longer. Theoretically, an extra ten minutes in the supermarket will add $7 to the cash-register tape. These figures can be used as a base for almost any retail outlet.

For this reason, POP signs and displays are growing in importance in the marketplace; they create a selling environment, gain the attention of and stop the consumer, create extra selling space, generate consumer excitement, provide product data for purchasing decisions, and—most important—close the sale.

The POPAI–Du Pont study also examined the effects of newspaper advertising, store circulars, couponing, and displays. It is no surprise that these devices all change the standard buying pattern of a product, but the study offers dramatic evidence that when advertising is used in conjunction with a display program, the ratio of sales increases significantly. For example, in the case of cookies, the combination of advertising and display increases sales 96 percent over what they would be using advertising alone. Oral-hygiene products respond equally to separate treatments of advertising or display. When both media work in tandem, sales are nearly tripled. Snack-food sales range from a sixfold to an eightfold increase; candy and gum sales show a 70 percent increase; and sales of canned vegetables have an approximately fourfold increase.

The POPAI–Du Pont study details seventy-four major product categories covering the full range of products sold in today's supermarket. Although the study reveals that consumers are using shopping lists more frequently today than in the past, it appears that these shopping lists are strongly oriented toward basic foods and household supplies. It is in the store that most shoppers decide to buy such items as cake mixes, pies, doughnuts, cookies, candy and gum, and crackers. The conclusion: Shoppers' good intentions regarding the foods they will buy come to naught when they see such products in the store. For the supermarket manager, this conclusion should be translated into more displays using these products.

The summary of the study proves anew that shoppers can be influenced greatly by what they see in the store, despite their best efforts to limit their purchases to the items they feel they really need. In truth, impulse buying is a great American pastime and is just about as popular as it ever was. And despite their protests to the contrary, consumers apparently love to be influenced in the store—and this shows at the cash register.

INNOVATIONS

The versatility of POP advertising in providing constant innovation is rooted in the ability of designers and model makers to continually change the materials, or combinations of materials, from which a display is made and to provide a unique appearance and unique features. A new material does not come along every day or every year to provide new construction opportunities. Probably the most recent is polyurethane, which has been used heavily in this industry for the last decade. Much of the innovation comes from a combination of materials, such as sheet metal and wood or plastics and wire, as well as from breakthroughs in POP technologies. These include thinner but stronger metal and better and deeper pigments of ink.

CHANNELS OF DISTRIBUTION

The primary difference between POP advertising and most other advertising media is that the other media take care of distribution for the advertiser. For example, when advertisers buy time on television, they give the network the commercial, and the medium broadcasts the message to the audience. With POP advertising, advertisers must distribute display units through their own channels or through a display installation house.

If an advertiser sells a product in different types of outlets, it is likely that more than one means of distribution will be used. There are three main channels of distribution: the company's own salespeople and/or detail crews; dealers' representatives and wholesalers' salespeople; and display installation houses.

Company Salespeople and Detail Crews

The company's own salespeople are most commonly used for distributing POP materials. Their presentation of these materials is critically important; the salespeople are the sole link between the advertiser and the retailer. A number of years ago, salespeople looked upon the distribution of POP materials as added work. But today, national advertisers expend great sums of money to properly train their salespeople in the philosophy that POP advertising benefits not only the corporation but also the salespeople themselves. Where detail crews are employed to back up the sales force, they actually deliver and set up the display.

Dealers' Representatives and Wholesalers' Salespeople

These people operate in much the same way that a company sales force does, except that they carry more than one product line. Thus, promotional programs may be used to gain their support. Contests and dealer incentives are used frequently to motivate these people and to gain their cooperation. Dealers' representatives and wholesalers' salespeople may work alone or help open retailers' doors by giving them advance notice of the company's program and the POP materials which will be coming.

Display Installation Houses

Hiring specialists to set up POP materials through their own channels is an efficient method of distribution, but it is rather costly. Thus, larger companies, particularly in the distilled spirits industry, are more prone to use this service. These companies often work on a local or regional (statewide) basis. They can arrange to receive the advertiser's displays and signs and physically set them up in the outlets specified and prearranged by the advertiser, or they will arrange for placement and installation directly with the stores. A feature of this type of service is that the advertisers receive affidavits stating where and when the POP material was set up.

Other Distribution Methods

Direct shipment is sometimes used when the display is relatively small. Direct shipment of a display may or may not be accompanied by the goods to be sold. Offers made by direct mail and trade magazines are another method for distributing POP materials. These methods are not very successful and are not recommended.

THE TRADE ASSOCIATION

The Point-of-Purchase Advertising Institute (POPAI) is a nonprofit industry association representing those who design, create, produce, and supply POP signs and displays, as well as those who buy and use them.

A group of lithographers and mounter-finishers (houses specializing in bonding printed sheets to reinforcements, die-casting, scoring, etc.) met in Chicago in 1938 for the purpose of establishing an association to represent this industry. The initial purpose was to foster a better understanding of POP materials as a vital part of merchandising and to provide an opportunity for an exchange of information that would further the use of signs and displays.

Since that time, POPAI has grown nationally and internationally, with chapters in France, Italy, and Japan and an affiliate in Great Britain. Where no organization exists, POPAI accepts individual memberships throughout the world. Today, POPAI is one of the most progressive and active trade associations in the marketing field.

Among its varied services, POPAI initiates objective research studies which supply answers to the many complex questions dealing with the impact of POP advertising; fosters ethical trade practices; develops educational materials and programs; promotes the entire industry in order to obtain the most effective and widespread use of POP materials; and circulates this information through an effective public relations, publicity, and advertising program.

9 Reaching the Public through Fairs, Expositions, Exhibits, and Demonstrations

ROBERT B. KONIKOW

Former Public Relations Counsel, Trade Show Bureau

According to an old adage, seeing is believing, and there certainly is a great deal of truth in this. What we experience firsthand is most likely to be accepted, and many manufacturers rely on sales promotion at a personal level, where they can explain the advantages of the product or service they are selling, obtain an immediate reaction to their sales story, modify or extend their sales arguments on the spot, and move quickly to a close.

Development of a full program along these lines, especially one involving sales demonstrations in the home, can be an expensive matter, however. It is time-consuming and thus is difficult to work into a full-scale sales program. The return on each sale may simply not be enough to warrant the time taken by a salesperson to make a single demonstration. And when you realize that you will probably have to make a number of demonstrations for each sale you achieve, the economic difficulties seem almost insuperable.

Under certain circumstances, of course, they can be overcome. Where the unit sale is large enough and the frequency of interest is high enough, home demonstrations are an effective means of distribution. Most encyclopedia sales are made through home demonstrations, and vacuum cleaners have been sold effectively in this way, in spite of the higher prices that must be charged. Cosmetics, with their intensely personal nature and their generally high markup, can be sold through in-home demonstrations, as the success of Avon illustrates.

Manufacturers of other products increase the potential return per hour of sales time by utilizing home parties, which succeed by enlarging the audience for each demonstration. Tupperware is the outstanding example, but there are many others. Success in this kind of distribution usually demands a constant recruiting effort, in which the sales representatives gain part of their income from the sales of those whom they have recruited, and even from those recruited by their recruits.

Like all direct selling, this process requires a special kind of individual, one who is able to maintain enthusiasm even after a high percentage of rebuffs. Much of the effort of sales management must be put into maintaining and building enthusiasm. Turnover is always a problem in these operations.

DEMONSTRATIONS

Demonstrations, of course, do not necessarily have to take place in the home. They can be given wherever there are potential customers, and that is literally everywhere. The old-fashioned hawkers are now part of American folklore. They used to set up portable tables on busy streets, attracting groups of passersby with vivid demonstrations. They had to tell their stories and make their sales quickly, before the police came around and sent them on their way.

Today's demonstrators are more responsible. They work for established companies, in recognized establishments, wherever enough qualified prospects can be found. Most commonly used for demonstration purposes are department stores and supermarkets, simply because they tend to carry more items with broader interest, but demonstrations are frequently held in specialized outlets, such as arts-and-crafts stores, camera shops, and stores that sell electronic organs.

There is no single format for such a demonstration, since the way in which it is set up depends upon the nature of the product and the nature of the store. Some demonstrations are held right at a counter, others utilize a special demonstration table set up within the appropriate department, and still others can be given in the store auditorium.

Some demonstrators go into a pitch whenever a passing shopper slows down for a moment, while others operate on a fixed and posted schedule. Some stores try to build traffic with advertising and promotion, including such media as bill stuffers, newspaper ads, radio commercials, handbills, and signs posted in the store, while others rely wholly on the passing traffic.

Almost all demonstrations are designed to lead to orders, which may be written up by the demonstrator, following store procedures, or by salesclerks assigned to the location. In supermarkets, an effort is made to place the product in the shopping cart, to be checked out normally. Often, a special offer is made to those who make a purchase during the demonstration or as a result of it.

FAIRS AND EXPOSITIONS

But there are often bigger and better audiences than those which happen to go into a particular store. Fairs and expositions attract such an audience, whose presence can be utilized to move a product. Before we get into a discussion of this important channel, we must be sure to make clear the difference between trade fairs and public fairs. Trade fairs, or trade shows, as they are usually known, are discussed in Chapter 19. They are designed to sell primarily to industry. Many of them, especially those sponsored by professional societies, do not even permit selling; rather, they are educational and informational in nature. But, essentially, they are designed to permit business to communicate to business. Attendance is limited in one way or another, and the general public is usually not welcome, or at least is admitted only during restricted "public" hours.

Public fairs and expositions, on the other hand, are directed toward the public, or at least toward a major segment of the public. They go to great effort to attract as large an audience as possible.

One of the major categories of public shows consists of state, district, and county fairs; these were originally almost completely agricultural in nature, but they have extended themselves into general consumer awareness. According to the industry association, the International Association of Fairs and Expositions (IAFE), there are approximately 3240 such fairs in the United States and Canada each year, and they attract an estimated audience of some 159 million. Somewhat more than half of this attendance is accounted for by the 350 major fairs.

These fairs, especially the state fairs, have impressive attendance figures. The State Fair of Texas reported that 2,868,062 people visited its 250-acre fairgrounds in Dallas in 1982. Its stadium holds 72,000, and its coliseum holds 7200. It offers 315,000 square feet of indoor commercial exhibit space, with another 55,000 square feet outdoors. It was topped by the fair in Columbus, Ohio, which drew 3,234,043 visitors. There are eleven other fairs that draw more than 1 million in attendance, and a total of thirty-eight around the country that pulled more than half a million in 1982.

We're talking big money, too. In 1982, IAFE estimated that the total gross income of all fairs in the United States and Canada was $702,335,412, of which 10 percent was spent on talent to help pull the crowds. Missouri alone had 138 fairs. Most fairs take place on their own permanent grounds, and many are operated by the appropriate state or county government, with some supervision from the legislature or other authorized body.

Special-Interest Shows

In addition to these agriculturally oriented events, there are a great number of special-interest shows: automobile shows, home and garden shows, sports shows, and the like. It is a little difficult to keep track of fairs in this category, since some of them are not held every year and others come and go as traffic supports them. They rarely operate in their own facilities, often using auditoriums and convention centers or renting state or county fair facilities. Many of them are well established and popular. Attendance at such a public show may often run over 100,000, with the Chicago Automobile Show normally claiming close to 1 million visitors in its two-week run, particularly before the recent economic crisis.

Admission to these shows, like admission to the fairs, is on a paid basis. To get people to come, the show managers resort to a variety of techniques. Publicity and promotion, of course, are heavy. Exhibitors are often enlisted in building attendance by selling discount tickets to their customers. And management builds in a program of events that occur within the hall to add to the excitement.

A special-interest show, by its very nature, draws an audience of people who are concerned with the subject area, who are knowledgeable, and who are likely to make a purchase, if not at the moment, undoubtedly within a reasonable time. It is an audience that, for the right exhibitor, is highly desirable.

A research study released by the Trade Show Bureau in July 1981 (RS 9) reports on some characteristics of the New York National Boat Show, which ran in the Coliseum from January 15 to January 25, 1981. About 400,000 people attended this show. Of these, 59.4 percent actually owned a boat, while 61.8 percent indicated that they would buy a boat, an engine, or an accessory within twelve months as a result of having visited the show.

PARTICIPATING IN A PUBLIC SHOW

Unlike trade shows, agriculturally oriented shows and special-interest shows are used for direct selling extensively, and sales promotional product demonstrations and hard sell are common. While major exhibitors tend to be more institutional, the smaller spaces are taken by companies which expect to sell enough on the spot to pay for their investment of time and money.

Both types of events are considered essentially local or regional, in contrast with trade shows, most of which are national or even international in nature, even if, in practice, those attending such shows tend to be drawn largely from within a 100- to 200-mile radius of the convention city. As a result, the actual exhibitor at a fair or exposition is likely to be the agent, the distributor, or the wholesaler for a national company, or perhaps a coalition of retailers handling a specific brand.

For example, let us look at the automotive shows, of which there were more than 100 in 1978. The major exhibitors at these shows were the automobile manufacturers, both domestic and foreign. But the space was almost always taken and operated by all the local dealers of a brand, who got together for this joint promotion, much as they would for a marketwide advertising or promotion campaign. They got assistance in various ways from the factories they represented, of course. Detroit may have loaned special display units to the group, may have brought in celebrities to boost interest in the show, and may have furnished other assistance, which is worked out each year. The terms have always been flexible and subject to negotiation. (From 1978 through the early 1980s, the economic situation severely depressed the auto market.)

In general, the home office—and this is true in most industries— furnishes the exhibit structure, while the local group pays for the space and supplies the personnel needed to run the booth. But the division of costs can vary greatly, depending upon the desire to participate. If a manufacturer is very anxious to extend its penetration into a specific market, it may be willing to absorb a greater share of the cost. There is no sacred figure.

Frequently, participation in appropriate shows and similar events is up to the local dealer or dealer group, supported by the manufacturer as part of its cooperative advertising program. Winnebago Industries, of Forest City, Iowa, a major manufacturer of motor homes, has a cooperative advertising plan for its dealers which is probably typical. It covers a number of forms of advertising, including shows and exhibits.

Each dealer has a cooperative advertising account, into which is credited a specific amount for each vehicle purchased from the factory. As long as they

FIGURE 9-1. On the floor at the Chicago Flower and Garden Show, a nontrade show, at McCormick Place.

follow certain administrative restrictions, dealers are permitted to spend this advertising allowance on any medium or combination of media they wish. The *Winnebago Retail Marketing Planner*, a loose-leaf guidebook, indicates that the company will reimburse dealers for 50 percent of what they spend at shows, provided that the show is a professionally organized recreational-vehicle show and that the space covered by the cooperative program is devoted to the exclusive display of Winnebago products.

This is the pattern generally followed, whether the actual exhibitor is a single dealer or a group of dealers. And it is the pattern followed by those exhibits which take up the most space at such shows and are the heart of the show. It is these exhibits that are the key to the success of the show, since they not only utilize the bulk of the space but also tend to give these essentially local shows their national feeling and since they are instrumental in attracting attendance.

These large displays, however, are not usually where sales are made. This is especially true where several dealers get together to exhibit as a group. In order to operate smoothly as a team, the dealers often adopt a rule that no orders will be taken on the floor, but that all those visitors who express an interest in buying will be given a complete list of the cooperating dealers and will be asked to return to any of them for the final buying step. But salespeople being what they are, and with the unit of sale being as large as it usually is at an automobile or boat show, one wonders how carefully the rule is observed with a prospect who is on the verge of signing up.

But the smaller booths, usually located on the fringes of the main display area, are quite different. They are almost always operated by individual companies, rather than a group of retailers, and there is no question of who is to gain from sales. The unit sale is likely to be smaller than sales in the other displays and is much more likely to be an impulse sale.

The ultimate decision on participating will be up to the local retailers, since they have the key responsibility for running the booth. Show managers will try to sell the idea of participation to manufacturers, and if they succeed, there will be pressure from the factory to get into the show. Often this pressure—or perhaps we should say persuasion—will take the form of absorbing more of the cost of participation. The factory can, for example, furnish a professionally designed and built booth background; it can give an extra discount on merchandise to be sold at the show; and it can pay the expense of special demonstrators. It all depends on how anxious the manufacturer is to get into this market and how good a bargaining position it finds itself in.

While earlier we distinguished between a trade show, which is devoted primarily to selling or reaching business, and a public show, which is aimed at the consumer, we should emphasize that this distinction is theoretical and is occasionally ignored by exhibitors. There is often a fine line between trade shows and public shows. People are people, and when a large group comes together at a show because of a common interest, there is no reason why a substantial number of those in attendance should not have other interests as well. Many of the shows in the health care field bring together a large number of individuals who share a common professional interest in such topics as surgery, radiology, and hospital administration. Most of the exhibits at these shows appeal to these special concerns. But those who attend have certain other characteristics in common. Their level of education is high, as is their income. This makes them a good target audience for certain general commodities such as encyclopedias and reclining lounge chairs, and some companies in these fields exhibit regularly at such shows to pick up serious leads or actual sales.

The same thinking can work in the reverse direction. Whenever you have assembled thousands of people, there are bound to be segments of the total with a common interest. Among the thousands or hundreds of thousands who attend a special-interest show or a state fair, there may be enough proprietors of small businesses, to take just one possibility, to warrant a display of cash registers.

FIGURE 9-2. Theme sections are used to create special-interest areas at fairs and other nontrade shows.

Should You Participate in a Show?

The decision to participate in a public show should be based on a calculated analysis of the costs and the potential benefits. As much as possible, you should set up measurable objectives for each show you are considering and see whether these can be achieved at a reasonable cost.

An analysis starts with the people who will be attending the show, and you want to know more than the raw numbers. You want to know their age distribution, their income distribution, where they live, whether they are homeowners, and all the other factors that might affect their interest in your product or service and their ability to purchase. Show managements have compiled these figures, to a greater or lesser degree, and you should ask for them. They are comparable to the circulation figures offered by newspapers and magazines or the audience figures supplied by radio and television stations. You need them to decide not only whether to enter a show but also what products you should display and what you should use as your major sales emphasis.

The state of the art is not as advanced in the area of show management as in the more familiar media, and you may have to do some insisting to get the figures you need. You may also find it necessary to go beyond the figures supplied to you by the show operators and do some checking with those who have exhibited in previous years. This is especially true of a newer show, which is likely to be less well established.

Remember that the total number of people attending is meaningless, except as a point at which to start your thinking. Not everybody who comes to the show is likely to be a prospect, and not all of those who are prospects will stop at your display, or even walk by it. There will rarely be enough information for you to develop a precise measurement of likely attendance at your booth, since to some extent this can be affected by what you do.

While you cannot do much to alter the total attendance and the audience's general characteristics, you can do a great deal to affect the traffic flow in your own booth. The design of your booth, the nature of what goes on within it, and the promotion you give your participation will all have some influence on how many people know about your exhibit and make their way to it.

What Are Your Objectives?

Now that you have a handle on the number of people who might visit your exhibit, you have to decide what you would like to happen. Are you looking for immediate sales? Are you trying to set up appointments for home demonstrations or to obtain leads for your salespeople? Perhaps you want people to sample your product during their visit and make their purchase later elsewhere. If you are doing market research, you might want to get consumer reaction to a new product or a new package. Or you might want to sign up new dealers or new representatives.

But whatever your objective, put it down in writing and give it a numerical value. Knowing what you want to achieve will give direction to the contents of your display area and will tell you how much you may be able to afford to spend and what kind of people should staff your booth. And it will permit you to determine whether you have reached your goal.

What Goes into Your Booth?

You have signed up for participation in a show in order to achieve a specific objective. You must now plan to utilize your space to achieve this objective. Doing this most effectively is a specialized skill, and you should avail yourself of the help of experts. If you are a retailer working with a national manufacturer, you should be able to get some help from your supplier, who is as anxious as you are to make sure that your effort is crowned with success. If you are completely on your own, you might call in a professional exhibit designer and producer; most of these people are members of the Exhibit Designers & Producers Association.

But you must always remember that a show or fair has its own special rules. Even if you try to transplant a retail outlet to the floor of a show, the public is not the same. The people who visit your exhibit may be the same kind of people who visit a retail store, but their mood is different. When people walk into a store, they are looking for something. They have taken, by themselves, the first step toward the completion of a transaction. At a show, visitors are there primarily to have fun. They have their special interests, of course, especially at a show that is built around a specific theme, but they are there for entertainment. Their attention must first be captured. They must be stopped as they walk down the aisle so that they can be exposed to your message. Like the headline in a magazine ad, your exhibit must have something that will grab people's attention, especially the attention of those who are most likely to be good prospects for whatever it is that you are selling.

Now is the time to utilize to the fullest the special characteristics of the exhibit. Unlike other promotional media, shows and fairs put you face-to-face with prospects. They can see your actual product, not just a picture of it. You can demonstrate how it works, let them see it in action, and perhaps let them handle it. You can get your prospects involved. They can ask questions and get immediate answers.

Your exhibit must be designed to allow this contact to happen as rapidly and as effectively as possible. It must do even more—it must encourage this contact. To achieve this, your designer must be familiar with what you are selling and how it is sold and must adapt the design of your exhibit to these circumstances. For example, if you are selling a new device to peel potatoes, you can demonstrate the gadget to a group of onlookers and make sales when you are at the right point in the demonstration. On the other hand, if you are selling a financial advisory service, you need more than a demonstration. You can use a demonstration to stop passersby and build an audience, and you can arouse curiosity and interest, but eventually you must end up on a one-to-one basis. You will want to arrange your exhibit so that a salesperson can talk in privacy with a qualified prospect. These two situations require different organizations of space and different exhibit designs, and they represent only two possibilities out of a whole range of activities that can be carried out at your booth.

How Can You Increase Traffic to Your Booth?

When you participate in a fair or exposition, you can rely on the show management to promote the total event. For its own success, the show will try to get as many people as possible to attend. This audience, which has come for the show in general, is the basis of the attendance at your booth.

You can let it go at that and rely simply on the traffic that flows past your booth. You can hope that enough people will see what you are displaying, and will stop, to make your participation profitable. Good design will help increase this number. If something interesting, something active, catches people's eyes during the second or two it takes them to walk by your booth, they may be persuaded to stop.

But there will be many who will walk by without ever looking in your direction. They may be looking the other way, or even looking straight at your booth without paying any attention. And then there are those who miss coming down your aisle. As far as you are concerned, these people were not even in attendance.

Taking some simple action can increase the traffic to your booth and thus add to the return on your investment. Spending just a little more on promotion can multiply the effectiveness of your participation.

Start by letting everybody know that you are participating in the show. By putting signs in your store or stuffers in your mail, you can let your customers, your suppliers, and all your contacts know that you will be at the show and that they should come and look for you. Get materials like posters and folders from the show management and associate yourself with the promotion of the show itself.

Try to find a special reason why people should come to visit *your* exhibit. Are you going to have a new and interesting product on display for the first time? Are you making a special offer for a purchase made at the show? Are you going to have a product expert on hand to answer questions or to demonstrate new techniques? Will a celebrity be there to give out autographed pictures? Do you plan to have some sort of a participation game for visitors? Can people enter a sweepstakes during the show? You can build attendance by giving people a good reason for putting *your* display on their "must" list.

Many exhibitors help build traffic through the use of advertising specialties. Giving away small gifts or souvenirs is a common practice at trade shows and expositions. People like to get something for nothing, and if the gift is useful, it will carry its advertising message for a long time as a constant reminder of the donor. If what you give away is too big to be put in a pocket or a purse, it will serve as a walking billboard around the fairgrounds. Such items as unusual balloons, inexpensive plastic shopping bags, lapel buttons with an amusing slogan, or hats with a distinctive shape or hatband serve to make an exhibitor very visible. They must be carried in full sight, and each recipient helps encourage more people to visit your booth in order to get a gift.

Who Should Staff Your Booth?

There is no simple answer to this question, because there are too many variables. What kind of a product or service are you showing? How well do people know your product? What are you going to do in your booth? What do you want to happen?

While you are likely to have members of your regular staff work at your exhibit, think through carefully how you can use each person at his or her top capability. If, for example, you have a large booth and expect large crowds to pass by, you need some people just for traffic control. These people need to know very little about your company and what it is selling, so it is a waste of talent to use sales personnel for this purpose.

At the other end of the spectrum are people who are technically knowledgeable. They, of course, are more important when your product or service is highly specialized and the purchase is a large one. Prospects will be more concerned about their buying decisions, will dig more deeply into the characteristics of the product, and will not be satisfied with superficial answers. You had better have somebody present who knows the answers and can give them with an air of authority.

In between are people whose activity is directly related to your product and those who bring a specialized skill to your booth. For example, magicians are often employed to help build a crowd at displays. It is obvious that you must have either a professional or a highly qualified amateur to play this role. You cannot take just any employee and say, "You are going to be our magician!" Similarly, donning a rented costume does not make an individual an effective clown.

The impact of a magician or a clown can be heightened if this person is able to work in direct references to your product and its selling points. Most professionals, especially those who have had trade-show experience, are used to doing this, but they need to be briefed far enough in advance to permit them to adjust their routines and have them down pat by the time they go into action.

Demonstrators should generally be professionals. It is often easier to train professional demonstrators in the techniques of handling your product than to take individuals who know your product and make polished demonstrators out of them. In most situations, demonstrators do not get into the closing of sales; they are merely giving a specified talk and going through a preestablished routine which illustrates the major points you want to get across. They must be smooth enough and theatrical enough to attract crowds and to hold their attention, as well as experienced enough to be able to gauge the audience's reaction and to handle the occasional wise guy or heckler.

In most situations, the final sale will be made by your people, who will make themselves available at the appropriate time or, better still, will keep an eye on those who are listening to the pitch and pick out the ones who seem to be the most likely prospects to approach at the right moment. Some demonstrators, with some products, will be able to go right into the final closing, in the manner of the Main Street hawkers. You will almost invariably have to go to the ranks of the professionals for such talent. Much of the charm of such a demonstration lies in watching a pro in action. It fascinates people, and you cannot expect an ordinary salesperson to put on that kind of performance.

There are agencies in most cities that can furnish people with these skills. You can find them listed in the yellow pages, usually under "Demonstrators." Again, allow time for the professional to work up a routine and become familiar with the subject to be covered. When you discuss the terms of employment with the agency or with the individual, be sure that there is a clear understanding about hours on duty, hours to be paid for, how often demonstrations are to be given, and so on. Dealing with large crowds over long hours, as must be done when working at a fair or exposition, is tiring, and you must give the people who do it adequate rest periods if you want them to be fresh and alert at all times when they are on duty. This applies to your own personnel, of course, as well as to outside specialists.

While there may be some people on your own staff who are capable of handling demonstrations at a show, if you are embarking on a program of demonstrations at retail stores, you will find that it is virtually essential to go to an agency that can handle the entire program for you. Even for a program that is limited to a single marketing area, you will probably need a number of demonstrators for maximum effectiveness. To gain as much impact as possible and to economize on the promotion of the event and make areawide advertising support possible, you will have to turn to multiple demonstrators. And if you plan to promote in many markets, there is probably no way you can handle this internally; to staff up for such a short-term operation is uneconomical and impractical for most companies.

The answer is to use one of the national temporary agencies, which have offices in most major cities. These companies supply temporary people, not only for manual and clerical tasks but for professional services as well. In the case of a national or large regional program, they are able to sit down with you, to discuss your needs and objectives, and to develop a working manual that will serve as a guide to the experienced demonstrators and salespeople whom they will furnish.

RELATED ACTIVITIES

A number of other opportunities for demonstrations and displays are very specialized in nature, may not occur very frequently, and are often limited in the ways in which participation is permitted; nevertheless, they are worth at least a mention in this chapter.

Most spectacular, and most limited, are *world's fairs*. A true world's fair must be approved by an international bureau, which places severe restrictions on the way in which it operates. It can run for no more than six months, must charge no space rental to foreign governments, and must limit commercial sales and souvenir shops to specific areas, even within its major pavilions. Such fairs are divided into category A fairs, which are general in nature, and category B fairs, which are built around a specific theme. A typical category A fair was Expo 67, held in Montreal in 1967. The New York world's fair of 1963–1964 did not get bureau approval, because its management did not wish to conform to the bureau's conditions. As a result, the foreign pavilions at New York were sponsored not by governments, but by groups of companies or importers from the participating nations. In addition, New York sold space in general buildings to smaller exhibitors, who were permitted to make sales in their display spaces.

Seattle, San Antonio, and Spokane all held category B events, based on specific themes, but they operated under bureau regulations, and thus there was limited commercial exploitation. A recent such event in the United States, with the official name of Energy Expo 82, took place in Knoxville, Tennessee, in 1982, and New Orleans hosted a world's fair in 1984.

Participation in either category of world's fair is a major investment; there is a six-month commitment, and usually it is necessary to design and construct a complete building to house the exhibit. Single-company participation is thus confined to major corporations. Smaller companies often participate through their industry associations or by cooperating in some sort of a tie-in with a major exhibitor. The objective, because of the restrictions placed on official world's fairs, is almost always stated in terms of public recognition and goodwill, occasionally leads, but almost never immediate sales.

The *theme park* is a rather recent addition to the American scene. Scattered all over the country, theme parks have developed from the familiar amusement park, which continues to exist. They feature rides and related attractions. An amusement park is often local in its attraction, or perhaps something that people visit as part of a vacation trip, while a theme park is large enough so that it often becomes the main objective of such a trip. Disney Land and Disney World are probably the best-known examples, but others, such as the Six Flags group and the Marriott Great America group, also attract vast audiences. The most recent innovations in this category are Disney's Epcot Center and the Disney park in Japan.

FIGURE 9-3. The Mill at Burlington House in New York City. This was an exhibit of textile-mill processes and products, open to the public. A moving walkway conveyed visitors through the three-level exhibit, which included demonstrations of fibers, yarn manufacturing, knitting, weaving, tufting, dyeing, and finished fabrics. More than 6 million people visited The Mill between 1970 and 1980. (*Courtesy of Burlington Industries.*)

Most amusement parks and attractions, from the local recreational facility (such as a swimming pool or picnic area) to the giant theme park, are interested in commercial cooperation, although each has its special requirements and limitations. These range from simple concessions, where souvenirs or curiosities are sold, all the way to permanent exhibits and attractions, very much like those erected at world's fairs.

Fairs and parks such as those discussed above must be explored individually to see how they might fit into your own objectives. They offer the advantage of furnishing large numbers of people who are open for amusement and who therefore may be an attractive target group.

A number of companies have used exhibit techniques to establish a sponsored *visitor center*, *exhibit center*, or *museum*, located either in a high-traffic area or in connection with a headquarters or major factory. One such exhibit center, called The Mill, was established by Burlington at its corporate headquarters in New York City. Such centers sometimes include retail outlets to sell factory merchandise. It is often possible to utilize the drawing power of these installations to extend the offerings. Such a center may warrant investigation as a possible opportunity for promotion.

ADDITIONAL SOURCES OF INFORMATION

The areas covered in this chapter are broad. Very little has been published on the subject of fairs, expositions, and demonstrations, nor is there a single publication which serves all segments of the industry. A number of the organizations listed in Appendix B publish, with lesser or greater regularity, material of interest to participants in these events.

Game-Show Giveaways:
A Low-Cost Way to Gain Nationwide TV Exposure

10

ROBERT A. ROBERTSON
President, Game-Show Placements, Ltd.

In early 1955, *Queen for a Day* gave away an Amana washing machine. It was one of TV's earliest game-show product promotions and was Amana's only form of national advertising. Today, almost thirty years later, Amana is still using game shows to promote its products, as are hundreds of other manufacturers. For anyone wishing to gain access to our most powerful national medium, these shows offer a unique opportunity.

Game shows now command 35 percent of the entire daytime television-viewing audience. For more than twenty-five years they have maintained an enormous popularity—despite a temporary setback following the game-show "scandals" of the late 1950s. They have survived heavy competition from the "soaps," the vagaries of American taste, and the fierce competitive strategies of the networks. In 1982, there were seven different network daytime game shows on the air, with more than twice that number in national syndication. Game shows are so popular, in fact, that in one record year they were estimated to have generated over $600 million, or 60 percent of the networks' total gross income![1]

AUDIENCE

A product or service that is given away as a prize during a single seven- to ten-second award segment on one of these shows will be seen by as many as 18 million American consumers. This enormous audience can be reached at a small fraction of the cost of regular commercial time. In addition, the cost of production, compared with the cost of producing a filmed commercial, is reduced to a bare minimum. Best of all, almost any promoter can afford this type of exposure, since there are no minimum-buy restrictions.

Some products obviously have more appeal than others and help enhance the format of the show. These are often favored by show producers when a number of products are available. But given the need for variety and the constant demand to fill award spots, almost any legitimate product or service can be promoted, subject to network and Federal Communications Commission (FCC) regulations. Game-Show Placements, Ltd., a Hollywood-based game-show prize broker, has placed products ranging from mousetraps to $20,000 mobile homes.

COST

The cost of this type of exposure is made up of a combination of product cost and cash fee. The amount of the fee is determined, to a significant degree, by the value of the product or award: the higher the retail value, the lower the cash fee. Most of the prizes awarded on game shows are in the low-retail-price category: packaged goods, food and grocery items, cosmetics, small appliances, sporting goods, and apparel. The retail value of the award must amount to at least $25. If the unit cost is less than this, multiples of that product or an assortment of the manufacturer's other, related products is added to reach the minimum figure. The typical cash fee for such a low-cost award on network shows is less than $800—quite a bargain, considering that a regular thirty-second commercial on these same shows can run as much as 20 times this amount. Additionally, regular commercials usually must be bought in minimum "flights"—multiple buys that amount to many thousands of dollars.

MECHANICS

The mechanics of game-show promotion on network and nationally syndicated shows are well defined by industry practice and regulation. Products are promoted separately as discrete "spots" within the program format. Each spot consists of seven to ten seconds of on-the-air visual exposure with twenty to twenty-five words of copy spoken by the program announcer. Almost all programs use "camera cards." These typically consist of an 11- by 14-inch photoprint with the product name or logo overprinted by means of composite photoprinting, color-cell overlay, or a similar method. As with regular commercials, the copy and the visuals are subject to network review and approval. Once approved, the copy is read by the show's announcer over the visuals, exactly as written.

A few shows use products "live," right on the set, instead of a camera card.

Usually, an attractive model is used to enhance the production value of the spot. She may sit on the sofa, open the freezer door, or model an item of clothing. *The Price Is Right* is the best known of these "live-prop" shows. Contestants try to guess the retail value of products featured. Whoever comes closest, without going over the correct amount, wins the products. This is a simple format, yet apparently an entertaining and engaging one, as the show's long-running success attests.

EFFECTIVENESS

Just how effective is this type of brief, but broad, exposure? As with most advertising, this is determined largely by such factors as frequency, the creative content of the copy and visuals, and the effectiveness of the sales message being delivered. In one study, conducted by Du Pont for its Teflon-

FIGURE 10-1. The success of *The Gong Show* expanded the boundaries of the traditional game show and opened new opportunities for prize promotions. (*Courtesy of Robert A. Robertson.*)

coated products, game-show spots were shown to be highly effective. A surprisingly high percentage of viewers could recall the products used as prizes twenty-four hours after seeing the show. Unaided, viewers could recall on the average of 12.5 percent of the prizes shown, while only 10 percent of products used on the commercials were recalled. The aided-recall results showed that, on the average, each of the thirty-three prizes offered on two game-show segments used in the survey was identified by 47 percent of the viewers. With few exceptions, prizes were identified by at least 25 percent of the audience, and in some cases by as much as 91 percent.

The report goes on to say:

> Viewers don't discriminate well between products used as prizes and those shown in regular game-show commercials. Recall of incorrect commercials averages only 13% among the viewers which again tends to verify their honesty.
>
> In both cases there was a direct relationship between perceived value or uniqueness of the product and the number of viewers who identified it.
>
> To further verify the communication value for prizes of TV game-shows, viewers and nonviewers of the show segments used in this study were asked if they had ever heard of certain brand name products used as prizes.
>
> The results were statistically significant . . . for the two brand names used, awareness among viewers was much higher than nonviewers: 48% vs 23% and 72% vs 44%.[2]

Demographically, game shows reach a surprisingly varied audience, according to viewer studies. Network daytime audiences are largely female. Syndicated shows with primarily evening time slots have approximately a 40 to 60 male/female viewer ratio. At least one popular show, *Family Feud*, reaches an uncommonly upscale audience, according to *TV Guide*. In an October 1981 article, *TV Guide* attributed the success of *Family Feud* (at that time it was the top-rated New York show in its important 7:30 P.M. time slot) to its sizable audience of sophisticated trendsetters:

> There is a secret cult of *Family Feud* fanatics among the ranks of sophisticated, intellectual Manhattanites. These passionate devotees of the all-American TV game show—"Feudophiles"—are highly educated, upwardly mobile professionals in their 20s and 30s. They are hip trend-setters who wear designer label sweat bands on their wrists and foreheads when they jog in Central Park.[3]

The show's popularity is attributed to the appeal of the game itself as well as to a fascination with the contestants, viewers either identifying with them or feeling smugly superior.

A basic factor in America's continuing fascination with game shows is not so much greed and desire for materialistic gain, but rather the opportunity to have a moment in the TV spotlight, either vicariously or as a contestant, according to Nancy Jones, producer of NBC's long-running *Wheel of Fortune*:

"The motivating factor is that people want to be on television. To be on television is, to most people, the ultimate American experience."[4]

Specialized Game Shows

In addition to general game shows, with their broad audiences and mass appeal, there are specific, vertically formatted shows that also accept ten-second promotional spots. One very specialized example is *Challenge Match Fishing*, a show syndicated to over ninety largely rural, recreational-area markets. Angler-contestants compete in landing the largest fish within the rather highly developed contest rules and time restrictions.

Car Care Central, which is syndicated to over seventy-five largely urban markets, deals entirely with proper automotive maintenance and use. The show accepts ten-second spots and is aimed at men as well as women and

FIGURE 10-2. One of the longest-running and highest-rated of all game shows, *The Hollywood Squares* **combined a mix of celebrities and witty questions and answers.** (*Courtesy of Robert A. Robertson.*)

teenagers—ideal for promotion of the many auto-related products being marketed.

A national dance-contest program, *Dance Fever*, features celebrity judges who select amateur dance finalists. The show is aired in over 100 U.S. markets as well as in Japan and eight other foreign markets and has a large youth-oriented audience.

The rapid expansion of cable systems has also opened numerous new opportunities for this type of product promotion. *The Shopping Game* is aired seven days a week on 369 cable systems reaching over 1000 local communities. Unlike network and syndicated shows, cable shows, with fewer controls, allow direct-response sales messages. *The Shopping Game* awards prizes to contestants but also sells the prizes to home viewers. As each contestant is awarded a prize, a ten- or thirty-second spot is run with a tag offering the home viewer the same product, which can be purchased by phone. A toll-free number is flashed on the screen, and viewers may call in credit-card orders or send for

FIGURE 10-3. NBC's *Wheel of Fortune* showcases numerous products, displaying them "live" as possible awards from which winning contestants make their selections. (*Courtesy of Robert A. Robertson.*)

FIGURE 10-4. Game shows that have been on network TV. (*Courtesy of Game-Show Placements, Ltd.*)

the product using a check or money order. The call-in procedure also allows measurement of the spot's effectiveness. As viewers call in to order, information is compiled for a monthly report including types of purchases made by people in different areas of the country. This information, combined with dollar sales of products for an individual company, can then be used to measure the response to particular products and sales messages. Specific markets may be selected within the broadcast schedule, and local dealer IDs may be inserted in the spot—a degree of flexibility not possible with network and nationally syndicated shows.

PLACING A GAME-SHOW SPOT

Game-show spots may be placed by negotiating either with the show producer directly or, more commonly, through a game-show prize broker. These brokers, who routinely place hundreds of products, can equip an entire show on short notice or supply specific items needed to meet a program format requirement.

It is the broker's job to determine which shows are right for a product, negotiate with producers, coordinate approval of spot content with the networks, help supervise program tapings, and notify the advertiser of when spots will air. After each spot airs, the broker will usually supply a certified proof-of-performance report (POPR). These POPRs contain a photo of the spot taken from the TV screen and a transcript of the audio copy. There are several independent companies whose primary business is to supply these reports.

An important additional benefit provided by game-show promotion is the "merchandising" of what amounts to a national television campaign to dealers and salespeople. Show logos and photos of the MCs, readily available through the prize broker, can be used in developing effective trade ads, flyers, news releases, and other publicity materials. Even a modest-sized campaign of ten spots can amount to over 100 million viewer impressions—a figure that salespeople are bound to find inspiring.

Designing an effective game-show spot involves certain creative considerations. Even though media and production costs are minimal, don't give short shrift to the design of your spot. Devote as much creative energy to it as you would to a high-budget commercial. Your spot will command a huge national audience sharing vicariously in the winning or losing of your product. Those seven to ten seconds of national television time are yours. Think of them as you would think of regular commercial buys. If used properly, ten seconds can be a long time. (In this regard, the J. Walter Thompson advertising agency predicts that regular TV commercials are likely to go to fifteen seconds.) Viewed another way, the game-show spot represents a rather long single "take," considering that the average thirty-second commercial contains as many as fifteen different takes, or individual scenes. So design exciting visuals, including an attractive photo of your product. Write audio copy that carries a simple, effective product sales message—one that can be repeated time and time again to millions of potential buyers.

Thanks to this low-cost, novel, but frequently overlooked medium, new products and services, as well as those with little or no advertising budget, can get exposure on national television.

"CASTING" CONSUMER PRODUCTS IN HOLLYWOOD FEATURE FILMS

Related to TV game-show placements are film placements in which consumer products are "cast," or used as props, in full-length Hollywood motion pictures.

Sales of Hershey's Reese's Pieces rose by 65 percent after the product appeared in *E.T.* In similar fashion, Diet Pepsi played a part in the film *Flashdance*, as did Wheaties in *Rocky III* and the 7-Eleven stores and their Big Gulp drink in *The Cannonball Run*. Other such appearances include Budweiser in *Tootsie* and Coke in *Missing*.[5]

There are a few firms specializing in the placement of products in films. One of them offers to get a product or service into at least five motion pictures for a minimum fee of $50,000.[6]

ENDNOTES

1. Judy Fireman, *TV Book*, Workman Publishing Co., New York, 1977, p. 89.
2. "Teflon Panorama," *Marketing Newsletter*, Du Pont, December 1975.
3. "The Secret Shame of New York Highbrows," *TV Guide*, October 1981.
4. Bob Greene, "The Fortunate," *Esquire*, July 1982, p. 19.
5. "Selling It at the Movies," *Newsweek*, July 4, 1983, p. 46.
6. Ibid.

Dressing Up for Sales Promotion:
Getting Your Logo Up Front

LAURENCE PETER STUART
Senior Vice President, Wembley Industries

What can make it possible for you to display your symbol of business, convey your advertising message, and create goodwill with fashion appeal and good taste? What will make consumers behave like walking billboards, wearing your corporate name or logo for all the world to see? The answer: corporate-insignia clothing.

THE OLD SCHOOL TIE GOES CORPORATE

Very quietly, and with little fanfare, companies are finding incredible residual value in having articles of clothing bear their symbols. From neckties to caps, scarves to shirts, blazers to sweaters, and windbreakers to bandannas, articles of clothing are being used as corporate gifts, as premium incentives for dealers, as rewards to sales forces for increased productivity, as quality "uniforms" for the personnel of America's best-dressed companies, and even as uniquely positioned items for sale directly to the consumer.

In the past, clothing used for displaying corporate logos was cheaply and poorly made, with no thought given to color harmony or to fashionable design. This has changed dramatically, however. Both manufacturers of the products and corporate management principals have realized that design and color considerations are highly important to the recipients of these gifts. They also realize that these products will be worn a lot more often if they can be easily coordinated with a person's everyday wardrobe.

This desire for fashion apparel by premium users and sales-oriented companies has necessitated a closer working relationship between the client and the manufacturer of the apparel item.

RELYING ON THE MANUFACTURER FOR FASHION ADVICE

As is generally agreed, the only constant in the fashion world is change. Therefore, you must be extremely careful to have clothing designed which will not become dated and thus have a reduced life expectancy. You should rely on the fashion direction of the manufacturers to lead you toward styles that will last and will continue to be worn, no matter what might take place in the volatile fashion world.

For example, consider the bow tie. Except for the black bow tie that is traditional for formal wear, bow ties are a fad. They appear on the fashion scene for perhaps six months to a year, and then they die a dismal death, almost overnight. If you have contracted for a rather novel bow tie, you could face serious inventory problems when the bow tie is no longer in vogue and nobody would be caught dead wearing one.

A clothing product should be developed that has the greatest potential for spanning all fashion changes. This is the only way to gain the maximum return on your investment and to realize the intended additional benefit of having your corporate name or message consistently worn for a long period of time.

John Moran, president of Hampton Hall Ltd., of New York, has discussed the problem of color in choosing a sales promotion clothing item that will have universal acceptance. "What is right for one area of the country is not necessarily correct for another. In New England, grey and navy in many tones are acceptable and on Wall Street they are practically the uniform of the day, while greens and browns are out. In the south and southwest, the reverse is true."

OTHER CONSIDERATIONS

Other factors besides color are important in the final decision-making process. For example, should the fabric be 100 percent polyester? Should it be a blend of polyester and silk or a blend of linen and wool? Should it be pure silk? Such decisions should be reached by determining the marketing objective of the gift item, and the lifestyles of the ultimate recipients.

If you are a manufacturer of accessory farm equipment and wish to reward your dealers with a premium incentive in the form of clothing, it is more than likely that you will lean toward a product such as a cap, a bandanna, or a work shirt. It is unlikely that your dealers would wear a color-coordinated pure silk tie to call on farmers in their area.

Picking the right clothing product to use as an incentive depends on:

1. The marketing objective of the company
2. The socioeconomic level of the recipients
3. The distribution of the product—local, regional, or national
4. The desired longevity of the product—whether it is intended for use at a July Fourth picnic, for example, or for everyday use

All these factors should be taken into consideration before making a decision to proceed with the design of a particular product. The fact that you are not familiar with the process of how your logo is made to appear on an apparel item does not mean that you are at the mercy of the manufacturer and must accept what is produced.

Price and Quality

"The bitterness of poor quality lingers far beyond the sweetness of low price." This is never more true than when we are dealing with clothing items. There are many ways to reduce the costs of producing an item of clothing that become apparent only after the product has been worn.

Don't make a decision to buy a gift clothing item on the basis of price. When choosing a manufacturer, pay particular attention to the company's reputation in the industry it serves. For instance, does the manufacturer also produce the particular garment for general consumer use through established retail outlets? Is the manufacturer's own name on the label? Does the company stand behind and guarantee the work?

Ask the manufacturer that you are considering to give you a quick education in the quality features of the product. Using your own general knowledge, or consulting with a local retail outlet, determine whether you are getting the real facts and the best possible product.

Never forget that when you give an item of apparel to a customer, you are giving a very personal gift. We all select our clothing to complement our personality and to make a statement to the world about our lifestyle, our attitudes, and our desire to be accepted by the peer group and social circle in which we travel.

You should also remember that the recipients of your gift clothing item will make a very objective judgment about the particular product that you are ultimately trying to sell, which is the reason you gave the gift in the first place. They will also feel that you, and your company, have made a value judgment about them.

For example, hamburger chains can easily get away with handing out little plastic games and toys because the marketing objective is to attract the children in the family: "Lets go to Dilly Burger, Dad, they give out spaceman games." The toy is not expected to last much longer than it takes you to grab your french fries and drive off in your car. In fact, it is probably designed not to last, for if it did, there would be no incentive for the kids to go back and get another one, unless the premium is one of a set to be collected. The situation is entirely different when it comes to selecting clothing as a corporate gift or premium item. Here you are dealing with the psychology of pride, prestige, and personal grooming.

Color and Design

After you have made your final selection of the item you wish to offer and have found a reputable manufacturer to produce it for you, you must spend some time considering color and design.

If you have decided to use a tie as your premium item, design, color, and accuracy of reproduction must be approved before production is started. Most neckwear fabrics are woven or printed in Europe under the most exacting specifications.

Consider choosing the background color of the fabric from among the basic clothing colors, such as navy, burgundy, brown, or bottle green. These colors will complement 90 percent of all suit and shirt colors. Avoid light background colors, such as sky blue, melon, and lighter shades of green and red. The background color is dominant and may be extremely difficult to coordinate with other items of clothing. The correct place for lighter, brighter colors in neckwear is in the pattern, which could be a fine line, a bar stripe, or your corporate logo woven throughout the tie and breaking up the solid background.

The most popular designs for neckwear to be given as corporate gifts are:

1. The club design. This is achieved by having your logo reduced proportionately and repeated in a pattern neatly and evenly all over the tie.
2. The club and stripe design. In this design, diagonal fine lines or bar stripes are spaced evenly down the tie, with your logo, in miniature, running between the stripes or lines on a diagonal.
3. The under-the-knot design. This is achieved by having your logo woven into the fabric one time in such a way that it appears approximately 3 inches below the knot when tied. This look is especially flattering when the tie is worn with a vest.
4. The bottom-panel design. In this design, your logo is placed in the cradle of the "V" at the bottom of the tie. This is the current trend in designer neckwear, such as that of Oscar de la Renta and Pierre Cardin.

WORKING WITH THE APPAREL MANUFACTURER

To help you in your final decision, the apparel manufacturer can make mockups of various designs. In the case of neckwear, the manufacturer can reduce your logo to the correct size and make an acetate layover, which can be placed on top of various pieces of fabric to show you how the design and color combination will look. The design will then be sent for weaving and will be resubmitted to you for final approval. At this point you will be looking at the actual design on the specific fabric you have chosen, so be critical and make sure that you are satisfied—this is your last chance! Bear in mind that while technology allows for many intricate designs, some colors and some very intricate detail work might be impossible to achieve, in which case you must settle for the best compromise.

Most manufacturers require a 10 percent overrun or underrun factor against your order, which allows for cutting errors and damage which might

FIGURE 11-1. Some recognizable corporate logos. (*Courtesy of Wembley Industries.*)

take place while the product is being made. Also, be sure to check minimum quantities required and price-break quantities. Generally, there will be an additional one-time setup charge for design work and loom weaving at the mill. These charges should not be made for any reorders.

If you have any doubts as to the effectiveness of clothing items designed specifically to be used as corporate gifts, as sales incentives, as premiums, or for any other sales promotion purpose, make some phone calls to prominent clothing manufacturers who have corporate-insignia design divisions and get a listing of the major companies for whom they have done work. You will be not only pleasantly surprised but also considerably impressed. And the recipients of the tie, sweater, blazer, or other item of clothing bearing your corporate logo will be too.

12 Special Promotions in Today's Marketplace

WILLIAM J. CORBETT, J.D., A.P.R.
Director, Public Relations, Avon Products, Inc.

Special promotions have always been an important public relations and marketing vehicle, but there has been a creative revolution in the public relations process in the last thirty years. This is the inevitable result of an age when mass communications have made a great leap forward from raw technology to a highly sophisticated machine that pervades every aspect of consumer life.

In the 1980s, there has been an abundance of innovative and challenging special projects designed by corporations which are determined to secure an extra dimension of positive visibility for themselves and their products. As in most business ventures, it is the additional dimension that reaps many dividends. A public relations professional must always be creative and innovative in squeezing every possible benefit for the client from any promotional endeavor.

A special promotion must enhance the company's image, and yet stretch beyond the textbook approach to maximize marketing objectives through efficient, cost-effective, and imaginative means.

DEFINING OBJECTIVES

Defining your objectives is the first step in today's highly charged and competitive market. You must zero in on the product or image that needs enhancement and aim at the demographic and marketing factors that will influence your current customers and other potential customers. In short, you must look for the method that best ties in with the product in a way that goes beyond the customary means of reaching the public, the press, or your in-house audience. In special promotions, the bottom line is always the exploration of the extra dimensions in addition to the primary target.

Throughout this chapter various techniques that have been employed at Avon Products, Inc., over the past decade will be cited as examples that can be adapted to many marketing and public relations sales promotions. For example, Avon laid the foundation for its special promotion events with a twofold objective which effectively set the style, tone, and logistics in motion for each event sponsored under an Avon banner.

The first consideration was Avon's corporate philosophy that promotes opportunity for women, at all social and economic levels, as the cornerstone of its business.

The next stipulation demanded that each event be conceived and executed in a manner reflective of the quality and care the public has come to associate with Avon products. The "law" explicit in every aspect of planning and production of each promotion program has always been, "Do it first-class or not at all."

Once your objectives have been clearly analyzed in order of priority, chart a course to enlarge upon the basics. Make the promotional package work for you in supplemental areas. Go for local, national, trade, and international publicity; enhancement of governmental and cultural relations; community involvement; and in-house personnel involvement. These added dimensions cost little or nothing compared with your major investment, and they often provide significant rewards.

WOMEN'S SPORTS

One of Avon's most successful sales promotion activities is the sponsorship of women's sports. You might question the role of the world's largest beauty and cosmetics company in the athletic area. Avon, however, discovered a valuable marketing and sales promotion vehicle in its involvement with sports. The events have proved to be of great significance in cementing the company's image with women worldwide. Market research has shown that these efforts are well received and well regarded by the women polled.

By channeling some of its corporate public relations energies to specific markets, Avon not only has appealed to an international spectrum of women runners, bowlers, and tennis players but also has received positive global publicity in a sphere which epitomizes the fitness, health, and beauty of the contemporary woman. The compatibility of fitness and beauty in selling Avon's products worked practically, as well as philosophically, and provided an important link in the company's promotional strategy.

In addition to the impressive indirect advertising and sales promotion achieved by the sponsorship of women's sports programs, the technical demographics of potential customers is awesome. The number of athletically oriented women has skyrocketed in the last decade; in the United States alone, there are over 20 million women tennis players, 30 million women runners, and 28 million women bowlers, from wide-ranging social and economic lifestyles.

Any company can profit immeasurably from press coverage of women's sports events; if planned and executed properly, this coverage can result in extensive exposure at a very reasonable cost. The Avon company name can be spotted in the headlines of sports sections around the country, as well as in feature articles on the beauty, women's, and society pages of national and international publications. In one month alone, Avon received almost 10,000 press clippings mentioning its sports programs. These translate into very effective sales promotion.

Constant local and national television and radio coverage round out the deluge of media coverage for a given Avon sports event; this is the type of coverage which you can achieve with a well-conceived program. All these variables of publicity—complemented by an upbeat, wholesome, and attractive image—have led Avon to conclude that the recognition received is considerably less expensive and covers a broader field than similar recognition gleaned through alternative promotional tactics would be.

Running

The Avon International Running Circuit has benefited from the global acceleration of interest in this form of athletics. Worldwide in both concept and implementation, this circuit attracts tens of thousands of women, from casual weekend joggers to more dedicated marathoners.

Avon's unique series of women-only long-distance races was designed to provide developmental opportunities, offer incentives, reward talent, and applaud fitness and health for women everywhere. Avon has received direct benefits from this. Runners who participate in the races receive an Avon running shirt as well as a gift of an Avon product, and every finisher receives an Avon International Running Circuit medallion. To date, since its inception in 1978 with the first Avon International Marathon in Atlanta, over 100,000 women of all ages have run in Avon-sponsored events. What a great sales promotion! Hundreds of thousands of physically fit women wearing shirts with the Avon name printed on the front and back. Tote bags imprinted with the Avon name are also used; these provide even better exposure since they last longer than the shirts. And each of these is a sales promotion item.

In addition to the twelve North American cities that host Avon races, the enormous popularity of road racing has extended the company's program to seventeen other countries. This provides the type of subtle and positive sales promotion that continues long after the event. The product samples given to the participants generate new customers and new independent sales representatives for Avon.

For each race scheduled in this country or abroad, a professional and dynamic press campaign is launched that covers most print and electronic media. From a marketing standpoint, clinics and makeup seminars are often incorporated into the fabric of the media offensive.

Local government officials are involved either in starting the race or in placing the laurel wreath on the winner at the finish line. Well in advance of an event, Avon asks national, state, and local government representatives to issue an official proclamation, with the attendant advance publicity; this helps promote the event.

The 1980 Avon International Marathon, staged in London, was a sales promotion coup with some unique aspects. Most notably, as far as could be determined, the city of London had never before closed its streets to allow a sporting event to take place. At first there was official resistance to closing the streets, especially in midsummer, at the height of the tourist season. However, because of the boycott of the Moscow Olympics and the fact that this event was for women only, an accommodation was reached that took into account the interests of all concerned parties, and governmental permission was granted for a race whose course would affect hundreds of vehicle crossings.

When the introductory press conference was held in late April in London, more than 100 press, radio, and television representatives attended.

It became apparent that the concept of women's running, the status of international competition, and the issues concerning the Olympics were all relatively new subjects for the London media. The areas of news, politics, lifestyles, and personalities were to be explored in depth and in fresh perspective.

An extensive public relations program was launched which involved everything from holding a beauty editors' luncheon at the Savoy (to promote running as a part of a beauty and fitness regimen) to setting up runners time and again in London's parks to run in front of television news cameras. A special reception was held introducing foreign correspondents to runners brought in from their home countries, and all the wire services were constantly fed with race updates.

Selecting the site for your event is extremely important. You should seek out a photographic locale. Avon's London race started in Battersea Park, continued across Westminster Bridge and down Victoria Embankment to the Tower of London, and eventually ended in the narrow courtyard fronting the 1000-year-old Guildhall, an important center of British civic and ceremonial activity that provided numerous excellent photographic opportunities.

Race-day promotional functions were in full force at the start of the race. On the course, an open-topped double-decker bus provided a firsthand view of the exciting action for more than sixty-five writers and photographers, and at the finish a complete international communications network was assembled at the Guildhall.

Highlights of the media exposure included major television features on both NBC's *Sports World* and BBC's *Grandstand* sports programs, shown nationally, as well as coverage by all major London television news programs and satellite news feeds to several countries.

Print coverage exceeded all expectations, with a summer-long series of feature articles in the sports and lifestyle sections of the major London dailies. Special-interest magazines and the publications of the London Tourist Board promoted the event as well.

In the United States, *People* magazine carried a double-page feature, and advance publicity appeared in major women's magazines such as *Vogue* and *Seventeen*. The race generated publicity in twenty-seven countries, with stories keying in on the runner from a particular country; in the United States, there was much local, hometown coverage of the American runners.

In addition to publicizing its corporate involvement in this sports event, Avon was able to carry its promotional message of opportunity for women, and the importance of fitness to good health and beauty, to millions of potential new customers.

It is important to try to measure the success of any promotional effort. In this case, the return on investment exceeded expectations, and the success of events such as the London marathon led senior management to view Avon's running program as an important component of the company's extensive, worldwide public relations and sales promotion operation.

Avon's objectives, therefore, continue to be met with a vehicle that not only increases the company's visibility but also improves community relations in the United States and abroad, while carrying its promotional message of fitness and beauty to millions. Additionally, the popularity of the running program paved the way for the acceptance of the women's marathon in the 1984 Olympic games in Los Angeles—a fact that can only enhance Avon's sports involvement right up through the 1984 summer Olympics.

Bowling

Branching out to a previously untapped reservoir of 60 million women bowlers around the world, Avon's senior management decided in 1980 to sponsor the prestigious Avon-WIBC Queens Bowling Tournament, which is held once a year in a different American city. The Women's International Bowling Congress has a membership of 4 million, and tens of millions of women are involved in league play in the United States, a substantial number of whom are Avon representatives, district managers, and customers; thus Avon's bowling endeavors dovetail nicely with its target group. Bowling may well be the largest organized participator sport in America and is open to everyone at a moderate cost. This nationally televised event features the largest first-place prize in women's bowling and has attracted hundreds of world-class bowlers vying for the coveted title.

Major women bowlers praised the Avon sales promotion during the televised event, and the hours of coverage were supplemented by heavy Avon identification in the form of banners, lane sweepers, and other mentions throughout the telecast—ending with the trophy presentation given by an Avon executive or a selected government official.

While the Avon sponsorship elicited a great deal of favorable publicity in the sports world at large, and in the bowling community in particular, thousands of press clippings around the country were a tangible yardstick for measuring the success of this sales promotion entry into yet another phase of women's sports.

Tennis

From 1977 through 1982, the company sponsored Avon tennis, a spectacular showcase which stands in the record books as a major contribution to women's tennis during the six successful years of Avon's involvement. The elite competitors in women's tennis were featured on the Championship circuit, while the Avon Futures tour changed the face of the sport with its unique developmental system, which created more depth in the sport. Known as the "prestige circuit," it was a unique catalyst in the international arena, providing a marketplace for the talents of the superstar as well as for those of the unknown challenger.

There were record-breaking crowds at Madison Square Garden for four consecutive years, from 1979 through 1982, when the Avon-sponsored events drew the largest attendance in the history of women's tennis. The positive publicity and acclaim were overwhelming. In a single three-month span, more than 30,000 newspaper clips were recorded, often mentioning Avon in the headlines. Although the tournaments were held exclusively in North America, international publicity in the form of wire reports and feature hometown stories on the foreign players were routinely generated by Avon's on-site press staff, with excellent sales promotional results.

To balance the glamorous, high-gloss image of professional women in sports, Avon launched a campaign aimed at providing opportunities at the grass-roots level, staging a series of inner-city and community clinics in each and every location on the tour. The campaign generated enormous publicity and had great sales promotion potential. It was important not to overlook the young people in each city who could profit from exposure to tennis—many for the first time. The local community involvement was an "extra dimension" of the program that cost very little.

With considerable attention to detail, Avon's team began to create an awareness that a major corporation, utilizing classic administrative procedures in conjunction with a systematic approach to public relations and sales promotion opportunities, could not only promote its own interests but also create considerable fanfare in an obviously upscale sport that was popular with a segment of the market which the company was interested in penetrating or in which it wanted to increase sales.

Spencer Conley, a Boston-based sports promotion consultant, and Alan Taylor, a New York City sports publicist, were selected to help Avon's in-house staff launch the effort. Ella Musolino and Bill Goldstein, of SportsEtcetra in New York City, were selected to help coordinate the company's major events at Madison Square Garden.

To underscore the relationship between Avon and women's tennis, a colorful logo was designed, and a bold color scheme devised. Banners, posters, flyers, counter cards, T-shirts, linesman's boxes and chairs, wristbands, and visors were designed—all bearing the Avon sports logo, and all of them very excellent sales promotion devices. Other important parts of the program included a weekly newsletter to an extensive national press mailing list and strong on-site publicity efforts aimed at supporting local media coverage of a tournament, with placements in sections other than the sports sections. Advance press conferences were also arranged, during which an Avon banner was prominently displayed behind the featured players.

An advertising offensive was designed to ensure that the tour and Avon were tightly linked in a wide variety of publications. The company utilized the services of a large ad agency (Ogilvy & Mather), as well as those of Howard Chalk (of Chalk, Nissen, Hanft Inc., a small New York group), with equal satisfaction. The details involved in meshing an ad campaign with a special promotion can be overwhelming, and unless your corporate ad department is geared to handle these details, you are well-advised to seek additional outside agency help. As part of your advertising campaign, it is often possible to trade off ad time and space for tickets, so do not hesitate to be creative.

Meetings were scheduled with the promoters of all twenty-two events so that the basic advertising strategies could be efficiently coordinated with ongoing local radio, television, and print-media schedules. Telecopiers were installed in the tournament office in each city to receive up-to-the-minute circuit information for distribution to the local press.

Keeping a handle on a program of this magnitude was a difficult but certainly not impossible task, and it was one that Avon had to accomplish if it was to meet its objective of producing only "first-class" events under the company logo.

Public relations affiliates were selected in each city. Instead of allowing these affiliates simply to free-lance publicity in their various markets, Avon insisted on a press game plan so that promotional efforts would be monitored and coordinated in each of the twenty-two cities.

The results, in the very first year of Avon Championship Tennis, were the largest audience ever to witness a women's tennis match at the Madison Square Garden finale and a press response that was epitomized by Britain's *Tennis World* magazine, which called the tournament "the best organized and best promoted event of its kind."

By avoiding "corporate clutter" (a variety of sponsors, presenters, and attendant signs and logos at the tournaments), Avon guaranteed that each event would reflect the quality control and topflight image that the company was determined to present. One basic color was used on all sales promotion graphics and decorations—lipstick red.

The corporation was proud to invite local and national political figures to attend the tournaments, and, if at all possible, to take part in the center-court prize presentations. Through the years, countless state governors, senators, members of Congress, and local political figures have participated in the closing portion of Avon-sponsored events. This, of course, has been excellent in terms of their visibility among local constituents, and it has also enhanced Avon's relationship with the men and women who are the prime movers in government affairs. It is simply good business, in this era of extreme regulatory swings, to get to know your representatives, and tennis was a vehicle that eased this endeavor in a relaxed setting.

The Avon Championship tournaments, held in Washington, D.C., provide an excellent example of how a company can gain additional exposure in the political sphere. In this case, a reception, featuring the top stars in tennis, was held for government figures. This was an extra dimension of benefit gained from the event. The Treasurer of the United States, Angela M. Buchanan, presented the winner's check and a bouquet of roses at the Avon Championships in New York City.

Since the success of Avon's products is closely aligned with the success of its 1.28 million independent sales representatives throughout the world, it made good business sense to involve them in the company's relationship with women's sports. This was done by giving the local Avon representatives a means of establishing a dialogue with another segment of the buying public— the active, health-minded athletic women who have created a market for sunscreens, foot powder, moisturizers, and other products that fit an outdoor, on-the-go lifestyle.

As incentives to the sales force, Avon arranged for on-site recognition of top sales representatives during the tennis events, tickets to a final event as a reward for outstanding sales in a district, preferred seating at any event and a reception with the athletes, participation in award ceremonies by district managers, and a drawing for a colorful supply of Avon products. In addition, each site was provided with impressive product displays to highlight the cosmetics behind the company name. In some cities, product samples and representative recruitment literature were distributed.

Every sporting event should have a program, and this can be successfully used for advertising, promotion, and corporate feature stories. This item is taken home by the fans and is a continuing promotion piece for your company.

In each city Avon involved a charity, for numerous reasons. First, this enabled the company to become involved with a worthwhile cause at each event, and it was also profitable to the charities involved. Second, it ensured Avon a large pool of volunteer workers to help run the event. Chapters of the Junior League in a number of cities were particularly helpful.

Avon's sports programs involved senior management officials in special events whenever appropriate so that they could see firsthand the efficacy of the corporate dollars in achieving the desired style and excellence. To further involve Avon in-house personnel in the tennis circuit, videotapes of previous final matches were set up outside the company cafeteria, and an extravaganza known as "Family Day" was arranged, which offered all personnel and their families an opportunity to attend the finals at Madison Square Garden, as well as a complimentary luncheon before the matches. The party was staged complete with tennis superstars who signed autographs and clowns and minstrels who performed in a festive, communal atmosphere that fostered and enhanced employee morale—another added dimension.

THE WOMEN'S SPORTS HALL OF FAME

The latest addition to the Avon sports contingent is the sponsorship of the Women's Sports Hall of Fame, a dynamic exhibit featuring the leading female athletes of the twentieth century. Items such as Chris Evert-Lloyd's first tennis racket, Janet Guthrie's racing helmet, and Peggy Fleming's Olympic-winning figure skates are highlighted for the entertainment and education of the public.

At a press brunch at New York's "21" Club announcing Avon's sponsorship of the Hall of Fame, there was standing room only for reporters from the print and electronic media, who lined up for an opportunity to talk with female Olympians such as Wilma Rudolph, Donna de Varona, Jo Jo Starbuck, and Wyomia Tyus.

The Women's Sports Hall of Fame is a traveling exhibit, and Avon currently is planning to show it in the lobby of the Empire State Building, at the International Tennis Hall of Fame, and in a Los Angeles site to maximize its visibility during the 1984 summer Olympics.

CORPORATE SPONSORSHIPS

Many other corporations sponsor women's sports activities as part of their sales promotion programs.

J&B scotch has the $100,000 J&B Gold Putter Award and the $200,000 J&B

Scotch Pro Am, both on the Ladies Professional Golf Association Tour. American Express supports Sportsman '82 and Women's Pro Skiing, Colgate provides New York City's girls and women with the Colgate Women's Games, Coca-Cola has launched a Women's Olympic Sports Tour, Manufacturers Hanover Trust Company sponsored a Women's Fitness Sports Conference, Mazda has made a major commitment to ladies' golf, Nabisco is involved in a promotion featuring Dinah Shore, Nautilus is taking part in a Sportsmedicine Symposium, Nike is sponsoring Women's Professional Racquetball, and Michelob Light supports a ski-racing tour, off-shore power-boat racing, and league tennis. Personal Products has a commitment to women's basketball through sponsorship of the Wade Trophy, honoring the top female collegiate basketball player; Rolex USA is sponsoring equestrian events; and Mercedes-Benz is backing a tennis tournament of champions.

Virginia Slims has once again become a major sponsor of women's tennis, and AMF sponsors the Bowling World Cup, the Pro Bowlers Tour, the Women's All Star Association Tournament of Champions, and the Western Women's Bowling Pro Tournament of Champions; it also cosponsors the AMF Hawaii Western Region PBA Championship.

The list of corporate sports sponsorship could go on for pages. This is just a small sampling.

PUBLICITY

Presentations

When planning almost any company sports event, it is usually possible to arrange at the production meeting held in advance of the event to have a spokesperson from your company interviewed on the air or videotaped in advance for inclusion in the broadcast. While this should not be overdone, at the very least you should arrange to have several senior members of your management identified on television in a close-up crowd shot during the event. It is good for the sales force to see the "chief." Be sure to provide the producer, in writing, with the executives' names and correct titles. Alert the executives to the possibility that they will be photographed so that they will maintain the proper composure. This will help prevent embarrassing incidents such as occurred during a CBS telecast of an important event, when viewers saw a person of great public stature picking his nose.

The final presentation ceremonies for any event must also be carefully planned and quickly executed. If TV is going to be used, you will find that everyone wants to get into the act. You should limit this involvement, lest your event appear to be cluttered and disorganized. Have a specific roped-off area for still photographers and advise them in advance of the ground rules.

The participants must also be briefed in advance so that their acceptance remarks are appropriate. I was aghast at a recent tennis tournament when a young tennis player, who was about to receive a $20,000 check from a member of senior management of a foreign-car company, announced on the telecast that she was going to use her prize money to buy a competitive brand of car, and even mentioned the other brand and model.

Photographers

It's also vitally important to hire the "right" photographer. In the case of sports events, insist on reviewing their published work in advance. Some photographers have valuable connections with various sports magazines and can actually help you with the placement of publicity photos. For example, Art Klonsky and Jane Sobel, of Janeart in New York City, who do most of Avon's sports work, are often called upon by sports magazines for artwork to support stories the magazines are preparing. If the photo provided to a publication happens to have your corporate banner in the background or if the sports figure is wearing your T-shirt, this is a nice extra return on your sales promotion investment.

Television

Before we move to another example of a special promotion, we must discuss the application of television to your promotional efforts.

The name of the game today is TV—be it network, syndicated, public broadcasting, or cable. For an event to be perceived as important and classy, it has to have TV coverage on either a live or a delayed basis. If you run an event, you can almost always count on local news coverage, but the extra dimension that pays dividends is a feature broadcast that will provide exposure of your company or your product to hundreds of thousands, if not millions, of people. You can seek this coverage yourself, rely on ad agencies to help you, or use outside consultants who "package" such shows. On some occasions, and with great success, Avon has arranged for TV coverage of an event without help. It is more costly to use outside help, but in many cases you will have no choice but to use an agency or "deal packager" to arrange for a special broadcast.

Before Avon representatives approached network TV officials responsible for the enforcement of TV codes and practices, they had heard all sorts of horror stories about how unreasonable, difficult, and arbitrary these people were. It was a very pleasant surprise to find that they were nothing of the sort, but were reasonable and gracious, as long as one approached them in a friendly, businesslike manner and did not become greedy in terms of requests (rather than demands) for exposure during a telecast. Of course you want exposure for your company or client, but, by the same token, TV officials cannot permit you to turn a legitimate sports event into one long commercial and thus detract from the legitimacy of the event.

It is customary, but certainly not mandatory, to purchase some commercial advertising time during the broadcast of your event. If you try to pull a "fast one" and sneak in extra plugs once you have reached an agreement, you can seriously jeopardize your success in having future events televised.

To provide an added dimension, you can also arrange to have your event shown on TV in countries outside the United States. There are companies with the proper contacts to help you achieve this. In this regard, Avon has been pleased with the work of Jack Butefish, of Group Dynamics in Los Angeles.

THE TOURNAMENT OF ROSES

In 1982, Avon entered a float in the world-famous Rose Parade for the fourth consecutive year. The company won the grand prize for its 1981 entry, entitled "Autumn Splendor," and for its 1982 entry, "Beauty of the Orient." The blue ribbons, however, were the icing on the cake, since just participating in these events was an opportunity tailor-made for Avon's objectives. It was the perfect fit of a wholesome event with Avon's clean-cut image.

The Pasadena Tournament of Roses Association has ninety-three years of experience and has amassed an army of facts designed to prove that its Rose Parade is "the world's greatest advertising bargain."

Over 100 million persons see the event on network TV and through newspaper articles, souvenir magazines, newsreel agencies, the Armed Forces Network, and official tournament films; in addition, there is an on-the-spot audience of 1½ million.

The 1979 Rose Parade, which marked Avon's debut in the event, had as its theme "Our Wonderful World of Sports." Avon entered a float featuring six female athletic champions: Tracy Austin, tennis; Linda Fratianne, figure skating; Kathrine Switzer, running; Enith Brighita, swimming; Barbara Ann Cochran, skiing; and Donna Capone Young, golf.

Each athlete was interviewed separately by the press corps, and two of them appeared on network telecasts for added coverage. Avon senior management saw the Rose Parade as the perfect opportunity to publicize Avon's dedication to women in sports. Obviously, the 1979 parade theme was made to order for Avon; the theme changes every year, however, and Avon has utilized all the creative means at its disposal to generate fresh and exciting angles.

To supplement its efforts, Avon employed the Sheffield Company, a small Los Angeles public relations agency with twenty years of experience working for clients in the Rose Parade. Each year, Avon's press blueprint was to cultivate publicity months in advance. The company did not wait to see whether it had won a prize; rather, enough press coverage was activated prior to the event so that its participation was well rewarded, whether it won first prize or no prize at all.

Foreign press receptions were held before the parade in Pasadena, California, to capitalize on international relations. The entire royal court of the Tournament of Roses was brought to Avon's Pasadena branch to involve the personnel and enhance their morale and pride, and beauty seminars were conducted on the site.

Avon has become the exclusive beauty consultant to the Rose Queen and her court, and to support this program it has retained Hollywood's Sue Cary, a former Rose Princess and a professional Hollywood makeup artist.

Cary's advice and expertise are in heavy demand by the Tournament of Roses. Additionally, she makes television appearances on behalf of Avon and does newspaper interviews in markets where there is great interest in the Rose Parade. She has also conducted makeup seminars on the Avon Tennis and Avon Running Circuits to acquaint the athletes with the company's products. The seminars themselves are a press photo opportunity and always generate media coverage.

On the national scene, Avon has reminded its customers to tune in and watch the parade on television through the use of corner tags in tens of millions of Avon brochures distributed during the sales campaign in late December. *Avon Calling*, a publication going to some half a million active Avon representatives in the United States, reminds them to tune in.

Once again, it is essential to know whether a given event will create the type of exposure necessary for a successful promotional relationship. The Rose Parade is not for every business, but Avon feels that it is the perfect vehicle for its company image.

INTERNATIONAL PROJECTS

Because Avon does business not only in the United States but also in thirty-one other countries around the world, the company is especially interested in promotional vehicles abroad that reflect its commitment to, support of, and regard for women.

The Avon Awards to Women, inaugurated in Japan in 1979, was created to recognize women from all walks of life who have made significant contributions to the status of women and to society in general. The program rewards special achievements by women in diverse fields of endeavor, and it helps focus international attention on exceptional women working at the grass-roots level as well.

The Avon Awards to Women is guided by a panel of distinguished women who lend their prestige and expertise in the final selection of winners. The year's search culminates in a banquet hosted by Avon for winners and their families, panelists, and representatives from government, society, the professions, and the arts.

Each winner of an award receives a cash grant, and a matching amount is donated to an appropriate organization or charity of the recipient's choice. A commemorative certificate and fine silverware designed to mark the occasion, from Tiffany & Co., an Avon subsidiary, are also awarded.

This continuing special promotion provides a unique method of interacting with the Japanese market. Receptions for dignitaries, press conferences, and a full media campaign are utilized to maximize Avon identity in a key overseas marketplace.

Against an international backdrop of women's struggle for higher social status and greater opportunities in business, the Avon Awards to Women has served to stimulate widespread interest in the concerns of women, as well as to achieve Avon's sales promotional goal. As a result of its success in Japan, several European countries are scheduled to implement this program.

In dealing with overseas operations in general, it is important to utilize information gathered by in-house personnel stationed on the site in order to get a sense of the customs and basic societal mores of each country. Tailor the particulars to the country involved to ensure success and always remember that what guarantees headlines in Los Angeles might hardly be noticed in London.

PLANT DEDICATIONS

It is always particularly gratifying when a corporate event can be turned into a special promotion by means of ingenuity and hard work. Such was the case in July 1981, when the dedication of a new manufacturing facility for Avon in Northampton, England, was transformed into a promotional spectacular by the appearance of Her Royal Highness Princess Anne.

The mystique that surrounds the royal family in England has no parallel in the United States, but it is a phenomenon that creates a media event whenever any member steps foot in general society. After the invitation to dedicate the laboratory was accepted, Avon's prime objective was to conduct the event in the most tasteful, yet most visible, way possible.

Following a private reception and the official dedication ceremony, at which the princess unveiled a commemorative plaque, a royal tour of the new factory was undertaken. The informal and up-close nature of the tour was perhaps the highlight of the visit for both photographers and Avon employees, whose pride in their company increased immeasurably.

A formal luncheon and press reception followed, but each portion of the program staged was carefully monitored to allow press coverage only when this was appropriate, tasteful, and approved in advance by the royal family. Nevertheless, the press response was enormous; full pressroom facilities were established, and there was a special press coach for transport from London.

The beauty, commercial, and financial media were areas of concentration; the aim was to entertain and impress representatives of these media and to elevate their concept of Avon as a company. Stories were placed, photos were sent, and contacts were made in a single afternoon during a carefully run media-conscious program. Again, Avon's promotional objectives were met with style and class. While local TV provided extensive coverage, the frosting on the cake was a nationally broadcast TV program entitled *A Day in the Life of Princess Anne*, which was seen as far away as Australia and was very favorable to Avon.

CONCLUSION

The examples given in this chapter are specific, but the principles of a successful marketing and special promotions package are general and can be used by any corporation looking for fresh ways to catalyze a marketing sales promotion program in today's business environment. There will always be an element of risk associated with a truly unique opportunity, but with clear-cut planning, quality products, and a dedicated staff, the rewards of special promotions will far exceed the liabilities, especially if you make an effort to seek out and implement the "extra dimension" of sales promotion.

Retailers' Sales Promotions to Consumers

There was a time when retail shopkeepers went out to the street and practically dragged customers into their stores. Fortunately, that day is behind us. Modern retailers have better ways of attracting business. For example, in October 1982, May department stores of California gave, with each purchase of $100 or more, two-for-one coupons good for flights on AirCal airline. At the same time, to encourage use of their automatic teller machines, banks gave out thousands of dollars in jackpots and contests. One method was to substitute $100 bills for $1 bills in the stacks of cash dispensed by the machines. Would you go back to an automatic teller if it gave you $100 or more than you expected? You bet you would!

For the most part, retailers' sales promotions to consumers are very similar to manufacturers' sales promotions to consumers. However, while manufacturers are concerned with the sale of *their own* products, retailers are interested in the sale of *all* products rather than those of a particular manufacturer. So, while manufacturers might offer premiums to the consumer for the purchase of their own branded products, retailers will offer premiums for overall purchases. That is, a retailer might give a premium—say, a dinner plate—for total purchases of $30 or more. (Each week the customer could get a different piece of the dinnerware set.) Retailers also use their own form of cents-off coupons, and a recent trend has been to offer double the value printed on a manufacturer's cents-off coupon. Games, sweepstakes, and contests are other types of sales promotions also employed by the retailer.

Another point of difference between manufacturers' and retailers' sales promotions to consumers is that manufacturers are not particularly interested in *where* their merchandise is sold, as long as consumers buy it. On the other hand, retailers don't care *which* manufacturer's merchandise a consumer buys, as long as the consumer buys it in their store or utilizes their particular services, in the case of retail service companies. Thus retailers' sales promotions are designed to bring customers into a particular store or stores. And trading stamps, cash-register tape plans, and other continuity promotions are employed to keep them coming back.

Trading stamps are a form of delayed premium; although they have certain similarities to manufacturers' proof-of-purchase seals, they are used exclusively by retailers. Specialty advertising is employed by retailers as well as by manufacturers. Manufacturers, for example, do send calendars and other specialty items to their dealers and wholesalers, and in addition they often favor them with business gifts. The latter practice is rarely followed by retailers. Like manufacturers' promotions to consumers, retailers' sales promotions are designed to pull merchandise through the marketing channels.

13 Inducing the Consumer to Action

FRED SHERRY, J.D.

Sales Promotion Consultant; Former Sales Promotion Manager, The Grand Union Company

In the retail business there is a constant stream of sales promotions. The customer is bombarded every day in every way by the supermarket, the drugstore, other retailers, and their suppliers. Every medium, every trick of the trade, is used.

SOME BASIC QUESTIONS

How do you raise your voice over the constant clamor? How do you bring customers to your store?

Your store—a supermarket, let us say—is filled with customers who are spending an average of 18 percent of their income on a vital necessity. How do you keep them coming back?

The supermarket on the next block is a good store. It is also filled with customers. How do you get some of them?

How do you get that supermarket's customers and your customers to spend more of their food dollars with you?

I shall try to answer these questions because they are elemental. Unless they are a part of the sales promoter's planning and execution, the promotion will fail. It will succeed, in whole or in part, in direct proportion to the attention to detail lavished on it at every stage, from inception to conclusion.

How Do You Bring Customers to Your Store?

First, you must show your customers how you evaluate what you are promoting. The confidence you display acts directly on your customers' confidence. You need not be concerned about the success or failure of the promotion. If you have properly planned a promotion and have properly expensed its cost by doing a pro forma profit-and-loss estimate, you do not have to be fearful of any adverse effect on your bottom line.

Then take aim and fire at your customers' most vulnerable targets: their emotions, pocketbooks, curiosity, greed, pride, sloth, love. Here are some examples.

A simple promotion that will pique customers' curiosity consists of "mystery specials," a group of unadvertised items. For this you need a big cardboard sign on which you paint the face of a clock and write the caption "Mystery Special." Two movable pointers show the time interval during which the item will be on sale. The bottom of the sign tells what the item is and gives its price. The merchandise is well displayed beneath the price. Just be sure that the item is something the customers want, that it is priced right, that the time interval is adhered to, and that the next item is ready to go when the previous one's time has elapsed. A loud alarm clock can signal the end of each time interval.

Is this corny? Yes, but even the most sophisticated customer likes a little corn now and then. I have used this promotion and it works. You can use it too, and many more like it.

To appeal to your customers' greed, you can print a list of winners of cash prizes every day. Signs can read: "Is your name listed in our Winners' Circle? You can win too. . . ."

Your customers' pride is important. For a dinnerware promotion, your advertising message could read: "Friends and relatives will compliment you when you serve dinner on this fine imported china—and each piece costs you only $0.22 with each $5 purchase."

The list of such promotions is long, and the variations are endless. Whether you are the operator of a single store or the promotion manager for a national chain, the basic elements for success are the same: the wanted item at the proper price, the correct emotional appeal, and the proper advertising to get the message across.

How Do You Keep Customers Coming Back?

To do this, you must appeal personally and directly to your customers and use your own organization. Within a week of the time I got my first job in the supermarket business, the boss invited me to visit some stores with him. We visited three stores, and I watched him very carefully as he made notes, greeted employees and customers, and looked at the books. On the way back to the home office, I reviewed in my mind all the things he had done. I had understood all but one. Why had he stood in the front of a store for three or four minutes without moving or saying anything? "I was imagining that I was a customer," he explained. "I was visualizing this store as the only one I would be able to shop at when I was hungry, and I asked myself if this store would satisfy my needs."

Well, how basic can you get? I had missed the whole point of the visit. Does the store, which is the very foundation of the promotion, appeal directly and personally to the customer?

Am I getting off the track and into the operations end of the business? No, what I am doing is making sure of your success as a sales promoter. There are three elements involved in bringing customers back to your store:

1. You must be completely convinced that what you are doing is right and that you are doing it the right way.
2. You must be able to convince the people in both merchandising and operations that you can bring the customers in and help bring them back. In other words, you make them equal partners in your concept so that they will have the incentive to make their stores more appealing.
3. You must execute your plan down to the last detail by continuing to sell your own people, even if this requires pushing your boss to get it done. Never let up.

Shopping for food and other merchandise week in and week out can be a chore and a bore, but it can be made interesting, exciting, and rewarding. The sales promoter's job is to keep it varied, keep it topical, and spice it up. Don't repeat yourself too frequently; there is a plethora of things to do.

Remember that the customer is being wooed on all fronts. Be sure that what you plan to do is filling a basic need. There is more to promoting than games, coupons, premiums, and gimmicks. After all, A&P's "Price and Pride" promotion did the company no harm.

If you want to bring customers back, know what your real strength is and use it, be it quality, price, convenience, variety, or personnel. Whatever you promise must be evident and available to the customers. Don't disappoint them; you can't get away with it.

If you have it, flaunt it. Everyone is trying to get the customer's attention. The sales promoter's job is to show customers that they were right when they decided to shop with you. Even if the customers hate you, they can learn to love you. It's rudimentary. Besides, the other fellow can't be *that* great.

How Do You Get Competitors' Customers?

You must be aggressive, unpredictable, and timely. The first kid on the block with the new toy gets the most attention. When trading stamps were new in the food industry, they were phenomenally successful. Although the approximate cost was 2 percent of sales, the volume increases were so great that it was not necessary to raise prices to make enough money to cover the added expense. By the time everyone had adopted trading stamps, nobody was getting any benefit from them. But the first stores to use them usually retained some of their increases. It is far better to be on the offense than the defense, and usually less costly in the long run.

There is an old saying that goes, "Fight fire with fire." In the supermarket business this is wrong! Fight fire with water. But be sure you have an ample supply of water on hand. That means keeping a file of tested sales promotions—ready to go. Plan ahead. (These are the two words you'll hear most often in any sales promotion job.)

If your competitors run a game, you run a tape plan offering free merchandise. Your competitors are appealing to their customers' emotions, their desire to get something for nothing. You are also giving customers something for nothing, but you are appealing to their acquisitiveness. The odds are in your favor. All your customers can win, and they can get something tangible. What you offer through your tape plan must be accepted as having real value, however, because your competitors' games can be exciting.

If your competitors run a price promotion, you run a coupon promotion. You do not have to be a creative genius to do something different; you just have to look at your ready-reference file and use or improve on pretested successful promotions. Of course, a little creativity helps a lot. When using someone else's idea, you must understand all the elements that went into making that idea a success. When improving on a sales promotion, it is better to augment, without unduly complicating, than to omit.

Use people. A good intelligence system will ferret out your competitors' weaknesses and make the job easier. Listen carefully to your field people and check out what they say by visiting both your stores and your competitors' stores. Follow your competitors' ads and try to anticipate them. Your suppliers are an important segment of the industry grapevine.

The trade periodicals in the retail business are good, although often repetitious. They use case histories from which ideas can be gleaned. There are times when there is just a slight inference that will stir up a stream of thought, and there are times when you find meaningful similarities to your situation.

In this highly competitive business, where every day presents a new competitive thrust, a new way to give away part of one's profit, a competitor often has to withdraw to the periphery of the arena. That is your opportunity to start something fresh. When competitors get tired, so do their customers, who are then prime targets for your well-planned promotion.

How Do You Get Customers to Spend More in Your Store?

You must confront your customers at every important point of sale. Impulse sales account for a large part of customers' purchases. Few customers bring a complete shopping list to the store. I have seen many lists, but few that are complete to the last item. Lists usually include things like salad items, vegetables, or enough meat for two meals. Some are long and detailed, but rarely do they include everything. How do you augment the list?

Think of it this way: The food business may be the largest industry in the country, and the supermarket its largest segment, but it is a business of penny profits. Few national or regional chains make a profit after taxes of more than 1 percent of their sales volume. Every sale helps the bottom line. None should be foregone.

A supermarket with sales of $72,000 a week (the approximate average throughout the country) makes 9000 transactions averaging $8 each week and has about 4000 customers. Thus the promoter has ample opportunity to induce customers to make impulse purchases.

The merchandise departments know when to promote the items they sell, as well as the prices at which they can afford to sell them, but you can be of inestimable help. You can augment displays with appealing point-of-purchase material. There are growers', manufacturers', canners', and packers' associations that are anxious to help you sell their merchandise, and their material is lively, professional, and often very attractive. There are times when you can prepare your own original material in-house. There are tie-in sales, locations that are better than others, and new items.

Figure it out: If you can get these 9000 transactions up $0.10, you have added $900 to the week's sales. You have increased the sales by 1¼ percent.

CONTINUITY PROMOTIONS

In the supermarket business a continuity of high volume per square foot of selling space is an absolute necessity. One of the tools most frequently used to attain this constant volume is the "continuity promotion."

A continuity promotion is what the term implies—a means of bringing customers back week after week to get a part of an entire unit or set. Some examples are sets of dishes, flatware, glassware, cooking utensils, tools, towels, or luggage. The customer buys these items on a "piece-a-week" basis, with cash and a specified amount of food purchases; they can be offered free with food purchases, or the customer may be required to save cash-register tapes to get the set.

These sales promotions can be bought completely packaged from a company specializing in supermarket promotions, or they can be pro-grammed in-house. The prevailing custom is to buy a packaged sales promotion tailored to the specific needs of the buyer, with a guarantee that the supplier will take back all unsold merchandise.

The precursors of this type of promotion were the United Cigar Store coupons, trading stamps, and "dish night" at the movies. In the food business this type of promotion started with the old door-to-door wagon routes of some of today's largest corporate food chains. So much for ancient history.

The best way to explain is by example. Therefore, let's run through one complete continuity sales promotion from its inception. This sales promotion, which is from my own experience, was a complex promotion involving every phase of retailing. Perhaps you will be critical of the detail, but this example covers every aspect I know of retail sales promotion.

The company for which I worked was using trading stamps. In fact, it was in the trading stamp business and was one of the first to use stamps in many of its markets. After several years everyone was using stamps, and much of their effectiveness had been lost. The problem was to come up with a smashing promotion of some duration that would create impetus sufficient to move the stores to a higher-volume plateau.

An analysis of our files proved that a good dinnerware promotion brought the best results, but not good enough to warrant repeating one of the prepackaged promotions available at that time. It must be said that prepackaged promotions then were not as desirable or sophisticated as they are today. Most "dinnerware deals" consisted of four- or five-piece place settings manufactured by domestic factories that gave little thought to style or design. Most were of the type that could be bought by the piece in variety stores or in 45-piece sets in discount stores.

When we used the answers to some of the previously posed questions, the solution became apparent, but complex in its execution, because many aspects of the proposed promotion had never been tried before by a supermarket chain. And much that had been done in this area was unfamiliar to me.

The sales promotion would consist of Japanese porcelain china sold on a piece-a-week basis over a period of 18 weeks. About a year earlier, a representative of a Japanese trading company had started selling packaged china promotions in boxed five-piece place settings to supermarkets and had left his card. This was the place to begin. I called him in and got all the information available. Then I wrote a complete description of what I intended to do and how I proposed doing it. We would buy the china at the lowest negotiable price so that we could sell it at a sensational savings and make money doing it. This, I believe, was a novel approach at the time and set a precedent for future supermarket and other retail sales promotions.

At a meeting with the merchandise manager of our general merchandise (nonfoods) department, with whom I had had several previous and encouraging conversations, we went over the plan, polished it, and set up a meeting with our immediate boss, the vice president of merchandising. He proved to be an ardent devil's advocate and later on our most powerful protagonist, although it took our combined personalities and selling power to convince him of the workability of the plan.

As the plan called for an investment of over $1 million, it required approval of the president, which our vice president championed at a combined meeting. Now there were partners at the senior management level.

At a second meeting the representative of the Japanese trading company was presented with the plan. During a quick trip to Japan, the price negotiations were completed and two patterns were chosen. It was decided that two patterns would appeal to at least 25 percent more customers than a single pattern would. Results showed the distribution of sales by pattern to be 65 percent and 35 percent, but we never did ascertain the percentage of additional customers we attracted.

A profit center was set up to handle the purchase and sale of the merchandise. This was funded by the company with a $1 million letter of credit and $50,000 of working capital to pay for some market research, display dies, photos, copy, ad layouts, etc.

The portion of the promotion that was visible to the customer was simplicity itself. During the first week we sold only dinner plates at $0.22 each with every $5 purchase (at that time the average transaction was under $5). During the second week we sold only bread and butter plates; during the third week, cups; during the fourth week, saucers; and during the fifth week, fruit dishes. These were the five basic pieces in a place setting. Each time customers wanted to buy a $0.22 piece of china, they would have to buy $5 worth of food.

During the sixth week of the sales promotion we started the cycle over, and again during the eleventh week. We had planned to stop there and give the customers three weeks to complete their sets. But, in fact, the demand was so great that we continued for a fourth cycle and had to give customers six more weeks to complete their sets. Thus the sales promotion lasted six months.

At the same time, we were selling 12 different auxiliary items and serving pieces, nine of which were available in department stores only in sets of high-priced china and were not available at all in comparable promotional-quality china. Those customers who were in a hurry could buy as many packaged five-piece place settings as they wished at approximately three times the price, but without any qualifying food purchase.

Another advantage we gave customers was the opportunity to replace broken dishes during a three-year period (at higher prices, of course). We engaged an experienced fulfillment house for this open-stock privilege. This was unheard of in lower-priced china and proved to be an important incentive to our customers. Ten years later we were still getting replacement requests.

If at this point you analyze the program carefully, you will see that it provides many of the answers to the questions previously posed.

The following will be more meaningful if you keep a hypothetical store in mind. This store handles 5000 transactions a week; its average transaction is $4.80, for a total of $24,000 a week. If you increase the average register ring-up by $0.20 to $5, you have added $1000 ($0.20 × 5000, or just over 4 percent) to your business. If, in this store, you sell 1665 dishes at $0.22 each, you will have added another $366.30, or $1366.30 each week. You are now doing $24,000 +

1366.30 = $25,366.30 each week. Multiply $1366.30 by 26 weeks and you get $35,523.80. You can easily compute the final results for a 500-store chain. The supermarket business is a penny business, but the total of $0.22 sales produced a final result in the multimillions of dollars.

The portion of the promotion that went on behind the scenes was complex and far less glamorous. Because of our multigeographic corporate structure and our outright ownership of the merchandise (what would we do with the remainders?), a method for projecting sales had to be found that could be used under any set of circumstances.

The method we devised was a projection based on units per $1000. Here's how it worked. The dinner plate, our lead item, was given an arbitrary number, in this case 150. This number was not pulled out of the blue but was related to prior experiences. In other words, we assumed that we would sell 150 dinner plates for every $1000 of weekly supermarket sales. Extending that number, we estimated that our hypothetical market, generating $24,000 in weekly volume, would sell 24 × 150, or 3600 dinner plates, during the course of the promotion. Each of the other items became a factor of the dinner plate. If the dinner plate was 150, the bread and butter plate was 80 percent of 150; the cup, 100 percent; the saucer, 90 percent; and the fruit dish, 75 percent. Now we had a basic way of determining sales. We would sell 150 dinner plates, 120 bread and butter plates, 150 cups, 135 saucers, and 112.5 fruit dishes. Comparably smaller sales were plugged into the 12 other items.

Next a test area was chosen. The company territory was divided into nine unequal segments. Each was an area that could be advertised with the least overlap into other areas and therefore the least amount of confusion to the customers. It was further decided that the test area should do no more than 10 percent of the company's total weekly volume. This was to ensure that if we had a flop, we would be able to sell any remainders of merchandise within the company. The weekly volume of the test area chosen was $1.2 million. Therefore, we projected sales of 1200 × 150, or 180,000, dinner plates and cups; 144,000 bread and butter plates; 162,000 saucers; and 135,000 fruit dishes. The other 12 items were projected to sell in much smaller quantities: soup plates at 12 percent, or 17,280; sugar and creamers at 5 percent, or 7200; etc. In total, 801,000 pieces of place-setting items were projected to be sold at $0.22 each, or $116,200. An equal number of dollars was projected for all the serving and auxiliary pieces. This particular proportion turned out to be exactly right, but we were not sanguine enough when we projected sales of our place-setting items.

The actual sale was just over $432,000—985,000 starter pieces at $0.22, or $216,700, and $215,500 in the rest of the line (these numbers are rounded to the nearest 100). Fortunately, we ordered 50 percent more than we projected selling. The test stores accounted for under 10 percent of our total weekly volume.

That brings us to a very important point about promoting premiums at the retail level: How does one project for maximum sales and minimum remainders? We set up a bell graph (Figure 13-1) and located our divisions by weekly volume, as a percentage of total sales, on the curve.

After getting our sixth week's report, we had to consider our position very carefully. We had a winner—or did we? The results were too good. And if our results were right, could we get sufficient merchandise? We decided to test another area and, at the same time, to place heavier orders to take care of the largest segment of our company (areas 3 and 4 combined).

Our second test was started before the first one was completed. It confirmed our success. It also gave more meaning to our internal product mix. We could now order in a more efficient way, as we had a pattern to follow. Even if we made a serious mistake in our 36 percent area, we had five more areas, making up 50 percent of the company, to go.

Think of it this way: If we overordered in our last area (Figure 13-1) by 50 percent, our remainders would be only 2 percent of our total purchases. In fact our last area was under 20 percent overordered, partly because we kept our pipeline filled and partly because of buying habits, a result of the area's ethnic mix. A good portion of this remainder was used to supply our open-stock fullfillment house. The rest was sold to a trading stamp company that was going into the business of packaging promotions for supermarkets.

Three basic forms were designed for the foregoing part of the promotion: a standard projection form, a store reporting form, and an area reporting form, on which the total of all store sales was entered each week, and weekly totals accumulated. Each item was given a number, and from that time on every form showed the number and the item in exactly the same sequence. The

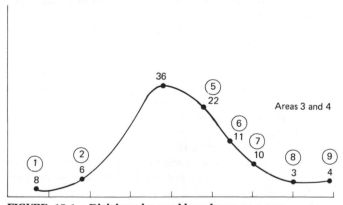

FIGURE 13-1. Divisions by weekly volume as a percentage of total sales.

sales promotion department kept a sales spread sheet showing each week's sales by item and total, by dollar sales of merchandise, and by area dollar volume. Pilot stores in other areas were set up to show percentage of dollar increase or decrease in the promoted area compared with increases or decreases in nonpromoted pilot stores.

The question of supplying the stores had to be carefully considered. Although a supermarket chain usually has large warehousing facilities, they would not be large enough to store this volume of merchandise at one time. For areas 3 and 4 we had to order 135 forty-foot containers. A container holds an average of 1300 cases, which amounts to over 175,000 cases, in addition to our remainders from the two test areas.

To facilitate getting the merchandise in and out of the warehouse, we devised two forms. The first was a container receiving form, which listed the quantities of each incoming item and all other pertinent information about each container (the steamship line, the name of the boat, the container number, seal numbers, the date of arrival, the location of the warehouse, and the customs broker—most of this information was available from the packing list). The second form was a store distribution form.

We made a spread sheet listing each store and its weekly volume. Since we were projecting in units per $1000, we distributed in the same way. Each store was assigned a specific quantity of each item. These were plugged into our IBM system, and copies were sent to the proper warehouse and store. This procedure ensured that the day a container arrived at the warehouse, the IBM system would be alerted to send information that would start its distribution to the proper store. Further, for some of the larger stores, we loaded a complete container for that store, bypassed the warehouse, and forwarded it from the pier to the store. In these instances the stores got the container receiving forms and sent them back to the warehouse filled out properly for entry into our IBM system.

An unexpected benefit was derived from this method of handling. It showed us a way of keeping a perpetual inventory system of what we owned in stores and warehouses. We knew our total receipts; all we had to do was subtract our weekly sales. Prior to this we knew only what was in our warehouses. The perpetual inventory made ordering quite simple. It also gave us a clear picture of the profit (or loss) in our profit center.

Speaking of profit centers, all this merchandise, you must realize, was bought by the sales promotion department with our $1 million letter of credit and sold to our warehouses at a profit to the sales promotion department. There were times when we needed more than $1 million, and this we also borrowed from the company at ½ percent per month. (Those were halcyon days for borrowers; the prime rate was low.)

Therefore, a bookkeeping system had to be devised wherein we could sell to, and buy from, the corporation. The sales promotion department made a profit, but it also guaranteed the sale. That placed the risk of overordering on the department, a responsibility we had to bear forever in future promotions. We had to do the bookkeeping and be examined by our outside auditors.

Now we had taken care of everything: the projections, the ordering, the financing, the receivings, the distributions, the reporting of sales, and the inventory control. Or had we? No! One afternoon we received a call from our Japanese representative. The yen, which had been steady at 359 to 360 to the dollar, was about to jump. His company had taken a multimillion-dollar position, and did we want a part of it? I had not bargained for being an expert in foreign currency, but knew I had to act immediately. First I made an appointment with our president for later that afternoon. Then I called our controller for an immediate statement of our account.

Here is where our attention to detail paid a real dividend. All our purchase orders had been entered on our spread sheets; every shipment made against them had been entered too. Therefore, we knew how much merchandise we still had coming. Our sales spread sheets were completed to the previous Saturday. Thus we knew how much we had sold, how much we would sell in the future, and what our actual inventory was, as of less than one week before.

Armed with this information and knowing how many areas remained to be promoted, we were able to extrapolate our future needs and make a respectable pro forma statement in about 1½ hours. Needless to say, our president said "yes" to the purchase of the yen, or our story would have ended here. It is important to note that the value of the Japanese yen could have dropped in relation to the dollar, in which case we would have bought the china at a lower cost.

Now let's go back to the beginning. Other aspects of the promotion were the advertising, display, and point-of-purchase materials; public relations; and internal communications.

Three complete sets of china in each pattern were ordered to be used for advertising photos and to present at "show-and-tell" sessions with our board of directors, senior officers, and field staff members. We also ordered 12 cases of dinner plates and one case of every other item, all in advance of our first container shipment. We would use these to design our displays and also to make a film to show at indoctrination meetings we were planning to have with store managers.

Our display stands, designed to show and sell merchandise, were complete even to a diagram (silk-screened on the display) showing where every item was to be located and how many of each item were to be placed in the assigned location. This display was to be set up in the highest traffic location in each store.

It was decided that the item of the week was to be displayed at the front end of each checkout stand, in the original overseas shipping cases. We wanted masses of merchandise at the location most convenient and accessible to the customer. (Anyone who has stood in line during a busy time in a supermarket knows how many impulse purchases people make while they're waiting to be checked out.) Signs were designed for all displays. In addition, the store was filled with multicolored signs. Nobody, even the most distracted, astigmatic customer, was going to leave a store without knowing that something *big* was going on.

A sizable advertising budget was planned, and a variety of one- and two-page ads were made up with tabloid-type headlines. The plan was to place a full-page ad (in color, where possible) on Sunday or Monday. This would be followed by a two-page ad on Wednesday, along with our regular weekly food ad. All the direct-mail circulars were to contain two pages in color. Starting on the Sunday of the first week, radio and television advertising was programmed, with saturation coverage consisting of 20-, 30-, and 60-second spots.

A complete public relations program was planned. This program was kicked off with a Japanese smorgasbord party held on the deck of the first ship to arrive with our dishes. We invited everyone, including our president, our warehouse managers, and all the other people who had, or would have, anything to do with the promotion. The shipping company and trading company executives were invited too; they all came with their wives and ate tempura from our new china. Luck was on our side, and the New York skyline stood out against a gorgeous June sunset.

Many press releases were written, but the one that got the most coverage was the one we sent out the week before the promotions started. This one was hand-delivered by a lovely Japanese model, wearing a kimono, to the editor of the woman's page of every newspaper involved. It contained an assortment of pictures, a variety of publicity releases, and two demitasse cups and saucers for the editor. All national services were included in the distribution. During the opening week of the sales promotion, a large percentage of our papers gave us excellent and valuable coverage.

The week before each area started its promotion, a sales indoctrination meeting was held. Each manager received a bulletin at the store, as well as a personal letter from the vice president, stressing the importance of attending the meeting. These were formal dinner meetings and included not only store managers but also field vice presidents, their staff, and many supervisory personnel. All those attending were given a large envelope containing a brochure detailing the promotion, copies of ads, publicity materials, forms to be used, and a stack of checker's manuals explaining fully the importance of their part in the sales promotion.

Each meeting had a master of ceremonies, usually the superintendent of the stores in the area, who spoke on the "why" of the meeting. The master of ceremonies introduced the main speaker, who went through the manager's brochure up to the point of the actual operation of the promotion in the store. At that point, our film, made after hours in a store, detailed every step to be followed in the back room, at the display, and at the checkout counter. Next, the person who was to monitor the promotion in that area explained the ordering and reporting of sales in full detail. A question-and-answer period followed.

Finally, the vice president made a speech exhorting the "troops" and telling them of the importance of this sales promotion. Everyone was to read the brochure at home, and thoroughly. Meetings were to be held with store personnel. Checkers, including part-timers, were to have separate meetings, at which the manager would go over the checker's manual. It covered everything from an outline of the entire sales promotion, including answers to possible customer inquiries, to a variety of sales pitches.

The vice president also announced a list of prizes for managers and checkers. These ranged from TV sets for winning managers to $25 bonds for checkers who performed best in relation to their weekly store volume. Managers also had to report sales promptly every week in order to qualify for a prize. A $0.50 booby prize for the poorest performance was to be announced.

At the end of each meeting, which took about 1½ hours, there was a cocktail hour, during which we found out about any mistakes we had made and also got a general feeling about attitudes toward what we were trying to do. This was followed by a four-course roast-beef dinner. As the managers left, they were given a five-piece place setting, in their choice of pattern, to take home to their families. From their selection of pattern, we knew that the sales proportions would be 65 percent and 35 percent. We changed our orders accordingly.

Basically, in this promotion, no customer was to get past the checkout counter, unless it was over the checker's dead body, without buying a dinner plate. And the plan worked. During the first week we sold an average of 62 dinner plates for every $1000 of food sales. That meant that for every 200 transactions, 62 plates were sold (80 actual customers at an average of 2½ shopping transactions a week).

This did not mean that three out of every four customers bought a dinner plate. Some bought two, and others bought four or five. Our store surveys showed that approximately one-third of our customers were participating. I always thought the figure was high. In addition, not every store sold the same amount. The figures in one area ranged from 19 to 138 dinner plates per $1000. I personally visited the two stores reporting these figures and found that the manager of the store that had sold 19 dinner plates was a complete dud (he was later demoted) and that the manager of the store with 138 sales not only had done everything required of him but also had used his imagination and supplemented our ideas with some very good ones of his own.

The cost of all this activity, including display stands, point-of-purchase materials, public relations, ad layouts and mats, meetings, and startup costs, was about $150 per store. Sales were over $15,000 per store.

TAPE PLANS

A tape plan is a "cost" promotion and a very effective means of bringing customers into the store many times. Using much the same kind of merchandise that is used in a straight continuity promotion, but with a little more leeway for bigger-ticket items, it works in the following manner.

An item, a group of items, or a set of items is placed on sale at a previously fixed retail price. All items are placed on sale at the start of the sales promotion. During the first week of the promotion every customer is given a flyer and an envelope.

The flyer displays all the items on sale, with their prices. (The usual format allows the customer either to buy the merchandise or to get it free with register tapes totaling a specified amount.) It also explains the way the sales promotion works and lays down the ground rules so that there are no questions in the customer's mind about how to fulfill the requirements of purchase. A date is set for the end of the sales promotion, and on the day the promotion starts, the color of the cash-register tapes is changed at all registers. This ensures that tapes saved will be those acquired during the course of the sales promotion.

The envelope contains a set of rules and a place to list and total the tapes stuffed into the envelope. It is very important to get one or more envelopes into customers' hands at the start of the promotion because, unless they have envelopes, it is hard to get them to start collecting. When enough completed envelopes are collected, customers present them for a premium.

It is not unusual for the promoter to include in the flyer or other advertising medium a coupon to get the customer started (one coupon per envelope or item, as the case may be). This is particularly effective when more than one envelope is required. Experience shows that the tapes in an envelope should total no more than $100 and that items calling for more should require more than one envelope. For example, if you are requiring $132 in tapes, you should ask customers to collect two $66 envelopes. As customers complete envelopes, they reach higher plateaus and are less likely to stop collecting.

Accurate projections are most important when running tape plans. The following simple formula can be used to determine what such a program will cost.

Let: C = cost of the item

V = volume of the store

R = redemption factor (35% is reasonable)

E = envelope value

Then

$$\frac{CVR}{E} = \text{average cost of promotion each week}$$

Example: C = $2

V = $24,000

R = 35%

E = $100

$$\frac{2 \times 24{,}000 \times 0.35}{100} - \frac{\$16{,}600}{100} = \$166 \text{ weekly cost}$$

$$\frac{166}{24{,}000} = 0.692\% \text{ weekly cost as a percentage of sales}$$

This promotion will run for 10 weeks and will cost $1660, or 0.692 percent of sales, plus the cost of advertising and miscellaneous expenses. These figures can and should be budgeted.

There is an absolutely erroneous rule of thumb that many supermarket managers use to determine how much of a volume increase is needed to offset the cost of a tape program. They say that one needs $10 in regular retail sales for every $1 given away. This method of figuring is as efficacious as counting beans in a bowl by observation alone. The only way to find out exactly what increase in sales is needed to offset the expense of a program is to use the already established profit and loss estimate. The promotional costs should then be entered where they would regularly appear as expenses. Depending on gross margins generated and fixed and variable expenses, the amount of sales needed could be from 4 to 15 times the expenses incurred.

Now let's run through a hypothetical sales promotion. (See Table 13-1.) We want to run a tape program in which we are going to sell and/or give away a group of five pots and pans. We are willing to spend about ½ percent or our current volume to achieve a sales increase. First we project and budget. Let's do both on one form for the sake of convenience. The projection is in units per $1000, that is, the number of units sold or given away per $1000 of weekly sales times the price. In this case it is also the total number of envelopes × the number sold × 13 (the total in column 7).

A reasonable length of time to run this particular sales promotion is 13

TABLE 13-1   Costs of a Hypothetical Continuity Promotion*

(1) Items	(2) Percent of sales	(3) Unit cost	(4) Total cost	(5) Unit retail	(6) Total retail	(7) Number of envelopes
1-qt saucepan	6	$1.75	$10.50	$1.99	$11.94	1
10-in. frying pan	4	2.77	11.08	3.99	15.96	2
2-qt saucepan	3	3.08	9.24	3.99	11.97	2
5-qt dutch oven	4	5.90	23.60	7.99	31.96	4
Tea kettle	3	5.25	15.75	7.99	23.97	4
Total	20		$70.17		$95.80	4800

* Projection: $1000 of total store sales × 13 weeks = $13,000.

NOTE: Profit if all sold, $25.63 (col. 6 minus col. 4); retail margin, 27.66 percent (total cols. 6 and 4 divided by 6); tape redemption factor, 37 percent ($4800/$13,000); cost of giveaway, $70.17 (total col. 4); cost as a percent of sales, 0.539 percent ($70.17/$13,000). In our $24,000 you would multiply 24 × $70.17 = $1684.08. $1684.08/24,000 × 13 = 0.539 percent.

weeks; this is sufficient time for a customer with a family of four to collect enough tapes to get several items free. If customers like them, they may buy one or more. They will also pick up a few tapes from the floor and the parking lot. These are included in the figures. It is assumed that customers are getting excellent value for their money even if they pay the full retail price.

When you consider that some merchandise must be sold—in this hypothetical case, perhaps 10 to 15 percent—you can readily see that the new cost of the promotion will be less than 0.5 percent (plus all expenditures for advertising above those already budgeted).

Theoretically, one should attract more customers if the envelope requirement is less. I have never been able to prove this by any scientific method, but I have always thought of 0.75 to 0.80 percent as a proper amount to spend for a tape plan. With some additional advertising, the total cost of a tape plan should be about 1.0 percent, which is a reasonable expenditure for a promotion of this type.

Here are some answers to questions that may have arisen in relation to the projection figures. None of the figures is forced. The percent of sales listed in column 2 of Table 13-1 is experiential. The 37 percent redemption rate is realistic. Although I have personally experienced a redemption rate of more than 50 percent, most redemption rates have been between 33 and 40 percent, and I consider 50 percent to be an anomaly.

The importance of accurate projections and careful budgeting cannot be overstressed. They are the key to profitable promotions.

At this point I believe we have answered the question, How can you give away something for nothing? You can do it if you make proper provisions for your giveaway in your budget. Trade-offs and other types of juggling are perfectly good business practices, but what if you are wrong? You must be wrong sometimes, no matter how brilliant you are. The more things you do, the more times you can be wrong. You are doing things right when you are prepared to be wrong, when you have previously expensed your promotion and are able to proceed with impunity.

Ideas are plentiful; proper execution is rare. Management confidence and cooperation are obtained as a result of good forecasting—no untoward surprises. Clever ideas that may or may not bring results are valueless.

RETAIL COUPONING

Coupons have been, over the years, a popular way for retail stores to promote price. Acceptance by customers has been cyclical. There are times when customers can't get enough coupons, and there are times when they all but ignore them. This cycle seems to be related to precipitous climbs to unattractive retail prices. For example, several years ago, when coffee leaped the $0.99 price barrier, coffee coupons became very desirable. Market-wise coffee buyers, who were able to anticipate this rise, jumped in, loaded their warehouses, and were able to coupon coffee at very attractive prices.

In fact, the price increases of the past few years have made couponing a desirable as well as a popular promotional tool. Couponing gives the retailer the opportunity to limit losses while advertising merchandise at very low prices. The limit is imposed, substantially, by the number of coupons proliferated. However, circulation is not the only measure of redemption. Type of circulation, type of market, regular movement of the item, seasonality, and purchase requirement tend to inhibit or enhance the desirability of the coupons and therefore the redemption.

In a large city with several newspapers, redemption is apt to be low in relation to circulation. In suburban areas, the same pattern is prevalent, partially because of the overlapping big-city circulation. In smaller cities where circulation in relation to population is very high, redemption is usually high, not only because of the higher circulation, but also because there is usually more interest and more participation, in all things, in smaller cities (as opposed to large metropolitan areas and their suburbs). Then, too, certain newspapers encourage more female readership with excellent women's pages, and this results in greater redemption.

Circulars mailed to the home encourage greater redemption, as a percentage of circulation, than newspapers do. Here again, it is hard to establish exact figures, as they are dependent on the complexity of the marketplace. It is safe to say, however, that a sale price without a coupon will produce greater results than the original price or a somewhat lower price with a coupon.

In recent times, supermarkets have been redeeming manufacturers' coupons at 2, 2½, and 3 times their face value. This may be a self-defeating promotion. It helps the manufacturer, but at great cost to the supermarket. What's more, the results are short-lived because supermarket owners, as stated before, have a penchant for fighting fire with fire. When a supermarket advertises this type of coupon, store traffic does increase, but the owner can be sure that before 24 hours have elapsed, one or more competitors will advertise the same value or a greater one. It is like paying the devil to witness your own suicide.

The value of a medium can be determined by coupon coding; this is discussed in Chapter 3. Suffice it to say that couponing is a tool supermarkets can use when considering new media or omitting competing media. But again, remember that it's only a tool, not the answer to every problem.

Then, too, there are mysterious forces at work. I recall a mailing piece sent out many years ago to a small group of supermarkets. This mailer contained a book of checks. The first check told the customer about the stores. The next four checks were dated; each one was redeemable during a specific week with a $10 food purchase. The checks were dated for redemption in this order: (1) a silver dollar, (2) a container of ice cream (a $0.99 value), (3) a pound of bacon (a $0.99 value), and (4) a watermelon (selling during that week for $0.99). Consider the following before you decide which coupon had the greatest redemption rate. In a series of coupons, there is a tendency toward maximum coupon redemption during the first week and toward declining redemption in later weeks.

As I said earlier, some results are hard to predict and may even reverse the rules. And that's what happened. The greatest redemption, by far, was of the watermelon coupon. (The weather may have been a factor.) The second and third coupons were redeemed in that order and at very much the same rate. Last, and way down the line, was the first week's coupon—the silver dollar (worth a full $1, in those days). Naturally, we had assumed that the order of redemption would be the order of the on-sale dates. Who can explain the vagaries of a customer's perception of value?

SWEEPSTAKES AND CONTESTS

There are several types of retail promotions I would like to discuss briefly as retail sales promotions. The first is the sweepstakes. I have never used one that I could call successful, including one in which the first prize was a two-week, all-expense-paid trip to Europe for two (with pocket money added). That does not mean that they cannot be successful. It merely means that from my own personal experience I cannot give you any glowing reports about their results. In my experience contests are also not an especially good way of spending big money, although I have used several low-cost contests successfully as a means of promoting good public relations. Consider the value of having schoolchildren compete in a Halloween window-decorating contest, with appropriate prizes for the winning class or school and something tasty for losers too. This is a contest that will endear you to parents and teachers. What's more, the decorations are attractive and will draw people to your store. They also produce good newspaper publicity, the kind you can't buy.

During late spring and early summer, dance contests in the supermarket parking lot cost very little and tend to bring out the crowds. They can be run from 9 P.M. on, depending on the neighborhood.

SPECIAL SALES PROMOTIONS

Special problems in individual stores can give rise to what may aptly be called special store promotions. Such a program can be used in the mix of events. For example, a display of paintings gathered from local artists and art associations, a bake sale for the benefit of a local organization or charity, or a series of demonstrations can be effective. These events can also be used to overcome customer resistance, whether due to a real or an imagined cause.

The following is an example of an elaborate special sales promotion that had a special goal. The store was doing good business, but the percentage of meat sales to total store volume was extraordinarily low, and we wanted to bring those sales up. It was felt that increasing meat sales might also increase overall sales.

To accomplish our goal, we staged a "cook-in." For this event we set up a 30-foot table and a large outdoor-style barbecue, which we vented to the outside of the store. We hired a chef and a person to keep things neat during the event. The chef made tubs of potato salad and coleslaw beforehand and then charcoal-broiled steaks and hamburgers. Suppliers helped us with a variety of condiments, paper products, soft drinks, cookies, and, in fact, everything we needed for a gala spread. This event went on for three days, during which time we ran a beef sale that would show off the store to the best advantage. The results were more than gratifying. Store volume went up dramatically, and a good portion held. Meat sales rose to a normal figure.

Another special promotion was absolutely free. One of our stores had an extension in the front of the building. We located a self-contained delicatessen and an on-premises bakery in this area, which had its own entrance and an entrance into the store proper. Business was spotty at first as we changed master bakers frequently, trying to find a good one. The one we were finally satisfied with became disgruntled because of the lack of volume.

One day the baker approached us with the suggestion that we keep the bakery and deli open on Sundays. (In this county, supermarkets were not allowed to be open on Sundays.) During the first two weeks business was not sufficient to pay for the labor, so during the third week we advertised this department as being open on Sundays in the body of our major weekly ad. No sooner had the newspaper hit the street than a zealous clergyman called the store and threatened the manager with dire consequences. Despite the admonition, we decided to keep the store open. Within 15 minutes after services were over, the store was jammed, and it remained that way every Sunday from then on.

One Sunday several months later I visited that store (for another reason), and the clergyman came up to me and introduced himself. He told me that some of his parishioners had complained about his position on the Sunday opening, and we had a good laugh over the incident. The moral is: Yes, you may have to work some Sundays.

GAMES

Games are another viable promotion in the retailer's bag of tricks. They should certainly be in the promotion mix. While games have been detailed elsewhere in this book and supermarket games are similar to all other games, they should be discussed in this chapter because they are important. Perhaps I should have said that they are the same as other games, but with a slight difference.

First, to my knowledge, probability games have rarely been successful in supermarkets, and I don't know why. A well-conceived probability game should be good. Bingo-type games, and bingo itself where it is legal, have been highly successful, partly because of the variety of tickets a bingo game affords.

Let us consider variety and its impact on the success of games. There are retailers whom the customer visits once a month. Gas stations are patronized about once a week. Supermarkets are shopped, on the average, more than twice a week. Therefore, customers pick up many more tickets in a supermarket game than in other retailers' games. If they continue to get the same losing tickets every time they shop, they become discouraged.

A good rule of thumb by which to judge the quality of a game is: The more ticket variety, the better the game. Judge, too, the game pieces themselves. They should be attractive and convey the idea of quality. This tends to increase customers' confidence in the game. If the game is not bingo, it should have an interesting theme and one that lends itself to interesting game pieces.

Supermarket TV games, like "Let's Go to the Races," have been very successful. This type of game has a lot going for it. There is an added bonus in the thrust of the TV advertising and programming. Therefore, it is more likely that your trading area will know that you are giving away something for nothing. But you must not neglect the print media. They are the bread and butter of supermarket advertising.

The prize structure definitely influences the customer. In supermarket games, cash prizes are best. The quantity of prizes is also important. An outstanding grand prize is very important, but most people have never won anything, and so it is also important to offer a large number of small prizes. I, for one, am very fond of Mr. Washington's countenance and the color green; many of your future customers will be too.

The experience and quality of the game company with which you are doing business are also important. As in many other promotions, the ideas are easy to come by, but how carefully the game is thought out is more important. Has your supplier covered you with the right forms, the proper mix of tickets, and a faultless method for securing about 70 percent of the winners seeded in the mix? Is there a true limit to the number of winners and the number of dollars? Can the customer understand how to win and what the chances of winning are? Is everything honest—no hanky-panky you can't control? You must be in control at all times.

Most important, however, is the way a game is run. The very best game can be throttled by an inattentive engineer, crippled by contemptuous checkers, or massacred by mindless managers. You, the promoter, have to make customers believe. In this day of casual concern and often total ennui, it is not an easy task to rouse people to do more than is called for or even to enforce minimum discipline. However, it can be done, though perhaps not to your ultimate satisfaction.

Analyze the game; visualize its assets and its potential problems. How can you get big winners' names and pictures in your ads so that people will know there are big winners? How can you tell whether people are winning anything or even getting their tickets? The better prepared you are to deal with the exigencies that are bound to arise and the better able you are to explain how your people can help you avoid them, the better results you will have.

Running a game is like running any sales promotion. It takes care and preparation—and it takes the guidance of your law department. Never consider running a game unless it meets with the approval of your lawyers. Government regulations on the national, state, and local levels present too many pitfalls. In addition, there is a complex contract and insurance policy to be read and agreed upon.

If you are not completely conversant with games and there are mathematical complexities involved, get help from someone who is. But be sure that, in the final analysis, you do understand the game. Perhaps you think I am being overweening. No, I am merely recalling the multimillion-dollar errors, the lawsuits, and the bad feelings that poorly conceived, poorly engineered, and poorly executed games have caused in the past.

Don't let any of these complexities deter you from running games, however. I have run many with varying degrees of success, from fair to excellent, and I have never run a complete dud. I can only caution you. Don't be late. Don't follow someone else. If you are going to run a game, run it when the competition least expects it. One last word of advice: A game works better where your business is on the upswing and when your share of the market is sizable.

CONCLUSION

A good sales promotion manager is the prime ingredient in a successful retail sales promotion. In large chain operations this is the sales promotion manager's only job. In smaller organizations the job may be among the other duties of a marketing or sales manager, an advertising manager, or a merchandising manager. Whoever it may be, the one who wears the sales promotion hat must have the following qualifications.

This person must be well-grounded in merchandising. A flair for numbers and their meaning is essential because the manager will forever be dealing with merchandisers. Feeling for the merchandise itself is essential because it will often be incumbent upon the manager to accept and/or interpret a buyer's ideas.

The sales promotion manager must have a well-rounded knowledge of marketing and advertising. Whether the manager executes these particular segments of the promotion or not, he or she must understand them. The manager must know who the customers are, who they can be, and how to present the case to them in the most advantageous way. It is not necessary to write the copy and draw up the layout, but if the manager cannot explain lucidly and forcefully what is wanted and cannot critique the outcome of this presentation, the job is being held by a "second stringer."

Of course, the advertising manager thinks that everybody wants to be an advertising manager. It is easy to criticize another person's ads. No, you, as the sales promotion manager, do not want the advertising manager to put the picture 2 inches nearer the left column and move the copy up to the top of the page. Anybody can do that and be just as wrong as anybody else. The advertising for your sales promotion should speak to the promotion and talk to the customer. It should present the promotion directly and in its most favorable light, and you should be the best judge of whether it does this. You are supposed to know more than anyone else about what you are doing and what you expect to accomplish.

The sales promotion manager must be a convincing public speaker and conversationalist. Ability as an orator or party wit isn't necessary, but the manager must demonstrate confidence and be able to deliver a speech that will capture and hold an audience's interest. The sales promotion manager must be able to present facts and figures that are meaningful to the listeners, whether these listeners are operators, merchandisers, or senior officers. If the manager can put on a boater and lead the parade down Main Street while twirling a baton, so much the better.

The sales promotion manager must become a shopper and be immersed in retailing. Department stores, auto accessory stores, hard goods and soft goods stores, and supermarkets are in the same business: retailing. The sales promotion manager will be called upon to participate with other retailers in shopping-center and other area promotions and must be able to evaluate the effort as it pertains to the business.

The individual responsible for sales promotion must be careful, thoughtful, and thorough and must follow through, because even the so-called experts make lots of mistakes. I could tell you about some of the brainstorms I've had (one, in particular, in which we sold genuine cultured pearls for $0.29 apiece with each $2 purchase and also gave out instruction booklets and the components for stringing them—about $40,000 down the drain), but I won't.

14 Trading Stamps

EUGENE R. BEEM, Ph.D.
Former Vice President, The Sperry & Hutchinson Company

THOMAS W. NETHERCOTT
Former Manager of Research Studies, The Sperry & Hutchinson Company

Few would dispute the clout wielded by the trading stamp as a promotional device. The little gummed sticker's promotional power per square inch gives it a special distinctiveness. The key to this power, as we shall see, is its continuity feature. The customer accumulates the stamps for future redemption in the form of cash or merchandise premiums, and is thus motivated to return to the issuer for more. The trading stamp's effectiveness can also be measured in terms of the controversy it has created resulting from concerted antistamp efforts on the part of nonusers. This, along with the economics and mechanics of the system, is what makes the brief history of trading stamps so fascinating.

Had Simple Simon been able to display a more imposing stature as a customer, he would probably have succeeded in inveigling a free sample from the pieman. Facts as well as folklore document the many means that merchants have used to attract and retain patronage over the centuries.

WHERE IT ALL BEGAN

Trading stamps did not appear on the American scene until the 1890s. Documentation of the earliest use is retained in the archives of the Edward Schuster Company (now Gimbels), a department store in Milwaukee, Wisconsin.[1] A firm called the Blue Stamp Company was issuing stamps as early as 1891, the year that Schuster's took them on. When the Blue Stamp Company went out of business in 1905, Schuster's took over the responsibility of redeeming the outstanding Blue stamps that it had issued to its customers and immediately initiated its own plan with the Schuster stamp. By this account, Schuster's operated the first "captive" trading stamp plan, and the Blue stamp was issued by the first independent trading stamp company. The term *captive* later came to be used to describe a trading plan that is owned and operated by its principal user.

Historically, the independent company which sells its trading stamp service to retailers and other users has accounted for the major portion of the industry's volume. Such companies undertake the entire responsibility of the trading stamp program except the issuing of the stamp to the saver. The Sperry & Hutchinson Company is the largest of the "independents" and has been dominant in the industry since its inception in 1896. A third form of trading stamp sponsorship is the cooperative ownership plan. This variant of the owner-user type of operation comes into being when a group of compatible merchants, usually within a common retail trading area, jointly sponsor a trading stamp plan on a per-share basis. Co-op plans have accounted for only a very minor share of total trading stamp volume.

WHAT THEY ARE AND HOW THEY WORK

The trading stamp systems of today have changed hardly at all from their forebears of the 1890s, either in their reasons for being or in the particulars of their operation. Users have three prime motives for adopting a trading stamp plan. First, they wish to increase their share of patronage in their trading area by building a stronger bond of loyalty among their present customers. Since customers must accumulate the stamps in order to redeem them in the future for a reward, a user expects customers to purchase a significantly larger portion of the items they need in that user's store. Second, users expect new business from nonpatrons who by word of mouth hear about the satisfaction obtained from the redemption process and the premiums. Third, users expect the increased sales volume from present and new patrons to generate a contribution to profit that will be more than sufficient to offset the cost of the stamps issued. In short, users expect the trading stamp plan to significantly contribute to the expansion of their businesses over the long term by creating the soundest competitive advantage for them in retailing and by building strong, loyal, and enduring patronage from an expanding base of stamp-saving customers.

The physical particulars of the typical trading stamp operation today are almost identical to those of operations in existence eighty years ago. In its lowest denomination (one unit) the trading stamp is slightly smaller in dimension than the typical U.S. postage stamp. Many users receive them from the issuer in pad form, as they have always done, but more users today prefer the roll form for machine dispensing. Since things cost many more dollars today than they did years ago, higher-denomination stamps (units of ten and fifty) are now predominant. The quantity and value of the stamps given to the customer are in direct proportion to the amount spent for the purchases, and the most popular ratio today is the same as it was at the turn of the century, one stamp for each $0.10 purchase.

The stamp saver moistens the gummed backs of the stamps and pastes them into a book. Generally, a book containing 1200 to 1500 stamps must be filled before it can be turned in for redemption. The saver can pick up a premium merchandise catalog from the stamp-issuing merchant or from the stamp company's redemption center. The retail value of the redemption merchandise will vary with the class of goods selected and the stamp plan. The higher the normal retail markup on the item, the better the value that can be passed on to the redeemer. Also, the larger the stamp system, the greater the bargaining power in purchasing the redemption merchandise. Today, the average retail merchandise value per book of 1200 S&H stamps is about $3, but this varies, depending on the item, from $2 to $4. The $3 value thus represents a 2.5 percent discount on purchases of $120 where the trading stamps are issued at the rate of one per $0.10 purchase.

Most of the major stamp systems offer the saver the alternative of cash redemption, and nineteen states require that the cash-redemption value be printed on the face of the stamp. These values generally range from $1.20 to $2 for a book of 1200 stamps. When Schuster's began issuing its own stamps in 1905, a 500-stamp book representing $50 in purchases was redeemable for $1 in merchandise or $0.70 in cash.[2] Thus, the discount on purchases for Schuster's customers at that time was 2.0 percent for merchandise and 1.4 percent for cash.

The cost of stamp service to the user is less than its retail-merchandise value to the saver. The stamp cost to the user is about $2.53 for the 1200 S&H stamps that fill a saver's book, which has a retail value of about $3. This represents a bonus to the saver of about 19 percent over the cost of the stamps to the retailer. The $2.53 cost for 1200 stamps converts to $2.11 per 1000, which in turn represents 2.1 percent of the user's sales, if the stamps are issued at the rate of one per each $0.10 purchase. However, few users strictly adhere to this practice. Most give their patrons bonus stamps for any number of reasons tied to their promotional strategies, and some give stamps only to those patrons who ask for them. Furthermore, the cost of the stamps varies with the issuing company and with the type of account. Currently, stamp costs vary from about $1.50 to $2.50 per 1000.

While in their fundamentals trading stamp systems have changed hardly at all since their inception over eighty-five years ago, their popularity and the extent of their use as a promotional medium have undergone extensive cyclical swings, as we shall see.

THE INDUSTRY'S EARLY GROWTH PATTERN

As an innovative promotional medium, trading stamps could not have come upon the scene in a more propitious era. The two decades preceding World War I were marked by steady economic growth. The population of the United States grew by 31 million persons, of whom almost half were industrious immigrants. Except during the recession of 1907–1909, per capita real gross national product, prices, and productivity per work hour were increasing at a 2 percent annual rate. In this comfortable environment, trading stamps brought a distinctiveness which increased the patronage of the merchants who used them. Thus, they were a valuable franchise.

Usually, with a department store as the hub, the other noncompeting "Main Street" merchants were able to form a family of stamp-issuing retailers, which enabled the stamp-saving households to accumulate quickly sufficient quantities of stamps to redeem for worthwhile premiums. Interestingly, it was the independent retailers who featured customer service, rather than the chain stores, that found trading stamps to be a most suitable promotional device. Montgomery Ward experimented briefly with a coupon plan from 1905 to 1908, and the Great Atlantic & Pacific Tea Company issued trading stamps from 1908 to about 1914.

Harold Fox observed that trading stamps are in heavy use when (1) the business sectors dealing frequently with consumers are so similar in terms of what they offer that they need promotional differentiation and (2) the consumer can accumulate enough stamps to make saving them worthwhile.[3] The first condition pervaded the retail scene in the years just prior to World War I, to the extent that large numbers of stamps were given out as double and triple bonuses.[4] This, along with their widespread use, contributed to 35 million in stamp industry sales volume by 1914. Wartime inflation and shortages of merchandise greatly reduced the need for sales promotion after that, so trading stamp usage went into a long decline, as shown in Figure 14-1 and Table 14-1.

An aggressive expansion of grocery chains in the 1920s, followed by the great depression of the 1930s, kept the retail sales of stamp users well below 1 percent of total retail sales. The A&P gradually dropped trading stamps along with other services when it converted its outlets to "economy" stores beginning in 1912. Trading stamp volume descended to its lowest level at the depth of the depression in 1934. At that point, personal consumption was so low and trading stamps were so scarce that the consumer could not accumulate enough stamps to make saving them worthwhile—the condition that supports Fox's second observation. Furthermore, it was a time of struggling for mere survival for almost all merchants, so trading stamps, along with most other promotional devices, became expendable.

The trading stamp industry might have experienced an earlier revival had it not been for World War II. Once again the economy was faced not only with material shortages but with rationing and price controls as well. Furthermore, merchandise items used as gifts and premiums are by their nature not among life's basic necessities, so premium merchandise was in particularly short supply. It was not until the war restrictions had been removed and consumer goods were once again in normal supply that the trading stamp industry began its years of phenomenal growth, which were to extend through the 1960s. During this period there was a distinct change in the nature of food retailing, which was fundamental in bringing this all about.

TRADING STAMPS AND THE SUPERMARKET

The most significant change in living patterns during the post-World War II years was the flight to the suburbs and the corresponding greater dependency upon the automobile. Food retailers who expanded outward from the urban center adapted their operations to the comforts of the suburban lifestyle. The "no-frills," King Kullen type of supermarket that typified the innovation in food retailing during the 1930s had no place among the merchants who

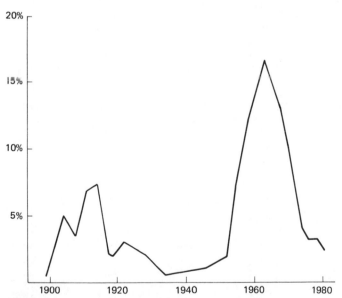

FIGURE 14-1. Share of retail trade made by merchants giving trading stamps, 1900–1980. (*Courtesy of The Sperry & Hutchinson Company.*)

integrated their operations within the vast retailing centers, which were designed to make the shopping experience a comfort and a pleasure.

The prime objectives of the postwar supermarket were (1) to draw as many customers as possible from a greatly enlarged surrounding shopping area and (2) to maximize the share it could take of the consumer's convenience-goods dollar. To do this, the selling area was expanded to accommodate specialty-food departments, such as meat and fresh-fish sections and on-premise bakeries and delicatessens, and later to provide space for health and beauty aids and general merchandise. Many customer services and conve-

TABLE 14-1 Share of Retail Trade Made by Merchants Giving Trading Stamps, 1900–1981

Year	Percent of retail sales	Year	Percent of retail sales	Year	Percent of retail sales
1900	0.4	1928	2.1	1955	7.0
1901	1.9	1929	2.0	1956	10.0
1902	3.2	1930	1.7	1957	10.5
1903	4.4	1931	1.4	1958	11.1
1904	5.3	1932	1.1	1959	12.3
1905	4.6	1933	0.8	1960	14.2
1906	3.6	1934	0.5	1961	15.0
1907	3.0	1935	0.6	1962	15.9
1908	3.9	1936	0.6	1963	16.8
1909	4.6	1937	0.6	1964	16.3
1910	5.3	1938	0.7	1965	15.2
1911	6.0	1939	0.8	1966	14.5
1912	6.8	1940	0.8	1967	13.7
1913	7.5	1941	0.9	1968	12.9
1914	8.0	1942	0.9	1969	12.0
1915	6.4	1943	0.9	1970	11.3
1916	5.0	1944	0.9	1971	9.5
1917	3.4	1945	0.9	1972	8.1
1918	2.0	1946	0.9	1973	5.6
1919	2.4	1947	1.2	1974	4.2
1920	2.6	1948	1.3	1975	3.7
1921	2.8	1949	1.4	1976	3.2
1922	3.1	1950	1.6	1977	3.2
1923	2.8	1951	1.8	1978	3.2
1924	2.7	1952	2.0	1979	3.3
1925	2.6	1953	3.0	1980	3.1
1926	2.4	1954	4.5	1981	2.9
1927	2.3				

SOURCE: The Sperry & Hutchinson Company.

niences were added in further competition for patronage, including check cashing, express lanes, and carry-out service. While adequate off-street parking was essential from the outset, evening openings were extended from one to six and even seven nights a week. Wide aisles, bright lighting, and air conditioning distinguished the newer suburban units from the older ones back in the inner city, and in-store conveniences were extended to include rest rooms, service desks, hostesses, and even play areas for children.

While the new specialty-food departments and the addition of nongrocery merchandise lines contributed to higher gross margins, the additional customer services and conveniences increased operating costs to the extent that net operating profits as a percentage return on sales declined during the 1950s. (See Table 14-2.) Furthermore, since much of the operating expense was fixed or increased only slightly by additional customer volume, the payoff on promotional investment that succeeded in bringing in new business was high. The better-established food chains with good store coverage in a trading area could profitably use newspaper, radio, and TV advertising to pull in the much-needed additional traffic, but for the smaller operator with limited coverage, the costs of these media were prohibitive. The smaller operator had to resort to premium promotions, sweepstakes, and circus-type entertainment events to attain distinction. In brief, the promotional objective was to gain a distinct competitive advantage in an environment where uniformity, not only of services and conveniences but also of nationally branded merchandise, was becoming predominant in the supermarkets' offerings. The customer with the mobility of the family car had more supermarkets to choose from, so the competitive bidding for customer patronage intensified throughout the 1950s and 1960s.

Trading stamps were not thought to be a practical promotional medium

TABLE 14-2 Gross Margin, Expenses, and Operating Profits for Nine Identical Food Chains, 1950–1958

Year	Gross margin, percent	Operating expense, percent	Operating profit, percent
1950	18.5	15.1	3.4
1952	18.0	15.2	2.8
1954	18.9	16.1	2.8
1956	19.1	17.0	2.1
1958	19.5	17.5	2.0

SOURCE: Wilber B. England, *Operating Results of Food Chains in 1958*, Harvard Business School, Division of Research, Boston, 1959, p. 8.

for the prewar supermarkets. With their significantly lower operating costs, they pulled in traffic with their prices, which were 10 to 15 percent below those of the service grocers, who were their only competitors at the time. However, in 1951 King Soopers, a four-store independent supermarket group in Denver, Colorado, took on trading stamps, and the Denver story set the pattern for what was to evolve as the trading stamp boom. The King Soopers stores' sales volume increased by 50 percent in the first year of trading stamp use and by another 50 percent in the second year. Moreover, within twelve months after the stores' move into stamps, three other independents countered with competing stamp plans. In 1953, the first major chain took on stamps, and by 1955 stamp-issuing supermarkets accounted for 36 percent of total food-store sales in Denver.

If the Denver supermarkets were the forerunners, those in the rest of the

FIGURE 14-2. Trading stamps are given at the checkout counter. (*Courtesy of The Sperry & Hutchinson Company.*)

nation did not lag far behind. The Supermarket Institute began providing a measure of trading stamp usage among its members in 1954. After the dramatic increases during the 1950s, the peak in stamp usage among this group came in 1962. But economic growth, inflation, and continued usage by many of the major food chains kept the total trading stamp industry sales volume in an upward trend through the late 1960s. (See Table 14-3.) It is of interest that, as in Denver, it was the independents that led the food retailing industry into and out of trading stamps. The major chains were usually the followers. The A&P did not introduce its Plaid stamps until 1961 and was the last major chain to join the movement.

The early stamp users could select the best from among the established trading stamp plans and effectively use them to differentiate their stores from their competitors' operations. Because of the exclusivity of the franchise, later users had to resort to less well established plans as a means of defense, and they often found them to be less effective in achieving their marketing objective of distinctiveness. Furthermore, some users adopted stamps in an attempt to compensate for basic deficiencies in the operation of their stores. Finally, the last of those to go the stamp route were the largest chains, many of whom already had a substantial share of the available patronage. Safeway already had 30 percent of the patronage in the city of Denver when it adopted its stamp plan in 1958, and this action drove stamp penetration to 88 percent of the retail food trade there.

From 1951 through 1960 food prices were very stable, increasing at an average rate of only 0.7 percent a year, and from 1960 through 1965 they increased at only a 1.4 percent average rate. But in the year 1966 alone food

TABLE 14-3   Percent of Food Marketing Institute Members Issuing Trading Stamps

Year	Percent	Year	Percent
1954	13	1972	31
1955	17	1973	23
1956	40	1974	17
1958	58	1975	12
1960	72	1976	10.5
1962	78	1977	11.6
1964	70	1978	13.0
1966	55	1979	14.7
1968	45	1980	11.0
1970	37		

SOURCE: *The FMI Speaks.*

prices jumped 5 percent, enough to bring about protests, demonstrations, and even boycotts of supermarkets in some cities. While stamp usage among all supermarkets never reached the proportions that it did among Supermarket Institute members, almost 60 percent of supermarkets were using them in 1966, and 49 million households were saving them. Since nonusers within the retail trade and some consumerists without have always claimed that the consumer pays for the cost of stamps with higher prices (a hypothesis which has never been conclusively proved and which will be covered in the section dealing with controversy), the hue and cry over food prices gave many longtime stamp users the opportunity they had been waiting for to drop their stamp plans and turn to other promotional means. Their new promotional theme became "we have dropped stamps and can now give you lower prices." While food prices continued to increase at a 4 percent annual rate throughout the remainder of the 1960s, they increased at an average rate of 8.3 percent per year in the 1970s, and the transition from nonprice to price competition picked up momentum as the era of supermarket discounting got under way.

Observing the most recent trend toward continuity promotions; then to contests, games, and sweepstakes; and finally to trading stamps, Steve Weinstein, of *Supermarket News*, observed that price and nonprice promotional emphasis runs in an endless cycle.[5] There also appears to be a rising trend in supermarket gross margins during the nonprice phase, followed by a declining trend in gross margins during the price phase; some of the underlying conditions that feed the cycle are shown in Figure 14-3.

The price phase of a food retailing cycle begins when a new type of store comes upon the scene. The innovation is such that it significantly reduces the store's operating expenses. This enables the store to reduce prices enough to disrupt the status quo in the marketplace. The A&P initiated such an innovation with its "economy" stores just before World War I. This limited-assortment, one-person operation dispensed with the traditional credit and delivery services along with trading stamps, and it converted the cost savings into prices that were 10 percent lower or more. A generation later, the King Kullen type of self-service food store appeared. In that depression-ridden era, these stores drew patronage from far outside their normal trading areas by offering a 10 to 15 percent saving on the family food bill. The most recent price phase of the cycle can be said to have begun with the appearance of the second-generation supermarket in the mid-1960s. Here the "all your shopping under one roof" theme engendered new store space of up to 50,000 square feet, or triple the area occupied by stores of the generation before. These stores had increased average transactions and the potential for significantly lower labor and management costs per dollar of sales.

While it might have been coincidence that these innovations occurred at unhappy times, the consumer is more attentive to cost savings when living standards are deteriorating because of inflation, as during World War I;

because of severe depression, as in the mid-1930s; or as a result of the "stagflation" of recent years. Imitation of the innovator seems the only course for survival in an environment with such critical operating ratios as food retailing. The last years of the price phase of the cycle have been characterized by price wars and, most recently, coupon wars. Gross margins usually drop to their lowest ebb as the industry enters its transition phase, as shown in Table 14-4.

One might assume from what is known about general economic and social conditions prior to World War I and again in the 1920s that the elements supporting nonprice phases of the food retailing competition cycle (i.e., relative price stability, economic expansion, and consumer optimism) were generally present. Reliable estimates of the food industry's operating ratios have been available only since the early 1950s, but it was at this time that evidence of the dire need for improvement in profits fostered the movement into the nonprice phase of the last cycle. It has been shown that the supermarkets' outstanding profile at that time was one of "sameness" and that

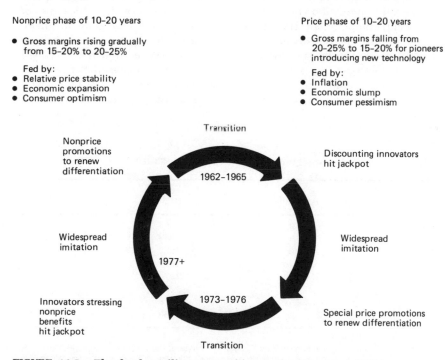

Nonprice phase of 10–20 years

- Gross margins rising gradually from 15–20% to 20–25%

Fed by:
- Relative price stability
- Economic expansion
- Consumer optimism

Price phase of 10–20 years

- Gross margins falling from 20–25% to 15–20% for pioneers introducing new technology

Fed by:
- Inflation
- Economic slump
- Consumer pessimism

Transition

Nonprice promotions to renew differentiation

Discounting innovators hit jackpot

1962–1965

Widespread imitation

Widespread imitation

1977+

Innovators stressing nonprice benefits hit jackpot

1973–1976

Special price promotions to renew differentiation

Transition

FIGURE 14-3. The food retailing competition cycle. (*Courtesy of The Sperry & Hutchinson Company.*)

the trading stamp gave a competitive advantage to the innovators mainly because of its distinctiveness as an inducement to consumers, which was difficult to imitate because of the exclusiveness of the franchise.

While the competition cycle has come around again to where it was in the early 1950s, the situation now is more complex than heretofore. There was a surge in economic growth from 1975 through 1980, but it was accompanied by an increase in food prices. Consumers are far from optimistic as they see their living standards eroded by inflation and taxation. Furthermore, marketing patterns in the food industry have become more diverse, as retailers have accommodated an emerging consumer segmentation with a broader variety of outlets. Two- and three-worker households support the current growth in convenience stores and twenty-four-hour supermarkets. Some households with children stretch their food-budget dollars by buying in bulk at warehouse stores. Finally, the trend toward "giantism" in store size appears to have passed its peak. Slower population growth increases the risk of not attaining the planned sales volume within a time frame that was feasible ten years ago.

Will trading stamps be outmoded in this new setting, as another nonprice phase of the competition cycle emerges? Shortly, we shall explore the basics of the stamp company operation to see what stamps still have going for them. The opportunities they provide will be assessed in the light of recent changes in consumer attitudes toward them. The controversies that have plagued them in times past may prove to be an even more formidable challenge in the new era of consumerism. These will be identified. Finally, the question of who should use trading stamps will be discussed from the potential user's point of view.

TABLE 14-4   Gross Margins for Food Chains, 1952–1980

Year	Percent	Year	Percent
1952	18.0	1966	22.2
1954	18.9	1968	21.5
1956	19.6	1970	21.4
1958	20.5	1972	20.9T
1960	21.6	1974	21.2
1962	22.1	1976	21.4
1964	22.5P	1978	21.5
		1980	22.0

P is peak; T is trough.
SOURCES: National Association of Food Chains, Washington, D.C.; Wilber B. England, *Operating Results of Food Chains in 1958*, Harvard Business School, Division of Research, Boston, 1959, p. 3; Gene A. German and Gerard F. Hawkes, *Operating Results of Food Chains*, Cornell University Press, Ithaca, N.Y., 1980, pp. 7, 9.

TRADING STAMP USAGE BY OTHER RETAILERS

Department Stores

Department stores were a mainstay of the trading stamp industry during the early days. Many, such as Schuster's, issued their own stamps. The May Company initiated Eagle stamps in 1904, and these are still the most widely used stamps in their strongholds in St. Louis and Cleveland. They were important in the industry because of the large sales volume generated in each store. They were important to stamp savers as the source of many of their "big-ticket" purchases. For these purchases, the shopper traditionally went "down-town" to the central business district, where the large department stores were clustered, often on opposite corners of a main intersection and rarely more than two short city blocks from one another. Comparison shopping among the major downtown stores, when important purchases were involved, was the common practice since it required so little extra effort. The department store relied upon the trading stamp to counter this practice somewhat by reinforc-ing store loyalty among savers. The stamp issuer often found that having a redemption center on the premises of its downtown store was beneficial as a traffic builder. Along with the supermarket, the department store followed the population drift to the suburbs. However, unlike the situation with the supermarket, the distances between a department store and its competitors' branches reduced the intensity of the interstore rivalry that had made the trading stamp so valuable to the store in its downtown location. Furthermore, the department store's suburban competition came mainly from the rapidly expanding branches of the national chains such as Sears, Montgomery Ward, and J. C. Penney and from the new breed of regional discount department stores. Some of the major department stores upgraded their institutional image and concentrated their merchandising at the higher end of their product lines. Most of these dropped stamps before the stamp boom in supermarkets got under way. Others chose to compete with the newcomers directly on price promotions. Enough of these stores felt that trading stamps continued to give them an effective competitive advantage, and so stamp sales to department stores continued to advance into the 1960s. However, the increase in the number of department stores was far less than the increase in the number of supermarkets and service stations, and their importance as stamp issuers within the industry markedly declined. (See Table 14-5.)

Service Stations

Service stations became a factor in the trading stamp industry during the 1930s. Even then they faced the promotional problem that was to confront the supermarket in the 1950s. They sold a uniform product and offered similar services, and in all but the most rural settings there were a number of them from which the motorist could choose. No other type of retailer has found it more difficult to gain a competitive advantage. For the stamp saver, they were an important secondary source of stamps, after the department store and, later, the supermarket.

Service stations retained their volume of stamp usage in the late 1960s and early 1970s, after supermarket usage had started to decline. Then in 1973 the fuel pumps dried up and the stamp industry lost about 90 percent of its service-station business. Since then the major gasoline and petroleum marketers have discouraged all but the lowest-key promotional measures, for fear of government intervention and public disapproval. Also, the tremendous increases in the prices of gasoline and other auto maintenance products have made consumers extremely cost-conscious and have driven them to self-service islands, private-brand discounters, and cut-rate gas pumps at convenience stores.

Drugstores

Drugstores have traditionally ranked fourth in the industry as stamp users. Like service stations, they benefited from being a secondary source of stamps to the saver throughout the stamp boom and on into the early 1970s. However, with the decline in the availability of stamps at supermarkets and the almost complete curtailment of their use at service stations, many drugstores felt their franchises had become less valuable, and they dropped stamps. Interestingly, when a supermarket comes back into stamps, the nearby drugstore is usually the first to join it.

TABLE 14-5 Estimates of Trading Stamp Industry Sales Distribution by Retail Store Type, 1954–1981, Percent

Retail store type	Year					
	1954	1958	1968	1972	1977	1981
Food stores	43	63	66	59	85	91
Service stations	29	25	23	30	3	1
General merchandise stores	10	5	4	3	2	1
Drugstores	10	3	3	3	2	1
All other stores	8	4	4	5	8	6

SOURCE: The Sperry & Hutchinson Company.

Specialty Stores

Another category of retailers encompasses hundreds of different types of specialty stores, many of which have used trading stamps as their only promotional medium. Therefore, they were the most reluctant to give them up. Because of their diversity, they have been the most stable stamp-user group in retailing. But among them a newcomer has emerged, the truck stop. Refueling an over-the-road rig is not a petty transaction. It averages $160 and is worth 1⅓ books of stamps. When stamps were first offered, enough truckers jumped at the deal to provide a solid new base for trading stamps, which has grown significantly over the past decade.

TRADING STAMP COMPANY OPERATIONS

The industry has always been characterized as having a few "big" companies and many small ones. At the top of the boom in the 1960s there were 350 to 400 stamp companies doing business. In 1981, there were fewer than 100, and the five largest companies accounted for almost 70 percent of the sales volume. About thirty or so of the small companies are independently owned and confine their operations to several cities and towns within a region. The remainder are user-owned. Many of these are operated by a single drugstore or supermarket or a two- to three-store chain. The redemption premiums for these plans are often regular store merchandise.

Closely allied to trading stamp plans are cash-register tape plans, hundreds of which are in operation at any time. These are usually active in a store for limited time periods, typically from two to four months. They have the same advantage of continuity that stamps do, since the tapes must be accumulated by the saver, usually to a minimum sum representing $20 in purchases. Sometimes the exchange entitles the saver to as much as $1 or $2 in regular merchandise and thus represents a 5 to 10 percent discount on past purchases. More often tape plans offer redemption options much like those of stamp plans, except that the saver's choice of premiums is more limited and the redemptions are made right at the issuing store. Savers collect tapes for a week or two and then go back to the store for their gifts. The advantage of the tape plan to retailers is that it does not require a long-term commitment to the promotion. On the other hand, more store personnel time is required to administer the program. Also, the bother of collecting and tabulating the tapes "turns off" many companies.

The number of trading stamp plans swells during the early years of an upward phase of the stamp promotion cycle because of the ease of entry into the business. The stamp company collects for its service when it distributes its stamps, but it does not have to redeem them until the saver has accumulated enough books of stamps to exchange for a premium. This time lag averages six to nine months, but can range upward to several years. Thus, very little initial capital is required to put a stamp plan into operation. Long experience has shown that almost all the stamps that are issued will eventually be redeemed. All the major stamp companies have redemption rates of 90 percent or more. Prudent accounting procedure requires that a reserve similar to a sinking fund be established for the future redemption costs, and this fund or float can be profitably used as an additional source of income.

The decision to issue trading stamps represents a substantial long-term commitment on the part of the user. Where an important retailer is involved, success of the promotion from the outset is earnestly sought by the stamp company as well, since the drawing power of the trading stamp is the basic service that the stamp company offers. When a major contract is signed, it is newsworthy in trade circles, and early performance is monitored by the trade press. At the earliest part of the talking stage, and sometimes even before, the stamp company will often conduct a feasibility study at its own expense. Today, the initial contract is usually for one year, and the package includes an assortment of kickoff costs that are borne by the stamp company. Sequentially, these include training the user's lower-level management; installing in-store, window, and outdoor displays; sponsoring and preparing mass-media advertising; and, of course, dispensing equipment and delivering stamps, saver booklets, and premium catalogs to all issuing locations. During the kickoff stage, the stamp company will conduct an intensive drive to sign up noncompeting retailers in the trading area. Finally, redemption centers will be set up, staffed, and stocked with premium merchandise.

Merchandising and Distribution

It is primarily the trading stamp company's merchandising operation that enables it to pass on to the saver a value in premium goods that is significantly greater than the cost of the stamps to the user. In its specialized functions of purchasing and distribution, it has been able to achieve efficiencies that exceed those of the largest retailers. There are a number of reasons for this, the foremost of which is the nature of premium merchandise.

As a reward for their patronage, the stamp issuer gives loyal customers a "gift." Ideally, this is an item that many people want but often cannot afford. It provides comfort or convenience and is durable, giving it long remembrance value. Despite an array of more than 1500 items in a typical premium catalog, the merchandise lines do not include essential nondurables such as basic apparel. This eliminates problems having to do with style and size assortment, as well as problems associated with fashion trends and cycles. A further constraint on premium selection involves the value of items offered for redemption. Items must be valuable enough to warrant a trip to the redemption center, but not so expensive as to require excessive time to accumulate the necessary stamps. The ordinary store prices for the most popular items of redemption merchandise are in the $6 to $25 retail range. Housewares, portable appliances, jewelry, personal items, toys, and gift items are the kinds of merchandise that best meet all these requirements. Since the saver can choose only from among the offerings in the catalog, the premium buyer can select the strongest brands and buy in great quantity.

The trading stamp company is somewhat similar to the mail-order house from the viewpoint of the vendor. Supply of the item ordered must be ensured for the life of the catalog edition, but little or no further servicing is required after delivery dates have been established. Bulk shipments are scheduled to regional depots, and the stamp company's needs for advertising and promotional aids are nil. The financial strength of the stamp company eliminates the need to use the vendor's credit facilities. Since all these cost savings to the vendor are considered in negotiating contract prices, the stamp company's costs for premium merchandise are significantly lower than those of the largest conventional retailers.

Further economies are achieved in the distribution process. Premium merchandise is by nature lighter, more compact, and more uniform in its packaged dimensions than the assortment of items carried by general-merchandise stores. This permits an extremely high degree of efficiency in warehousing at the regional depot and in delivery to, and stock handling at, the redemption center. Computerized reordering and inventory control have now been refined to a point where they contribute close to optimum efficiency in these operations. Furthermore, the redemption center operates more like a commissary than a retail store. The saver-customer has usually preselected the merchandise, which can be chosen only from among the items shown in the catalog; thus there is no selling involved. In the past, clerks at the redemption center usually brought the goods to the customer from the stockroom. While some of the newer, larger centers have placed greater emphasis on self-service, there is still significantly less breakage, less wear and tear to display merchandise, and less opportunity for pilferage than in a retail store. Customer services and conveniences are fewer. Consumer credit facilities are not required. Delivery, gift wrapping, rest rooms, and lounges are not the rule. There are many fewer merchandise returns and exchanges. In summary, the redemption operation is much more stripped down than the conventional retail store, and thus productivity per employee and per square foot is much higher. While off-street parking is required, prime retail locations are not, so occupancy leases are negotiated on favorable terms. Finally, the redemption center can serve more households in a wider trading area with shorter business hours to further increase productivity and reduce utility and labor costs.

The stamp saver has the alternative of redeeming by mail order. A mail-order blank is printed on the back page of each saver book. The stamp company also maintains catalog order offices in lower-volume trading areas, where no premium merchandise is stocked. While only a small portion of trading stamp redemptions are handled by mail, the stamp companies' mail-order facilities have provided them with a means of diversification.

Diversification

To compensate for a lower utilization rate of their vast merchandising capacities after the peak in stamp usage in the late 1960s, stamp companies sought out other users. The major credit-card companies entered into long-term fulfillment contracts with them for their ongoing premium promotions. Shorter-term agreements include contracts with banks and other financial institutions to provide gift merchandise for their new-depositor drives. Some supermarkets use them as suppliers of cutlery, dishware, and books for their commodity continuity programs.

A major diversification for stamp companies has been the sponsorship of incentive programs to meet the diverse motivational needs of American business. Trading stamp awards are used in programs to encourage peak performance in a number of activities. They boost sales; reduce absenteeism; encourage suggestions; improve service, safety, and quality; and lower accident rates. Here, the gift certificate representing trading stamps in multiples of hundreds of stamps—100, 300, 500, 600, 1200 (one book), etc.—is the usual award. Awards for major sales contests are certificates of special imprint for larger numbers of books. Luxury-gift catalogs offer selections of higher-value merchandise for these programs. The contributions to operating revenues from these newer ventures have done much to enable the larger companies to maintain the basic redemption value of their trading stamps throughout the recent years of lower-level usage.

Scope of Operations

In addition to the estimated $570 million in current sales volume, the following figures make the scope of stamp company operations more readily comprehensible. In 1981 the industry issued some 340 billion stamp units along with 50 million premium catalogs and 130 million saver books to 20,000 retail stores. The industry employs some 6000 people and is distributing annually premium merchandise with a retail value of $680 million to 22 million stamp-saving households.

AVAILABILITY, SAVING, AND CONSUMER ATTITUDES

According to the Sperry & Hutchinson Company, which, since 1957, has sponsored consumer surveys measuring the extent of availability of trading stamps and consumers' saving habits and attitudes, only one out of four households currently saves trading stamps, but where they are available, better than six out of ten save. During the peak years of usage by retailers, stamps were available virtually everywhere, and eight to nine out of every ten households saved them. These peak levels prevailed from 1962 through 1968.

Consumer attitudes remained in a narrow range, from 72 to 78 percent favorable to stamps, until 1965. Then the trend turned downward to a low point of 61 percent favorable in 1968. During these years, important stamp users turned to discounting and promised lower prices instead of stamps. Furthermore, the trend toward significant increases in the prices of consumer goods, especially food, began in 1966 and has been with us ever since. By 1978, despite persistent inflation, consumer sentiment favoring stamps had returned to the 72 percent level, and where stamps are available, saving continues at a high rate. Also, more savers today say they would be disappointed if their supermarkets stopped issuing them than in 1968. (See Table 14-7.)

TABLE 14-6 Availability, Saving, and Consumer Attitudes toward Trading Stamps

	Percent of households				
	1957	1962	1968	1978	1980
Behavior					
Currently save stamps	64	84	78	35	27
Stamps available where I shop	87	97	95	46	40
Saving based on availability	74	87	82	76	62
Attitudes*					
Favorable (+1 to +5)	78	72	61	72	70
Unfavorable (−1 to −5)	14	22	33	28	30
Don't know	8	6	6	—	—
Total	100	100	100	100	100
Most favorable (+4 and +5)	47	39	34	40	39
Most unfavorable (−4 and −5)	8	13	24	16	19
Ratio	5.9	3.0	1.5	2.5	2.1

*Based on responses to the question, "On this card is a scale running from +5, meaning something you like very much, to −5, meaning something you dislike very much. Please pick the one which best describes how you feel about trading stamps."
SOURCES: Benson & Benson, Inc., Princeton, N.J.; Opinion Research Corporation, Princeton, N.J.

TABLE 14-7 Consumer Attitudes toward Trading Stamps*

	Percent responding	
	1968	1980
Very disappointed	33	28
Somewhat disappointed	25	43
Somewhat pleased	7	4
Very pleased	11	6
Don't know	24	19
	100	100

* Based on responses to the question, "If your food store stopped giving stamps, how would you feel?"
SOURCES: Benson & Benson, Inc., Princeton, N.J.; Opinion Research Corporation, Princeton, N.J.

The principal reasons for consumers' consistently favorable attitudes toward, and participation in, trading stamp plans appear to be (1) the value, both intrinsic and personal, that they place upon the premium and (2) the self-esteem and personal gratification derived from the saving and redemption process.

To some, the thought of saving stamps for a new $15.95 steam iron might seem trivial, but to many more, it is a practical means of replacing an item that is now beyond the limits of the household budget. Current inflation rates, combined with the tax structure, have reduced the standard of living of many people in their most productive years, and for those on fixed incomes the situation has been much worse. Even in better times people have sought out painless ways to save. Series E savings bonds, which have a payroll withhold-

TABLE 14-8 Consumer Responses to Statements Concerning Trading Stamps, 1980 Survey

Statement	Percent agreeing	Percent disagreeing	Percent with no opinion
"Stamps are a really good way to get extras you want."	66	28	6
"In general, trading stamps benefit consumers."	58	32	11
"I really like to save trading stamps."	47	43	10

SOURCE: Opinion Research Corporation, Princeton, N.J.

ing feature, have maintained their popularity, despite their inferior yields. For many years, Christmas clubs paying no interest were a boon to banks.

The people who have the most favorable attitudes toward stamps are apparently those with the least amounts of discretionary income. As Table 14-9 shows, these are people under age 45, those with incomes below $15,000, blue-collar workers, the less well educated, and those with larger families.

While unfavorable attitudes toward stamps have dropped back from their 1968 highs, they are still at twice the level they were in 1957. The predominant reason for the unfavorable attitudes is the belief that stamps cause higher prices. Other reasons are the effort and inconvenience involved in pasting the stamps into the books and the necessity of making a trip to the redemption center.[6]

The perceived net value of the trade-off between the reward and the effort required to attain it appears to be the basis on which consumers select their preferences from among the inducements offered to them in sales promo-

TABLE 14-9 Variance in Attitudes toward Trading Stamps by Demographic Sector, 1978*

	Index
Sex	
Male	39
Female	115
Age	
Under age 45	110
45 and older	87
Family income	
Under $15,000	120
$15,000 and over	79
Occupational level (male head)	
Professional and managerial	64
Clerical and sales	96
Skilled and semiskilled	119
Service and labor	119
Education	
Grammar school	119
High school	108
College	58
Size of household	
One to two persons	90
Three to four persons	104
Five or more	116

* Index: 72 percent favorable attitude toward trading stamps by all respondents = 100.

SOURCE: Opinion Research Corporation, Princeton, N.J.

tions. Of the six promotional practices used most frequently by retailers to induce greater patronage, reduced price specials are the most preferred by consumers.[7] Consumers cite as benefits the immediate saving, the chance to stock up, and the fact that they have to make only minor, occasional compromises in terms of brand or quality. Consumers' second preference is for cents-off coupons. Here again, the immediate saving is the benefit, but at higher perceived costs. The consumer misplaces the coupons, forgets to take them to the store, and considers them a bother and a nuisance. Trading stamps are the third choice; their pros and cons from the consumers' point of view have been discussed. Sweepstakes rank a poor fourth in consumer preference. The lure of the big prize is diluted by the low probability of winning. Also, one in five consumers thinks that sweepstakes are dishonest or rigged. Commodity continuity programs rank fifth. While they are considered to offer good value and have an installment-payment characteristic, the consumer often is unable to complete the set or complains that it takes too long to do so. Contests are rated the lowest. They are perceived as having all the unfavorable characteristics of games and sweepstakes and as requiring considerable time and effort besides.

THE ISSUES OF CONTROVERSY

Convincing attestations as to the ineffectiveness of trading stamps are replete in the eloquent and often vituperative prose emanating from the nonstamp competition. George Meredith unearthed the following from a pamphlet entitled *Anti-Stamper—Story of the Trading Stamp Swindle*, published by the Anti-Stamper Association in New York in 1904: "The Trading Stamp system is the meanest, most invidious and by all odds the most contemptible fraud ever perpetrated upon honest trade."[8]

Such indignation was not completely unjustified in the early days of trading stamps. The ease of entry and the absence of regulation prompted some unscrupulous operators to sell stamps with no intention of redeeming them. More common was the low-valued and shoddy merchandise that was sometimes offered as premiums.

Unfair Competition

Even in the early days of stamp usage, most of the protests were voiced by merchant groups who felt that the use of trading stamps constituted unfair competition. Under the general charge of "unfair competition" commercial opponents of trading stamps have over the years subjected the industry to frequent legal and legislative attacks. These have usually taken the form of statutes specifically prohibiting stamps, limiting their use with restrictive regulation, or discouraging their use with prohibitive or discretionary taxation. Where enacted, these measures have usually been stricken down in the courts as excessive use of police power or as violations of equal-protection and due-process clauses in the federal and state constitutions.

Trading stamps may at present be issued legally by retailers throughout the United States. In Kansas, however, they can be redeemed only by the stores issuing them for cash or regular store merchandise. Wisconsin and Wyoming have somewhat similar statutes. The state of Washington imposes a prohibitive license tax on issuance of stamps and redemption of merchandise, which, in effect, restricts issuers to cash redemptions. A number of states require that each trading stamp company disclose basic information about its operation and financial condition and that it provide a bond or other evidence of financial stability to ensure redemptions.

Economic Issues

Of greater concern to the marketer are the economic issues: Must trading stamps increase prices, and who bears the cost of stamps? Consumers have always been subjected to a heavy barrage of "stamps raise prices" messages from the nonstamp competition and also from stores that drop stamps and promise lower prices instead.

There have been no authentic research findings to support the claim that stamps raise prices. In a comprehensive analysis of trading stamps and prices, Albert Haring and Wallace Yoder stated, "The charge that adoption of stamps will raise the level of prices in a store or even in a community appears to be completely unsubstantiated."[9] The U.S. Department of Agriculture, in a three-year study of prices in stamp and nonstamp food stores in twenty-one cities, did find a 0.6 percent difference favoring nonstamp stores, but reasoned that this small difference may have been caused, at least in part, by the fact that nonstamp stores lower food prices to compete with stamp stores. The study also concluded that consumers who save and redeem stamps can more than recoup any difference between prices in stamp versus nonstamp stores in the value of the premiums.[10]

So who must bear the merchant's cost of using trading stamps? The cost of doing business—be it games, sweepstakes, media advertising, wages, salaries, or shoplifting—must be covered in the gross margin. If trading stamps or any other promotional practice will increase sales volume sufficiently, the consumer pays for the promotion, but the promotion cost is offset by the greater store productivity.

WHO SHOULD USE TRADING STAMPS?

Trading stamps are a way of gaining distinctiveness for a marketer when basic offers among competitors are quite similar in the eyes of customers and when there is excess capacity for the marketer. The differentiating power of the trading stamp lies in the exclusive franchise, which restricts the use of a given stamp brand to only one issuer in a particular line of trade within a defined trading area. From here the task is to narrow down the prospective users to those for whom stamps are most effective and profitable.

Among retailers with similar product, service, and price offers, stamps have worked best for those whose customer purchase cycles are frequent—for example, supermarkets, service stations, drugstores, and car rental agencies serving regular business travelers. Frequent customer buying speeds up stamp-saving rewards and reinforces the stamp-saving habit. But in communities with a high incidence of stamp use among retailers of the types listed above (and therefore a high percentage of stamp savers in the total population), stamps have also worked well for less frequently visited retailers who are weakly differentiated. Successful users have included bowling alleys, dry cleaners, jewelry stores, and garden centers.

Other important factors in how well a retailer may do with a stamp promotion are discussed below in the context of a supermarket operator's decision and are summarized in Table 14-10.

The Supermarket Case: Criteria for Self-Appraisal

We shall look in depth at supermarkets, for they are the major stamp issuers by virtue of their similarity in the eyes of consumers and the frequency of customer shopping trips. It has been observed that a typical suburban shopper has four or five supermarkets within easy reach by car. Even in the central cities, there are usually two or three within walking distance. Many shoppers favor one market and do most of their grocery shopping there, but many more express little preference for one of several supermarkets that are within easy reach. Where this is the case, it is the supermarket management's task to capture the major weekly shopping trip by offering the most exciting promotion.

Despite the fact that trading stamps have been the most effective promotional device ever used by many supermarkets, they are not the most suitable promotion for all supermarkets. The go–no-go decision is especially critical since supermarkets' gross margins and net profit ratios are, on the average, lower than those of most other retail stores. Typically, supermarkets have to achieve a 15 to 20 percent increase in sales to absorb the 2 percent cost of the stamp program before operating profits will improve.

The element of risk in making a decision about whether to use stamps can be greatly reduced by objectively appraising the store's external and internal operating environments and matching these to the capabilities and limitations of a trading stamp program. In appraising the external environment, one must take into account the store's present share of patronage within its own trading

TABLE 14-10   Considerations for Retailers Deciding Whether to Use Trading Stamps

Favorable	Unfavorable
Retailer differs little from direct competitors in terms of product, price, or service offer, but may have moderate location handicap.	Retailer has basic problems with what is offered—inferior products, inferior service, or price level higher than justified on basis of products or services provided. Or, retailer's product, price, or service offer is distinctive in the eyes of most shoppers—for example, exclusive specialty stores or stores distinctive by virtue of price discounting.
Retailer can absorb extra sales with little extra operating cost.	Retailer is operating near capacity—extra sales would require more or less proportionate extra cost.
Retailer does not dominate the trading area—enjoys less than 30% share among customer targets within reach of the establishment. Therefore, can experience substantial sales gain by diverting only a little of the competitors' business.	Retailer dominates the trading area and therefore has limited growing room.
Retailer's strategy emphasizes shopper pleasures—decor, friendliness, and other shopper "extras."	Retailer predominantly emphasizes price.
Retailer has many fewer stores than competitors and is therefore at a cost handicap compared with competitors in terms of advertising expenditures in mass media.	Retailer has stores available to virtually all consumers reached by mass media and therefore has a competitive advantage in efficient use of advertising.
Prospective customers are primarily low- and middle-income people for whom stamp extras are significant rewards.	Prospective customers are primarily high-income people for whom stamp extras are trivial.
Customer targets are enjoying increasing affluence and thus tend to be "gain-oriented" in their buying.	Customer targets are economically squeezed, are acutely anxious about their jobs or inflation, and thus tend to be predominantly "price-oriented" in their buying.

area (among households within reach) and its extent of coverage in the entire retail trading area as defined by the local advertising media. The store's internal operating environment is the major determinant of its type of patronage. This is the patronage mix consisting of those who do most of their shopping at the store, those who do some but not most of their shopping there, and the nonpatrons who do not shop there at all. The mix is the result of the store's image, in terms of its prices and the overall quality of its basic operation, in the eyes of its present customers and of noncustomers in its area of dominance. These criteria for self-appraisal should be examined one by one.

Present Share of the Market. The first criterion is the store's present share of the market among households within reach. If, for example, the store commands a 50 percent market share and if stamps bring in another 4 percentage points from competitors, the sales increase is 8 percent (4/50). However, if the store has only a 20 percent market share and gains 4 percentage points, the sales increase is 20 percent (4/20). Thus, the lower the original market share, the greater the gain from stamps.

Coverage of the Retail Trading Area. The second criterion is the extent of the store's coverage of the retail trading area as defined by the

TABLE 14-11 Effect of Sales Increases from Stamp Use on Supermarket Operating Performance with No Change in Gross Margin Ratio

	Before stamps		Change after stamp use		
	Percent of sales	Weekly sales	10 percent increase	20 percent increase	25 percent increase
Weekly sales	100	$100,000	$110,000	$120,000	$125,000
Cost of goods sold	78	78,000	85,800	93,600	97,500
Gross margin	22	22,000	24,200	26,400	27,500
Operating expense	20	20,000	21,000*	22,000*	22,500*
Stamp cost	2	0	2,200	2,400	2,500
Pretax profit	2	2,000	1,000	2,000	2,500
Change in profit			−1,000	0†	+500

* Operating expenses on incremental sales are assumed to increase at half the rate of increase in sales; e.g., if sales increase by 20 percent, operating expense increases by 10 percent. The division between fixed and variable expenses will vary by supermarket, but our implied estimate of a 10 percent variable expense ratio and a 12 percent contribution to overhead and profit on incremental sales is conservative. Many operators estimate 14 percent or higher.

† Break-even point.

SOURCE: Cornell University annual studies of supermarket performance (rounded).

advertising media. The less adequate the coverage, the greater the waste of promotional dollars spent on media advertising. One of trading stamps' greatest strengths is in reducing a store's dependence on media advertising when this is an element of competitive disadvantage.

Potential of Stamps to Improve the Patronage Mix. The third and most important criterion for self-appraisal is the degree to which trading stamps can improve the store's patronage mix. Once again, the objective of a trading stamp promotion is to capture, again and again, the major shopping trip of the customer who rates a store and its strongest competitors equally well. The continuity feature of the promotion stresses value that cannot be matched by the competition because of the exclusivity of the stamp contract. The customer must rate the store equally well on overall basics (products, services, price); in other words, on total value. The store need not be perceived as offering lower prices than its competitors (whether this is actually the case or not), but it does need a total value image that is as strong as its major competitors' to attract extra patronage with stamps. No stamp plan works as a crutch to offset inferiority in terms of the overall basics.

Only the most avid savers will accept compromises in the quality of the store's basic operation, whether in the form of discourtesy from the personnel, lack of cleanliness, inferior quality of the perishables, or any combination of shortcomings that downgrade the store's overall image. Symptoms of inferiority can be ascertained during an average transaction that is significantly unsatisfactory. If the meat, produce, or dairy department is below par in terms of share of total store volume, it is probably selling products of inferior quality. After all, there is little a store can do to downgrade its nonfood items and dry groceries except not to restock the shelves. Par values for store operations are reported periodically in the trade publications. It should be noted here that a store need not be outright superior to its competition to benefit from the pulling power of trading stamps. The objective of the promotion is to get more of those patronage dollars that are "on the fence" between a store and its competition.

If the prospective user can meet the standards outlined above, trading stamps can convert a significant number of "sometime" shoppers into "most-of-the-time" shoppers and can bring some new shoppers into the store. More important, the store's current gross margin is held down by the present proportion of those who do only some of their shopping there. Among this group are the bargain hunters who systematically hunt for the weekly price specials. Trading stamps strongly induce the customer to shop the whole store since the reward is directly related to the total on the tape. Thus, more of the higher-margin merchandise winds up in the shopping bag. It is not uncommon for a successful trading stamp program to increase the user's gross margin by 1 percentage point, if the prestamp margin was below par. In effect, this consideration reduces the risk associated with the decision concerning whether to use stamps. An additional percentage point in gross margin goes directly into net profit and can bring about a profit improvement with an 8 to 10 percent increase in sales, as shown in Table 14-12.

The potential retail user must be mindful of the demographic composition of the trading area. It has been shown that stamps are favored most where the premiums have the strongest meaning, and that is among the lower-middle- and middle-income population.

BENEFITS AND DRAWBACKS OF STAMP PLANS

Ancillary Benefits

The stamp user can maximize the effectiveness of the program by judiciously investing a portion of the store's promotional budget in bonus stamps. Offering bonus stamps on the slowest days (usually Monday, Tuesday, and Wednesday) can do much to even out the weekly traffic flow and cut down on

TABLE 14-12 Effect of Sales Increases from Stamp Use on Supermarket Operating Performance with 1 Percent Increase in Gross Margin Ratio

	Before stamps		Change after stamp use		
	Percent of sales	Weekly sales	10 percent increase	20 percent increase	25 percent increase
Weekly sales	100	$100,000	$110,000	$120,000	$125,000
Cost of goods sold	78	78,000	85,800	93,600	97,500
Gross margin	22	22,000	24,200	26,400	27,500
Operating expense	20	20,000	21,000*	22,000*	22,500*
Stamp cost	2	0	2,200	2,400	2,500
Pretax profit	2	2,000	1,000	2,000	2,500
Change in profit			−1,000	0†	+500
Increase in gross margin of 1%			1,100	1,200	1,250
Increase in profit	2	2,000	2,100	3,200	3,750
Change in profit			+100	+1,200	+1,750

* Operating expenses on incremental sales are assumed to increase at half the rate of increase in sales; e.g., if sales increase by 20 percent, operating expense increases by 10 percent. The division between fixed and variable expenses will vary by supermarket, but our implied estimate of a 10 percent variable expense ratio and a 12 percent contribution to overhead and profit on incremental sales is conservative. Many operators estimate 14 percent or higher.

† Break-even point.

SOURCE: Cornell University annual studies of supermarket performance (rounded).

the weekend crush. Bonus stamps reduce the markdown cost on slow-moving merchandise because it takes fewer of them to move the goods than a markdown equivalent in cash.

Similarly, selective merchandising of weekly price specials with bonus stamps requires a smaller markdown than a cash equivalent. Furthermore, it eliminates the expense of physically marking the merchandise down and later marking it back up to the regular price at the end of a sale. Less apparent but most worthy of consideration is the conservation of the management's time and effort spent in planning, preparing, and trying to outguess the competition on weekly price specials. The effectiveness of competitors' price specials is reduced as more and more stamp-saving customers shop the whole store. Thus, the management can devote more of its time and effort to further improvements in the store's institutional image and to its internal operation.

Major Drawbacks

In addition to the basic cost of a stamp program, most potential stamp users are concerned chiefly about (1) the additional promotional cost of launching the program, (2) the relatively long-term commitment, (3) the cost of getting out of the program, and (4) the loss of the current patronage of "stamp haters." None of these concerns can be dismissed as unimportant. However, they become much more significant toward the end of the nonprice phase of the retail competition cycle than at the beginning of it. By then, the effectiveness of a trading stamp promotion has been reduced by widespread imitation.

The additional promotional cost of entry is of relatively short duration and is normally absorbed by the gains achieved in the first year of successful operation. The long-term commitment, by contrast, is ordinarily for one year, but the real cost of getting out depends upon the proportion of avid stamp savers that the user has accumulated over the course of the promotion. The user may have to offer a dramatic new benefit in lieu of stamps to keep total sales from falling.

Some customers consider trading stamps an imposition. Table 14-6, presented earlier in this chapter, shows the ratio between most favorable and most unfavorable attitudes to be 2.1 to 1.0. But the pragmatic issue for the potential stamp user is: How will the stamp-hostile shopper react when offered stamps? Sperry & Hutchinson gave particular attention to this issue in its 1978 consumer survey. Only 2 percent of the respondents indicated that they would go out of their way to *avoid* stores that offered stamps, as shown in Table 14-13. Taking this statistic at face value, but making allowances for sampling error and demographic variance for any particular clientele, it would seem reasonable to expect the loss of patronage from stamp haters to range from 1 to 5 percent. Reviewing Table 14-13, it would appear that at the outset, trading stamps will generate significantly more sales volume from about 31 percent of households within reach (statements 1 and 2), about the same volume of sales from about 63 percent (statements 3, 4, 5, and 8), and some reduction in sales from 6 percent (statements 6 and 7).

Thus, a supermarket that takes on stamps is likely both to divert some patronage from competitors and to lose some patronage to competitors. The following example illustrates the process:

Present sales per week: $100,000 (20 percent of market served)
Competitors' patronage within reach of stamp adopter: 400,000
Diversion from competitors by stamp promotion: 20,000 (+5 percent)
Loss of present patronage to competitors: 5000 (−5 percent)
Net gain in sales from stamps: 15,000 (+15 percent)

SUMMARY AND CONCLUSION

Trading stamps came upon the retailing scene as a deferred discount to customers. The root of their popularity lies in the fact that they represent a painless way to save for discretionary extras. They work by reinforcing

TABLE 14-13 Summation of Consumer Attitudes toward Trading Stamps, 1978

Statement	Percent agreeing
"I think trading stamps are great, and I wish every store offered them."	16
"I am highly in favor of trading stamps, and I prefer shopping at stores which offer them."	15
"Trading stamps are OK, and I take them when they are offered to me."	29
"I don't care one way or the other about trading stamps. It makes no difference to me whether stores offer them."	24
"I am not in favor of trading stamps and would prefer that stores not offer them."	9
"I dislike trading stamps, but I will still trade at stores which offer them."	4
"I hate trading stamps so much that I would go out of my way to avoid stores that offer them."	2
No opinion	1
Total	100

SOURCE: Opinion Research Corporation, Princeton, N.J.

customer loyalty. Furthermore, the exclusivity of the stamp franchise gives the user a significant long-term competitive advantage that is difficult to imitate. Generally in the past, stamp use has expanded during eras of "good feeling." Periods of national peace, economic growth, full employment, and improvement in living standards engender widespread goodwill and optimism among merchants and consumers alike. Nonprice competition thrives in such times, and premiums are viewed as additional comforts of life. By contrast, stamp use has held (at best) or contracted in periods of consumer and retailer "squeeze" and pessimism.

Trading stamps will probably come into broader usage again as the current nonprice phase of the retailing competition cycle evolves, but the greater diversity of lifestyles among consumers and the higher degree of specialization among merchants seeking to meet their demands may mean more selectivity in future promotional practices. The challenge for the trading stamp industry is to seek out those potential users for whom the stamp service is most productive. Premiums, along with all other promotional practices, are in the public interest only when they generate economic gains for both marketers and the consumers whom they wish to induce to buy their products. In the future the motivating power of trading stamps may justify their use outside the traditional areas of retailing and sales incentives. These would include areas where it is in the public interest to induce conservation and civic responsibility.

ENDNOTES

1. *Keeping in Touch*, Edward Schuster Company, Milwaukee, Wis., 1922.
2. Harvey L. Vredenburg, *Trading Stamps*, Indiana University School of Business, Bureau of Business Research Report no. 21, Bloomington, 1956, p. 14.
3. Harold W. Fox, *The Economics of Trading Stamps*, Public Affairs Press, Washington, 1968, p. 59.
4. Sumner H. Slichter, *Alexander Hamilton Institute Report on Coupons, Trading Stamps and Premium Systems*, Alexander Hamilton Institute, New York, 1916, p. 2.
5. Steve Weinstein, "Games, Stamps, Coupons Alternate in Endless Cycle," *Supermarket News*, Oct. 24, 1977, sec. 2, pp. 8–10.
6. *Consumer Attitudes toward Sales Incentives*, Ladies' Home Journal, August 1977, p. 60.
7. Ibid., p. 4.
8. George Meredith, *Effective Merchandising with Premiums*, McGraw-Hill Book Company, New York, 1962, p. 145.
9. Albert Haring and Wallace O. Yoder, *Trading Stamp Practice and Pricing Policy*, Indiana University School of Business, Bureau of Business Research Report no. 27, Bloomington, 1958, p. 225.
10. U.S. Department of Agriculture, *Trading Stamps and Their Impact on Food Prices*, Marketing Research Report no. 295, December 1958, p. iv.

15 Promotional Impact through Specialty Advertising

RICHARD G. EBEL

Vice President, Specialty Advertising Association International

A company in Highland Park, Michigan, was relocating and wanted clients to know about it—the sort of thing that happens every day, and who pays attention for long? In this case, the firm was a specialty advertising distributor, and its business was to make people sit up and take notice. Instead of mailing a traditional announcement that would possibly be noted and probably discarded, the distributor mailed to 500 clients a lighted 2- by 2-inch slide viewer containing a color slide of the new building with the address printed underneath.

"We wanted to utilize what the firm was known for—packaging, distribution, and promotion—and we wanted to give something of value that would be remembered," explained an account executive.

In essence, he was describing the function of specialty advertising.

The function of the medium is often a mystery to many marketers, even those who may be using it regularly. The words of one marketing educator, written in 1973, still hold true:

> The use of specialty advertising has been increasing at a rate faster than most segments of the promotional mix. Even so, the industry's fragmented structure, its lack of public identity, misunderstanding about the role of specialty advertising, its lack of acceptance as an important part of the total promotion mix by professional advertising people, failure to realize the full influence it can play in personal selling activities, and the inadequate significance attached to it by marketing practitioners, all suggest that specialty advertising is neither fully understood nor appreciated. In fact, even an acceptable definition of the term "specialty" has been difficult to achieve among industry members.[1]

If an agreement on terminology is difficult for practitioners, one can imagine why persons outside the industry may be confused.

To keep things simple, let us just say that specialty advertising is a medium of advertising and sales promotion that employs advertising specialties to help accomplish marketing objectives. Advertising specialties have three principal characteristics: (1) They are *useful* articles of merchandise; (2) they are *imprinted* with an advertiser's name, logo, or message; and (3) unlike premiums (with which they are often confused), they are *given away* to the target audience. One doesn't have to buy anything or do anything to earn them.

This last point deserves elaboration, because the absence of obligation on the part of the recipient is really what distinguishes advertising specialties from premiums. This fact is not always recognized, undoubtedly because advertisers often find it convenient to use the same article of merchandise as either a specialty or a premium, depending on which better suits their purpose and budget.

So, one might think of advertising specialties as advertising gifts. However, business and executive gifts are in a separate category. They differ from other advertising specialties in that they often bear no advertiser's imprint. The Internal Revenue Service defines them even more narrowly by placing a limit (presently $25, but inflation makes this subject to change) on what a donor may deduct as a business expense.

On one thing there is no limitation. That is the number and types of firms and entities that use specialty advertising. Banks and financial institutions are among the biggest and best-known users, but the medium is employed by industrial firms of all kinds, retailers of all sizes, politicians campaigning for public office, labor unions seeking to build membership or advance a cause, and churches trying to fill pews. In short, anyone who has a promotional message to transmit to a specific audience will find specialty advertising— when implemented properly—to be an effective means of doing so. How specialty advertising accomplishes this goal will be described later.

One of the ironies of contemporary marketing is that specialty advertising is often relegated to the "miscellaneous" section of corporate advertising budgets. Perhaps this is because the significance of these advertising-imprinted articles of merchandise has not yet sufficiently impinged upon the consciousness of marketing people. Yet the volume of billings for this medium and its accelerated growth rate tell another story. In 1972, specialty advertising billings accounted for a little over $1 billion of the $23 billion in billings for all media. Ten years later, when total media billings reached $57 billion, the volume for specialty advertising nearly quadrupled.

Comparing specialty advertising sales volume with that of other media can be misleading, however. Specialties are often used for situations unrelated to marketing. As a Specialty Advertising Association International publication points out:

> Many companies use specialties internally to promote employee safety, to obtain money-saving suggestions, or to motivate and recognize performance. Indeed, awards programs, involving trophies, plaques and other mementoes of recognition, are important elements of many [specialty advertising] distributors' businesses.[2]

ORIGINS OF THE SPECIES

No one knows for sure when specialty advertising came into being. Some trace its origins back to the Middle Ages, when artisans who made armor for knights distributed suitably inscribed pegs upon which their martial customers could hang shields, broadswords, and poleaxes. One can imagine the slogan possibilities: "Lancelot trusts his life to Alcuin Chain Mail."

In the United States, politicians were among the earliest users of specialty advertising. William Henry Harrison catapulted from hero of the Indian wars to occupant of the White House in 1840 with the help of buttons and badges imprinted with the slogan "Tippecanoe and Tyler Too." The idea caught on and has been perpetuated. More than 100 million buttons were distributed by candidates in the 1980 presidential election.

In 1845, an insurance salesman in Auburn, New York, was having trouble persuading merchants to display his business announcements in their shops. When he attached a calendar to his signs, he experienced a much better reception, and thus is credited with coming up with one of the earliest genuine advertising specialties outside the political arena:

> This salesman, whose identity has been lost, unwittingly capitalized on an axiom which is basic to the specialty advertising industry: Give the recipient a sign (representing your ad or imprint) and something of value (the calendar), and you obtain exposure of your message throughout the entire course of the year represented on the calendar and perhaps even beyond.[3]

Coshocton, Ohio, is generally recognized as the cradle of the industry, and even today it remains an important center of specialty advertising. In 1879, after witnessing a schoolboy drop his books in the mud, Coshocton newspaper publisher Jasper F. Meek came up with a practical item in the form of a schoolbook bag. He ensured a sponsored distribution by having it imprinted, "Buy Cantwell Shoes." So successful was the response that he gave up the newspaper business to start the first specialty advertising firm, which became the Tuscarora Advertising Company after he merged with a competitor, H. D. Beach.

The first advertising specialties, then, were really developed to solve problems as well as to meet promotional needs. In that respect, nothing has changed very much today.

ANATOMY OF THE INDUSTRY

The number of articles of merchandise used as advertising specialties is estimated at between 15,000 and 20,000. A few of these are shown in Figure 15-1. Production of most of these items is concentrated in some 800 to 1000 firms in the United States and Canada. These companies, known as *suppliers*, range in size from very small, family-owned operations to corporate giants whose names and products are household words. Each company usually specializes in products made of a specific material: paper, metal, plastics, vinyl, wood, fabric, glassware, or clay. Although many suppliers manufacture the products, a large number of these firms are primarily assemblers. Suppliers also do the imprinting of the advertiser's name and message. This is done by a variety of printing and engraving processes such as letterpress, hot stamping, silk screen, photoetching, and laser engraving.

Suppliers generally have no communication with advertisers other than

FIGURE 15-1. Some of the thousands of different articles circulated as advertising specialties.

what is involved in shipping the specialties, which are ordered through specialty advertising distributors. Independent businessmen and business-women, these distributors (often referred to as *counselors* and sometimes as *jobbers*) run businesses of all sizes—from small, family enterprises to firms employing hundreds of salespeople and operating in many states. There are approximately 4500 distributor firms in the United States and Canada. Equipped with catalogs and samples offered by many suppliers, distributors and their salespeople serve advertisers in two primary ways: They recommend and secure the appropriate specialty advertising articles for the advertisers, and they design the campaigns which employ the specialties.

This emphasis on campaign development is, in most instances, as important as product procurement; as Herpel suggests:

> Specialty advertising is concerned with ideas, not merely goods. The advertising specialty itself can only transmit and apply the message of the campaign; it cannot constitute the promotion in and of itself. Just as in any other applications of advertising media, the optimum use of the specialty advertising medium requires a high level of originality, ingenuity, and resourcefulness. A top specialty advertising counselor must be the same kind of creative and dynamic formulator of ideas as the successful advertising agency account executive.[4]

Distributors and advertising agencies have much in common. As one distributor explains:

> There are a lot of correlations between the ad agency and the specialty advertising distributor. What we really have to sell is our talents. Now, the agencies have creative talent to sell, and they book and place media. We have creative talent to sell and we book and place products as media. So there is a great deal of similarity.[5]

There are a lot of differences, too. In addition to the fact that distributors confine their interests to specialty advertising, premiums, sales promotion, and perhaps direct mail, their operations tend to be far less compartmentalized than those of ad agencies. Distributors' account executives, or salespersons, are "jacks-of-many-trades," securing and placing orders, writing their own copy, perhaps doing their own client and audience research, and sometimes even preparing their own rough art. If this multifunctioned method of operation has its shortcomings, it at least has the advantage that the right hand knows what the *right* hand is doing.

One other industry component deserves attention. This is the direct selling house. Although few in number, direct selling houses are among the largest firms in the industry. Most originated as calendar manufacturers, but their product lines today include scores of other articles. Unlike other suppliers, the direct selling house maintains its own national sales force, which is likely to consist of several hundred persons. To provide these salespeople with a competitive portfolio of specialties, direct selling houses often augment their lines by buying products from suppliers.

CHARACTERISTICS OF THE MEDIUM

Any discussion of the merits of using specialty advertising should commence with the understanding that specialty advertising is primarily a *targeted* medium, not a member of the mass-media fraternity. Although used successfully in national consumer marketing, the medium produces a satisfactory cost per impression only when market segmentation has been developed. Indiscriminate distribution of specialties in a saturation campaign has a way of overreaching promotional budgets and negates one of the advantages of using the medium: the ability to direct a communication to a pinpointed audience. Just as in direct mail, advertisers can aim specialty advertising to as narrowly defined an audience as they wish. Budgets do not have to absorb the circulation waste that occurs when a message goes to nonprospects.

Inasmuch as the target audience is known—and is usually of limited size—advertisers in many instances find it practical to personalize the specialties they give by imprinting on them the names of the recipients. Such personalizations greatly enhance the appeal of the specialty and increase recipients' appreciation of the donor. At a time when marketing is consumed by numbers, the ability to recognize buying prospects as something other than impersonal ciphers is definitely an advantage worth looking into.

Because specialty advertising tends to complement direct mail, which also shares the targetability characteristic, the latter is often used as the vehicle to distribute the specialties. For that matter, specialty advertising is often used in conjunction with many other forms of advertising, so it has the versatility of application to single-element strategy or to a multiple-weapon offensive.

Although there are any number of considerations which come into play when advertisers make their media choices, there are two things they invariably will strive for. They will want to capture attention and try to hold onto it. All media, given the right creative engineering, have the ability to make a dramatic impression. Prolonging it is quite another story.

Multiple insertion is the traditional method of message extension, additional billing coming with each additional space and time purchase. A strong argument for specialty advertising is that it offers a lot of mileage without running up the meter.

What advertisers would not be elated to have their advertising signs carried around continuously by the people they want to sell to? Some contend that an advertising specialty is no more than an advertising sign—albeit a portable one.

"All we are doing," remarks Fred O. Coble, past board chairman of Specialty Advertising Association International, "is putting signs in front of people where they work, where they live, where they play, where they travel. It adds up to the fact that we are first, last and always in the sign business."[6]

The key here is that these advertising "signs" are useful, and therefore recipients tend to hang onto them. They rely on a wall calendar to tell them the date, and each reference to the calendar is a concomitant exposure to the advertiser's message on it, a message that in this case gets repetitive exposure for twelve months. Although the intensity of discernment may vary, the same principle applies to the advertisement on the key chain each time the car ignition is switched on and to the message on every type of ad specialty. Even though virtually impossible to compute, the cost per impression must be minuscule.

While advertisers are seeking long-lasting exposure, they know they must operate within the confines of their budgets. Often their budget limitations are such that certain media are beyond their reach. Not so with specialty advertising. With specialty products priced from a few cents to several dollars apiece, advertisers have, in this enormous range of selection, what amounts to thousands of options.

People involved in specialty advertising are fond of characterizing their medium as the one form of advertising that says "thank you." It is a goodwill medium that expresses appreciation for patronage, but it also induces prospective customers to think highly of the sponsor. Studies have indicated that persons who have received specialties from one firm and not another prefer to do business with the former, other things being equal. The psychology of this has been examined only superficially. The reason for the preference is not clear, and it is hoped that further research can establish something more substantive than the prevailing speculation that "people just like receiving gifts."

Physical retention of the advertising product ensures a memory and reinforcing role for specialty advertising. Buyers' attitudes and behavior predispositions are often temporary; unless reinforced, they're subject to change. Herpel suggests that the "reinforcing role of specialty advertising could be its biggest role in the promotional mix."[7]

Against this array of positive characteristics of the medium must be noted some limitations. One has to do with the space available for printing a message. Obviously, a key chain, cigarette lighter, or letter opener, for example, does not provide enough space for much more than an advertiser's name, logo, address, and slogan. These would not be the right items to tout the benefits and describe the operation of a centrifugal compressor.

Reasonably astute specialty advertising distributors can circumvent this obstacle in one of two ways. They can distribute the specialty with companion literature that tells the whole story, or they can use the visual characteristics of the specialty to provide a graphic portrayal of the message. A cartridge manufacturer, for example, distributed a shot glass to gun dealers. Silk-screened on each glass were representations of the different pellet sizes of the company's line of ammunition. A four-page catalog sheet of shot sizes would not have been so effective.

A second consideration is the absence of suitable response measurement in many situations. When a specialty is distributed with a response card in a campaign designed to produce leads, this problem doesn't exist. However, specialty advertising is often used simply to generate goodwill or to encourage a delayed response, sometime down the road when the recipient is ready to act. The advertiser may accumulate thank-you letters, and salespeople may notice if the specialty is on display or is being used when they make calls, but the thing that every advertiser wants to know—the number of orders stimulated—often is not ascertainable.

Such deficiencies in measurement, of course, certainly are not limited to the specialty advertising medium.

A MEDIUM WITH ALMOST UNLIMITED APPLICATIONS

Specialty Advertising Association International has isolated seventeen marketing problems which the medium is adept at solving. *Problems* is probably the wrong term; a look at the list indicates that they are more like opportunities and could probably be more safely described simply as situations:

- Promoting branch openings
- Introducing new products
- Motivating salespeople
- Opening new accounts
- Stimulating sales meetings
- Developing trade-show traffic
- Balancing an improper product mix
- Activating inactive accounts
- Changing names or products
- Using sales aids for door openers
- Motivating consumers through premiums
- Moving products at the dealer level
- Improving client or customer relations
- Building an image
- Motivating sales department employees
- Promoting new facilities
- Introducing new salespeople

This list can be contracted, for examination clearly indicates instances of duplication and overlapping. It could also be expanded, for the applications of specialty advertising are multitudinous, if not infinite. To list seventeen problems, then, serves only to remove some of the more customary applications from the abstract and marshal them into a tangible formation for convenient identification. For our purposes here, we will reduce the list to six marketing situations and enhance their descriptions with a suitable example of promotions applied to each.

Developing Leads

In the mid-1970s, the TelComm department of the 3M Company embarked upon a campaign to generate new sales leads. Actually, there was a dual objective, for the department also wanted to present an image of dedication to the telephone industry. A direct-mail specialty advertising promotion (Figure 15-2) was targeted to 1631 persons in independent telephone companies and other firms.

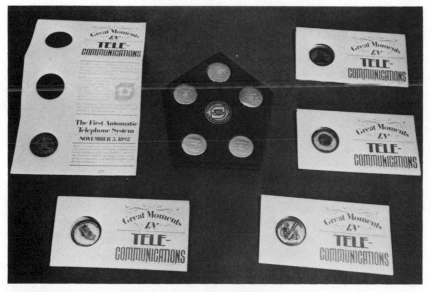

FIGURE 15-2. A campaign built around collecting commemorative coins helped demonstrate 3M's TelComm department's dedication to the telephone industry and produced sales leads.

TelComm employed serial distribution, a technique somewhat akin to pulsing in mass media. One form of this is the *array*, in which unrelated specialties are circulated at various intervals to extend target-audience interest after the initial exposure. TelComm, however, chose the *collection* approach, whereby the recipient is periodically issued articles that are of no real value unless and until a complete set has been accumulated. This offers the marketer the advantage of building anticipation for the next delivery.

The department's first mailing consisted of an introduction letter and a wood plaque containing a coin bearing the advertiser's logo in the center and surrounded by five empty slots. The slots could be filled in by subsequent mailings of limited-edition commemorative coins, each depicting a "great moment in telecommunications," such as the invention of the telephone or the laying of the first transatlantic cable. Copy accompanying each mailing gave a short synopsis of the great moment and also a soft sell about a comparable great moment for the advertiser. A prepaid postcard for requesting product information was enclosed with each mailing.

Thirty-five percent of the plaque recipients responded one or more times. By the time the promotion was wrapped up, TelComm had received 879 inquiry cards to act upon.[8]

Opening Doors

Unless business prospects are really prospects by virtue of having a compelling need for a specific product or service, they often are unwilling to be charitable with their time to see salespeople. How, then, can a salesperson get into the seemingly impregnable office for five minutes of the prospect's time?

In a field dominated by competitors, Furnas Electric Company was finding it difficult to get its salespeople past the receptionist. A mailing list of 200 purchasing, engineering, and management personnel was assembled, and the specialty advertising distributor devised a series of three mailings, each one containing a wooden nickel (Figure 15-3). The first mailing also contained the advertiser's catalog and a letter stating: "Wooden nickels and strangers' catalogs: many people accept neither. And yet, upon close examination, both can be windfalls." The letter went on to explain that recipients could redeem the three wooden nickels for a socket-wrench set as a gift from Furnas. If recipients didn't choose to wait for the subsequent mailings, they could pool the nickels that others in the company had received, or they could request a call from a salesperson, who would deliver an extra nickel.

In the campaign, budgeted at less than $2500, the Batavia, Illinois, electrical equipment company secured 244 interviews, many of which produced subsequent business.[9]

Providing Goodwill or Favorable Remembrance

Goodwill advertising is really latent sales generation. Little is expected at the time of the giving, but these courtesies have a way of evoking reciprocity in the form of continued patronage or fresh purchasing response at an appropriate later date. The idea is to convey the impression of being an appreciative vendor, although many vendors are neither appreciative nor true believers in the efficacy of goodwill advertising. If such cynical management employs goodwill advertising, it does so only because the competition is doing so. Unfortunately, the less-than-enthusiastic advertiser may be missing some of the benefits that could be gained from a more wholehearted approach.

Often the goodwill approach is not as effective as it could be because it is too methodical and too predictable. On the other hand, it is still possible to impress prospective buying influentials with something as conventional as a desk pen set—but a little imagination helps.

Using the desk pen set as an example, we can assume that in selecting such an item we must deal with the likelihood that the recipients already have one. Naturally, it would be nice if we could give our promotional gift features

FIGURE 15-3. Wooden nickels, symbolic of worthlessness, earned recipients a socket-wrench set; they also gained Furnas Electric salespeople some of their prospects' time.

that would endear it to the recipients at the expense of whatever similar item they might have.

This thought occurred to R. W. Summers Railroad Contractor Inc. when it was looking for something to remind managers of various southern railroads about the Bartow, Florida, firm's services. With this in mind, the specialty advertising distributor created a custom desk set which involved the assembling of a miniature railroad track junction and frog switch. To do it right, the distributor had to paint the crossties with a hypodermic needle. The junction trackage was subsequently embedded in Lucite to form a handsome desk set (Figure 15-4) that was meaningful to top-echelon managers of railroads on Summers's account list.

Undoubtedly, the thank-you letters that ensued would not have been so enthusiastic had the distributor simply relied on something out of the catalog.[10]

Introducing New Products, Services, or Facilities

There may be, as expressed in Ecclesiastes, nothing new under the sun, but that's no reason to discourage marketers from evoking curiosity with every major or minor novelty or alteration that comes along. With every new product or service there is an appeal or benefit to be embellished upon; with every new edifice or new anniversary of an old one there is attention to be captured.

Scarcely a day goes by without a newspaper announcement of a grand opening at some new business location. To attract traffic to the opening of one of its branches, Fidelity Mutual Savings Bank of Spokane, Washington, employed newspaper and radio advertising to announce that visitors would receive several advertising specialties. These included a letter opener, a tape measure, and a shopping bag. In addition, not underestimating the irresistibility of a teaser, the bank management mailed small plastic disks, imprinted with the corporate symbol (a rose) and name, to 13,000 persons, who were told that the disks were part of a useful article, for which they could be redeemed. Few people had any idea whàt the disk was, let alone what it was part of. Eleven thousand individuals—85 percent of those on the mailing list—were sufficiently curious to visit the bank, where they learned that what they had received in the mail was the lid to an inexpensive but useful tape dispenser.[11]

Motivating Employees

There may be some dispute over whether bigness or smallness is beautiful, but any business operation that remains static soon becomes moribund. From time to time, it is necessary to stimulate employees' adrenaline, to propel them to more sales activity, to draw attention to plant safety, to encourage them to produce more things while making fewer mistakes, or simply to raise ebbing morale.

Sales motivation often is in the form of quotas and incentives. J. M. McDonald's Company, of Hastings, Nebraska, chose as an incentive a trip to Spain for store managers who met their quotas. "The year of the bull" was the theme of the campaign undertaken by the chain of seventy-seven department stores, the idea being that it would be a bullish financial year for the firm if all store managers put forth their best efforts. Badges reflecting the theme were affixed to managers' lapels when they came to a managers' meeting where the campaign was announced. Monthly mailings (Figure 15-5) to the managers contained a sales quota chart, a figurine in the shape of a bull, a scroll promulgating the campaign creed, and a paperweight. Adhesive seals were to be placed on the sales charts, with an arrow pointing up when sales in a store were up, and pointing down when the quota wasn't met. Failure to meet a monthly quota required a $1 remittance from the store manager, and the penalty was doubled if the report was late. The money went into a pool to be divided among the twenty-five winners for use as spending money in Spain.

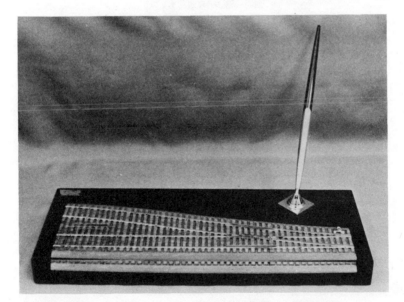

FIGURE 15-4. A desk pen set, which featured a miniature track junction and was sent to railroad executives, illustrates how creative thinking can transform a useful but conventional advertising gift into an appreciated remembrance item.

Incentive strategy often includes involving the salesperson's spouse. Presumably, the spouse will profit from his or her mate's achievement and will encourage—by one means or another—the salesperson to achieve the goal. Spouses of McDonald's managers received notes from the store president, calling attention to an enclosed luggage tag that was to be used when the couple went to Spain.

In the case of McDonald's promotion, the increase in sales among the stores ranged from a low of 8 percent to a high of 20 percent above the preceding year's figures.[12]

Renewing Interest in Existing Products or Services

This is often one of the most difficult aspects of advertising and sales promotion because older products must compete with newer ones whose appeals are projected with fresh promotional onslaughts. Aside from reputation, which should never be taken lightly, established brands must rely on

FIGURE 15-5. Designed to help people get more from their purchase of fresh pineapple, a specially curved knife stimulated pineapple sales.

innovation in theme or market use if they are to draw increased buyer attention.

This was the problem of Castle & Cooke Foods, which wished to increase domestic sales of its Dole brand of fresh pineapple. The advertiser believed that people who used conventional knives weren't getting all the fruit and that any assistance offered them would result in additional sales. A knife was developed with a specially curved blade that would help remove all the "meat" of the pineapple. To provide a secure and comfortable grip on the knife handle, impressions were taken from clay that consumers in several cities had been asked to handle in the same way they would handle regular kitchen cutlery.

Eighteen hundred of the knives, with the Dole brand name etched into the blade, were issued as advertising specialties to consumers at pineapple-cutting demonstrations in Los Angeles and Chicago supermarkets (Figure 15-6). The promotion was supported by television, radio, newspaper, and point-of-purchase advertising.

Castle & Cooke found that people were pleased with the pineapple knife, which, as the product manager stated at the time, proved to be "a tremendous value—more than doubling the sales of fresh pineapples in many areas."[13]

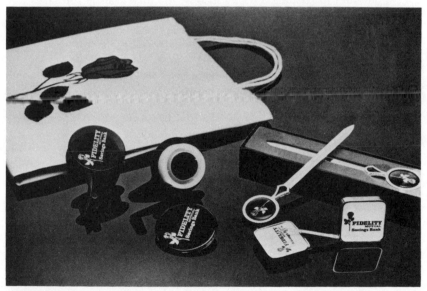

FIGURE 15-6. Advertising specialties distributed by a bank to attract traffic to the opening of one of its branches.

THREE SELLING AND BUYING ORIENTATIONS

As these examples show, some specialty advertising promotions are highly conceptualized and coordinated pieces of strategy. Other promotions are elementary. The type of promotion which is developed depends on the client's needs and on the capabilities of the distributor's salespersons.

Russell H. Woodlief, sales executive of a major west coast distributor, classifies distributors' salespersons according to item, idea, and program orientation. This categorization is generally accepted in the industry.

The *item* salesperson acts in situations "where the sale is completely dependent on the emotional presentation of the item, or the customer wants that particular item and the salesperson sells it."[14] This may well be the most common transaction situation: The advertiser's needs are clear-cut and uncomplicated, and the salesperson, armed with samples, solicits the order and sees that it is fulfilled.

The *idea* salesperson "develops a number of ideas—it might be a birthday plan, store traffic idea, a convention item—and then merchandises the idea to many firms, thinking more in terms of the idea and less in terms of the specific marketing needs of the client."[15]

In addition to creating a desire to buy, the idea salesperson takes into account the target audience (the people who are to receive the specialties), the distribution alternatives (how the specialties are to be delivered), and the ad copy to be printed, as well as what is supposed to be accomplished by the specialty distribution. The principal difference between the idea salesperson and the item salesperson is that the former must accompany the presentation of the idea with a *reason* to buy.

More ingenuity and research are required of the *program* salesperson, "who seeks out the marketing needs of a client and develops a series of ideas to fill one or more marketing needs."[16]

Many salespersons combine all three ways of selling. "In each of the categories, there are people highly professional, well respected and earning money commensurate with their abilities," Woodlief observes.[17]

These salesperson orientations have parallels among advertisers. As a result, item salespersons are most likely to gain acceptance from item-oriented clients, who will often make price the paramount consideration, offering their business to the lowest bidder. Such business is apt to be eschewed by program salespersons, who are selling their creativity and expertise as well as items.

The program orientation deserves further elaboration here; not only is it the most complex of the three, but it also implies a predisposition for thought-out campaign development.

CONSTRUCTING A CAMPAIGN

It can be said that developing an advertising campaign is like writing a story; many of the same elements are involved, such as conflict resolution or plot (the objective), theme, and delineation of characters (the audience). Campaign authors, however, are not able to write an ending, but ideally they will have done their work so well that the denouement will be a happy one for them and their clients. At least five things must be attended to in campaign development, and this is when the salesperson becomes a counselor, advising the advertiser on the objective, the target audience, the distribution plan, the theme, and the selection of the specialty advertising article.

Definition of Objective

Clients presumably know what they want to accomplish through advertising, and salespersons ought to share this knowledge. To say that execution of the campaign should be keyed to a concrete objective may seem to be belaboring the obvious, but the purchase and distribution of specialties that are unconnected to any clearly defined goal have always been a too common occurrence in what passes for "marketing." The client, in effect, fits the objective to specialty advertising and other media, instead of the other way around.

Audience Selection

Proper audience selection is critical to the success of any medium, but particularly to that of targeted media. If the message isn't going to the right people—and only the right people—the advantage of using targeted media is nullified. In a promotion conducted a few years back, shapely models (are there any other kind?) handed out specialties indiscriminately to passersby in front of the John Hancock Building in Chicago. Everyone within reach was given an aluminum token stamped with the schedule of the Chicago Bears and the name of the scotch being promoted. How does one isolate scotch drinkers from the rest of the sidewalk crowd?

If sales promotion is the "silent salesperson" of marketing, one must make it work by taking a leaf from the book of vocal, flesh-and-blood salespeople and see which prospects they concentrate on. Input from sales personnel is often valuable in circumscribing the target audience. Companies frequently make up their audience manifests by asking salespersons to list a specified number of buying influentials who they feel are their best prospects. The subsequent promotion is directed to this audience.

Method of Distribution

When the right audience is known, attention must be directed to the method of distribution. Frequently, specialty advertising is delivered by mail or by salespeople making calls, is enclosed in convention registration kits, or is simply placed on the sales counter. In one instance a state agency at the municipal level served as the willing transmitter of a marine products supplier's imprinted vinyl permit case, distributing it to persons purchasing boating or fishing licenses. And advertisers have been known to enlist Boy Scouts to deliver message-carrying items, making a donation to the troop in return. A good argument can be made for adopting a distribution system in which the recipient personally receives the specialty advertising article.

Theme

The theme is what ties the promotion together. As in 3M TelComm's "Great Moments in Telecommunications," it is a statement of the agenda for the advertiser's monologue to the audience.

Theme selection is often the product of group brainstorming, the outcome frequently suggesting that the "storm" was more of a mild breeze than a tempest. Campaign themes should be on a high note, but often they are lofty or pretentious or promise too much. When imaginations go rampant, the theme often becomes esoteric—the audience doesn't understand what the advertiser is talking about. When imaginations aren't working, the theme is pedestrian—you've heard or seen it six times in the last six months.

From where do themes emanate? Among the most popular sources are song titles and successful motion pictures. One can only guess how many promotions promised "an offer you can't refuse" and blessings of the galactic "Force," these following on the heels of such movie blockbusters as *The Godfather* and *Star Wars*. The theme may also be a parody of a familiar entity or be derived from a play on words. Generally, it should be timely so that members of the target audience can associate it with something in their own lives. Most important, however, the theme must relate to the idea that the advertiser is attempting to convey.

Selection of the Specialty Item

The final stage of the game plan is the selection of the specialty advertising article. Because price (usually) and quality (often) are considerations, the client must rely on the distributor's counsel in computing an acceptable equation out of budget, audience size, and article desirability. The distributor's salesperson, one can ordinarily assume, knows where the specialties can be obtained, how much they cost, how much lead time is required to fulfill the order, which suppliers are likely to do the best job of imprinting, and which suppliers can be relied on to provide on-time delivery. These may seem like minor points, unless one has had the experience of an advertiser's logo that was printed out of register or of door prizes that were delivered a day after the grand opening.

The usefulness of the specialty is another consideration. The wooden nickels in the Furnas Electric promotion, discussed earlier, were completely useless to the recipients, once they had obtained their socket-wrench sets. Yet the nickels were the instrument used to carry out the theme of the campaign and arouse attention. At the other end of the use spectrum, the socket-wrench sets quite obviously had an appreciable value to the recipients. They were retained and used, guaranteeing a long run for the impression of the advertiser that they conveyed.

Frequently, then, the specialty may have usefulness only to the advertiser: it creates a desired impact but does nothing more. If advertisers seek to create a long-lasting impression, they should choose articles which recipients are more likely to retain.

To increase the likelihood that the specialty will be retained, the distributor can recommend an item that relates in some way to the recipients and their occupations. To ensure that the impression of the advertiser will be perpetuated, the article selected should be one which bears a natural relationship to the advertiser, to the product or service being offered, or to the theme of the promotion.

In a recently published reference book directed to owners of small businesses, the author cursorily dismisses specialty advertising by telling readers that ballpoint pens won't do them much good and that calendars are too expensive to be worthwhile, unless, of course, the calendars are placed in barber shops or other places where they can get some exposure. Such casual advice misses the point. Any advertising specialty will be of marginal value unless it is employed with forethought and discrimination. And no type of advertising specialty is devoid of worth. Like a humble baseball team, on a given day and in a given situation it'll beat the best in the league.

What really needs to be taken into account is this: "Look at the big picture. Companies are not in business to give things away. They're in business to sell goods and services. So item and distribution should first be considered in terms of the results the client is looking for—not simply what would be clever, cheap, or nice."[18] This suggestion, offered by Dan S. Bagley III, advertising professor at the University of South Florida, is directed to distributors, but it has relevance to the corporate user as well.

SUPPORT STRUCTURE OF THE INDUSTRY

As an industry, specialty advertising tends to be somewhat inward-looking, not terribly concerned about what the other media are doing. Some of its proponents even view specialty advertising as not being in competition with other media, although in instances where all purchasing allocations are drawn from the same ad budget, this argument is hard to sustain.

In recent years, there have been some signs of departure from this self-imposed isolation, as many industry members—particularly the younger ones—have become affiliated with, and assumed leadership roles in, ad clubs, local chapters of Marketing Communications Executives International, and premium organizations.

Among themselves, specialty advertising practitioners for the most part have a zeal for education, are dependent upon external sources for information about products they must include in their portfolios, and are usually willing participants in the exchange of ideas. Practitioners are characteristically independent; distributors fit the entrepreneur role to a T, and relatively few suppliers obscure their identities in conglomerates. Despite this independence, there is a strong propensity for organization, and the organizations to satisfy this inclination do exist.

All three industry components—distributors, suppliers, and direct selling houses—are represented by Specialty Advertising Association International (SAAInternational), located in Irving, Texas. Formed in 1903, this organization sponsors twice-yearly conventions and expositions, which constitute the only national marketplace for the industry. Although closed to the public, these events may be attended by nonmember practitioners. SAAInternational also conducts several educational programs for its members, most notably the week-long executive development seminars at the University of Houston. It sponsors the annual Golden Pyramid Competition, an awards program that recognizes—and publicizes—outstanding specialty advertising promotions. Association membership services also include extensive public relations, research, and legislation-monitoring programs.

In an industry offering 15,000 to 20,000 different types of products, to what part of the haystack does one go to locate a specific needle? Providing source information is one of the principal services performed by the Advertising Specialty Institute (ASI), a private publishing enterprise in Langhorne, Pennsylvania. Its services, which include a consolidated catalog indexing virtually all suppliers and their products, are purchased by distributors through subscriptions.

In addition to these organizations, there are twenty-four local and regional associations located in major cities.

Practitioners are also kept informed in print. Two publications—*Specialty Advertising Business*, issued to members of SAAInternational, and *The Coun-*

selor, put out by ASI for its subscribers—appear monthly. For buyers of specialty advertising, SAAInternational publishes a quarterly, *Ideasworth*; ASI offers *Imprint* four times a year; and Lakewood Publishing Co., in Minneapolis, circulates *Potentials in Marketing* monthly.

THE INDUSTRY HOROSCOPE

As marketers become more familiar with what specialty advertising can do for them, the medium seems assured of securing a more prominent role in the marketing mix. This means continuation of an already substantial growth pattern for the intermediate term. Conjecture for the long term is like an "air ball" on the basketball court—really a futile business.

Some problems may be prophesied, however. One has to do with material shortages. As certain resources become scarce (most plastics are made from oil) or exorbitantly expensive, distributors and their suppliers will have to look for substitutes. This will probably be primarily an internal problem; to advertisers, it will mean at worst that their favorite widgets, which they have ordered for fifteen years, have been priced out of the market.

Buyer reception to business gifts, which constitute an important market for some distributors and suppliers, is uncertain. Believing that acceptance of gifts, no matter how inexpensive, compromises their employees' integrity, some companies have adopted policies forbidding the receiving of goodwill executive gifts. Whether such professed ethical purity has merit or not, it should be noted that many of the same companies issue gifts to *their* clients. Corporate policies proscribing acceptance of business gifts are by no means a recent phenomenon. And there is no indication that this practice is either growing or reversing itself.

One trend bears watching. Many specialty advertising practitioners and premium sellers have found it mutually profitable to explore each other's markets. Aside from the selling structure, there are few fundamental differences between the advertising specialty and the premium. But one is given away, and the other must be earned—remember? The problem is to make that difference understood by legislative bodies, however. Specialty advertising, because it does not obligate the recipient to do anything, has escaped some of the restrictions that have been placed on premiums, such as federal and state regulations concerning the use of premiums by banks and savings and loan associations. As specialty advertising and premium people draw closer, it is in the interest of the former to be sure that this distinction isn't blurred.

Inflation and its effects upon advertising and promotional budgets must be considered too. Increasingly, marketers who are trying to hold the line on budgets are asking what they are getting for their media expenditures. The best answer seems to be a lot of research, and media are attempting to supply it. Specialty advertising practitioners, sometimes as much to their relief as to their sorrow, have never had to wallow in a morass of supporting statistics. The time may be coming when they will have to begin doing so.

The time *is* coming for a number of opportunities destined to benefit users and practitioners alike. One worth mentioning is an event, or an advent: the coming of metrification to the United States. Although adoption of the metric system has been proceeding so far with the speed of a somnambulant snail, marketers have found that the advertising specialty, useful item that it is, can provide a metric conversion table, for example. Doubling as an educational tool makes it twice as useful as an advertiser's message carrier. One can anticipate many promotional opportunities, or as *Marketing Communications* puts it, "Metric converters can lead the way to the bank if a specialty advertising campaign is carefully designed and executed. Just don't ask how many kilometers away the bank is—figure it out for yourself."[19]

And finally, there is evidence that the public, which is subjected to a steady bombardment of advertising impressions, is growing both irritated and numbed by much of what it sees, hears, or reads in a commercial vein. Advertisers trying to cope with the "yawn" factor probably will have to find some means of personalizing their communications. Specialty advertising happens to be rather adept at that sort of thing.

SUMMARY

Specialty advertising, defined as a medium employing useful articles of merchandise that are imprinted with an advertisement and are distributed without obligation to customers and prospects, is one of the oldest forms of advertising. It is also one of the most ubiquitous; examples are to be seen every day and in almost every location. Rare is the individual who does not own at least one advertising specialty—perhaps an imprinted cigarette lighter, a key chain, or a ballpoint pen. Equally rare is the home or place of work that is without a wall calendar or one of the other 15,000 to 20,000 articles used as advertising specialties. Despite the fact that billings for specialty advertising place it among the largest media, it is not nearly so well understood as most other types of advertising and sales promotion.

The medium has a number of characteristics which make it of interest to marketers. As opposed to the mass media, it is a targeted medium. Advertisers can direct a specialty advertising campaign to as narrowly defined an audience as they want, without squandering their money on wasted circulation. Because the specialties are useful, they tend to be retained by customers and prospects, who are then exposed to the advertiser's message for as long as they keep the specialties. And with so many types of specialties available, there is a wide price range to fit any advertiser's budget. Although specialty advertising can be used to stimulate decision making in the desired direction, advertisers find the medium to be an excellent reinforcing mechanism.

The medium is applicable to any number of marketing situations, but advertisers have found it to be particularly effective in developing sales leads; opening doors for salespeople; providing goodwill or favorable remembrance; introducing new products, services, or facilities; motivating employees; and renewing interest in existing products or services.

The distribution chain of a specialty advertising promotion begins with the supplier who manufactures the item and proceeds to the distributor's salesperson (or direct selling house) who sells the order and plays an important role in developing the campaign, assuming one is to be developed. In constructing a campaign, the salesperson is called upon to be a counselor who will be involved in such things as helping the advertiser focus on the marketing objective, determine the target audience, develop a distribution scheme, create a theme, and, ultimately, select the appropriate advertising specialty. Decisions made in this process are often based upon what's clever, cheap, or attractive. These considerations, however, should be overshadowed by a much more important one: What is likely to produce results?

Although the medium has its limitations, the fact that it is an unobtrusive means of transmitting an advertiser's message makes it deserving of additional consideration by marketers in the future. Because the receiver of the message carrier (the advertising specialty) takes actual possession of it, the specialty has a personal quality that is lacking in much advertising and sales promotion today. The result of this lack of personalization is that too many messages are being transmitted to unreceptive eyes and ears.

ENDNOTES

1. George L. Herpel, *A Study in Industry Marketing Structure, Problems and Image*, Specialty Advertising Association International, Irving, Tex., 1973, p. 1.
2. Richard G. Ebel, *Preference Building: The Dynamic World of Specialty Advertising*, Specialty Advertising Association International, Irving, Tex., 1982, p. 2.
3. George L. Herpel, *Specialty Advertising in Marketing*, Dow Jones–Irwin, Inc., Homewood, Ill., 1972, p. 27.
4. Herpel, *A Study in Industry Marketing Structure, Problems and Image*, p. 2.
5. Steve Sellers, "Viewpoint," *The Counselor*, December 1977, p. 135.
6. Fred O. Coble, "The Sign Story," *Specialty Advertising Business*, November 1977, p. 19.
7. Herpel, *Specialty Advertising in Marketing*, p. 104.
8. *Winners' Circle*, Specialty Advertising Association International, Irving, Tex., 1974, p. 6.
9. *24-Karat Specialty Advertising*, Specialty Advertising Association International, Irving, Tex., 1977, p. 16.
10. *Ideabook*, Specialty Advertising Association International, Irving, Tex., 1980 supplement, p. S-67.

11. *Championship Specialty Advertising*, Specialty Advertising Association International, Irving, Tex., 1978, p. 18.
12. *24-Karat Specialty Advertising*, p. 2.
13. *Winners' Circle*, p. 7.
14. "Marketing Plan Is Path to Increased Professionalism," *Specialty Advertising Business*, December 1976, p. 12.
15. Ibid.
16. Ibid.
17. Ibid.
18. Dan S. Bagley III, "Building Long-Range Profits," *The Counselor*, June 1977, p. 180.
19. "Making Metric Memorable," *Marketing Communications*, October 1977, p. 46.

16 Display Is Visual Merchandising

JEROME HAMBERGER
Vice President, David Hamberger Inc.

Display, or visual merchandising, as it is now called, is not a science, but an art form, whose purpose is to provide that link between the customer and the merchandise which will result in the final selection and purchase of the product.

It is sales promotion. Display can create excitement, set a mood, spotlight a product, focus on a new or unfamiliar item, or, in today's market, with its great emphasis on customer self-selection, act as an informative sales aid.

If need were the buyer's only motivation for purchasing a product, the display person's job would be simple: laying out the merchandise in neat lines, lighting it sufficiently, putting on easily readable price tags with the lowest possible prices, and waiting for customers to come in and select the items they want. However, a large part of any retailer's trade consists of impulse buying by customers who have been drawn into the store by something they saw in the window. This is where the display person's art becomes important.

TYPES OF DISPLAY

There are two types of display, according to Lisa Ulanoff, an award-winning professional display artist. One, which she calls a "right-brain" display, appeals to the side of our brain associated with creativity, intuition, and nonverbal communication. In contrast, a "left-brain" display appeals to the side of our brain associated with logic, order, and language.

The left-brain display shows, in a logical manner, a sample of every item available for sale, with prices carefully marked. For example, a display would show ten ski sweaters in the colors and patterns in which they are available. The right-brain display might show only three of the ten sweaters, placed in a window with a spinning wheel, a rocking chair, and skeins of wool in colors to match the sweaters. In response to a right-brain window, people enter the store without knowing why. There was something they liked, they were reminded of a story, they love antiques, etc. But somehow they end up inside the store, where it is up to the salespeople to sell the merchandise.

Although merchandise is sometimes sold in a logical, straightforward manner, romancing the customer with an imaginative presentation is usually more effective, and it is this facet of display on which this chapter will focus.

ELEMENTS OF A GOOD WINDOW

Color.   Of the elements that go into making a good window, color is probably the first that is noticed by the window-shopper. In selecting a color scheme, a strong, positive statement should be made. For example, if red is the featured garment color, doing the entire window in shades of red will dramatize and emphasize the importance of the color. On the other hand, if a range of merchandise colors is shown, repeating these colors in backgrounds or props will reinforce the color scheme and establish it in the buyers mind at a glance.

Lighting.   Lighting is of prime importance in any window. Incandescent lights, spotlights, and floodlights—rather than fluorescent lights—should be used; they lend warmth and sparkle and, when properly placed, provide interesting highlights. Lighting levels must be adequate, but contrast through the use of "pin spots" or similar high-intensity lights provides a sense of drama.

Composition.   Good composition is one of the qualities that differentiate mundane art from memorable art. In trimming a window or painting a picture, balance and symmetry should be taken into consideration. The focus of a window must be on the merchandise; however, the use of props creates interest and calls attention to the merchandise, as well as aiding in the overall composition of the window. Following are the elements which enter into the composition of a window. Many of the examples cited are from *Store Windows That Sell*, edited by Martin Pegler.[1]

LINE.   Employ some elements to lead to or frame your merchandise. For example, arrange a group of fake I beams to point to and partially frame a group of mannequins.

SCALE. Use outsized or undersized props to accent your merchandise. For example, place your wool sweater near a ball of yarn that is 3 feet in diameter, or put your mannequins of children next to a set of 4-foot-tall crayons. Conversely, surround your custom-tailored suit with Lilliputian tailors climbing all over the mannequin on ladders and scaffolds.

DRAMA. Create a theatrical setting that will put your merchandise on center stage. For example, build a proscenium arch around your window using natural or artificial branches.

HUMOR. Create an outlandish scene. For example, fill a window with arms stretched to ridiculous lengths, each holding a suitcase at a different height from the floor.

REALISM. Dress your window to show a real-life vignette. For example, create a living room in which family members are putting presents under a tree, or show a skating-rink scene in which one mannequin has fallen on the ice.

REPETITION. Duplicate one setting over and over in a window. For example, set up a row of mannequins, each in the same pose but wearing a different bathing suit and stepping out of identical dressing rooms.

SHOCK. Do something entirely unexpected. For example, show a nude mannequin sitting primly in a bathtub while a spouse models a bathrobe. (Salvador Dali did this many years ago in a Fifth Avenue window.)

ASSOCIATION. Tie in your window with a recognizable figure from the stage, movies, television, comic strips, etc.

MOTION. Provide motion through the use of turntables or mechanical figures. Test windows have shown a significant increase in viewers when a mechanical display is placed in a window.

SOME HISTORY

Although there have been great changes in the style and emphasis of window displays over the decades, the last few years have brought about a change in the entire structure of the display industry.

Display as we know it today in the United States probably originated in the mid- or late-nineteenth century. General merchandise and dry goods stores, such as Lazarus Co. in Dayton, Wanamaker's in Philadelphia, Macy's in New York, and other predecessors of our present-day merchandising giants, grew into large department stores as our cities grew, acting as a nucleus for "downtown" shopping-center hubs. Marshall Field in Chicago placed tremendous emphasis on its windows, spurring a flourishing display industry in that city. By 1893, so much interest had developed in the display profession that the periodical *Harmon's Journal of Window Dressing* began publication. This was followed in 1897 by *Show Window*, and in 1903 by *Window Trim and*

Merchant Advertising. In 1905, these publications were joined to form the *Merchants Record and Show Window*, the journal of the International Association of Display Men (IADM). This organization acted as the official voice of professional display people until the 1940s, when it became inactive. It was succeeded by the National Association of Display Industries (NADI).

Since the downtown areas were the primary shopping centers, the principal stores in the towns found themselves acting as the "sales promotion departments" of their areas. Christmastime saw beautiful and elaborate displays of lights and animation. Animated figures were at first imported from Europe; later, some of the finest were built in Chicago by George Silvestri and in New York by Metropolitan Display and Al Bliss. Smaller stores augmented the promotions, and the cumulative effect was to attract crowds of shoppers to the area.

Every season had its theme. Cruise-wear or Palm Beach displays followed Christmas. (The window trimmers worked all night to have the windows ready on the day after Christmas.) The cruise-wear displays ran concurrently with the animated Christmas displays. A small New Year's window featured evening gowns and tuxedos. January white-sale displays reminded housewives to restock their linen closets, and as soon as these windows were vacated, Valentine displays took up the slack in the lingerie, hosiery, jewelry, cosmetics, and candy departments. March meant that spring was just around the corner, and window displays reminded one and all that the spring wardrobe had to be replenished. April, of course, meant Easter, with bunnies, chicks, and eggs. Beautiful displays of carnations signaled the arrival of Mother's Day, which for most stores meant sales figures rivaling those of the day before Christmas. June brought promotions for graduation and Father's Day. July Fourth sales of vacation wear and bathing suits preceded the "back-to-school" promotions and provided sufficient sales volume to offset some of the fear of having a poor Christmas. August meant that autumn and cold weather were coming, and displays featured winter coats and other cold-weather gear. September meant football promotions, Thanksgiving day marked the beginning of the Christmas season, and the cycle started all over again.

In order to direct the rapidly changing promotions, the display department worked together with, or under the supervision of, the advertising and sales promotion department, which in turn was responsible to the merchandise manager. In many of the small and medium-size stores, the display manager doubled in brass as the advertising manager. Since the dates and subjects of major promotions were predetermined, it was possible to make budgetary allocations a year in advance.

Windows were the prime area for displaying merchandise. Large stores maintained banks of windows, usually dedicated to specific departments.

Women's fashions, menswear, children's wear, furniture, and household items had their assigned positions. In addition, windows were used for institutional purposes. At Christmastime, the animated display window rarely contained merchandise; the nativity display, of course, was never commercialized. July Fourth promotions could include a picnic window, but often they were built around a patriotic theme, such as the Liberty Bell or the Constitution. Many of these windows made a real contribution to the community's knowledge of United States history.

Store interiors were generally divided into discrete departments. Women's blouses were kept in one location, as were women's skirts, scarves, and other fashion apparel, with each major classification of merchandise remaining in its assigned area. Accessorizing was accomplished through the use of mannequins or dress forms on the ledges within a department or in the show windows. Coordinating a wardrobe was at best difficult, since it involved moving from department to department, sometimes even to different floors. Our current "shop" concept is a vast improvement over this system and is a great convenience to customers, in that they can now more easily assemble and coordinate a wardrobe.

Interior store displays normally consisted of decorations attached to columns, ledges, elevator banks, and stairwells. The excitement of an Easter flower show, with its elaborate displays of real or artificial flowers, often accompanied by cages full of singing birds, did indeed provide a lift to the shopper after the cold winter. Incidentally, the only season still treated in this elaborate manner is Christmas, the one season in which retailers are sure of showing a reasonable profit.

The exterior of the store was normally enhanced with lighting displays at Christmastime. The marquees over the store entrances contained tableaux at Christmas and floral displays at Easter.

Recent Developments

The post-World War II era brought a vast change in lifestyles and an equally vast change in the display field. The rapid growth of suburbia resulted in the development of shopping centers; at first these were in the form of open malls, which were soon superseded by enclosed centers in which the stores were almost always facing inward. Customers, after leaving their cars, head directly toward the mall entrance, and therefore outside windows are superfluous. In addition, although the specialty stores in the malls still retain relatively large windows, the anchor stores have considerably less window space than their old downtown locations provided. It is therefore no longer possible to showcase every department in the store, so it is more vital than ever that these windows be powerful enough to accomplish their purpose. Visual merchandisers have but a few brief moments in which to tell their story. They must catch the customer's eye, present the merchandise attractively, and arouse enough curiosity to induce the customer to come into the store.

Among all the changes that have taken place in store display in recent years, none has been more dramatic than the change in store interiors. Whereas stores were formerly laid out as decorated warehouses, with rows of racks and shelves arranged to be serviced by salespeople or clerks, today, because of higher labor costs and lower markups, there are fewer salespeople available to help the customer make a selection. It has therefore become necessary to arrange merchandise so as to make selection as simple as possible. Many departments have become shops, such as junior shops, teen shops, and sports shops, featuring not single items of apparel, but rather a whole range of related and coordinated merchandise, thus enabling the customer to select an entire wardrobe more easily.

In order to display the merchandise offered, the perimeter area around each shop is set up as an extension of the windows. Here are placed islands with merchandise displayed on mannequins and props, serving to get the attention of customers and make them aware of the contents of the shop. A whole new generation of display racks and fixtures has been developed to open the merchandise to view. Waterfall displays and displays that face out, quadruple and triple racks, and slat-wall and grid systems are all designed to show off the front of the merchandise, rather than just the sides. An excellent analysis of this concept is contained in a training manual prepared by Cecil Bessellieu, visual merchandising director of the Belk Stores Services Corporation, excerpts from which are presented below.[2]

Visual Merchandising: A New Dimension in Selling

Visual Merchandising is another name for merchandise presentation. It is psychological selling created by utilizing the proper techniques of Display with that of creative merchandising within a department. It is done in order to achieve a unified look within a department, a floor, a store.

Our objectives are to:

- Increase sales
- Update the look of the store
- Achieve a group look of unity
- Create an updated fashion image
- Facilitate suggestive self-service selling
- Concentrate on customer ease in shopping

It is imperative that fashion looks and merchandising classifications have impact, that they have logical placement and logical priorities. We must always put ourselves in the shoes of the customer, and analyze our merchandise presentation from the consumer point of view.

Advertising gets the customer's attention and it is up to us to do the rest.

Upon entry into the store, the initial store and merchandise impact must be powerful. It must make the customer fully confident in Belk taste and knowledge of merchandise presentation. The key is that your merchandise must speak first.

Visual merchandising must create, by whatever means necessary, the desire to buy.

Departmental Anatomy

The retail store is a stage for merchandise presentation. It is the job of the visual merchandiser not only to direct the designing of sets, lighting and props, but to choreograph the movement of the star performer—the merchandise—on stage.

In the 70s, visual merchandising took on a new dimension by uniting the best visual technique with creative merchandising concepts to create the desire to buy *visually*. Visual merchandising orchestrates the use of fixtures, mannequins and props to bring the merchandise into the spotlight.

This focus on merchandise has created the concept of in-store media; an exciting and productive method of presentation which leads today's retailer to a new dimension in selling.

The objectives of visual merchandising are, first and foremost, to increase sales by creating the desire to buy.

Secondly, visual merchandising is a tool to achieve a consistent fashion image within a department, a store or a partner group.

Thirdly, visual merchandising relates our fashion statement to the current life-styles of our customers.

Ultimately, visual merchandising facilitates ease of selection and self-service.

These basic objectives are met by thorough knowledge of merchandise presentation. Visual merchandising begins with an understanding of the anatomy of a department. Each department has three distinct divisions:

- The *Window on the Aisle* or main aisle
- The *Bread and Butter* or central core
- The *Vista Wall* or back and side walls

The customer's eye should be drawn into the department by careful attention to the positioning of fixtures and the creation of definite focal points within a department. Let's analyze each of these divisions in detail.

Windows on the Aisle

The *Window on the Aisle* emerges from the concept that the customer "window shops" the aisle.

Therefore, Window on the Aisle fixtures and merchandise must make a strong fashion statement and provide immediate interest and excitement. It is the *most* important merchandising presentation area.

Key points to remember include:

- Keep fixtures low in height to allow a view into the department.
- Make sure merchandise is "facing out" to the aisle.
- Use this area for fashion impact to Trend Emphasis merchandise.
- Use costumers alone or with mannequin groupings.

- Limit stocks on these fixtures and always have coordinated outfits out front on each fixture.

Bread and Butter

The center or core area of a department is referred to as the *Bread and Butter* area. This area is used for the mass merchandising of large coordinate groups, major classifications of goods and promotional items. Fixtures in this area should include rounders, 4-Way and 3-Way, designed for the greatest stock capacity.

Varying the heights of these fixtures makes this area more visually interesting. Have the lower height level nearest the front of the department.

- Merchandise on these fixtures should be color coordinated and then sized within the color groups.
- Coordinate outfits at ends of racks wherever possible.
- Size merchandise when stocks are broken.
- As stock quantities decrease, fixtures in this division may be removed.
- Position sale or promotional racks in this division to draw customers into the department. Make sure these racks are well signed.

Vista Walls

The back and side walls are known as *Vistas* and they make up the second most important merchandise presentation area in a department. Vistas must be seen from the vantage point of the customer standing in the aisle. They must be exciting enough to entice the customer into the department.

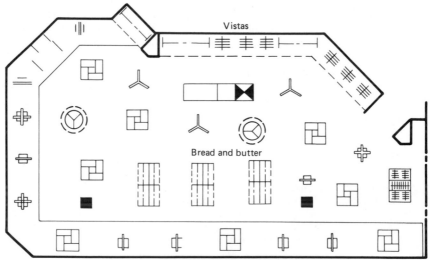

FIGURE 16-1. The divisions of a department.

Vistas must have variety:

- Intersperse face out waterfalls and straight bar hanging.
- Vary the height on a wall of straight bar hanging and avoid one-level presentation.
- Create focal points.
- Balance is essential. Avoid off-center arrangements.

CURRENT TRENDS

The trend toward total emphasis on merchandise in window and interior displays has minimized the use of seasonal trims, institutional promotions, and displays based on special events formerly handled within the windows and the store interiors. With the advent of the closed mall, it was recognized that these functions of display would still be needed to help draw the large crowds necessary to keep the mall profitable but that they would have to be provided by the entire center. This job was at first done by voluntary merchants' associations, but it soon became apparent to mall developers that a much more formal arrangement was needed if they were to protect their long-term investment. Today, most merchants' associations are set up as a

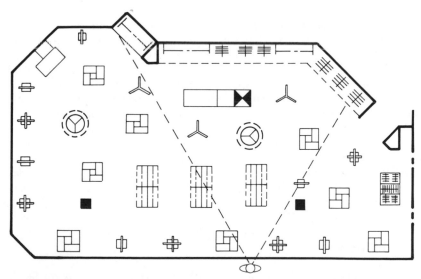

FIGURE 16-2. Vista walls, the second most important merchandise presentation area in a department.

division of mall management, and mandatory contributions to the association are collected along with the rent.

Under the direction of the International Council of Shopping Centers (ICSC), annual promotion seminars have been organized to provide a forum for the exchange of ideas in this exciting new display field.

The mall has in effect become an extension of the display window, taking over and expanding two of the major display roles: creating excitement and setting a mood.

Since almost 30 percent of retail earnings are generated within the last six weeks of the year, the major expenditure for decor occurs during this period. The animated Christmas displays have been taken from the store windows and put onto the floor of the shopping center, where they become "Santa lands." Often the cost of these displays is partially or completely borne by the photo area, in which kids have their pictures taken with Santa Claus. Banners, garlands, trees, lights, etc., are used to carry the theme throughout the mall. This theme, which is an extremely important promotional tool, is often selected to reflect the degree of sophistication of the mall's clientele. A group of animated figures arranged to tell a story, with an overall theme such as "a visit to Santa's kitchen," "the twelve days of Christmas," or "the palace of the Snow Queen," has a greater impact in a promotion than a random group of decorations or displays. The moving figures also make great subjects for television spots or for artwork for newspaper ads or mailers.

Although Christmas and Easter are the times for high-budget promotions, the need to create excitement exists all year long. Fashion shows, flower shows, children's art shows, etc., have all become part of the mall's promotional functions. In addition, many promotions that are rarely utilized by department stores, such as auto shows, boat shows, home repair shows, and antique shows, have been developed to attract shoppers.

The field of shopping-center promotion is relatively new and is still evolving. Most centers do not yet employ a full-time display department; rather, they farm out the "display package" to contractors or installers, who submit proposals and then supply the material and supervision and, sometimes, the installation crew to put up the display. Recently, some of the larger developers and operators have begun hiring their own designers, and the day may not be far off when a display department will become a part of the mall management structure.

CONCLUSION

The field of decorative display, in which I have worked for most of my life, is unique in today's business world. A display factory is probably closer in organization to the Renaissance studio of Michelangelo or Leonardo da Vinci than to a modern factory. The range of materials used is vast, and quite often the display industry, because of its high visibility to the public, serves to introduce new products to the market. Among those which come to mind are such widely used materials as styrofoam, fiberglass, foam core, polyurethane, and the preexpanded foam which is currently used to make millions of insulated coffee cups but which was earlier used by display manufacturers to mold bust forms to display bras and blouses. The miniature white lights that now are imported by the millions from the Orient to brighten our Christmas trees were originally a display idea. Display sculptors and mold makers use many of the same techniques used by ancient Egyptian and Chinese artists, and they direct the movements of the resulting figures with computers.

Display is an extremely stimulating and satisfying field of work, which, by its nature, is constantly changing. As long as the right side of the brain influences creativity, intuition, and feeling, there will be a place for display in the field of marketing.

ENDNOTES

1. Martin Pegler (ed.), *Store Windows That Sell*, Retail Reporting Corp., New York.
2. Cecil Bessellieu, *Visual Merchandising Training Manual*, Belk Stores Services Corporation.

Manufacturers' Sales Promotions to Retailers, Distributors, and Sales Forces

IV

Sales promotion has two broad functions. The first, which is to induce or persuade consumers to buy, is generally considered to be its only job. The second is hardly known by those who don't practice it. It is to motivate salespeople to sell.

Whereas sales promotion's first function, along with consumer advertising and publicity, is designed to pull merchandise through the channels of distribution, its second function's reason for being (together with trade advertising and publicity) is to push that same merchandise through the channels. It does this by providing sales personnel with incentives to sell. These include sales contests, prizes (cash, merchandise, and/or travel), dealer premiums, trade allowances, and push money, along with trade shows. Other incentives are advertising specialties and business gifts.

One of the most effective sales promotions to dealers was that of the Chevrolet division of General Motors. In the face of drops in sales of close to 15 percent registered by Ford Motor Co. and 17 percent by American Motors, dealer incentive contests sponsored by Chevrolet boosted total GM sales 6 percent, raising its share of the domestic market to 61.4 percent, 5 points above the previous year. An article describing this promotion appeared in *The Wall Street Journal* of October 25, 1978. The headline and subheading read:

New-Car Sales in Mid-October 2.1% below 1977
But GM Achieved 6% Gain Due Largely to Contests for Its Chevrolet Dealers.

Again in 1979 the two largest automobile manufacturers, Chevrolet and Ford, ran practically identical promotions in newspapers and on radio. In essence, they informed consumers that because of "special incentives" given to their dealers, buyers would save "hundreds of dollars" on car and truck purchases.

Interspersed with direct rebates to consumers, in 1982 Chevrolet once again provided special "factory incentives" of $400 per car to its dealers and boldly announced this promotion to the public through ads in the mass media. Other auto manufacturers followed suit.

While manufacturers of consumer goods put a considerably greater share of the sales promotion dollar into consumer promotions to encourage purchases at the retail level, a substantial sum is pumped into the marketing system to motivate sales personnel and resellers. These promotions are designed to push merchandise through the channels of distribution and are another way to sell the manufacturer's products. And, like consumer sales promotion efforts, they come in a number of diverse forms—a few of which are similar to those used to encourage consumers to buy. Principal among these are premiums, contests, exhibits, and demonstrations.

On the other side of the coin are those sales promotion devices which are employed exclusively to induce the manufacturer's salespeople, and the resellers and their sales personnel, to sell more of the manufacturer's wares. Generally speaking, the manufacturer's salespeople compete with one another or, more likely, with themselves. Goals are set for each salesperson beyond the previous year's total, and the incentives offered for exceeding these goals usually include merchandise prizes, cash awards, and/or travel.

Resellers and their sales forces present a different problem. While the manufacturer's sales personnel sell only that manufacturer's merchandise, resellers and their employees sell the competing wares of many manufacturers. So, in the case of the dealer, the manufacturer's aim is to have that reseller sell more of the goods produced by the manufacturer's company. The manufacturer does this by offering one or more different trade allowances, many of which, in effect, are a form of discount. Manufacturers also try to motivate resellers by offering premiums, which might be given to dealers to encourage them to use point-of-purchase displays.

In some industries, sales personnel of resellers are given push money which is an extra cash allowance provided by the manufacturer in addition to the salesperson's salary and is given directly to the individual who sells that particular manufacturer's merchandise. And like the manufacturer's sales force, these salespersons, along with the resellers, can be given realistic goals to reach or exceed, in which case they will win prizes.

Stimulating Manufacturers', Wholesalers', and Retailers' Sales Forces

17

RICHARD I. TOPUS, M.B.A.

Assistant Professor of Management and Marketing, C. W. Post Center, Long Island University; Former Vice President of Marketing, Friendship Dairy Products, Inc.

DANGLE THE CARROT!

In a capitalistic free enterprise society such as ours, reward rather than fear of punishment is the basis of a successful business enterprise. *Dangle the carrot*! People who are striving for a better position in the corporate hierarchy or who just want to know that their efforts are appreciated will give that little something "extra" if they can have a tangible reward to show for it. This basic fact often escapes the sales or marketing executive. There are many ways to dangle the carrot. A business that has seasonal highs and lows can even out its sales or production forecasts by providing the necessary incentives to its employees or customers. The retail store is just as concerned with offering incentives to its customers as a manufacturer or distributor is. Premiums, trading stamps, coupons, price reductions, contests, and sweepstakes are only some of the many ways the retailer competes in the marketplace for customers.

Almost everyone, from manufacturers', wholesalers', and retailers' sales forces to the ultimate consumer, is "turned on" by a prize. It is this psychological stimulus that creates additional sales for the business enterprise. A salesman, for example, is proud to relate to his friends and family how he entered a contest and won a gift or a trip to a distant land. The supermarket that offers a free set of dishes to consumers for cash-register tapes totaling a certain amount not only creates store loyalty but also generates additional purchases. Therefore, considering the freedom of choice offered in the marketplace and the close similarity between products and services, it is essential that business create additional sales not by price alone. All the incentive plans discussed in this chapter employ merchandise, cash, and/or travel as the award. This chapter will attempt to elaborate on some of the programs made available by manufacturers to wholesalers, to retailers, and to their own sales forces.

THE INCENTIVE INDUSTRY

Let us begin by examining the incentive and premium industry as a whole. The 1981–1982 *Incentive Marketing* magazine "facts issue" shows that users spent a total of more than $3.8 billion on merchandise and travel incentives for dealers and sales personnel in 1981. Travel incentives for dealers and salespeople cost more than $1 billion, compared with merchandise award and business gift purchases of over $2.7 billion in 1981. It is estimated that in 1982, spending for travel incentives amounted to more than $1.2 billion and that over $2.8 billion was spent for merchandise promotions.[1] These statistics tell only a part of the story. Generally speaking, in early studies, marketing executives in various industries indicated that the cost of incentive programs averaged 3 percent of sales.

The incentive industry seems to be expanding at a fast pace, and we should examine the rapid growth of certain user industries challenging the ranking order. Two charts appearing in the *Incentive Marketing* issue mentioned above indicate the rank of the top ten industries using merchandise and travel incentives.[2] The charts also show the actual dollars spent by these industries for these incentives. They clearly indicate that the top-ranking industries in both categories are the overall top spenders for dealer and sales-force incentives.

Heading the list of the top ten merchandise incentive users was the automobile parts, tires, and accessories industry, which spent $264,187,000 for merchandise incentives and $92,380,000 for incentive travel, for a combined figure of $356,567,000. The insurance industry, the leader among the travel incentive users, with an expenditure of $136,130,000, also spent $130,415,000 for merchandise incentives, making a grand total of $266,545,000.[3]

Accordingly, it is estimated that in 1982 American businesses spent a record amount of more than $10 billion on every type of sales promotion. Another chart shows the generally steady, dramatic growth of usage of all categories of sales promotion, including consumer promotions, from 1969 ($3.7 billion) to the present.[4] Although there are certain unknown factors that make forecasting less than an exact science, it certainly appears that the use of trade incentives will continue to grow.

MERCHANDISE AND CASH INCENTIVES

Offering merchandise awards to a manufacturer's trade customers, in recognition of good performance, is not a new or unique concept. In 1960, Friendship Food Products, a manufacturer of quality dairy products, was having difficulty getting retail store personnel to rotate its products when they arrived from the distributor. The rapid growth of the supermarket industry did not allow time for proper training of store employees. In many cases, a pair of hands to put the merchandise out on the shelf was all that was available, let alone experience. Friendship Food Products was also faced with a shortage of trained merchandising personnel to assist the retail stores. It required an incentive program that would be economically feasible and would also motivate store personnel to handle these products with "loving care" and to increase sales.

The Friendship award program, consisting of a type of dealer loader, was instituted. It was an ongoing program that offered retail store personnel a choice of gifts from several categories; coupons were packed in each case of merchandise and could be redeemed for the gifts. Each coupon had a specific point value, depending on the type of product purchased. A description of the program was put into a colorful folder that also included catalog sheets showing the brand-name gifts available in each category, the rules, order forms, and category values. Award recipients were able to establish the value of the gifts they selected in any retail store carrying these name-brand items. Redemption was handled by an incentive redemption company, which submitted recipients' names for approval to the marketing department of Friendship Food Products before the gifts were shipped, in order to avoid possible errors. The result of the program is now part of the success story of this dairy company, which today enjoys the honor of having the largest share of sales in its marketing area.

Companies in the automotive parts industry, which ranked first in use of incentives and which spent more than $170 million on them (particularly before the recent auto industry crisis), have to be especially sophisticated in order to compete in the marketplace. Fram Corporation's incentive programs have played an important role in motivating dealers and sales personnel for many years. This company manufactures filters, PCV valves, and windshield wipers and is also a marketer of Autolite spark plugs. An incentive program required special characteristics that would appeal to different groups of the corporation's thousands of dealers. Recognizing that tastes differ, the company offered clothing items in many styles, colors, and fabrics. Jo-Ann Barclay, assistant sales promotion manager of Fram at that time, stated:

> To motivate salespeople, a good program should enable the majority of them

to obtain at least a small incentive item, while motivating the more successful to earn costlier items. This is accomplished by using incentives which have logical increments on a value basis. For example, Fram recently completed a windshield wiper promotion which allowed our sales force as well as our distributors to earn their choice of General Electric incentives. Included were several items, ranging from home sentry lights to a color television. Fram also has an ongoing gift program devoted to the "something for everybody principle."[5]

The program has been in operation for approximately twenty years and employs a form of trading stamps redeemable for nearly 1000 items pictured and described in a catalog. This particular program is handled by an in-house department; the Fram Corporation understands that its customers are looking for values and not necessarily gimmicks. The company incentive program emphasizes simplicity and uses a central computer for handling incentives. It stresses simple systems for greatest efficiency, and the company tries to use single-source suppliers of all incentive items.

There are many directions that a gift incentive program can take. By offering rewards, a manufacturer can effectively encourage a better sales approach on the part of the salespeople in retail stores handling its products, where both technical data and courteous service must be more effective.

The Bell & Howell/Mamiya Co. had a program that was planned to run for a five-month period. The program was directed to approximately 5000 retail store personnel handling its photographic equipment. The salespeople could select their gifts, each worth $25, from a catalog by following a relatively easy set of rules, which required answering sales training quizzes and making and reporting Bell & Howell equipment sales promptly for each monthly period.

Joe Kazimer, the manager of market planning, indicated that it was important to convince the general public that photography is a rewarding and gratifying hobby. He felt that the photo equipment industry was competing with industries catering to other recreational activities. He regarded retail salespeople as the best means of influencing consumers concerning the merits of, and joys that can be experienced from, photography. According to Kazimer, six brochures were sent out on a monthly basis. The brochures were designed to help salespeople better perform these functions, and they included several solutions to problems that regularly occur in selling photographic equipment, as well as techniques for identifying buying signals and for ultimately closing a sale.

Of the six brochures, only two involved products. A $25 retail-value award was offered to the salespeople for answering correctly true-or-false questions relating to the six brochures. The manager of market planning noted that "a great number of the participants were regularly sending in answers that were usually all right. He also added that some dealers allowed their people to participate only in that particular part of the program."[6]

Most Bell & Howell dealers enrolled their employees in the program, and it became apparent that more people were involved than had been expected. Every piece of communication, in the form of a computer letter, was sent directly to the individual through the premium marketing headquarters.

A program kit, which included the 1000 merchandise awards and a pocket record notebook, launched the program. The merchandise awards were displayed in a custom-art catalog issued by the premium marketing headquarters; the catalog included an eight-page insert that announced the program and the rules. All sales and sales data were to be listed in the pocket notebook. At the end of each month, the participants wrote down their sales on score cards and had them approved by supervision for mailing to the premium marketing headquarters for actual award credit.

Each entry was automatically recorded by computer and credited to the individual's account. This program left no stone unturned and kept the participants informed each month by mail as to the status of their prize bank accounts.

Sales training for retail store employees is another form of sales promotion. However, it does not purport to promote a specific manufacturer's products in a retail store—unless that manufacturer is conducting the training program. Additional incentives are necessary to accomplish this.

TRADE DEALS AND ALLOWANCES

Trade deals and allowances are sales promotion devices designed to induce resellers to purchase more of a specific product and/or to motivate them and their salespeople to give greater effort to its sale than they ordinarily would or, more important, to give greater effort to its sale than they would give to the sale of a competing brand. These allowances are above and beyond the regular commission paid to sales personnel, and they are in addition to the customary profit margins that are a part of the price structure of each product category. (Under normal circumstances, bigger and more costly products and slower-selling and less frequently purchased merchandise carry the larger profit margin for the retailer, and, conversely, faster-moving, more frequently used products offer a smaller percentage of profit.) Trade deals provide an additional incentive.

Like all manufacturers' promotions aimed at resellers and sales forces, trade deals serve to push merchandise through the channels of distribution. Specifically, they can accomplish a number of marketing functions. The principal one, of course, is to sell more merchandise because of the greater profit or other reward incentive offered by the manufacturer. Sales can also be increased because of the advertising allowance or the discount provided to the retailer for using a display or for putting it in a choice location. In addition, deals can help a manufacturer who is overloaded with stock to move it to wholesalers' warehouses and dealers' shelves. They can also be used to enhance a consumer promotion by gaining greater retailer support and cooperation.

Generally speaking, trade deals can be more easily and quickly implemented, despite the fact that other, more complex consumer sales promotions might better accomplish the task. By the same token, they can resolve marketing problems that the consumer variety cannot. And, though the money and merchandise allowances can be quite expensive, trade deals are often less costly than consumer sales promotions.

According to Luick and Ziegler, there are three basic categories of sales promotions to the trade, each of which has a number of subdivisions.[7]

Deals or Merchandise Offers. These are designed to encourage resellers to buy and sell the products of a specific manufacturer in exchange for additional sums of money or merchandise.

Buying allowance. A buying allowance is usually associated with the introduction of new products and serves to cover the costs of handling them. It is also employed with older products that are suffering from the sales promotion efforts of the competition. In effect, it is a short-term promotion offering a price reduction for the purchase of a specified amount of goods.

Count-and-recount promotion. In this promotion, the manufacturer offers resellers a stipulated sum of money for each of the manufacturer's products moved from the reseller's warehouse within a certain period of time. A count-and-recount promotion serves to encourage restocking and also clears the way for new and improved versions of the product.

Buy-back allowance. This is always employed as a backup to another type of trade deal to prolong and enhance its value, e.g., to replace the merchandise moved from the warehouse in an earlier count-and-recount promotion. Again, a stipulated amount of money is offered to the reseller for each of the manufacturer's products purchased within a specific time period.

Free-goods offer. This is simply the substitution, for the cash incentive, of additional amounts of the merchandise being promoted. Additional merchandise could replace the monetary allowance in each of the deals discussed above.

Advertising and Display Allowances. These reward resellers for advertising and displaying the manufacturer's products.

Merchandise allowance. This is compensation given to resellers, under a temporary agreement, for including or featuring the manufacturer's wares in their displays or in their advertising.

Cooperative advertising. Unlike a merchandise allowance, cooperative advertising usually involves a long-term contract. The retailer is given an allowance for each unit or case of the manufacturer's goods purchased. The retailer receives that money, dollar for dollar (up to the amount earned), only as reimbursement for actual advertising, mentioning or featuring the manufacturer's wares, that the retailer does, according to rigid standards set by the manufacturer. One toy manufacturer gives retailers an advertising allowance of 3 percent on their purchases. The retailers receive this money as reimbursement for "qualifying advertising" and "upon presentation of the necessary and proper documentation."[8]

What does advertising have to do to qualify, and what is the required documentation? The manufacturer will reimburse the dealer, not exceeding the advertising allowance earned, for 100 percent of the cost of an ad or commercial that features its products *exclusively*. Where other manufacturers' products are in the ad or commercial, the company will pay only for the actual time and space devoted to its own products. Some of the additional requirements are that the corporate logo, no smaller than 3/16 inch square, be shown in newspaper advertising and that, in the case of broadcast media, the product be mentioned at least twice (one time being a *full* identification of the product) in a thirty-second commercial and at least once in a ten-second spot.

All this must be properly documented with actual copies of the ad torn from the newspaper, scripts of broadcast commercials, and copies of paid bills.

Use of "alternate media," such as outdoor advertising, direct mail, handbills, flyers, and shopper's guides, may also be allowed, with special authorization from the manufacturer.

In most cooperative advertising programs the manufacturer makes the actual preparation of the ad very easy for the dealer. The manufacturer provides a variety of finished ads or mats, prepared by its advertising agency. On receiving the dealer's order, all the local newspaper has to do is set the dealer's store name and address in type and insert these into the space provided in the manufacturer's prewritten ad, along with the price the dealer wants to charge for the item. The manufacturer usually also provides radio scripts with plenty of thirty-second and ten-second commercials from which the dealer can choose. All the radio announcer needs to do to customize the commercial is fill in the blanks with the local dealer's name and address.

Dealer listing promotion. This is advertising by the manufacturer in which the virtues of the product are extolled and in which are listed the names (and sometimes the addresses) of retailers who buy a specified minimum amount of the manufacturer's merchandise. In dealer listing promotions, the listing itself is the retailer's allowance or remuneration.

Direct Stimulants of Resellers and Their Salespeople. These consist of compensation over and above regular salaries or commissions for the sale or purchase of a specific manufacturer's products.

Push money. Push money (also called *spiffs* and *PMs*) consists of a cash bonus or a discount on merchandise offered to retail store employees. In effect, PMs amount to an additional commission paid by a manufacturer to retail salespeople for promoting that manufacturer's products.[9]

PMs are also used to stimulate the wholesaler's sales force. Quite often, the sales forces of jobbers who distribute many lines of competing items are offered special incentives for promoting specific product categories of any one manufacturer. The manufacturer foots the bill and is basically promoting the sale of certain product lines. The Kaywoodie Company employed a graduating scale of extra money to be paid to retail salespeople for selling its line of pipes. This technique provided added incentives for pushing the company's high-priced line at the retail level.

Although PMs can be useful in a particular situation, recent developments have caused manufacturers to question paying these extra bonuses. The employment of PMs or any incentive program may also be legally restricted and is not allowed in some states. As a result, manufacturers utilizing a PM program generally insist upon reciprocal "extras" from the sales desks. It is almost mandatory to restrict PMs to those retailers who are exclusive agencies of the manufacturer. In addition, retailers are usually asked to sign a written contract spelling out their willingness to participate in the program and to perform additional services.

There are some difficulties involved in evaluating the results of a PM program. Once it has been established, it becomes an ongoing practice, and most manufacturers dare not try to discontinue it for fear of losing goodwill at the retail level. There may also be repercussions when other manufacturers whose brands are sold in the same retail store begin to offer a greater amount of money.

Despite the foregoing caveats, PMs are a useful tool at a most important level in the channel of distribution. However, the manufacturer contemplating employing them must evaluate whether they will accomplish what is expected of them and whether they are economically feasible.

Sales contests. Contests are an additional inducement offered by a manufacturer to resellers and their salespeople. When sales contests are properly executed and when realistic goals are set, everybody can be a winner. If winning is based upon the amount of increase in sales over the previous year, small retailers and neophyte salespeople will have a chance to walk off with a top prize, along with experienced salespeople and the owners of big stores.

Dealer loaders. These are premiums given to retailers in return for the purchase of a stipulated quantity of goods. There are two types: *buying loaders* and *display loaders*. A buying loader is another form of buying allowance, in which a premium is substituted for cash or additional merchandise. In the case of a display loader, the premium serves as an actual component of the display. At the end of the promotion, the dealer keeps the premium, for example, a fiberglass canoe that was used as a dump bin for cans of tuna fish during a promotion. Such a display can be multipurpose, lending itself to consumer promotions as well. In this case the canoe might be offered as a self-liquidating premium, or it might serve as a prize in a sweepstakes or contest.

MANUFACTURERS' SALES PROMOTIONS TO RESELLERS IN ACTION

A Floor-Tile Manufacturer

A detailed trade incentive plan was presented to the manufacturer of do-it-yourself floor tiles by its advertising agency. The major objective of the plan was to increase sales of the tiles through increased sales pressure at the distributor and dealer levels. The ad agency hoped to tailor the incentive program to fit different sales and marketing situations, and it approached the distribution and dealer problems somewhat differently.

At the distributor level, the objective was to persuade distributors to devote more of their energies and those of their salespeople to developing the market for the floor tiles. The ad agency recognized that distributors and their salespeople are not primarily consumer- or retail-oriented. The solution to this problem was to point out that putting added sales pressure behind the company's brand of floor tiles would help ensure it a share of the fast-growing do-it-yourself market. The agency also pointed out that these were "clean" sales and did not involve selling adhesives or solving installation problems. Naturally, the manufacturer had to "dangle the carrot" by providing specific rewards for greater efforts. The incentives decided upon were money, allowances, and prizes.

At the retail level, the objective was to persuade dealers to give more space and attention to the floor tiles at the point of purchase. Dealer problems included space limitations, competitive pressure, lack of interest, and lack of sales pressure. The solutions to these problems were to increase sales pressure and promise higher returns for sales of the tiles. As noted above, the tools used included money, allowances, and prizes, and retailers employed traffic builders and made an effort to increase consumer demand.

Toyota

Toyota, a Japanese auto manufacturer, combined a winning consumer promotion with a travel incentive promotion for its American dealers.

As everyone would agree, including Toyota, nobody buys a car to get a $100 gift. But if you're already in the market for a car or truck, an attractive premium just might bring you in. Hot prospects (preselected) and a "Celebration/77" theme helped Toyota toward the goal of retaining its position as number one importer of foreign cars, achieved as early as 1976.

For six weeks during the normally cold and quiet months of January and February, Toyota offered a choice of seven incentives, each with a value of $100 or more, to the buyer of any of its twenty-seven car and truck models. The result was record-breaking sales—double the rate of the preceding two-week period.

The "Celebration/77" campaign earned a Premium Showcase award for Richard Harwood, of Toyota Motor Sales U.S.A., and for Helen Olsen, of H. Olsen & Co., who supplied the incentives and handled the fulfillment. The appeal was simplicity itself: "Buy a Toyota—Toyota buys you a gift." The prime target was males between the ages of 18 and 34, and the premiums were chosen for appeal to this group. They included a Skil power-tool set, Tasco zoom binoculars, Samsonite luggage, a LeJour man's or woman's watch, and a Minolta automatic 35-millimeter camera. There were two pieces of luggage and two watches to choose from, making a total field of seven items.

"Just one winner saying thanks to another," Toyota called the campaign in its promotion to dealers. The first mention of the offer came at a dealer meeting in Hawaii in October. The occasion was appropriate to the group of winners of the travel award, since the January and February promotion period also coincided with the beginning of dealer promotion for another trip—another travel incentive.

When dealer agreement forms were sent out, they combined the consumer premium program and an "eighty days to go" travel campaign for the dealers. Bonus points toward the travel awards were given for January and February sales. A series of four dealer bulletins helped keep interest high.

A strong schedule of advertising, prepared by Dancer Fitzgerald Sample, was planned for the consumer offer. About two-thirds of Toyota's TV time in January, and half of its TV time in February, was devoted to the promotion. Ads ran in *Sports Illustrated*, *Newsweek*, *People*, *Time*, *TV Guide*, and other magazines, as well as in major-market newspapers. For local dealer use, Toyota supplied newspaper ads and radio commercial copy.

A customer who bought a car or truck was asked to complete a five-part certificate form and was given an envelope in which to mail it directly to H. Olsen & Co., in Chicago. Toyota emphasized that dealers would get all the credit but not be burdened with paperwork or handling premiums. Participating dealers had to sign up formally for the program in advance, and the form included what amounted to a pledge not to inflate the car price to pay for the premium—with a reminder of FTC guidelines concerning "free" offers.

The cost of the premiums was rounded to $57 each, of which the dealer was required to pay $39.90. Toyota and the distributor each paid 15 percent, or $8.55 per unit.

Dealer display materials included wall posters, window banners, buttons, and car toppers, plus materials for local radio and newspaper advertising. The program was kicked off with dealer meetings the week of January 10, when dealers were shown a slide presentation, were given all the promotional materials, and were filled in on the details of Toyota's national campaign.

To keep Toyota out in front as the number one import, dealers were reminded constantly of the prime competition—Datsun—and were given facts to use in the battle against that company and other competitors. Toyota's "Hot Sheet" newsletter pointed out its current edge in price over Datsun. For an extra push, dealers were urged to use the consumer premiums as incentives for salespeople, and it worked. All around it was working: Of the total dealer organization of 1013, 85.5 percent participated. They enjoyed an average increase of 55 percent over sales in the same period of 1976, while the sales of nonparticipants declined 8 percent. "Celebration/77" set out to move 51,319 cars and trucks. The actual count came to 62,732; this was 22.2 percent, or more than 11,000 cars, over the objective. Toyota increased its market share of imports by 2 percentage points. And what about its principal competitor, Datsun? No increase in share.

The most popular premium in the promotion turned out to be the Minolta camera, chosen by over 32 percent of the customers. And of all redemptions, between 30 and 40 percent were made by women, who evidently play an important role in car-buying decisions.

For Toyota, a long, cold winter had been heated up. "Celebration/77" had achieved its bluntly stated goal: to "steal purchase-ready traffic away from our direct competitors."[10]

Pentel

Pentel, originator of the felt-tip pen, introduced a new liquid-ink ballpoint pen in the spring of 1976; this was its first entry into the ballpoint market.

Pentel's new Rolling Writer was launched with a retail price of $0.89, in a market dominated by ballpoint pens costing from $0.19 to $0.49. To gain rapid penetration and awareness, Pentel used a dual incentive offer for the stationery trade and commercial users of pens. The promotion won the Premium Showcase award for Wally Kaiser, of Pentel, and Roy Thomas, of Premium Marketing Corp., the National Premium Sales Executives (NPSE) member who entered the program, in conjunction with another NPSE member, Alan Wigod, of Teledyne Water Pik.

The main objective was to sell 1 million Rolling Writers in a ninety-day period and to expand the American introduction of this unique writing instrument. The incentive goal was to increase unit purchases and to identify and segment target audiences. These target audiences included corporate and institutional buyers, small offices, and secretaries, as well as stationery dealers, wholesalers, and distributors.

Two premiums were selected for purchases of different quantities. The items were chosen because they had high perceived value, because there was advertising support to enhance acceptance, and because they matched Pentel's customer demographics in terms of product appeal. The first offer, for buyers of eight dozen pens, was an Equity travel alarm clock. For larger-volume orders—eighteen dozen Rolling Writers—Pentel offered a Water Pik shower massage.

Program support was developed through trade advertising, merchandising materials, and year-end advertising. Trade ads appeared as full-color pages in the March and April issues of the most widely read and widely distributed publications in the stationery industry. More than two-thirds of the ad space featured the incentives, with the rest devoted to product copy on the Rolling Writer.

Other promotional support materials were developed for the dealer's use, in each case featuring the Rolling Writer heavily, but still giving at least half the space to the premium offers. These included selling sheets with details of the promotion, window banners provided for in-store merchandising, counter cards for use at the point of purchase, large free-standing in-store display pieces, and statement stuffers for dealers' use in promoting the offer to large trade customers.

To back up the appeal to these customers, Pentel used print ads in five general business publications: *Business Week*, *The Office*, *Modern Office Procedures*, *Office Product News*, and *The Wall Street Journal*—publications read by people who influence the purchase of office products in volume. The effect of this advertising helped create a demand which was the catalyst that filled the trade pipeline. Business buyers of volume office supplies were also reached through radio commercials scheduled to coincide with commuting periods.

Pentel called the results of the program "phenomenal." The original forecast was for 6200 travel alarm clocks and 2500 shower massages to be used in the ninety-day promotion. The actual results were close—about 6000—in the case of the clocks. But the large-volume purchases to earn the shower-massage premium totaled almost 5 times expectations, or 12,000 units. The product sales target of 1 million pens looked very conservative in the end; more than 3 million pens were sold. Pentel had planned a ninety-day promotion, but the success of the incentive offer was such that the promotion was stopped after sixty days.

Pentel's original promotional budget was allocated as a gross-margin reduction against a percentage of sales. As sales increased, the budget increased concurrently.

What were the marketing benefits? By specific measurement of the program, the objective of 1 million pens was met 3 times over—with sales of 3 million—and in two-thirds the projected time.

The fact that the smaller eight-dozen purchase unit pulled approximately as forecast, while the eighteen-dozen package outsold the smaller assortment by a wide margin, suggested to Pentel that a larger promotional package can be sold effectively if the premium has strong appeal.

In the postpromotion period, sales continued almost at the same pace, indicating that the pump-priming effect of the incentive campaign had gained real market penetration and higher awareness of the Rolling Writer.

In looking to the future, Pentel has concluded that incentive promotions are a prime vehicle for generating increased sales of its products, and programs for additional and larger premium offers are being studied, including an offer of another Water Pik product.

In fact, as a result of the success of the shower-massage promotion, Pentel has charted a course of using an annual trade incentive promotion to stimulate sales of the Rolling Writer.

Pentel's biggest, and now most successful, premium program has made a lasting impression on this company's marketing philosophy.[11]

Colgate-Palmolive

A unique incentive program in which consumers, salespeople, and dealers all had a chance to participate was offered by the Colgate-Palmolive Company. The program used sports and travel holidays to strengthen the company's brand image. Trips to foreign countries were awarded as top sweepstakes prizes, and weekend trips to local resort areas were also provided for runners-up. Sales, by the dealers and by sales personnel, were well above expectations. Purchasers of Ajax were offered an opportunity to obtain free tickets to sporting events, such as the NBA games. A proof of purchase of either Ajax liquid or Ajax powder cleanser was required. The consumer would purchase one ticket to a local game and be able to get the other tickets free. The sales staff also used the tickets as handouts when they made retail sales calls.

Often, the sponsor of an incentive program is able to get the merchandise or travel free or at a reduced cost from the manufacturer or travel company. This can play a very important role in cutting overall costs for the program. Naturally, the company providing the free goods on travel must be compensated by the advertising of its products or services in the major media as a trade-off for the prizes or awards furnished. This practice, however, is more common with consumer promotions, which are more likely to be advertised in the mass media.

Ramada Inn

The Ramada Inn nationwide chain of motels launched a $1 million advertising campaign in order to increase the number of reservations made on its computerized "room finder" reservation system. It offered an employee incentive program for a three-month period to achieve a fourfold increase over a similar period the previous year.

All employees at the inns who reached the goal received, as an additional bonus, nightshirts imprinted with "I'm building a reputation." The slogan related to the theme of the Ramada campaign, "We're building a reputation, not resting on one." The actual prizes for plateaus reached ranged from a set of monogrammed drinking glasses to AM-FM digital clock radios. To add impact to this program, Ramada presented each inn manager with a specially made Ramada Inn license plate with the Ramada logo.

TRAVEL INCENTIVES

Travel incentives are probably the most effective sales promotion tool a company can use to create extra sales and goodwill for the future. The glamour and excitement of visiting a far-off vacation spot appeal to the entire family. Incentive travel "turns people on," especially if there are choices of destination for different levels of achievement.

According to John T. Tyner, incentive travel planners must answer the "five W's": who, what, why, when and where?[12] The Conn Organ Corp., a manufacturer of electronic organs, has been answering these five questions for eight successful years with incentive travel programs. The question of "who" must be tailored to the type of people you want to motivate. The Conn Organ Corp. realized that its dealers consisted mainly of husbands and wives who operated music stores, although there were dealers in different age groups and with varied interests. In order to satisfy the needs of such a diverse group, the company sought the services of a professional incentive organization. The "what" was also determined by the professionals. It had to be a trip that included interesting side trips, cocktail parties, leisure shopping time, fun, relaxation, and excitement. The "why" was an opportunity to meet with other dealers who had similar travel interests in a social and relaxed atmosphere. In deciding on the "when" and "where," the company tried to coordinate the best time and place, in terms of introducing a new line of products or a new sales campaign. The trip also had to take place when the winners could be away from their businesses. Naturally, the trip also had to be to a place that would have the right kind of weather at the right time of year. In other words, if it's cold at home, a tropical vacation spot is in order.

Bob Kohn, the director of advertising who coordinated the trips, lists several "musts": (1) Hire a professional incentive travel planner, (2) give the trip universal appeal so that it meets the needs of every group, (3) get feedback and do a checkout trip in advance, (4) do not establish a rigid all-day and all-night schedule, and (5) leave some free time.[13]

At the General Motors Corp., travel incentives have been a way of life for many years. These travel incentive programs are massive, and Chevrolet leads the list. According to E. K. Roggenkamp III, national manager of sales promotion, travel incentives are not used solely for competitive reasons at the Chevrolet division; they "motivate people to do things that they wouldn't do, even for money." These incentives recognize effort and stimulate friendly competition. Most of the Chevrolet dealers are relatively comfortable financially and can usually buy what they need. The incentives are used to help move backlogs of cars in slower periods and to even out the peaks and valleys of automobile sales.[14]

Cadillac, another division of General Motors, though not a big user of incentive programs, does employ them to meet specific needs or solve certain problems. In the spring of 1974, when gasoline shortages had threatened the big-car market, Cadillac launched its first major incentive promotion in more than ten years—and the first promotion ever directed at salespeople. The results proved that quality selling techniques *can* overcome obstacles.

The "Challenge of Excellence" campaign, created by the Sperry & Hutchinson Company (S&H), offered merchandise incentives to salespeople and their managers and a trip to Hawaii to dealer principals. The campaign ran from March 21 to July 21; the main qualification period ended May 31.

During this time, 7800 salespeople, 1120 sales managers, and 1460 Cadillac dealers regularly received materials to stimulate their interest in the campaign and keep their enthusiasm up—a total of 110 different promotional pieces in all, each planned to reflect Cadillac's quality image. The prime motivating factor was a selection of highly desirable awards, including a trip for dealers and their spouses to Mauna Kea, Hawaii; deluxe merchandise selected by sales managers and salespeople from the S&H "Challenge of Excellence" catalog; and prestige gifts from Tiffany for sales managers and dealers. Awards were based on assigned unit sales objectives.

Every aspect of the campaign was covered, from necessary forms and kickoff meeting banners to elaborate announcement kits, follow-up mailings, and attractive gold package stickers. To dramatize the travel award, an eight-minute film was presented to the Cadillac dealers at regional kickoff meetings just prior to the program's official opening.

Before these meetings, the dealers received a teaser brochure linking Hawaii with such Cadillac attributes as elegance, beauty, style, quality, and excitment; the purpose of the brochure was to motivate the dealers to place among the top thirty in their group and earn the trip. The dealers also received an order form and a Tiffany catalog featuring jewelry, silver, and the like, which they could earn by placing in the top fifty in their group.

An official campaign reference source explained the program in detail. A brochure highlighted the awards and acted as a wraparound for a separate twelve-page booklet of rules. Each sales manager received an embossed gold box stamped with the program logo. Inside, fitted into a die-cut velour bed, were the Tiffany catalog, the announcement brochure, a merchandise redemption form, and a deluxe book of awards, in a high-gloss black cover stamped in gold.

The book of awards contained 154 pages of luxury merchandise that could be earned by managers at the rate of $6 per unit sold after reaching their objective. The enclosed "Challenge of Leadership" brochure set the stage for

FIGURE 17-1.   The merchandise incentive award program for Cadillac sales personnel. (*Courtesy of National Premium Sales Executives Foundation.*)

follow-up mailings to the sales managers and outlined contest rules and awards for them and their salespeople.

The salespeople's announcement brochure was brightly illustrated with merchandise awards and contained motivating text material. Salespeople earned $51 worth of merchandise per unit sold. Regular mailings were sent to all participants. Sales managers received a series of four brass-plated plaques in a folder embossed with the "Challenge of Excellence" logo. Plaques and folders related to the accomplishments of the Apollo astronauts, John F. Kennedy, Theodore Roosevelt, and Vince Lombardi, drawing parallels between the challenges they faced and those faced by Cadillac sales managers. Salespeople received brochures dealing with the challenges met by Michelangelo, Paul Revere, Stradivari, and Cadillac founder Henry Leland. Sales managers received a modified version of each.

The spouses of dealers were involved in the program by means of special mailings to their homes, which included a brochure and a personal letter from the manager of the Mauna Kea Hotel; a record of Hawaiian music and a Time-Life illustrated book, both with cover letters; and an orchid corsage. A book, *The Tiffany Touch*, went to dealers' and sales managers' homes, as did personalized letters from the regional sales managers.

Meanwhile, back at the salespeople's homes, mailings of merchandise-award postcards kept interest high. When the program was over and the sales tallied, the results spoke for themselves. Cadillac's objective had been the sale of 41,500 new cars. Actual sales were 28 percent higher—53,120 new cars were sold during the period.

All salespeople earned some award, since credits were given from the first unit sold. Among sales managers and dealers, 83 percent qualified, with 212 of the dealers earning the Hawaii trip. The top fifty of each group also got Tiffany awards. Significantly, Cadillac's competitors in the luxury-car field did not have increased sales during this period. Cadillac alone recorded an increase, going from a fifty-eight-day inventory to virtually zero and ringing up the best May sales record in Cadillac history!

The "Challenge of Excellence" proved the ability of a well-planned and well-executed motivational program to increase sales. The dramatic results were enough to convince Cadillac to operate its second incentive program in 1975.[15]

Connie Goldstein, in an article published in *Successful Meetings* magazine, states that the spouse, still usually a woman, can motivate her mate in ways that are better than anything an employer can devise in an incentive program. And for incentive travel, directing the pretrip publicity to the wife is a must. Most women want a warm climate, exciting things to see, shopping, evening entertainment, and fine food. They also seem to be very much concerned that their husbands be able to relax, attend and participate in business sessions, and have free time. Balance is the key.

Goldstein points out the need for considering the wife's wardrobe as well as the possible expense of child care. When both husband and wife are on a trip, these factors cannot be overlooked, and they are important considerations for management when planning a promotion. Another point that should be taken into account is the possibility of offering an alternative when the winners are unable to get away at a particular time. This can be a problem when attendance at the planned time and place is an important part of the sales promotion.[16]

CONCLUSION

Any award earned in an incentive program is a form of recognition, a status symbol, and a proof of job proficiency. Merchandise gifts, cash bonuses, and travel awards appeal to almost anyone you strive to motivate. They can have a range of appeal to the individual as a business person, a hobbyist, or a parent who can use the award in the home, on the job, or as part of a better way of life, as in the case of incentive travel. While the primary purpose of dealer or sales-force incentive programs is to induce or stimulate participants to sell more, there are many additional goals that management can accomplish or make easier by offering incentive programs:

1. Overcoming routine selling
2. Introducing new items
3. Broadening channels of distribution
4. Boosting full-line sales
5. Securing new accounts
6. Gaining more facings
7. Stimulating selling
8. Highlighting special deals
9. Thwarting and slowing competitive promotions
10. Increasing the company's market share
11. Getting secondary displays
12. Stimulating routine selling performance
13. Evening out sales periods
14. Getting the cooperation of retail personnel

In summary, merchandise awards are not as effective as travel awards. However, it must be noted that travel awards can and often do create problems in terms of time away from the job. In order for incentive travel awards to be economically feasible, they are usually offered in the off-season, which can cause difficulties for people with family and school commitments. Regardless of whether the incentive is a merchandise, cash, or travel award, it is the author's opinion that everyone who participates in the program should win some type of prize. After all, the company sponsoring the program wants to build a favorable attitude toward its product, service, or goal in the minds of all participants, not generate negative feelings.

ENDNOTES

1. "The Incentive Field at a Glance," *Incentive Marketing*, December 1982, p. 45.
2. "Top Ten Merchandise Users (1981)" and "Top Ten Incentive Travel Users (1981)," *Incentive Marketing*, December 1982, pp. 46, 47.
3. Ibid.
4. "Total Dollar Volume of Incentive Usage," *Incentive Marketing*, December 1982, p. 44.
5. Jo-Ann Barclay, "Incentives Need Dealer Appeal to Get past Fram's Screening," *Incentive Marketing*, January 1978, pp. 19–21.
6. Nancy Ferer, "Bell & Howell Training Retail Salespeople via Catalog Program," *Premium Incentive Business*, February 1978, p. 10.
7. John F. Luick and William F. Ziegler, *Sales Promotion and Modern Merchandising*, McGraw-Hill Book Company, New York, 1968, pp. 99–115.
8. *Retail Advertising Kit and Co-op Program*, GAF, p. 6.
9. Alfred Gross, *Sales Promotion*, The Ronald Press Company, New York, 1961, p. 176.
10. George Meredith and Robert P. Fried, *Incentives in Marketing*, National Premium Sales Executives Education Fund, 1977, pp. 458–460.
11. Ibid., pp. 451–453.
12. John T. Tyner, "The Whats and Wheres of Conn Organ Incentive Travel Programs," *Successful Meetings*, June 1978.
13. Ibid, p. 70.
14. "Chevrolet: The Best Seller, the Biggest Incentive User," *Incentive Marketing*, May 1978, pp. 44–48.
15. Meredith and Fried, op. cit., pp. 442–443.
16. Connie Goldstein, "Ask Wives What They Really Want," *Successful Meetings*, February 1978.

18

How to Run a Dealer and Sales-Force Incentive Program

HAROLD J. DeVESTERN
Eastern Sales Manager, Premium and Incentive Sales Division, Bulova Watch Company, Inc.

Incentives are the motivating forces that enable us to cope with the mundane responsibilities we must all face every day of our lives.

When your alarm clock rings at 6 A.M., why do you bother to get up at this ungodly hour? Because you have an incentive to do so. Think about it. Any one of us can probably compile a long list of incentives that motivate us to respond to that little mechanism that starts our day.

OK, what's next? You shower, brush your teeth, and comb your hair. Why? You can compile another list of incentives to do these things: to look good, to feel clean, and to avoid offending the people with whom you will come in contact during the day. Why are you putting on that clean shirt? Why did you have your shoes shined? Why did you just pay $80 for that new dress? We could go on like this forever, but by now you are getting the message. Everything we do is done because of an incentive, that little carrot that is held out in front of us, and makes us run like a rabbit trying to reach it.

Actually, this striving to reach a goal is instilled in us when we are infants and continues throughout our entire lives: "Better be good, or Santa won't bring you any presents." "Eat all your vegetables so that you'll grow up to be big and strong." "Study hard in school so that you'll get good grades." "Invest your money wisely, and you'll have a nice nest egg when you retire."

Is it any wonder that the incentive and award business has grown into a multibillion-dollar industry in relatively few years? The reason for this growth is the strong desire in all of us to get that "pat on the back" for a job well done. We all have a need to be recognized for our efforts. (See Figure 18-1.) The numerous ways in which these efforts are rewarded are what constitute the lucrative giant known as the *incentive industry*. One would be hard-pressed to come up with the name of a manufacturer who is not in some way involved in incentives.

WHY WE USE INCENTIVES

Incentives are used to motivate company salespeople to sell more merchandise, to get new accounts, to reactivate old accounts, and to make more calls. In turn, the company will offer its salespeople, or authorize them to offer, an incentive to their accounts to increase sales. As a result, the accounts may offer an incentive to their customers to help move the accounts' inventory, or the manufacturer may offer incentives to end users. The cycle goes on, creating increases in sales for all sellers involved and ultimately benefiting the end user, as well.

Don't get the idea that incentives are used just to sell more merchandise. The types of incentives are almost endless, as are the ways in which they are used. They come in the form of account-opener premiums, bounce-backs, box-top offers, business gifts, contest prizes, continuity promotions, coupon plans, credit-card offers, dealer incentives, dealer loaders, and in-pack premiums, to name only a few.

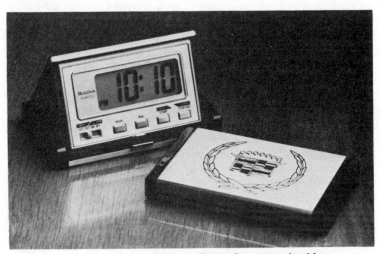

FIGURE 18-1. Some incentive awards can be customized by means of silk screening or engraving a corporate logo or monogram or a special message to the recipient. (*Courtesy of Bulova Watch Company, Inc.*)

THE INCENTIVE MARKETING DEPARTMENT

Where does one start with incentives? How are the costs, advantages, and feasibility determined?

Most manufacturers offering products used as incentives maintain separate departments assigned to merchandising and selling to corporations and organizations. These departments, operating almost as separate entities, prepare their own sales material, employ advertising agencies, and have a sales force and a network of stocking distributors and representatives.

The pricing structures of premium and incentive departments do not correspond to retail price structures; here, success is predicated on high sales volume rather than the single-unit sale in the retail forum.

Let's look into the activities and operations of an incentive sales department that can be counted on to be productive. The sales material consists of:

• Incentive catalogs containing pictures and information on quantity pricing (Figure 18-2)

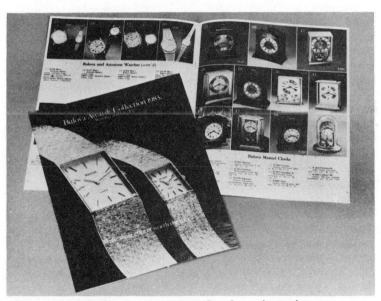

FIGURE 18-2. Most manufacturers that have incentive or premium departments publish annual awards catalogs. These catalogs, often in full color, illustrate the companies' lines of products that can be used for incentives, premiums, business gifts, and prizes. (*Courtesy of Bulova Watch Company, Inc.*)

- Full-color picture sheets
- Color transparencies for reproduction
- Artwork
- Brochures, booklets, etc., giving information on product personalization, drop-shipping charges, and program planning

The advertising agency is responsible for:

- Planning ads for trade publications
- Supplying mailers to the trade
- Creating ads geared to generate potential leads to be followed up by sales personnel
- Providing feedback on which type of ad creates most end-user excitement

The sales force is responsible for:

- Contacting potential accounts
- Presenting the product to customers
- Suggesting programs
- Following up leads
- Directing the network of representatives and distributors
- Providing general counsel to customers

The distributors and representatives are responsible for:

- Taking inventory of products
- Calling on potential customers
- Fulfilling program orders
- Suggesting programs
- Following up leads
- Supplying feedback to the manufacturer on customer requests

STARTING AN INCENTIVE PROGRAM

An incentive program is a well-structured plan designed to generate enthusiasm among, and increase the performance of, the participants in a project. But realistic objectives are essential from the outset. For example, your sales-force objective might be to increase dollar sales by 10 percent over the same period last year, which means $10,000 more in dollar sales per salesperson. Alternatively, you might be determined to increase unit sales by, say, 5 percent over last year, which means selling 5000 units more per salesperson than in the same period the previous year.

Other sales-force objectives include upgrading existing accounts, either by increasing average dollar sales per account or by converting existing accounts to higher-ticket merchandise; opening new accounts; and increasing dealer participation in company goals, through such methods as in-store promotions. (See Figure 18-3.)

Each of these programs necessitates a budget, and, especially when the objectives represent an entirely new direction or a greatly expanded one, the amount of money appropriated to see it through must be arrived at realistically.

If the objectives are unrealistic—or downright unattainable—or if the reward is simply not worth the effort, the program is sure to fail. Yet a realistic approach is not in itself a sure predictor of succcess. We at the Bulova Watch

---

Goal: Increase dollar sales.

Objective: Increase dollar sales by 10% over same period previous year.

Performance level: $10,000 more in dollar sales per man than same period previous year.

Goal: Increase unit sales.

Objective: Increase unit sales by 5% over same period previous year.

Performance level: 5,000 units more sold, per salesman, than same period previous year.

***Goal: Upgrade existing accounts.**

Objective: Increase average dollar sale per account for all accounts doing under $10,000 annually.

Performance level: $1,000 increased sales per account for all accounts presently doing under $10,000 annually.

***Goal: Upgrade existing accounts.**

Objective: Convert existing accounts to higher ticket merchandise.

Performance level: 20% more sales of $10 units, replacing $5 units, per account, over same period previous year.

Goal: New account openings.

Objective: Increase present active account roster by 3%.

Performance level: 3 new accounts opened per man over previous quarter.

Goal: Increase dealer participation in company goals.

Objective: 10% more dealer participation in in-store promotions.

Performance level: 20 more dealers per salesman signed to participate in in-store promotion over same period previous year.

---

*Note: The same overall goal may be tacked by specifying different objectives, and performance levels.

FIGURE 18-3. A sample work chart of typical sales-force objectives and performance levels.

Company have thoroughly studied the correlation between thorough pre-evaluation of sales-force objectives and performance levels and have developed proven techniques to build business and increase profits by getting salespeople to sell more—and dealers to buy more. That information, including excellent ratios and formulas to use in determining a favorable mix of budget and objectives, is provided in this chapter. The techniques are applicable to all businesses, large and small.

Developing a Budget

Three basic elements make up the overall incentive budget:

1. Administration
2. Promotional materials and services
3. Prize awards

Generally speaking, a modest program run internally requires no more than 10 percent of the budget to be allocated for combined promotion and administration. For complex programs or for those demanding elaborate promotional materials, the allocation may go as high as 30 percent.

The cost of prize awards can be either a fixed or a variable cost. In a "closed-end" budget, the sponsor determines in advance what the maximum expenditure will be, either by allocating funds arbitrarily or by fixing a percent of anticipated sales. An "open-end" budget is required for any incentive plan which encourages unlimited improvements in performance level (e.g., a plan that offers a reward for every new account opened, with no cutoff point after a fixed number has been reached). In this case, the number and value of the awards given are a function of performance levels achieved.

Traditionally, between 1 and 7 percent of anticipated additional gross sales can be applied to the cost of a sales incentive program. While 3.5 percent is the average, higher or lower budgets are determined by a variety of factors, including salaries, participants' commissions, program length, and individual business considerations.

Award values must be consistent with participants' earnings. It's important to point out that there is a definite correlation between participants' earnings and the value of the awards that will motivate them to achieve more.

When running a program to *increase sales*, award-value amounts must be set. These are the earnings the participant can win at the top performance level, generally falling between 3 and 8 percent of salary or commission within the period of the program.

The present wages or commissions of the participants are a good basis for evaluating what those award amounts should be. Obviously, a higher-value award is required to motivate an individual earning $1500 a month than to motivate someone earning $500.

When running a program to *improve efficiency*, it is also necessary to determine award-value amounts at the start; these earnings at the top performance level usually fall between 1 and 7 percent of the individual's salary. However, although the percentage range is a useful guide, actual amounts should be related as accurately as possible to the sponsor's performance-level value.

Longer programs require better awards. Finally, for those incentive programs lasting sixty days or less, higher-value awards per performance level are mandated. These short-duration programs frequently fall in the "special-emphasis" category, which means they are intended to effect rapid changes in some temporarily critical aspect of the sponsor's business. Also called "spurt programs," these activities are suitable for such goals as new-account acquisition or the introduction of a new service or product, or they can be used for something as simple as a campaign to lower the incidence of "gone-fishing" sick days during the summer.

Reduction of program length can also be utilized as a budget-stretching mechanism. In the event that a budget allocation is inadequate to the task of awarding sufficient bonuses to participants, the smartest solution is to shorten the program's duration.

A Hypothetical Situation

Here's a hypothetical situation involving the creation of an in-plant incentive program using the guidelines discussed above.

ABC Company desires to increase sales in the first quarter of the year by 10 percent over the same quarter last year, when sales totaled $3,635,000. An anticipated sales increase of 10 percent would equal $4 million (in round numbers), a total dollar increase of $365,000. Using the guidelines outlined in this chapter and knowing that this period is a difficult one for sales, the ABC Company decides to allocate fully 6 percent of the anticipated increase in sales to achieve its objectives:

$$\$365,000 \times 0.06 \ (6\%) = \$21,900$$

Now the theoretical budget for the ABC Company's incentive program is $21,900.

Eighteen salespeople and two regional managers will participate in the program. The eighteen salespeople earn an average of $35,000 per year in commissions. Thus, each has an average salary during the first quarter of the promotion (three months) of $8750. The regional managers each earn $38,000 per year, or $9500 per quarter.

By multiplying the average salaries (commissions) by 3 percent and 8 percent, we can see the minimum and maximum award budgets based upon income guidelines. (See Table 18-1.)

TABLE 18-1 Costs of a Hypothetical Incentive Program

Participants	Minimum award budget (3% × 0.03)*	Maximum award budget (8% × 0.08)*
Eighteen salespeople with salaries of $8750 per quarter = $157,500	$4725	$12,600
Two regional managers with salaries of $9500 per quarter = $19,000	570	1,520
Total	$5295	$14,120

* Based on income guidelines.

Since the salespeople and the regional managers are high earners, the ABC Company decides that it will utilize the full 8 percent maximum based on salary for awards to motivate them. For administration and promotion, which will be handled internally, the company calculates that 15 percent of the budget, or $3285, will be necessary:

$14,120 (award) + $3285 (administration and promotion) = $17,405

This is $4495 less than the amount predicted in the theoretical budget.

The ABC Company can now decide whether to reduce its budget accordingly or to designate the additional moneys to other areas that will strengthen its program. For example, the company may decide to add a dealer sweepstakes to the program, which will further increase the chance for success, or it may decide to add the customer relations in-plant personnel to the program, since these are people whose backup services affect sales. Or the company can simply lop off $4495 of the projected budget and still anticipate success.

Dealer objectives and performance levels, like those of a sales force, are goal-oriented. (See Figure 18-4.) They may be designed to increase units purchased; to increase dollar volume; to increase dealer participation in company goals through store sales, co-op and clerk educational programs, or dealer-created promotional ideas; or to increase product exposure at the dealer level. Whatever the goal is, it must be monitored for performance level, no matter how modest that may be. For instance, if the goal is to increase product exposure at the dealer level by 20 percent, that may mean allowing 2 additional feet of counter, floor, or aisle space in the store. If the goal is to generate dealer-created promotional ideas, then it's essential to maintain a performance level which takes into account the creation and implementation of an in-store promotion or advertising campaign, verified by photographs, advertising tear sheets, and other publicity.

The Schedule

Scheduling is also extremely important; the dates and times that are chosen for the program depend on the kind of program it is as well as its magnitude. Needless to say, a small, self-contained, single-goal program conducted at a small plant will not entail the planning necessary for a program that is of considerably larger scope, in which many participants and a complex organization, perhaps consisting of multiple plans running concurrently,

---

Goal: Increase units purchased.

Objective: Increase units purchased. per dealer, by 10% over same period previous year.

Performance level: 100 units more purchased per dealer over same period previous year.

Goal: Increase dollar volume.

Objective: Increase dollar volume per dealer by 15% over same period previous year.

Performance level: $1,500 more spent by dealer with your company over same period previous year.

---

*Goal: Increase dealer participation in company goals.

Objective: Increase dealer participation in in-store sales programs. co-op programs and clerk education programs.

Performance level: One additional area of participation. per dealer. over previous quarter.

Goal: Increase product exposure at dealer level.

Objective: Increase display area by 20% per dealer.

Performance level: 2 feet additional counter (floor. aisle) space for product exposure over previous quarter.

---

*Goal: Increase dealer participation in company goals.

Objective: Generate dealer-created promotional ideas.

Performance level: Creation and implementation of one in-store promotion or advertising campaign, verified by photographs. tear sheets. etc.

---

*Note: The same overall goal may be tacked by specifying different objectives, and performance levels.

FIGURE 18-4. A sample work chart of typical dealer objectives and performance levels.

require a different level of scheduling expertise. But, whether the program is large or small, there is no substitute for a written calendar of the events that mean so much to the campaign.

You'll need at least thirteen weeks prior to the commencement of your program to allow for preparation of applicable materials, to mesh individual schedules, and to arrange for conference times, if necessary.

The Theme

In the preprogram phase, a theme should be shaped that ties together the promotion and the incentives to be used.

For instance, a company that manufactures a line of cleaning compounds and desires to use watches as incentives could choose "time to clean up and watch profits shine" as a theme.

The Award and the Supplier

As a rule of thumb, the item used as the award should be a brand-name product which recipients would want to buy for themselves and which cannot be purchased in discount stores. The product should be of good quality, befitting the achievement for which it is awarded. It should also be a useful item and something that will serve as a reminder of the goals achieved. (Note, however, that travel is often used as an award.)

Now that you have chosen the award, you must start checking on the supplier. The supplier should be truly committed to the incentive business. Make certain that availability of the product is assured and that the supplier will guarantee on-time delivery and provide product support services and aids to assist in the overall operation of the program. There are many fine companies that meet these criteria, making it possible for you to select an incentive award that best suits your company's budget and objectives.

Merchandise vs Cash. While some companies still give cash awards, the disadvantages of cash are clear: It has no lasting value, and offers no satisfaction of recognition. Since the company can purchase award merchandise at below the retail price, its value is greater than that of cash. The recipient is also given a range of gifts from which to choose. The greater the efforts or accomplishment, the greater the award.

Presenting the Awards. Besides the program results, one of the most important factors in an incentive plan is awarding the merchandise. On-time delivery is a must! Don't keep prizewinners waiting for their rewards. They didn't disappoint you; now don't disappoint them.

19 The Trade Show: *Dynamic Tool of Marketing*

ROBERT LETWIN

Publisher, Successful Meetings *Magazine; Vice President, Bill Communications, Inc.*

SOME HISTORY

The trade shows and industrial shows that we know today are descendants of the ancient bazaar. The trade show originated in biblical times at the places where ancient caravan routes crossed. At these junctures traders would display their goods for barter. Throughout the Middle Ages, major city-states developed trade fairs, where goods from wide areas could be displayed, sold, or traded.

During the Middle Ages these major fairs became annual events. Leipzig was the site of an annual fair that still exists today after 800 years. As city-states grew into nations, international fairs came into vogue. And today, throughout Europe particularly, annual international fairs take place at which goods from all nations may be examined and ordered. These events are also called *sample fairs*, because only samples are exhibited; buyers must place orders for items to be delivered later.

The first world's fair, which was open to the general public, took place in 1851 in London. The aim of the British at the time was to boast of the achievements made by the British Empire, then at its zenith. The first commercial fair in the United States was held in 1814. Trade shows and industrial shows, however, did not come into their own until the age of mass production.

Instead of focusing on general merchandise put on display, trade shows and industrial fairs developed along industry or professional lines. Such shows include automobile shows, premium shows, shows for the chemical industry and for the metal industry, technical shows, and even shows centering on medicine and engineering.

General merchandise fairs are on the decline; now specialties and subspecialties are the basis for trade shows and industrial shows. With each new scientific development, a new discipline emerges, along with a trade or technical show to promote the sales of products in the new field; atomic energy shows and computer shows are examples.

THE PLACE OF TRADE SHOWS AND INDUSTRIAL SHOWS IN THE ECONOMY

Trade shows and industrial shows are valuable tools for the economy because they fit the buying patterns of industry. Industry does intensive "comparison shopping" for the products and services it buys. There is no better way to see and compare a variety of products and methods—often in operation—than at a trade or industrial show. Most of the major suppliers usually exhibit their products at an industry show.

Multiple purchase decisions are another characteristic of the buying patterns of industry. A trade or industrial show offers the many decision makers in a company the opportunity to see, examine, and compare a variety

FIGURE 19-1. Well-run trade shows draw big crowds of potential buyers. (*Courtesy of Thalheim Expositions, Inc.*)

of products in which they are interested. These buyers can see, analyze, and test products in a short span of time, which facilitates their buying decisions.

A major need of buyers in industry is for technical information. At trade shows and industrial shows, buyers have an opportunity to probe deeply for facts because exhibiting companies generally staff their booths with technicians, chief engineers, and sometimes their top executives, as well as sales representatives.

No other marketing method or event serves the buying needs of industry as well as the professionally managed and promoted trade or industrial show.

While trade shows and industrial shows—the supermarkets for industry and the professions—are among the most effective marketing tools available today, they are not used to their optimum. Unfortunately, few industry executives have ever been schooled in the exhibit medium, and therefore they do not know what works and what should be avoided. In the course of experimentation, much time and money are lost.

PLANNING FOR EFFECTIVE PARTICIPATION

For trade-show participation to be effective, the exhibitor must think of the experience as a *super sales call*. It is an opportunity to provide the salesperson

FIGURE 19-2. Potential customers talking business at the New York Premium Show. (*Courtesy of Thalheim Expositions, Inc.*)

with a dynamic instrument to attract prospects and make a sales presentation dramatically. While a good exhibit is dramatic, it is not "show biz" in the theatrical sense. It is not entertainment. An exhibitor who enters a show with the thought of producing an entertainment vehicle usually will fail.

Analyzing the Expected Attendance

To exhibit effectively at a trade show, you must take several important steps. The first is to analyze the expected attendance. What kinds of people will attend? What percentage of these will be your prospects? You should make estimates of how many people will attend and of their level of sophistication.

Trade-show attendance data are provided by the show management. The more reliable the show management, the better the data. Approximately forty shows currently have their attendances audited by outside organizations to authenticate the accuracy of the figures and, in most cases, to monitor registration procedures. The number of audited shows has risen very slowly because the average exhibitor makes no demand for more accurate attendance data. Most exhibitors do not appreciate the value of precise figures, which provide the best basis on which to plan exhibit participation intelligently. When you have good data on show visitors, you are able to analyze a show's attendance and determine how many of your best prospects you can expect to visit the next show.

Setting an Objective

Your second step in exhibit planning is to set an objective. An objective for an exhibit should be in the form of a figure or figures that tell exactly *what you expect to happen as a result of your participation*. An objective would not be, for instance, "to show the new line" or "to introduce a new product." This kind of objective is too nebulous and will prove a poor basis for planning. Instead, an objective should contain a number indicating how many prospects you want qualified at the show by your salespersons, how many sales you expect to make, how many follow-ups you anticipate, or how many dealers or distributors you hope to sign. Until you can focus on real numbers, you are building sand castles, isolated from marketing reality.

Attracting the Right Audience

Once you have put figures in your objective, you can start the creative part of your planning. This involves the techniques for attracting those persons to your exhibit who are your *prime prospects*. An exhibit should never be planned simply to attract crowds. Seldom is every show visitor a prospect for a particular exhibitor's products or services.

A wise exhibitor wants to talk only to those show visitors who are prime prospects. When you attract crowds to your booth, you merely put buffers between your prime prospects and your salespersons. It is because you want a distilled audience that you avoid any element which will attract everybody. For instance, magicians, caricaturists, and photographers will attract huge audiences to an exhibit, but these crowds are not responsive to sales presentations. In fact, they inhibit the salespersons on duty from making valid contacts to qualify prospects.

Another approach often used to attract a large audience is to give away advertising specialties and samples. These giveaways are often counterproductive because they attract large audiences but do not discriminate between serious prospects and the shopping-bag element who gravitate to anything offered free. However, serious prospects can be qualified.

The aim for planning an effective exhibit is to create a message that appeals directly to your best prospects' business or professional interests. This usually is in the form of a solution to a problem currently experienced by your prospects. If the message of your exhibit promises a solution to a major problem, you are well on your way to attracting the right audience.

Every good exhibit should have a "headline" message that tells prospects what's in it for them—why they would be wise to stop and talk to your sales personnel. It is an advantage to use technical terms in your message if you want to reach technical people. In addition to attracting the technical people you want to speak to, such terms discourage nontechnical people who are not prospects from coming into your booth and wasting precious time.

Demonstrations.   One of the most valuable techniques for an exhibitor is a demonstration of the product's use or special qualities. Nothing beats a technical demonstration for attracting a quality audience, providing that the demonstration is aimed strictly at the prospects' interests. The goal of a demonstration should be to show the product's quality or special attributes. For instance, a demonstration can prove that a product is resistant to damage, versatile, or stable or that it operates better than a competitor's product in terms of speed or endurance. The best demonstrators in an exhibit are the salespersons or technicians who know the equipment or products best. Their presentations are most believable, and these demonstrators are able to answer technical questions from the audience. For some demonstrations, professional actors may serve well. But use professionals only to demonstrate a set procedure with a rigid script. Sales and technical personnel should be on hand to answer technical questions from those who are attracted to the demonstration.

Exhibit Design. The aim of an exhibit's design is to attract those members of the audience who are your real prospects. The decor of your exhibit should create an atmosphere that tells visitors you are serious about their needs and interests. Avoid a design which is frivolous, unless this is the kind of atmosphere you use in your business. Be wary of too severe a design, one that's so "modern" that it might be uninviting or even forbidding. If you display products or processes, be sure that visitors can touch, handle, or lift the material. Engineers and technical people, particularly, appreciate being able to turn dials, flip switches, and operate equipment.

Avoid free-form shapes in exhibits, since they tend to blend, rather than stand out. Circles, squares, rectangles, and octagons—common geometric forms—are the best shapes to use in exhibit design.

FIGURE 19-3. Visitors to a technical trade show want to handle equipment, push buttons, and operate levers. This is one of the main reasons they visit a trade show. (*Courtesy of* Successful Meetings *magazine.*)

The human eye is caught by motion against any kind of background. Therefore, some type of animation in your exhibit will create interest. The motion need not be complex. Its purpose is to catch the eye. The colors used in an exhibit should complement the products on display. It is best when the products are in contrast to the background colors so that the products will stand out.

All products and messages within an exhibit should be well lighted. However, avoid light aimed at the visitors' eyes; all light should be focused on the products and the message.

Audience Participation. Audience participation in an exhibit is valid only if the visitor becomes involved with your products or selling message. Games of chance and skill that have nothing to do with your products or service should be avoided. They attract people with time to kill, rather than serious prospects. With participation devices use short, clear instructions. Copy such as "Flip this switch," "Feel this flex," or "Press this diaphragm" should be used with any exhibit element that invites participation.

DEVELOPING LEADS AND MAKING SALES

Exhibits have proved to be the most valuable tool for developing valid inquiries. A study made some years ago by Westinghouse Electric Co. showed that exhibits can produce quality inquiries that can be converted into sales. In the Westinghouse study, 7000 inquiries were analyzed over the period of a year. Of the inquiries, 50 percent were the result of public relations releases, 35 percent were prompted by advertising, and 15 percent were generated by trade-show participation. It would appear from this analysis that trade shows do not do well in terms of inquiries. However, when you look at the sales conversion rate, trade shows do remarkably well. Of the inquiries prompted by public relations, only 10 percent resulted in sales. Inquiries developed by advertising were converted to sales in 50 percent of the cases. However, inquiries stimulated by trade-show participation developed sales in 80 percent of the cases.

SELECTING AND MANAGING BOOTH PERSONNEL

Since the ultimate aim of any exhibit should be sales, the key element in any exhibit is booth personnel. Booth personnel should be selected carefully on the basis of their product knowledge and their skills in handling dialogues with more than one person at a time. Trainees or inexperienced salespersons should never be used in an exhibit booth because prospects make judgments about your company on the basis of the answers they get from your personnel. Nothing freezes a prospect faster than inadequate information or incompetent personnel in an exhibit. Show visitors expect to garner the latest, most authoritative information available when they step into an exhibit. They resent having to deal with unqualified representatives of exhibiting companies.

To get the most effective use of booth personnel, assign duties realistically. Nobody should be required to be on duty in a booth for more than four hours at a stretch. Working in a booth is hard and tiring. Booth personnel should never sit down; they must remain standing and alert to greet visitors. Booth personnel should be motivated and excited about the prospect of conversing with more prospects in a day than they usually talk to in a month or more. Booth personnel should be trained in preparation for the trade-show experience.

Your booth personnel should be advised of the quotas that you have developed (based on your original objectives). For instance, if your original objective was to sell 100 units at the show, break this down so that each salesperson knows how many of those 100 units he or she is responsible for. To appeal to the competitive spirit of booth personnel, let everyone know how well the company did at previous shows. This allows personnel to understand the difference between past and present objectives and sets up the challenge to beat previous results. Your salespersons should be told the strategy developed for the exhibit effort. They should know how to take advantage of the products and props on hand. Before the show opens, your exhibit personnel should practice using demonstration materials and should role-play conversations with show visitors. The aim is to have the personnel appreciate the difference between trade-show activity and one-on-one discussions in a prospect's office.

All booth personnel should be adequately identified by means of special badges (in addition to the normal show badge), jackets, hats, or special insignia. This allows show visitors immediately to identify a source of information in your booth.

The minimum number of exhibit personnel for an exhibit is two persons per 100 square feet. Thus, for an exhibit booth which has an area of 100 square feet and which runs eight hours a day, you would need a minimum of four persons (preferably six), two on at a time. For effective exhibiting, company executives should be on hand, in addition to sales personnel. Show visitors like to talk to the executives of the companies with which they do business or contemplate doing business. A show is also an ideal place for company executives to get firsthand feedback from the marketplace. If two executives are going to be at the show, make sure that they are not both there on just the first day. They should be on hand through most of the run of the show so that there will be somebody in a position of high authority who is available to meet and talk to good prospects and customers.

One aim of sales personnel in the booth is to qualify all visitors by recording their names, positions, affiliations, addresses, and product interests. A special form should be prepared for sales personnel so that they can quickly enter pertinent data about visitors that can be translated into clear follow-up instructions. The follow-up can be done either through direct mail or by making visits in the field.

A debriefing session should be held each day after the show closes. This allows booth personnel to compare notes and plan strategy changes that might be required for the next day. It also provides an opportunity to assign follow-up chores at the show—to contact prospects again who were seen previously in the exhibit.

PROMOTIONAL AND PUBLIC RELATIONS TIE-INS

In addition to actual contact with prospects and customers during show hours, there are many opportunities to tie in promotional activities with trade-show participation. In advance of the show, sales personnel can hand out printed invitations during their sales calls to interest customers and prospects in attending your exhibit. Invitations to your exhibit should also be sent to the people on your prospect list. Two or three months in advance of the show date, your advertising should make mention of your show participation. Publicity should be sent out to tell what new or interesting products or information will be available at your exhibit.

A target list of prospects or customers should be made up, and this list should get special attention. The aim is to try to set up appointments with these key customers and prospects during the show. Most show visitors come with special problems or interests. The exhibitor's aim is to make sure that customers and prospects arrive at the exhibit expecting to find solutions. Preshow publicity and advertising are valuable to the exhibitor, since show visitors plan ahead to get facts, ideas, and information. Make sure that they have your exhibit on their list of "musts" to see at the show. Promotion during the show should include a hospitality or technical suite. The aim of maintaining a suite in addition to the exhibit is to have a private area for thorough discussions with customers and prospects. In the suite, you might have pieces of equipment, product samples, special literature, or information to further your objectives. Make certain that personnel are specifically scheduled to be in the suite so that there will always be competent people on hand to answer visitors' questions.

Depending on the size of your exhibit and the total investment in marketing at the show, you might consider other media tie-ins such as billboards, radio and TV spots, taxi signs, newspaper advertisements, and leaflets distributed outside the show building.

Make sure that someone is assigned public relations responsibilities at the show. Every trade and industrial show attracts a large corps of media representatives. These reporters and editors are looking for new products, new ideas, and new trends. It is worthwhile to contact editors in advance if you have newsworthy information and to make appointments for interviews at the show. It is easier to get publicity at a show than anywhere else, since members of the press are looking for ideas for articles, facts on trends, and new developments in the field.

As a further promotional tie-in, an exhibitor can make a mailing of photographs of the exhibit to current customers and prospects to illustrate the effectiveness of a product or process. An exhibitor can also tie in with other exhibitors. For instance, an exhibitor might supply other exhibitors with his or her product to use in their exhibits and provide signs indicating where facts on this product can be obtained at the show. If a customer is also participating in the show, the supplier might want to mention this fact in the exhibit; this is another way of making show visitors aware of the company's activity and acceptance.

EXHIBIT COPY

Trade-show exhibitors make one of their biggest mistakes in the area of the handling of exhibit copy. The two worst errors are to have copy that is too long and to have copy that is not slanted to customer benefits. The general practice of featuring the name of the company dramatically and of subduing all other messages is wrong. The message concerning customer benefits should be the most prominent copy in the exhibit, with the company name secondary. You should try to fashion a message that promises to solve a customer's problem or presents a special benefit to intrigue your prime prospects.

All captions used in an exhibit to explain charts, graphs, or photographs should be short. Visitors will not read long copy. (And incidentally, copy in an exhibit is expensive and can boost the cost of an exhibit well beyond its value.)

If you are holding a demonstration in your booth, it is well to consider short, punchy copy to call attention to it. This copy should be intriguing; for example, "Hard to believe!" "Test it!" "Compare!" "Watch it happen!" "It's all new!"

When three or more claims can be made for your product or service, do not scatter these claims throughout the exhibit in your copy panels. Consolidate them so that all the product benefits and qualities that are important to your prospects are in one spot. Research has shown that trade-show visitors are able to recall more of this kind of information when it appears in one spot than when it is spread throughout an exhibit area.

"SHOW SPECIAL"

There often is an advantage in making plans for a show special. Your show special might be a discount for a volume purchase, a free item with a purchase, or a special price for any order placed during the run of the show. This prompts on-the-spot decisions. It is particularly effective at a trade show attended by dealers and distributors.

EVALUATION

After each day's debriefing of booth personnel, an objective evaluation of booth activities should be made. Decide whether to continue to operate the booth in the same manner the following day or to change the basic plan. During an evaluation session, you may make a decision to rearrange the elements in the booth to take advantage of special interests shown by visitors. You might want to give a product more prominence or more space or to eliminate elements that do not attract any attention. Never consider your exhibit set in concrete. Be prepared to make changes that will produce better results the following day.

CONCLUSION

To get the most out of your exhibit participation, think of it as a major sales campaign. Apply the same creativity to it that you would devote to a major effort. When you have a large audience of prospects coming to you, seeking you out, it is incumbent upon you to be thoroughly prepared to make the most of this marketing opportunity. When well planned and executed, there are few marketing tools more effective than exhibits. When poorly planned and ineptly managed, there are few marketing activities more expensive and more wasteful.

For further information, see Appendix A.

20 Incentive Travel

NANCY ZIMMERMAN
Managing Editor, Incentive Travel Manager *Magazine and*
Association & Society Manager *Magazine*

According to Webster, an *incentive* is something that tends to incite one to determination or action. So it is with incentive travel (or IT, as it is known in the trade), which is employed by hundreds of manufacturers and other kinds of companies to motivate their employees and stimulate their sales personnel to increase sales.

Long before it was recognized as a field unto itself, IT was motivating salespeople to achieve and surpass quotas set by their companies or suppliers. As recently as the mid-1980s, IT was just one of the several motivational tools employed by companies, sharing the billing with cash prizes and merchandise awards offered to top sales producers who exceeded the established sales goals.

It was well known, even in the days before popular psychology and behavior modification methods gained widespread acceptance, that most salespeople (especially those working for straight commission) work just hard enough to ensure that they earn a comfortable living, but rarely exert themselves beyond the level necessary to maintain the standard of living they have selected for themselves. For example, if a salesperson can earn $30,000 a year by working a thirty- to forty-hour week and if this amount is sufficient to meet his or her financial needs, there is simply no motivation to earn, say, $50,000 a year. Not only would taxes consume a large portion of the additional income, but also the trade-off of time and effort necessary to make the additional sales might not be perceived as worthwhile. Enter the motivational field, offering a number of approaches to boosting sales efforts by rewarding the high achievers, among them IT.

IT programs operate on the premise that employees will be motivated to

359

produce more if the increased production brings a reward of high perceived value. Through long years of experience, motivation experts have learned that the opportunity to travel excites and motivates a vast majority of people, and thus IT lends itself well to company-sponsored programs designed to increase productivity. A company offering an IT prize to its top salespeople therefore selects destinations that offer as many favorable characteristics as possible; then it devises a program of activities for the group of winners that will further excite and motivate them. Traditionally, "sun and fun" resorts top the list of favorites among IT qualifiers, followed closely by foreign sites with an exotic or sophisticated image.

Regardless of the destination selected, however, IT planners agree that the most important aspect of any trip is the manner in which the winners are treated; they must be given red-carpet treatment at every stage, from checking in at the airport to checking out at the hotel, and everything in between. As a high-budget operation, the IT experience must never give the impression that corners were cut or that expenses were minimized. Winners are to be pampered in such a way that they understand that the company recognizes the importance of their contribution to its success.

In achieving this end, IT planners find that it is essential to include in the itinerary activities that the participants could enjoy only through an IT program, rather than activities that they could just as easily provide for themselves. The trip must be memorable if it is to serve as a motivator, and the participants must come away from it feeling that they have had an experience that couldn't be duplicated under any circumstances or for any amount of money.

ADVANTAGES OVER CASH AND MERCHANDISE

That travel is an effective motivator is now a given, but in order to employ it with maximum benefit, it is still important to understand just how and why it surpasses cash and merchandise.

Cash awards are probably the best-known and most frequently used incentives, since cash promotions are the simplest to execute. But while extra cash is rarely unwelcome, even in affluent households, many corporations have found that the lure of a cash prize is not always sufficient to generate the enthusiasm necessary to earn it.

The psychological pressures of home and family to use any additional income for serious purchases or expenses can erase the element of fun connected with winning a prize, thereby eliminating one of the important parts of any motivational effort. A prize should be perceived as something special, as an added bit of excitement or entertainment that is the direct result of one's accomplishment. But if the cash prize is used to finance the children's orthodontic work or to pay off a loan taken out during leaner times, the psychological benefit of having earned the prize can easily be lost. If the prize money is used for a purchase of a frivolous nature more in keeping with the notion of a prize, the winner often feels a sense of guilt for not having used the money in a more practical way, and again the sense of having won an award is negated. Thus the power of cash to motivate employees to produce is minimal.

Pride in accomplishment is another aspect of winning that should be underscored by the prize itself. Winners should be able to boast about having won and to elicit favorable responses from family and friends concerning their proven success. This, of course, is difficult to do when the proof of one's worth is in the form of cash, since in our society it is generally considered boorish to discuss one's salary or to specify amounts of earnings.

A merchandise award thus does not have some of the negative aspects of a cash prize. Presented with a color television set or a microwave oven, the winner cannot possibly use the award to pay bills, for example, and is free of the guilt associated with spending money on luxury items. The congratulations of family and friends can also be enjoyed, as it is certainly acceptable to point to a prize one has been awarded in a contest, even if it is improper to talk of one's income.

But as with cash prizes, the motivational power of a merchandise award is limited. The qualifier may not have a need or desire for the offered prize or may already own or have won the same prize or a similar one in a previous promotion. If the perceived value of the award is low, the participants in the promotion will simply not be motivated to work for it. This is especially true of repeat winners, whose homes are full of appliances, stereos, and sporting equipment won through company sales contests. Once salespeople have accumulated a variety of such items, the motivational power of a merchandise offer diminishes.

It is because of the inherent problems with cash and merchandise awards that IT enjoys a favored position in the motivational field. As with merchandise prizes, the winners cannot be tempted to direct the winnings toward household needs rather than enjoying them, nor is there any guilt associated with their enjoyment. Peer approval is greater than that generated by merchandise prizes; winners find that friends and neighbors are uniformly impressed at the prospect of being sent by one's company on an all-expense-paid luxury trip.

But unlike merchandise promotions, IT programs are virtually free of the problems of duplicate prizes and low perceived value. Even if qualifiers are offered a trip to a destination they have already visited, the fact that no two travel experiences are alike tends to keep interest levels high. In many cases, the chance to return to a certain destination can even be an added incentive, as winners who enjoyed a positive experience on a previous trip are often eager to go back. Golf clubs and bicycles take up space and have limited use, but memories of pleasurable events can live forever and are easily stored.

Besides being free of some of the negative aspects of cash and merchandise promotions, IT claims some less tangible benefits that result nonetheless in real benefits for the sponsoring company. Most IT planners agree that travel by a group of winners who have shared the many facets of the job and who then are able to enjoy the common experience of the trip engenders a special kind of camaraderie that in turn encourages loyalty to, and concern for, the company. The combination of a luxurious setting, VIP treatment, the adventure of travel, and the sharing of the experience with respected colleagues rarely fails to contribute to a positive working environment. There is thus a cumulative effect of the IT program; winners are encouraged by memories of past trips to continue to qualify for subsequent trips.

The trip also affords winners the opportunity to become personally acquainted with the executives of the company in a relaxed, low-pressure setting. Such an experience strengthens employees' identification with an organization; they feel that they are more than just a number or a name on the payroll roster, and this increases their motivation to perform. Management personnel find the experience equally beneficial, since it enables them to obtain valuable feedback from their employees; to get to know their tastes, characters, and philosophies in general; and to reveal themselves to these employees as approachable and interested.

Additional benefits of the IT experience include the motivating effect that returning winners have on other employees who failed to qualify. IT managers note that often their salespeople respond to the photographs, slides, and comments of those who made the trip by working to qualify for the next one so that they can share in the excitement and recognition.

As for the winners themselves, the travel experience invariably serves to broaden the scope of their experience, increase their level of sophistication, and enhance their understanding of their place in the overall scheme of the company and its goals. Such an education can have only positive effects on their subsequent performance as salespeople, as they return to the job not only with renewed vigor but also with increased awareness and a strong motivation to continue to succeed. IT programs take them to places that they might never visit on their own and provide them with experiences that no amount of money could buy for them, thus giving them the best kind of motivation to succeed.

A GUIDE TO INCENTIVE TRAVEL PLANNING

Site Selection

Even before establishing the contest rules and determining the length of the qualifying period, the planner must select the destination that is to be promoted. Factors to be considered in the site-selection process are the size of the IT budget, the length of the trip, and, above all, the tastes and preferences of the qualifiers themselves. Additional considerations can affect a planner's choice of destination as well; the size of the group, the travel season, and the availability of scheduled and charter air service all play a part. An IT manager may find, for example, that the trip to Tahiti that appeared to be out of reach of the budget can actually be managed quite easily if the travel dates are shifted to take advantage of off-peak rates for hotel accommodations and airfares. Sometimes increasing the size of the group can entitle them to greater discounts on airfares and hotel rates; cutting a five-day trip to four days can mean the difference between selecting a site close to home and choosing one farther afield.

Most IT experts rely on polling their potential qualifiers to ascertain the group's preferences. They consider as well the age group and the level of education of the participants, and then they attempt to match the destination to the resulting profile. The next step is a site inspection, during which the destination is examined firsthand to determine its suitability as an IT prize. After weighing all the factors and selecting an appropriate site, the planner is ready to mount the promotion and begin making the actual travel arrangements.

Establishing the Rules and Promoting the Contest

The next step in planning the IT contest is to establish the rules. There are two basic types of contest: the open-end contest, which allows as many people as achieve the quota to be included in the trip, and the closed-end contest, in which only a specified number of participants, based on sales figures, are accepted. There are variations and combinations of these contest types, including buy-ins that allow salespeople who haven't attained the quota to purchase all or part of the program on their own. IT planners devising contests that attract participants from diverse territories with differing levels of potential usually adjust the quotas to reflect reasonable expectations, since impossible quotas can be counterproductive, actually serving as a disincentive.

Once the contest rules are established, the promotion stage begins. Contests are usually announced amid a great deal of fanfare in order to generate as much excitement as possible among potential qualifiers. A favorite time to announce the IT prize for the coming year is at the dinner held to celebrate the end of the previous incentive trip; winners are still reveling in the pleasure of their hard-earned reward and are especially motivated to become repeat winners.

One such announcement that proved particularly effective was made in Lucerne, Switzerland, to a group from the Seattle-based Northern Life Insurance Company. The participants, who were expecting their final-night entertainment to include the usual Swiss yodelers dressed in lederhosen, were surprised and delighted to behold a stage full of grass-skirted hula dancers swaying to the accompaniment of live Hawaiian music. The incongruous sight of hula dancers in Switzerland marked the kickoff of the next IT contest, eliciting an enthusiastic response to the Hawaii trip. For potential qualifiers not present at these banquets, announcements can be made by memo, through the company newsletter, or at specially called meetings.

After the initial announcement is made, the follow-up stage begins. The frequency and intricacy of follow-up announcements will vary according to the length of the qualifying period, the IT budget, and the planner's imagination. Mailers are a popular means of maintaining interest levels, and these can include any number of "teaser gifts" designed to encourage participation. The same company that kicked off the Hawaii contest in Switzerland used an equally creative approach in the promotion of its Hong Kong trip, which it announced by mailing out chopsticks, fans, and a colorful brochure explaining the contest rules.

Jerry Johnson, sales promotion manager of Lindsay Co., a manufacturer of automatic water conditioners in Woodbury, Minnesota, boosts participation by sending out teasers every two weeks. For a recent trip to Acapulco, he started by sending a brochure. As the contest progressed, the mailings became increasingly elaborate, featuring bags of white sand accompanied by notes reminding participants that they could soon be enjoying Mexico's sandy beaches. Next, qualifiers received Mexican-made onyx paperweights.

For a trip to the Bahamas, Bob Reiser, of Continental Insurance, New York, sent out 3500 coconuts, along with cookbooks featuring coconut recipes. For his Acapulco promotion, mailings included tin masks, onyx burros, and clay piggy banks.

Whatever the contents, planners agree that to be successful the mailings should be frequent and must always go to the home. They have observed that spouses have a great deal of influence on the qualifiers and that involving them in the promotion through mailings makes the participants more likely to work for the IT prize.

Other promotional ideas that have been used with success include circulating photo albums containing shots of IT winners in action on previous trips, presenting travel films of the featured destination at sales meetings, and sending out coupons redeemable for cocktails while on the trip. Creative planners tailor their ideas to the destinations they are promoting as well as to the overall profile of the contestants, continually finding new and different ways to generate excitement.

ON-SITE ARRANGEMENTS: PLANNING AND EXECUTING THE TRIP

Negotiating favorable rates with suppliers is an acquired skill, and many planners prefer to turn some or all of the travel arrangements over to professionals. They may opt for a travel agency to handle reservations and tickets, or they can consult an incentive house to handle all stages of the trip, from site selection to reservations to activity planning and promotion. Even when relying on these professionals, however, the planner must remain involved in all stages of the preparations to ensure the success of the trip.

After hotel and transportation arrangements are made, the next major step is to prepare a schedule of activities that will keep the winners interested and active without wearing them out, on the one hand, or leaving them bored, on the other.

"One common problem with inexperienced planners is that they tend to overschedule activities," says Bob Dauner, director of incentive sales for Hyatt Hotels Corporation, in Chicago. "Not only does this cost more, but your people won't appreciate being run ragged."

At the same time, planners must be careful to offer enough entertainment to their winners, the nature of which should be consistent with the perception that these are high-status people deserving of the best. Equally important is the understanding that the experiences must be of the sort that the individuals would be unable to duplicate on their own. Since most IT qualifiers earn an excellent living and are quite able to afford travel apart from the company-sponsored trip, merely providing lavish accommodations and gourmet meals, while pleasant, is not enough. The most important aspect of any planned activities is creativity.

Theme parties are a perennial favorite, as they allow planners to evoke whatever mood, period, and setting they feel will excite and entertain the participants. Roaring twenties, casino night, Mardi Gras, and the old west are just a few of the possible themes an IT manager can try, and most hotels used in IT programs have a full repertoire of events they can stage.

Other activities can also be built around meal periods; "dine-arounds," which allow the travelers to sample their choice of restaurant and cuisine, are easily arranged and very well received. To fill in the time between meals, sightseeing excursions, side trips, and recreational activities can be arranged according to the locale, taking advantage of points of interest and local lore.

A look at some successful promotions executed recently will underscore the importance of creativity in an IT program.

The Swiss Road-Rally Incentive: "See Switzerland by Mercedes"

What does a company that is known for its innovative and exciting IT programs do for an encore? For the Central Air Conditioning Division of the General Electric Company, the answer was a Swiss road rally that allowed participants to tour one of Europe's more scenic regions in their own brand-new Mercedes sedans. Les Brown, manager of advertising and sales planning for the company (now a subsidiary of the Trane Corporation), knew he was dealing with a sales force of experienced travelers and devised the program to appeal to participants who were especially sophisticated and not easily entertained.

Brown explains that the exact details of the IT program vary from year to year, depending on the goals of the company, but it is generally based on dealer purchases over a ten- to twelve-month period. Dealers receive award credits for their purchases, and these credits can be used in a variety of ways: for merchandise, for individual trip options, or for the national dealer trip, the latter being by far the easiest to promote and the most exciting of the three.

To introduce the Swiss road rally, Brown prepared on audiovisual presentation to deliver during the company's trip to Rio de Janeiro the previous year. He followed up this introduction with a series of promotional mailings until seven months prior to the departure of the first group of participants, by which time he had determined the actual number of participants and was ready to finalize arrangements with hotels and airlines. About 1300 dealers and their spouses participated in the trip, many more than in previous years.

"We were particularly gratified by the enthusiastic response," he says, "because the economy that year [1982] was not all that good. We were afraid that the economic climate would affect the number of qualifiers, and I believe it was a tribute to the appeal of the trip itself that this did not occur." But the large number of qualifiers did present some logistical challenges, as Brown was able to obtain only forty new Mercedes sedans that had all the features he wanted. By placing two couples to a car and limiting individual groups to 160, Brown was able to accommodate everyone in a series of nine back-to-back trips.

The itinerary was to take the winning drivers through some of Switzerland's most scenic countryside, allowing time for tours of the three cities where they stayed overnight. At the outset the participants were flown to Geneva, where they were greeted at their hotel (the Geneva Inter-Continental) by Swiss flag throwers and Alpine horn blowers. After being left on their own to rest during the afternoon, they were entertained that evening at a welcoming party prepared by the hotel. The next day was devoted to touring Geneva, including a cruise across Lake Geneva to Évian, on the French side. The group lunched at a French restaurant in the medieval village of Yvoire and then returned to Geneva for afternoon shopping and dinner at one of several restaurants in a section of the city known as Old Town. No special activity was planned for after dinner, as the rally was scheduled to begin the following day.

In the morning the participants were briefed on the rules of the road trip and were given rally guidebooks, albums, and Polaroid cameras for recording rally sites. They also received the first of three cassettes to play during the outing; these gave further instructions as well as hints about the destination for the next year's trip.

"We scheduled the rally so that there would not be all that much driving at any one time," notes Brown. "They could take things at a leisurely pace and stop off and enjoy themselves along the way, with plenty of time before the group got together again."

The first leg of the trip took the group to the famous cheese center of Gruyère, where they stopped for lunch. That afternoon they drove on to Interlaken, where they stayed at the Hotel Victoria Jungfrau, and that night they attended a formal dinner party in the hotel's ballroom.

The following morning the group drove through the Bernese Alps to Stechelberg, where they took a cable car up to the peak of Mount Schilthorn, the mountain featured in the James Bond film *On Her Majesty's Secret Service*. They lunched in the mountain village of Murren and then spent the afternoon at the resort of Grindelwald. Evening festivities included a cocktail

FIGURE 20-1. IT winners are welcomed by a member of the Sperry & Hutchinson Company motivation and travel staff, prior to embarking on a Pan American clipper for a trip to the Caribbean. (*Courtesy of the Sperry & Hutchinson Company.*)

reception in the hotel, followed by a dine-around at several of Interlaken's restaurants.

The following morning the group set off on the last leg of the rally, driving to Lucerne, where they had time for shopping. Lunch was served at the Hotel Furigen, just outside Lucerne, after which the travelers made the short drive to Zurich, where they turned in their Mercedes sedans. Before departing, they had a full day to explore Zurich, with an optional bus tour that made stops at the fashionable Bahnhofstrasse, with its elegant shops; the lakeside promenade; Old Town and its historic houses; Grossmunster Church; and the university.

On the final evening a banquet was held at the Hotel Zurich. A gourmet meal accompanied by fine wines was served, there was music and dancing, and the festivities ended with the rally awards ceremony. Prizes were given for obtaining the correct kilometer readings on the cars' odometers and for photographing all the sites listed in the guidebook. The following morning the group departed, while another group arrived to begin the rally in reverse order, starting in Zurich and arriving in Geneva, where the next wave of participants would begin their trip.

Brown considers the program an unqualified success. "The idea of a road rally was well received," he says. "They enjoyed the cars themselves, as well as the freedom of movement that allowed them to feel that they were exploring the country on their own. The key to the success of the program was that the trip was highly structured, and yet it gave participants a feeling of freedom as they explored the country. Also, touring the country in private cars gave them an opportunity to see things that they never would have been able to see otherwise."

New York City: The Cosmopolitan Incentive

Although resorts and foreign cities usually top the list of favorite destinations, IT planners can also find a wealth of possibilities closer to home that generate an enthusiastic response among qualifiers. One advantage to such site selection is the reduced cost of transportation, leaving a larger share of the budget to devote to activities, accommodations, and some of the small but important touches that make a trip special.

Jim Dittman, president of Lancer Communications, a New York City incentive house, planned a successful promotion for Art Carved Rings, a New York–based company. A four-month sales contest open to all the company's sales divisions nationwide featured a five-day, four-night trip to New York City as the prize. Entitled "The Golden Apple," the contest was mounted without using any gimmicks; the lure of the city itself proved to be enough of an attraction to invite participation. Mailings were sent out describing the exciting itinerary planned for the winners, along with menus from some of the city's finer restaurants.

The trip began when the group of thirty winners arrived at the airport and were met by Dittman and a trail of Cadillac limousines that escorted them to the Grand Hyatt, in the heart of Manhattan. The group had been preregistered there to simplify the checking-in process, and they were ushered quickly to their rooms, where they found a welcome kit awaiting them complete with maps, an itinerary, a guide to shops and restaurants, and sightseeing tips from the New York Visitors and Convention Bureau.

That evening the participants were taken, again by limousine, through Manhattan, Chinatown, Wall Street, Little Italy, and Harlem. On the next day, lunch was at the Rainbow Grill at Rockefeller Center, with the afternoon left free to roam Fifth Avenue's shops.

The evening's activities included a cocktail party at the hotel followed by a Broadway show. The evening continued in the traditional theatergoing vein with a late supper at Sardi's and dancing until dawn at a local discotheque. The next day's itinerary included a walking tour of the galleries and artists' lofts of Greenwich Village, with lunch at the Front Restaurant. During the rest of the day the participants were free to wander about the Village or return to the hotel to rest.

That evening they were taken to Club Ibis, an intimate nightclub where they were entertained with a dinner show featuring a well-known New York comedian. After the show the group continued to Studio 54, where they bypassed the long lines of people outside and entered immediately for another night of dancing until dawn.

The final day's plan included a visit aboard a nineteenth-century schooner at the South Street Seaport, where lunch was served. The afternoon was reserved for more sightseeing so that the winners wouldn't miss such old favorites as the Statue of Liberty, Radio City Music Hall, and the Empire State Building. The final night's dinner was at the glass-enclosed Tavern on the Green in Central Park, preceded by a wine and cheese party prepared especially for them by the management. Dancing that night was at the Red Parrot, where the group stayed until closing time. A farewell brunch was offered in the morning prior to returning the weary but satisfied winners to the airport for the flight home.

"What's important about a trip to New York," observes Dittman, "is that you have to be willing to involve yourself in the fast pace. You should have as much energy as the city and move with the flow."

THE FUTURE OF INCENTIVE TRAVEL

IT has been lauded as one of the few truly recession-proof businesses, and with some qualification this observation is essentially correct. IT budgets are allotted according to the amount of sales surpassing a specified number, and thus these programs tend to be self-liquidating.

Manufacturers and suppliers to the tourism industry alike find that IT programs not only weather difficult economic times but also can be instrumental in helping related businesses weather them as well. Recent recession-induced cutbacks have caused many companies to trim their IT budgets in a variety of ways: planning shorter trips, traveling to destinations closer to home, increasing quotas for qualifiers, and traveling during off-seasons. But even with reduced budgets limiting some of the more lavish tendencies of travel planners, IT remains a lucrative field for all affected by it. Hoteliers welcome incentive business, knowing that their rooms will be filled by high-budget groups with large discretionary incomes who will also make use of meeting facilities, banquet rooms, and restaurants. Ground operators are kept busy arranging and conducting sightseeing tours, while local merchants benefit from the inevitable shopping sprees indulged in by the winners.

All this means that IT will continue to grow, just as it will continue to be a prime motivator for salespeople in a wide variety of fields. In fact, recent interest in the field of motivation, coupled with an increased interest in enhancing productivity at a variety of levels in many different areas, suggests that IT is emerging from its purely sales orientation to encompass a wider range of applications. Decreasing profits are causing businesses of all types to examine productivity levels, some for the first time, to determine ways to increase productivity while cutting back on waste of time and materials.

One company that has recognized the potential of IT in this regard is APA Transport of North Bergen, New Jersey. As part of the company's thirty-fifth anniversary celebration, all employees were invited to participate in a three-day cruise aboard the *Queen Elizabeth II*. Making the trip even more rewarding for the employees was the fact that each person was allowed to bring a guest.

"Everyone goes," said Arthur Imperatore, president of the company, "from the porter to the president. We like to build memories. For the most part our people are working people, family people who ordinarily wouldn't experience anything like this."

According to Imperatore, IT programs have virtually eliminated employee turnover. Many people come to work at APA as their first place of employment and stay until retirement. "The IT reward creates happy people," he says, "people who care about our company. We build bonds."

Another area of business with IT potential is employee safety, as attested to by Sig Front, vice president of the Sheraton Corporation. "Back in 1957, when I was with a hotel in Miami Beach, I sold incentives based on safety rewards to a company. The premise was, 'If you can cut accidents down, we'll send the plant supervisors to the hotel.' We still do that at Sheraton. Do you know how many injuries take place in a hotel kitchen? Thousands!"

Front also suggests that IT could supply the means for reducing overhead. "The company president could say that if heat, light, and power costs were reduced 10 percent over a given period, the company would send the supervisors to, say, Hawaii. This approach can be used with the Boy Scouts, with church groups, and even with union members. You can put something into a union contract that says that if people work for the same company for five years, they get a three-day weekend in Florida. If they work ten years, they get a week in Europe, and so on."

The potential applications of IT are thus limitless. Any business with the ability to quantify productivity, sales, or employee performance of any sort can use IT to motivate its staff. The prizes can range from a weekend getaway awarded to the department that saves the most money on supplies to a lavish ten-day foreign fling for top-producing salespeople or company VIPs; the variations of the program and its applications are limited only by the imagination of the company executive in charge of motivating employees.

THE FOCUS ON PROFESSIONALISM

As the field expands, the need for professional recognition among IT planners has emerged. To foster a professional approach as well as to monitor the growth of the industry, the Society for Incentive Travel Executives (SITE) was born. Annual premium and incentive trade shows are including more travel-related presentations, and IT expositions featuring exclusively the travel side of incentive marketing are now planned for 1984 and beyond. SITE has also founded the University of Incentive Travel, which offers a course of study leading to the professional designation of Certified Incentive Travel Executive (CITE).

This new focus on professionalism, coupled with industry's trend toward incorporating IT into a variety of new motivational programs to increase productivity, should result in continued growth in the IT field. In these times of "no-win" situations, a "no-lose" program that fosters employee loyalty, increased sales, and higher productivity is a welcome change.

V Special Personal Sales Promotions

Most types of sales promotion are designed for the mass market, and generally they are promoted through the mass media, including direct marketing. Possible exceptions are advertising specialties, which may be distributed on a more selective basis. However, they can be dispensed in relatively large quantities, for example, anyone who enters any of the 200 branches of a particular bank receives an imprinted plastic pocket calendar or ballpoint pen.

Closely related to specialty advertising are business and executive gifts, which are given on a much more limited and selective basis. Their relationship to specialty advertising stems from the fact that they are distributed by specialty advertising counselors, and often they are also manufactured by the same companies that produce advertising specialties. On the other hand, business and executive gifts are considerably more expensive than advertising specialties. They may or may not carry an imprinted advertising message, however, and they usually are given "with no strings attached." As was stated above, they are given more selectively, to executives in appreciation of past business or in anticipation of future business, often as Christmas gifts. Because such gifts tend to be expensive, the Internal Revenue Service has placed a ceiling on the tax-deductible amount that can be spent on them.

21 Executive Gifts as Promotional Tools

LYNN I. HALBARDIER
Manager of Media Relations, Specialty Advertising Association International

Webster's New Twentieth Century Dictionary defines *gift* as "that which is given or bestowed; anything which is voluntarily transferred by one person to another without compensation; a donation; a present."

While mention of the word *gift* may initially call to mind visions of holiday celebrations, with all recipients under the age of 8, gift giving has also earned a place in the structured echelons of business. In fact, it was estimated that more than 50 million business gifts would be distributed in 1982, for a total expenditure of $926 million.[1]

And, according to a study conducted by the advertising faculty at the University of Florida, the majority of companies presently employing an executive gift program consider the practice effective and plan to continue it.[2]

There is nothing new in the custom of giving gifts; many instances of gift giving are recorded in the Old Testament. Down through the centuries, gifts have been given to rulers, other leaders, and business acquaintances to cement relationships and create a favorable atmosphere in which business discussions can be held.[3]

The caricature of a glad-handing sales representative picking up tabs and passing out bottles of scotch at Christmas to generate business is an overblown stereotype. In reality, astute purchasers usually make their buying decisions on the basis of price, quality, and service, and the sales force of any company has to be knowledgeable and professional in manner as well as personable. However, it is always good business to let customers know that their patronage is appreciated, and gifts play an important role in the company-client relationship. In commenting on its gift policy, a Louisiana firm says, "We accept gifts from companies that we already do business with. These gifts do not determine whether or not we do business with these firms. Service and competitive prices are the criteria that we and most firms in our industry use."[4]

PURPOSES OF GIFT GIVING

Gifts are given to businessmen and businesswomen for the purpose of expressing appreciation and generating future good relationships.[5] This nearly billion-dollar business practice may be classified as a corporate activity, public relations, advertising, or sales promotion, depending on an individual company's policy. Sophisticated executives consider gift giving one facet of a good customer relations program which is carried on throughout the year. A gift supplements the regular sales calls, the business lunches, and other activities undertaken in a constant effort to strengthen the relationship between a firm and its audience.

A Saint Paul manufacturer says that his firm uses gifts as a "communication device to reflect appreciation for attention—past, present, and future."[6] An oil company executive claims that a gift "develops a stronger relationship with the customer" by acting as a reminder.[7] Another approach is that the rite of gift giving is an extension of the advertising function, or so states the advertising manager of one of Union Carbide's Canadian subsidiaries.[8]

Business gift giving then, you could say, enables a company to advertise, thank a customer, and reinforce a continuing relationship at the same time.

RELATIONSHIP TO SPECIALTY ADVERTISING

Business or executive gifts are ordinarily categorized as one aspect of the specialty advertising industry. Although technically not advertising specialties (for one thing, they are usually not imprinted), business gifts constitute an important market for the industry. Executive gifts accounted for 15.7 percent of the more than $3.8 billion in sales for specialty advertising in 1981.[9] Retail stores and other sources accounted for millions of dollars in additional sales.

Though the articles presented as gifts may be imprinted with the giver's name, generally they are not. This lack of a donor imprint would take them out of the category of specialty advertising.[10] By definition, a useful article of merchandise imprinted with the advertiser's name or message is a promotional vehicle distributed with no obligation to the recipient. See Chapter 15 for additional information.

Even though business gifts may carry no imprint, their relationship with the specialty advertising industry has most likely come about because the majority of companies which practice executive gift giving seek specialists to do their shopping for them, especially if they buy in quantity. These specialists are specialty advertising distributors, individuals or companies which develop promotions for clients.[11]

In a University of Florida study, 61 percent of the respondents reported purchasing executive gifts through specialty advertising distributors or premium representatives, 33 percent said they dealt with retail and wholesale outlets, and 20 percent reported using other sources. Preferences for specialty advertising distributors by type of responding firm ranged from 81 percent, in the case of service organizations, to 50 percent, in the case of wholesaler firms.[12]

DEVELOPING A GIFT PROGRAM

The specialty advertising distributor may be viewed as an expert in the area of executive gift giving, partly because of the nature of specialty advertising, which is a targeted medium of advertising and promotion, as opposed to mass-media advertising. Some small firms with limited gift lists may elect to shop for individual gifts, but a large corporation giving hundreds of gifts would not be likely to consider this either practical or economical. Yet both large firms and small businesses want the gifts they present to be perceived as personal in nature. Specialty advertising counselors are adept at dealing with the direct, personal aspects of promotion, and thus they can assist a firm with an effective gift program.

The specialty advertising counselor works with the client to ensure that all elements of an executive gift program will lead to the desired results. This includes such steps as determining the audience; deciding whether one gift product is suitable for all recipients on a list, whether there should be any imprinting or personalization, and how and when the gifts will be distributed; and, of course, selecting and ordering one or more appropriate articles to be used as gifts.

RECIPIENTS OF EXECUTIVE GIFTS

Customers

In line with the philosophy that gifts are part of a customer relations program, customers are the most favored recipients for a majority of firms. About one out of every three companies includes employees on its gift list, fewer than two out of ten include prospects as recipients, and only 5 percent give to stockholders.[13]

The term *customers* is a broad generalization which connotes small groups in some industries and very large groups in others. For example, retailing firms might be hard-pressed to furnish gifts for all individuals patronizing their establishment. Thus, one firm may elect to practice some selectivity by restricting a gift list to "major customers," while another may give to those individuals classified as "important buyers" or "buying influentials." Still others may practice two-level giving by sending higher-ticket items to top buyers and cheaper gifts to lesser personnel or companies.

Employees

For some companies, the decision-making role of the recipient is a primary consideration. As a Berkley, California, manufacturer says, "Many of our gifts are given to employees who work with our products, and it helps to reinforce our quality and name with them."[14] An Ohio manufacturer targets its gift program to the management personnel of its distributors, commenting, "These are usually owner-managed, having 25 employees or less. Our small gift is intended to express appreciation without involving it in any buying judgments."[15]

POPULAR GIFT PRODUCTS

With thousands of specialty advertising products to choose from, is there one product category which fits companies' gift needs more than another? Yes, in companies of all sizes, a gift for the office is far and above the most popular

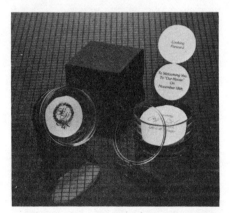

FIGURE 21-1. A desktop accessory serves as part of an invitation to an executive party. (*Courtesy of Specialty Advertising Association International.*)

choice. According to a survey by *Incentive Marketing* magazine, desk sets and accessories led a list of thirteen product categories compiled by respondents. Falling into this classification are pens and pen sets, diaries, calendars, briefcases and portfolios, paperweights, business-card cases, and address books. Runners-up in popularity were practical or decorative items for the home, electronic items, and food.[16]

A New York City hotel, the Halloran House, had a dual-purpose program, with promotional as well as appreciative aspects. The hotel used a desk accessory as part of an invitation to a holiday party it was staging for corporate accounts and potential customers. The gift was an acrylic box for desktop use. The hotel crest was embossed on the lid, and a printed reminder of the party was inserted inside the box. The invitees were shown not only that they would be welcome at the party but also that their business was important to the hotel management.[17] (See Figure 21-1.)

COSTS OF EXECUTIVE GIFTS

The most popular executive gifts cost less than $25, according to the respondents in the University of Florida study.[18] A gift in this price range permits a firm to express its appreciation without creating an awkward situation for the recipient, as could be the case with a lavish gift. A West Virginia wholesaler expressed a common sentiment: "It is not the size of the gift that counts but the fact that the customer was remembered."[19]

A number of factors determine the amount a company budgets for an executive gift program, one of which is company policy. Another is the general condition of the economy. In lean times, a company makes its dollars go further by maintaining its current gift list but spending less per gift or by paring its total list and sending more expensive gifts to fewer recipients. When the economy is running at full steam, there is more latitude for gift selection.

IRS Guidelines

Another source of direction in executive gift planning is the Internal Revenue Service, which allows a maximum annual deduction for a business gift of $25 per person.[20] The IRS permits business gifts to be made directly or indirectly to an individual, but the total cost of business gifts during the tax year to any one individual may not exceed $25. Incidental expenses, such as the cost of engraving, packaging, insuring, and mailing or other means of delivery, are not generally included when determining the cost of a gift.

As of 1983, the $25 rule still held, although legislation has been proposed to increase the amount. Most organizations conform, finding suitable products at or below this limit to fill their gift needs. Others, however, are willing to absorb the loss of deductibility to present more expensive gift items.

What Companies Spend

Overall, companies which employ executive gift programs spend less on them than one might think. Small companies—those with annual sales under $1 million—spend an average of $1000 per year to express their appreciation to customers. Medium-sized firms (with sales from $1 to $10 million) spend an average of $3600; large firms (with sales from $10 to $50 million) invest an average of $12,000 in gifts; and giant firms (with sales of $50 million or more) spend just under $20,000 on the average each year for gifts.[21] It appears that the practice of giving fur coats or expensive jewelry is undocumented, if it exists at all.

WHEN AND WHERE TO GIVE GIFTS

Corporate gift givers feel that timing is another important aspect of an effective program. For the majority of firms, Christmas is still the most popular gift-giving time, according to the University of Florida survey, but other occasions are gaining favor, such as company anniversaries, Thanksgiving, and individual birthdays.[22]

Fig. 21-2. An executive gift from the National Football League to thirty sportswriters (*Courtesy of Specialty Advertising Association International.*)

Some firms present their gifts in face-to-face situations, such as at trade shows, during plant visits, and at sales meetings.[23] According to a company spokesperson, one manufacturing giant in Pittsburgh takes this approach and also chooses gifts which are related to the product line: "We use gifts to key customers basically when they visit our plant. We try to give them an item that will remind them of their visit and an item they can take home. Steak knives are an excellent gift for us because they are made out of our material. On sales calls we give selected purchasing people stainless steel pens. The imprint reminds them of our company constantly, and it is a quality pen they are proud to carry and use."[24]

The National Football League presents gifts primarily as mementos of occasions associated with a sports event. For example, during the week of Super Bowl XV festivities, the NFL presented a special gift to thirty sportswriters and announcers who had covered all fifteen games. The NFL's specialty advertising counselor designed a walnut desk set which featured a notepaper holder, a pen, and a small electronic clock. The lid was illustrated with football helmets of the AFC and the NFC, the two conferences represented by the competing Super Bowl teams. Flanking these colorful illustrations were laser-engraved representations of the NFL shield and the Lombardi trophy (which is presented to the winning Super Bowl team). Inside the lid was a brass plate on which were engraved vital statistics for all fifteen Super Bowl games.[25] (See Figure 21-2.)

The reaction from the recipients of the Super Bowl XV desk item was universally favorable, and NFL management labeled the promotion a success. Is this a typical reaction? How do those with authority for executive gift programs view the practice?

EFFECTIVENESS OF GIFT GIVING

Of the respondents in the University of Florida study, 47 percent said they felt that executive gift giving was either "very effective" or "effective" in achieving the goals of thanking customers for their patronage and developing business by building goodwill; 39 percent said they believed the practice to be "somewhat effective." Only 2 percent reported feeling that the practice was "ineffective."[26]

Measurement of effectiveness can be difficult at best, whether one is evaluating a mass-media advertisement or a gift program. The NFL was not seeking to increase sales with its gifts as some companies might wish to do. The effectiveness of any gift program ties back to the original objective, which is most often saying "thank you."

A small manufacturer in Texas perhaps spoke for others, too, when he summed up his philosophy in these words: "I think effectiveness depends almost entirely on how useful the gift is to the receiver. If it is something that clutters the desk and is never used, it probably has negative value. If it is something that is used quite often, the customer probably will think of the person or company which gave it many times throughout the year."[27]

Effectiveness is a secondary consideration for some companies in evaluating executive gift programs. Perhaps because of the benevolence associated with the practice they approach gift giving in human terms and state, very simply, that the custom gives them pleasure.[28]

CRITICISMS OF GIFT GIVING

There is another side to the coin, however, and the practice of gift giving does have its critics. The question they pose is, When does a gift cease to be an expression of appreciation and become an actual bribe for future business? On the question of ethics, a faculty member of Southern Methodist University, in Dallas, says: "It's hard to say what is right and what is wrong. A sales rep comes around and gives a fifth of Scotch, and it can be viewed as a normal part of doing business. But let that sales rep give five cases of Scotch and you've got something else. The dividing line between black and white is a fuzzy one."[29]

Unfortunately, the dictionary definition quoted earlier does not shed much light on this aspect of gift giving. What a gift is can be determined only by the parties involved. The personnel vice president of a Fortune 500 company says, "If there is no compromise of business or personal interests by either party in the exchange, it is a gift."[30]

POLICIES AGAINST GIFT GIVING

"No-Gift" Policies. As a protection for executives and employees, some companies set blanket policies which state that acceptance of any gifts or gratuities is not permitted. Big companies, such as IBM, Xerox, and Mobil Oil, send potential donors an annual letter explaining company policy against receiving gifts.[31]

While most of these letters simply request that no gifts be sent, the U.S. Postal Service distributes its prohibition against gift giving in press-release form. It says that "an employee will not solicit or accept any gift, gratuity, favor, entertainment, meal, loan, or other thing of value from any person who has, or is seeking to obtain, contractual or other business or financial relations with the Postal Service. . . ."[32]

Other Policies. Many discerning companies are adopting policies spelling out what an employee can and cannot accept. This more prudent approach has the benefit of acknowledging that their employees with purchasing responsibilities are capable of making ethical judgments and are not inherently susceptible to bribery. As a matter of fact, some companies have relaxed their no-gift positions and permit acceptance of legitimate business gifts. They have perceived the distinction between these traditional expressions of appreciation and undue attempts to influence buyers.[33]

Policy Waivers. A small percentage of companies waive their policies on executive gift giving. According to the University of Florida survey, of the companies which gave gifts, 27 percent did not permit their own employees to accept gifts. Of the firms which did not give gifts, 22 percent permitted their employees to receive gifts.[34]

DONORS' VIEW OF POTENTIAL INFLUENCE

A no-gift policy has its roots in the conception that executive gift giving is improper per se, regardless of the value of the gift or its potential to influence a buyer. Do recipients feel that the donor of a gift is trying to influence them? There is a possibility of this, stated 8 percent of the respondents in an *Incentive Marketing* survey. However, a large majority, 92 percent, took a stand for the proper use of business gifts. Of executives surveyed, 97 percent denied that their gifts had ever improperly influenced a customer's buying decision.[35]

Gift giving is a way of showing "commercial appreciation." Obviously, there is always an attempt to influence, in the sense that donors want recipients to think favorably of them. It would be naive to assume that companies give gifts purely out of purposeless generosity. They do so because the practice usually fits in with a corporate marketing objective. The difference between legitimate gift giving and attempts to influence improperly is that the former does not obligate the recipient.

GUIDELINES FOR MAKING A GIFT PROGRAM EFFICIENT

These suggestions from Specialty Advertising Association International should be of help in ensuring that your gift program works as efficiently as possible:

1. Keep your gifts of modest value in relation to the importance of each recipient as an employee, prospect, or customer. Extravagant gifts can be offensive.
2. Choose gifts individually, considering the tastes of each group of recipients, or, preferably, of each individual recipient. It is helpful to maintain a file in which bits of information on the firm or individual are kept. This can be of great assistance when it comes time to select a gift.

3. Give some thought to when you will send the gift. Most business gifts are sent at Christmas, but the gift has a chance to stand out more and make a greater impression if it is sent at some other time of year.
4. Select only high quality gifts that are useful and durable.
5. Personalize each gift, if possible, with the recipient's name or initials.
6. Be sure that all gifts are attractively packaged.
7. Accompany each gift with a personalized note to the recipient.
8. Deliver each gift with a flair, personally or by messenger if possible. Deliver it to the recipient's home rather than the office if the gift is for family use.[36]

ENDNOTES

1. Frank N. Pierce, *Incentive Marketing*, University of Florida, 1982, p. 24
2. *Business and Executive Gift Giving Attitudes and Practices*, Specialty Advertising Association International, Irving, Tex., 1980, p. 11.
3. George L. Herpel, *Specialty Advertising in Marketing*, Dow Jones–Irwin, Inc., Homewood, Ill., 1972, p. 18.
4. *Business and Executive Gift Giving*, p. 79.
5. William N. Kincaid, Jr., *Promotion—Products, Services, and Ideas*, Charles E. Merrill Books, Inc., Columbus, Ohio, 1981, p. 231.
6. *Business and Executive Gift Giving*, p. 66.
7. Pierce, op. cit., p. 30.
8. *The Season for Business Giving*, Specialty Advertising Association International, Irving, Tex., 1979, p. 2.
9. *The Case for Specialty Advertising*, Specialty Advertising Association International, Irving, Tex., 1982, p. 3.
10. Herpel, op. cit., p. 17.
11. Lee Ballard, "Seasons Givings and Fruitcake Alternatives," *DALLAS Magazine*, 1981, p. 19.
12. *Business and Executive Gift Giving*, p. 37.
13. Pierce, op. cit., p. 25.
14. *Business and Executive Gift Giving*, p. 65.
15. Ibid., p. 84.
16. Pierce, op. cit., p. 28.
17. *Capital Campaigns*, Specialty Advertising Association International, Irving, Tex., 1982, p. 17.
18. *Business and Executive Gift Giving*, p. 17.
19. Ibid., p. 72.
20. "Business Gift Giving Covered by IRS Rules," *Ideasworth*, Specialty Advertising Association International, Irving, Tex., 1982, p. 1.
21. *Business and Executive Gift Giving*, p. 27.
22. Ibid., p. 45.
23. Pierce, op. cit., p. 26.
24. *Business and Executive Gift Giving*, p. 70.
25. *Ideabook*, vol. 2, Specialty Advertising Association International, Irving, Tex., 1981 supplement, p. NR-68.

26. *Business and Executive Gift Giving*, p. 51.

27. Ibid., p. 71.

28. Pierce, op. cit., p. 31.

29. Ballard, op. cit., p. 17.

30. Kathleen Reardon, *International Business Gift-Giving Customs*, The Parker Pen Company, Janesville, Wis., 1981, p. 27.

31. Ballard, loc. cit.

32. *Postal Employees Cautioned Not to Accept Customer Gifts*, U.S. Postal Service, 1982.

33. George L. Herpel and Steve Slack, *Specialty Advertising: New Dimensions in Creative Marketing*, Specialty Advertising Association International, Irving, Tex., p. 189.

34. *Business and Executive Gift Giving*, p. 40.

35. Pierce, op. cit., p. 29.

36. *Specialty Advertising Report*, Specialty Advertising Association International, Irving, Tex., 1978, p. 1.

VI The Management of Sales Promotion

Whereas the overall subject of sales promotion has heretofore received little attention from book publishers, even less notice has been given to its management.

The next few chapters will cover in detail the various aspects of the sales promotion department, the preparation of the specialized sales promotion budget, and other areas concerned with the management of sales promotion.

22 Planning a Sales Promotion

WILLIAM A. ROBINSON
President, William A. Robinson, Inc.

In the past decade sales promotion registered a steady climb in terms of both dollar expenditures and share of the corporate marketing budget. It became a more attractive option in the marketing mix, while advertising saw some of its glamour and share of marketing dollars erode away.

As the budget grew, so did the demand for a more professional, sophisticated approach to developing sales promotion plans. More and more marketers began to apply the same high standards to judging sales promotion programs that they had applied to marketing and advertising plans for years. Marketing executives wanted justification for putting more dollars into sales promotion, and they wanted assurance of maximum effectiveness and efficiency.

The result has been a remarkable growth in professional sales promotion planning—the work that precedes a creative director's and marketing manager's sitting down and creating a specific concept. The old shoot-from-the-hip, often patchwork development of a program is giving way to long-term analytical thinking and scientific evaluation. This is essential, not only for getting the best results in the field but also for selling programs to corporate or marketing management.

Like advertising or overall marketing planning, sales promotion planning requires that you determine where you want to go and, in general terms, how you're going to get there before you begin the actual creative development of the program. Usually there are six steps that you'll want to take during the planning stage:

- Reviewing the market situation
- Identifying problems and opportunities

- Setting the overall sales promotion budget
- Setting the sales promotion objectives
- Developing strategies
- Scheduling

At each point in this process, you should also note how sales promotion plans integrate and coordinate with overall marketing, advertising, and sales plans.

The starting point is a review of the market situation, which is analyzed to identify sales promotion problems and opportunities.

REVIEWING THE MARKET SITUATION

The situation review contains the data that tell you where your product or service marketing stands now and where it's going. Most professional planners use a standard format for working up a situation review. This includes data on both the product or service and its category, including trends and sales projections.

Many, if not all, of the data needed for sales promotion planning are identical to the data used for marketing and advertising planning. In a case where marketing, advertising, and sales promotion plans are combined, one situation review, covering problems and opportunities, serves all three.

For example, a situation review for a typical consumer product covers the following areas:

Category Situation

1. **Size:** What does the product category or subcategory generate in sales?
2. **Trends:** Is it a growth category, or is it declining?
3. **Seasonality:** Is usage restricted to a particular season, as with a snow shovel? Do sales peak in a particular period?
4. **Demographics:** Who are the people using the product?
5. **Psychographics:** How do people feel about the product category?
6. **Geographics:** Are sales stronger in one area than another? Is the product available only in certain areas?
7. **Pricing and margins:** What are the price and marketing ranges within the category? What are their positions in the overall marketplace?
8. **Distribution chain:** How is the product delivered to the consumer—by direct sales by the manufacturer to the retailer or by broker or wholesaler intermediates?
9. **Major brands:** What are the shares and sales of the competitors, and what are their marketing activities?

Brand Situation

1. Description: What are the brand lines and sizes?
2. Positioning: How is the brand positioned in terms of usage and quality?
3. Sales and shares: What is the brand's past performance, and where is the brand headed?
4. Trends: Is the brand growing or declining? Why?
5. Seasonality: Is usage of the brand restricted to a particular season? Do sales peak at a certain time?
6. Demographics: Who uses the brand?
7. Psychographics: How do people feel about the brand?
8. Geographics: Are sales of the brand stronger in one area than another? Is the brand available only in certain areas?
9. Pricing and margins: What are the price and marketing ranges within the brand? What are their positions in the overall marketplace?
10. Distribution chain: How is the brand delivered to the consumer—by direct sales by the manufacturer to the retailer or by broker or wholesaler intermediates?
11. Marketing activities: What trade and consumer sales promotion programs are planned, and what will they cost?

Doing a comprehensive review at least once a year will serve as a basis not only for year-long marketing, advertising, and sales promotion planning but also for specific, short-term sales promotion planning. For example, the review can be updated and focused for a plan to counter a competitor's sales promotion program in a given market.

Not doing a thorough review, on the other hand, means that you risk developing objectives and promotional executions that totally miss the mark—the real needs of the brand in the marketplace (see the marketing data checklist below).

Typical Marketing Data Checklist

This checklist is used by a large grocery products corporation to develop a synopsis of the marketing situation from all available data.

1. Category volume
2. Category penetration (household and population)
3. Brand share
4. Geographic share ranges: high _____ percent; low _____ percent
5. Brand penetration (household and population)
6. Sizes (percent of sales)
7. Pricing (ranges)

8. Demographics
    a. Sex
    b. Age
    c. Income
    d. Marital status
    e. Education
    f. Size of household
    g. County size
9. Psychographics
10. Consumption data

	Percent of users	Frequency of use	Frequency of purchase	Percent of consumption
Heavy users				
Average users				
Light users				

11. All commodity volume (ACV) distribution levels (by size): food _____ percent; drugs _____ percent; mass merchandiser (M/M) _____ percent; other _____ percent
12. Geographic ACV distribution ranges (by size): high _____ percent; low _____ percent
13. Trial levels: _____ percent of households or the population have tried the brand within the past _____
    (time period)
14. Conversion levels: _____ percent of new users become regular users
15. New-user worth: $_____ per year
16. Average retail sale: $_____
17. Everyday retail profit margin (ranges): _____ percent
18. Cost of goods to wholesale profit margin: _____ percent
19. Current marketing objectives
    a. Consumers
        (1) Inducing trial
        (2) Inducing conversion
        (3) Maintaining current users
        (4) Loading
        (5) Countering competitors
    b. The trade
        (1) Getting new distribution
        (2) Maintaining current distribution
        (3) Gaining shelf space and position
        (4) Loading
        (5) Getting display space

(6) Advertising

(7) Price feature

   c. The sales force

      (1) Creating awareness

      (2) Creating emphasis

      (3) Training

      (4) Motivating

20. Past and present promotion performance

   a. Type

   b. Spending level

   c. Evaluation

IDENTIFYING PROBLEMS AND OPPORTUNITIES

When listing problems and opportunities, many planners make the mistake of failing to be specific and/or of stating the obvious. Saying that "distribution is 40 percent below average west of the Mississippi" doesn't help much in setting up promotional objectives. Statement of a general problem must be accompanied by a statement of the causes, if your objectives are to address brand problems in a meaningful way. The more you narrow down and zero in, the easier it is to develop an effective plan.

This detailed analysis of the market situation is essential for planning major, year-long programs. But even in the case of a small, tactical sales promotion program—a retailer's July Fourth weekend specials, for example—the whole job is easier when you have clearly defined in writing the problems to be solved and the opportunities to be exploited.

SETTING THE OVERALL SALES PROMOTION BUDGET

Most major marketing firms go into year-long planning with a predetermined budget, including a contingency reserve. In such a case, planning the sales promotion budget consists of breaking the total budget down for separate programs and then breaking each program budget down into components, such as distribution media, creative possibilities, redemption liabilities, and production. Budget breakdowns are then more properly considered part of the development of strategies. In fact, they may be a major factor in the selection of a strategy.

Some marketers use a different approach—the "objective-and-task" method. Here, overall marketing and sales promotion objectives precede the budget. With a new brand, for example, where the budget can't be keyed to previous sales performance, the brand manager sets an objective of, say, a 20 percent share of market in the first year. With this goal, it is possible to determine fairly accurately what it will take in terms of sales promotion and advertising spending to take those share points away from the competition.

With this method, you will fine-tune the objectives and spending requirements simultaneously and come to a budget that optimizes results without
eliminating profits. It is by far the more difficult budgeting method, but it is the
one that lets you base the budget on the job to be done, rather than the other
way around.

SETTING THE SALES PROMOTION OBJECTIVES

Sales promotion objectives are the keystone of professional planning. And if
you don't set objectives before you start work on executing a sales promotion,
you can spend a huge amount of time and money for a very glitzy program
that won't move you an inch toward the solution of your marketing problem.

Sales promotion is usually defined as a short-term inducement to buy
that deviates from the normal marketing mix of price, product, and packaging.

The most common deviation is in pricing—the techniques of cents-off
coupons and refunds, for example.

Generally, consumer and trade sales promotions can accomplish the
following:

- Gain trial users
- Hold current users
- Load current users
- Increase usage and consumption
- Induce consumers to trade up
- Introduce new products and services
- Reinforce brand-sell advertising
- Increase brand awareness
- Gain trade support
- Build trade inventories
- Gain distribution
- Increase on- and off-shelf merchandising space and improve position
- Create trade awareness for new products

   Generally, a sales promotion cannot:

- Change a negative consumer attitude
- Turn around a long-term declining sales trend
- Create an image for a brand
- Motivate consumers to buy a product over a long period of time

Writing Down Objectives

It pays to put your objectives down in writing, whether you are doing a major,
national year-long program or a one-shot weekend retailer clearance sale.

Writing down objectives may seem like a simple step; it's often overlooked because it is assumed that everyone knows what the objectives are. Unfortunately, that is seldom the case if you have meaningful objectives, generated by a careful analysis of the market situation and of problems and opportunities, or if more than one person is involved in the sales promotion.

For that reason, everyone involved in planning and executing the sales promotion should be able to see and agree on clear-cut, specific, written objectives. If you don't write them down, you'll have a hard time evaluating whether you're going in the right direction and, at the end, whether you got where you were supposed to go.

The first problem arises when the people who are actually creating the sales promotion get some vague or casual direction from the marketing manager; for example, "We need a couple of ideas for the salespeople to take out in September." If the brand manager and the creative director had known that sales needed a low-budget program to counter a competitor's coupon drop and hold trade interest until a major advertising program was introduced in October, they would stand a far better chance of developing a promotion that would go to the heart of the problem. Vague, general objectives get you into the same mess. Too often each person involved with a project will come up with a totally different interpretation of a vague objective. And, again, there will be a lot of thrashing around, and money will be wasted.

The second risk is that you will not be able to gauge the results of the promotion accurately. If you don't know where you were supposed to go, how do you know whether you got there?

Setting Specific Objectives

Keeping in mind the general goals that sales promotion techniques can and cannot help you attain, as well as your review of the market situation, with its problems and opportunities, set objectives that are as specific and detailed as possible.

Most marketers begin with a sales objective; however, saying that the objective is "to sell more" won't win you any plaudits from the professional planner. Be specific as to the amount of unit or dollar sales or the share of the market that you are aiming for. If you are using the objective-and-task method of budgeting, be extremely careful, because this first objective will determine how much money you will have to spend.

Be specific as to the type of sales you want. Are you looking for trial sales? Do you want to load current users? If you're a retailer, are you looking for a loss leader that will increase traffic and thus also increase impulse buying of nonsale merchandise?

Specifically target your geographic and demographic goals. Demographically, spell out ethnic markets and age and income groups, as well as the size of the audience you want to reach in each demographic segment.

Specify how the sales promotion should be coordinated with advertising, public relations, and sales-force drives.

Set your media objectives and your creative objectives: If you want a blockbusting attention-getter to build brand-name awareness rather than immediate sales, lay it all out.

Clearly define and distinguish between the consumer and the trade objectives of the promotion. Even the same sales promotion may have two different purposes. For example, the consumer objective for a match-the-label instant-winner sweepstakes might be to juxtapose the consumer and the product, since you know that when the consumer is next to the product, sales can go up 400 to 500 percent, especially if the product is off the shelf. But your trade objective in this case might be to force off-shelf display of the brand, to load the dealer, or to give the dealer an incentive in the form of a proof-of-performance display allowance.

State any time objectives you have. Do you want a program for winter and summer? Do you have time limits? How many programs do you need for fixed periods, and how many "floating" programs do you want?

And if you haven't already done so, put down your budget objectives.

Following is a checklist for determining measurable objectives.

Checklist for Determining Measurable Objectives

One multibrand packaged goods manufacturer separately lists objectives when results can be precisely measured. The list provides not only very specific goals but also the method of evaluation. Use whatever mix of the following objectives may apply.

1. To achieve the following sales volume goals (as measured by the marketing department):

Brand	Dollar volume	Number of weeks of business adjusted for seasonal index	Incremental increase, dollars

2. To increase individual brand share levels (as measured by Nielsen) as follows:

Brand	Current share	Desired share

3. To achieve the following display levels (as measured by field sales or Burgoyne Syndicated Service):

Store size	Number of stores	Number of cases displayed	Total number of cases displayed

4. To achieve the following advertising or feature objectives as expressed in percent of ACV volume featuring the promotion (as measured by Majers or promotion payments):
   a. _____
   b. _____
   c. _____
   d. _____

5. To achieve any desired incentive program results at the regional, divisional, or individual field sales levels, as expressed in percent of participants reaching or surpassing set goals (as measured by the sales department)

6. To increase ACV distribution levels from _____ to _____ (as measured by Nielsen)

7. To increase trade inventories as expressed in week's supply from _____ to _____ (as measured by Nielsen)

8. To reduce out-of-stock levels from _____ to _____ (as measured by Nielsen)

DEVELOPING STRATEGIES

The basic sales promotion techniques you use in developing your strategies can be reduced to two general types. The first is a short-term deviation from regular pricing: coupons, price-off packs, trade allowances, bonus packs, etc. The second uses an incentive unrelated to the normal product marketing mix: premiums, sweepstakes prizes, etc.—in other words, an added value.

These two broad categories can be broken down into ten basic building blocks that you use alone or in combination.

1. Sampling
2. Couponing
3. Value packs
4. Premium packs
5. Mail-in premiums
6. Refunds
7. Contests and sweepstakes
8. Continuity programs
9. Trade incentives
10. Special events

Before you despair of having an adequate arsenal to work with, consider that these ten building blocks can be combined in close to 8 million different ways to develop your strategies. And that's not taking into account the infinite variety of headlines, copy, graphics, mechanical details, and distribution media that you can employ, not to mention combinations with brand-sell advertising, public relations, sales-force drives, and trade programs.

Each of these techniques has well-defined strengths and weaknesses in terms of helping you achieve specific objectives. If you have developed realistic, meaningful objectives, the job of selecting and combining the techniques into a strategy is not that formidable.

For example, if your objective is to increase sales by x percent over the previous period and if your primary strategy is a modest cents-off offer, your promotion ad might get lost in today's blizzard of high-value coupons.

But for a modest increase in the budget, you can combine the coupon offer with a sweepstakes, which we know will increase ad readership or attention to a point-of-purchase display. This in turn will increase the coupon redemption rate, the number of proofs of purchase you receive with sweepstakes entries, and trade cooperation. Thus it is possible to achieve your sales objective without a budget-busting increase in the face value of your coupon.

Following are the advantages and disadvantages of commonly used sales promotion techniques; you need to be aware of these in order to create the most effective strategies.

Sampling. This technique involves delivering a free sample of the actual product or service to the consumer for trial. It is used primarily to introduce new or improved products, to open new markets, and to reach new users.

Sampling new products most commonly involves giving a trial-size package to the consumer. This is done by door-to-door delivery, through the mail, by means of field intercepts (the person who hands you a four-pack of cigarettes in the shopping mall, for example), and at point of sale. In the case of services and products for which an actual sample is impractical, the most common device is to provide a "taste." The consumer gets a free session at a health spa or test-drives a car, for example. Free samples are also delivered by store demonstrators, in response to mail or telephone requests, and by print media, or they can be in the form of an on-pack premium.

The advantages of sampling are:

- It is the strongest and quickest trial device, especially when combined with a coupon.
- It can force distribution with the retailer.
- It can gain off-shelf display.

The disadvantages are:

- It is extremely expensive.
- It can be very wasteful if the product has no mass appeal.
- It can be disastrous if the product is inferior to competitive products or has no real appeal to consumers.

Couponing. For giving an instant lift to sales, couponing is the most commonly used technique by far, and its share of the marketing budget continues to grow at a mind-boggling rate. In the simplest form of couponing, a manufacturer agrees to reimburse a retailer for discounting a product and also to pay a small handling charge. Variations are (1) the in-ad store coupon, a device declining in favor, in which retailers place the manufacturer's coupons in store ads for a fee, and (2) the trade coupon, in which retailers provide a price cut but pay for it themselves. Most of the impressive figures you see concerning couponing's enormous share of the promotion budget are based on manufacturers' coupons. The costs of in-ad store coupons and trade coupons are next to impossible to measure.

Coupons are delivered mainly by print media, including run-of-press newspaper ads, solo and co-op mailings, free-standing inserts in Sunday supplements, and magazines. Solo and co-op mailings are growing in popularity. In-pack and on-pack coupons, especially the on-pack coupons that can be used immediately, are used to reward current users. Retailers deliver trade coupons by means of flyers and store ads.

Couponing is used to reach a large number of objectives, alone or in combination. It's an excellent way to generate trial, to reach a mass audience more economically than is possible with sampling, to load regular users or induce them to trade up to larger sizes, to increase consumption by regular users, to counter competitors' sales promotions, and to increase distribution, inventories, and display space, in the case of the trade.

Couponing's overwhelming dominance as a sales promotion technique is due to the fact that it is the cheapest, simplest, and most reliable way for a manufacturer to deliver savings to the consumer. This suggests that couponing should be the first strategy you look into. It's hard to beat.

The advantages of couponing are:

- It has a very strong ability to pull a product through the channels of distribution.
- It can increase distribution, facings, flooring, and loading.
- It ensures that the manufacturer's discount is passed along to the consumer.
- The results are easily predicted.

The disadvantages are:

- Proliferation and clutter reduce the impact of coupons.
- There are opportunities for misredemption.
- The trade complains about the massive handling chore.

Value Packs. This technique is divided into bonus packs and price-off packs. Bonus packs provide more of the product at the regular price. Price-off packs provide the regular amount at a marked-down price. In either case, the unit cost is reduced.

Value packs are used to generate trial use, reward and load current users, get off-shelf display, build traffic, and quickly counter competitors' sales promotions. They are the second most popular consumer promotion technique, after couponing, used by manufacturers. For retailers, they are probably the number one technique, in the form of sale-priced merchandise.

Value packs are delivered at the point of purchase, but they usually have heavy advertising and display support.

The advantages of value packs are:

- They load the trade.
- They load consumers.
- They provide retailers with a traffic-building advertising event that increases overall sales.

- They provide a display event.

  The disadvantages are:

- They don't enhance the product image.
- They can be pilfered by the trade (twin packs, for example).
- They don't produce loyal new users.
- They provide only a temporary increase in market share.
- The trade does not always pass along the full manufacturer's discount.
- There is trade resistance to manufacturers' value packs because of duplicate inventories with stock-keeping-unit control systems.

  Figure 22-1 shows a typical bonus pack.

  Premium Packs. This technique is divided into in-pack, on-pack, near-pack, and container premiums. Premiums add to the perceived value of the product and are useful for gaining new users as well as for rewarding current users. They can stimulate multiple purchases, thus loading the consumer; they can help reinforce the brand image; they can make advertising and point-of-purchase displays more attention-getting; and they can help load the trade and force off-shelf display.

  Mail-in premiums and premium packs together account for the third largest expenditure by manufacturers on consumer sales promotions.

FIGURE 22-1. A Hefty bonus pack. This plastic-bag value-pack provides twenty-four bags for the price of twenty.

The advantages of premium packs are:

- They are a strong display device.
- They help differentiate between similar products.
- They can be designed to be self-liquidating.

The disadvantages are:

- They can actually reduce sales if the premium is undesirable.
- They can create trade resistance.
- They may involve problems with inventory and logistics.
- They can be abused by the trade.
- They may promote pilferage, in the case of on-pack or near-pack premiums.

Figure 22-2 shows a typical on-pack premium.

Mail-in Premiums. The subcategories of mail-in premiums are self-liquidators, free mail-in premiums, and speed-plan premiums. With the speed plan, the more proofs of purchase the consumer provides, the lower the cost of the premium. Mail-in premiums are especially effective in reinforcing a brand's image and making advertising and displays more attention-getting. They can generate trial, especially free mail-in premiums; they can load the consumer; and they can get trade support and off-shelf display when the premium is also offered as a dealer loader.

One of the clear-cut trends in sales promotion is the increase in self-liquidating collections—a wide range of exclusive, customized items offered to the consumer over a long period of time. Collections are especially effective in reinforcing brand image, while appealing to a broad spectrum of users because of the variety of items and prices.

The advantages of mail-in premiums are:

- They are powerful attention-getters for an ad or display.
- They require a proof of purchase.
- They do not have the stigma of discounting, as coupons and price-off packs do.

The disadvantages are:

- Self-liquidating and speed-plan premiums won't generate trial.
- Mail-in premiums do not provide an immediate reward.
- It is often difficult to measure precisely the impact of mail-in premiums on sales.

Refunds. A refund or rebate is one of the old reliables of sales promotion, especially for manufacturers who want to create an advertising price event while cutting redemption liabilities to a minimum. Because most refunds require the consumer to write directly to the manufacturer, the reward is delayed, which is not the case with a coupon or a price-off pack, where the discount is provided at the time of purchase. For that reason, redemption rates for refunds are considerably lower than those for coupons, even when the amount of the discount and the product are identical.

However, in times of economic stress, refund redemption rates tend to climb. And packaged goods manufacturers' recent trend toward offering coupons rather than cash has allowed the manufacturers to increase the amount of the discount, which also increases the redemptions.

Refunds are used to generate trial and to reward current users. They are good for loading the consumer when multiple purchases are required. Like

FIGURE 22-2. A Benson & Hedges 100s on-pack premium. The company is a long-time user of on-carton premiums, offered in a special floor display. (*Courtesy of Philip Morris U.S.A.*)

coupons and price-off packs, they are excellent traffic builders. They are especially useful in building the total amount of an offer—when used with a coupon, for example—without incurring the redemption costs that a coupon offer alone would involve.

The advantages of refunds are:

- They are a low-cost sales promotion tool, compared with couponing.
- There is good trade acceptance for displays featuring refunds.
- They provide a basis for traffic-building advertising.
- They are a good sales-force incentive.
- The manufacturer is assured that the savings are passed on to the consumer.

The disadvantages are:

- The trade would rather see coupons and allowances.
- The results are sometimes difficult to measure.
- They are weak in terms of generating trial, compared with coupons and price-off packs.

Contests and Sweepstakes. Sweepstakes dominate this category of sales promotion techniques, and in recent years there have been a number of refinements in sweepstakes that have made them far more effective in building sales. The problem with sweepstakes is that proof of purchase cannot be required with entry, and thus the number of entries has nothing to do with sales.

For that reason, a sweepstakes strategy has been used most often to meet objectives such as increasing ad readership, increasing awareness of a tandem promotion (e.g., in combination with coupons), creating trade excitement and display events, and reinforcing a brand image.

However, there are ways to tie sweepstakes entries to purchase of the product or to increase the chances of a purchase. The in-pack game-piece sweepstakes—in which a game card is placed inside the package—forces purchase. A match-the-label or match-the-display-symbol instant-winner game forces the player to come to the point of purchase and the product. Another device is to combine the coupon and the sweepstakes entry form. When consumers redeem the coupon, they are automatically entered. This too stimulates purchase.

There is a trend in sweepstakes design toward the "everybody-wins" concept. This strongly stimulates participation. The top levels of prizes are usually the standard high-ticket inducements, but the lowest-level prizes are frequently coupons for the brand. This device reduces liabilities while boosting sales in the postsweepstakes period.

Contests, in which skill rather than chance determines the winners, are also growing more popular. (See Figure 22-3.)

Contests and sweepstakes are used to increase ad readership, to extend or reinforce a brand image, to build store traffic, to force purchase, and to create a display event.

The advantages of contests and sweepstakes are:

- They allow control of costs (compared with a refund or coupon offer, in which redemption liabilities will vary).
- They generate traffic.
- They increase attention for advertising and display.

The disadvantages are:

- They can't produce mass trial.

FIGURE 22-3. J&B scotch contest. The company uses a crossword puzzle to educate the consumer concerning the product's unique points. Because winners are chosen on the basis of skill rather than chance, this is a contest, rather than a sweepstakes. (*Courtesy of Paddington Corp.*)

- There is a high percentage of proof-of-purchase facsimiles.
- There are many professional entrants.
- They can result in proliferation and clutter.

Continuity Programs. There is a wide variety of continuity programs. The most common form is a trading stamp program, in which stamps are collected and redeemed for merchandise. Continuity plans differ from other consumer sales promotion techniques in that they are long-term.

Continuity programs are used to stimulate repeat purchases; to generate traffic; to add distinctiveness to a product that is competing with many other, similar products; to create brand loyalty; and to reward regular customers.

The advantages of continuity programs are:

- They increase frequency of purchase.
- They increase frequency of store visits.
- Their effectiveness is easy to measure.
- They create a purchase habit that may extend beyond the promotion period.

The disadvantages are:

- They may have limited appeal.
- A long-term program won't gain trade support.
- They can't generate off-shelf display.
- There are opportunities for misredemption, especially of stamps.

Trade Incentives. Most of the consumer techniques can be used with the trade. But there are special devices peculiar to the trade: allowances, free products, and premium loaders. Trade incentives are the largest single element of promotional spending, and they are the basic "push" device for packaged goods.

They are used to build trade inventories, gain distribution, gain shelf space, get off-shelf display, encourage price and ad features, and launch new products.

Every major consumer sales promotion sponsored by a manufacturer should be backed up with trade incentives.

The advantages of trade incentives are:

- They get trade action.
- They can have a performance requirement.
- Costs are easily controlled.

The disadvantages are:

- They can be extremely expensive for slow-moving brands.
- They can't be offered selectively.
- There is no consumer involvement.

- In the case of price allowances, the savings are not always passed on to the consumer.

Special Events. The special-events technique involves sponsorship of sports, entertainment, cultural, public service, and educational events. In some cases, the event is free to the consumer; this creates brand-name awareness, goodwill, and brand-image enhancement. As a sales promotion technique, the event may be attended at no cost or at a discount with a proof of purchase. It is also used as a vehicle for other sales promotion techniques, such as sampling and couponing.

Special-event sponsorship is an increasingly popular marketing device, involving everything from tennis tournaments to rock concerts.

The advantages of special events are:

- They can generate extensive publicity for the brand.
- They can preempt the competition.
- They can get free media space or time for the brand.
- When celebrities are involved, they can constitute endorsement of the brand.
- They can be used as a vehicle for other promotional techniques.

The disadvantages are:

- Logistics may be a problem.
- Their impact is difficult to measure.
- Sometimes they generate weak trade support.

Figure 22-4 shows how a special event can combine brand-sell advertising with promotional inducements.

Combining strategies. When you are developing strategies, especially for large programs, remember that the ten basic techniques can be put together in 8 million different combinations. The trend today is toward gaining a synergistic effect by combining two or three techniques in one program. The most common combination are (1) coupons and mail-in premiums and (2) coupons and sweepstakes. The sweepstakes, for example, will increase readership of the promotion ad and redemptions of the coupons, while the coupons will increase the number of proofs of purchase accompanying entries.

Remember also that two or three techniques may work equally well in achieving your objectives. Keep all the options open until you begin creative development.

The third opportunity to note is that you can extend a consumer strategy into your trade promotion. A through-the-mail self-liquidator offer to the consumer can be used as a trade loader as well. A consumer sweepstakes can be run in conjunction with a parallel trade sweepstakes.

Distribution and Media Strategies

The second most important element in creating strategies is defining media. Distribution or media costs can take the largest share of the budget for a particular program. For example, when you run a sweepstakes-coupon combination nationally with free-standing inserts and special store displays, the media cost can easily exceed the cost of prizes or coupon redemptions. If

FIGURE 22-4. The Kool jazz festival. As the Kool jazz festival moves across the country, local promotion can tie in with free tickets for both consumers and the trade. (*Courtesy of the Brown and Williamson Tobacco Corp. Reprinted by permission; all rights reserved.*)

your technique strategy requires this type of distribution—as it would with an instant-winner match-the-display game card—you may want to change the technique to meet budget goals.

Your media strategy will also control redemption and fulfillment liabilities. For example, featuring a black-and-white coupon in a run-of-press newspaper ad results in a much lower redemption rate than featuring a coupon in a free-standing insert in the same paper. Therefore, the strategy planner can juggle the media and the face value of the coupon to arrive at the most efficient combination for a fixed budget. Media strategy should also include how you are going to reach specific demographic or geographic targets. Following is a media checklist.

Distribution and Media Checklist

Use this checklist when you are planning media strategies to be sure that you have looked at all the media that can communicate your sales promotion message or distribute your promotional material, such as a coupon or a sweepstakes entry form.

- ☐ Ad mats and slicks
- ☐ Ad reprints
- ☐ Advertising specialties
- ☐ Anniversary and birthday programs
- ☐ Annual reports
- ☐ Attire and uniforms
- ☐ Audiovisual techniques
- ☐ Booklets
- ☐ Brochures
- ☐ Business awards and gifts
- ☐ Catalogs
- ☐ Closed-circuit TV
- ☐ Comic books
- ☐ Consumer testing
- ☐ Contests
- ☐ Continuity programs
- ☐ Contracts
- ☐ Couponing
- ☐ Coupon plans
- ☐ Credit-card promotions
- ☐ Customer relations
- ☐ Dealer loaders
- ☐ Demonstrations
- ☐ Direct mail
- ☐ Educational programs
- ☐ Ethnic market programs
- ☐ Executive meetings
- ☐ Field services
- ☐ Fulfillment (offers and bounce-backs)
- ☐ Graphic design
- ☐ Grocery bags
- ☐ Handbills
- ☐ House organs
- ☐ Incentive programs (premiums and travel)
- ☐ Industrial development programs
- ☐ Industrial exhibits
- ☐ Industrial shows
- ☐ In-store displays
- ☐ Internal communications programs
- ☐ Logos
- ☐ Magazines
- ☐ Mail orders
- ☐ Management fact books
- ☐ Marketing plans
- ☐ Market research
- ☐ Matchbooks

☐ Motion pictures
☐ Multimedia shows
☐ Newsletters
☐ Outdoor billboards
☐ Package attachments
☐ Package design
☐ Package flags
☐ Point-of-purchase displays
☐ Posters
☐ Premiums
☐ Promotion analysis and evaluation
☐ Prototype packages
☐ Publicity
☐ Public relations
☐ Radio
☐ Referrals (using the user)
☐ Retail promotions
☐ Sales-force promotions
☐ Sales incentives
☐ Sales meetings
☐ Salespersons' presentations

☐ Sales training
☐ Sampling
☐ Selling materials and kits
☐ Skywriting
☐ Slides
☐ Special events
☐ Speech writing
☐ Stationery
☐ Storyboards
☐ Sweepstakes drawings
☐ Teasers
☐ Telephone solicitation
☐ Television
☐ Trademarks
☐ Trade relations
☐ Trade shows
☐ Trade testing
☐ Trading stamps
☐ Transit advertising
☐ Translations
☐ Truck advertising

Strategy Guidelines

In addition to technique and distribution strategies, be sure to cover these areas:

- Creative strategy. Set the creative tone of the sales promotion and determine how it will reinforce brand image, if that's an objective.
- Coordination strategy. Explain how the sales promotion coordinates with advertising, sales drives, and other activities.
- Scheduling strategy. If necessary, explain how the timetable will help achieve goals.
- Budget strategy. If several programs are involved under one total budget, explain how the budget is broken down for each program.
- Evaluation strategy. Just as it is important to agree on objectives for evaluation before launching a sales promotion, it is wise to get the strategy down on paper as well.

Be sure you have covered not only consumer but also trade strategies and specify nonpromotional support strategies such as selling aids for the sales force and trade advertising.

SCHEDULING

There are two big reasons why scheduling every step of the sales promotion is the key to professional planning. You must be certain that the promotion hits at the right time for the target consumers. And you want to have sufficient time to execute the plans properly.

When you have blocked out your promotion strategies, you are usually able to rough up a reliable timetable. The logical progression is to work backward from the program's in-field period.

Use the following guidelines.

In-Field Period. Selecting in-field dates is usually part of developing objectives and strategies. At this point, in addition to considering whether the period is right for the consumer and trade audience, consider the nonpromotional logistics. For example, a sale price on skis in June will beat the competition, but will retailers have sufficient inventories to meet demand, or will out-of-stock situations nullify the money you've laid out?

Also, double-check the length of the promotion. A refund offer, for example, may be designed primarily to get off-shelf display at retail stores. You'll get a display up at the beginning of the promotion, but then the trade will replace the display. If the refund offer is good for six months instead of one month, you may fail to meet your display objective for the last five months, while incurring redemption liabilities.

Development Time. Working backward from the in-field period, do you have sufficient time for planning, creative execution, legal and market research, distribution and media buys, print and audiovisual production, shipping, and sell-in? Not allowing for all these steps results in errors, less-than-perfect creative executions, whopping overtime charges from suppliers, lack of trade support, and even missed deadlines.

Retailers' Scheduling Procedures. Many retailers—especially food and drug chains—do their advertising and promotional planning from three to six months in advance. If your sales promotion depends heavily on retailer advertising and in-store displays, make sure to take the retailers' lead-time requirements into account. One way to make sure that you sidestep these pitfalls is to do your scheduling along with the development of the promotion strategies.

BENEFITS OF PLANNING

Whether sales promotion is getting more and better planning because of its larger share of the marketing budget, or whether it is getting more of the budget because of better planning is a question you could debate for years.

There is no question, however, that thorough preliminary planning means better sales promotions.

If you follow the six preliminary planning steps before you begin creative, premium, or prize selection and before you start production and field implementation you are bound to end up with more effective and efficient promotion plans, to know when and why you've achieved your goals, and to be able to sell your program to corporate executives and financial officers much more easily.

23
Promotions Cost Money:
Don't Overlook the Budget

ROBERT N. ZOUL
Manager of Marketing Expense and Control, Kraft, Inc.

Promotion and *budget* are two readily identifiable but not easily definable words. The following discussion will focus on definitions and, it is hoped, will provide food for thought, which should equate to a good budget.

SOME DEFINITIONS

Webster's Ninth New Collegiate Dictionary defines *promotion* as "the further-ance of the acceptance and sale of merchandise through advertising, publicity, or discounting."

The Random House Dictionary of the English Language gives some useful definitions of the word *budget*: "an estimate, often itemized, of expected income and expense . . . for a given period in the future"; "a plan of operations based on such an estimate"; "the total sum of money set aside or needed for a specific purpose."

These definitions include some of the key terms and phrases used in budgeting: *in the future, itemized, for a given period, for a specific purpose*, and *plan*. An understanding of the way these terms and phrases relate to the elusive word *promotion* can be helpful when building a promotion budget.

When we speak of a promotion, do we mean a consumer promotion, a promotion aimed at the trade, or a promotion designed to motivate a retailer's or manufacturer's sales force, or does the word encompass all these forms of promotion? In this chapter we will assume that it includes all forms of sales promotion. The fact that there are different forms of promotion is important only insofar as we acknowledge that they exist.

What Is Sales Promotion?

First, sales promotion should not be confused with advertising. It seems that everyone knows what advertising is and what is included in advertising expense. In fact, most sales promotion people would readily claim to be experts in the field of advertising, and most would agree that it consists of sponsored, or purchased, communications of product or service benefits to consumers via the mass media: the broadcast media (television and radio), the print media (magazines, newspapers, and supplements), and the outdoor media (such as billboards). The cost of production of the materials used for ads in these media is generally included as a part of advertising expense.

Is it more difficult to define *sales promotion*? Probably not; in fact, it may be easier. Many in the industry define it as all forms of sponsored communications other than advertising, personal selling, and publicity. This is a simple definition. However, it may be a primary cause of the frequent neglect of promotion budget planning and control; advertising budgets do not suffer from such neglect.

TYPES OF PROMOTION

So much for definitions. Let us now look at the specific types of promotion and the audiences to whom they are directed.

Among the most common types of promotion are point-of-purchase displays, premium promotions, contests and sweepstakes, couponing, refunds, and sampling. These are generally directed to three primary audiences: (1) the consumer, (2) the trade, and (3) the sales force. (Promotions to the trade and promotions to the sales force are sometimes considered to constitute one category of promotion.)

Although these classifications of promotion types and target audiences are straightforward, controlling them under a budget system is not easy. Some promotions are directed to all three target audiences; others are not. Should the budget and expense classifications change, depending on the target audience? The answer depends on company policy. The classification of promotion types is more a matter of company policy than of strict accounting principles. Therefore, it is necessary to determine company policies in this area before putting budget preparation into motion.

CLASSIFYING PROMOTION EXPENSES

Each company should clearly identify which activities are to be classified as promotion expenses. As stated above, classification of promotion types will vary from company to company. It is not important that all companies classify promotions in a similar manner, but it is important that each individual company determine its own classification of expenses. Without such a classification, the preparation of a budget and the recording and reporting of promotion expenses will be meaningless.

Earlier we mentioned such forms of promotion as point-of-purchase displays, premium promotions, contests, sweepstakes, couponing, refunds, and sampling. We also indicated that such promotions are generally directed to one or more of three target groups: the consumer, the trade, and the sales force. Generally, each target group represents a separate expense category.

Consumer promotions are commonly referred to as *sales promotions*, and their costs are frequently considered to be a part of advertising expense (or are assigned to a similar expense category). Consumer promotions are those activities which "speak" to the consumer. Promotions designed to enlist the cooperation of the working professionals in a business or industry are considered to be trade promotions; the costs of such promotions are not usually considered to be an advertising expense and are carried in a different expense category. Those programs designed to elicit some special effort from the sales force are usually considered to be incentive promotions; their costs are a part of administrative expense. All three types of promotion, however, come under the overall sales promotion umbrella.

Identifying the specific elements of a promotion does not ensure proper budgeting and control; there must also be an effort to report all charges that fall into the designated promotion categories. All categories must be clearly defined as to what expense items are to be included in them. For example, if a consumer premium promotion offer involves a design alteration of an existing package or label, company policy must determine, before the budget is finalized, whether the extra design and production costs are to be part of the promotion expense. Similar policy decisions should be made concerning the proper handling of bonus packs, special coupons or package inserts, and bottle collars. Company policy must state how production costs for such promotions are to be handled. Frequently such costs are charged to packaging expense, manufacturing expense, sales expense, and/or marketing administrative expense. Company policies may vary, but a decision must be made as to how such expenses are to be charged. In order to exercise proper control over promotion expenses, it is important to realize that all such related expenses are part and parcel of the promotion and should be charged accordingly. The rationale is that without the promotion, such expenses would not have been incurred.

An Example from Industry

The preceding discussion has covered definitions and classifications in general terms. Now I would like to discuss the promotion budget philosophy of a company with which I am most familiar, Kraft.

First let us take a look at the philosophy of promotions and the reason for this philosophy at Kraft. Inflation, escalating prices, and a depressed economy have worked toward shaping a new consumer group, the "value seekers." The emergence of value seekers is responsible for an increase in the number and type of promotions currently being used at Kraft. Consumer dollars are scarce, and manufacturers and retailers need to use all the tools available to them to move products off store shelves.

Promotions, if properly planned, will motivate the cost-conscious consumer and retailer. The goal of any promotion is to reward both the consumer and the retailer; one that offers "good value" will accomplish this goal. At Kraft a successful promotion must have (1) a perceived value to both the consumer and the retailer and (2) the ability to pull a product off the shelf. Whenever possible, Kraft creates a promotion which will also reward the sales force. The successful promotion must have the ability both to push the product on the shelf and gain display space and to pull if off the shelf. (These are not the customary marketing uses of the words; promotions to the trade and to sales force push merchandise through the channels of distribution, while promotions to consumers pull it through.) A promotion that motivates only one of the main parties (the consumer or the retailer) will fail.

At Kraft the marketing objective of a promotion is of primary importance. The most obvious objective of most promotions is to sell a product at a fair profit. Another objective can be to obtain either short-term or long-term results. The promotion selected must be one which can meet such objectives. Other objectives include (1) introduction of a new product or package, (2) increased product awareness, (3) increased market share in a particular area, and (4) support advertising or other scheduled promotions. Obviously, different promotions will have different objectives, but the objective of a particular promotion should always be set beforehand. Without an objective, the promotion is destined to fail.

In accordance with Kraft's philosophies and objectives, a sales promotion group has been established to handle promotions in cooperation with the marketing groups. The sales promotion group consists of a number of sales promotion managers who work directly with marketing managers and who have specific product brand and/or corporate promotion responsibilities. Promotion is an in-house activity at Kraft. It is the responsibility of this in-house group to integrate the promotion effort with the advertising plans (in conjunction with the advertising agencies, the marketing staff, and the advertising staff). At Kraft the departmental costs, including the salaries of the sales promotion staff, are not classified as a promotion expense; they are considered a marketing administrative expense.

THE IMPORTANCE OF PROMOTION

Promotion has been gaining in importance in the marketing of products for many years. Not only is this trend continuing, but it also appears to be accelerating, possibly as a result of the present depressed economic conditions and the success of promotions under such conditions. In order to obtain their share of retail shelf space, companies are encouraged to try new techniques which are more efficient and which will result in faster consumer response.

Companies are now tailoring their promotions to fit their marketing objectives. Since large sums of money are involved, new or untested promotion techniques should and can be tested in several control markets to ascertain their effectiveness. There is no reason why a single promotion must be national in scope; different promotions can be used simultaneously in different markets.

Promotion Spending

Promotion spending has increased among companies that have always utilized promotions as a marketing tool and among companies that are experimenting with different types of promotion techniques. The widespread use of promotions as a competitive edge is another factor contributing to increased promotion spending. Promotions have gained wider acceptability as viable marketing tools because more executives are better qualified in this area. The brand management structure of many companies dictates quick returns by brands, and promotions are more responsive to this need than media advertising. These factors make it more important than ever to examine your company's budget planning, reporting, and controls in the promotion area.

How Much to Spend. The increased importance of promotions raises the question of how much to spend. Before a dollar amount is arrived at, a promotion plan should be structured by setting goals and objectives by product. These goals should then be converted into a series of promotions by type: refund offer, premium, sweepstakes, store display, etc. The specific activities can then be converted into cost estimates; however, this is usually done concurrently with the planning of the specific goal of the promotion. Each phase of the promotion budget should be "costed out" as accurately as possible.

Although very few promotion budget expenses are of the type that can be estimated from published rate cards (as in media advertising), most promotion costs can be determined on the basis of good purchasing procedures and policies. A company's own records reflecting the costs of similar promotions launched in the past are a good source of cost data if the materials used in these promotions were bought using good purchasing procedures, including competitive bidding and component pricing.

After establishing the goals and objectives of the promotion and making sure that the aforementioned criteria are met, a company must still determine how many total dollars are to be invested. The methods used fall generally into two categories: (1) those based on a desire to achieve the marketing objectives of the promotion and (2) those based on a need to make a predetermined profit. A balance of both types should be considered. However, I suggest that the dominant philosophy should be one of achieving marketing objectives within the affordability of the brand.

The responsibility for budgeting rests with each of the groups involved in the promotion process. How much to spend should be determined, however, on the basis of company goals and objectives and the success of previous promotions. Promotion budgets should be a reflection of goals translated into dollars, and goals should be a reflection of objectives to be achieved. In essence, the promotion budget should be set on the basis of a "priced set of goals," not a predetermined allocation of funds.

WHAT IS A BUDGET, AND WHY SHOULD WE HAVE ONE?

It is said that budget preparation, administration, and control is an integral part of every successful business, whether this budget function is in the area of marketing and sales, sales operations, production, distribution, or any other segment of the business. Advertising, which is usually a function of marketing, is no exception to this rule; however, there is frequently one exception, and that is the area of promotion.

At this point in our discussion of budgets, it may be a good idea to recall some of the key terms and phrases in the dictionary definition: *itemized, for a given period, for a specific purpose*, and *plan*. Budgeting promotions is nothing more than planning. It is an expression of a systematic advance plan for each itemized promotion activity for a given period of time in dollars and for a particular purpose. The budget control system consists of:

1. An advance, formal, itemized plan which serves as a tool to management for allocating company resources to the various promotion activities during a period of time
2. A dollar plan by activity relating to marketing goals and objectives
3. A formal system within which adjustments can be made to meet changing conditions.
4. A basis against which actual performance can be measured

If budgeting is an integral part of every successful business, why is promotion, which is a major area of marketing expense and represents a multibillion-dollar industry, so often overlooked when it comes to budget planning and control? The promotion budget receives far less attention than it deserves. Often the promotion budget is put together "on a wing and a prayer." I believe that promotion has an identity problem; that is why promotion budgeting is so frequently neglected.

The Budgeting Process

The budgeting process forces the responsible personnel to plan, and it enables management to exercise judgment concerning a recommended course of action. The budgeting process also provides for the allocation of funds to various promotions and for an orderly expenditure of these funds. In addition, it provides a means for measuring results.

Since few people view the budgeting of a promotion as a frivolous pastime, we must address ourselves to the preparation of a meaningful budget and to the question of what a promotion budget is and how it should be put together.

A major responsibility of business life is the process of planning, administering, and controlling corporate funds. The primary tool for meeting this responsibility is the budget. Promotion funds obviously are corporate funds and must be subject to the same disciplines that apply to all other corporate funds. As with any project, the setting of objectives is of primary importance; this is certainly the case when establishing a budget. These objectives should include:

1. Improving ways to determine the amount of funds needed for the promotion, the way in which these funds will be allocated to products, and the type of promotion that will be launched
2. Ascertaining that the greatest value is obtained from budgeted funds
3. Controlling budgeted funds
4. Keeping management advised at all times of the current status of the budget

Budgetary Control

Budgetary control can be defined as the tracking of expenditures against the plan and the measurement of actual performance against the plan. The promotion budget can be viewed as the plan, and the method of measuring actual performance against the plan can be thought of as budgetary control.

Good budgetary control provides a continuing awareness and understanding of the current status of the plan, and it also provides for accountability to management. The ability to switch plans if new conditions arise that require changes and the ability to note problems when they occur are also part of good budgetary control.

Assembling a Budget

I have some definite ideas as to how a promotion budget should be put together. Just as there is no one definition of *promotion*, there is no one answer to the question of how a promotion budget should be assembled. The following are some of my thoughts and observations concerning methods which have proved successful and which form a workable approach.

Budgeting can never be misdirected if marketing goals and objectives, including profits, are determined in advance. These goals and objectives need to be considered both in terms of the overall company and in terms of individual brands. Remember that your company is in business to sell products at a profit; all planning must be done with this goal in mind. The task of budgeting is to establish what the job of a promotion will be; from this will follow what kind of promotion is required and how much it will cost. First the objective of the promotion is delineated, and then the budget is assembled.

A first step toward more efficient planning and control is to identify those activities whose costs are to be classified as promotion expenses. The next step is to identify all expenses that are a part of these promotion activities. Once this has been accomplished, an effective budget planning process can be started.

Other steps which need to be taken in planning and controlling promotions include:

1. Establishing the company's promotional objectives: what the funds allocated can do for sales and profit
2. Defining objectives and strategies so that the solutions arrived at will meet the company's goals
3. Determining the amount to be spent
4. Having regular status reviews so as to be flexible in the face of changing conditions
5. Providing a disciplined, formal structure from which to operate

It is important to have certain data on hand as you approach the promotion budget. You should have available to you a review of past years' promotions and their effectiveness and of what these promotions accomplished in terms of product objectives and sales. You should also be knowledgeable concerning the current position of the product and the current corporate and marketing objectives, opportunities, and targets. Be sure that you are familiar with any recommendations concerning strategies for meeting these objectives through specific types of promotions, the way they are to be implemented, and the dollars needed to execute them.

It is also important to clearly define the responsibilities of the various parties involved in the promotion and, if possible, to prepare a multilevel budget for management review—one that provides for maintenance of the present position, moderate growth, and substantial growth.

PREPARING THE BUDGET

Because promotions and budgets are frequently misunderstood and do not get the attention they deserve, much of this chapter has been devoted to defining and classifying promotions, explaining the role of promotions, and outlining the purposes of, and the proper approach to, budgeting. Proper preparation and control of promotion budgeting depend on a complete understanding of these areas; if you cannot identify a subject, you cannot control it.

There are four steps in the budgeting process: (1) holding preliminary meetings, (2) assigning responsibilities, (3) preparing and administering the budget, and (4) establishing budgetary control.

Holding Preliminary Meetings. The budget process should start early in the year with preliminary meetings. These meetings should deal with the results of promotions launched during the present year and previous years, the outlook for the next year's promotions, sales objectives and how they relate to promotions, and precise problems to be solved and suggestions for solving them. With this background, marketing and sales promotion personnel prepare the promotion strategy and cost it out. These meetings should include, at one time or another, all the personnel who will be involved with the promotion.

One major factor that must be considered during the preliminary meetings is the budget time span. Usually, a budget is planned for each year; however, budgets should always be made in the light of future plans, extending out at least two years and up to five years.

The preliminary meetings should also include a review of the track performance of previous promotions in terms of company and marketing objectives. Such performance reviews of past promotions should enable you to make necessary adjustments to the current year's plans. Make sure that a promotion has been given sufficient time to perform before making an adjustment.

A quality assessment should be made of the promotions that are to be budgeted. Creativity in promotion plans must be encouraged, if the company is to stay ahead of the competition, and the budget must not stand in the way of such creativity.

Planning, if properly done, will require no contingency or reserve funds. Planning should provide for promotion activities and needed funds during all time periods in which promotions will be under way. Thus, if a new promotion activity is undertaken during the year, the funds can come from those allocated for a planned promotion, which will be replaced by the new one.

During the preliminary meetings, ascertain that all promotions are within the ability of company personnel to implement. A promotion that is implemented at a time when it is not needed is not a good promotion, nor is a good promotion idea of any value during a time period when the sales force does not have the time to put it into effect. The simple rule here is to take advantage of the company's human resources to implement a plan, to consider both the retailers' and the product's need for such a plan, and to present a promotion plan which offers outstanding value.

The preliminary meetings should address each product's profile in relation to the promotional vehicles which could be used. Products that are very similar to competitors' products need different promotions from those used for products that are distinctive. In the case of the former, using promotional tools to maintain and/or stimulate sales will be much more effective than using the established advertising media; premium offers, contests, and sweepstakes are some of the techniques that can be used to increase the sales of such products. In the case of products with distinctive profiles, effective use can be made of advertising media and/or promotional tools which encourage trial, such as coupons and sampling.

A particular promotion may not be suitable for all products. For example, a trade promotion "best-display" contest might do well for a dry grocery product but be inappropriate for a refrigerated product, since major displays of such a product would be impossible to put up inside a refrigerated case and would be a disaster outside the case. In such an instance, a contest or sweepstakes based on a random drawing would be more appropriate. The responsiveness of each product to a particular promotion is a key consideration during the preliminary meetings.

The timing of promotions is another vital consideration for discussion during these meetings: Should a promotion be conducted when the brand is enjoying good movement, in order to increase sales even more, or should a promotion take place when the brand is relatively inactive, in order to generate new usage?

Assigning Responsibilities. The responsibilities for the various stages of a promotion, from budgeting to implementation to control, should be clearly established. All parties involved should fully understand their areas of responsibility. The role of advertising and/or promotion agencies, marketing personnel, sales personnel, and financial personnel should be clearly defined.

Preparing and Administering the Budget. The preparation of the actual budget is the culmination of all the preliminary discussions as well as a reflection of company policy concerning the definition and classification of promotion expense. As mentioned before, the preparation of the promotion budget must start with definitions of the subject at hand, since promotions are a loosely defined part of the marketing arsenal. Promotion can be thought of as all sponsored communications which are not advertising; although this is an accurate description, it is too general to provide a meaningful base for budget preparation and control.

The delivery of a promotion to the three different target audiences (consumers, the trade, and the sales force) must be addressed, and the expenses that are chargeable to each type of promotion must be determined. Definitions, distinctions, and allocation of expenses will vary from company to company. The most important thing is that promotions be defined and classified by company policy in such a way that the budget preparation can proceed in an orderly, systematic, and consistent manner.

The final budget is simply the "fine tuning" of all the data discussed and decisions reached during the preliminary meetings; it is the commitment of these decisions to paper. The steps in preparing the final budget include:

1. Determining the overall company goals and the marketing and sales goals.
2. Setting out brand strategies and goals in terms of specific promotions and specific time periods. Any goal should be subject to measurement; if it cannot be measured, it is not specific enough.
3. Costing out the plan.
4. Preparing a formal budget in such a way that it will lend itself to periodic reviews against actual commitments. Measurement of results against goals should be conducted so that over a period of time, the effectiveness of various promotion techniques may be evaluated.

Establishing Budgetary Control. Budgetary control can be separated into (1) commitment control, (2) expenditure control, and (3) management control. Where approved budgets leave off, budget control takes over. The real control is established at the commitment stage, or purchasing stage (we shall discuss the area of purchasing in more detail later). Ultimate control over promotion expenditures occurs when the promotion plan is formulated and the promotion tools are selected. This is the real commitment stage.

Management control consists of the review and evaluation of the entire promotional effort as it relates to current marketing conditions and programs. To exercise such control, management must assemble complete cost information. Cost data are needed to determine the appropriateness of funds being committed, in view of market conditions and promotion results to date, and to determine whether any budget adjustments are necessary. Cost data also permit management to know, on a continuing basis, the extent of commitments and disbursements.

Expenditure control ensures that all valid charges have been submitted and accounted for before the end of the budget period. Expenditure control is not just a mechanical function; it requires a knowledge of the budget items, of the promotion plan, and of company purchasing and billing practices.

The details of an effective control system will vary from company to company, depending on the complexity of the promotion plan, the size and capabilities of the promotion group, and the company's internal accounting requirements. The basic elements of an effective control system include:

1. Establishing responsibility for proper authorization of all expenditures
2. Estimating costs for management approval prior to commitment
3. Holding periodic status reviews of expenditures while the promotion is in progress in order to keep abreast of any deviations from the budget

4. Establishing standard procedures for planning and commitments which cannot be varied without management approval

A good rule to remember is that the control over the total promotion budget can be no more effective than the control exercised over each part, no matter how small.

Kraft's Budgeting Program

The preceding has been an examination of budgets in general. Now let's take a look at the way Kraft handles the budgeting process.

Kraft has an annual advertising budget which is made up of the following elements: (1) media advertising, including production costs; (2) publicity; (3) point-of-purchase materials; (4) sales promotion materials; (5) premiums; (6) sweepstakes and contest prizes; and (7) coupon-carrier media. The costs of media advertising, publicity, and point-of-purchase materials are normally classified as a promotion expense. At Kraft, these include activities which entail communications to the consumer, to the trade (except premiums), and to the sales force.

Coupons, which are one of the company's primary promotional tools, are not included in the list above. The costs of media carriers of coupons (including direct mail) are considered an advertising expense; however, the redemption of coupons is considered an action of the consumer in response to the advertising and is handled as a trade-deal expense outside the advertising budget.

Kraft's promotion budget addresses not only the definition and classification of promotions but also the reporting of all related expenses on a consistent basis. The preparation of the company's budget and the reporting of expenses against the budget are consistent from one year to the next, and therefore the items reported are meaningful. Kraft's program captures all expenses against a promotion, and it plans and reports them in the budget year in which the promotion takes place—not in the year when the promotion elements are produced or when payment is made.

PROMOTION PURCHASING

The act of purchasing the promotion marks the end of the planning and preparation stage and the beginning of the execution of the promotion plan and the budget. Purchasing is the commitment of funds to the company's promotion plan. It is the responsibility of the purchasing function to ascertain that full value is received for each dollar spent. It is critical that sound purchasing policies and procedures be in place to ensure that the promotion's objectives are met.

The basic principles which are applied to the purchasing of promotion materials are no different from those which are applied to the purchasing of any other materials and/or services. The basic principles include:

1. Establishing detailed specifications of the item or service to be purchased in order to have a means of measuring receipt
2. Dealing only with vendors who are capable of providing materials and services of the quality desired and who can be trusted to perform within the time frame allowed
3. Making sure that fair value is received for the monetary investment
4. Measuring purchasing commitments against the achievement of marketing goals, not against the availability of funds in the budget
5. Ensuring that the item or service to be purchased is in the plan and has been approved by authorized management for purchase at the time the commitment is made

The next question is, Who is to do the actual purchasing? This will vary, depending on the company's organizational structure. The responsibility can rest with the company's corporate purchasing department, the promotion department, or a financial control group. A simple solution is to give this responsibility to the group most qualified to perform this function.

Purchasing is a specialized function, and buyers should be trained to assess not only price and quality but also the reliability of the vendors. Assigning a purchasing function to a buyer outside the promotion group will free up the members of this group to devote more time to the job for which they were hired—the creation of promotions. This can be done if clear lines of responsibility and approval are set up in advance and if the individual who does the purchasing fully understands the promotion's needs and objectives.

Unfortunately, the services of a trained corporate purchasing department are frequently bypassed when it comes to the purchasing of the various promotional items. This occurs because many of the items to be purchased are creative in nature and the members of the promotion group are reluctant to entrust such purchases to people whom they envision as experts in the purchase of nuts and bolts. It is true that some promotional items are unique and cannot be readily assessed using normal purchasing criteria; also, in some instances the purchasing department is not familiar enough with the needs and objectives of the promotion to do a proper purchasing job. In addition, many of the items are geared to a unique promotion and are not identical to those used in any previous promotions. However, even when a promotion is highly creative and involves one-time purchases, using sound purchasing techniques will help get full value for all dollars spent. Trained professional buyers who take the time to familiarize themselves with the promotion at hand can efficiently and effectively purchase any item, creative or not.

Many areas of a promotion program are clearly not of a creative nature, and there is no reason why such areas should not be turned over to the purchasing department, with little input from the promotion group. Printed point-of-purchase materials, premiums, contest and sweepstakes prizes, and refund fulfillment services are some examples. Many company purchasing departments have graphic arts buyers to handle these areas. In some instances a strong case can be made for placing such an individual in the promotion group and/or in the advertising department. If the purchasing department is properly staffed, it can be given the entire purchasing responsibility, subject to the approval of the promotion group.

The primary function of the members of the promotion group is to plan and create; whenever possible, they should leave the responsibility for buying to the purchasing department. However, selecting and buying creative work cannot take place without input from the promotion group. Even if the members of the promotion group are not responsible for the actual buying, they must have input into the selection of suppliers who can perform the necessary tasks, and they must be the final judge as to whether the vendor has delivered a satisfactory product. The purchasing department should also be asked to submit suggestions as to potential suppliers and/or promotion methods and to offer assistance in coordinating the solicitation and review of competitive quotations. In other words, it is important that the members of the promotion group have input into the selection of creative sources; however, it is not essential that they perform the work involved in soliciting bids or that they handle the actual details of the purchasing function, including issuing purchase orders and obtaining authorized approvals for purchases.

Cost Control

Control over the spending of promotion funds must be established at the time the purchase request is made. In order to ensure proper control, all purchases should be fully documented in writing via a purchase order or contract, and all purchases should be approved by properly authorized personnel before the commitment is made. All the necessary specifications, as to the work to be done, price, quality, quantity, delivery instructions, and other pertinent matters, should be contained in the written document.

Always visit major suppliers to view their facilities and evaluate their capabilities. Ascertain that suppliers are financially sound and are capable of producing according to your specifications and time schedules. Find out whether they will do the entire job or whether part of it will be subcontracted; major subcontractors should be reviewed in the same manner as the prime supplier.

A key to cost control is to ascertain that full value is received for every dollar spent. There may be inefficient spending in the case of rush jobs that result in premium payments, although proper planning should eliminate most such instances. Rush commitments do not allow for the application of proper purchasing techniques and may result in the selection of poor and/or expensive suppliers as well as overtime charges.

Inefficient spending can also result if price quotations are received before a job is awarded and if you repeat previous promotions, using the same suppliers, without exploring new techniques and promotion vehicles or new, more efficient suppliers. If you find it necessary to pay a premium for creative work, have some assurance that it will add value to the promotion.

In summary, be a planner, not an improviser. Avoid poor and hastily conceived work and missed due dates.

Purchasing Techniques

Use the most efficient and up-to-date purchasing techniques. Although many promotions are sold to the client as a "package," the concept of "component purchasing" lends itself very well to the promotion area. Most promotions include varied elements of work, such as creative development, creative implementation, printing, fulfillment services, distribution, storage, binding, and engraving. A sophisticated purchaser will avoid the package buy and switch to component purchasing; this approach should result in substantial cost savings and also give you greater control over your job and a better understanding of the makeup of promotion projects. Over the long run, component buyers should do a consistently more efficient job as they become more familiar with those techniques and with promotions in general. Component purchasing usually furnishes a cash-flow advantage as well, since payments are made only as each component of the promotion is completed; package buys usually require substantial up-front payments.

SUMMARY

Promotion budgets should be approached with the same attention and sophistication accorded to advertising budgets. It should be recognized that promotion is a major area of marketing, requiring vast financial resources and much strategic planning, and that promotion and advertising should interact with each other to produce higher sales than either one could achieve alone. This requires the establishment of clear, quantitative marketing objectives. It also requires an integration of promotion and advertising planning by the company and its advertising agency.

Budgeting a promotion should be carried out using the same strict cost-effectiveness criteria that are applied to advertising budgets. Each promotion should be examined to ascertain that it meets both short- and long-term marketing objectives. Information should be compiled as to planned expenditures, actual expenditures, and the effectiveness of the promotion; that is, not only should budgeting provide a system for planning and measuring promotion expenditures, but it should also provide a means of measuring the return on the company's investment in this area.

Remember that the promotion budget must be subdivided by product, by type of promotion, by period in which the promotion will take place, and by sales territories. In effect, a promotion budget must be a "project" budget.

Questions that need to be answered in budgeting promotions are:

1. How can promotion activities help achieve marketing objectives?
2. How much promotion is required?
3. Is the promotion selected right for the marketplace? Is it appropriate for giant retail organizations, as well as for those of moderate size? Does it lend itself to storewide application, as opposed to application in departments within a store?
4. Is the promotion designed to be fast-acting and to produce short-term results, or is it designed for long-lasting results which will build market share?
5. Is the promotion designed to convince consumers of the product's desirability and therefore move the product off the shelf, or is it meant to motivate the retailer to stock, feature, and display the product?

The fact that such questions were asked when the budget was assembled provides some assurance to management that the plan was put together using the proper amount of thought, analysis, and data.

The Big Event and the Sales Promotion Campaign

24

JOSEPH S. MAIER
President, Joseph S. Maier & Associates, Ltd.

Sales promotion has been around since ancient times. The streets of early Greece and Rome were filled with barkers, town criers, and sign carriers, all promoting their goods and services. But it wasn't until the nineteenth century, when the inimitable Phineas T. Barnum came upon the scene, that sales promotion acquired true excitement and flair (though, admittedly, sometimes with an element of deceit). Old Barnum humbugged and flimflammed his contemporaries with a promotional zest never equaled, before or since.

Many tried to imitate Barnum's style, but few could match it. Unfortunately, most of the sales promotion approaches in the early twentieth century consisted of a lot of fluff, but not much stuff—not much substance. However, as marketers gained more sophistication, they started to realize that sales promotion is more than just a bagful of tricks—that it is a viable marketing tool. Marketers knew that they *should* promote, but often they didn't know how to do it, or they thought of sales promotion as something they'd get around to "when they had the time."

It was only about ten years ago that marketers began to use sales promotion with any degree of real sophistication. So, while sales promotion has been around for centuries, we've only begun to scratch the surface in terms of sophisticated marketing and research. This chapter is intended to help you scratch that surface just a little bit deeper.

A Sales Promotion Philosophy. I have a sales promotion philosophy. It's not unique to me—a lot of sales promotion and marketing people are thinking this way today. I think that it really reflects how smart marketers view modern-day sales promotion.

429

- Sales promotion should be an *integral part* of each brand's marketing mix. You can't isolate it from all the other elements of the marketing mix: advertising, packaging, sales, pricing, etc. It's a key ingredient in the total marketing process.
- Sales promotion should be used as an *offensive weapon* in the brand's marketing arsenal, not merely as a defensive reaction when a problem arises.
- Sales promotion should *extend* and *reinforce* the brand's advertising and positioning, whenever possible. This synergy will help build the brand's franchise and will result in a more efficient and effective use of the available marketing dollars.
- Sales promotions should be developed as *campaigns*, not as single, unrelated events. We shouldn't use sales promotions merely to provide a short-term bump in sales. If we plan sales promotion campaigns that reinforce the brand's advertising and positioning, those short-term bumps will develop into a long-term strengthening of the brand's franchise.
- Good sales promotions are built upon *sound strategic planning*. You've got to know your market, identify your problems and opportunities, and develop some specific sales promotion objectives. Then build your strategy—a single-minded, focused one—to attain those objectives.

When it comes to execution, lots of sales promotion devices are available to us. I call them my "bag of bones." These bones represent all the sales promotion tools (coupons, refunds, premiums, trade allowances, sales incentives, sweepstakes, and so forth) that we can call upon to build a sales promotion plan.

With the proper strategy, we can put the right bones together to form a strong, solid sales promotion, one that is strategically sound. But we must not stop there. We must look for that extra creative spark, perhaps a clever overlay, that will reinforce our advertising positioning and make our sales promotion appealing to the consumer—and uniquely our own.

Macro Sales Promotions. One more thought. Just as economists deal in macroeconomics and microeconomics, I believe that you can approach sales promotion planning in terms of broad, long-range results (macro sales promotion) or in terms of a specific, single event (micro sales promotion). Until recently, most marketers limited themselves to micro sales promotion planning. They ran a series of isolated, unrelated sales promotion events, hoping for short-term sales increases. Often, their promotions were defensive in nature and did little or nothing to reinforce the brand's advertising and positioning.

Today, however, smart marketers are taking the macro sales promotion approach. They are developing sales promotion campaigns, taking an offensive promotion stance, seizing upon opportunities, and using sales promotion as an important and integral part of their marketing mix. That's how I hope you'll approach your sales promotion planning. Think of sales promotion in the macro sense. Plan sales promotion campaigns, not merely unrelated, individual sales promotion events.

The individual sales promotion is a *micro* event, but when it's integrated with other events into each brand's overall promotion and marketing mix, it becomes part of a broader, *macro* sales promotion plan. So remember that, regardless of the success of individual sales promotion events, the true success of any sales promotion is measured by the extent to which it strengthens the brand's franchise over the long term. And that is the result of strategically sound macro sales promotion planning.

THE BIG EVENT

My favorite subject is the *big event*, an exciting and impactful multibrand macro sales promotion that creates tremendous interest in, and volume for, the participating brands. What really constitutes a big event? Well, if you live in Chicago, it might be seeing the Cubs win a pennant, or even a ballgame, for that matter.

In the promotional sense, big events are the spectacular, usually multibrand, sales promotions that command consumer attention and stimulate strong trade support. They usually involve several brands, most often within the same company. Of course it is possible to develop a big event with compatible brands from different companies, but the sales promotion is logistically simpler, and usually more successful, when it involves the brands of a single company.

It's true that not every company has the brands and the resources to create a spectacular big event. But nearly every company should be able to put that extra magic and impact into a sales promotion that will make it special and successful. So if you're saying to yourself, "I don't have the volume or the resources to create a big-event sales promotion for my brand," think again. With creativity, a little innovation, and the right tie-in partners, you can turn an ordinary sales promotion into an extraordinary sales promotion. You can create your own big event for your brand. A little later, I'll describe how a small-budget company did that very thing.

A Case History

First, I want to share a successful case history with you. It involves Purina cat foods. Purina is the leading manufacturer of cat foods, with entries in three different segments of the market: dry, moist, and canned cat foods. There are many Purina brands in each segment. Cat owners are known to feed a variety of cat foods to their pets, across all three market segments. This presented Purina with a real opportunity. Since it was the market leader, with more brands in more market segments than any of its competitors, Purina realized that it could benefit by encouraging consumers to choose Purina cat-food brands to fulfill all the various feeding needs of their cats.

Traditionally, single-brand sales promotions of cat food have received little off-shelf trade support. But a major, multibrand effort with strong advertising support could provide that extra incentive for the trade to climb aboard. Purina wisely decided to cash in on the opportunity and to stage the largest, most spectacular sales promotion event in cat-food history.

The company set three objectives. First, it wanted to stimulate dramatic consumer purchasing and loading. Second, it wanted to generate combination purchase and usage of Purina cat-food brands. If consumers were going to feed their cats multiple brands, Purina wanted those brands to be its own. And, finally, Purina wanted the sales promotion to encourage strong trade support in the form of multibrand displays and features.

To accomplish these objectives, Purina created the "Circus of Savings" sales promotion, which was a high-powered, multibrand event that delivered a variety of coupons and rewards to consumers for purchasing Purina brands across all three market segments. This three-ring extravaganza included dynamic in-store support material, and it was backed by strong, concentrated advertising support. The "Circus of Savings" theme was selected over one that was more closely tied with cats in order to encourage broader retail support. It could easily be extended to a storewide promotion that the retailer could use to move items other than cat food.

The traditional three rings of a circus were quite appropriate for this sales promotion. There were three basic consumer offers, in the form of coupons, a sweepstakes, and a refund. The three rings also represented the three categories of Purina cat foods involved in the sales promotion: dry, moist, and canned. As a further tie-in with the theme, there were three targets of the promotion: the consumer, the trade, and the sales force.

The "Circus of Savings" was advertised in a six-page four-color free-standing insert (FSI) distributed to 42 million homes. It contained nine coupons worth $1.35 and announced a $100,000 sweepstakes and a refund offer.

The coupons were the core of the sales promotion. A total of 378 million coupons were distributed. These coupons were sequentially numbered and positioned in the insert to minimize misredemption and gang cutting. The refund offer could save consumers up to $2. A $0.50 refund was offered for a purchase in each of the categories, but consumers who purchased cat food in all three categories were entitled to a $0.50 bonus, for a total savings of $2. A $100,000 sweepstakes made up the third leg of the offer. All consumers who responded to the refund offer were automatically entered in the sweepstakes. The prizes were all circus- or cat-related; the top prize was a one-week trip for two to Circus Circus in Las Vegas and a brand-new Mercury Cougar automobile. In all, 1463 prizes were offered, and the insert looked as exciting as a poster announcing the arrival of a real circus in town.

The promotion was backed by seven concentrated days of network TV advertising leading up to the FSI drop. In-store collateral materials carried the FSI visuals over to the point of purchase. Some stores even dressed their employees up in "Circus of Savings" T-shirts in a storewide promotional effort. Over-the-aisle and end-of-aisle point-of-purchase display pieces brought the circus theme to every participating store.

Trade ads and selling brochures announced this three-ring spectacular to the trade. The final target of the sales promotion, the sales force, also received the circus treatment. A multimedia sales meeting, complete with a ringmaster, a juggler, a magician, and clowns, created real enthusiasm and excitement among members of the sales force.

The results were well worth the effort. This single big event moved some *35,000 tons* of cat food—over 6 million cases. More than 9 million coupons were redeemed, and the refund rate was over 1.0 percent. Two-thirds of the consumers who responded to the offer sent in proofs of purchase from two or more categories. And there were 1.2 million sweepstakes entries.

That was a big event.

BIG EVENTS AND WORTHY CAUSES

Procter & Gamble

Within the last few years, more and more large manufacturers of packaged goods have focused their big events on worthy causes. One such company is Procter & Gamble, which has run four sales promotions in connection with Special Olympics; the first was launched in January 1981, and the most recent in January 1984.

Special Olympics is a nonprofit organization dedicated to providing the mentally handicapped with a means for physical, social, and psychological development through sports. The organization conducts Olympic-style competitions on a continuing basis, and special summer and winter international sports events are held every four years. There are over 17,000 local Special Olympics chapters, with more than 325,000 dedicated volunteers, providing programs for over 1 million retarded athletes.

As a prelude to its involvement with Special Olympics, Procter & Gamble had been distributing coupons in the Publishers Clearing House mailing for several years. This is one of the largest single private mailings, reaching over 50 percent of U.S. households. Only Donnelley's Carol Wright and the Internal Revenue Service send out larger mailings each year.

While coupon redemptions through Publishers Clearing House had always been good, Procter & Gamble wanted to find ways to improve the overall results. The company felt that an overlay with strong consumer appeal would give the mailing greater impact and thus increase response and trade appeal. The basic objectives of the proposed overlay were to increase coupon redemptions and stimulate increased trade support. The strategy focused on providing the consumer and the trade with added incentives to respond by tying the promotion in with a worthy cause.

After much searching, Procter & Gamble selected what it felt was the ideal partner: Special Olympics. This organization has a positive, upbeat, hopeful, family image—the type of image that Procter & Gamble wants for its products. It just so happened that the 1981 International Winter Special Olympics Games were scheduled to be held in Smugglers Notch, Vermont, just two months after the Publishers Clearing House mailing. That provided a rallying point for the 1981 promotion.

All recipients of the mailing were told that Procter & Gamble would donate $0.05 to Special Olympics for every coupon redeemed within a three-week period. Details of the offer were included in the direct mailing. During 1981, local chapters of Special Olympics could earn additional money to help send their athletes to the games through a label-saving offer.

In 1982, this portion of the program was changed to a matching-donation offer; Procter & Gamble announced that it would match any personal donation to Special Olympics dollar for dollar up to a total of $250,000 nationally. Consumers could pick up matching-donation certificates at any participating store. To this end, the Procter & Gamble sales force and Special Olympics volunteers worked together to encourage retailers to build mass point-of-purchase displays on a large scale. The more displays that were built, the more matching-donation certificates would reach potential contributors, and the more donations would flow directly to local Special Olympics chapters.

The promotion was supported by twelve days of concentrated network TV advertising, which was kicked off by Procter & Gamble's complete sponsorship of a made-for-TV movie, *The Kid from Nowhere*. This heartwarming film about the growth and accomplishments of a Special Olympics athlete starred Beau Bridges, Susan Saint James, and Ricky Wittman, himself a mentally handicapped Special Olympian.

Procter & Gamble also used real Special Olympians in its commercials—first in 1981, along with Olympic speed-skating champions Eric and Beth Heiden, as well as in the commercials of subsequent years. Procter & Gamble's association with Special Olympics was an unqualified success. Virtually every participating Procter & Gamble brand registered shipment and share gains, and trade merchandising was at a high level. Each year the company reached its overall goal of creating an impactful big event.

These sales promotions had another very important result: the financial aid, support, and joy that Procter & Gamble's efforts brought to these very special athletes. There are no losers in Special Olympics events—only winners. All Special Olympics athletes are winners because their participation provides hope and personal development. These were big events for Procter & Gamble, and for Special Olympics, and were certainly deserving of a gold medal.

Bristol-Myers

Another major company that recently ran a sales promotion focused on a worthy cause was Bristol-Myers. This company chose United Cerebral Palsy as its partner. Like Procter & Gamble, Bristol-Myers saw such a sales promotion as an opportunity to stimulate consumer purchasing via increased coupon redemption and in-store merchandising. At the same time, it could help a wonderful organization.

This particular sales promotion had two key commercial objectives: to generate consumer purchase of a wide variety of Bristol-Myers products and to stimulate broad trade support. It was truly a big event for the participating Bristol-Myers brands, some of which would not have had the volume or resources to generate sufficient promotional impact on their own.

A two-page FSI carried coupons for eleven different Bristol-Myers brands, with values ranging from $0.15 to $0.20. In total, over half a billion coupons were distributed. That was equal to about 0.5 percent of *all* coupons that were distributed by *all* companies in 1981.

Bristol-Myers told consumers that it would donate $0.05 to United Cerebral Palsy for every coupon that was redeemed, up to a total of $100,000. The offer, which ran in the first quarter of 1982, also included a sweepstakes as well as an appeal to consumers to make further personal donations to United Cerebral Palsy. An interesting aspect was that all sweepstakes entries and donations were to be sent directly to United Cerebral Palsy. This apparently freed Bristol-Myers from the burden and cost of handling. In many cases, the organization chosen can provide volunteers and other support for the sales promotion tie-in. Be sure to take advantage of this possibility where it exists.

Other Companies

The Campbell Soup Company, with its ongoing label-saving campaigns on the behalf of schools, has been a leader in the growing use of sales promotions tied to a worthy cause. Other companies include General Foods, which has developed a strong affiliation with the Muscular Dystrophy Association; Kimberly-Clark, which recently ran a big-event sales promotion that benefited the American Heart Association; and Lever Brothers, which has come up with a sales promotion that will raise money for The March of Dimes, while generating volume for its ALL brand of detergent products.

All the big events discussed above were run by major, multibrand companies. However, in the spring of 1982 a sales promotion focusing on a worthy cause brought together products from several different companies for a major effort to benefit Easter Seals. This coincided with the national Easter Seals telethon, featuring entertainer Pat Boone. A Sunday "big Easter Seal event" featured several brands, including Morton doughnuts and honey buns, Yardley of London liquid soaps, No Nonsense panty hose, Swift Brown 'n Serve sausage and Sizzlean breakfast strips, and Chef Boy-Ar-Dee canned pastas.

This event, which was spearheaded by Sunday Comics Co-op Corporation, provided an excellent opportunity for smaller brands with limited budgets and for companies that did not have a broad-enough product line to conduct a big event on their own. If that sounds like your company, you might want to consider such an Easter Seal promotion for next year.

A WORLD SERIES BIG EVENT

When it comes to sports-related sales promotions, Gillette is the master of the big event. The company's sports tradition dates back to 1910, when Gillette first used the endorsement of baseball players. But it wasn't until 1939 that the company made its first major commitment to baseball by purchasing the broadcasting rights to the World Series. For a fee of approximately $100,000, Gillette got not only the sponsorship of the entire World Series on radio but also full promotion rights. Today, you couldn't even buy a thirty-second TV commercial during the World Series for $100,000.

As the costs of network advertising and sponsorship have increased, the role of consumer sales promotions has become more significant for Gillette. The company seeks to transfer fan interest and loyalty to the retail level with two major annual sports-related consumer sales promotions. One is the "All-Star Election," and the other is a World Series sales promotion.

Beginning in 1977, Gillette joined the forces of two of its divisions, the Safety Razor Division and the Personal Care Division, in a big-event World Series sales promotion. The company has four key objectives in mind for its major sports-related sales promotions. First, it wants to capitalize on, and enhance, the tremendous sports image that it has developed among consumers and the trade. Second, it hopes to generate high levels of consumer awareness, interest, and involvement, as well as increase store traffic. Third, it wants to encourage trade support over a longer period than normal. And finally, Gillette wants to maximize in-store display and feature price support.

The basic strategies that Gillette uses to accomplish these objectives include providing strong incentives for the trade to display and feature Gillette products and providing meaningful incentives for consumers to come to the point of purchase, the retail outlet.

Gillette's 1981 big event was its "Everybody Wins in the Gillette World Series" sales promotion, which included coupons good toward the purchase of several Gillette products, as well as an instant-winner sweepstakes. A full-page FSI and a two-page spread in *Reader's Digest* distributed the coupons and announced the sweepstakes. Each coupon included an instant-winner baseball-related symbol, such as a baseball cap, a bat, or a catcher's mask. Consumers were asked to take their coupons to the Gillette display at their favorite store. If the symbols on their coupons matched the symbols on the display, they were instant winners. The top prize was a Ford Escort and $25,000 in cash. There were five second prizes of $1000 and an RCA TV and videocassette recorder, and there were 50 million guaranteed winners of at least a PaperMate Eraser Mate 2 pen plus $2 in Gillette coupons, which was a nice sampling technique for some other Gillette products.

Of one thing you can be certain: Gillette never forgets the trade. It ran a Gillette World Series batter-up display contest for retailers. All retailers who entered the contest by submitting photos of their displays were guaranteed to win at least a Braun travel clock, and they were eligible to win one of forty-one other prizes, including a 1982 Ford Escort.

As most companies do when launching big events, Gillette backed this sales promotion with strong advertising support, both in print and on TV. Gillette's effort paid off. Over $90 million worth of Gillette products were moved during this promotional period, and trade support was excellent. Each year, Gillette expects its major brands to do 25 to 33 percent of their annual volume during this one concentrated period, lasting from forty-five to sixty days. Gillette's World Series sales promotions look sharp, and they do their very best!

A SINGLE-BRAND BIG EVENT

Now I'd like to discuss a sales promotion that was a big event for a single brand, in combination with compatible brands. My hope is that some of you who work for smaller companies or on smaller-budget brands will be inspired to stretch your imaginations and develop some high-impact big-event promotions for your brands.

The sales promotion was launched by Welch Foods, which produces juices, drinks, jellies, and jams. The brand involved in the sales promotion was

Welch's jams and jellies. And what are more natural companions for jams and jellies than bread and milk? The target users are similar, and the products are compatible—ideal sales promotion partners.

This is the story of the "Free Milk from Welch's" sales promotion, in which a relatively low-budget single brand seized upon a compatible tie-in opportunity to fashion its own big event. The company had two main objectives: to load its existing customers and to stimulate new trial among users of competitive brands. The strategy that it employed to achieve these objectives was to offer consumers a higher-than-normal coupon value and to give them some multiple proof-of-purchase incentives.

Here's what the Welch company did. It lined up a bread company (Quality Bakers of America, which markets several different brands in various markets) and the American Dairy Association as tie-in partners. Then it put together a multifaceted sales promotion, consisting of a coupon good for a free half gallon of milk, a $0.20 coupon in a Sunday comic-strip section with a circulation of 30 million, a soccer-ball offer at the point of purchase, and a competitive trade allowance.

The Sunday coupon ad highlighted the free milk offer; the illustration and the name of the bread were changed according to which market the ad appeared in. In those markets where Quality Bakers of America did not have distribution, the offer was made for any brand of bread. The ad also allowed space for dealer listings. The coupon offered $0.20 off on Welch's grape jelly, grape jam, or strawberry jam. Consumers were required to submit three proofs of purchase from the Welch's products and one proof of purchase from a loaf of bread in order to receive a coupon good for a free half gallon of milk.

Tear-off or "take-one" pads at the point of purchase also featured the milk offer, plus a premium offer of a Pelé soccer ball, worth $27, for only $11.95 and two Universal Product Codes from Welch's jams or jellies. To help stimulate retail support, a trade display contest offered a Nassau vacation for two, in addition to 500 Pelé soccer balls.

This was a very successful single-brand effort. That's why I've classified it as a big event. It achieved big results for the Welch company. The sell-in to the trade exceeded the forecast by 30 percent, and the brand experienced an increase of 3.9 share points. This increase was maintained for two 4-week reporting periods. There were twice as many in-store displays as had been originally estimated, and the promotion received heavy display treatment at the dairy case. The featured price displays with bread and milk were considered to be very instrumental in boosting sales.

So, as you can see, you *can* make a big impact and achieve significant sales results even if you are working with a smaller brand and have a limited budget. The answer might be to find some compatible sales promotion partners for your brand. This was a big event for a brand of modest size.

A NONCONSUMER BIG EVENT

A final big event that I'd like to share with you was different from those discussed above in that it didn't involve a packaged goods product. Rather, it was a big-event sales promotion involving a line of International Harvester eighteen-wheel trucks. This was the "IH–NFL All Pro-motion," a sales promotion that captured the excitement of the National Football League and tied in with the image of the rugged, dependable linemen who do the job but get little of the glory. In a way, the big, burly linemen of the NFL might be likened to the rugged and dependable International Harvester trucks.

The sales promotion evolved from International Harvester's desire to expand its media coverage beyond truck publications, truck-stop posters, and all-night truckers' radio stations. The company and its advertising agency felt that it could reach target truckers and truck-fleet buyers through CBS radio coverage of NFL football on Monday nights. International Harvester purchased one-quarter sponsorship of these CBS broadcasts and looked for ways to extend this sponsorship via a big-event sales promotion that would generate showroom traffic and dealer enthusiasm.

The sales promotion's objectives were to generate traffic for dealers in trucks and truck parts, to reinforce International Harvester's number one position in the truck industry, and to provide a comprehensive merchandising program for dealers.

The strategy was a very thorough, yet simple, game plan that would tie in with the NFL, with particular focus on the rugged and dependable offensive and defensive linemen, and maintain continuous excitement about, and enthusiasm for, the program among truckers, dealers, and company sales personnel. A secret "playbook" took this game plan and turned it into a victorious promotion for International Harvester.

Sponsorship of Radio Coverage. The first play consisted of International Harvester's sponsorship of NFL football on the CBS radio network. A total of thirty-six games were involved, including the Super Bowl and the NFL Pro Bowl. As part of this effort, CBS broadcasters Hank Stram and Jack Buck selected the International Harvester lineman of the game for each Monday-night contest. The number one lineman was presented with a plaque and a $1000 check to be donated to his favorite charity.

Purchase of Promotion Rights. The second play consisted of the purchase of the exclusive promotion rights from NFL Properties. This tie-in arrangement allowed International Harvester to inaugurate two new awards to be presented to the NFL's number one offensive lineman and number one defensive lineman of the year. The winning linemen were selected by votes from football fans and truckers across the nation. The winning linemen of 1982—offensive tackle Anthony Munoz, of the Cincinnati Bengals, and defensive tackle Randy White, of the Dallas Cowboys—were presented with trophies and with checks for $5000 to be donated to their favorite charities at the NFL Pro Bowl in Honolulu. A replica of the trophy, with the winners' names inscribed, was placed in the NFL Hall of Fame in Canton, Ohio.

As an adjunct to the voting, International Harvester ran a $60,000 "NFL Linemen of the Year" sweepstakes; the top prize was a trip for two to the 1982 NFL Pro Bowl in Hawaii. All sweepstakes entries had to be deposited at International Harvester dealerships, a requirement designed to stimulate showroom traffic.

Advertising Support. The third play consisted of gaining advertising support. *PRO*, the magazine of the NFL, carried ads for the balloting but did not mention the sweepstakes. The NFL wanted a lot of fan participation, but International Harvester did not seek traffic from nontruckers. Ads in truckers' magazines and truck-stop posters mentioned both the balloting and the sweepstakes and encouraged truckers to bring their entries into an International Harvester dealer.

Dealer Support. The fourth play was a critical one: getting strong dealer support. First, the company ran a weekly "guess-the-winner" contest for dealers' salespeople. This kept them involved and interested in the program throughout the season, while providing some fun and prizes along the way. A selling brochure provided dealers with complete details of the sales promotion, and showroom collateral pieces, such as a dangler, carried the theme and excitement right into the dealerships. Window posters, counter cards, a dynamic four-sided display piece, and entry forms were made available to every International Harvester dealer. Outdoor posters proclaimed that each dealer's showroom was a balloting headquarters.

A co-op advertising program was offered to dealers, and copies of the NFL publication *Monday Night Preview* were provided to dealers to give away to their customers. A sales motivation program, the "IH/NFL '81/'82 Touchdown Club," provided incentives for dealers' salespeople to increase their sales of trucks and truck parts. Dealers and important buyers were invited to NFL games and to pregame cocktail parties and buffet suppers, where they could meet CBS broadcasters Hank Stram and Jack Buck. The entire details of the sales promotion were described in the official playbook. This was used by International Harvester's sales personnel in presenting the program to dealers and their salespeople.

The whole program succeeded in helping International Harvester maintain its number one position in the market in the face of recessionary and financial problems the company was facing. Truck sales increased over the same period a year earlier, dealer enthusiasm for the program was strong, and company sales personnel considered that the sales promotion was the most comprehensive and exciting program that International Harvester had ever run.

CONCLUSION

I hope that I've whetted your appetite for big events. They require a lot of planning and hard work, but if they are properly developed and executed, they can produce some very dramatic increases in sales volume.

If you think that your brand or company could execute a big event, be sure to consider these three points:

- Develop a *focus* for your event, a theme or cause that is compatible with the positioning of the participating brands.
- Be certain that the focus or theme will create a positive impression on your target consumers and the trade.
- Look for a cause or a theme that you can make uniquely your own.

Do all these things, pay attention to details, and then sit back and enjoy watching the sales roll in. You've just succeeded with a big event!

25 Advertising the Sales Promotion

EDWARD D. MEYER
Senior Vice President and Director of Promotion Services, Dancer Fitzgerald Sample, Inc.

The main difference between an advertisement that sells a product only and a sales promotion advertisement is timing. The straight product-selling advertisement is usually part of an overall campaign that can take several months or more to create impact with consumers. The sales promotion ad must achieve results quickly. Within days or weeks after the sales promotion is launched, consumers must react by purchasing the product or products in order to receive what is being offered, whether it is a coupon, a refund, or a premium.

The one point to remember when communicating a sales promotion idea is that the actual sales promotion is a creative effort. The coupon, the refund, the sweepstakes, and the premium are all departures from the normal advertising of a product. Each is a unique offer not found in a straight product-selling advertisement, so each should be designed in a special way when being communicated to consumers.

Not every sales promotion should receive advertising support. Advertising is expensive, and therefore it should not be utilized unless it will create additional sales or increase store traffic immediately. Advertising support for a sales promotion is most appropriate when the objective is to move heavy volume quickly, as in a coupon drop; to create increased store traffic for special retail outlets, such as fast-food restaurants; or to hold consumers in a franchise, as in the case of refunds and free premiums. Another, less important reason to use advertising support is to reinforce a product's image through the premium or sweepstakes offer.

The "Call to Action." Thus the primary objective of the sales promotion advertisement is to spur consumers to action—to motivate or induce as

443

many readers of the advertisement as possible to respond quickly and positively to the offer being made. This action might consist of purchasing a product with a coupon, sending in for a premium with multiple proofs of purchase, or even reading a sweepstakes ad and immediately entering that sweepstakes in the hope of winning a prize.

How to Motivate Consumers. The first thing to remember when designing a sales promotion advertisement is that if it does not explain the sales promotion to consumers in a simple, straightforward way, they will miss it. They will turn the page quickly, whether it is in a magazine, a Sunday supplement, a daily newspaper, or even a cluttered free-standing insert. You don't want this to happen; the moment you have failed to sell a sales promotion, you have lost a potential customer.

Now, assuming that you have a well-thought-out sales promotion, the key to its success is communicating it to the consumer, from headline to body copy to layout to graphics. Each element of the ad must be part of an overall design that results in a sale. The headline should immediately make the consumer interested in the offer. It can be provocative, but should not be abstractly creative, or readers will surely lose interest. It must lead the reader directly into the body copy, which should explain the details of the offer so clearly and easily that within seconds the consumer can understand the offer and be ready to make a decision as to whether to participate in it. The layout and graphics must be uncluttered and easy to follow. The layout should clearly lead the reader from headline to body copy to entry device. Ease of consumer involvement is the key.

Following are several examples of print-media advertisements for sales promotions and one example of television advertising support for a sales promotion. In each case, the techniques are explained, and specific examples and guidelines are presented that you can follow in creating your own advertisement for a sales promotion.

ADVERTISING A COUPON

A coupon is designed to induce consumers to purchase a product immediately. Except for the actual delivery of a product sample to the home, couponing can create trial more rapidly than any other sales promotion technique.

Example

The Sales Promotion. Consumers are offered a coupon worth $0.50 toward the purchase of a new household pack of Bounty paper towels.

Headline. "Save Big." This directly announces the savings on the new, larger package size. The copy has two meanings: "Big" relates to both the savings and the new jumbo-size package.

Visual. A large photograph of the product tells what the new package size is all about.

Subheading. "Save $0.50 on Bounty's New Household Pack." This immediately tells consumers how much they can save and the specific product involved in the offer.

Body copy (lower left). This reinforces the headline, the product, the photograph, and the subheading with specific reasons for buying the product.

Coupon with spokesperson. The spokesperson, television personality Nancy Walker, directs the consumer to the well-designed, easy-to-understand product coupon in the lower left corner of the ad.

Guidelines for Advertising a Coupon

• Use an attention-getting headline.

FIGURE 25-1. An advertisement for a coupon good toward the purchase of a new jumbo pack of Bounty paper towels. (*Courtesy of The Procter & Gamble Company.*)

- Make the savings offer as quickly as possible.
- Show a large photograph of the product being couponed.
- Use short body copy that quickly highlights the attributes of the product.
- Design the coupon in either dollar-bill or half dollar-bill size. Utilize bold type that clearly emphasizes the savings and the product and package size for which the coupon is redeemable.
- Show the product package on the coupon.
- Place the coupon in the upper or lower outside corner of the ad so that it is easy to remove.

ADVERTISING A REFUND

A refund is designed to hold consumers in a product franchise over a short period of time. Consumers are offered cash, coupons, or both in the mail in return for proofs of purchase from a specific product.

Example

The Sales Promotion. Consumers are offered a total savings of $2.75 on Solo—$0.50 immediately with a coupon and $2.25 in coupons or cash when they send in proofs of purchase from a 1-gallon container of Solo.

Headline. "Buy Big, Save Big . . . Up to $2.75. Go Solo!" This gets directly to the point. It tells consumers that they can save and save big when they buy Solo.

Visual. A picture of a 1-gallon container of Solo strongly reinforces product identity and shows the consumer which size to purchase.

Subheading 1. "Here's How to Save on Solo." A simple, step-by-step explanation of the offer follows, with special emphasis on the expiration date.

Subheading 2. "Save Up to $2.75 on a Deep-Down Clean and Fluffed-Up Soft." This induces the consumer to action—to use the refund and the coupon.

Mail-in certificate and coupon. These should be positioned together at the bottom of the ad, making it easy for the consumer to remember both.

Guidelines for Advertising a Refund

- Announce a combined refund and coupon savings in the headline.
- Follow up the headline with a clear explanation of what the consumer must do to get the savings.
- Identify the product with a good, clear photograph.
- Place the mail-in certificate for the refund and the store coupon together at the bottom of the ad.

• Use any of the print media to advertise the offer.

ADVERTISING A SWEEPSTAKES

A basic sweepstakes should focus on a product's selling points, such as an improvement in the product or a new package design, or on an advertising theme.

Example

The Sales Promotion. Consumers are offered the chance to enter a sweepstakes and win cash prizes to use for grocery purchases. The sweepstakes is sponsored by the Florida Citrus Orange Growers.

FIGURE 25-2. An advertisement for a refund on Solo detergent and fabric softener. (*Courtesy of The Procter & Gamble Company.*)

Headline. "Orange You Smart to Try to Win $10,400 to Buy Groceries." This strongly reinforces the advertising theme, "Orange You Smart to Drink Orange Juice from Florida," and it offers a very practical, "smart" grand prize of $10,400 in cash.

Visual. A picture of a woman surrounded by groceries and pointing to her head carries out the "Orange You Smart" theme. This is an excellent tie-in reinforcing the ad campaign and the "smart" prize structure.

Subheading. This lists all the prizes—cash or shopping certificates. They are all "very smart" prizes, relating to the theme and to the grand prize.

Sweepstakes rules and entry form and coupon. These are a must. The entry form is easy to read, and the coupon is appropriate, since this sweepstakes is designed to reinforce the image and move the product.

FIGURE 25-3. An advertisement for the "Orange You Smart" sweepstakes. (*Courtesy of the Florida Department of Citrus.*)

Guidelines for Advertising a Sweepstakes

- Create a theme that accomplishes a specific objective, such as the "Orange You Smart" theme, which relates to the product and to the prizes offered in the sweepstakes.
- Offer an exciting grand prize (and show a picture of it, if possible) and quality secondary prizes.
- Advertise the sweepstakes in a color medium (magazine, free-standing insert, or Sunday supplement).
- List all the rules.
- Include an easy-to-fill-out entry form and a product coupon together at the bottom of the advertisement.
- Mention or show the product as often and as tastefully as possible.
- It is not necessary to use the word *sweepstakes* in the headline.

ADVERTISING A MATCH-AND-WIN GAME

A match-and-win game builds traffic by encouraging consumers to take a media-delivered card with a symbol on it to the stores and try to match it to a symbol shown either in a special display or on the product package to see whether they have won a prize.

Example

The Sales Promotion. A match-and-win game run by Old Spice directs consumers to take a card showing the Old Spice sailing-ship logo from a free-standing insert and try to match it with an in-store display card to see whether they've won a prize.

Headline. "Sail an Old Spice Tall-Ship Match-and-Win Game. Every Card a Winner." This boldly identifies the product and the theme, gives directions for playing the game, and tells the reader that every card is a winner.

Body copy. All prizes relate to the sailing theme. Since all players will win at least a set of posters, consumer involvement in the game is increased.

Entry form and coupons. The entry form directs consumers to in-store displays, and the coupons offer them an inducement to save on the Old Spice line.

Guidelines for Advertising a Match-and-Win Game

- The headline should announce that it's a match-and-win game.
- The grand prize should be pictured, and secondary prizes should be strongly emphasized.

- Consumers should be shown how to use the match-and-win cards by means of pictures and/or words.
- Coupons should always be included and placed next to the match-and-win symbol.
- The game should be advertised in magazines with a pop-up card or a free-standing insert to allow for seeding of different logos.

ADVERTISING A FREE PREMIUM

A free premium is another excellent way to keep consumers in a franchise and to move heavy volume quickly. Consumers are sent a free premium in the mail in exchange for proofs of purchase.

FIGURE 25-4. An advertisement for an Old Spice match-and-win game. (*Courtesy of Shulton Incorporated, U.S.A. Division.*)

Example

The Sales Promotion. Consumers are offered a free video game in return for proofs of purchase from Kool-Aid.

Headline. "Free Kool-Aid Man Video Game with 125 Proof-of-Purchase Points and Mail-in Certificate Below." This clearly announces the premium, states the requirements for obtaining it, and tells the consumer how to send in for it.

Visual. A picture shows someone actually using the premium. Also included are a picture of the premium package and a picture of the product, Kool-Aid. Showing a premium being used is an excellent way of selling it to consumers, and including a picture of the product creates strong product awareness.

FIGURE 25-5. An advertisement for a free premium, offered in return for proofs of purchase from Kool-Aid. (*Courtesy of General Foods Corporation.*)

Secondary copy. "Made by Mattel Electronics." This strongly reaffirms the quality of the premium.

Mail-in certificate and coupon. These should be clear, easy to read, well identified, and simple to remove from the page.

Guidelines for Advertising a Free Premium

- Announce the premium and the fact that it's free in the headline.
- Immediately state how many proofs of purchase are required to get the premium.
- Picture the premium being used, list its best qualities, and show the product package and name several times.
- Place the mail-in certificate next to the coupon at the bottom of the advertisement.

ADVERTISING A SELF-LIQUIDATING PREMIUM

The self-liquidating premium (so called because it pays for itself) is used primarily to reinforce a product image or advertising message and is usually accompanied by a purchase incentive such as a coupon.

Example

The Sales Promotion. Instant Nestea offers consumers a self-liquidating premium consisting of a set of four glasses.

Headline. "Enjoy the Clear, Clean Taste of Nestea Glass after Glass after Glass." This direct statement sells the product along with the premium.

Visual. A picture shows iced tea being poured into a glass with the Nestea identification on it, as well as a jar of the product. This illustrates the premium and its end use perfectly.

Mail-in certificate and coupon. Both are clear, easy to read, well identified, and simple to remove from the page. The mail-in certificate has a photograph of the glasses printed on it. Dotted lines connect the coupon and the mail-in certificate, tying the two together.

Guidelines for Advertising a Self-Liquidating Premium

- Utilize a headline that creates enough excitement to get consumers to read the ad.
- If possible, select a premium that relates to the product (in the case of Nestea, the glasses are perfect).
- Show a picture of the premium in use and make this an integral part of the ad.

- List the characteristics of the premium.
- State the retail price of the premium so that consumers will know how much they are saving.
- Advertise the offer in a color medium, such as women's magazines or Sunday supplements.
- Insert a mail-in certificate that gives all ordering details, and always include a store coupon.

ADVERTISING A SALES PROMOTION ON TELEVISION

Television advertising is used primarily to support advertisements of a sales promotion run in the print media or shown on a product package. Since a television commercial does not directly offer a specific incentive to purchase a

FIGURE 25-6. An advertisement for a self-liquidating premium offered by Instant Nestea. (*Courtesy of The Nestle Company Inc.*)

product, manufacturers were skeptical at first concerning its effectiveness in enhancing a sales promotion in another medium. Since television commercials can create strong product awareness by repeatedly showing the product, manufacturers have begun to use TV to announce a sales promotion aimed at creating large-volume movement of a product.

Example

The Sales Promotion. Procter & Gamble offers consumers $2.25 in coupons and a Little Red School House premium. The free-standing insert advertising the sales promotion, placed in newspapers on heavy shopping days, is supported by a TV commercial announcing the insert.

TV commercial copy. The commercial effectively sells the sales promotion by repeating the offer three different ways, each time announcing the coupon savings and the premium offer. The primary job of this commercial is

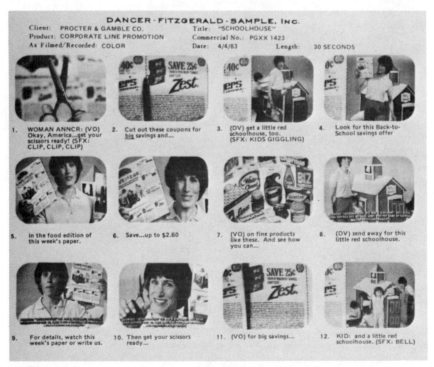

FIGURE 25-7. A coupon and premium offer, which was supported by television advertising. (*Courtesy of The Procter & Gamble Company.*)

to announce the offer clearly and simply, to tell consumers how they can take advantage of it, to create a call to action by telling consumers to look for the sales promotion in the food edition of their newspapers, and to repeat the message enough times to create strong product awareness.

Guideline for Advertising a Sales Promotion on Television

- Get viewers' attention with an impactful visual, like the scissors in this commercial.
- Announce the offer clearly by talking directly to the audience.
- Create a call to action by telling consumers how they can participate in the offer.
- Repeat the offer at least twice during the commercial.
- Repeat the commercial often before advertising the sales promotion in the print media.

OVERCOMING CLUTTER

Every point made thus far relates to the most effective means of advertising sales promotions so that consumers will immediately act on an offer. However, in recent years, even sales promotions that have been effectively advertised have been jeopardized by the multitude of offers that are made each week by manufacturers. This clutter of coupons, refunds, sweepstakes, etc., in weekly newspapers, free-standing inserts, Sunday supplements, and monthly magazines has created confusion among loyal consumers, to the point where they respond to sales promotions more because of the savings than because of their loyalty to a specific product.

To solve this problem, we're going to have to design advertisements for sales promotions that will stand out from the clutter, whether these are placed in free-standing inserts, in newspapers on best food days, or in quality magazines.

Following are some suggestions for making your sales promotion advertisement stand out from competitors' advertisements and for overcoming the problem of clutter.

Create big, bold headlines that grab the reader. Sales promotion advertising must sell the product strongly and quickly. Be direct and get the consumer's attention; most important, make sure that what you say is going to be of interest to the consumer.

Be provocative if necessary. How can you be provocative in a coupon advertisement, besides shouting "Save $0.50"? Well, you can sell a meaningful attribute of the product, such as the fact that it will give the consumer "fantastic whites." Then tell consumers that they can save $0.50 if they buy your detergent.

Whet the consumer's appetite right away. In the case of a sweepstakes, immediately announce the most exciting thing involved, whether it's the grand prize, the fact that everyone wins, or a million-dollar prize list.

Use visuals with lots of impact. Illustrate the grand prize in a sweepstakes boldly and clearly. Show a free premium being used in a setting that's as realistic as possible. And, in the case of a coupon, show a photograph of the product package so that consumers won't forget it.

Make the layout clear. Make the bold headline, the simple directions, the impactful visuals, and the easy-to-follow instructions flow together naturally.

Don't use too many typefaces. You want to induce consumers to action; therefore, the easier it is for them to read the offer, the better the chance that they will buy your product. Too many typefaces are confusing.

Consider the media attributes and restrictions and use them well. When using a black-and-white newspaper ad on a best food day, use lots of white space. When using a free-standing insert, make the most effective use of color.

A Final Thought

Always design your sales promotion advertisements so that they are easy to understand and so that they make the offer easy to participate in. Good luck!

How to Use Research to Make Better Sales Promotion Marketing Decisions

26

ROBERT L. KLEIN
Senior Vice President, Management Decision Systems, Inc.

The use of coupons is continuing to grow at a rapid rate. The A. C. Nielsen Co. reported that over 103 billion coupons were distributed by manufacturers to American households in 1981. That works out to over 100 per month per household! Nielsen also reported that between 1975 and 1980 the number of coupons distributed increased by 65 percent, that the average coupon's face value increased by one-third during this period, and that in 1980 the handling charge paid to retailers increased 40 percent. The cost of couponing for manufacturers increased by over 120 percent in the five years between 1977 and 1982. And this has led a number of marketing managers to ask with increasing frequency, Do coupons really work?

WHY MANUFACTURERS USE COUPONS

There are many reasons for using coupons: to create awareness of a new product, flavor, etc.; to communicate product benefits; to motivate trial of a new product; to get trade support for a product or for a promotion; to increase the probability that consumers will switch to a manufacturer's product or brand; to lessen the incidence of switching away from a manufacturer's brand; to speed up consumer purchasing of a brand; and even to mess up a competitor's new-product introduction. Sampling, refunds, contests, etc., are used for the same reasons.

The real objective behind all these sales promotion vehicles is to increase sales, and yet when people evaluate a sales promotion, they look only at the costs of the promotion, the redemption rate, or the number of responses to the offer or contest. They do not look at the effect on sales. Why is that?

One reason given is that costs and redemption rates are easy to measure. We can thank the accountants and the coupon clearinghouses for that. Another is that costs and redemption rates are easy to communicate to marketing management and easy to use in budgets and forecasts. But this focus on redemption rates reminds me of the old joke about the drunk who lost a quarter on a dark street, but went looking for it under a lamppost because the light was better there!

EVALUATING A SALES PROMOTION

To evaluate the effectiveness of a sales promotion, we have to measure what that promotion was designed to do. If we are really trying to increase sales (and who isn't?), we should measure incremental sales. A quick definition: The incremental sales due to a coupon drop, a refund offer, etc., are the sales which would not have occurred otherwise.

SOME MYTHS

Many sales promotion people have some deeply held beliefs about coupons: how they work, what's good to do, and what's bad to do. When you look at what these people are actually doing, you get an idea of what their beliefs really are. First, they apparently believe that all coupon redemptions are incremental sales. That certainly can explain the preoccupation with redemption rates. But if all redemptions are by consumers who would have bought the product anyway, the result is zero incremental sales. Redemption rates really do not have anything to do with incremental sales. For example, think about distributing a coupon worth $0.50 toward the purchase of any drink at a local bar after work today. A lawyer would probably advise against offering coupons for alcoholic beverages, but pretend you gave one to everyone in the place. You know that the redemption rate will be very high, but you don't expect any incremental sales because people can drink only so much. No incremental sales are expected, no matter how high the redemption rate, because the customers would have bought anyway.

Second, sales promotion people apparently believe that coupon users become loyal users. This may be true if the coupon motivates trial of a product that is significantly different from competitors' products. But what about the Folger's coffee user who gets a $0.50 coupon for Maxwell House and redeems it at the store? Is this person going to become a loyal user of Maxwell House? Think about it. We have taught consumers to use coupons and to switch brands. And just when they prove that they have learned the lesson, we expect them to forget it!

Sales promotion people also seem to believe that incremental consumer purchases due to a coupon drop cannot be measured. Well, this used to be true, but it isn't any longer, because of a revolution that is under way in supermarkets.

MEASURING INCREMENTAL SALES

The Universal Product Code (UPC) symbol is the key to measuring incremental sales. Almost every item sold in a supermarket is marked by the manufacturer with a unique UPC symbol. The clerk takes an item out of the shopper's basket and passes it across a glass-faced slot in the counter. A low-powered laser under the glass recognizes the UPC symbol, decodes it, looks up that eleven-digit number in its memory, retrieves the price and product information, prints the register tape, and updates its own internal record of how many units of that item has been sold. Scanners count everything the supermarket sells. There are more than 12,000 items in an average supermarket, and these sales data have never been available on such a wide scale before. Today over 5000 supermarkets are equipped with scanners, and the current rate of installation is over 1500 per year.

Scanner panels are a more recent development for measuring consumer response. Families residing near scanner-equipped stores are offered a discount on all their purchases in those stores. All family members are given ID cards, which they show at the checkout counter. The checker keys in the card number, the scanner rings up the sale, and the computer keeps track of everything that family buys in every category on every shopping trip.

Instrumented Markets. In seven different cities across the United States, several different research companies had established instrumented markets by the end of 1981. In these markets all stores are scanner-equipped. In each market, 2500 families are members of scanner panels. Split-cable TV to the member households permits control of the actual advertisements delivered, and split-run newspapers can target individual neighborhoods. In-store monitoring of displays, as well as actual in-store collection of the coupons redeemed, provides complete measurement of all marketing activities and of consumer response.

And now, incremental consumer purchases can be measured. Two identical groups of people who are scanner-panel members are chosen. They have the same demographics, they shop at the same stores, and they see the same advertising, the same sale promotions, the same prices, and the same shelves. But one group gets coupons and the other group doesn't, and the scanners in the stores measure the effect.

THE METRIC COUPON LABORATORY

This idea was used to develop the Metric Coupon Laboratory. At the laboratory, we split an instrumented market into three groups, balanced in terms of demographic characteristics and shopping behavior. Each group is mailed a packet of "valuable coupons." Group A gets $0.10 coupons, for example; group B receives $0.20 coupons; and group C is the control group. As many as a dozen different tests in different categories can be run with one mailing. One client's test group is another's control group, so everyone gets an envelope filled with valuable coupons, but the envelopes are all different. To date, we have tested almost fifty different coupons for products ranging from antacids and toothpaste to cookies and coffee and with face values of from $0.07 to $1.50.

At the Metric Coupon Laboratory, we measure the difference in consumer purchasing between the test and control groups. Figure 26-1 shows the week-by-week difference between the test and control groups for one test—and these are real data! There are short-term variations that naturally exist between the test and control groups, and this is the background noise against which any effect must be measured. Statistical tests can tell us whether any

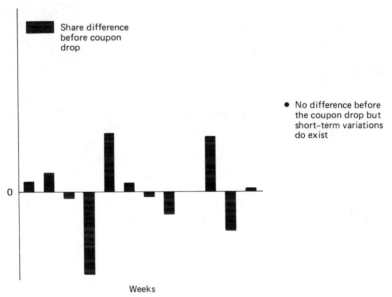

FIGURE 26-1. The test and control groups behave the same before the coupon drop.

significant change has occurred after the coupons have been dropped. But fancy statistics really aren't necessary.

Figure 26-2 shows how it worked with a $0.35 coupon for a dishwashing liquid. Sales and market share increased quickly and peaked after only three weeks. At this point, sales in the test group were 4 times what they were in the control group. But by the tenth or twelfth week, things seemed to be back pretty much where they had been at the beginning, with no difference between the test and control groups.

Another way to look at this is to count up the total incremental sales each week. If a bar is above the line, it adds to the incremental sales, and if it is below the line, it subtracts from them. Doing that (Figure 26-3), we see that the line for cumulative incremental sales levels off at about twelve weeks. There are no more incremental sales after that time. But for this twelve-week period the market share increased by 8.2 points on a base of 12. That is a 75 percent increase for a twelve-week period due to a single coupon drop!

Two brands in the same category can respond very differently (Figure 26-4). Here again we are looking at cumulative incremental sales, this time of two different brands of a snack food. One group got $0.10 coupons for brand S, the other got $0.10 coupons for brand T, and the control group got nothing; we are measuring incremental sales for each of the two test groups against the control group. Notice that the control group's incremental sales occurred during the first four weeks. After that time, there was really no change in the level of incremental sales, but brand S was 50 percent higher than brand T.

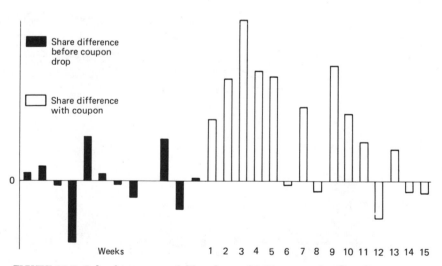

FIGURE 26-2. Sales increase quickly when a $0.35 coupon is offered.

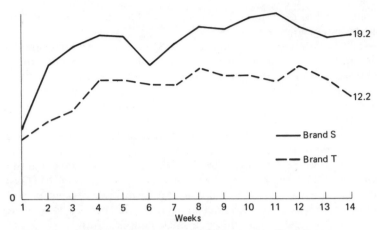

FIGURE 26-4. Brands in the same category can respond
differently.

Sometimes the short-term increment disappears completely. Figure 26-5
shows what happened in the case of a coupon good toward the purchase of a
laundry detergent. After only seven weeks, the coupon drop would have been
seen as a success, and yet all the short-term increment had disappeared by

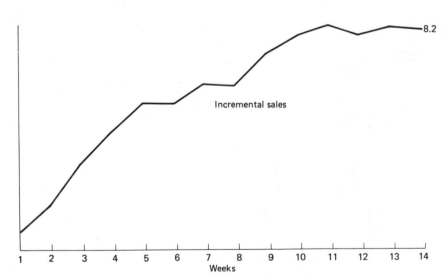

FIGURE 26-3. The total effect is all over in twelve weeks.

the seventeenth week. All the early sales increase was borrowed from later time periods, and the result was zero incremental sales.

A coupon with a sample can be much more effective than a coupon alone. Figure 26-6 shows results using a $0.45 coupon for an instant coffee with a single-serving sample and results using a $0.45 coupon alone. Incremental sales in each case are measured against the same control group. You can see the significant difference in incremental sales generated by including the sample with the coupon.

Different face values can produce different levels of incremental sales. Figure 26-7 shows the results using the same product, but two different face values. Incremental sales in the group that got the $0.30 coupons were almost 50 percent higher than incremental sales in the group that received the $0.20 coupons.

But incremental sales are really only part of the story. What about the cost-effectiveness of coupons? Cost-effectiveness is the incremental sales per dollar of promotion expenditure. I have shown how you can measure incremental sales. Dollar amounts are easy to determine because we collect the coupons in the stores. That means that we know how many people redeemed the coupons each week and who they were. And since we have their prior purchasing histories, we also know which are new users and which are not. So while higher face values can get you more incremental sales and more new users, they may be less cost-effective in total and for the new-user

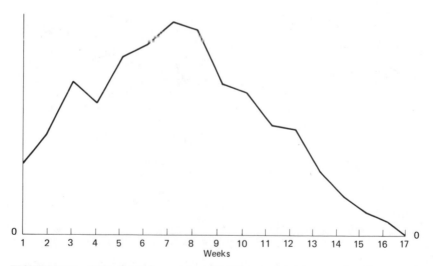

FIGURE 26-5.   Some brand response can be very short-term and end up at zero.

group. Remember that cost-effectiveness is measured by incremental sales per promotion dollar. We have seen a $0.25 coupon generate more incremental sales, but be less cost-effective, than a $0.15 coupon for the same product. The $0.25 coupon resulted in more sales, but at too high a price.

WHAT WE HAVE LEARNED

Following are some of the things that our Metric Coupon Laboratory experiments have taught us.

Incremental sales are harder to get for bigger brands. Brands with high market shares and high penetrations have a lot of people who are already buying them. Most of the redemptions will be by people who would have bought the brand anyway, and so the only thing that gets incremented is the coupon cost.

Incremental sales are easier to get for smaller brands. This follows rather naturally from the first point. When no one is buying your brand, almost all the valid redemptions are going to be incremental sales. For example, coupons can quickly create incremental sales of a new product.

High redemption rates can be very costly. High redemption rates are almost always associated with people who would have bought the product anyway, and we already know what they are worth in terms of incremental sales. The clearinghouses tell us that the highest redemption rates are for in-

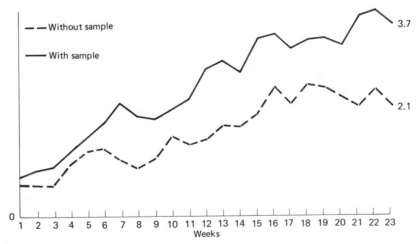

FIGURE 26-6. A coupon with a sample can be almost twice as effective as a coupon alone.

pack coupons. Is there an easier group to identify who would have bought anyway than those who just did without receiving a coupon?

The earliest redemptions are the incremental sales. People who put coupons in a file until they need them are obviously in the "would-have-bought-anyway" category when they finally use them. But the early redemptions are much more likely to be associated with purchases that would not have happened anyway. And these are the purchases that contribute to incremental sales.

Shorter purchase cycles mean shorter-term effects. Frequently purchased products are going to show all their incremental sales very quickly. If people go shopping for products in a certain category every week, the effect is all over much more quickly than if they buy only once every six or eight weeks. With cookies or crackers it is all over in four weeks. There are no more incremental sales beyond that time. Although the coupons keep being redeemed, they don't contribute to incremental sales. Instant coffee has a much longer purchase cycle, and it shows incremental sales for up to twenty weeks after the coupons have been dropped.

Current purchasing habits can be profitably exploited. We recently found that coupons can effectively take advantage of current consumer purchasing patterns. If your product is normally bought in multiples (bar soap is a good example), a coupon good on one bar is really all you need. People will still buy two or three bars at a time, but all you are paying for is one coupon.

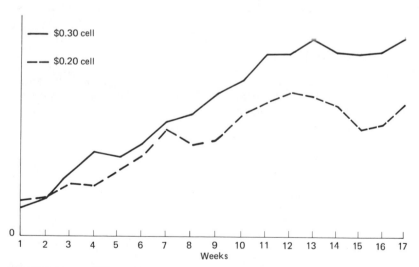

FIGURE 26-7. Different face values produce different incremental sales.

Trade-offs

Now all the important trade-offs associated with coupons can be made using real data. Should it be a $0.10 or a $0.20 coupon? Which copy should be included with the coupon? Should you include a sample with the coupon? Should you include a coupon with the sample? Which brand should get the coupon, brand X or brand Z? Or should any brand get the coupon? Should there be a refund overlay with the coupon or coupon overlay with the refund?

Measuring Other Sales Promotions

Many of these same questions can be answered, and the same trade-offs made, in relation to other types of consumer sales promotions. Refunds and rebates provide the easiest illustration. The test group receives the announcement and the refund form, the control group does not, and the scanners measure the effect! The same goes for self-liquidators and mail-in premiums.

Contests, games, and sweepstakes are a tougher problem. Legal restrictions on the actual awarding of sweepstakes prizes may make small-scale testing of a specific game impractical. Instrumented markets, however, do permit an easy evaluation of any actual promotion of this sort. First, identify the scanner-panel members who would actually receive, say, the sweepstakes announcement. Now drop half of those people, chosen at random, from the mailing. The result is a valid experimental design which will use the scanners to measure the impact of an actual contest, game, or sweepstakes on sales.

THE STATE OF THE ART

Technology has opened a new era in sales promotion evaluation. It is an era that will be marked by more professional management of sales promotion budgets, more productive marketing, and more profit. Technology lets us throw away our crystal ball and make better sales promotion marketing decisions.

VII

The Creation and Distribution of Sales Promotion Items and Services

Most of the products and services which are used as premiums and which serve as prizes for contests, sweepstakes, and games are the regular consumer goods and services purchased by all of us. These range from homes, cruises, automobiles, and TV sets to T-shirts and ballpoint pens. In most cases they are sold by the manufacturers directly to the companies that are using them in a sales promotion, or they may be sold by special marketing departments or incentive marketing departments.

Advertising specialties, on the other hand, are often manufactured by companies which serve the specialty advertising market on an exclusive basis. For example, there are companies which manufacture ballpoint pens solely for use as advertising specialties. They do not sell to the consumer market. Their normal channel of distribution is to sell through specialty advertising counselors, who, in a manner of speaking, constitute their sales forces. In the normal course of events, however, the counselors are resellers. They take title to the merchandise that they sell to companies which use the advertising specialties in their sales promotions.

27 The Specialty Advertising Supplier

JAY K. SHAPIRO
Vice President, Hand Tip & Novelty Co., Inc.

The generally accepted industry definition of a specialty advertising supplier is that it is a company that manufactures, imports, assembles, converts, imprints, or otherwise processes advertising specialty items or executive gifts for sale to specialty advertising distributors.

Two points should be stressed. First, specialty advertising suppliers, in contrast to other, similar companies, imprint their products with an advertising message. Second, specialty advertising suppliers sell their products *only* through specialty advertising distributor firms. Their marketing thrust is therefore directed specifically at this network of national or international distributors (and their sales personnel, known as *counselors*) and not toward the advertiser or ultimate user of the merchandise.

There are reportedly over 1000 specialty advertising suppliers operating in the United States. Some are engaged exclusively in the specialty advertising market, and some have other divisions or operations, most commonly aimed at retail markets. Some are small companies that specialize in one or two products, and some are large, nationally recognized firms with long lists of various product lines.

SOME HISTORY

The specialty advertising industry as we know it was born about 100 years ago in the town of Coshocton, Ohio, in the mind of Jasper Meek, publisher of a small weekly newspaper. In order to bolster his struggling enterprise, Meek began printing the name of his paper on burlap schoolbags, which he gave

469

away. The idea took hold, and soon local merchants were ordering bags imprinted with their names. The schoolchildren who carried the bags around town were also carrying advertising messages to the local consumers.

Henry Beach, another Coshocton newspaper publisher, followed his competitor's lead, and by 1890 he was using his press to print advertising messages on wooden yardsticks, flyswatters, and paint mixers. Beach also tried printing on metal signs and trays with limestone plates, using a technique that was a forerunner of today's offset lithography processes. The rest, as the cliché has it, is history.

HOW ADVERTISING SPECIALTIES DIFFER FROM OTHER PRODUCTS

Basically, the specialty advertising supplier faces the same problems and enjoys the same successes or endures the same setbacks as any other manufacturer, importer, or assembler. However, as was mentioned above, the product carries an advertising message, and it is marketed through a network of independent distributors. Those two differences are the subject of this discussion.

The injection-molding process that turns out plastic coffee makers also produces advertising key rings, molded badges, and hundreds of different advertising specialties. Other injection-molded plastic items, such as mugs, ashtrays, and ice scrapers, are produced directly for the retail trade as well as for advertising specialty use.

Stamped metal parts are basic to the manufacture of both automobiles and advertising or campaign buttons. Extruded plastic may end up as a tabletop or as a giveaway desk caddy. Metal castings become machine parts or emblematic jewelry or belt buckles. Cutting and sewing cloth is as fundamental in the production of award ribbons or imprinted T-shirts as it is in the manufacture of designer jeans. The same wooden slat that keeps your seat cushion in place might have been a ruler bearing an advertising message. The newspaper you read this morning could have become a deck of playing cards that an airline would give to a passenger.

The list of everyday items that are similar or identical to specialty advertising products is endless. They differ from advertising specialties only in that the specialty items have been imprinted with an advertising message. You might have bought your ballpoint pen in a stationery store, or you might have been told to keep it by the waiter who gave it to you to sign your check with last night. The difference, of course, is that the restaurant pen tells you to "Eat at the Eatery."

PRINTING PROCESSES

The specialty advertising industry makes use of all the traditional printing techniques:

- Letterpress, in which ink is transferred directly from raised type or half-tone cuts onto the surface to be printed, is used on paper, metal, and plastic.
- Photo-offset uses photographically prepared plates to transfer ink to another surface, from which it is then transferred to the item to be printed. This process is used most often for printing on paper or thin sheets of metal.
- Hot stamping is a means of imprinting cloth or plastic by using heated raised type or dies to melt colored foil or metallic leaf.
- Silk screening, which can be used to imprint virtually any surface, is a process in which ink is forced through a fine cloth screen with a squeegee. Areas of the screen that are not to be printed are masked out with a prepared stencil.
- A heat transfer is a decal that is either prepared photographically or printed. It is a finished product in itself, but it can also be affixed to another surface by applying heat and pressure. Heat transfers are often applied to T-shirts with a simple household iron.

Two of the newer printing processes that have found use in specialty advertising are flexography and pad printing. Flexography uses liquid ink, a rotary letterpress, and flexible rubber plates to imprint paper, vinyl, or Mylar.

Pad printing is a form of offset in which ink is transferred from engraved type or cuts to a foam pad and then to the surface to be printed. It can be used to imprint almost any material; more important, however, it can print on surfaces of almost any shape, no matter how rough or uneven. Pad printing has been used successfully to imprint walnuts and golf balls.

Nontraditional Printing Processes

There are other methods of "imprinting" that are part of the manufacturing process itself and do not require printing. By using the techniques of etching and engraving, an imprint can be carved into metal or plastic without ink. Copy and artwork can be incorporated into the casting of metal shapes and the molding of plastic items; color can be added later by filling in the appropriate areas.

Perhaps the most recent innovation in the advertising specialty field is laser engraving, in which advertising messages are burned into the surface of wooden specialties with laser beams.

MARKETING TECHNIQUES

Catalogs

Specialty advertising suppliers have devised a number of successful approaches to marketing their products. All suppliers provide counselors and distributors with printed catalogs of some sort, ranging from a one-page price sheet to a comprehensive full-color compendium of sixty pages or more. Catalogs generally show list prices, that is, the distributor's selling prices, along with coded indications of the distributor's discounts, so that they can be used by the distributor in dealing with customers.

There are also a number of industrywide catalogs published by various companies in which suppliers can buy space to advertise their products. These catalogs encompass a wide range of products and lines and are given out by distributors to their customers.

One company that publishes many of the industry catalogs is the Advertising Specialty Institute (ASI). ASI also publishes a trade magazine, in which suppliers can advertise to distributors, and another magazine specifically for users of specialty advertising. In the latter publication, suppliers advertise to specialty users in order to generate leads for their distributors.

Trade Shows

Not to be confused with ASI is the Specialty Advertising Association International. This is the national trade association of the specialty advertising industry, and it publishes trade journals, sponsors periodic educational forums both for distributors and for suppliers, and—possibly most important—puts on biannual national trade shows. These shows, which are closed to the public, give suppliers the opportunity to display their lines, introduce new items, distribute new catalogs, and meet face-to-face with distributors they may have known previously only through the mail or over the telephone.

Many local and regional trade associations have developed in various parts of the country. Each of these carries out many of the same functions as the national organization, tailored to the more specific needs of a smaller membership. Several local associations put on their own trade shows; some are closed to the public, and others are open to everyone so that distributors can bring their customers in and expose them to various suppliers and their lines.

Some distributors even put on their own small shows for their clients, inviting selected suppliers to set up displays to help in the education of their customers and the eventual sale of their products.

Sales Representatives

Despite the frequency of specialty advertising trade shows, suppliers have found that it is often only the distributor's principals who can attend. In an attempt to establish closer contact with distributors' salespeople and counselors, suppliers may hire sales representatives to carry their lines in different areas of the country. Sales representatives may handle more than one supplier's line and are responsible for maintaining the visibility of all their lines to the distributors in their area.

Traveling Sales Seminars

A new marketing approach, used very successfully in the past decade or so, is the traveling sales seminar, in which several suppliers combine their talents and resources, map out an itinerary, and invite distributors to attend meetings in their own parts of the country. These seminars usually last a full day and include a sales presentation by each supplier, sometimes with an elaborate audiovisual show, a question-and-answer period, and time for socializing and a meal. Traveling sales seminars have been put on in as many as sixty cities around the country in the course of a year.

Incentive Travel

Another relatively new marketing technique used by specialty advertising suppliers is incentive travel. Distributors who reach sales quotas set by suppliers or by groups of suppliers are rewarded with trips to different parts of the world.

The Supplier's Own Products

In addition to all the marketing and advertising techniques discussed above, specialty advertising suppliers have another obvious, if sometimes overlooked, approach available to them. Specialty advertising suppliers who do not use their own products as a means of self-promotion are not practicing what they and their industry preach.

THE SEQUENCE OF EVENTS

What is the typical sequence of events in filling an order for an advertising specialty? As an example, let's look at what happens when a retail customer orders advertising buttons from a counselor. First, the distributor relays all details of the order to a supplier—usually a supplier who is known to produce a quality product at a fair price and in time to meet a customer's deadline. The supplier promptly acknowledges receipt of the order to the distributor and simultaneously starts the manufacturing process.

If camera-ready artwork did not accompany the order, such artwork is prepared and photographed, and an offset printing plate is made. Printers then produce the required number of copies of the imprint, and the printed sheets are laminated to clear plastic sheets and die-cut in the appropriate size and shape. While all this is being done, metal shells and collets are being stamped out. Laminated prints and metal parts are then assembled and pinned, and the finished buttons are packed and shipped from the supplier, under the distributor's label, to the retail customer.

THE PARTNERSHIP

The specialty advertising distributor and counselor sell ideas, ways of solving marketing problems. The vehicles that are used to carry these ideas are produced by the specialty advertising supplier. It is, at its best, a symbiotic relationship, with each partner feeding ideas and solutions to the other. Given the existence of such partnerships, it is not surprising that new advertising specialties and new ways to use older specialties are constantly being developed.

In the final analysis, however, the specialty advertising industry should be viewed as a three-cornered partnership. First is the customer, who has a promotional need that must be filled; then there are the counselor and the distributor, who can suggest appropriate ways to meet that need; and finally there is the supplier, who can provide the means for doing so. Like any partnership, it succeeds best when all partners contribute the full range of their imagination, experience, and skills.

28 The Incentive Marketing Department

PETER D. SMITH
Director of Incentive Marketing, Consumer/Professional and Finishing Markets Division, Eastman Kodak Company

Organizing an incentive marketing department is similar to planting bulbs in the fall, which requires a great deal of digging, careful ground preparation, placing the bulbs at the correct depth, plenty of the right fertilizer, judicious watering, a kind winter, a sunny spring—and luck. If all the factors work properly, or properly enough, the blooms will burst forth and give color to the drab leftovers of winter. The same degree of preparation and nurturing is required during the gestation period of an incentive marketing department. The main difference is that the spring flowers will often bloom much faster than an incentive marketing department will make a profit.

Some Questions

Before a company starts to organize an incentive marketing department, it must ask a very basic question: Should the company go into the business of selling premiums? In order to answer that question, it must look at a number of areas and ask further searching questions, whether the company is contemplating selling a product or a service. (For simplicity, the word *product* will be used in this chapter to signify both products and services.)

1. What is the present direct competition in the incentive marketing field for the firm's products? Are the competitive products the same or quite different? What about price comparisons? Premium buyers look for good value, i.e., the best quality possible at the lowest price. If the competition has the incentive market to itself, how might it react to another firm's entry into the field?

2. What is the market potential for the firm's products? How will the products be sold? Will this upset the firm's current channels of distribution? Will the products be the same as current products or "premium" versions? How about the prices of these products, compared with the prices of products currently in the firm's channels of distribution?

3. Do the products planned for premium use fit the various incentive markets? Will the products have an immediate perceived value in the premium buyer's eyes? Does the nature of the firm's products limit them to certain users or markets only? For example, a $10,000 automobile would not be a good candidate for a consumer self-liquidator program, but neither would a $0.19 ballpoint pen.

Many other topics must be covered before starting to organize an incentive marketing department, but these questions are a start.

A Few Definitions

Some people tend to use the words *incentive* and *premium* interchangeably. In this chapter, *incentive* will refer to the concept of motivating, while *premium* will refer to the product or service itself. An incentive program to motivate salespeople, for instance, requires the reward of a premium to accomplish its purpose. An incentive marketing department is organized to sell premiums, though it may also advise user companies on incentive programs.

Advertising Specialties

The business of advertising specialties is beyond the scope of this chapter. Advertising specialties are items on which an advertising message (or name, slogan, logo, etc.) is imprinted and which are then given away for the purpose of keeping the giver's name in front of the recipient. The items range from pens to T-shirts and from golf tees to balloons, but generally they are relatively inexpensive and are passed out to recipients at no charge. Their use in an incentive program is incidental to the true motivational purpose of the program. Everyone who enters a sweepstakes may receive an advertising specialty bearing the sweepstakes sponsor's logo, but each person is entering in the hope of winning the grand prize or one of the other major prizes, such as a television set, a camera, or cash.

A Premium Representative Looks at Potential Incentive Suppliers

Robert F. Sanford, president of the Robert F. Sanford Company, a premium representative organization located in New Jersey, asks a number of questions of suppliers who are interested in going into incentive marketing. His questions are in George Meredith and Robert P. Fried's *Incentives in Marketing* (National Premium Sales Executives Education Fund, 1977).

1. Does your company have a corporate commitment to the incentive market?
2. Do you have a full-time premium department, or is it a shared responsibility?
3. Do you have a full-time Special Markets Manager? Does he have an involved assistant who can answer the phone when he is traveling?
4. Does he report to a Marketing function, rather than a Sales Manager? (Relates to the need to communicate with manufacturing, etc.)
5. Does he have the necessary authority commensurate with his responsibility? .
6. Is your literature premium-oriented, or just ordinary retail copies?
7. Is your line properly priced for Special Markets distribution?
8. Have you established real policies re: sampling, returns, etc., or is it a case of dealing with each as they arise?
9. Can you accelerate credit clearances for Special Markets accounts or do they bog down in the system, delaying sampling, etc.?
10. Do you have the capability of altering standard packaging when necessary?
11. Is your management aware of the necessary gestation period in this market, and the fact that they can't realize revenue for 9 to 12 months?
12. Is your management sufficiently familiar with that gestation period that they can project pricing and availability for a year or so?
13. Do you have an organized program to generate leads, as well as one to effect an efficient follow-up in the field?
14. What does your management *really* expect from their Special Markets/ Premium/Incentive Division? More than 10% of their total billing? Merely incremental sales? Additional advertising exposure paid for by users? Manufacturing burden absorption? Are their expectations realistic?

These questions should provoke the potential incentive marketing manager into doing a great deal of homework prior to asking for management commitment to the establishment of the department.

NEED FOR MANAGEMENT COMMITMENT

For a marketing department to launch an incentive marketing division without top-management commitment would be foolhardy. Management must understand that there will be a long gestation period before there is a positive impact on the bottom line, that there will be (or may be) an impact on the regular product line in terms of both numbers and profitability, and finally that there is an initial expense involved in setting up such a department. Incentive programs for users often are planned one to two years in advance of their actual implementation. This is particularly true of very large programs, for which tremendous quantities of premiums are needed. Such preplanning is an advantage for production planning purposes, but it may also necessitate that the supplier be locked into a price for a program that is two years away.

At the other end of the scale, often a user will need a product immediately because a marketing situation demands it. This requires that the company keep inventory on hand above and beyond that needed for other programs. Management must be made aware that premium programs can impact regular product lines. In extreme cases they can become more important than the regular product line, and this can affect the profitability of the corporation.

Finally, there is the initial expense of setting up the incentive marketing group. People will have to be hired for the home office, as well as a sales force, if the corporation decides to go that route. Also, a premium product may be different from the regular product line, and this will mean additional inventory, at a minimum, and possibly added engineering and tooling costs as well.

To obtain the management commitment needed, sales projections must be established by premium product; expense budgets must be forecast for sales, advertising, sales promotion, and commissions; and quotas should be set up for a sales force, and ways of motivating that sales force to achieve its quotas should be decided on.

TABLE 28-1 Advantages and Disadvantages of Manufacturing Special Premium Products

Advantages	Disadvantages
The consumer cannot compare the premium version with the retail version to see whether the premium offer is a good value. This is particularly important if the retail models tend to be heavily discounted in the marketplace.	Two inventories are necessary, one for the regular product line and one for the premium product.
There is less chance of upsetting the current distribution channels if the premium version is used. The manufacturer is not then competing with the retailer for customers.	There will be additional engineering and tooling costs of producing a premium version of a product.
The manufacturer may be able to price the premium version differently from the way the retail model is priced, probably lower. Obviously, a legal opinion should be sought as to whether the premium version is sufficiently different from the retail version to permit such different pricing.	

Special Premium Products

There are advantages as well as disadvantages to manufacturing special products, different from the retail versions, for premium sales. These are listed in Table 28-1.

It is also possible to manufacture both special products and retail products, as has been done at Kodak. Special premium models can be used in all incentive programs, including self-liquidator programs, while the retail products are made available for all programs except those using self-liquidators, such as programs involving sales and dealer incentives, business gifts, safety awards, and productivity awards.

THE SALES FORCE

A major decision that must be made concerns how to sell to the incentive market. Selling can be accomplished by using an internal sales force or by using outside selling organizations, which in the incentive marketing area are known as *premium* or *incentive sales representative organizations*. There are numerous advantages and disadvantages to using either method, and it is also possible to combine them.

An Internal Sales Force

When considering an internal sales force, it must be decided whether it will be made up of people concerned only with incentive marketing or whether it will include people with other sales and marketing functions. The advantages and disadvantages of using an internal sales force are listed in Table 28-2.

Makeup of an Internal Sales Force.   If an internal sales force is to be used, then, as mentioned above, the company must decide whether it will be made up solely of people involved with incentive marketing or will include people with other sales and marketing functions. The advantages and disadvantages of the former type of internal sales force are listed in Table 28-3.

Outside Selling Organizations

Using outside selling organizations, such as premium representative organizations, also has advantages and disadvantages. These are listed in Table 28-4.

A company that is just starting out in the incentive marketing area would probably do well to work with an outside selling organization to begin with. That gives the company immediate access to the marketplace through a

TABLE 28-2 Advantages and Disadvantages of Using an Internal Sales Force

Advantages	Disadvantages
There is control of an internal sales force in terms of cost as well as direction of effort. Changes initiated by the home office can be immediately implemented since the sales force is under the control of the corporation. A meeting can be called at a moment's notice, and the sales force will show up; this may not be the case when an outside selling organization is used.	The cost of an internal sales force is fixed, regardless of sales. Salaries and company cars must be maintained, whether programs have been sold or not.
The selling efforts of an internal sales force will be devoted completely to the company's product, not split with the products of other companies.	It takes time for a new sales force in the incentive marketing area to learn the marketplace and how to sell to it.
An internal sales force will have a more complete knowledge of the company's products and procedures than people from an outside organization.	More supervision is required for an internal sales force than for an external one.
Changes in territories and coverage of customers can be determined easily from corporate headquarters.	

knowledgeable group of people who are familiar with the users and know how to sell to them. In the meantime, as the business grows, it might be well to build an internal group to act as supervisors or coordinators for the external sales force.

TABLE 28-3 Advantages and Disadvantages of an Internal Sales Force Whose Members Are Involved Solely in Incentive Marketing

Advantages	Disadvantages
The sales force will understand and learn the market more quickly and more thoroughly.	The long gestation period of an incentive marketing department means that the sales force must be kept motivated while seeing no real results.
The sales force will devote all its efforts to incentive marketing.	Compensation must be on some basis other than commission if the sales force is to stay motivated.

An Example from Industry. Like the programs of many other companies, Kodak's premium sales program has gone through several phases. Initially, the company had a director of premium sales and an internal sales force consisting of people concerned solely with premium sales. Outside organizations which brought premium business to Kodak were paid a finder's fee for their services. As the business changed and grew, the cost of the large internal sales force, which represented a fixed cost (salaries plus benefits and

TABLE 28-4 Advantages and Disadvantages of Using Premium Representative Organizations

Advantages	Disadvantages
The company has immediately available to it a force of trained salespeople who are knowledgeable about the marketplace and the premium users.	Premium representative organizations handle many lines. A number of factors will influence which manufacturer's product a representative will pull from a sales tool kit—for example, the commission paid on the product, how long it has been on the market, and whether another company in the potential user's same line of business has recently used the product or a similar one.
Selling costs are tied to results because commissions are paid only after a sale is made. There are very few fixed costs involved for the manufacturer.	It is more difficult to train premium representatives than an internal sales force because they establish their own priorities for attending sales and training meetings. Each company they represent must compete for their attention.
The hiring and firing of a premium representative organization is as simple or as complex as the contract agreement. Depending on the product, obtaining the best premium representative organization may be easy or difficult, although the company's reputation will be a strong factor.	An outside organization is less likely to be knowledgeable about the company's policies and procedures and is more likely to make sales which are contrary to company practice.
	Territorial coverage is a problem, since most premium representative organizations want exclusive territories, which may or may not be in the best interest of the company. Exclusive territories mean that there is no dissension among the premium representative organizations as to which one should be calling on an account. It should be asked, however, whether an organization will work as hard to make calls when it has exclusive rights to all the business in an area.

company cars), was deemed unnecessary, and premium representative organizations were substituted. Today, Kodak divides the United States into four zones, and a Kodak incentive marketing zone manager, located in the field, is responsible for each zone.

Within each zone there are between three and six premium representative organizations with nonexclusive territories, and they are paid on a commission basis. The Kodak incentive marketing zone managers coordinate the activities of the premium representative organizations, do the training, and assist them in complying with the company's policies, procedures, and paperwork. They also travel with premium sales representatives as they make calls to keep abreast of the needs of the marketplace and the key premium users.

CONVINCING TOP MANAGEMENT

Probably the biggest task facing any marketing department is convincing top management that selling in the premium market will not adversely affect current channels of distribution. If the argument to be used is that most large manufacturers of consumer products sell both through retailers and to the premium market, some market research may be in order. One question that should be asked is, What percentage of the people who obtained a product through a premium offer would have bought the product at retail? At one point Kodak conducted research and discovered that 60 percent of the people who got Kodak cameras through premium channels of distribution were not in the market for a retail camera at the time they got the premium camera. From the retailer's standpoint, every camera that gets into a consumer's hands expands the market for film, processing, and accessories such as camera bags and lenses.

Broadening distribution is only one argument that can be presented to management. There are others. Many times the user of a premium product will do significant advertising of the item used as a premium, and this exposure for the supplying company is free and often broad. Companies using premiums will often print the premium offer on millions of packages or bags. This kind of advertising would cost the company supplying the premium thousands of dollars. Selling in the premium market often allows companies to fill slack production times for regular products with schedules for premium products.

Another argument to present to management is that an incentive marketing department can add substantially to the company's bottom line through its normal activities and also can act as an excellent conduit for closeout items.

ORGANIZING THE DEPARTMENT

The Reporting Relationship

The incentive marketing department should report as high up in the general marketing organization as possible. The person to whom the department reports should be one who fully understands the unique nature of incentive marketing.

The incentive marketing department has a strong need for management clout when production resources are tight. Once committed to, premium programs do not wait for the production problems of the supplier company to be corrected. Failing to meet premium users' deadlines is a sure method of never being asked to bid on a program again. In order to function efficiently and effectively, the department also needs access to the various other resources of the company in such areas as estimating, production planning, business planning, pricing authority, engineering, manufacturing, distribution, advertising, and sales promotion.

Line or Staff? If the reporting relationship is effective and if sufficient authority is vested in the incentive marketing group, whether it is a line or a staff group is immaterial. Often this depends on the way the company itself is organized. The important thing is the group's ability to get things done quickly, both at the home office and in the field.

In a line organization, the head of the incentive marketing department would probably be a sales manager or a manager of incentive marketing or markets, of special markets, or of premium sales. In a staff organization, the same person would be a director of special markets, of incentive marketing, or of premium sales. In a line organization, the internal sales force would report to the manager of incentive markets, while in a staff organization, the sales force might well report to the regular line organization with final responsibility to the director of incentive marketing. The organizers of an incentive marketing group should know whether line or staff orientation would work better in their company.

Staffing the Department

Start small. All that is necessary to get this kind of department going is a manager or director, an assistant, and secretarial help, assuming that the department has access to all the other departments whose help it will need to function properly, such as the advertising, sales promotion, legal, and distribution departments.

The Manager.   What qualities should be looked for in a manager? First and foremost, the person should be sales-oriented. In addition to selling user companies on the product, the manager also sells sales reps on pushing the product, premium representatives (if used) on carrying and promoting the product, and management on continuing to fund the department. The manager should be a good communicator, a good trainer, a good supervisor, and a good motivator. The manager must also be willing to travel extensively (and have the budget for it), be patient (it will be a while before the results are translated to the bottom line), have a thorough knowledge of the company's policies and procedures, and be able to work with other company depart-ments as needed to get the results desired. If such a person does not exist within the company, it may be necessary to hire someone from outside; however, it should be recognized that a person hired from outside will not be company-oriented at the beginning and will have to establish all the relation-ships and earn the respect that a person from within the company would already have.

The assistant in the department should have the same qualities as the manager, since the assistant will take over when the manager is away. In addition, the assistant should be extremely well organized and capable of giving great attention to detail, since keeping track of programs and products is essential in running a successful incentive marketing department.

A Word of Caution.   A large incentive marketing department may give the manager a sense of power and success, but it does not necessarily build sales. In some successful companies the incentive marketing department consists of one manager and one secretary. The best way to achieve incentive marketing success is probably to start small and build on accomplishments. (Also, there won't be so much to take apart, should it fail!)

THE PREMIUM PRODUCTS

Retail Products for Premium Usage

It must be determined which products are to be used in premium programs. Using regular retail products has both advantages and disadvantages; these are listed in Table 28-5.

Special Premium Products

Using special premium products which are separate and distinct from retail products offsets the disadvantages listed in Table 28-5 but turns the advan-tages listed in the table into disadvantages. There is a way to minimize these disadvantages; this will be discussed later.

If special products are to be used, how should they be different from retail products? This is partly a legal question, and competent legal advice should be sought. Certainly, some product features must be different, and it is helpful to have differences in appearance as well. Another difference may be in the pricing of the premium product.

Pricing

Pricing is absolutely critical in the premium area. Premium users want to be able to get a product at a price substantially below the retail price of a similar product; they want to believe that they got good value. Prices to users may depend to some extent on whether volume discounts are offered. The number of price levels that are established may be based on how the product is sold (direct to users, through jobbers, by drop shipment, etc). It must also be decided whether there will be a discount off invoice, based on volume, or whether discounts will be effected through rebates at the end of the program.

Long lead times on user programs demand stable pricing. A lead time of from six months to one year is needed for advance notice on price changes, particularly in the case of self-liquidator programs in which the user has advertised a product at a certain price. For the manufacturer to raise the price of that product in the middle of a program would be disastrous for the user. The same consideration must be given to products sold to trading stamp companies or incentive houses that issue catalogs good for a certain time period. It will be recognized by those selling to catalog showrooms that this is a problem faced in the retail area as well.

Minimum Quantities

The manufacturer must decide whether to establish minimum quantities. These can be in units or dollars. Not to do so often results in requests for one item, which the potential user really wants for his or her personal use.

TABLE 28-5   Advantages and Disadvantages of Using Regular Retail Products in Premium Programs

Advantages	Disadvantages
There are no additional engineering, manufacturing, or inventory costs. The product is already being advertised and promoted.	The dealer organization already selling the retail product may react adversely when the manufacturer competes with it with the same product. Consumers can find out what the retail price of the premium is. The premium product may seem less valuable to the consumer if it is heavily discounted in the retail marketplace.

Return Policy

Another area for consideration is return policy. When an incentive program is over, should the manufacturer take back any unused products at full price, or should there be a "restocking" charge? The user should certainly pay the return transportation charges. Some manufacturers do not take back products at all. One disadvantage to this policy is that the products may end up on retail dealers' shelves and disturb the market for regular retail products. At Kodak it has been the practice to accept unused products back at the end of a program, as long as they are returned in factory-sealed cartons and are usable for other programs. There is no restocking charge to the user. The relative value of the premium product may be a factor in determining whether there should be a restocking charge.

Packaging

Packaging for premium products should be different from retail product packaging. Depending on the kind of program, it may be better to use a display box which will advantageously show off the product, rather than a mailer package. However, when a drop-shipment program is sold to a user, packaging will have to be devised which will convert the display box into a mailer pack. Packaging must also be considered in terms of weight, as the drop-shipment cost can rise significantly if the packaging adds to the weight of the product.

Inventory

The most difficult job of the manager of the incentive marketing department is forecasting when a premium product will be needed. It is essential that a premium be available when the user wants it, since the user has spent advertising and sales promotion dollars to get consumers to want to buy his or her product. The premium is intended to induce consumers to buy that product. If the premium is not available, consumers become angry with the company that offered it, not with the company that manufactured it. The result is a very unhappy premium user and a premium supplier with a bad reputation.

The incentive business is not like the retail business, in which seasonal buying patterns are common. There are distinct peaks and valleys in the sales of premium products too, but they may not be so predictable. Production must be geared to accommodate them. This can be an advantage if a company is willing to inventory premium products, since their production can be scheduled along with that of retail products to fill in the slack periods of production of retail products.

One final word of advice: Never commit yourself to a program for a major premium user if there is any possibility that production cannot keep up with demand. It is better to be candid about the ability to supply a product than to hope that production will be on time. The user of a successful program this year is one of the best potential prospects for programs in the years to come.

PREMIUM REPRESENTATIVE ORGANIZATIONS

Assuming that premium representative organizations will be used, what steps must be taken to motivate these organizations to promote your product over that of another manufacturer? These organizations do tend to carry ten to twenty major lines and a number of minor ones as well. They may also be involved in the advertising specialty business.

Commission

Commission is probably the key to getting the premium representative's attention. Most manufacturers establish a regular commission which is paid on all programs sold. Many manufacturers do not pay the commission until the user has paid for the product. There are also special commissions which may be more or less than the regular commission, depending on circumstances. Closeouts on specially priced merchandise may demand a lesser commission because the product is considerably less profitable to the manufacturer. However, it can also be argued that a higher commission should be paid since this merchandise may need a harder sell. It is also possible to increase the commission when the manufacturer wants to put emphasis on certain products. Perhaps the premium representatives are not paying sufficient attention to a particular line, and this is one way to point it out to them. Commissions can be budgeted just as other expenses are, or they can be charged as a cost of goods sold.

Training

Perhaps one of the best ways to train the members of premium representative organizations is at a sales meeting. Sales meetings can have many functions, but the three most valuable are motivating, educating, and offering a reward. If the premium representatives leave a sales meeting knowledgeable about a company's products, enthusiastic about mentioning those products on every call, and happy that they attended the sales meeting because it was fun and they knew they were appreciated, the objectives of the sales meeting were met. One question always arises: Who pays for the representatives to attend sales meetings? One possibility is to offer a free trip to a sales meeting for a certain amount of sales of the company's product. In the case of a brand-new premium representative organization, one member might be allowed a free trip to make sure that the organization gets off on the right foot with the company's product.

Territories

One sticky question is that of "exclusive" territories. Representatives often want exclusive territories so that they will automatically get all the leads generated in a given area. Many claim that they work much harder when they know they are going to get the business. This must be weighed against the question of whether representatives will make as many "cold" calls or work as hard when the business in a territory is automatically going to fall to them. It is strongly recommended that a supplier have exclusive representatives and not employ an organization just because it comes in with a potential program. This will demotivate the regular premium representative organizations that handle the product.

Contracts

A legal contract with each premium representative organization is advisable. Conditions such as commission, lead follow-up, and geographic area for leads can be spelled out, as can the conditions under which the contract is declared null and void. Thirty days' notification is normally sufficient, though representatives should be paid commissions on any programs they generate prior to the nullification of the agreement with the manufacturer.

Leads from Other Sources

Inquiries regarding the premium product can come from many sources, including jobbers, advertising specialty representatives, advertising agencies, and the potential users themselves. Unless the manufacturer has established jobber prices as well as user prices, each situation will have to be dealt with on an individual basis. One solution might be to pay a finder's fee for any business generated by someone other than the regular premium representative organizations under contract. The premium business is one in which everyone has "friends" who think they can do a better job of selling than the regular organizations in the business.

Final Thought

One final thought on premium representative organizations: A supplier should travel with premium representatives on a regular basis to be sure that they are up to date in terms of product knowledge and pricing, that their samples are in good order, and that they are showing the product to the best potential users. This also demonstrates that the manufacturer is interested in how well they are doing. Premium representative organizations have many different manufacturers' products to sell, and part of the job of the director or manager of the incentive marketing department is to make sure that each organization representing the company's products is pushing those products on every call possible.

INCENTIVE PROGRAMS

There are numerous kinds of incentive programs, including self-liquidator programs, sales or dealer incentive programs, and programs involving business gifts, productivity awards, and safety and merit awards. Each program has its own objectives, and the premiums used are designed to help the program reach those objectives. Self-liquidator programs often have the highest visibility because they are usually heavily advertised consumer programs in which the consumer is asked to send in money plus a proof of purchase in order to receive the premium advertised. The money sent in normally covers the cost of the product plus the drop-shipping charges. It is true that in the automobile aftermarket, dealer incentives are partial self-liquidators. In other markets as well, the user of the premium may pick up part of the cost of the product. Generally, though, the cost of a self-liquidator is borne entirely by the person who receives the premium.

Use of a Premium Product

In considering whether to sell a program to a user, the use to which the product is going to be put must be taken into account. Does the user want a retail product or a premium product? In the case of a retail product, is it going to be used as a self-liquidator, which means that the consumer may be paying the same price for it that the retail dealer pays? This establishes competition between the premium user and retail dealers. In the case of a premium product, does the manufacturer want to keep it from going to dealers who sell regular retail products? Most premium manufacturers do not want their premium products sold on retail shelves next to their retail products.

Trademarks and Trade Dress

Once a program is sold, the manufacturer must be careful about how the user treats the manufacturer's trademarks and trade dress. The premium supplier should demand the right to approve all mailings by users to see that trademarks are properly depicted, as well as to approve all point-of-purchase materials, literature, and packaging. This is often difficult, since the user faces deadlines and may not want to take the time to get the manufacturer's approval. However, it is a point that should be insisted upon for the manufacturer's own protection.

Exclusivity

Once a user has picked a product for a program, the manufacturer should, if the user asks for it, try to give the user exclusivity of the product for the duration of the program. This is particularly important in the case of programs within the same kind of market, e.g., banking, the automobile aftermarket, or frozen desserts. There is generally no harm in having a product used as a sales incentive for one type of market (insurance sales representatives, for example), as a dealer incentive for another market (automobile shock absorbers, for example), as a consumer self-liquidator in a third market (breakfast cereals, for example), and as a productivity, safety, or merit award in any number of industries. Disaster strikes, however, when two banks which are across the street from each other end up offering the same premium for new accounts. The supplier is going to have some difficult explaining to do to two bank marketing departments!

Probability That a Program Will Succeed

As programs funnel into the incentive marketing department, one of the assistant's responsibilities is to keep track of the programs and of the availability of products. Many times, programs will come in which are "iffy," and it may be well to establish degrees of probability that a program will come to fruition. As the premium representatives, the internal sales force, and the assistant become more expert in the field with the product line, the accuracy of the probability predictions will increase. One very good reason for keeping track of programs is to prevent two users whose own products compete from signing up for similar programs.

Terms and Conditions

It is important that the terms and conditions of doing business be firmly established. It may be that the manufacturer's credit department will have the final say, but marketing certainly wants to make its feelings known.

ADVERTISING AND PROMOTING

Buyers

Who are the best potential buyers for the product? Is the product something that will go to banks because of its price, which is within the legal limits that banks can spend? Is it a product that will interest sales managers for sales contests or for dealer incentive purposes? Does the product have universal appeal, or is it limited to certain categories of end users?

Buyers can be divided into three groups: (1) those who are very knowledgeable about the premium marketplace, who demand the newest and most innovative products, and who must be the first user in the market with the latest gadget or gimmick; (2) those who are also experienced but do not mind being second in the market with the latest product, who are steady purchasers of premiums, and who consider well-priced options as long as there are no conflicting programs; and (3) those who are inexperienced in the field, who have never set up an incentive program, and who need help establishing a program as well as selecting a product.

Reaching Potential Buyers

These different groups of buyers (decision makers) can be reached in a variety of ways. How to reach them will be determined to a large extent by which group of buyers is being zeroed in on. Very experienced buyers must be communicated with directly, either through the supplier's own sales force or through premium representatives. These buyers will also attend the premium trade shows. It may be worthwhile to have a drawing for valuable prizes or to use a clever gimmick to attract these buyers to exhibit booths.

Trade shows also attract less experienced buyers, but these buyers are not so visible. They generally read the business and premium publications, so ads in those magazines are useful. Direct mail is another very effective vehicle, if used properly. The "rifle-shot" approach can be used with specific decision makers, if the proper mailing list is utilized.

Inexperienced buyers are more difficult to find. One day they aren't there, and the next day they are. One new medium which has promise in terms of reaching inexperienced buyers is specialized cable television. Through choice of market and choice of show, specific target audiences can be tapped. Vertically integrated publications which cater to specific markets, such as the automobile aftermarket, banking, insurance, or publishing, can be effectively utilized. The supplier's advertising agency can also be a great help in directing efforts toward the most appropriate media.

Premium Shows

There are two major premium shows each year: the National Premium Show and Incentive Travel and Meeting Executives Show, which is held in Chicago in the late fall, and the New York Premium Show and Incentive Travel Show, which is held in New York, usually in May. The New York show centers mainly on merchandise premiums, although some incentive travel companies are represented, while the show in Chicago is fairly evenly split between merchandise and travel. Most manufacturers who are interested in the premium market exhibit at one or both of these shows. The advantage is that the buyers for user companies, as well as the premium representative organizations, are represented at these shows. The shows provide an opportunity for potential suppliers to reach buyers for their products and to make contacts with premium representative organizations.

Associations

There are a number of associations for people in the premium business. The three most prominent are National Premium Sales Executives, Inc. (NPSE), the Premium Marketing Association of America (PMAA), and the Incentive Manufacturers Representatives Association (IMRA). Each of these has a slightly different philosophy, but each can provide valuable advice on establishing a business. Further details on these associations can be found in Appendix B.

Co-op Advertising Funds

Co-op advertising funds are not as widely used in the premium business as in retail business. Many manufacturers choose to price their premium products at a level which does away with much of the normal sales, advertising, distribution, and administration (SADA) cost. This often means that no co-op advertising funds are available for the user. When co-op advertising funds are made available to the user, they are generally credited as a percent of the price of the premium itself and are given as a discount off invoice. Some companies do not offer co-op advertising credit to premium users, although such programs are available to their retail dealers. Likewise, companies may have different payment terms (e.g., eliminating cash discounts for early payment of invoices). Not using co-op funds may raise questions if suppliers are trying to deal with catalog showrooms or trading stamp companies in the same way that they deal with premium users. The permissibility of offering co-op funds or different payment terms to one class of trade and not to another should be thoroughly reviewed by the supplier's legal adviser.

Leads

Few things are more devastating for a manufacturer than failure to follow up on an inquiry. It is important to have a system of establishing leads which can be turned over to whoever is going to make the personal call on the potential user. A four-part lead form can be generated in the home office. Part 4 remains at the home office, while parts 1, 2, and 3 are sent to the sales representative (internal or external). Once the follow-up has taken place, information regarding the outcome can be put on the lead card; part 3 is retained by the sales representative, while part 1 is returned to the home office with information on what happened. Part 2 can be sent to the source of product literature or advertising materials, if that is appropriate. In this way the home office knows whether the sales representative is following up on the leads that the various kinds of advertising are generating.

An 800 Number

One excellent way of getting immediate response to ads is through the use of an 800 number, or WATS line toll-free number. If the company has a telemarketing department, the personnel can handle inquiries, send out literature and case histories if appropriate, qualify prospects, and send out lead cards if warranted. Otherwise, a coupon should be used in the ad, with a space for the inquirer's name, title, and company address or space for attaching a business card.

Case Histories

One very effective way to communicate a company's ability to meet a user's needs is to write up case histories of past successes. There should be case histories for companies of different sizes and for various kinds of programs. It is useful to have case histories on programs involving self-liquidators, sales incentives, dealer incentives, and safety, service, and productivity awards. The premium representative organizations, if that kind of selling group is used, are eager to feed in the information for case histories since mention of the organization's name in the writeup is good advertising for them. Often the user of a successful premium is delighted to have the company's success story told, since this is good publicity for the company. Telling potential users about a past success with a company whose problems were not too different from their own is very effective advertising.

SALES PROMOTION

There are numerous kinds of support for the sales organization and the user organization which should be considered.

Samples

A sample program should be established. Questions that must be answered include the following: Should an unlimited number of samples be provided to the premium representative free of charge, or should a "reasonable" number be sent at no charge, and the balance at a low net price? Should the supplier send samples to potential users when they request them, or should this be done only by the premium representative organization (assuming that one is used)? Will samples be sent free to users, or will users be memo-billed, and a credit issued when the product is returned? If samples are sold to premium representative organizations, will a commission be paid on those products? On that subject, often the premium representatives will take care of small programs through their own "sample accounts," and it probably makes sense to pay a commission on all products sold, whether directly to the user or to the premium representative organizations.

Price Lists

If the supplier is offering both premium products and retail products to the incentive market, it may be best to have two price lists. One would be for the premium products only and would cover the terms and conditions of sale, as well as any restrictions on those products, while the second would cover all the retail products and any unique terms and conditions applicable to them. If multiple pricing levels are used, such as two-step pricing for users and jobbers, any number of price lists may have to be produced. Prices change, and it is important to alert the incentive market to price changes at least six months before they go into effect.

Selling Sheets

Often it is difficult to send or take samples to potential users, or users may wish to alert their sales forces or dealers to the premium product being offered. All this makes selling sheets very important for both the supplier and the user. It is recommended that only one product be described on each sheet, since the user may not be buying more than one item. Presenting a family of products on a sheet can cause complications. Selling sheets should be provided free in reasonable quantities, although large quantities are frequently offered at cost. Information which is important to a user includes the weight and cubic measurements of the product in a shipping carton and also case dimensions for warehousing.

Line Art and Photographs

Some users will want color or black-and-white photographs of products they plan to use in their campaigns. They may also want line art which is camera-ready. Finally, there is the possibility that they will ask for color transparencies. The supplier must decide whether to provide these free of charge or to memo-bill users for them. Except for color transparencies, which are expensive and reusable, it is recommended that such items be furnished free in small quantities. Users can be memo-billed for color transparencies, and their accounts credited when the transparencies are returned.

PAPERWORK

In the incentive marketing area, paperwork becomes all-important. The supplier needs a lead response form, a listing form for users, a fulfillment form if the product is to be sent to the ultimate user through a fulfillment house, internal credit approval forms, a product return form if the supplier takes products back, and a form for canceling the user's account when the program is over. In addition, the supplier may need a form on which the sales representative can write up a case history if the supplier wants to publish it. It is also recommended that a thank-you letter be sent to the user at the end of the program, particularly if the program was successful. It is also important to thank the premium representative and the members of the internal sales force, if they are used.

Internally, forms may be used to keep track of programs, to keep track of inventory, and to notify the internal sales force and the premium representatives of programs that are currently in existence. Another means of keeping in touch with these people is through a newsletter, published on a regular basis, which tells them the kinds of programs booked for the future for various categories of users so that they may avoid selling similar programs to competing users. It is probably sufficient to tell the premium representatives that a cereal company is using product A during a given time period, for example, rather than to be specific about which manufacturer is using the product. There is intense competition within some industries, and it is obviously poor business practice to tell one potential user what another is planning to do.

FURTHER INFORMATION

No chapter such as this can provide all the information on the many intricacies of incentive marketing. It is recommended that anyone who wishes to establish an incentive marketing department consult other sources, such as the various organizations for people in the business of selling premiums, books on incentive marketing, and the publications which cater to the premium marketer and user. A number of these sources are listed in Appendixes B and C.

29 Fulfillment Services

DONALD A. ADLER
Chief Operating Officer, Promotion Fulfillment Division, Carlson Marketing Group, Inc.; Vice President, Carlson Marketing Group, Inc.; Former President, Maple Plain Company, Inc.

Although promotion fulfillment may appear to be a simple matter, it is in fact very complicated and possibly the least understood function performed by sales promotion people. The proper fulfillment of a program depends upon complete communication between the fulfillment company and the company that is developing the program. It is the purpose of the fulfillment company to fulfill orders in accordance with established guidelines and to communicate variations in the procedure to its client, whereupon decisions will be made to deal with such variations. The initial steps in promotion fulfillment are outlined below.

1. Within a minimum of thirty days before the starting date of a promotion, management should provide the necessary information for the fulfillment of the promotion to the product promotion department or liaison person, who will handle the contact with the fulfillment company.

2. A promotion specification sheet (see Figure 29-1) should then be completed and sent to the fulfillment company for quotation. On the basis of the information provided on the specification sheet, the fulfillment company will develop its quotation for the program and forward it to the client company.

3. Upon acceptance of the quotation, the client company will request the fulfillment company to rent a post-office box, the number of which will be assigned to the particular promotion. The client company will also provide the fulfillment company with ad reprints, premium samples, and any data that relate to the media being used for the promotion. It is important that any revisions of the specifications be communicated to the fulfillment company as soon as they are approved and confirmed in writing.

Promotion Fulfillment Division
PROGRAM SPECIFICATION FORM

12755 State Hwy. 55
Plymouth, MN 55441

Computer Processing ☐ MPC ☐ NB Acct. Exec. Phone_____ EST. NO._____

Manual Processing ☐ MPC ☐ NB Date Quote Need By_____ Custom Programming ☐ Yes ☐ No

Date_____ Account Executive_____ Account Coordinator_____

Client_____ Promotion #_____Contact_____

Address_____Title _____

City_____State_____Zip_____Phone No._____

Type of Offer: ☐ Refund/Rebate ☐ Coupon ☐ Premium ☐ Sample ☐ Label Stage ☐ Sweepstakes ☐ Other

☐ FTC Regulated ☐ Free ☐ Paid ☐ Paid Amount_____

Media/Circulation: ☐ On Label_____M ☐ Point of Sale_____M ☐ Newspaper_____M

☐ Magazine _____ ☐ Sunday Sup_____M ☐ FSI_____M ☐ Other_____M

Territory Limitations: ☐ National ☐ Regional ☐ Canadian ☐ APO - FPO Limitations

Name of Offer_____Total Estimated Volume_____

Offer Description _____

_____

_____

_____

_____

Note: UPC Code Verification ☐ Yes ☐ No How Many Digits?_____

Start Date_____Expiration Date_____Close Offer_____

P.O. Box #_____ Special Consumer Service P.O. Box ☐ Yes ☐ No ☐ P.O. Box 9000

Order Form ☐ Yes ☐ No Order Form Required ☐ Yes ☐ No ☐ P.O. Box 9___ Dept___

Accept No Pays ☐ Yes ☐ No Part Pays ☐ Yes ☐ No If Yes, Amount Accepted_____

Accept No Proofs ☐ Yes ☐ No Part Proofs ☐ Yes ☐ No If Yes, Amount Accepted_____

Order Form Requests: ☐ Forward to Client ☐ Process Under Separate Promotion

☐ PFD Will Handle, Explain_____

Retain Source Documents _____Months After Expiration

Computer Dupe Elimination ☐ Yes ☐ No Quantity Limit_____ Print Label For Duplicates Eliminated ☐ Yes ☐ No

Reply to Duplicated Consumer ☐ Yes ☐ No ☐ Reply W/ Proofs ☐ Reply W/O Proofs

Unqualified Letters: ☐ PFD Generic ☐ W/Microfiche ☐ W/O Microfiche ☐ Client Custom

Refund/Rebate Details:
☐ Checks (Check Two)   ☐ Coupons (Check Two)   ☐ Cash
  ☐ PFD Generic   ☐ Computer Printed - Continuous Form   ☐ Currency
  ☐ Client Generic   ☐ Non-continuous Form - Requires Cheshire Label ☐ Coin
  ☐ Self Mailer   ☐ Self Mailer
  ☐ Insertable   ☐ Insertable
  ☐ Special Order Check   ☐ Fold Coupon ☐ Yes ☐ No
                               Explain _____

Special Inserts: ☐ Yes ☐ No Description _____

How To Mail: ☐ UPS/PP ☐ UPS Only ☐ 3rd Bulk ☐ 1st Class ☐ Comingling ☐ Other_____

Premium Sample Offer: ☐ Bulk ☐ In Mailer ☐Sample Attached ☐ Sample Due Number of SKU's_____

Dimensions _____ x _____ x _____ Weight _____

Physical Description_____

Packaging Materials: Supplied by ☐ Client ☐ PFD

Materials Required_____ Inserts_____

FIGURE 29-1. A promotion specification sheet.

Client Name _____ EST NO. _____

Name of Offer _____

COMPUTER PROCESSING

1. Labels
   - ☐ Cheshire
   - ☐ Pressure Sensitive
   - ☐ Red MPC
   - ☐ Black NB
   - ☐ PFD
   - ☐ Client _____
   - ☐ Blank 3x3

2. Checks
   - ☐ PFD
     - ☐ Self Mailer
     - ☐ Insertable
   - ☐ MPC
     - ☐ Self Mailer
     - ☐ Insertable
   - ☐ NB
     - ☐ Self Mailer
     - ☐ Insertable
   - ☐ Client
     - ☐ Self Mailer
     - ☐ Insertable
   - ☐ Custom Form

   Describe_____
   _____

3. Print duplicate labels or list during regular run ☐ Yes ☐ No
   - ☐ Plain white 3x3 label
   - ☐ 2-Part listing

4. Label Processing Code
   - ☐ Label for each item requested
   - ☐ Label for total like items requested
   - ☐ Label for total combined items req.

5. ☐ Print check register during regular run

6. ☐ Print UPS proof of shipment mailing list

7. ☐ Save all data captured on personalization system

8. Automatic Voucher Balancing

   Qty. variance percentage _____

   Dollar variance percentage _____
   Hashing ☐ Yes ☐ No

RECEIVING INFORMATION:

Date of Receipt_____

Designated Plant _____

Medium of Shipment _____

No. Per Carton _____

☐ Floor Loaded

☐ Palletized

Comments: _____
_____
_____
_____
_____
_____

KEYING

1. ☐ Key
   - ☐ 3 Name line and address
   - ☐ Item or quantity code
   - ☐ Variable refund amount
   - ☐ Telephone number

2. ☐ Verify
   - ☐ 3 Name line and address
   - ☐ Item or quantity code
   - ☐ Variable refund amount
   - ☐ Telephone number

3. ☐ Key 1-digit media code

4. Personalization
   - ☐ Store name only
   - ☐ Store street, address & zip

5. Capture POP
   Average number_____

6. Key Other · Explain in comments

1. Activity Reports mailed to:
   Name _____
   Company _____
   Address _____
   City_____ State_____ Zip_____
   Number of copies required _____

2. Receiving Reports mailed to:
   Name _____
   Company _____
   Address _____
   City_____ State_____ Zip_____

3. Consumer correspondence not related to offer to be sent to:
   Name _____
   Company _____
   Address _____
   City_____ State_____ Zip_____

4. Send Invoices: ☐ Weekly ☐ Bi-weekly ☐ Monthly ☐ Other
   Name _____
   Company _____
   Address _____
   City_____ State_____ Zip_____

5. Label Stage · Send labels to:
   Name _____
   Company _____
   Address _____
   City_____ State_____ Zip_____

Merchandise/Checks to be mailed from:
Howard Lake ☐ Maple Plain ☐ Litchfield ☐ New Brighton ☐ ☐ Other_____

REPORTS

1. Standard Activity Report
   - ☐ Weekly ☐ Bi-monthly ☐ Monthly

2. 3-Digit Zip Report/Area Report
   - ☐ Monthly ☐ End of Offer

3. Name and Address Listing
   - ☐ Monthly ☐ End of Offer

4. State Report
   - ☐ Monthly ☐ End of Offer

5. Proof of Purchase Report
   - ☐ Weekly ☐ Monthly
   - ☐ End of Offer

6. ☐ Unqualified Report · Monthly Only

7. ☐ Media Report only

8. ☐ Special Report · Explain in Comments

9. ☐ Tapes
   - ☐ Weekly   ☐ Bi-monthly
   - ☐ Monthly   ☐ End of Offer
   - ☐ 1600 BPI   ☐ 6250 BPI

499

OFFER EXECUTION

Promotion offers should be designed to minimize consumer confusion and problems, thereby increasing the promotion's effectiveness. The promotion offer should be stated clearly and honestly. It also must comply with all legal requirements. General guidelines include:

1. Mail-in offers should be understandable to the average consumer. All terms of the offer should be clearly stated prior to the consumer's initial response.

2. Copy, layouts, and mechanicals for all promotion offers, regardless of execution, proof-of-purchase requirements, etc., should be reviewed by the promotion department, the brand manager, the legal department, and the sales department.

3. Approving mechanicals for promotion offers should be the responsibility of the product promotion department, the product manager, and the sales department, who will ensure that all legal requirements are contained and satisfied; that the details of the offer are clear, concisely stated, and easily understood; that all corporate guidelines, if any, have been followed; and that the appropriate post-office-box numbers, zip codes, and expiration dates have been verified.

ORDER-FORM GUIDELINES

Order forms are required for all mail-in offers where practicable. They include certificates in magazines, tear-off certificates, etc. Order forms should be designed according to the following guidelines:

- Any legal restrictions must be prominently stated on the order form, e.g., "Void where prohibited by law."
- A clear statement of the offer must be made.
- A premium or refund offer should be presented in a manner which is informative and not misleading to the average consumer; i.e., the appropriate terminology should be used, and dimensions, performance characteristics, etc., should be included. Brand-name identification or other qualifications should be provided if these would normally be considered by consumers in evaluating the item.
- Any visuals must represent and properly position the item's value.
- The expiration date of the offer should be clearly stated.
- The amount the consumer must pay for the premium must be stated; the term *free* can be used if no payment is required.
- If the consumer must pay a postage and handling fee, this should be clearly stated.

- There should be a clear statement of any product purchase requirements: brand, product size, etc. If the premium is available in a limited quantity, this should also be stated.
- The expected delivery time should be stated, e.g., "Please allow eight to ten weeks for delivery."
- Sufficient space, appropriately identified, should be provided for the consumer's name and address. This is very important and reduces the cost of data capturing.
- Any limitations in terms of returns per name or address must be stated in order to control liability, e.g., "One refund per family, group, or organization."
- A statement should also be made concerning assigned rights, e.g., "Your refund rights may not be assigned or transferred to any other individual, group, or organization."
- It should be clearly stated that the order form may not be mechanically reproduced.
- If the program is assigned to a certain territory or state, it is important that this be clearly indicated on the order form. Generally, any geographic limitations will be in terms of the boundaries of a state or, possibly, a sales territory.
- It is recommended that the order form include a consumer receipt feature, which consumers remove and retain for their records. The receipt should include a restatement of the offer, a special correspondence address, a statement of delivery time, and a space in which the consumer can record the date the order form was mailed in.

An order form which does not meet these criteria must be cleared by the promotion department, the product manager, and the sales department.

ADVERTISING GUIDELINES

All advertising of mail-in offers should be reviewed by the legal department. Advertisements should present the promotion in an honest, favorable, understandable, and meaningful manner. Television and radio advertising supporting mail-in offers cannot effectively communicate all the terms of the offers. However, such advertising must include the following:

- A clear statement of the refund or premium offer
- The fact that it is a mail-in offer
- The expiration date of the offer
- Any payments and/or proofs of purchase that are required
- A clear statement of actual purchase requirements or an identification of multiple purchase requirements in the case of complex offers

- A statement telling consumers how to get additional information, such as by visiting a participating store or writing the company for further details

Print-media advertising of a mail-in offer should give the full details of the offer or tell consumers where the details can be obtained.

Any in-store materials other than tear-off pads must include a mailing address to which consumers can write for further details. Materials communicating the complete details of the offer (tear-off pads) will probably state the important conditions. In addition, special copy is required to inform consumers where to mail in for certificates and to state the last date on which they can be sent in; this should be four weeks prior to the expiration date of the offer. A separate post-office box number is usually assigned for this purpose.

Qualified consumer requests for premium offers will automatically be honored if they are postmarked within one month of the stated expiration date. This, however, may vary, depending upon the specifications outlined in the program. Refund offers are usually honored for fifteen days after the expiration date, but again this depends upon the specifications outlined for cutting off fulfillment.

Checks are usually used for refunds, although refunds may also be in the form of coupons or cash. Duplicate requests are generally permitted in the case of self-liquidating premium offers. Other offers are usually limited to one per family, group, or organization.

RECEIVING PREMIUM MERCHANDISE

It is imperative that the fulfillment company establish standard procedures for receiving, inspecting, handling, and reporting incoming premium merchandise. These procedures can function only if there is advance communication with the client company regarding the type of merchandise, the proper distribution of the sponsoring brand, the offer number, the offer description, etc. It is also extremely important to verify quantities and report any shipping charges back to the client. All checks and coupons must be stored in a locked area, and counts must be maintained and reconciled upon removal and return. It is the usual practice to permit the fulfillment company a percentage of shrinkage or loss for damages due to handling and also minor pilferage. This percentage is usually established at about 0.5 to 1 percent of total receipts, depending upon the value of the merchandise.

PACKAGING AND EXECUTION OF FULFILLMENT

Parcel Post and United Parcel Service (UPS) test mailings are conducted to ensure that the premium is adequately packaged to prevent damage during transit. Prior to the beginning of a promotion, the fulfillment company packages and ships the premium to the promotion manager, the promotion purchasing department, and the product manager in the same package in which it will be sent to consumers. In some cases several other test mailings are made in order to get a better idea of the condition of the package when it is delivered to the consumer. The fulfillment company provides notification of a premium test mailing to each individual specified, advising that a specific premium item has been mailed. Those who receive it inspect the package and its contents, taking note of any damage, and then forward the notification of the premium test mailing to the various people responsible for the promotion.

Procedures are also established for verifying that the fulfillment company is properly executing the fulfillment of all cash-refund, coupon, and premium offers. Preselected individuals respond to the offer to verify that fulfillment is properly executed. They respond to the offer as consumers would, writing down their names and addresses, enclosing proofs of purchase, etc. When they receive the refund or premium, they forward their comments on the fulfillment to the individuals responsible for handling the promotion.

Before a promotion is launched, a check of the key elements is made. All parties concerned have spent many hours carefully planning and preparing for the promotion, and it is imperative that a definitive checklist be devised for confirming that every detail has been properly attended to. Before an offer begins, the manager of client services reviews the promotion checklist with the individuals and departments directly concerned. (See Figure 29-2.) If an oversight is discovered, there will be adequate time to rectify the situation.

Although the majority of people who respond to promotion offers satisfy the requirements of the offer as stated, some do not. It is believed that most of these people respond to an offer in good faith, but, either because of a misunderstanding of the exact requirements or because of an oversight, they fail to comply with the requirements as stated. In the interest of good consumer relations, the company usually makes the decision to fulfill the requests of such well-intentioned consumers, while discouraging the small percentage who fraudulently misuse offers. Tolerance guidelines are established for the fulfillment company to follow. These are based on two primary considerations: the value of the premium or refund offer and the nature of the offer requirements that are not fully satisfied. In general the greater the value of the offer, the less tolerance is permitted. The following are guidelines for establishing fulfillment tolerances.

For refund offers with a value up to $3, honor:

- Requests containing proofs of purchase from a package of the incorrect size
- Requests containing proofs of purchase from the incorrect portion of the package
- Requests containing proofs of purchase totaling 80 percent of the number required
- Requests from out of the designated area

The Maple Plain Company

Sequence # _____

Plant Location:
- ☐ MPC Maple Plain
- ☐ MPC Howard Lake
- ☐ MPC Litchfield
- ☐ MPC Watertown
- ☐ MPC Portland
- ☐ MPC Other

#

Amendments:	Sec. Letters	Date	Reason	Initial

Client: _____ **(A)** Job Name: _____

Promotion # _____

Secondary Promotion # _____   Free Offer ☐   Paid Offer ☐   Employee Order Allowed ☐ Yes ☐ No

Offer Description: _____
_____
_____
_____
_____
_____
_____
_____
_____

Box Numbers _____

Start Date _____ Expiration Date _____ Close Offer _____ Close Box # _____ Est. Vol. _____

Brand Code _____ Event Code _____ Account Code _____ FTC Yes☐ No☐ Del. Time _____

Territory Limitations _____

Order Processing Responsibility (B)

	Yes	No		Yes	No
Accept No Pay	☐	☐	Accept No Proofs	☐	☐
Accept Part Pays	☐	☐	Accept Part Proofs	☐	☐
Minimum Amount: _____			Minimum Amount: _____		
Accept Canadian	☐	☐	P.O.P. Save Bulk		☐
Accept APO - FPO	☐	☐	Qty. to be saved _____		
U.S. Holdings	☐	☐	P.O.P. Save with Order		☐
Accept Other	☐	☐	Save Order		☐
Explanation: _____			How Long _____		
			Source Returned To: _____		

Automatic Voucher Balance   ☐ By Item
                                      ☐ By Voucher

Qty. Variance Percentage __ __ __ . __ __

Dollar Variance Percentage __ __ __ . __ __

Max. Ref. Amount _____ Qty. Limit Per Order _____

Computer Dupe Yes ☐ No ☐

Order Form Requests

Process Under Promotion # _____
- ☐ Consumer Service will have a supply
- ☐ Consumer Service will reply
- ☐ Forward to Client
- ☐ Disqualify - No Reply

P.O.P. Codes		Media Codes	
01. _____	A. _____		
02. _____	B. _____		
03. _____	C. _____		
04. _____	D. _____		
05. _____	E. _____		
06. _____	F. _____		
07. _____	G. _____		
08. _____	H. _____		
09. _____	I. _____		
10. _____	J. _____		

Comments: _____
_____
_____

A/E _____   A/C _____

Sorting Department Responsibility (C)

	Yes	No		
Insurance Req.	☐	☐	Label Stage Orders Sent To:	
Transmittal Letters	☐	☐	_____	
Label Stage	☐	☐	_____	
Duplicate Labels	☐	☐	_____	
Label Type _____				
Duplicate List	☐	☐	Duplicate Labels ☐	
Receipt Requested	☐	☐	Duplicate List ☐	
Other: _____			Send To: _____	

No. of Copies _____   No. of Copies _____

Consumer Service Responsibility (D)

- ☐ MPC Maple Plain
- ☐ MPC Howard Lake
- ☐ MPC Litchfield
- ☐ MPC Watertown
- ☐ MPC Portland
- ☐ MPC Other

- ☐ P.O. Box 9__ __ __ Dept. __ __ __
- ☐ P.O. Box 9000
- ☐ Client Letterhead
- ☐ Client Envelope
- ☐ MPC Letterhead
- ☐ MPC Envelope

Form Letter Copy by ☐ Client   ☐ MPC
                                  ☐ with Approval ☐ w/o Approval

Form Letter Printed by ☐ MPC   ☐ Client

Dupe Elimination:

No Reply ☐ With Reply/No Proofs ☐ With Reply/Ret. Proofs ☐

Other Comments: _____
_____
_____

Mail: First Class ☐   Third Bulk ☐

Comments: _____
_____
_____
_____
_____
_____
_____
_____
_____

FIGURE 29-2.   A promotion checklist.

504

- Requests arriving fifteen days after the expiration date
- Mechanically reproduced certificates on order forms
- Requests not accompanied by official order forms

For refund offers with a value up to $3, do not honor:

- Requests containing proofs of purchase from competitive products
- Requests sent in by groups or organizations
- Duplicate requests

For refund offers with a value over $3, honor:

- Requests containing proofs of purchase from a package of the incorrect size, if equivalent
- Requests containing proofs of purchase totaling 80 percent of the number required
- Requests arriving fifteen days after the termination date

For refund offers with a value over $3, do not honor:

- Requests containing proofs of purchase from the incorrect portion of the package
- Requests containing proofs of purchase from competitive products
- Requests coming from outside the designated area
- Duplicate requests
- Requests from groups or organizations, except with the approval of the client company

Similar criteria can be developed for use with self-liquidating offers, partially liquidating offers, free premium offers, and coupon offers.

DATA PROCESSING

Data processing plays a key role in the performance of fulfillment services. Before any information can be processed on data processing equipment, it must be recorded for this type of processing. This can be done using (1) cathode ray tubes, (2) key-to-tape equipment, and (3) optical scanning devices. Typewriters are rarely used.

A state-of-the-art fulfillment company usually uses all three types of data processing equipment because it must be able to handle a large volume of information and must be versatile when promotion programs become very complicated, in terms of the information that the client company requires. A state-of-the-art system can also make it possible to edit various documents, correct zip codes, and look up zip codes if they are not provided. Systems of this type also provide the fulfillment company with the necessary controls to prevent and correct errors.

PROMOTION FULFILLMENT DIVISION
CARLSON MARKETING GROUP 12755 STATE HIGHWAY 55
MINNEAPOLIS, MN 55441
WEEK ENDING 5/27/83 REPORT NUM

CLIENT   MPC CORPORATION
PROMOTION   PO NUM.
CUSTOMER

MPCRP155   PAGE   1
BRAND   ACCOUNT   EVENT

ESTIMATED VOLUME   1 BRAND
0 PROMOTION PERIOD -

ESTIMATED MAIL RECEIVED

BOX	CURRENT	CUM/MONTH	CUM/OFFER
	0	0	0
	0	0	0
	0	0	0
	0	0	0
	0	0	0
	0	0	0
	0	0	0
	0	0	0
	0	0	0
	0	0	0
	0	0	0

MAIL PROCESSED

	CURRENT	CUM/MONTH	CUM/OFFER
QUALIFIED REQ	0	0	0
FREE	0	0	0
PAID	0	0	0
TOTAL ITEMS	.0	.0	.0
MULT FACTOR	.0	.0	.0
PART/NO PAYS	.0	.0	.0
UNQUAL. REQ	0	0	0
DUPS ELIMINATED	0	0	0

MONEY RECEIVED

	CURRENT	CUM/MONTH	CUM/OFFER
PART PAYS	.00	.00	.00
CURRENCY	.00	.00	.00
CHECKS	.00	.00	.00
TOTAL	.00	.00	.00

ITEMS MAILED

	CURRENT	CUM/MONTH	CUM/OFFER
CONSUMER	0	0	0
HOUSE	0	0	0
REPLACE	0	0	0
OTHER	10,800	10,800	1,627,850
TOTAL	10,800	10,800	1,627,850

POSTAGE

	CURRENT	CUM/MONTH	CUM/OFFER
1ST CLASS	.00	.00	.00
3RD BULK	.00	.00	.00
3RD REG	.00	.00	.00
4TH CLASS	.00	.00	.00
PSTG DUE	.00	.00	.00
UPS	.00	.00	.00
OTHER	.00	.00	.00
TOTAL	.00	.00	.00

OTHER TOTALS			

INVENTORY NUMBER	INVENTORY DESCRIPTION	PTD RECEIVED	RECEIVED	ADJUSTMENTS	PTD MAILED	UNMAILED CONSUMER	WORK-IN PROCESS	ENDING INVENTORY
75-004-00-00 NB CARTON STOCK		.0	0	0	0	0	0	0

506

75-004-01-00 NB KRAFT ENVELOPES

Item	Description						
01 10	9X12 B/K OS	452.000	0	0	0	0	70.003-
01 12	9 X 12 B/K OE TS	100.000	0	771-	19.200	0	63.043
01 23	6.5 X 9.5 B/K OE TS	354.592	0	274.782	0	0	312.548
01 29	12 X 15.5 B/K OE TS	0	0	782	0	0	500
01 34	9.5 X 12.5 B/K OE TS	56.100	0	1.104-	0	0	57.889
01 50	4 X 5.5 B/K OE TS	0	0	0	0	0	316.227
01 51	4.5 X 6.75 B/K OE TS	0	0	0	30	0	109.756
01 52	4 1/8 X 9 1/2 B/K OE TS	0	0	0	0	0	357.374
01 53	5.5 X 7.5 B/K OE TS	0	0	926-	0	0	3.258-
01 54	6 X 9 B/K OETS NB/RET BULK	0	0	7.758-	0	0	170.122-
01 55	7.5 X 9.5 B/K OE TS	0	0	278.480-	21.530	0	883
01 56	7.5 X 10.5 B/K OE TS	0	0	0	0	0	48.000
01 57	7.5 X 12.5 B/K OE TS	0	0	0	0	0	43.000
01 58	7 X 13.5 B/K OE TS	0	0	0	0	0	0
01 59	10 X 16 B/K OE TS	0	0	0	0	0	3.750
01 60	15 X 18 B/K OE TS	0	0	0	0	0	1.000
01 61	7 X 12 B/K OE TS	0	0	0	0	0	0
01 62	7.5 X 10 B/K OE TS	0	0	0	0	0	0

Item	Description						
03 60	7 NB RET BULK	1.094.500	0	6.747-	1	0	28.008-
03 61	7 NB RETURN	105.000	105.000	7.621-	0	0	92.518
03 62	7 WD NB RET 1ST CL	795.000	0	11.378-	0	0	364.086
03 63	10 NB RET BULK	262.500	0	215-	0	0	306.508
03 64	10 NB RET	306.900	0	522-	10.800	0	56.330
03 65	10 WD NB RET	242.500	0	0	396	0	234.604
03 66	10 WD W/OLD SPOTTS LOGO	0	0	0	0	0	32.000
03 67	7.5 X 4.5 SPEC WD	0	0	0	0	0	159.973
03 68	7 WD NB RET BULK	1.442.000	0	280-	0	0	254.330
03 69	6.5 X 3.75 PLAIN	0	0	0	0	0	20.500
03 70	7 WD W/OLD SPOTTS LOGO	0	0	0	0	0	0
03 71	6.5 X 3.75 PL NB/RET BULK	0	0	0	0	0	1.813
03 72	6.5 X 3.75 WD NB/RET BULK	0	0	0	0	0	0
03 73	7 WINDOW NB RETURN	102.800	0	0	0	0	92.732
03 74	#11-WD-PMD RETN	276.300	0	4.090-	0	0	112.100
03 75	10 OLD SPOTTS LOGO	0	0	0	0	0	5.300

RECEIVING DETAIL

DATE	QUANTITY	REFERENCE
5/25/83	105.000	76525
	0	

HOUSE ORDER DETAIL

DATE	QUANTITY	REFERENCE
	0	
	0	

OTHER SHIPPING DETAIL

DATE	QUANTITY		REFERENCE
5/25/83	10.800	0	46972

FIGURE 29-3. A sample report generated by computer.

507

Data processing in a fulfillment company is very different from data processing in other companies. Data processing in a fulfillment company includes zip-code sorting and the printing of checks and mailing labels. Also, software programs can be used to report to client companies on the progress of their programs. Data processing also makes it possible to put every name and address directed to the company on microfiche so that in case of a consumer complaint, the name and address can be retrieved and verified. Once all the names and addresses are recorded, marketing data can be obtained for the client company for use in special reports, such as a sales territory analysis. With proper software, territories can be reduced to counties and states in which the product was purchased or consumers responded to the offer.

Some companies ask that consumers include their telephone numbers on their requests. This makes it possible for the marketing department of the company to verify consumer satisfaction as well as to obtain additional marketing information.

REPORTING SERVICES

It is the responsibility of the fulfillment company to institute and maintain an accurate reporting procedure for all consumer promotions. The information in these reports should be so structured that it will relate to the client company all promotion activity on a weekly basis, or as otherwise specified.

In addition, the fulfillment company should issue a monthly report documenting the handling of consumer complaints, and, when necessary, this report should be broken down by type of complaint processed. A monthly report should also be prepared on the status of all premium and refund offers presently being handled by the fulfillment company, and an evaluation should be generated at the conclusion of each program, as specified by the client company.

The fulfillment company should issue a quarterly report indicating gross dollars expended on a client's behalf for postage, fulfillment services, consumer correspondence, packaging, premium procurement, and refund activities. This report serves as a management tool for the fulfillment company's sales department and also as a summary document for the client company.

All standardized reports should be sent to the promotion department of the client company and should contain information on reporting procedures and an analysis of consumer complaints. A sample report generated by computer is shown in Figure 29-3.

A monthly report on consumer complaints can be generated indicating the total volume of consumer correspondence handled and detailing the reasons why orders did not qualify. Reports of this nature are provided by the

CUSTOMER SERVICE DEPT. UNQUALIFIED & REPLACEMENTS

PROMOTION

* UNQUALIFIED ORDERS *

NOTE - 99 PERCENT IS WRITTEN 99.000

CURRENT	PROM TO DATE	PERCENT OF REQUESTS	CODE	REASON FOR NOT QUALIFYING
1	1	.002	2	PART PAYS
44	44	.078	11	NO PROOFS OF PURCHASE
162	162	.286	12	WRONG PROOFS OF PURCHASE
933	933	1.650	13	INSUFFICIENT PROOFS OF PURCHASE
5	5	.009	15	NO CERTIFICATE
34	34	.060	16	NO SPECIAL CERTIFICATE
2	2	.004	19	
180	180	.318	22	LIMIT
2	2	.004	25	NOT OUR OFFER
3	3	.005	29	PREVIOUS REQUEST, LEFT SOMETHING OUT
4	4	.007	31	RETURN EXTRA P.O.P. OR SALES SLIPS
				REPLACEMENTS OR REFUNDS
3	3	.005	57	ORIGINAL REQUEST REPLACEMENT
1	1	.002	59	LATE AND CORRECTED

TOTALS FOR PROM 263-033　GRT PARTS& CAR GIVEAWAY $8. R TOTAL REQUESTS = 56,547

	CURRENT	TO DATE	PERCENT
UNQUALIFIED =	1,370	1,370	2.423
REPLACEMENT =	3	4	.007
TOTAL CONSUMER MAIL =	1,373	1,374	2.430

FIGURE 29-4. A quarterly report generated by computer.

fulfillment company upon request and at an extra charge. They are an excellent tool for evaluating a program and also provide design information for the next program or promotion. This information can be carefully examined to prevent dissatisfaction among consumers whose orders did not qualify.

A quarterly report is sometimes generated at the client company's request covering gross dollars expended, billings for postage, consumer correspondence, packaging, premium procurement, etc., for use in measuring activity based on total media circulation. A report of this nature is for supplemental use by the client company and the fulfillment company. (See Figure 29-4.)

CONSUMER SERVICES

All promotions involve various types of consumer correspondence, which are addressed as description or reason codes. (See Figure 29-5.) Each situation and procedure may differ, depending on the requirements of the individual

---

FIGURE 29-5.   A description of reason codes for a consumer-mail summary report.

Group I   Money

01   No Money
No cash or check received on an offer requiring money. If coin mail, there is no imprint of coins on envelope.

02   Part Pays
Money received is not enough to cover order or orders and is not within stated allowance.

03   COD
Consumer requests sending out merchandise on a COD basis which is not an authorized procedure on the promotion.

04   Unsigned Check, Verify Signature, Check Not Made to Correct Company, etc.
Check as received is not negotiable for one or more reasons: Not signed; signature not decipherable; signature is a name different than name imprinted on check; check made payable to a company or other name that we are unable or unauthorized to endorse for deposit.

05   Wrong Date on Check
Date written is too old or predated; also includes checks that have been altered. Check must be replaced.

06   Wrong Part of Money Order
Consumer has submitted a copy of the money order instead of the negotiable portion.

07   Not Responsible for Money Sent through the Mails
Consumer states he or she sent cash for more than $3. We find no record of handling order.

---

08 No Stamps Accepted on This Offer
Consumer submits stamps instead of money on an offer; we are unable to exchange the stamps for money.

Group II Proof of Purchase

11 No Proofs of Purchase
One or more proofs of purchase are required, but none have been included with order.

12 Wrong Proofs of Purchase
Proofs are from another product from same company, wrong part of the package, too small portion of proof.

13 Insufficient Proofs of Purchase
Not enough proofs for order.

14 Competitive Proofs of Purchase
Proofs are from a product produced by some other company.

15 No Certificate
Certificate or coupon from original ad or display is required but has not been submitted.

16 No Special Certificate
Certificate or coupon from controlled source; i.e., packed with certain product or merchandise.

17 Short Points

18 No Points
These reasons apply to promotions which assign point values to various proofs and a certain number of points are necessary to comply with requirements of offer.

Group III Information

20 No Choice, Item, Color, Size, etc.
Offer requires a selection by the consumer.

21 Out of Area (Also Canadian or Foreign Requests)
Requests from unauthorized states or unauthorized areas and requests from Canada and/or other foreign countries when not acceptable on a promotion.

22 Limit
Consumer has requested more than the stated limit on an offer.

23 Insufficient Name or Address
Offer requires that we have a name—cannot be sent to "occupant" or "householder." Original order is returned to consumer requesting more information.

24 Special Letters
Special situations that require a letter to the consumer; i.e., consumer states that he or she sent a check or money order for more than $3, and we have no record of servicing the order—we write requesting a copy of canceled check or replacement of money order.

FIGURE 29-5 (Cont.)

25 **Not Our Offer**
Mail or requests for offers not handled. Original request returned to consumer.

26 **Offer Is for Refund Only**
Consumer requests product, usually submitting money, instead of requesting refund on a refund promotion. (For example, "Enclosed is $2, please send me a turkey on a refund offer of $2 off on purchase of a turkey.")

27 **Personalizing Information Needed**
Offer requires an indication from the consumer for a name, initials, or other personalized information. Request as submitted may be blank (we require an "OK" from the consumer to leave blank), too long, or have unavailable characters or symbols.

28 **Serviced Our Portion of Order—Part of Order to Another Company**
Consumer requests containing multiple requests—part of which is serviced by us and part not our offer which must be returned to consumer.

29 **Previous Request, Left Something Out**
We have previously returned a request to the consumer which has now been resubmitted but is still incomplete or incorrect and must be returned a second time for additional information, etc.

Group IV   Special

30 **Information Wanted**
Consumer has requested additional information prior to submitting request. Questions include "How large is the item?" "Is a certain size and/or color available?" "Can item be sent to a particular place or sent by a certain time?" etc. The information is requested before consumer sends in the actual request.

31 **Return Extra POP, Sales Slips, Extra Money, etc.**
Proofs may be returned to consumer when he or she submits more than required, usually on a promotion which requires multiple proofs and consumer has submitted noticeably more proofs than required. Also consumer may request return of a sales slip proof which is necessary for records, or we may have to return some money if consumer has submitted too much for an item ordered.

32 **Directions Wanted**
Responses to consumer requests for use directions not found packed with merchandise; what are proper qualifiers or portions of qualifiers for a promotion; what is needed to order a certain item, etc.

33 **Certificate Request**
Consumer is requesting a certificate for a specific promotion, and we have the forms to send to the consumer.

34 **Replacement or Refund Letter**
Correspondence to the consumer regarding replacement or refund. May be instructions to consumer to return merchandise; may be note stating refund or replacement is in the process or on its way.

35 Not Received, Parts Missing, etc.
Correspondence with consumer that we are aware of the inquiry and the problem will be handled from another office; or the order has been shipped recently so please allow more time.

36 Offer Expired
Request returned to consumer with note that offer has expired and merchandise or refund is no longer available.

37 Offer Expired but Available for Limited Time
Response to request from consumer that they may submit order within a specified time frame while inventory is still available; requests filled on offers that are no longer current or advertised but we still have stock available—offer is no longer on regular reporting system.

38 Merchandise Temporarily out of Stock
Notification to consumer that shipment on the request may be delayed.

39 Miscellaneous
May be used for any unusual circumstances not covered by other specified reason code. For example, correspondence with consumer who states he or she sent a previous response but forgot part of the order, part of the qualifiers, or some other information and ask that we retrieve the order—usually not practical.

Group V Coding Only

[Use of codes in this group indicates that these responses have been forwarded to the client for further handling. There are no consumer labels produced and no record of individual consumer names and addresses.]

40 Complaints and Thank-Yous
Comments pertaining to client's products or services.

41 No Certificate—Can't Return
Requests for certificate from consumer normally handled but we have not received supply or our supply is depleted.

42 Special Offers—Client Wants to See
All source material forwarded to client per its request.

43 How to Handle Information
We require additional instructions from client on how to handle unusual requests or situations.

44 Not Our Offer
Requests for offers not handled by us but are an offer from client—request forwarded to client.

45 Mail Returns, Lost Mail
Empty wrappers, loose labels returned from post office—forwarded to client for handling.

46 Second Time Around—Incorrect
Request forwarded to client for further handling.

FIGURE 29-5 (Cont.)

47 Certificate Requests (Client Supplies)
   Requested certificates are forwarded by client.

48 No Name or Address
   Request not serviceable because of missing name and address information.

Group VI   Replacements

50 Merchandise Received Broken

51 Order Received Incomplete

52 Wrong Merchandise Received
   Wrong item, color, size, amount, etc.

53 Customer Dissatisfied with Quality
   Defective merchandise—doesn't run, etc.

54 Item Not Received—Replacement Sent
   Applies to merchandise, coupons, or checks (refunds).

55 Change of Address
   Reshipping because of address correction by post office or consumer.

56 Postal Damage
   Reshipping of items lost from containers by handling by postal service.

57 Original Request Replaced
   Expired jobs—new orders processed as replacements.

58 Expired Check or Coupon Replaced

59 Late and Corrected
   Unqualified requests that have been returned corrected after promotion has been
   expired or closed.

Group VII   Refunds

65 Refund: Overpayment
   Consumer has submitted $3 or more than the amount required for the order.

66 Refund: Merchandise Returned
   Consumer has returned wrong, unwanted, or defective merchandise—does not
   want replacement.

67 Refund: Merchandise No Longer Available
   Consumer order has been processed and check or cash deposited.

68 Refund: Merchandise Temporarily out of Stock
   Consumer requests refund rather than wait for shipment.

69 Refund: Limit on Quantity
   Consumer has requested more than the allowed quantity—we must deposit the
   check or cash to cover portion of order processed.

70 Refund: Postage
   Consumer is reimbursed for postage spent in returning merchandise, etc.

71 Refund: Not Received
   Consumer requests refund rather than have item reshipped.

offer and the way in which the consumer has responded to these require-ments.

The consumer services department of a fulfillment company tries to handle each inquiry or situation in a prompt and completely informative manner, realizing that the primary purpose of any promotional offer is to gain new customers and satisfy old ones, as well as to increase sales. A detailed flowchart (Figure 29-6) outlines the flow of mail through the checking of orders that are not qualified, through the consumer services department, through data processing, and finally into the mail. The expedient handling of consum-er inquiries is of the utmost importance to both the fulfillment company and the client company. The client company spends millions of dollars to obtain a customer base, and one mishandled consumer complaint could result in the loss of a consumer.

Because of the large volumes of mail handled by a fulfillment company, form letters are often utilized in replying to consumers. In most cases, these letters suffice, although sometimes an individual letter must be written. (See Figures 29-7, 29-8, and 29-9.)

Special attention is paid to inquiries from consumer agencies; these mean either that a consumer did not receive a reply from the fulfillment company or that the action taken by the fulfillment company was unsatisfactory. All inquiries from better business bureaus, the offices of attorneys general, etc., are logged by a secretary in the consumer services department. They are then routed to a consumer services team supervisor for research and handling. A personal letter of reply is prepared. Letters of this nature are reviewed by the department manager and are signed and mailed under his or her direct supervision. All copies of correspondence of this nature are filed for future reference.

It is also extremely important that any letter which is directed to the fulfillment company but which relates to the product be forwarded immedi-ately to the client company so that it can begin follow-up. This allows such an inquiry to bypass the regular mail-handling procedures and results in speedier communication with a dissatisfied consumer.

MAILING PROCEDURES

The delivery costs involved in a promotion program represent a major financial obligation to the company sponsoring the promotion, and thus fulfillment companies tend to standardize mailing procedures as much as possible. The procedures cover the mailing of coupons, refunds, premiums, records, books, etc. Generally, in order to reduce costs to its clients, the fulfillment company, through the use of computer technology, has programs for sorting mail according to how it will be delivered. Following is an overview of mailing procedures.

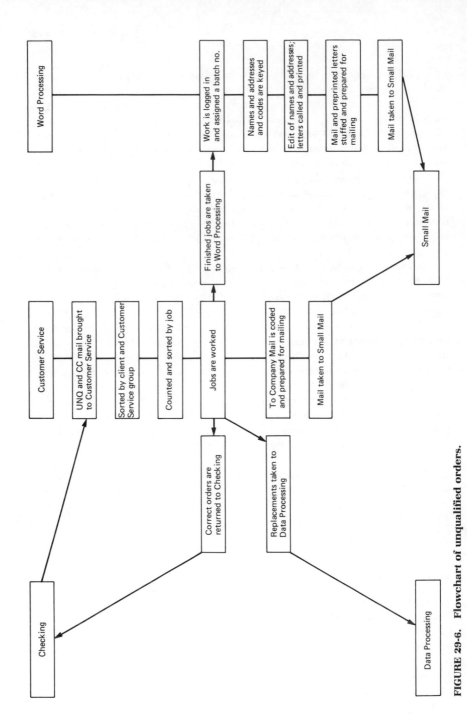

FIGURE 29-6. Flowchart of unqualified orders.

First-Class Mail. First-class mail should be used for all consumer correspondence or when specified by the client company.

Third-Class Mail. Third-class mail should be used for all merchandise and printed materials when rapid receipt is not a critical factor. Third-class bulk-rate mail should be used for premium items weighing 16 ounces or less and when the shipment consists of more than 200 items or weighs more than 50 pounds and the items are sorted by zip code; for coupons and refunds, unless the client company specifies otherwise; and for books that include advertising but do not weigh more than 16 ounces.

The only time regular third-class mail is used is when the volume requirements for third-class bulk-rate mail cannot be met. Regular third-class mail should be used for test mailings of premiums and books or records if they do not weigh more than 16 ounces.

Date:

Dear Consumer:

Thank you very much for your recent submission to one of our offers. Unfortunately, your request is being returned to you because the materials submitted do not meet the requirements of the offer for the reason(s) below.

We regret having to return your request, but in fairness to our customers who have sent in the proper material, we must ask for strict adherence to the terms of the offer. We hope you will continue to participate in future offers.

code: Maple Plain, MN 55348

MONEY	PROOF OF PURCHASE
01 ☐ No money received. Should be $	11 ☐ No proof(s) of purchase enclosed.
02 ☐ Not enough money. Should be $	12 ☐ Wrong proof(s) of purchase.
04 ☐ Check or money order not signed/dated.	13 ☐ Short proof(s) of purchase.
09 ☐ Check or money order made out to wrong	15 ☐ No Order Form enclosed.
company.	16 ☐ No Sales Slip enclosed.
☐ Other:	19 ☐ Original Order Form required. (No photos accepted)
	23 ☐ Name required.

IF YOUR REQUEST WAS RETURNED FOR ANY OF THE ABOVE REASONS, PLEASE CHECK THE REQUIREMENTS OF THE OFFER AND RESUBMIT IN THE PROPER MANNER. ENCLOSE THIS FORM WITH YOUR RESUBMISSION TO THE ABOVE ADDRESS WITHIN 30 DAYS OF THE DATE OF THIS NOTICE.

DO NOT RESUBMIT YOUR REQUEST IF IT HAS BEEN RETURNED FOR ANY OF THE FOLLOWING REASONS:

21 ☐ Valid in U.S. only.	31 ☐ Order Serviced. Over remittance
22 ☐ Duplicate request. Offer is limited to	enclosed.
One per family or address.	36 ☐ Offer Expired.
25 ☐ Not our offer.	☐ Other:

FIGURE 29-7. A form letter used to reply to consumers.

Dear Consumer:

Thank you very much for your order for the Colorsilk Refund Offer. Unfortunately, we are unable to service your request for the reason(s) checked below:

_____ There are no proofs of purchase enclosed with your request. Please check the requirements for the exact proofs of purchase needed.

_____ One or more of the proofs of purchase enclosed is not correct. Please check the listed requirements for the correct proofs of purchase.

_____ There are not enough proofs of purchase enclosed. Please check the requirements.

_____ One or more of the proofs of purchase enclosed is not from a Revlon product. Please check the requirements for the brand names from which proofs are required.

_____ One of your requests is being processed and will arrive in the near future. As is the case with most of our offers, this one is limited to one request per name or address as stated on our advertising for the promotion. Therefore, your extra proofs of purchase are enclosed.

_____ This offer requires a complete name and address for delivery and your name is either missing or not readable on your request.

_____ This offer is restricted to the 50 United States. Therefore, we are returning your order to you.

_____ Because this offer has expired, we are returning your request. The interest which prompted your writing is sincerely appreciated.

_____ Other:

To avoid a possible misunderstanding, the requirements of the Colorsilk $2.50 Refund II Offer are:

"Send a salon formula Colorsilk boxtop plus a cash register tape circling the Colorsilk purchase price. Void where prohibited, taxed or restricted. Good only in U.S.A. Offer expires August 31, 1982. Limited, one per household or address."

If you wish to resubmit, according to the requirements of this offer, we will be happy to process your order. Please note: If this offer has expired, this letter serves as authorization to resubmit. However, it is important to mail your corrected order, along with this letter, to the *new* address given below.

Thank you very much for your interest in Revlon products.

> Colorsilk
> Department 081
> P.O. Box 9047
> Maple Plain, MN 55348

047-081

FIGURE 29-8. A form letter used to reply to consumers.

047-081

Dear Consumer:

Thank you very much for your order for the Free Minute Maid® Apple Juice Offer. Unfortunately, we are unable to service your request for the reason(s) checked below:

_____ The required original certificate is not enclosed.

_____ There are no or not enough proofs of purchase enclosed with your request. Please check the requirements below for the exact proofs of purchase needed.

_____ One or more of the proofs of purchase enclosed is not from Minute Maid Frozen Concentrated Apple Juice.

_____ This offer requires a complete name and address for delivery and your name is either missing or not readable on your request.

_____ One of your requests is being processed and will arrive in the near future. As is the case with most of our offers, this one is limited to one request per name or address as stated on our advertising for the promotion. Therefore, your extra proofs of purchase are enclosed.

_____ This offer is restricted to the 50 United States and Puerto Rico due to the difficulties involved in sending merchandise into other countries. Therefore, we are returning your order to you.

_____ Other:

To avoid a possible misunderstanding, the requirements of the Free Minute Maid Apple Juice Offer are:

"Send certificate and three (3) plastic opening strips from any size can of Minute Maid Apple Juice. Please allow 6 weeks for processing. Offer good in U.S.A. only. One free coupon per family per address. Void where taxed, prohibited or otherwise regulated. Offers submitted without the form or by clubs, organizations, etc. not accepted. Facsimiles of the order form will not be honored. Mail strips per postal regulations. Offer expires October 15, 1982."

If you wish to resubmit, according to the requirements of this offer, we will be happy to process your order. Please note: If this offer has expired, this letter serves as authorization to resubmit. However, it is important to mail your corrected order, along with this letter, to the *new* address given below.

Thank you very much for your interest in Coca-Cola Company Food Division products.

> Free Minute Maid Apple Juice
> Dept. 076
> P.O. Box 9104
> Maple Plain, MN 55348

104-076
"Minute Maid" is a registered trademark of the Coca-Cola Company.

FIGURE 29-9. A form letter used to reply to consumers.

Fourth-Class Book-Rate Mail. All records and books which weigh more than 16 ounces and which do not contain advertising material should be mailed under this rate classification.

Parcel Post (U.S. Mail) and UPS. Whenever possible, items weighing more than 16 ounces should be shipped via UPS, as opposed to parcel post, because UPS provides automatic insurance coverage of $100. In addition, any item can be verified for delivery, which is not possible using parcel post.

Most major fulfillment companies provide optimum sorting of mail in order to realize postage savings for their clients. The promotion service manager and the marketing director of a company that is launching a promotion must investigate the fulfillment company carefully to be certain that it can provide savings in postage and UPS charges and that it has the capability of routing drop shipments and truck shipments.

Truck Shipments. All truck shipments of bulk inventory must be properly routed, and a copy of the bill of lading should be forwarded so that both the parties receiving the shipments and the client company are aware that the merchandise has been shipped as requested.

FEDERAL TRADE COMMISSION RULING

Promotion fulfillment programs are subject to the same Federal Trade Commission (FTC) ruling that covers mail-order sales in which the consumer is required to submit cash, a check, or a money order. This ruling went into effect on February 2, 1976. The major provisions of the ruling are:

- If a mail-order seller is unable to ship merchandise within the time stated in the offer (or, if no time is stated, within thirty days after receiving an order), the seller must notify the buyer of the delay and give the buyer an option to cancel the order.
- The buyer must be provided with a cost-free way to cancel an order, such as a postage-paid card or envelope.
- If the buyer so requests, the order must be canceled.
- If the buyer fails to respond to the delayed-delivery notice, it will be assumed that he or she has consented to an additional thirty-day delay.
- If there is a delay longer than thirty days, the buyer must expressly consent to the delay; otherwise, the buyer's money must be refunded.
- If the seller or the fulfillment company realizes that there will be a delay but cannot determine its length, the consumer can be asked to agree to an indefinite delay. However, any customer agreeing to such a delay can later request a refund.

- Sellers of mail-order merchandise must have a reasonable basis for claims they make about shipping time.

This FTC ruling is presented in more detail in Figure 29-10. Obviously, if insufficient inventories of merchandise are ordered initially for promotions which require payment on the part of the consumer, it will be necessary to offer options or to give refunds.

In the event that out-of-stock conditions or problems having to do with quality occur, the fulfillment company must act quickly to restock the merchandise or solve the problems. It must identify problems before processing requests for offers which require a payment on the part of the consumer. The fulfillment company will check the inventory in such situations to determine whether there is sufficient merchandise to fill the requests to be processed. When there is not sufficient merchandise, the processing is accomplished by retaining the proof of purchase submitted, along with the order. In the event that a refund is requested or required by the FTC ruling, the fulfillment company retrieves the consumer's proof of purchase and returns it along with the refund check.

When the out-of-stock condition is first recognized, the fulfillment company should immediately notify the client company by telephone so that additional inventories may be ordered, and a delivery date established. This delivery date will determine the type of option that is offered to the consumer. Delay forms will be prepared by computer and mailed after determination of the option offer.

CONSUMER OPTION OFFERS

If shipment cannot be made within thirty days after receipt of the consumer's request and if the revised shipping date is no more than thirty additional days away, the fulfillment company must:

- Offer the consumer the option to consent to a delay or cancel the order and receive a refund. (See Figure 29-11.) A postage-paid card must be provided for the consumer's response.
- Inform the consumer that if no response is received, it will be assumed that the consumer consented to the delay.

If the revised shipping date is more than an additional thirty days away, the fulfillment company must:

- Offer the consumer the option to consent to a delay or cancel the order and receive a refund. A postage-paid card must be provided for the consumer's response.
- Inform the consumer that expressed consent for the delay must be received.

FIGURE 29-10. The FTC ruling governing mail-order sales.

In connection with mail-order sales it constitutes an unfair method of competition and an unfair or deceptive act and practice for a seller:

(a) (1) To solicit an order unless reasonably sure shipment can be made
  (i) Within the time stated or
  (ii) Within 30 days of receipt of order

(b) (1) Where seller is unable to ship within applicable time [(a)(1)] to fail to offer an option to consent to a delay or cancel and receive a refund. Offer to be made within reasonable time but no later than applicable time [(a)(1)].
  (i) Offer should fully inform buyer regarding right to cancel and obtain a prompt refund, and shall provide a definite revised shipping date. If no reasonable basis for a definite revised shipping date, the notice shall inform the buyer that seller is unable to make any representation regarding the length of the delay.
  (ii) Where the definite revised shipping date is 30 days or less later than the applicable time [(a)(1)] the offer shall inform the buyer that unless he specifically cancels the order prior to shipment and prior to the revised shipping date it will be considered that he has consented to the delay.
  (iii) Where the definite revised shipping date is 30 days later than the applicable time [(a)(1)] or where the seller is unable to provide a revised shipping date the offer should inform the buyer that his order will automatically be cancelled unless:
    A) The order has been shipped within 30 days of the applicable time and notification has not been received cancelling the order or
    B) The buyer has consented to the delay. Where the seller is unable to make any representation as to the length of the delay, the buyer shall be expressly informed that he has a continuing right to cancel his order at any time after the applicable time, prior to actual shipment.
  (iv) A seller who provides a definite revised shipping date may request, simultaneously with or at any time subsequent to the offer of an option, the buyer's consent to a further unanticipated delay beyond the revised shipping date. The buyer shall be expressly informed that should he consent to an indefinite delay he has a continuing right to cancel his order at any time after the definite revised shipping date, prior to actual shipment.

(2) Where the seller is unable to ship merchandise on or before the definite revised shipping date to fail to offer a renewed option either to consent to a further delay or cancel and receive a refund. Offer to be made within a reasonable time, but no later than the definite revised shipping date. Where the seller has already obtained the buyer's consent to a further unanticipated delay [(b)(1)(iv)] until a specific date beyond the definite revised shipping date or to a further delay until a specific date beyond the definite revised shipping date, that date shall supersede the definite revised shipping date.
  (i) Offer of renewed option shall provide the buyer with a new definite revised

shipping date. If no reasonable basis for a new definite revised shipping date, the notice shall inform the buyer that he is unable to make any representation regarding the length of the delay.

(ii) The offer of a renewed option shall inform the buyer that unless the seller receives notification consenting to the further delay, prior to the expiration of the old definite revised shipping date or any date superseding the old definite revised shipping date, the order will be deemed to be cancelled if the seller is in fact unable to ship prior to the old definite revised shipping date or any date superseding the old definite revised shipping date. The notice shall inform the buyer that he has a continuing right to cancel the order.

(iii) This paragraph will not apply where a seller has previously obtained consent to an indefinite extension beyond the first revised shipping date.

(3) The buyer must be provided with adequate means, at the seller's expense, to exercise any of the options.

A seller, when he is unable to make shipment, may decide to consider the order cancelled and provide the buyer with a notice of the decision and a prompt refund within a reasonable time after he becomes aware of his inability to ship.

(a) To fail to deem an order cancelled and make a prompt refund when:

(1) The seller receives notification of cancellation prior to the time of shipment.

(2) Where consent to a delay is required and has not been received.

(3) The seller has notified the buyer of his decision to cancel the order.

(4) The seller fails to offer the required option and has not shipped the merchandise within the applicable time.

(d) To fail to have records or other documentary proof establishing the use of systems and procedures which assure compliance, in the ordinary course of business, with any requirement of paragraphs (b) or (a).

If no response is received, it will be assumed that the order has been canceled, and a refund will be made.

- Inform the consumer that if the delay is consented to, the consumer still has the right to cancel the order at any time prior to actual shipment.

If there is no reasonable basis for a revised shipping date, the fulfillment company must:

- So inform the consumer and offer the option to consent to a delay or receive a refund. A postage-paid card must be provided for the consumer's response.
- Inform the consumer that unless the order has been shipped within thirty days, expressed consent for the delay must be received. If no response is received, it will be assumed that the order has been canceled, and a refund will be made.
- Inform the consumer that if the delay is consented to, the consumer may still cancel the order at any time prior to actual shipment.

FIGURE 29-11.   A sample thirty-day-delay notice.

THE MAPLE PLAIN COMPANY INC.
ONE INDUSTRIAL DRIVE
MAPLE PLAIN, MINNESOTA 55359

IMPORTANT
PREMIUM DELAY NOTICE
—READ CAREFULLY—

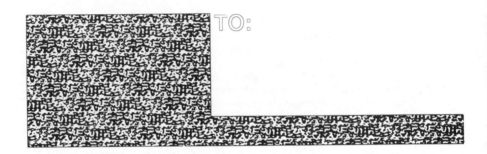

Dear Customer,

A new regulation has recently been established requiring companies that sell merchandise through the mail to advise their customers if for any reason, they are unable to ship merchandise within the time stated in the offer or if no time is stated, within 30 days after receiving a customer's order. It further states that we must provide you, our customer, with a postage paid device enabling you to consent to a delay in the processing and shipping of your order or to request a refund.

There are many other technical parts of the regulation but the purpose of the business reply post card is to allow you to inform us how you wish us to handle your premium order.

We are sorry that the availability of merchandise has occasioned the necessity of corresponding with you about your order. However, we would appreciate your promptly returning the business reply post card which indicates how we are to handle your order.

THE MAPLE PLAIN COMPANY, INC.

Dear Customer,

We appreciate your interest in responding to our offer indicated below, but regret to have to advise you that there will be a delay in the shipment of your order.

We are trying to solve this problem as quickly as possible, and expect to be able to ship your order (on the date indicated below). You may either consent to this delay or you may cancel your order and receive a prompt refund.

You may consent to this delay by detaching and mailing the business reply postage paid post card. If we have not received this post card and the merchandise is not available by the cancellation date shown below, your order will automatically be considered cancelled, and a refund will be mailed to you. If we find that we are able to ship your merchandise prior to the date indicated below, and we have not received any correspondence from you, we will, of course, ship your merchandise.

If you consent to the delay and decide at a later date that you do not wish to wait any longer, please let us know, and we will cancel your order.

NOTE: If necessary to write us at a later date enclose this form with your letter.

THE MAPLE PLAIN COMPANY, INC.

CANCELLATION DATE
ANTICIPATED SHIP DATE
ITEM ORDERED

CODE:

DEAR MAPLE PLAIN COMPANY,

PLEASE SHIP MY ORDER FOR THE PREMIUM MERCHANDISE SHOWN BELOW.

CHECK ONE
☐ BY THE DATE SHOWN BELOW

☐ WHENEVER POSSIBLE

I UNDERSTAND THAT IF AT A LATER DATE I DO NOT WISH TO WAIT ANY LONGER FOR MY ORDER, I CAN LET YOU KNOW AND THEN CANCEL IT.

DATE

SIGNATURE

CANCELLATION DATE
ANTICIPATED SHIP DATE
ITEM ORDERED

CODE:

FIGURE 29-11. (Cont.)

POSTAGE
WILL BE PAID
BY
ADDRESSEE

NO
POSTAGE STAMP
NECESSARY
IF MAILED IN THE
UNITED STATES

BUSINESS REPLY MAIL
FIRST CLASS PERMIT NO. 2   MAPLE PLAIN, MINN.

THE MAPLE PLAIN COMPANY, INC.

ONE INDUSTRIAL STREET

MAPLE PLAIN, MINN. 55359

Record keeping for programs which fall within the FTC ruling is extremely important because fines can be levied by that agency. The fulfillment company must prepare a computerized listing by promotion of the names and addresses of all consumers who have been sent an offer option. This listing should be maintained at the fulfillment company until all consumers have been sent either a refund or the merchandise. The appropriate information—refund or merchandise—should be indicated on the listing, and a copy should be sent to the consumer products manager of the company originating the promotion.

In order to be in a position to respond promptly to consumers when an offer option or refund is required, the fulfillment company must have sufficient forms on hand to handle requests.

SELECTION OF A FULFILLMENT COMPANY

The selection of a fulfillment company is of extreme importance and should be done very carefully. There are several ways of selecting a fulfillment company. One is to contact other business organizations that have used a particular fulfillment company to ascertain whether they were completely satisfied with the company's work.

The promotion managers of the company seeking fulfillment services should visit at least three fulfillment companies. During the visit to a fulfillment company, many questions must be asked in order to make a proper evaluation. Some of these are discussed below.

Experience. How long has the company been in business? Who are some of its major clients? This information will provide the opportunity to call several existing clients to determine their degree of satisfaction with the fulfillment company. When evaluating another company's experience, it is important to speak with management people at the executive level as well as with those who work in staff positions. These interviews will clearly indicate the expertise of first-level management and second-level supervisors.

Financial Strength. Does the company have the financial strength to perform the services? If something were to go awry with a program, it is necessary to ascertain that the company would have the financial stability and adequate working capital to carry through the contract. In discussing the company's financial situation, be certain to find out whether it has adequate insurance coverage.

Systems and Procedures. Does the company use the proper systems and procedures? A review of company systems and procedures should be made, and documentation for them requested. Ask to see a flowchart of the processing methods and procedures.

Security Systems. Does the company have the proper security systems in place in order to prevent losses?

Plant Capacity and Location. Does the company have adequate storage space and mailing area to handle the promotion? The location of the facility as it relates to adequacy of a good labor force, postal rates, UPS rates, and trucking and rail facilities is also important.

Data Processing. Does the company have state-of-the-art data processing equipment and the necessary software resources? Is the software documented, and are the data processing tapes stored off the site to prevent any loss of data? It also should be determined whether there is a retrieval system allowing consumer requests to be retrieved up to six months after the program ends.

Equipment. Does the company have adequate equipment for material handling, storage, picking, packing, shipping, labeling, and automatic inserting?

Accounting and Billing. Are the accounting and billing departments able to perform the necessary reporting services, inventory control, and financial control of moneys received and disbursed?

Inventory Locator System and Consumer Services Department. Does the company have an inventory locator system? Is the company's consumer services department adequate and well trained in the handling of consumer complaints?

Turnaround Time. Does the company have tracking methods to follow a program completely, i.e., from the time the consumer's request is received to the time the premium or refund is mailed? If the consumer does not receive the refund or premium in the shortest period of time possible, the client company could lose a customer.

Bids

A company that is going to launch a promotion usually requests bids for fulfillment services from more than one company. The lowest bid is normally accepted. This can be a dangerous practice. If this bid is much lower than the other bids, the service could be inadequate. One must keep in mind that the company sponsoring the promotion has spent large sums of money for the promotional material, for the premium, and for advertising; when selecting a fulfillment company, why should it take a chance if only a few dollars per 1000 units are involved? The consumer's only contact with the promotion is through the fulfillment company, and the services rendered can make the difference between winning or losing many customers. Consumers get the best impression of the company sponsoring a promotion when their requests are fulfilled promptly and satisfactorily.

VIII Sales Promotion and the Law

The Funk & Wagnall's *Standard College Dictionary* defines *law* as "a rule of conduct recognized by custom or decreed by formal enactment, considered by a community, nation, or other authoritatively constituted group as binding upon its members."

What does this have to do with sales promotion? Well, the dictionary goes a little further, stating that law is also "the body of authoritatively established rules relating to a specified subject area, or activity subject to legal control"—which, in this case, is sales promotion.

Generally speaking, the statutes relating to sales promotion are part of the body of laws pertaining to business and, more specifically, part of the laws governing the marketing of products and the promotion of business.

Our economic system is based upon competition, which has been fostered and protected by the Congress and the U.S. Supreme Court. The first major legislation in this area was the Sherman Anti-Trust Act of 1890; it was followed by the Clayton Anti-Trust Act of 1914, the same year that the Federal Trade Commission (FTC) was established. These were followed by the Robinson-Patman Act and the Wheeler-Lea Amendment. Many of these statutes pertain to sales promotion.

Most laws involving sales promotion are enforced by the FTC. In addition, there are applicable state, municipal, and local laws which are administered by those jurisdictions. At the end of December 1982 the attorney general of New York State sued Eastern Airlines and Eastman Kodak for deceptive advertising of a joint sales promotion. No action was taken against a similar promotion by Delta Airlines and Poloroid.

While commercial bribery is in no way related to sales promotion, some may associate it with the subject because of its similarity, however remote, to business gifts, trade allowances, push money, and other legitimate sales promotion practices. In other parts of the world, commercial bribery, as defined in the United States, has for years been an accepted way of life and the means of doing business. And some large American firms have stooped to the practice in order to compete with foreign corporations. The case involving the Lockheed Aircraft Co. made headlines for months. It toppled governments in Japan and Italy, and its tentacles reached into the pockets of Prince Bernhardt, husband of the former Queen of the Netherlands.

Toward the end of the last decade two other large American companies announced that they, too, had been involved in the practice. Westinghouse Electric Corp. pleaded guilty to charges that it had neglected to disclose payments of $332,000 to an official of a foreign government. McDonnell Douglas Corp., another aircraft manufacturer, admitted that it had made foreign payments related to airplane sales, in the amount of about $18 million, in more than a dozen countries. The company spokesman said that some of the money had gone to foreign government officials. Violations of the Foreign Corrupt Practices Act, enacted in 1978, come under the jurisdiction of the U.S. Department of Justice, the Securities and Exchange Commission, and the FTC, as well as the foreign government involved. Within the United States, commercial bribery comes under the jurisdiction of the FTC.

Most laws involving sales promotion, however, are covered by the Robinson-Patman Act but are enforced by the FTC. Sweepstakes, contests, and games come under the aegis of the FTC as well, and they are also covered by state and local statutes.

By the same token, even a small, seemingly harmless sales promotion can run afoul of the law. Many years ago a manufacturer of ice-cream popsicles placed special marks on the sticks of a limited number of his products. This mark indicated that the purchaser had won a prize, usually, a free popsicle. The mark was hidden by the ice cream and was exposed only after the ice cream had been eaten. This promotion, catering principally to children, was declared to be an illegal lottery by the courts, and the company was forced to discontinue the practice.

30

The Laws Affecting Marketing and Promotions

MYER S. TULKOFF, J.D.

Attorney, AT&T Technologies, Inc.; Former Assistant Regional Director, New York Office, Federal Trade Commission

The necessarily brief treatment given here to the laws affecting marketing will not make anyone a legal expert. Many volumes have been written on the laws affecting business, not to mention antitrust law, which is a major subject itself. This chapter is intended only to alert marketing people to those areas—legal pitfalls, if you will—in which company counsel should be consulted. Many legal decisions and judgments turn upon fine or vague lines of distinction, depending on the facts of the particular case. Even experts in business law, including the judiciary, often disagree, and cases are constantly evolving which promulgate new interpretations of the law. The reader might well be mindful of the age-old pronouncement that "a little knowledge is a dangerous thing." Some of the topics treated in this chapter have antitrust implications. It has been observed that no other field of law approaches antitrust law in terms of proliferation of writing on the subject.[1]

This chapter deals primarily with federal requirements, that is, laws and regulations enforced by the federal government. No attempt is made to cover, even in summary fashion, state and local requirements. All businesses, however, must take into consideration not only federal laws and regulations but also those of the states in which they are located or do business. This requires consultation with counsel familiar with the statutory enactments pertaining to business in the various states. While federal laws generally preempt state laws where a conflict exists, in many situations a business must meet both federal and state requirements.

SUPPLIERS' PROMOTIONAL PROGRAMS FOR THEIR CUSTOMERS: EQUALITY OF TREATMENT UNDER THE ROBINSON-PATMAN ACT

Suppliers, whether they are manufacturers or distributors, must be cognizant of the requirements of the Robinson-Patman Act with respect to any promotional programs they set up for their customers in the vertical distribution system, namely, their wholesalers or retailers and dealers.[2] The Robinson-Patman Act (which is Section 2 of the Clayton Act) is enforced by the Federal Trade Commission (FTC).[3] It is applicable to so-called services and allowances provided by a supplier to its customers in connection with the latters' resale of the supplier's product. Section 2(d) applies to those services or allowances which are provided by the customer for the supplier and for which the supplier pays or shares the cost. Section 2(e) applies to services and allowances provided to such customers and paid for by the supplier. Examples are advertising (including cooperative advertising), handbills, window and floor displays, demonstrators and demonstrations, catalogs, display materials, special packaging, prizes or merchandise offered in promotional contests, and push money (PMs).

In general, we can say that compliance with the Robinson-Patman Act is necessary if the supplier sells identical products or goods of like grade and quality across state lines (interstate commerce) to competing customers, at or about the same time, and if the supplier provides any of the services or allowances mentioned above to these competing customers. (See Figure 30-1.)

Some Examples

Under the Robinson-Patman Act, the primary rule is that any such promotional benefits must be offered to all competing customers on proportionally equal terms. For example, assume that the Acme Company, an appliance manufacturer, wants to promote its products in Philadelphia by sharing the advertising cost with department store A. It offers to pay 50 percent of the advertising cost if the department store will advertise Acme products in local newspapers. There are other retailers in Philadelphia who are purchasing the same appliances from Acme and who compete with department store A. The Robinson-Patman Act requires that Acme offer the same promotion on proportionally equal terms to *all* competing dealers in the Philadelphia area.

Acme also wants to motivate department store A's salespeople to sell Acme products by offering them PMs; it will give each salesperson $5 for every big-ticket appliance sold. Under the provisions of the act, Acme must offer similar PMs to the salespeople of competing dealers.

Continuing our example, the Acme Company decides to give cooperative advertising allowances to a major department store in the Boston area and offers to pay for 50 percent of the cost of newspaper advertising up to 3 percent of the customers' purchases. Acme also offers this program to its other, smaller customers in Boston. The company knows that the purchases of the smaller customers are too small for them to obtain a sufficient accrual in advertising allowances to enable them to engage in newspaper advertising in Boston. Under the requirements of the Robinson-Patman Act, Acme must offer these smaller customers alternative forms of promotional benefits that will in fact fill their needs. These may be in the form of counter displays, mailing pieces, window displays, or similar promotional materials.

As another example, assume that the Beauty Cosmetics Company, a cosmetics manufacturer, decides to promote its line of products by furnishing demonstrator models to its major department-store customers in Atlanta. The

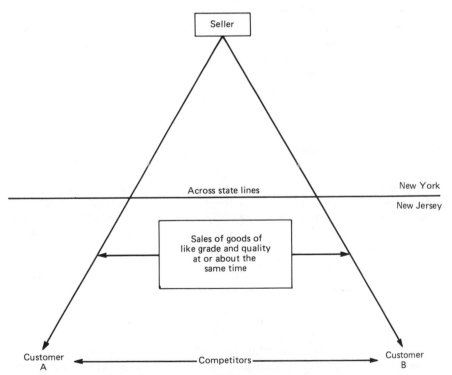

FIGURE 30-1.   A depiction of factors that invoke requirement, under the Robinson-Patman Act, of availability of promotional programs on proportionally equal terms.

models will spend a week at each department store behind the cosmetics counters demonstrating Beauty's products to prospective customers. Beauty also sells its products to small competing boutiques in Atlanta, for which this type of promotion is not appropriate. According to the Robinson-Patman Act, Beauty must furnish these smaller customers with alternative forms of promotion, such as counter displays, promotional literature, and window displays.

The requirements of the act become more complex if the supplier sells direct to dealers as well as to distributors, who in turn sell to other dealers who compete with such direct purchasing dealers.[4] In such circumstances the supplier must offer promotional programs on proportionally equal terms to *all* dealers.

Continuing our example, the Beauty Cosmetics Company sells its line of products to both retailers and distributors. In the Atlanta area it sells to retailers A, B, C, and D. It also sells to distributor X. Distributor X in turn sells to retailers E, F, G, and H, who compete with retailers A, B, C, and D. Beauty embarks on a promotional program in which it will give cooperative advertising allowances to all its direct purchasing retailers (A, B, C, and D) and will pay 50 percent of their newspaper advertising costs up to 5 percent of their respective purchases from the seller. The Robinson-Patman Act requires that Beauty make the same promotional program available on proportionally equal terms to retailers E, F, G, and H.

Methods of Compliance

The methods of compliance with the Robinson-Patman Act described in the examples above are covered in the FTC's *Guides for Advertising Allowances and Other Merchandising Payments and Services*, which was issued May 29, 1969, and amended August 4, 1972. (Copies are obtained from the FTC.) The initial problem is to inform dealers purchasing through distributors of the availability of the promotional program, since the seller normally would not know who they are and would not have any contact with them. This required notification may be accomplished in several ways. One method is to disseminate some sort of written notification in the product packaging (inside or on the label). Another method is to publicize the program in a trade publication that is widely read by the retailers in the particular product market.

Of course, the distributor can be enlisted to handle such notification of its dealers, if it is willing to do so. The next problem is administering the program, that is, checking dealers' advertising performance by examining the newspaper advertisements and media bills. Finally, there is the matter of making disbursement of the seller's share of the cost. Here, again, the distributor can be utilized if it has no objection to becoming involved in these administrative details. If the distributor is not willing to become involved, the seller has no choice but to notify all retailers (purchasing through distributors) of the promotional program in the ways indicated.

As to administering the program, the seller will have to require such retailers to submit advertisement copies and media bills directly to it. Of course, the seller may wish to avoid such administrative details itself, in which case it can hire a third-party firm to check eligibility for reimbursement and to disburse advertising and promotional funds under the program. There are firms that offer such services.

BRIBES, PAYOFFS, BUSINESS GIFTS, AND "SPECIAL" PRICES

The term *commercial bribery*, as used by the FTC, applies

> ... to the practice of sellers of secretly paying money or making gifts to employees or agents to induce them to promote purchases by their own employers from the sellers offering the secret inducements. The vice of conduct labeled "commercial bribery," as related to unfair trade practices, is the advantage which one competitor secures over his fellow competitors by his secret and corrupt dealing with employees or agents of prospective purchasers. . . .[5]

A person who makes any payment which can be characterized as a bribe, payoff, or substantial business gift in order to "buy" business thus opens up a Pandora's box of potential legal problems—in both the domestic and the international business arenas. Sellers are well-advised to avoid such pitfalls and compete solely on price, quality, and service. On the federal level, multiple federal agencies may invoke enforcement action for unlawful payments by bringing criminal or civil actions against the offender who is discovered.

The FTC, for one, can bring a civil action pursuant to its broad mandate under Section 5 of the Federal Trade Commission Act, which prohibits unfair methods of competition in or affecting commerce.[6] Commercial bribery, payoffs, or substantial gifts to the officers or employees (the decision makers) of a potential customer, the purpose of which is to induce them to buy or to reward them for doing so, constitute the violation. Customers are supposed to buy on the basis of merit (price, quality, and service), and not because of payments by a seller who has a "deep pocket" and thus takes unfair advantage of competitors who sell only on the basis of merit.

Bribes and Payoffs Abroad

In recent years hundreds of domestic companies have made significant payments, in the millions of dollars, to foreign officials as bribes or payoffs to obtain business abroad. Legally, it is beside the point for American firms to contend that this is the "only way" to get business abroad. There have been significant developments in the legal arena to discourage and penalize such payments, which can subject a firm to tax implications, disclosure by the Securities and Exchange Commission (SEC), criminal prosecution, and even extradition to face prosecution by foreign governments, as well as to a charge by the FTC that the firm engaged in unfair competition.[7]

The Foreign Corrupt Practices Act, which became law at the end of 1977, makes it a criminal offense for a corporation to bribe a foreign government official or an official of a political party for the purpose of gaining or retaining business in a foreign country.[8]

The act is enforced by both the SEC and the Department of Justice, and it provides for civil and criminal penalties. (Under criminal sanctions a corporation can be fined up to $1 million; an individual officer can be fined up to $10,000 and sentenced to five years in prison.) Business firms registered with the SEC are under the jurisdiction of that agency for purposes of enforcing the act, while the Department of Justice is responsible for all firms not subject to SEC jurisdiction.

According to the Foreign Corrupt Practices Act, it is a criminal offense for a corporation or its employees to "corruptly" influence foreign officials. The law is applicable to any payment when there is reason to believe that even part of it will be turned over to a foreign official. Therefore, there is risk even if an independent agent of the seller pays over all or part of its sales commission to an official with the knowledge of the seller. At this writing there is insufficient case precedent, so it is not known what will be deemed "knowledge" on the part of the corporation. The corporation that does business abroad should institute safeguards by keeping proper records (required by the new law anyway) and by making certain that it knows the reputation of the foreign agent with whom it does business.

Special Prices

Special or lower sales prices or discounts to a favored customer may under certain circumstances cause the FTC to bring an action against the supplier under Section 2(a) of the Robinson-Patman Act, which prohibits price discrimination.[9] Special prices can also result in a lawsuit by an "unfavored" customer for treble damages. This provision applies only to domestic sales.

The following would constitute a violation: sales of goods of like grade and quality across state lines to competing customers, at or about the same time but at different prices, with the result that the competitive position of the unfavored customer is damaged.

As an example, assume that the Jones Company manufactures, sells, and ships widgets throughout a multistate area. Its current price is $100 per dozen. The company is located in New York City and sells to five dealers in New

Jersey, who compete with one another. Jones decides to favor a large dealer, dealer A, by lowering the price to $90, or by granting a "special" discount of $10 per dozen. Dealers B, C, D, and E are charged the higher $100 price. As a result, either they suffer competitive injury, or such injury is highly probable, while dealer A gains a competitive advantage. The Jones Company may be charged with a violation of Section 2(a) of the Robinson-Patman Act.

It is important to note that the customer who is given a special price or discount may also violate Section 2(f) of the act by accepting the lower price.[10] Thus, dealer A in our example may be vulnerable. (This can be advanced as a reason for refusing a customer who seeks special prices or discounts that are not available to the customer's competitors.)

It should be noted, however, that the Robinson-Patman Act does provide two defenses to a charge of price discrimination: (1) that the lower price was granted only to meet the supplier's competition and (2) that the lower price was justified as a result of a savings to the supplier in terms of sales, delivery, or manufacturing costs—due to a quantity purchase by the customer—and that the lower price merely reflected this savings.[11]

For example, the Jones Company also sells widgets to three retailers in Philadelphia. Jones's current price is $100 per dozen. The Smith Company, Jones's competitor, approaches one of Jones's customers and offers to sell widgets to that customer for $90 per unit. Jones learns of the competing offer and believes that it will lose the customer to the Smith Company as a result. Jones may lower its price to that customer to $90 to meet Smith's competitive offer while continuing to charge $100 to others.

The Meeting-Competition Defense. In order to establish the meeting-competition defense as a valid basis for giving a lower price to a purchaser, several requirements must be met.

1. The seller may meet *but not beat* the competitor's price. Therefore, in the above example, Jones may meet Smith's price of $90 but may not go below it, e.g., to $85.

2. The lower competitive prices met must be actually available to the seller's customers individually or areawide. In the example above, if the Smith Company subsequently withdraws its offer to sell widgets to Jones's customer or to customers in that marketing area for $90 per dozen, Jones cannot continue to sell to that or other customers for $90 since the competitive necessity no longer exists.

3. The seller must make its best "good faith" effort to ascertain the identity of the competitor and the precise amount of the competitive price it must meet. Preferably this will be in the form of a written offer, price list, etc., given by the competitor to the seller's customer, if the customer is willing to furnish such proof. If the customer is not willing to, then the seller's salesperson should submit a salesperson's call report or similar written evidence concerning the competitive offer. Such items of proof should be retained by the seller in the event of an FTC investigation into price discrimination or in the event of a civil lawsuit by a nonfavored customer for treble damages.

The Cost-Justification Defense. Offering a lower price to one of several competing customers may also be legally justified and defended on the basis that the lower price merely makes due allowance for the seller's lower cost of manufacturing, sales, or delivery, which was the result of that customer's quantity purchases. The most common problem sellers have in trying to establish the cost-justification defense is that it was not worked out in advance. In many instances, sellers who are charged with price discrimination will attempt to establish retroactively that a lower price to a favored customer was cost-justified, only to discover that the price difference exceeded any cost savings to them. This is tantamount to closing the barn door after the horse has escaped. Seldom do sellers succeed in ex post facto establishment of this defense.

In the case of sales or delivery costs, it may be relatively easy to determine—in advance—that a customer's quantity purchases will afford the seller a given amount of savings in freight or sales costs. These savings may be passed on to the customer in the form of a lower price.

For example, assume that a seller has three customers in St. Louis: customers A, B, and C. Customer A always buys in truckload quantities, while customers B and C buy in less-than-truckload quantities. The seller does not charge for delivery to the customers' premises. Truckload freight charges are less than less-than-truckload freight charges by $0.10 per case. The seller may lower the price to customer A by $0.10 per case, reflecting this savings.

Continuing with this example, the seller utilizes a salesperson to call on customers in St. Louis. The salesperson makes weekly calls on customers B and C since they normally purchase in small quantities. Since customer A purchases in truckload quantities, the salesperson needs to visit this customer only once per month. The seller may pass on the resulting savings in sales expenses to customer A.

Savings in manufacturing costs also may be passed on to a customer in the form of a lower price to the extent that the savings can be directly attributed to the quantity purchased by, and manufactured for, that customer.

A word of caution. Both the meeting-competition and the cost-justification defenses are very technical. A seller is well-advised to consult counsel in connection with any pricing questions or problems, including volume or quantity discounts.

PMs

The Code of Federal Regulations makes the payment of PMs to customers' salespeople an unfair trade practice under certain circumstances.[12]

1. When the payment is made without the knowledge and consent of the salesperson's employer
2. When the payment is dependent on a lottery
3. When the payment is made to "unduly and intentionally" hamper the sales of a competitor's products
4. When the effect of the payment may be to substantially lessen competition or create a monopoly
5. When such a payment does not comply with the requirements of the Robinson-Patman Act (discussed above)

FALSE ADVERTISING OF SAVINGS AND BARGAINS: OFFERING "SOMETHING FOR NOTHING"

Offering "free" merchandise and offering merchandise at special prices are promotional devices frequently used to attract customers. Everyone loves a bargain, and thus it is not surprising that offering mechandise free or at a reduced price has been utilized as a marketing tool. Unfortunately, however, many sellers have exploited consumers' love of a bargain by representing an offer as a bargain when in fact it is not. The FTC has been very active over the years in challenging advertising and promotional practices that deceive customers into believing they are getting a bargain when such is not the case. This FTC activity has taken the form of cases, guides, and regulations.

The language and terms used in such advertising usually include, for example, *free*; *buy one—get one free*; *two-for-one sale*; *50 percent off with purchase of two*; *one-half off*; *special price*; and *comparable value*.

Use of the Word *Free* and Similar Representations. An FTC guide covers the use of the word *free* and similar representations.[13] According to this FTC guide, if an item is represented as free with the purchase of another item, the customer must pay nothing for the free item and no more than the regular price for the purchased item. Furthermore, the seller must not immediately recover the cost of the free item by marking up the price of the item which must be purchased. In other words, the cost of the free item cannot be hidden in the cost of the purchased item.

Regular price is defined as the price at which the seller of the product has sold it in the marketplace or trade area in which the free offer is made, in the regular course of business and for a reasonable period of time before making the free offer, such as thirty days. The FTC deems it improper to use *regular price* or *free* if no substantial sales have been made.

Also, where the term *free* is used, any special conditions or obligations on the part of the consumer should appear in close conjunction with the offer of the free merchandise.

Introductory Offers. According to the FTC guide, the term *free* should not be used in connection with the introduction of a new product or service offered for sale at a specified price unless the seller expects to discontinue the free offer after a limited time and then to start selling the product or service at the same price at which it was promoted with the free offer.

Cents-off and Related Offers. Regulations issued by the FTC in 1972 cover cents-off offers on certain packaged consumer products, such as soaps and detergents, in accordance with the Fair Packaging and Labeling Act.[14] Similar regulations covering food, drugs, and cosmetics are issued by the Food and Drug Administration.

Deceptive Pricing. The FTC has also published guides concerning deceptive pricing; these cover a variety of the forms of such advertising.[15]

LOTTERIES, SWEEPSTAKES, CONTESTS, AND GAMES

What distinguishes lotteries from sweepstakes and games? In the case of a lottery, consideration (payment) is required, there is a distribution of awards or prizes, and the prizes or awards are given out on the basis of chance. In the case of a game or a sweepstakes, consideration is not required; that is, the consumer does not have to make a purchase in order to participate. While lotteries, games, and sweepstakes are based on chance, a game or a sweepstakes differs from a lottery in that no purchase is required.

Contests are often judged on the basis of skill or ability rather than chance. In such cases the "best" entry wins. Since chance is not a factor, consideration can be required. For this reason, contests, games, and sweepstakes are generally deemed to be legal, while lotteries are not. However, since even contests, games, and sweepstakes are unlawful in a few jurisdictions, promotional literature for these events should include such caveats as "Void where prohibited by law."

Lotteries. As long ago as 1934 the United States Supreme Court affirmed an FTC decision holding that the use or sale of lottery schemes or devices in connection with the marketing of products is an unfair method of competition and a deceptive practice.[16] Both the FTC and the courts have held lotteries to be contrary to public policy. In numerous instances, the FTC has prohibited suppliers from selling punchboards and similar lottery devices which involve selling merchandise to the public through games of chance.[17]

Games. In 1969 the FTC issued a trade regulation rule specifically covering games of chance in the food retailing and gasoline industries.[18] While this rule is limited to supermarket chains and the gasoline retailing industry, nevertheless it establishes a standard by which such games in other industries may well be measured or judged as to legality by the FTC. The rule declares the following to be unfair and deceptive:

1. Misrepresenting a participant's chances of winning a prize
2. Making reference to prizes without disclosing:
    a. The exact number of prizes to be awarded in each category and the odds of winning each prize
    b. The geographic area covered by the game (e.g., whether it is being conducted nationwide or only in the New York City metropolitan area)
    c. The total number of retail outlets participating in the game and its scheduled termination date
3. Failing to mix, distribute, and disburse all game pieces solely on a random basis throughout the game program and in the geographic area in which the game is being conducted
4. Promoting, selling, or using any game which is capable of being solved or "broken," making it possible to preidentify game pieces

The rule also contains provisions for posting the names and addresses of winners at the conclusion of each game and for allowing a certain amount of time to elapse between games.

MAIL-ORDER MERCHANDISE: SHIPMENT-TIME REQUIREMENTS

An FTC trade regulation rule specifies time limitations on the delivery of merchandise purchased by mail. Basically, shipment by the seller must be made within thirty days of receipt of the order. If unforeseen circumstances make shipment within this time period impossible, customers must be given the opportunity to obtain an immediate refund, unless they wish to grant a specific extension of time to the seller. Mail-order sellers should be thoroughly familiar with the requirements of this rule, which was issued by the FTC as a result of numerous complaints by consumers concerning slow delivery and nondelivery of merchandise ordered by mail.[19]

DOOR-TO-DOOR SALES

An FTC trade regulation rule imposes certain cancellation requirements in connection with door-to-door sales involving transactions of $25 or more. Basically, this rule gives a buyer a three-day cooling-off period in which to cancel the transaction.[20]

SHIPMENT OF UNORDERED MERCHANDISE

The shipment of unordered merchandise for which payment is expected is prohibited by Section 3009 of the Postal Reorganization Act.[21] Exceptions are samples labeled as such and merchandise from charitable organizations; however, even in the latter case, payment cannot be required. Recipients may keep unordered merchandise and use or dispose of it as they please, without any obligation to pay. While this prohibition applies only to shipments made by mail, the FTC deems any such activity, regardless of how shipment is made, to be an unfair trade practice.[22]

WARRANTIES UNDER THE MAGNUSON-MOSS ACT

Sellers of merchandise are not required to offer a warranty to consumers. However, once a seller, whether it is the manufacturer or the retailer, undertakes to warrant a product, the requirements of the Magnuson-Moss Warranty Act are triggered.[23] The requirements of the act, as further defined by FTC implementing rules, are very technical and must be carefully studied. Only two types of warranties are prescribed: full and limited. The act prescribes what must be offered by the seller under a full warranty.

A significant ruling is the so-called lemon provision, which requires a seller giving full warranty to replace the purchased item or refund the purchase price if an excessive number of repairs are required. FTC rules prescribe what is deemed excessive.

MERCHANDISE CERTIFICATES AND COUPONS

FTC policy prescribes certain general requirements respecting the use of merchandise certificates, in-pack coupons, and similar promotional techniques. The redemption time for coupons or certificates should not be unreasonably short. The terms and conditions of the offer should be disclosed on the product package, e.g., whether the coupon or certificate is good toward a price reduction on the purchase of the same item or on the purchase of a different product or whether any charges are involved. The coupon or certificate must also present an honest description of the merchandise for which it can be redeemed.[24]

LEGALLY SENSITIVE ISSUES IN SUPPLIER-CUSTOMER (DISTRIBUTIONAL) RELATIONSHIPS

Sellers should be aware of the legally sensitive aspects of imposing restrictions on their customers. A supplier (especially a relatively large company) should consult counsel before employing any of the sales practices discussed in this section in connection with the marketing of its products. If these practices are found to be anticompetitive or injurious to competitors or customers, they may result in lawsuits by injured competitors or customers or in prosecution by the Department of Justice, the FTC, or even state authorities.

Exclusive Dealing. This is the practice of selling to distributors or retailers on the condition that they will not buy from other suppliers.

Tying Arrangements. These require that customers buy products they may not want in order to buy those which they do desire to purchase. For example, the manufacturer of a unique new copying machine that is in great demand might require that purchasers of the machine also buy copying paper from the manufacturer, although copying paper of a similar quality is readily available from other suppliers.

Requirements Contracts. Under requirements contracts, customers agree to purchase all their product requirements from a supplier. Such contracts may be deemed anticompetitive if a significant volume of business is foreclosed to competitors for an unduly long period of time.

Territorial Restrictions. These are restrictions on distributors or retailers as to the territory in which they may resell a manufacturer's products. For example, a supplier might set up exclusive distributors and prohibit them from selling outside their assigned territories.

Restrictions on Resale. These are restrictions on customers in terms of purchasers to whom they may resell. For example, a distributor might be prohibited from reselling to large chain or department stores while being permitted to make sales of the manufacturer's products only to small retailers, such as mom-and-pop stores.

Restrictions or Agreements on Resale Prices. These require distributors or retailers to resell at prices set by the supplier or to enter into agreements with the supplier concerning sale prices. These practices, known as *resale price maintenance* or *vertical price-fixing*, are extremely risky under the antitrust laws.

CONCLUSION

One final word of caution: This chapter is not intended to take the place of a legal adviser. Its main purpose is to alert the businessperson to areas of legal "thin ice" or legal sensitivity in the marketing process. A wise marketer will constantly consult and seek the advice of counsel and will have counsel that is knowledgeable in such areas as marketing plans, pricing methodology, advertising and promotional programs, and distribution plans.

The law and its interpretations are constantly changing, especially in the field of antitrust and trade regulations. Violations are diligently prosecuted by the Department of Justice, the FTC, and many state attorneys general. Competitors or customers may bring lawsuits and will be awarded treble damages if they prove injury as a result of antitrust violations. Such damage awards can reach astronomical proportions.

"An ounce of prevention is worth a pound of cure." This may be a trite old adage, but it is particularly applicable in the area of sales promotion and the law.

ENDNOTES

1. *The Antitrust Bulletin*, vol. 22, no. 4, 1977, p. 915.
2. 15 U.S. Code, sec. 13.
3. 15 U.S. Code, secs. 12 ff.
4. *FTC v. Fred Meyer, Inc.*, 390 U.S. 341, 358 (1968); see Jerrold G. Van Cise, *Understanding the Antitrust Laws*, Practising Law Institute, New York, 1976, p. 75.
5. *American Distilling Co. v. Wisconsin Liquor Co.*, 104 F. 2d 582, p. 585.
6. 38 Stat. 719 (1914), as amended; 15 U.S. Code, sec. 45.
7. *Antitrust & Trade Regulation Report*, The Bureau of National Affairs, Inc., no. 812, pp. A-7, A-8.
8. Amendment to Securities Exchange Act of 1934, Public Law 95-213 (effective Dec. 19, 1977); 15 U.S. Code, secs. 78dd-1-2, 78m(b), 78 ff.
9. 15 U.S. Code, sec. 13(a).
10. 15 U.S. Code, sec. 13(f).
11. 15 U.S. Code, secs. 13(a), 13(b).
12. *Title 16: Commercial Practices, Code of Federal Regulations*, sec. 14.7 (covering push money).
13. *Title 16: Code of Federal Regulations*, sec. 251.
14. 15 U.S. Code, secs. 1451–1461.
15. *Title 16: Code of Federal Regulations*, sec. 233.3. For proposed revisions of pricing guides, see *Federal Register*, vol. 39, 1974, p. 21059.
16. *FTC v. R. F. Keppel & Brother, Inc.*, 291 U.S. 304 (1934).
17. *Trade Regulation Reporter*, Commerce Clearing House, Inc., paras. 7939.90–7939.93.
18. *Title 16: Code of Federal Regulations*, sec. 419 (effective Oct. 17, 1969, as amended), 46 *Federal Register*, 36840-1 (effective Aug. 17, 1981).
19. *Title 16: Code of Federal Regulations*, sec. 435 (effective Oct. 27, 1975).
20. *Title 16: Code of Federal Regulations*, sec. 429, 1974.
21. 39 U.S. Code, sec. 3009.
22. *Antitrust & Trade Regulation Report*, The Bureau of National Affairs, Inc., no. 849, pp. A-32, A-33.
23. 15 U.S. Code, secs. 2301–2310.
24. *Trade Regulation Reporter*, Commerce Clearing House, Inc., para. 7625.

BIBLIOGRAPHY

Antitrust & Trade Regulation Report, The Bureau of National Affairs, Inc., no. 812, 1977; no. 849, 1978.

The Antitrust Bulletin, vol. 22, no. 4, 1977.

Code of Federal Regulations, National Archives and Records Service, General Services Administration, Washington, D.C.

Guides for Advertising Allowances and Other Merchandising Payments and Services, Federal Trade Commission, May 29, 1969; amended Aug. 4, 1972.

Trade Regulation Reporter, Commerce Clearing House, Inc.

Van Cise, Jerrold G.: *Understanding the Antitrust Laws*, Practising Law Institute, New York, 1976.

United States Code Annotated, West Publishing Company, St. Paul, Minn.

Trade Shows:
A Checklist

JAY THALHEIM
Chairman of the Board and President, Thalheim Expositions, Inc.

PLANNING, DEVELOPMENT, AND IMPLEMENTATION

Trade shows don't just happen by themselves. They are the product of many years of planning, development, and implementation on the part of professional exposition management specialists.

Steps in Planning a Successful Trade Show

1. Establish a need for the show.
2. Conduct proper research and development to determine the reactions of both potential suppliers and prospective attendees.
3. Establish a qualified organization of exposition professionals.
4. Determine the best time and site for the show.
5. Enlist the support of industry associations and of leading firms and personalities serving the industry for which the show is planned.
6. Sell the concept of the show.
7. Ensure that enough suppliers will be exhibiting and that enough buyers will be attending.
8. Develop ways to attract potential exhibitors. The trade-show management must convince suppliers of the advantages of exhibiting. Keep in mind that trade shows are truly unique. Buyers do not normally visit a single supplier, but they welcome the opportunity to attend trade shows because they know that they can see several hundred potential suppliers of their needs. Nowhere else are so many lines of products presented under one roof at one time, and nowhere else can buyers find their established sources of supply and also see so many new and unique products.

547

9. Convince potential exhibitors of the advantages of exhibiting, which include opportunities to:
   a. Meet current customers
   b. Find potential new customers
   c. Develop an image and reputation for a certain product
   d. Test-market new products
   e. Communicate with manufacturers' representatives or salespeople
   f. Exchange ideas with other suppliers in the field
   g. Keep pace with industry developments
   h. Find out what the competition is doing
   i. Meet potential customers as well as current accounts face-to-face
   j. Resolve any differences with current accounts or representatives

Participation in trade shows is the most effective and economical way for suppliers of products to meet and sell their merchandise to current and potential customers.

Why Buyers Attend Trade Shows

1. To see their current sources of supply
2. To determine industry trends and product innovations
3. To define new and profitable products
4. To discover new suppliers or resources
5. To see under one roof and at one time a complete industry presentation
6. To exchange views and ideas with other merchants in the same field
7. To attend seminars held during the show

How to Attract Exhibitors

1. Determine the important suppliers within the industry.
2. Make a comprehensive list of other potential exhibitors within the field the industry serves.
3. Prepare an exhibitor prospectus outlining the complete details relating to participation in the show.
4. Mail the exhibitor prospectus to all potential exhibitors.
5. Visit as many potential exhibitors as possible to explain the nature of the show and to get commitments for their participation.
6. Conduct a telephone follow-up of the mailing.
7. Continue a series of innovative mailings to arouse the interest of suppliers.
8. Place advertisements announcing the show in industry publications.
9. Develop a full-time public relations campaign.
10. Enlist the support of industry associations.
11. Maintain constant contact with potential exhibitors by means of personal visits, phone calls, and mailings.
12. Promote, advertise, and promote more.

How to Attract Buyers

1. Determine who the potential buyers are.
2. Develop mailing lists of potential buyers.
3. Advertise in trade and business publications.
4. Use a series of aggressive direct-mail announcements and invitations.
5. Develop a publicity and public relations campaign.
6. Enlist the cooperation of exhibitors in promoting the show to their own customers.
7. Enlist the cooperation and support of publications.
8. Develop ancillary activities such as seminars, social events, and a program for the families of attendees.

Servicing Exhibitors after They Have Signed Up for Space

1. Make exhibitors feel "at home"—that they are part of a family of other suppliers who share the same needs and concerns.
2. Prepare an elaborate exhibitor manual containing instructions and information relating to all aspects of the show.
3. Spell it all out. Outline all matters relating to show activities in complete detail.
4. Prepare exhibitors by means of a series of communications well in advance of the show. Keep reminding them of what they should be doing at different stages of the preshow planning.
5. Offer to assist in solving every type of problem—and be able to do it.
6. Establish a contact within the show management to serve each and every exhibitor.
7. Ensure that the show management will have personnel on hand during the setup of the show to assist exhibitors in every way possible. Develop an organization of "floor managers" who will be on the exhibit floor constantly during the setup period, while the show is in progress, and during dismantling to accommodate all the needs of exhibitors.
8. Enlist the cooperation of service contractors and union personnel to assist exhibitors.
9. Make sure that exhibitors and buyers know where all facilities within the show site are located.

Helping Exhibitors Get the Most from Their Participation

1. In advance of the show, inform exhibitors as to the "dos" and "don'ts."
2. Remind exhibitors of helpful hints for minimizing problems, including advance planning for hotel accommodations, staffing of exhibits, filling out order forms for various requirements to avoid overtime rates, and anticipating needs prior to the show, rather than "scrambling around" once it has begun.
3. Encourage exhibitors to promote their participation by way of preshow advertisements and mailings to their customers.

4. Provide exhibitors with a complete list of all registered buyers.
5. Suggest to exhibitors who are not members of the trade associations that they explore the advantages of joining these organizations.
6. Encourage exhibitors to have top-management people on hand at some time during the show.

Assisting Buyers

1. Establish advance registration procedures whereby buyers can receive their admittance credentials in advance of the show so that they will not have to wait in line to register.
2. Provide an advance listing of exhibitors so that buyers can review it prior to arriving at the show.
3. Provide a year-round "where-to-find-it" service for buyers who are looking for a particular product.
4. Assist buyers in finding appropriate hotel accommodations.
5. Establish a program of nonshow activities for the families of buyers.
6. Set up group-rate travel plans for out-of-town buyers.
7. Ensure maximum comfort at the show by providing food and beverage facilities, lounges, and informational services.

THE FUTURE

After centuries of various forms of trade fairs and expositions, the outlook for the trade-show industry has never been brighter. The trade show benefits suppliers, buyers, and the industry they serve, as well as the people within the city where the show is held. Trade shows are truly the most effective and economical way to generate business and keep abreast of industry developments.

Organizations and Associations Involved in Sales Promotion

American Association of Advertising Agencies
666 Third Ave.
New York, NY 10017

Association of National Advertisers
155 E. 44th St.
New York, NY 10017

Council of Sales Promotion Agencies
2130 Delancey Pl.
Philadelphia, PA 19103

Direct Marketing Association
6 E. 43d St.
New York, NY 10017

Direct Selling Association
1730 M St., N.W.
Washington, DC 20036

Exhibit Designers & Producers Association
521 Fifth Ave.
New York, NY 10017

Exposition Service Contractors Association
P.O. Box 16004
Cleveland, OH 44116

Incentive Manufacturers Representatives Association (IMRA)
7912 Ardleigh St.
Philadelphia, PA 19118

International Association of Amusement Parks & Attractions
7222 W. Cermak Rd.
Suite 303
North Riverside, IL 60546

International Association of Convention & Visitors Bureaus
702 Bloomington Rd.
Champaign, IL 61280

International Association of Fairs & Expositions
1010 Dixie Hgwy.
Suite 103
Chicago Heights, IL 60411

International Association of Sports Show Producers
3539 Hennepin Ave.
Minneapolis, MN 55408

Marketing Communications Executives International
1831 Chestnut St.
Philadelphia, PA 19103

Meeting Planners International
3719 Roosevelt Blvd.
Middleton, OH 45042

National Association of Exposition Managers
334 E. Garfield Rd.
P.O. Box 377
Aurora, OH 44202

National Association of Public Exposition Managers
Charlotte Merchandise Mart A-30
Charlotte, NC 28205

National Premium Sales Executives Inc. (NPSE)
1600 Rte. 22
Union, NJ 07083

National Trade Show Exhibitors Association
4300-L Lincoln Ave.
Rolling Meadows, IL 60008

Point-of-Purchase Advertising Institute
2 Executive Dr.
Fort Lee, NJ 07024

Premium Industry Club
307 N. Michigan Ave.
Chicago, IL 60601

Premium Merchandising Club of New York
1605 Vauxhall Rd.
Union, NJ 07083

Promotion Marketing Association of America (PMAA)
420 Lexington Ave.
New York, NY 10017

Sales & Marketing Executives International Inc.
330 W. 42d St.
New York, NY 10036

Savings Institutions Marketing Society of America
111 E. Wacker Dr.
Chicago, IL 60601

Society of Company Meeting Planners
1555 E. Flamingo Rd.
Las Vegas, NV 89109

Society of Incentive Travel Executives (SITE)
271 Madison Ave.
New York, NY 10016

Specialty Advertising Association International
1404 Walnut Hill Ln.
Irving, TX 75062

Trade Show Bureau
49 Locust Ave.
New Canaan, CT 06840

Trading Stamp Institute of America
1600 Rte. 22
Union, NJ 07083

Travel Industry Association of America
1899 L St., N.W.
Washington, DC 20036

Western Fairs Association
2500 Stockton Blvd.
Sacramento, CA 95817

Periodicals Related to Sales Promotion

Advertising Age
740 N. Rush St.
Chicago, IL 60611

Advertising/Communications Times
121 Chestnut St.
Philadelphia, PA 19106

Advertising World
150 Fifth Ave.
New York, NY 10010

Amusement Business
1717 West End Ave.
Nashville, TN 37203

ANNY-Advertising News of N.Y./ADWEEK
820 Second Ave.
New York, NY 10017

Canadian Premiums & Incentives
481 University Ave.
Toronto, Ont., Canada M5W 1A7

Creative—The Magazine of Promotion and Marketing
37 W. 39th St.
New York, NY 10018

Direct Marketing
224 Seventh St.
Garden City, NY 11530

Exhibits Schedule
633 Third Ave.
New York, NY 10017

Imprint
P.O. Box 427
Langhorne, PA 19047

Incentive Marketing
633 Third Ave.
New York, NY 10017

Incentive Marketing and Sales Promotion
Davis House
69-77 High St.
Croydon, England CR9 1QH

Incentive Travel Manager
825 S. Barrington Ave.
Los Angeles, CA 90049

Journal of Advertising
School of Journalism
University of Georgia
Athens, GA 30602

Journal of Advertising Research
3 E. 54th St.
New York, NY 10022

Journal of Marketing
222 S. Riverside Plaza
Chicago, IL 60606

Journal of Marketing Research
222 S. Riverside Plaza
Chicago, IL 60606

MAC Western Advertising News
6565 Sunset Blvd.
Los Angeles, CA 90028

Madison Avenue Magazine
369 Lexington Ave.
New York, NY 10017

Marketing Communications
475 Park Ave. S.
New York, NY 10016

Marketing & Media Decisions
342 Madison Ave.
New York, NY 10017

Meeting News
1515 Broadway
New York, NY 10036

Meetings & Conventions
1 Park Ave.
New York, NY 10016

Meetings & Expositions
22 Pine St.
Morristown, NJ 07960

Official Meeting Facilities Guide
1 Park Ave.
New York, NY 10016

Potentials in Marketing
731 Hennepin Ave.
Minneapolis, MN 55403

Premium Incentive Business
1515 Broadway
New York, NY 10036

Sales & Marketing Management Magazine
633 Third Ave.
New York, NY 10017

SAM
16 W. Erie St.
Chicago, IL 60601

Signs of the Times
407 Gilbert Ave.
Cincinnati, OH 45202

Specialty Advertising Business
1 Crossroads of Commerce
Rolling Meadows, IL 60008

Successful Meetings
1422 Chestnut St.
Philadelphia, PA 19102

The Counselor
Langhorne, PA 19047

The Specialty Advertiser
731 Hennepin Ave.
Minneapolis, MN 55403

Tourist Attractions & Parks
327 Wagaraw Rd.
Hawthorne, NJ 07506

Visual Merchandising Magazine
407 Gilbert Ave.
Cincinnati, OH 45202

World Convention Dates Magazine
79 Washington St.
Hempstead, NY 11550

Glossary

This glossary is based on POPAI's *Glossary of Point-of-Purchase Terms*; NPSE's *Premium Dictionary*; the glossary from Bulova's *Everything You Ever Wanted to Know about Running an Incentive Program (But Didn't Know Who to Ask)*; and the editor in chief's *Advertising in America: An Introduction to Persuasive Communication*.

A board: A curb sign used by the oil industry. The two sides lean together at the top and are connected by a cross brace, forming an "A."

account-opener premium: A premium given by a bank or savings and loan association to a person who opens a new account.

add-on (bonus) award: An award or award credit issued for a performance-level achievement, such as exceeding a quota or increasing sales volume in an incentive program.

ad-reprint holder: A framing device, usually displayed on a counter containing reprints of advertisements.

advance premium: A premium given to new customers on the condition that they will earn it by making later purchases. The technique was originated by home-service firms and door-to-door sales companies.

advertised brand: A brand which is advertised nationally to consumers and the trade and which is distributed by the competing wholesalers and stocked by the competing retailers.

advertising: A tool of marketing used to communicate ideas and information about goods or services to a group. It employs paid time or space in the media or uses other communication vehicles to carry its message, and it openly identifies the advertiser and the advertiser's relationship to the sales effort. It is one of the elements of the promotion mix, along with publicity, personal selling, and sales promotion.

advertising specialty: A useful item bearing an advertising imprint and given freely, with no strings attached. It is a close cousin to the premium.

affixed merchandise: Merchandise that is glued or otherwise fastened to a display so that the display will remain intact.

aided recall: A research technique used to measure the level of advertisement perception. The interviewer gives respondents a clue to refocus their attention on the original exposure situation.

air-rights display: A display hanging from overhead, above store traffic and merchandise.

aisle jumper: An overhead wire that reaches from one aisle to another, jumping the space between them. Flags and pennants announcing advertising messages are draped over the wire. It differs from an arch in that it consists of just the frame.

altruistic display: A display featuring the products of advertisers other than the advertiser who pays for the display. Also, a storewide program featuring seasonal products which includes the advertiser's product but does not specifically name it.

animation: Motion used in displays.

apron: The open area of a filling station or other retail outlet where displays and/or signs are in evidence and/or where merchandise is sold.

arch: A display designed to go from one gondola to another, above the aisle.

assortment display: A display designed to offer the customer a choice of size, color, type of item, etc. Also, a display offered to the retailer with the purchase of a product assortment.

attach-to-merchandise display: A display which may be larger or smaller than the merchandise it advertises, which usually includes some informational copy, and which is attached directly to the product or to a grouping of products.

audience: The total number of people who have the opportunity to see or hear a promotional message.

audioprint: A process which combines sight and sound for unusual display impressions.

audiovisual display: A display that uses sound as well as images to convey an advertising message.

award credits: Points issued to participants in an incentive program to represent the accumulated value of awards earned.

award-credit system: A system for measuring performance-level achievements and administering an incentive program efficiently, using award credits.

award vehicle: The actual prize that a participant in an incentive program gets for the achievement of goals.

back-bar display: A display designed to be used behind a bar or on the mirror behind a bar or fountain.

back card: A card unit attached to the back of a dump bin, floor bin, or counter merchandiser which projects above the merchandise and presents the advertising message at eye level.

backlighted display: See *transparency*.

balancing features: Features such as special handicaps and proper formulation of quotas, used primarily to "equalize" the opportunity for everyone to win in an incentive program.

banded premium: A direct premium that is attached to a product package by a band of paper, tape, or plastic film; an on-pack premium.

banner: A piece of plastic, cloth, or paper, usually in the shape of a rectangle or triangle, suspended from windows, walls, or ceilings. An outdoor banner is usually printed on heavy canvas, has metal grommets for stays, and is suspended from rope or wire stretched between two poles.

basic award: An award earned for individual or group performance that meets the performance level set by the sponsor in an incentive program.

basic material supplier: A manufacturer who supplies component parts or materials to the producer or supplier of point-of-purchase advertising materials.

Ben Day process: An engraving process which results in the production of halftone or color effects by adding dots, lines, or other patterns over the original art.

bin: A holder for bulk merchandise. It can be made of wire, wood, corrugated paperboard, sheet metal, etc.

black and white: A photograph without color.

blank dummy: A mock-up; a full-size serviceable model of a display with no printing or art.

blanking area: The area between the outside edge of a poster and the inside edge of the molding which is covered with white paper and serves as a mat for the poster.

bleed: The part of the original artwork which is carried beyond the illustration or background so that when the finished unit is cut or die-cut, no unprinted border or portion shows.

bonus award: An award earned for performance-level achievement that exceeds the level set by the sponsor in an incentive program.

bottle glorifier: A display designed to fit on a bottle or to serve as a background for a bottle, usually with a cut-out area or recess to hold the bottle in place.

bottle pourer: A plastic or metal configuration, carrying an advertising message, which fits over the opening of a liquor bottle and is used to facilitate pouring or to pour a specific quantity.

bottle topper: A cardboard display, smaller than a bottle glorifier, designed to encircle the neck of a bottle and carrying an advertising message.

bounce-back: An additional offer mailed with a self-liquidator. Several items may be offered, frequently related to the first. Also, a cents-off coupon placed in a package to encourage an additional sale of the product.

brand consciousness: Consumers' awareness of a particular brand.

brand ID: Brand identification. Also, a brand trademark and the signs used to call attention to a brand name.

brand image: The qualities, real or imaginary, that consumers associate with a particular brand.

brand loyalty: Consumers' faithfulness to a brand, measured by the length of time they have used it or the regularity of their use.

brand name: A name selected by the advertiser to identify a product to the consumer and to set it apart from all other products.

brand selection: The selection made by a customer who seeks a particular item but has no brand preference or who has two or more brands in mind. Brand selection that is made in the store is called *in-store brand selection*.

brand switching: Buying a brand that is different from the brand the customer usually buys. A brand switch may be planned prior to store entry, or it may be made at the point of purchase, usually as the result of some form of in-store stimulation.

bubble maker: A machine that produces bubbles and ejects them into the air. The bubbles are sometimes scented.

bubble-up: A hollow glass rod or tube with a ball on one end which contains a gas and a liquid. Warmth activates the gas, causing a steady movement of bubbles within the tube. Bubble-ups are used on Christmas trees to add sparkle and in beer mugs or glasses in displays to give the beer a look of freshness.

business gift: A gift presented to a customer, stockholder, employee, or other business friend, usually at Christmastime, as an expression of appreciation. Also called *executive gift*.

cart: See *mobile floor stand.*

car topper: A display that is attached to the top of a car or truck. It can be for either permanent or temporary use, as in a showroom.

cart wrap: An advertising message printed on paper, light cardboard, etc., designed to wrap around a shopping cart.

case divider: A strip of material, carrying an advertising message, that fits in a display case or freezers and helps the retailer organize the case or freezer.

case strip: A plastic or cardboard strip designed to snap into the channel molding of food cases or shelving.

case wraparound: A decoration or sales promotion sheet designed to wrap around a case of merchandise. It is used as a display or as the base for a display.

cash-register display: A display designed to be mounted on a cash register at the checkout stand in self-service stores. It is usually designed to hold impulse items such as candy, gum, and razor blades. Also, a sign, usually illuminated, mounted on the cash register on a bar.

catalog items: Merchandise, offered in a catalog, that can be redeemed for stamps or coupons, for example.

cents-off coupon: A certificate distributed to the consumer in, on, or near the product package; in magazines and newspapers; and by direct mail. The consumer can redeem the coupon for a savings of a specified amount on a particular product. Both retailers and manufacturers use coupons. Also called a *price-off coupon*.

chair easel: A point-of-purchase vertical riser held in place by a chairlike projection in front and dependent upon the weight of the merchandise for stability.

changeable-letter sign: A sign which, in addition to providing identification, allows the advertising message to be changed by the use of removable letters.

change holder: A rubber or plastic mat with a nubbly surface to keep coins from rolling off the counter when the sales clerk puts them down for the customer. It usually carries an advertising message.

change pad: See *change holder*.

change tray: A receptacle on the cashier's stand for holding customers' change, usually featuring an advertising message.

checkout-counter piece: A point-of-purchase device, placed at the checkout counter, which performs a consumer service (dispensing matches, giving the time, etc.) and contains an advertising message to stimulate impulse buying.

checkout stand: A stand at which purchases are checked out and bagged in a self-service store. The cash register is a feature of the checkout stand.

cigar-store Indian: A wooden image of an American Indian brave, formerly used for advertising in front of tobacco shops and said to be the first instance of point-of-purchase advertising in this country. The Point-of-Purchase Advertising Institute uses this symbol for its Outstanding Merchandising Achievement Award statuette, presented to winners in its annual merchandising awards contest.

clean display program: A display program which involves minimum effort on the part of the retailer. No paperwork, special pricing, or special handling is involved.

closed-end budget: A budget based on arbitrary allocation of funds, percent of anticipated savings, or percent of anticipated profit, for example. The sponsor of a program knows in advance what the maximum expenditure can be.

collar: A flange which encircles another piece or section and which stands up to protect or hold the other piece or section. Also, a flat printed piece carrying an advertising message and designed to encircle the neck of a bottle in a display.

collotype: A direct, screenless printing process which reproduces continuous tones with maximum fidelity. It allows facsimile reproduction of any original copy or artwork, monotone or multicolored. This method is used for printing point-of-purchase transparencies and posters on paper and vinyl. The printing plate is a special metal plate covered with a thin film of chemically treated gelatin.

colorama: A giant-size color transparency, usually photographic.

combination feature: An offer in which two or more products can be purchased together for the price of a single unit.

combination plate: An engraving plate which combines line and halftone reproduction.

combination sale: A tie-in of a premium with a purchase at a combination price. Sometimes the premium is a self-liquidator; often an on-pack premium is used.

comprehensive ("comp"): A finished or semifinished piece of art; a drawing or model.

container premium: A direct premium that consists of a reusable container, which serves as the product package. All or part of the extra cost of the packaging may be added to the price to make the promotion self-liquidating. Also called *secondary-use container*.

contest: A competition, based on skill, in which prizes are offered. A proof of purchase is usually required for entry. Compare *sweepstakes*.

continuity credits: Award credits issued for consecutive periods of high achievement or outstanding individual accomplishment over and above the performance-level quota set in an incentive program.

continuity program: A self-liquidating (or profit-making) plan, run most often by supermarkets, in which a set of related items is offered. The consumer can get one item a week for a period of six to fifteen weeks.

co-op contract: A cooperative display contract between an advertiser and a retailer. It may constitute a violation of the Robinson-Patman Act unless it is offered on equal terms to all retailers.

copy: The printed advertising message.

copy platform: The formulation of the basic ideas behind an advertising campaign and the designation of the importance of the various selling points.

copy slant: The style in which a selling point is presented. Copy is usually said to be "slanted" toward a particular audience.

copy testing: Research performed to evaluate the appeal and/or clarity of a proposed selling message.

cost-per-1000 method: A method of determining the cost of 1000 exposures of a promotional message to potential customers for a product. Most advertising media utilize this means of cost measurement.

counter card: A card, showing a brand name and giving product information, designed for use at the checkout or service counter. It may be placed with the purchased merchandise to serve as a reminder.

counter mat: A mat placed on the checkout counter and bearing an advertising message.

counter stand: A small display piece designed to fit on a store checkout counter.

coupon pad: A deck or pack of coupons that can be torn off easily. It usually features a mail-in premium or a refund.

coupon plan: A continuity program offering a variety of premiums for coupons, labels, or other proofs of purchase from one or more products.

credit-card offer: A merchandise offer mailed direct to credit-card holders. Originally this was a self-liquidating device; now a profit may be involved.

crow's-feet: A pair of metal brackets which fit into pole slots at right angles to each other and form feet for a pole display.

customer profile: An estimate of the number of people and their demographic or geographic characteristics who will probably buy a given brand. It may also include their purchasing patterns.

cut case: A shipping carton designed to be cut into shelf trays; the trays hold the product and carry an advertising message.

Day-Glo: The trademark for fluorescent paint or ink used in advertising.

deal: An advertiser's offer of a free display, free merchandise, cash, or other considerations to a retailer, in return for which the retailer uses the display, buys a specified quantity of merchandise, or performs other functions.

dealer copy: The retailer's name, price, or other message appearing on an advertiser's sign or display.

dealer incentive: See *dealer premium*.

dealer loader: A premium given to a retailer in return for an order of a specified amount. There are two types: In the case of a *buying loader*, the retailer receives a gift; in the case of a display loader, the gift, or premium, is a part of the actual display that the retailer keeps when the promotion is over. See *display premium* and *dealer premium*.

dealer premium: A premium given to a retailer in return for a specified purchase of one or more products or for coupons or purchase credits accumulated over a period of time.

dealer's privilege: A two-sided point-of-purchase unit which carries an advertisement on one side and a message from the dealer to the customer on the other side, e.g., "Thank You, Call Again," or "Please Pay when Served."

dealer survey: A survey of proprietors or managers of retail stores.

debossed sign: A sign in which all or part of the copy area is recessed, or pushed in, from the flat surface.

decal: A printed plastic or specially treated paper sign, either water-immersible or pressure-sensitive, usually affixed to windows, doors, products, or any smooth surface.

decalcomania: See *decal*.

demographic characteristics: The vital statistics of a population group or a derived sample: age, sex, education, etc.

demonstration stand: A display stand which allows a product, such as a vacuum cleaner or an electric orange-juice squeezer, to be shown in use.

demonstrator: A manufacturer's representative, trained and paid by the manufacturer, who demonstrates products in retail stores.

demonstrator display: A display which shows the function of a product.

demo-sticker: A self-adhesive sticker or card that points out product features and is usually attached to the sales-floor demonstration model.

die-cut sign: A sign cut in other than a rectangular shape for purposes of design.

die-cutting: The process of cutting out special shapes by means of a die made for the purpose.

diorama: An elaborate color display of a scenic nature, which is almost always three-dimensional and illuminated. Motion is often included.

direct premium: An item that is given free with a purchase. It may be an on-pack, in-pack, near-pack, or container premium.

direct shipment: The shipment of point-of-purchase materials direct to the dealer, either automatically, as part of the complete merchandise order, or at the special request of the dealer. This type of shipment is employed extensively by smaller advertisers with limited sales forces.

discount: A reduction in price that may more properly be considered a part of pricing, rather than promotion, in the marketing mix. Discounts are related to refunds and rebates, but are taken off the price before the consumer makes the purchase.

discount coupon: See *cents-off coupon*.

dispenser: A sign or display containing product literature or a tear-off pad. Also, a merchandise display containing a stock of merchandise for active selling.

display: A window display or other point-of-purchase display.

display allowance: An allowance given to a retailer by a manufacturer in return for the retailer's use of a special display of the manufacturer's product.

display card: A piece of display advertising, printed or mounted on cardboard, for attachment to a display of merchandise. See *shelf talker*.

display carton: A carton that can be folded out into a display without removing the product.

display loader: See *display premium*.

display premium: A form of dealer incentive which is part of a point-of-purchase display. It may be a sample of a consumer premium or a functional element of the display itself.

divider: See *case divider*.

door-opener premium: A relatively inexpensive premium given by a door-to-door salesperson to induce a prospect to listen to a sales presentation.

double-face display: A display that carries a sales message on both the front and the back.

double-face sign: A board sign that is finished on both sides.

drop shipment: A timed shipment of small batches of a large order or the simultaneous shipment of items to multiple destinations.

dummy: A mock-up of a finished sign or display, rough or finished.

dummy merchandise: Empty packages, bottles filled with colored water, etc., used instead of the real merchandise for display purposes.

dump bin: A bin-shaped holder, designed to stand on the floor, containing merchandise that is dumped in from the case.

duomounting: The process of laminating printed sheets to both sides of a piece of cardboard.

dynamic system payoff: A system of award credits that uses progressively higher volumes of credits for each successive performance-level achievement in an incentive program.

easel: A free-standing floor unit made of wood, plastic, or metal that supports signs, large cards, and frames; a support attached to a display card to enable it to stand.

easeling: The process of attaching point-of-purchase signs and displays to easels.

electric spectacular: An outdoor sign in which lighting forms the design.

electrotype: A duplicate of the original engraving plate.

embossed sign: A sign on which all or part of the copy area is raised so that it stands out from the flat surface.

embossing: The process of raising prints, designs, patterns, etc., above the flat surface of a sign or display.

end display: A mass display stacked against the end of a gondola or tier of groceries.

end-of-aisle display: A display, accommodating a large group of product units, that is built specifically for placement at the end of a store aisle.

exhibit: A display at a trade show or theme park (e.g., Disney World); a special display set up by a company in a permanent location of its own, such as those of Eastman Kodak, IBM, and Burlington Mills.

expanded metal: Sheet steel which is slotted and stretched to form a geometric pattern.

exposed merchandise: Merchandise that is visible to consumers on shelves and counters and is readily accessible to clerks and customers.

exposure: The individual consumer's visual contact with a point-of-purchase unit or other advertising medium.

exposure frequency: The number of times that an individual point-of-purchase sign or display is exposed to consumers within a specified time period.

extruded aluminum: A finished piece of aluminum whose shape has been formed by passing it through a die.

eye-beam display: An unmounted display, based on a unique construction principle, which can be rolled and shipped in mailing tubes and yet will be rigid when set up.

eyeletting: The process of punching small holes, which may or may not be reinforced, for the purpose of lacing or tying parts of a display together or attaching hooks, cords, etc.

fabric banner: An advertising banner made of woven or knitted cloth, usually suspended from a horizontal pole and fringed on the bottom and sides.

face: A style of type. Also, the front of a display.

facings: Items at the front of the store shelf.

factory-pack premium: A direct premium attached to a product. In-pack, on-pack, and container premiums are factory-pack premiums.

FCC: See *Federal Communications Commission*.

feature: A product that is given a special sales promotion.

Federal Communications Commission: The U.S. government agency responsible for the regulation of electronic or broadcast media.

Federal Trade Commission: The U.S. government agency responsible for the regulation of promotions.

feet: Display stands, in various styles, made of wire or corrugated board. See also *crow's-feet*.

fixative: A chemical substance applied to signs to give permanence and to prevent fading.

flange: A projecting rim around a sign or part of a display that holds it in place.

flange sign: A sign made so that it can be mounted vertically to the surface of a wall, building, or post, from which it projects. It carries an advertising message on both sides.

flasher: A light that flashes on and off at timed intervals to attract attention.

flexography: A variation of rotary letterpress in which flexible rubber plates and fast-drying fluid inks are used. Also called *flexo printing*.

flexo printing: See *flexography*.

flocking: An electrostatic spraying process that produces a velvety finish on any surface.

floor bin: See *bin*.

floor mat: A mat of any type carrying a product message. Also, a step-on mat used to trigger sound, motion, etc., in a display.

floor pyramid: A display of merchandise, rising from the floor, in which products are stacked in the form of a pyramid.

fluorescent ink: An ink that has high light-reflecting properties and hence is attention-getting. It is most effective when surrounded by black or a very dark color.

flush: Vertically aligned. Copy may be spoken of as *flush left* or *flush right*, meaning that it is vertically aligned on the left or right side. Copy that is aligned vertically on both sides is called *adjusted*.

four-color process: A printing process using four colors—red, yellow, blue, and black. When printed one over the other, they give the effect of natural color.

free: A "magic" word with some strings attached. Its use is not so severely restricted as it once was, but an advertiser should still be sure that an item really is free if the advertising says it is. The conditions of the free offer should be clearly stated.

free-standing insert: A promotional piece inserted loosely into newspapers, often containing cents-off coupons.

FTC: See *Federal Trade Commission*.

game: A device for encouraging consumers to visit a particular retailer or to purchase a specific product or service frequently.

giant replica: An oversized reproduction of a product or trademark.

giveaway: A low-cost item given out freely. It is akin to an advertising specialty or a traffic builder. Also, a direct premium.

glow panel: A luminous lighted panel bearing an advertising message.

gondola: A set of shelves that are open on both sides, commonly used in self-service stores.

gondola end: A display, usually large, designed for use at the end of a gondola in a self-service store.

gondola topper: A two-sided display that rests on top of a gondola in such a way that it can be seen from both aisles.

gravity-feed merchandiser: A merchandiser that uses the force of gravity to bring more merchandise into view when that which was on view is sold. A single unit or a quantity of units can be fed in succession.

gravure: See *photogravure*.

gripper edge: The area along the edges of a printing sheet which allow mechanical fingers to pick up the sheet and carry it through the printing or die-cutting press.

grommet: A metal eyelet used for fastening.

halftone printing: A printing technique for reproducing artwork with tonal variation. The original artwork is photographed through a screen which separates the design into small dots of various sizes, producing the tonal variation.

hanging sign: A point-of-purchase sign which hangs from a mounting bracket that usually projects from a wall, building, or post. It usually features copy on both sides.

hardboard: A fabricated board material often used in displays.

header: A message board projecting above a display and giving the headline or the advertising message. It is usually larger and more intricate than a riser.

heat motor: A small rotating element which is operated by the heat of an inside light. It may be used to give the illusion of falling water, blowing drapery, etc., in a display.

hollow lumber: Square cardboard tubes for display construction.

honeycomb: Material made of sheets of tissue paper glued together in such a way that it stores flat but opens into a honeycomb configuration. It is used to make three-dimensional bells, balls, etc.

hook-up: A plastic button with a metal hook and a sticky back, used to hang small signs or displays.

horizontal arrangement: The stocking of a line or variety of products along the full length of a single gondola or wall shelf.

hostess gift: A gift given to a housewife who allows a demonstration party to be conducted in her home. She usually gets value in proportion to the sales made at her party (e.g., a Tupperware party).

I beam: A metal sign whose vertical section is in the shape of an "I."

ident: The identification of a brand name, as on a sign.

identification sign: A sign, furnished by the advertiser, that bears the name of the retailer, bank, etc., in addition to an advertising message. Also, a sign showing only the name of a place of business.

illuminated display: A display that uses light in any form.

illuminated sign: A sign that uses light in any form.

imprinting: Reproducing letters, symbols, marks, etc., by pressing.

impulse buying: Making an unplanned purchase.

impulse item: A product that the consumer buys on impulse; an item that the consumer did not plan to purchase.

impulse sale: A sale that would not have taken place except for the display of the impulse item, which caused the consumer to make an unplanned purchase.

incentive: A reward offered for desired performance; often used as a synonym for *premium*.

incentive program: An established plan of action to generate and recognize performance that is involved with specific management goals.

incentive travel: A trip, for a group or for an individual, offered to sales personnel and dealers who reach or exceed a sales quota. It is often tied in with sales meetings at a resort area.

inducement: See *incentive*.

inflatable: An item which assumes three dimensions when filled with air or gas. It may be used as a premium or as an integral part of a display.

injection molding: The process of shaping plastic pieces inside a mold.

inner supports: Supporting pieces of a display, such as a dump bin or floor stand, which is designed to hold merchandise or is subject to stress.

in-pack premium: A direct premium enclosed in a product package as an incentive for consumer purchase.

insert: An advertisement packaged with retail merchandise.

insert cards: Display cards that can be inserted in a permanently mounted frame.

installation service: A service offered by a company which contracts to place displays in retail outlets for an advertiser at a certain price per unit.

instruction sheet: A sheet of printed instructions for setting up a display.

intaglio printing: Printing from a depressed surface. The lines to be printed are cut below the surface of the engraved plate. When flooded with ink and wiped clean, only the inked design remains. Photogravure is a form of intaglio printing.

integration: The coordination of point-of-purchase advertising with advertising in media—television, radio, newspapers, magazines, etc.

island: A free-standing display on which merchandise is available from all sides.

island floor stand: A floor stand designed so that it is accessible from all sides.

IT: See *incentive travel*.

itinerant display: An expensive display or exhibit which is moved from one retail outlet to another.

J hook: A hook which projects from a shelf and on which a display of merchandise is hung.

jumble basket: A container, similar to a dump bin, into which articles for sale are tossed willy-nilly. A jumble basket usually contains many different kinds of products, while a dump bin contains only one.

jumble display: A loose arrangement of items in a display container.

KD display: A display that is shipped partially assembled, or "knocked down," for reasons of economy in shipping, storage, or actual production. A KD display is assembled at the spot where the display is to stand.

key line and pasteup: A set of drawings, one for each color that will appear in the finished print, which are keyed to one another for successive printing runs. Usually the drawings are pasted down on a board with overlaying plastic sheets on which other elements intended for different colors are pasted.

kick strip: A strip, usually dark in color, that is placed at the bottom of a floor stand to protect it from accidental scuffs, kicks, mopping stains, etc., when in use in a retail outlet.

lagniappe: A gift or present given by a merchant to a customer.

laminating: The process of spreading a clear, bright, thin coat of plastic over a printed surface to give it a high degree of brilliance and protect it against wear.

lamp pulls: See *light-cord hangers*.

latex: A material made by suspending fine particles of rubber and/or synthetic rubber in water.

Latex 61-1000: A special form of latex.

lazy-Susan display: A display turned by hand or push-button motor on a turntable base.

lead time: The time between the arrival of signs and displays at their intended destinations and the date the promotion is due to begin.

ledge display: A display designed to go behind the counter on the top of a bar or shelving (in which case it is flat in back) or on top of a gondola (in which case it is round or two-sided).

lenticular display: A display in which a three-dimensional effect is created.

letterpress: A printing process in which ink is transferred from a raised surface to paper, board, etc.

licks: Tabs that secure sections or pieces of a cardboard display in the correct position.

light box: A box-shaped display unit in which a backlighted transparency forms one face of the box.

light-cord hangers: Cardboard advertising messages suspended at the end of a lamp chain or cord.

light stealer: A display which has no illumination of its own but which seems lighted because of the use of transparencies seen against a store light source or because of the use of reflective surfaces which trap and focus light.

linecut: A photoengraving of a line drawing, without tonal variation.

line screen: See *screen*.

linkage: The connections from the motor to the moving parts of a motion display. It can be more or less complicated, depending upon the type of motion wanted.

literature holder: A display that holds product or service brochures at the point of purchase.

literature rack: A floor or counter holder designed to stimulate use of sales brochures or to sell periodicals or books.

lithography: A printing process in which the art is photographed on a sensitized metal, plastic, or paper plate that will accept ink only in those areas on which an imprint is desired. This method is based on the principle that oil and water don't mix; the design is put on the surface with a greasy material, and then water and printing ink are successively applied. The greasy parts, which repel water, absorb the ink, but the wet parts do not. This type of printing is used in offset lithography, offset printing, photooffset, photolithography, and planography.

live merchandise: The actual product on display. When the display is in a position where it is vulnerable to pilferage, small items such as pens and razor blades are sometimes cemented or otherwise affixed to the display.

loader: See *dealer loader.*

logo: An advertiser's stylized name or trademark used repeatedly in advertising and sales promotions.

logotype: A printing plate used to reproduce an advertiser's logo.

lottery: A plan, generally illegal in sales promotion, which awards prizes on the basis of chance and requires consideration (purchase or payment) to enter. It becomes a sweepstakes when consideration is not required or a contest when prizes are awarded on the basis of skill or ability. (Lotteries authorized or run by state and other governments are legal.)

magic base: A floor display with a device that elevates the back product area.

mail-in premium: A premium that is offered through the mail. It can be either a self-liquidator or a free offer in return for multiple proofs of purchase.

make ready: Prepare for the production of materials by setting up production facilities, making special adjustments, etc.

makeup: The arrangement of printed messages on signs and displays.

mandatory copy: Copy that is required by law. Also, copy that the advertiser requires to appear in every advertising message.

Market-Diser: The trademark for a battery-operated, transistorized, message-repeater device which adds the impact of sound to displays.

marketing: A major component of business, concerned with the movement of goods and services through the channels of distribution, from the manufacturer, or source, to the ultimate consumer. It consists of four basic elements: product, price, promotion, and place. These make up the marketing mix.

marketing mix: The four basic elements of marketing: product, price, promotion, and place. Sales promotion is a component of promotion.

Masonite: The trademark for panels made from exploded wood chips pressed into dense boards.

mass display: A display featuring a sizable grouping of the product, plus the advertising message.

mats: Carpets or mats bearing an advertising message which are placed on the floor immediately in front of a product or leading to and from a store entryway. See *floor mat.*

mechanical: See *key line and pasteup.*

mechanical book: A motion display consisting of a giant book whose pages turn automatically. The pages are mounted on a horizontal cardboard cylinder that revolves slowly and continuously from back to front, like a Ferris wheel. Power is provided by a small alternating-current motor.

media support: Television, radio, magazine, and newspaper advertising used to back up a sales promotion.

memo-changer: A compact checkout-counter piece with room at the top for the customer's change and for memo paper, usually located next to the cash register in liquor stores. The back of the unit functions as a handy storage compartment.

merchandiser: A display containing merchandise for immediate sale.

merchandising: The promotion of advertising to an advertiser's sales force, wholesalers, and dealers and the promotion of a product to consumers through the use of point-of-purchase materials, in-store retail promotions, and guarantee seals or tags.

merchandising kit: A display kit promoting a general event or a selected group of related products, consisting of different types of display units to be used throughout the retail outlet.

message repeater: An endless film or sound tape, used in some form of indoor or outdoor box display, that repeats a message. The film is usually backlighted.

miniature: A small-scale model of a large and/or expensive display. Also, a very small, usually rough sketch.

mobile: A display consisting of several counterbalanced pieces suspended in such a way that each piece moves independently in a light current of air.

mobile floor stand: A floor stand which has wheels so that it can be moved from one area to another. Also called *cart*.

mock-up: A facsimile sample of a proposed point-of-purchase sign or display.

modular display system: A system that permits the building of a variety of displays from a few basic units.

molds: Patterns or forms from which metal or plastic sign and display elements are produced.

motion display: A display with moving elements to attract attention.

motivate: To stimulate salespeople to sell more through a program that recognizes achievement by awarding merchandise or travel prizes. Motivational techniques are also used to encourage consumers, retailers, and wholesalers to make purchases or perform in other ways.

mounting and finishing: Bonding a printed sheet to reinforcement, die-cutting, scoring, etc.; joining parts in subassembly or assembly.

movable merchandiser: A merchandiser, usually made of metal, with two or more wheels to allow the retailer to move the entire display without disturbing the merchandise. Such displays are often constructed on the hand-truck principle.

moving-letter sign: A horizontal panel sign having many lights. The successive lighting of these lights in pattern makes the letters seem to move.

multideck fixture: A display fixture with a vertical shelf arrangement.

Mylar: The trademark for a colorless or colored metallic finish, often applied to signs and displays. It is also used as a film base.

national brand: A brand that, because of its universal distribution, is familiar to consumers throughout the country.

neck extender: A pole extension with a sleeve fitting on one end and an adapter connection on the other. One or more neck extenders may be used between the top and bottom sections of a pole display.

noncommit situation: A situation in which an advertiser who is not sure how many point-of-purchase units will be needed places the risk on the supplier who produces and stocks the item, selling it to the advertiser as ordered, a few pieces at a time, at a higher cost to the advertiser.

novel paper stock: Distinctive paper (iridescent, textured, or patterned) mounted on cardboard.

off-pack display: A display containing a product and premiums, not physically connected to each other, or containing just premiums.

offset: A printing process in which impressions are transferred from the engraving plate to a rubber blanket and then printed on paper. See *lithography.*

on-pack premium: A direct premium attached to the exterior of a product package or, sometimes, riding with it in a special sleeve, carton, or film wrap. See *banded premium.*

open-end budget: An estimated amount required for an incentive plan which encourages unlimited performance-level improvements. Program sponsors generally benefit from this type of budget because the higher the level of performance, the greater the potential profit accruals.

out-pack premium: See *on-pack premium.*

out-pack shipper display: A prepacked group of premiums in a shipper display device, placed alongside stacks of the product; the consumer is on the "honor system," taking both the premium and the product to the checkout counter.

outsert: Separate printed matter attached to a package.

overlay: A sheet of paper fastened on the printing surface of a press to make a heavier impression.

over-pack: A product package containing one or more items packed together. Also, a product plus a display.

overrun: Additional copies of printed material beyond the number ordered. This is necessary whenever more than one operation is required to produce the final product. The printer must gamble on how many pieces will be required to offset accidental damage during each process so that at least the number ordered will be produced.

over-the-wire banner: A long rectangular piece of paper with the product message printed twice (head-to-head) on one side of the paper. When thrown over a wire, the messages are back-to-back and can be seen from either side. Frequently, a series of smaller banners are placed over one wire.

package band: A strip of paper or plastic attached to a product package announcing a premium offer; a special advertising message wrapped around a package.

package enclosure: See *in-pack premium.*

painted wall: An outdoor advertisement painted on a wall that is visible from a shopping area in which there are many shoppers.

painter's guide: A line drawing in which the colors to be used are indicated on the various elements of the design.

panel: An outdoor or indoor poster.

paper sculpture: Cut-out and folded paper figures that give the illusion of being three-dimensional.

part-cash redemption: An option, often included in coupon plans, permitting the consumer to get premiums faster by redeeming fewer coupons with a cash amount; it may be self-liquidating.

pegboard: A board, perforated with rows of holes, designed for the suspension of pegs or hooks to hold displays or product samples; sometimes the holes are specially and specifically located.

pegboard hooks: Hooks, usually made of wire, suspended from pegboard holes to hold displays or product samples.

peg tube: A paper tube that accommodates hooks and fixtures.

pencil rough: A preliminary pencil drawing of a proposed sign or display, usually done in a loose style. Roughs can also be produced by other implements, such as chalk.

penetration: The degree of effectiveness of advertising in terms of its impact on the public.

pennant: A banner in the shape of a triangle.

perforated metal: Sheet steel or other metal that is die-cut in an all-over geometric pattern.

performance level: The fundamental element around which incentive plans are designed, developed, and structured. The company's objectives are achieved when the participants' performance reaches the desired level.

permanent display: A display, such as a large outdoor sign, designed for use for an indefinite length of time (often defined as one year).

personalized display: A display that includes the retailer's name, address, etc.

photogelatin process: See *collotype.*

photogravure: A printing process using an intaglio plate prepared by photographic methods.

photo stamps: High-gloss photographs in postage-stamp form reproduced from photographs, negatives, or artwork. They are made available in sheets with gummed backs and are perforated.

pilfer-proof display: A counter display which shows the product to the customer but which is accessible only to a clerk behind the counter. Pilfer-proof displays on the floor sometimes have ingenious locking devices. The product itself is locked onto a card or into a container. Most such displays are actually pilfer-resistant, not pilfer-proof.

placement: The use and acceptance of a display offered by an advertiser.

plaque: A message or figure mounted on a backing of a regular shape and having a more or less formal appearance.

plastic transparency display: A display unit showing the body of a product; transparent slides are dropped in various combinations to show the different colors available. The most commonly used products in this display category are automobiles.

plate: A metal or plastic sheet engraved with the reverse image of material to be printed.

Plexiglas: The trademark for acrylic plastic sheets.

point-of-purchase advertising: Advertising that tells the product or brand-name story to customers at a retail outlet.

point-of-purchase advertising agency: An agency that creates, programs, and supplies point-of-purchase advertising materials. The agency operates without manufacturing facilities, but has creative facilities geared to meet clients' needs.

Point-of-Purchase Advertising Institute: The trade association representing the point-of-purchase advertising industry.

point-of-purchase advertising materials: The devices or structures located in or at the retail outlet which identify, advertise, and/or merchandise the outlet, a service, or a product, as an aid to retail selling.

point-of-purchase display: A professional display prepared by a manufacturer to promote products at the retail level. Also, a retailer's own display.

point-of-purchase material supplier: A supplier of point-of-purchase advertising materials. The supplier may or may not own production facilities or have the creative facilities for supplying point-of-purchase materials.

point-of-sale advertising: See *point-of-purchase advertising*.

pole: A round cardboard tube, usually in several sections, used to hold a display above a stack of merchandise. Also, a metal pole on which a display or sign is erected.

pole cat: A one-piece telescoping pole support for displays and lights.

pole display: A display, mounted on a footed pole, designed to be used with massed merchandise and to be seen above it. The pole is mostly hidden in use.

pole sign: A single- or double-face sign attached to poles at gasoline stations and other outlets.

pole topper: The display part of a pole display.

polystyrene: A clear, colorless plastic material used for molding sign faces, trays, parts of displays, etc.

polyurethane: A material used in making foams, coatings, and adhesives.

polyvinyl acetate: A vinyl polymer used for coatings and adhesives.

POP advertising: See *point-of-purchase advertising*.

POPAI: See *Point-of-Purchase Advertising Institute*.

pop-up display: A display that is set up automatically when it is opened.

pop-up bin: A corrugated display bin constructed so that it can be set up with one motion.

porcelain sign: A sign made of porcelain on metal, usually printed by the silk-screen process, each color being applied and fused separately onto the metal. Extremely durable and long-lived, these signs are used extensively by companies whose advertising approach remains constant for extended periods of time.

portable display: A floor display that has folding legs and is easily transportable.

portable reefer: A refrigerator case on wheels which can be moved to various locations.

POS advertising: See *point-of-purchase advertising*.

postdisplay testing: Testing consisting of a store audit or other research technique to determine whether a display has increased sales or brand awareness.

poster: A printed plastic, paper, or cloth banner or sign for window or interior use.

poster frame: A frame for use with posters or blowups of an advertisement. Layers of ads may be mounted on one frame, whereby the top ad can be torn off to reveal a new one.

pourer: See *bottle pourer.*

predisplay testing: Testing consisting of a few displays to determine their effectiveness before an entire order is placed. The testing can be misleading if the display sites are not carefully selected.

premium: An article of merchandise offered as an incentive to perform a specified function or take a specific action.

premium representative: A specialized manufacturer's representative serving premium users; a commissioned salesperson representing different manufacturers.

premium show: A show featuring displays of incentive merchandise suppliers. Two premium shows are held annually, one in New York and one in Chicago.

premium test: A method of measuring the appeal of a premium in advance of an offer. Frequently the test is done by means of personal interviews and sometimes by means of a mail "ballot" or split-run advertising in newspapers.

prepack display: A display designed to be packed with merchandise by the advertiser and shipped as a unit; a more refined version of a shipper display.

preselected winner: A person who holds a winning number or game piece selected in advance. A plan in which there are preselected winners may be deemed a deceptive practice unless a drawing is also used to award unclaimed prizes.

press run: The total number of copies printed.

pressure-sensitive material: An adhesive material, usually available in strips or sheets used to affix signs, etc., where desired.

price-off coupon: See *cents-off coupon.*

price sign: A sign carrying a price.

privileged copy area: The part of a display that is for the private or exclusive use of the retailer.

prize: Reward given to a winner in a contest, sweepstakes, game, or lottery. Also, a salesperson's incentive award.

product identifier: A miniature printed plastic sign (self-sticking) or label affixed to the product itself. It gives product information and usually carries the brand name.

product-in-use display: A demonstration-type display showing how the product is to be used by the consumer.

product spotter: A small sign or device designed to call attention to a particular product or brand that might otherwise be missed.

product switching: Buying an item that is different from the one whose purchase had been planned.

program: A planned, coordinated series of displays.

promotion: The element of the marketing mix that is used to inform and persuade consumers concerning the merits of a product, a service, or an idea. It employs advertising, personal selling, publicity, and sales promotion to achieve these ends.

promotional display: A display which is designed to be used only for the duration of a particular promotion, as opposed to a display which is designed for use for an indefinite period (although, in a broad sense, all displays are promotional). See *permanent display* and *semipermanent display*.

promotion mix: The basic elements of promotion: advertising, personal selling, publicity, and sales promotion.

proof: A trial impression taken at each stage of the printing process.

proof of purchase: A boxtop, label, trademark, Universal Product Code, or coupon from a product which qualifies a consumer to receive a premium or a refund.

publicity: News or information about a person, company, product, service, or idea that is communicated to the news media by an interested party in the hope that the media will use it as a regular news item. It is an element of the promotion mix as well as a component of public relations.

public service display: A display that gives information, such as the time, the temperature, or baseball scores, which is of interest to customers but is not necessarily related to the product. The advertiser is clearly identified.

pump topper: A display used on top of a gasoline pump.

purchase-privilege offer: A food-store promotion, similar to a tape plan or continuity program, often using trade cards. The term is little used today.

push money: A commission paid to a salesperson to push a particular product or line of merchandise.

pylon: A tall identifying sign.

Q tabs: Stand-up pressure-sensitive fixtures used to hold flash messages, shelf talkers, and attention-getters in place.

rack: A floor stand featuring shelves, pockets, or hooked arms, usually made of wire, designed for the special display of a group of related items—sometimes in a subdepartment—for customer self-selection and/or self-service. A rack may or may not also carry an advertising message.

rebate: The return, by the manufacturer to the consumer, of part of the purchase price of a product. It is similar to a refund except that it is usually offered on higher-priced merchandise and involves a larger sum of money.

redemption center: A store maintained by a trading stamp company where customers can redeem filled stamp books for premiums.

redemption coupon: A coupon which, when mailed to the advertiser or presented to the dealer, entitles the consumer to acquire the advertised product at a discount or without charge.

redemption reserve: Funds put aside by a trading stamp company or the user of a coupon plan to pay for the cost of merchandise for future redemptions, which may come several years after the original issue of the stamps or coupons.

referral premium: A premium offered to a satisfied customer who refers the seller to another person who purchases the product or service. Also called a *use-the-user plan.*

refund: See *rebate.*

related display: A single display combining several related products. Also called *related-item display.*

reminder sale: A sale that takes place when in-store stimulation causes the customer to remember a product for which a conscious intent to buy has been established.

revolving display: A turning, motor-activated display.

riser: The part of a display which projects above the merchandise presentation. Also, a sign or display which rises from the top shelf of an aisle or is placed on top of a pole and thus is visible from other parts of the store.

riveted display: A metal display, the parts of which have been finished and decorated in the flat and assembled by means of rivets.

robotape: An audio sales-message repeater which automatically operates a product or display for a self-animated sales demonstration.

rotating display: A hand-turned display or one turned by pushing a button.

rotogravure: A printing process in which the surface to be printed is etched on a copper cyclinder.

rough: See *pencil rough.*

rubber-plate printing: The process of reproducing from rubber plates, usually on corrugated board. It eliminates the need to print on lithographic paper and then mount it on the board.

run long: See *overrun.*

run short: See *underrun.*

sales contest: A sales incentive program. The word *contest* is used less today than previously, since direct competition among salespeople is not as common as it used to be.

sales incentive: An award to a salesperson for performing above a specified level, signing new accounts, reopening accounts, selling specified products, or achieving other stated objectives.

sales promotion: All promotion activities, other then advertising, personal selling, and publicity, that encourage the consumer to purchase by means of such inducements as premiums, advertising specialties, samples, cents-off coupons, contests, sweepstakes, games, refunds, rebates, trading stamps, exhibits, displays, and demonstrations. It is also employed to motivate retailers', wholesalers', and manufacturers' sales forces to sell, through the offer of such incentives as prizes (merchandise, cash, and travel) and through various trade shows.

sample: A free trial size of a product sufficient to allow the potential customer to use it and appreciate its benefits. The manufacturer hopes the sample will induce purchase of the full size.

sconce: A wall bracket for holding signs, displays, lights, mirrors, etc. Usually a pair of sconces is used.

scoring: A partial cut through cardboard or a crease made to allow for bending the cardboard.

Scotchlite: The trademark for outdoor sign letters with great light-reflecting properties.

screen: A transparent plate with two sets of parallel lines running at right angles to each other, used in the photoengraving process. The more lines per square inch, the finer the reproduction.

secondary-use container: See *container premium.*

self-liquidating point-of-purchase unit: A display unit for which the retailer pays in whole or in part.

self-liquidator: A premium offered at a price which makes the premium plan entirely consumer-supported.

self-selector display: A display containing merchandise organized in such a way that the customer may readily select color, size, style, etc.

self-sticker: A pressure-sensitive sign or product spotter.

semicommercial display: A display or merchandising aid that gives the retailer or salesperson benefits over and above the advertiser's goal.

semipermanent display: A display sturdy enough to be used for a seasonal promotion, such as at Christmastime, but not intended for indefinite use. It would customarily outlast several short-term displays and would serve as the encompassing carrier of a seasonal theme.

semispectacular: A painted outdoor bulletin with special effects, cutouts, lighting, or animation.

shadow box: An illuminated transparency holder with a forward-projecting frame, frequently with a provision for changeable messages and concealed interior illumination.

sheet-fed press: A printing press which uses paper cut into separate sheets before printing.

shelf extender: A display in the form of a small tray, designed to be fastened or clamped to a shelf and to project from it, thus extending the space of the shelf. It is usually used for related-item sales.

shelf miser: A small display designed to be attached to a shelf and to hold more units than would ordinarily fit on the shelf. It frequently has a spring or gravity-feed arrangement to keep the front of the facing full.

shelf strip: A device made of tag stock, plastic, wire, or other material and pressure-fitted into the price railing under a product. It is used as an attention-getting device.

shelf talker: A printed card designed to lie on a shelf under a product and project out and down to carry an advertising message which will call attention to the product. The flap end is frequently die-cut. It is sometimes held in place with pressure-sensitive adhesive.

shipper display: A display that is usually larger and more elaborate than a carton display. All parts are included in one shipper display, along with the prepacked merchandise.

side guide: A device employed in printing to pull the sheet to a certain spot on the printing plate. Printing and die-cutting are performed using the side guide and the gripper edge as the point of reference.

sign: A device which identifies a company or a product and/or carries an advertising or directional message. A sign may be a separate entity or an integral part of a display.

silk screen: A method of printing one color at a time through a stencil securely affixed to a porous surface on a silk screen. The color used in this process is a paste, which, when pushed through the pores of the silk, leaves an even coating on stock placed under the screen. All parts of the design not to be printed are rejected by an impermeable substance.

silver-colored foil: A foil used extensively in combination with cardboard to produce interesting optical and attention-getting effects. Silver-colored foil can be dyed any color or can be purchased in other colors. It is mounted to cardboard for printing and die-cutting.

single-face sign: A sign made of corrugated board with one smooth face, usually printed on the corrugated side; any sign or display finished on one side only.

slip sheet: A paper sheet used between sections of a display or placed between the display and the carton when packing for shipment. Also, a sheet used between freshly printed sheets to prevent rubbing.

snapper: An extra incentive used to stimulate consumer purchase of a particular product.

sniffer display: A display which uses odor to attract attention or enhance the product.

solid matter: Lines of type set without spacing between them.

sore-thumb display: A display designed to attract immediate attention by virtue of its size or unique style.

special display space: The space allocated for the promotion of a product other than its regular shelf space.

specialty advertising: See *advertising specialty*.

spectacular: A large, permanent outdoor sign equipped with special lighting and motion effects. Also, a large indoor display designed either to stand free or to be used in a free-standing stack of merchandise, often incorporating elements of light and/or motion.

spiffs: See *push money*.

spinner sign: A sign with a wall-mounted bracket, designed so that it is revolved by the wind.

spot display: A prominent display of merchandise, accentuated by an extraordinary attention-getting device.

spot-welded display: A metal display, the parts of which have been fabricated and assembled by means of spot welding and then finished and decorated.

spreader: A device to hold a display, customarily shipped flat, in an open position.

spring pole: A spring-tension, floor-to-ceiling pole used for a display.

spring wire: Wire which produces motion without electricity. Vibrations and air currents cause it to quiver. It can be used for floor, wall, counter, and shelf displays.

spurt program: A short-duration incentive program in the "special-emphasis" category, designed to effect rapid changes in some temporarily critical aspect of the sponsor's business.

stabile: A display suspended from the ceiling, similar in some respects to a mobile, and sometimes reaching from the ceiling to the floor. Unlike a mobile a stabile does not have moving parts.

stacker display: A display that permits projecting or suspending an advertising message from stacked merchandise.

standard art: See *syndicated art.*

static system payoff: A system of award credits in an incentive program in which each level of achievement is rewarded with the same volume of credits.

stereotype: A duplicate printing plate cast from a paper matrix.

stiffener: A hem strip which folds back to strengthen the edge of a display.

stirrer: A long stick used for stirring drinks. It carries an advertising message and is usually made of plastic.

stirrer holder: A receptacle for holding stirrers, napkins, and other bar accessories, used on a bar or fountain. It carries an advertising message, frequently on a riser.

stitching: Fastening parts of displays to each other or to holders with heavy wire staples.

story: See *theme.*

streamer: A printed plastic, paper, or cloth banner for window or interior use.

stringing: Stretching signs on one wire in an orderly row, usually spelling out an advertising message.

supplier: See *basic material supplier* and *point-of-purchase material supplier.*

sweepstakes: A promotion which awards substantial prizes on the basis of a chance drawing. It is similar to a contest, but it requires neither skill nor consideration (purchase).

syndicated art: Low-cost point-of-purchase material supplied to various advertisers for different brands of a commodity in separate market areas.

tab: A small flap fastened to the edge of a display, sometimes conveying an extra advertising message or reminder.

table tent: See *tent card.*

tacker: A small metal sign.

tacker sign: A sign made so that it can be tacked or nailed to a building, a fence, etc. It has copy on one side only.

tag stock: Thin, flexible cardboard.

take-one pad: A pad used as part of a sign or display. Customers tear off sheets from the pad.

talker: See *shelf talker.*

tape plan: A continuity promotion run by a supermarket in which a variety of premiums are offered in return for cash-register tapes totaling a specified amount and, most often, cash sufficient to make the promotion self-liquidating or even profitable.

taping: Applying a cloth or plastic binding.

tap-maker display: A display that is attached to a bar or fountain tap handle for a particular brand of beer or soft drink.

tapper: A motorized device for tapping a window or making another sound to attract attention.

T bar: A T-shaped bar used to hang two signs or to hold a large paper poster which can be draped over it and thus seen from both sides.

tear-off pad: See *take-one pad.*

tent card: A single-fold card, resembling a tent, for use on counters, bars, or tables and carrying an advertising message. Frequently messages appear on both the front and the back of the tent card.

test store: A retail unit where tests of product sales are made to determine buying and merchandising practices.

theme: The basic idea around which a promotion is built.

thixotropy: The property of a gel of becoming fluid when agitated. Using a thixotropic resin, a vertical surface can be painted on without running.

three-dimensional display: See *lenticular display.*

thumbnail sketch: A miniature sketch.

ticky-tack: A very rough model put together for the purpose of judging size and overall looks.

tie-in: A cooperative advertising effort featuring multiple products together in one display unit, usually at a money-saving combination price, e.g., a toothbrush and toothpaste or a razor and after-shave lotion. The products are sometimes manufactured by different companies.

tip-on card: A special card which is attached to a display to call attention to a special sale or other feature.

tooling: The process of readying productive facilities for mass production of point-of-purchase materials. Also called *tooling up.*

topper: The part of a pole display that tops the pole. See *pole topper.*

trade card plan: A plan, little used today, in which a retailer punches the amount of a consumer's purchases onto a card. When purchases total a certain amount, the customer is entitled to buy a premium at a self-liquidating price.

trademark: The registered name of a company's product.

trade name: The name by which a product is known to the public. It may be used and protected as a trademark.

trade show: A place where manufacturers and other members of a particular industry display or exhibit their wares and introduce and demonstrate new products to the trade: retailers and wholesalers (their customers). Trade shows are usually held annually at the same time of the year and usually at the same location.

trading stamp: A gummed stamp given by a retailer, usually for each $0.10 worth of purchases. The stamps are pasted in a "saver book," and the consumer redeems them for premiums illustrated in the stamp company catalog.

traffic builder: A relatively low-cost premium offered free as an inducement to visit a store, sometimes where a demonstration will be held.

traffic count: The number of potential customers passing a display during a specific time period.

Trans-Lite: See *transparency*.

transparency: A backlighted photographic print on film which depends on the light behind it to bring out the full color. Also, a material applied to glass that is backlighted. See *collotype*.

travel incentive: See *incentive travel*.

traveling display: A display designed to be shipped from place to place and reused in various retail outlets.

traveling-tape sign: A sign, usually illuminated, in which an advertising message, brand identification, and pictorial elements appear on a tape which moves across the open face of the sign, with the motion generally supplied by power from an electric motor.

tray: The part of a display which holds the merchandise or customers' change. It may be separate or an integral part of the display.

triple-message sign: A sign with rotating triangular louvers which turn in unison and present a different message as each of the three faces is exposed.

truck topper: See *car topper*.

turntable: A rotating table used to display all sides of a single piece of merchandise or a selection of various pieces. It may be turned mechanically or by hand.

two-for-one sale: A sale in which two units of a product are offered for the price of one.

underrun: The number of displays or pieces of printed material short of the number specified in the order. See also *overrun*.

unselfish display: A unit which accommodates related-item merchandise not sold by the advertiser. Also, a storewide program which does the same. See *altruistic display*.

use-the-user plan: See *referral premium*.

vacuum-forming process: An inexpensive process by which plastic signs and displays are shaped into three-dimensional figures by the use of vacuum machinery.

valance: A long, narrow sign or display designed to be used above eye level.

Velox: The trademark for a photographic process in which small black dots in a white field represent highlighted areas, and small white dots in a black field represent shadow areas. Also a screened photoprint.

Verplex: The trademark for a process that simulates the effect of an oil painting through special embossing.

Versa-Panel: The trademark for a type of sign having a four-panel screen for bulletin display.

vertical arrangement: An arrangement in which a line or variety of products are stocked on shelves above and below each other.

Vue-More: The trademark for a mechanical turntable.

wagon merchandiser: A movable wagon designed to hold merchandise and carry an advertising message.

wall banner: A large advertisement placed on a wall or suspended from a wire and stretched across a store.

web-fed press: A printing press in which a roll of paper is printed and then cut into separate pieces.

window display: A display placed in the window of a retail outlet, facing outside to attract the attention of pedestrians passing by the establishment.

window streamer: A long, narrow advertisement attached to a store window.

window strip: An advertising message placed at the bottom of a window.

wire wobbler: A spring-steel wire extended to hold a display card. It oscillates with light air currents caused by store traffic.

wobbler: A lightweight display that hangs from a wire over a frozen-food case or in other locations and bobs and turns with light air current.

wood-grain finish: A woodlike finish that is applied to metal, paper, and other materials.

wraparound: A roll of continuous printing, usually on single-face corrugated cardboard or heavy, soft sheets, designed to decorate the space between a counter or tabletop and the floor. Also, a display card of special design that "hugs" or wraps around a product.

wrinkle finish: A decorative baked-enamel finish that is characterized by a pattern of wrinkles.

Index